LUCIUS Q. C. LAMAR

✻

JUSTICE LUCIUS Q. C. LAMAR

LUCIUS Q. C. LAMAR

Secession and Reunion

BY WIRT ARMISTEAD CATE

Chapel Hill
THE UNIVERSITY OF NORTH CAROLINA PRESS

*The University of North Carolina Press, Chapel Hill,
N. C.; The Baker and Taylor Company, New York;
Oxford University Press, London; Maruzen-Kabushiki-
Kaisha, Tokyo; Edward Evans & Sons, Ltd., Shanghai;
D. B. Centen's Wetenschappelijke Boekhandel, Amsterdam*

To

ALLAN NEVINS

➤➤➤ ✳ ⟨⟨⟨

PREFACE

⠿✱⠿

THIS BIOGRAPHY represents an attempt to make use of much recently accessible material (particularly letters in a score of MS collections) in the portrayal of the career of Lucius Q. C. Lamar—perhaps the most gifted statesman that the South gave to the nation from the close of the Civil War to the turn of the century, and the man to whom was due, more than to any other, the death of sectionalism and the healing of the wounds of the fratricidal war.

One of America's few authentic political philosophers, Lamar's career touched every phase of post-Civil War life, and in his constructive and liberal statesmanship he anticipated the future in a wide diversity of fields. A product of the pre-war South and one who went with his people in their attempt to found a new nation, he lived to have a major part in delivering them from the horrors of carpetbag rule, and, as the first truly reconstructed statesman either North or South, to become the leading exponent of fraternalism between the sections. His character and personality, indeed, combine everything that was best in the Old South with a liberalism that is timeless because its virility had its inception in an attitude of mind (the only true liberalism) and not in a mere body of beliefs which, however progressive in one generation, tend to seem conservative or even reactionary in the next. A great teacher, orator, legislator, administrator, and jurist, Lucius Quintus Cincinnatus Lamar placed his impress upon four decades of American life.

The original and constructive quality of his thinking was never more strikingly evident than in the decisive part (here fully told for the first time) which he played in the settlement of the disputed presidential election of 1876; in his exhaustive discussion of the Matthews Resolution and the Bland Silver Bill, the constitutionality of both of which he conceded while oppos-

vii

ing their passage from considerations of sound public policy; and in his enunciation and development of that most important contribution to the philosophy of history—the theory of the influence of the frontier on the evolution of our political system, a concept which was later to be popularized by Professor Frederick J. Turner, who is commonly but erroneously credited with its authorship.

Distinguished as was his public career, Lamar is equally to be honored for the purity and nobility of his character and for his remarkably gifted personality. "Some twenty years later [after the war], in the shifting search for the education he never found," says Henry Adams of himself, he "became closely intimate at Washington with Lamar, then Senator from Mississippi. ... [He was] quite unusual in social charm...he had tact and humor; and perhaps this was a reason why Mr. Davis sent him abroad with the others, on a futile mission to St. Petersburg. He would have done better in London, in place of Mason. London society would have delighted in him; his stories would have won success; his manners would have made him loved; his oratory would have swept every audience; even Monckton Milnes could never have resisted the temptation of having him to breakfast between Lord Shaftesbury and the Bishop of Oxford." Socially at home in the most exclusive circles in America and Europe, Lamar's friendships included a number of the most interesting and influential figures of two continents.

Finally, let it be said that to understand the problems Lamar faced in his rôle of the Great Pacificator, one must bear in mind something of the history of the reconstruction régime which he had so large a part in overthrowing. Hence it has seemed desirable to discuss in some detail the course of reconstruction in Mississippi—with the "redemption" of which state he was particularly concerned.

Throughout the preparation of the study, the author has found particularly helpful Edward Mayes' *Lucius Q. C. Lamar: His Life, Times, and Speeches.* Mr. Mayes (Lamar's son-in-law) presented a sympathetic and altogether admirable work, written at the request of the immediate family of Lamar, and growing out of long years of intimate association with him. The present author, however, has used a great deal of material made accessible during the almost forty years since the appearance of the latter. In addition he has attempted to present Lamar against a broader national background from a vantage point of greater perspective than was possible to Mr. Mayes.

In his labors incident to the publication of this biography, the author is indebted to a wide circle of friends and acquaintances for more help than he has space adequately to detail. Particularly does he desire to acknowledge the kindnesses of Chancellor Alfred Hume, of the University of Mississippi; Mrs. John Trotwood Moore and the late Mrs. Pearl Williams Kelly, of the Tennessee State Library; Professor John Donald Wade, of Athens, Georgia; Judge A. K. Nippert, of Cincinnati; Mr. A. C. Lunsford, of Covington, Georgia; Dr. Dunbar Rowland, Director of Archives of the State of Mississippi; Miss Ruth Blair, Georgia State Historian; Miss Annie A. Nunns, of the Wisconsin State Historical Society; Dean Frank R. Reade, of the Georgia State Woman's College; the authorities of the Library of Congress, particularly Mr. Jameson, Chief of the Division of Manuscripts; Mr. A. W. Cozart, of Columbus, Georgia; and Mr. Oliver Orr of Macon, Georgia.

To many of Lamar's descendants and relatives is he obligated for assistance in the collection of unprinted material and for other favors, particularly to Miss Laura Lamar, of Montgomery, Alabama; Mr. A. Longstreet Heiskell, of Memphis, Tennessee; Mr. George H. Lamar, of Washington, D. C.; Mr. A. Melrose Lamar, of West Palm Beach, Florida; Mr. W. W. Lamar, of the United States Navy; and Miss Decca Lamar West, of Waco, Texas.

The author owes an especial debt to Chancellor James B. Newman and Miss Margaret Cate of Nashville, Tennessee, and to Professor Allan Nevins, of Columbia University, each of whom read and criticized the entire manuscript. To them is he obligated for encouragement and advice throughout the whole course of his efforts.

Finally, the author's thanks are extended to the following

publishers who have kindly permitted him to quote from books of which they hold the copyrights: to the Macmillan Company; Houghton Mifflin Company; D. Appleton-Century Company; G. E. Stechert and Company; Doubleday, Doran and Company; Minton Balch and Company; and Charles Scribner's Sons. .

W. A. C.

Nashville, Tennessee,
February 1, 1935.

CONTENTS

xi

ILLUSTRATIONS

⟫*⟪

LUCIUS Q. C. LAMAR

❧※❧

eulogy of the man who, more than almost any other, had been an enemy to all for which the South had stood; who was regarded as perhaps her most uncompromising foe; and whose dying whispers had been a plea for a bill which was designed to place the ex-slave and his former master in the same class in respect to all civil privileges. That a Southern leader should speak in honor of such a man was as incomprehensible to his own friends as to the radical Republicans, and neither expected more than a purely perfunctory performance, a grudging and superficial tribute to a dead enemy such as might be demanded by civilized usage. None of them understood that the incident signalized a new day in the history of the nation, that, for the first time since Appomattox, had been heard a voice capable of conciliating all sections, and that there had emerged a new and commanding figure upon the national stage.[6]

Lamar paid eloquent tribute to Sumner's culture, his scholarship, his breadth of knowledge, his powers as an orator and logician, his intellectual superiority, and his high moral qualities. He dwelt understandingly upon the "instinctive love of freedom" that had prompted the dead statesman to espouse the cause of Negro liberation, and to champion a crusade for Negro social and political equality.[7] Departing from his formal eulogy, Lamar began to speak out of the fullness of his heart. Extemporizing in that fashion of which he was so brilliantly the master and referring to Sumner's famous resolution of 1872, "that the names of battles with fellow-citizens shall not be continued in the Army Register, or placed on the regimental colors of the United States,"[8] he said:

[Southerners] cannot but cherish the recollections of sacrifices endured, the battles fought, and the victories won in defense of their hapless cause. And respecting, as all true and brave men must respect, the martial spirit with which the men of the North vindicated the integrity of the Union, and their devotion to the principles of human freedom, they do not ask, they do not wish the North to strike the mementoes of her heroism and victory from either records or monuments or battle flags. They would rather that both sections should gather up the glories won by each section: not envious, but proud of each other, and regard them a common heritage of American valor.

Let us hope that future generations, when they remember the deeds of heroism and devotion done on both sides, will speak not of Northern prowess and Southern courage, but of the heroism, fortitude, and courage of Americans in a war of ideas; a war in which each section signalized its consecration to the principles, as each understood them, of American liberty and of the constitution received from their fathers.

It was my misfortune, perhaps my fault, personally never to have known this eminent philanthropist and statesman. The impulse was often strong upon me to go to him and offer my hand, and my heart with it, and to express to him my thanks for his kind and considerate course toward the people with whom I am identified. If I did not yield to that impulse, it was because the thought occurred that other days were coming in which such a demonstration might be more opportune, and less liable to misconstruction. Suddenly, and without premonition, a day has come at last to which, for such a purpose, there is no to-morrow. My regret is therefore intensified by the thought that I failed to speak to him out of the fullness of my heart while there was yet time....

But the central theme of Lamar's address was a plea for mutual trust and understanding between the two sections of the nation:

Charles Sumner, in life, believed that all occasion for strife and distrust between the North and South had passed away, and that there no longer remained any cause for continued estrangement between these two sections of our common country. Are there not many of us who believe the same thing? Is not that the common sentiment—or if it is not, ought it not to be—of the great mass of our people, North and South? Bound to each other by a common constitution, destined to live together under a common government, forming unitedly but a single member of the great family of nations, shall we not now at last endeavor to grow *toward* each other once more in heart, as we are already indissolubly linked to each other in fortunes? Shall we not...lay aside the concealments which serve only to perpetuate misunderstandings and distrust, and frankly confess that on both sides we most earnestly

3

desire to be one; one not merely in community of language and literature and traditions and country; but more, and better than all that, one also in feeling and heart?...

The South—prostrate, exhausted, drained of her lifeblood, as well as of her material resources, yet still honorable and true—accepts the bitter award of the bloody arbitrament without reservation, resolutely determined to abide the result with chivalrous fidelity; yet, as if struck dumb by the magnitude of her reverses, she suffers on in silence. The North, exultant in her triumph, and elated by success, still cherishes, as we are assured, a heart full of magnanimous emotions toward her disarmed and discomfited antagonist; and yet, as if mastered by some mysterious spell, silencing her better impulses, her words and acts are the words and acts of suspicion and distrust.

Would that the spirit of the illustrious dead whom we lament to-day could speak from the grave to both parties to this deplorable discord in tones which should reach each and every heart throughout this broad territory: "My countrymen! *know* one another, and you will *love* one another."

Unmoved, the vast assemblage had heard the resolution and tribute of the Hon. E. R. Hoar of Massachusetts. But as Lamar continued, it was apparent that an event of the first magnitude was occurring. The packed chamber became deathly still. It was observed that tears coursed down the averted face of Mr. Blaine, the Speaker, while Democrats and Republicans alike wept openly. With his last words: "My countrymen, *know* one another, and you will *love* one another," the assemblage remained oppressively quiet; then from the Republican side of the House, spreading throughout the hall and to the galleries, there swept a tremendous burst of applause.[9] This time there was no attempt on the part of the Speaker to quiet the tumult. "My God!" exclaimed Lyman Tremaine, of New York, to Pig-iron Kelley, of Pennsylvania, with tears in his eyes; "what a speech! and how it will ring through the country!" Said another spectator subsequently, "Those who listened sometimes forgot to respect Sumner in respecting Lamar." "The orator ceased," reported a third. "For a time the chamber was as silent as a mausoleum....For the first time in twenty years the peace of God, which passeth all understanding, seemed to pronounce its blessed benison upon the Congress of the United States." Under the spell of the witchery of Lamar's oratory, the Hon. S. J. Randall, Chairman of the Congressional Democratic Executive Committee, wrote to the editor of the *Jackson* (Miss.) *Clarion*: "Lamar has just finished his Sumner speech. It was a wonderful success. He said exactly what ought to have been said. The House was electrified. *All parties are pleased*, because it kindled a sentiment that rises higher than party passion. It will do us a great deal of good."

Lamar's only fear had been that the South might misunderstand the motives that had prompted his speech. On the 29th of April he wrote to his wife: "I never in all my life opened my lips with a purpose more single to the interests of our Southern people than when I made this speech. I wanted to seize an opportunity, when universal attention could be arrested, and directed to what I was saying, to speak to the North in behalf of my own people.... I did not aim at rhetorical or personal success, so earnest and engrossing was my other object; but the rhetorical triumph was as prodigious as it was unexpected." [10] A few "Bourbon" Southerners professed to think that he had surrendered his early principles, and several newspapers, particularly the *Canton Mail*, the *Meridian Mercury*, and the *Columbus Democrat*, of his own State, attacked him savagely. But by the great body of well-informed and thinking Southerners he was hailed as the dominant spokesman of their interests.

That Lamar, so soon after the war, had taken a precariously advanced position was realized by many of his contemporaries. George F. Hoar of Massachusetts, who followed Lamar with his tribute to Sumner, wrote that no other man could have delivered the eulogy and gone back to Mississippi to live, but his words, said Hoar, "never shook for a moment the love for Lamar of a people who knew so well his love for them." [11] A day or two after the memorial meeting Lamar attended a circus with Senator Thurman. In the midst of the performance a woman apparently lost her perilous balance on the flying trapeze but managed to grasp another as she fell from a great height.

"Lamar, that reminds me of you," said Senator Thurman. "How so?" said the Colonel. "About your speech, you know. You caught all right; but if you had missed, you'd have broken your neck." [12]

The unanimous verdict of historians accords with the belief of Rhodes that the eulogy was "one of the most remarkable ever delivered in Congress" and that it was a tremendous factor in the "redemption of Mississippi" from carpetbag rule. [13] "That a southerner, presumed to be of the fire-eating type, should find anything to approve in the Massachusetts Senator, save possibly his death," says Dunning, "was a fact to arrest instant attention through the length and breadth of the land. The note of charity and patriotism which Lamar skillfully infused into his address struck a responsive chord on both sides of Mason and Dixon's line. In the North it strengthened greatly the hands of the reforming element among the Republicans; in the South it perceptibly checked a growing movement among the whites to overthrow a growing radicalism by a ruthless suppression of the negro vote." It was of prime importance, Dunning thinks, "for the intellectual and spiritual reunion of the sections." [14] Savoyard, after a long life-time spent in Washington as a critic of national affairs, characterized it as "the first and the loftiest plea for union, the union of hearts. The dying song of Grady was but its echo. It awoke a responsive chord at the North, and even the bloody shirt was dipped in admiration and applause." [15]

The prestige and deference accorded Lamar after this event left no doubt that a new figure of national importance had appeared. He was not unaware of this himself, as is shown by a letter of May 5th, written to his wife: "My eulogy has given me a reputation that I have never had before. The whole world is my audience. No one here thinks I lowered the Southern flag, but the Southern press is down on me. That is unfortunate, for what they say will be copied by the Radical press of the North as evidence that the South still cherishes schemes of secession and slavery. I do not blame the Southern editors. ...Our people have suffered so much, have been betrayed

6

so often by those in whom they had the strongest reason to confide, that it is but natural that they should be suspicious of any word or act of overture to the North by a Southern man. I know *for once* that I have done her good, that I have won friends to her side who were bitter enemies, that I have awakened sympathies where before existed animosities. If she condemns me, while I shall not be indifferent to her disapprobation, I shall not be cast down or mortified or resentful. I shall be cheered and consoled by the thought that I have done a wise and beneficial thing for her. It is time for public men to try to *serve* the South, and not to subserve her irritated feelings, natural and just as those feelings are. I shall serve no other interests than hers, and will calmly and silently retire to private life if her people do not approve me." [16]

But they did approve of him, and henceforth, as his fame broadened through successive steps as United States Senator, Cabinet member, and Associate Justice of the Supreme Court, he was never to be without an audience and a devoted following.

II

THE LAMAR FAMILY

THE HISTORY of the Lamar family is peculiarly susceptible to accurate tracing because in every generation extensive land holdings have left indelible records in the Land Offices of several States. Despite a tradition among the Lamars of Georgia that their family was of Huguenot origin, and was planted in Maryland by four brothers who fled from France in the exodus consequent upon the revocation of the Edict of Nantes on October 17th, 1685, we know from authentic records that, though the Lamars were, in truth, of Huguenot origin, they left France about the middle of the century and had acquired extensive holdings in England and America by 1663.[1] As a matter of fact, they had left their native land in anticipation of the trend of events that finally resulted in the revocation of the Edict of Nantes rather than in consequence of that event.[2]

The ancestral home of the Lamars was near the small village of Wicre, not far from Lille, in Flanders.[3] Slightly before the middle of the century, the Protestant branch of the family, including Thomas and Peter "Lamore," moved to England where it shortly acquired considerable wealth as is proven by the will of Thomas, probated in Maryland in 1714 sometime after his death, wherein he bequeathed to his widow during the period of her life all his valuable "lands and moveable estate, both here and in England."[4] A part of the family, however, had become so rooted in Hampshire that they were content to remain there. Under the name of "Delamare" this branch still exists as a family of wealth and prominence.[5] But Thomas and Peter Lamore emigrated to Virginia where they did not remain long enough to become naturalized before they moved to Maryland. This last shift was occasioned, as the application

8

for naturalization shows, by the favorable conditions instituted by Lord Baltimore in 1649. Since Maryland was an English colony under English laws, it had been impossible up to that time for any emigrants to hold lands in fee except such as were of British nationality. In the year in question, Lord Baltimore issued a statement to the peoples of Germany, France, and other continental countries to the effect that any individuals who might join the Maryland colony would be granted favorable concessions and would be accorded all rights granted to those of English birth.

On September 14th, 1663, the Maryland Provincial Assembly approved the petition for "Pattents of *Dennizacõn* to Thomas Lamore and Peter Lamore of french descent," and on the 17th of the following November, Lord Baltimore granted a certificate of naturalization, the original now to be seen in the Annapolis Land Records, this stating that,

"Whereas Thomas and Peter Lamore, *late of Virginia*, and subjects of the crown of France, having transported themselves into this province here to abide, have besought us to grant them, the said Thomas and Peter Lamore, leave to here inhabit as free denizens, and freedom land to them and their heirs to purchase, Know ye, that we, willing to give encouragement to the subjects of that crown, do hereby declare them, the said Thomas and Peter Lamore, to be free denizens of this our province of Maryland...." [6]

On November 8th, 1664, Peter and Thomas Lamore bought and were deeded "a parcell of land lying upon Petuxent river on the south side and binding upon St. Steuens Creeke as by pattent appeare to be three hundred and fifty acres," [7] where they immediately set about acquiring more land and assumed the positions of the most prominent and wealthy planters of Calvert County. On November 24th, 1665, Thomas Lamar was petitioning for a grant of land such as would indemnify him for the expense of transporting "himself and his wife, Mary, into the province of Maryland," [8] this being granted on the day that it was submitted. Thereafter there appear in the records of Calvert County many deeds and land grants to Thomas and

Peter Lamar, as the name now commonly came to be spelled, most of these grants referring to tracts lying in that part of Calvert which was subsequently to be added to Prince George County.

It is an interesting fact that in the same records the name appears variously as Lamare, Lamore, Lamaire, De La Maire, Leamire, Lemarre, Lemar, La Mar, Le Marr, Lamare, and finally in its present form Lamar, according to the taste of the individual scribe. This latter form is not encountered in public documents before 1697, though it was then applied, in various legal instruments, to the same Thomas and Peter Lamore who had arrived in Maryland at least by 1663. This easy flexibility of spelling is to be expected in a current *milieu* where lawyers and public officials were none too well educated, as a rule, and at a time when modes of spelling had not crystallized as at present. Family records and letters indicate, however, that from the earliest period in this country the members of the family uniformly used the spelling "Lamar."

Light upon the ultimate origin of the name is not far to seek. The clue is found in the mermaid that appears on the crest of the colonial Lamars in America, and upon the arms of that branch of the original French family which did not emigrate, this indicating that the "De La Mar" was derived from "De La Mer," "of the sea." [9] Of the branch of the family that remained in France, the most gifted representative was the poet Lamartine, who evinced a decided interest in the American Lamars. When L. Q. C. Lamar was in Paris as special envoy of the Confederate States to the Court of France, Lamartine, who was greatly attracted by his magnetism and social charm, entertained him and explained that the suffix "tine" had, at a comparatively recent date, been added to the name to denote the younger branch of the family. [10]

In 1674, Dr. John Lamaire, a physician of Anjou, France, probably a brother of Thomas and Peter Lamore and possibly emigrating at their persuasion, was naturalized in Maryland whence he had come direct from his native land. [11] He patented a tract of land at Port Tobacco in Charles County, which he named Hispaniola, and soon he had married Margaret Waghoque who brought him a large land dower and considerable other wealth.[12] His quick rise to prominence is shown by the fact that soon the minutes of the Provincial Assembly are referring to him as one of the "Overseers" of Port Tobacco County, and he is frequently being voted large grants of tobacco for public services.[13] With his descendants, however, we are in no wise concerned.

Peter Lamar lived and died in Calvert County, where his will was probated March 31st, 1694. This instrument shows that he had acquired large holdings which he divided between his wife, Frances, and his daughters, Ann, Mary, and Margaret.[14] Though he had no sons, and hence the name of Lamar did not persist as the surname among his descendants, he had many grandchildren who perpetuated his line.

It is with the descendants of Thomas the emigrant that we are specifically concerned.[15] Like the other two emigrants he prospered greatly, and acquired a number of plantations. The deed to one of them is an interesting old document that is typical of all the others. It reads:

"Charles, Absolute Lord and Proprietary of the province of Maryland and Avalon Lord Baron of Baltimore, &c.

"To all persons to whom these presents shall come, Greetings in our Lord God Everlasting.

"Know ye that we for and in consideration that Thomas La Mare of Calvert County in our said province of Maryland hath due unto him fifty acres of land within our Province ...upon such conditions and terms as are expressed in the Conditions of Plantation of our late father Cecelius of noble memory under his greater seal at Arms bearing date at London the second day of July in the year of our Lord 1649....

"Do hereby grant unto him the said Thomas La Mare all that parcel of land called *The Fishing Place* situate lying and being in Calvert County on the West side of Patuxent River and the North side of Trent Creek....To have and to hold the same unto him the said Thomas La Mare, his heirs and assigns forever—to be holden of us and our heirs at our receipt

I I

of St. Marie's at the two most usual feasts of the year, vizt:
at the feast of the Annunciation of the Blessed Virgin Mary
and at the feast of St. Michael the Arch Angel by even and
equal portions the Rent of two Shillings Sterling in Silver or
Gold....

"Given at our city of St. Marie's under the great seal of our
said Province of Maryland the fifth day of April in the second
year of our dominion over our said Province Annoque Dom^m.
One Thousand Six hundred seventy seven." [16]

Thomas took as his family seat the Fishing Place, situated
as described in the above quoted instrument and adjoining other
lands already in his possession.[17] The records show that prior
to 1696 he owned much property in the province, and had
retained extensive holdings in England, all of which, as we
have seen, he left to his wife during her life, with the provision that it should eventually go to his two sons.[18] That
he was married before he moved to Maryland is proven by
the fact that he petitioned for land for himself and his wife,
Mary. Upon her death, however, he married Ann Pottinger
who survived him and who, in addition to inheriting a life
interest in his property, was made executrix of his will, which
was probated May 29th, 1714.[19] At his death Thomas was
buried in that part of Prince George County which had been
carved out of Calvert.

The eldest son of Thomas the emigrant, also named Thomas,
increased his inheritance until he became one of the most influential planters of the province. Among the extensive tracts of
land which he possessed and which he left to his descendants
were a number which bore curious names, among them "Joseph
and James," "Two Brothers," "Valentine's Garden," "Conclusion," "The Pines," and "Hunting Hill." [20] This Thomas, of
the second generation in America, married Martha Urquhart,
a sister of the Reverend John Urquhart, Director of All Faith
Parish in Saint Mary's County.[21] Thomas made her the executrix of his will, dated May 11th, 1747, and probated January
31st, 1749 "in the presence of Robert Lamar, Heir at Law."
He died in 1748, leaving his property to his wife and to his

six sons and two sons-in-law by name. This consisted largely
of the plantations already mentioned, these involving thousands of acres located in the section between Rockville,
Gaithersburg, and Hunting Hill.[22]

For seven years after the death of Thomas Lamar of the
second generation, and after the dividing up of his immense
holdings, the family continued to live upon the ancestral plantations. But the intensive farming, particularly the raising of
tobacco year after year without the scientific fertilization of a
later day, had so impoverished the land that in 1755 there
was held a general family conclave, as a result of which, Robert,
Thomas, John, Samuel, and their brother-in-law, Clementius
Davis, decided to dispose of their holdings and with their families and numerous slaves to move to a newer country further
south. Two of the brothers, together with the other brother-
in-law, remained in Maryland where they were the progenitors
of a large family connection, some of whom still dwell in the
same vicinity.

The records show that on January 25th, 1755, the four
brothers and Clementius Davis disposed of their broad acres
to their uncle, the wealthy divine, John Urquhart, and a few
days later set out on their journey to the southward, into
South Carolina and Georgia, settling at Beach Island near
Augusta and on the Georgia side of the Savannah River.[23]
Eventually, as was to be expected, the families became more
widely separated, the greater part of them settling in Beaufort
County, South Carolina; in Edgefield, Richmond, Lincoln, and
Putnam Counties, Georgia; and subsequently becoming widely
disseminated throughout Georgia, Alabama, Tennessee, and
Missouri. It is perhaps worthy of note that Justice Joseph Rucker
Lamar, appointed by President Taft to the Supreme Court of
the United States in 1910, was a great-grandson of the Robert
who moved to Georgia, while Justice L. Q. C. Lamar, the
subject of this study, was of the same generation in descent
from the younger brother, John.

It is, then, to the line of John that we must briefly devote
our attention. The second son of John, and Rachel his wife,

was John Lamar of the fourth generation in America. He, too, had a son, John, who married his first cousin, Rebecca Lamar, also of the fifth generation and daughter of Thomas Lamar. She bore him a number of children, nine of whom reached maturity and two of whom attained real distinction: Lucius Quintus Cincinnatus Lamar, judge of the highest court of Georgia and father of Justice L. Q. C. Lamar of the Supreme Court of the United States; Mirabeau Buonaparte Lamar, second President of the Republic of Texas, as well as major-general, Attorney General, Secretary of War, Vice-President of the Republic, founder of the public school system of Texas, and United States minister to the Argentine Republic and to Costa Rica and Nicaragua; Jefferson Jackson and Thomas Randolph, both respected citizens of Georgia; and five daughters.[24]

Something should be said of the unusual names which were accorded the sons of John Lamar. "With the family," writes William Preston Johnston, lived a "brother, Zachariah, who, without any particular occupation, was a devotee of history and literature. So when son after son was born to the head of the house, this bookish enthusiast claimed the privilege of naming his infant nephews after his favorite of the moment, and the amiable and doubtless amused parents consented. Thus Lucius Quintus Cincinnatus, Mirabeau Buonaparte, Jefferson Jackson, Thomas Randolph, and Lavoisier Legrand (a grandchild) indicate how his interest shifted from history to politics, and from politics to chemistry."[25] There is a tradition among the Georgia Lamars that this naming was done by their uncle, Colonel Zachariah Lamar, a wealthy slave-owner of Milledgeville and father of Mrs. Howell Cobb. This identification can be discounted, it seems, in view of the fact that his own children received no such appellations.[26]

It should be noted that by this time members of the Lamar family had begun to figure prominently in public life. For the first hundred years after the arrival in America the colonial records show that they had been large land owners, none of them living within towns or cities, and few of them showing any particular interest in the affairs of the provincial govern-

14

ments. But with the Revolutionary War the descendants of Thomas the emigrant begin to appear in public life. General Maximillian Lamar played an active part at the battle of Saratoga where he lost his life; Major Mareen Lamar was killed at Parle Tavern; and Colonel William L. Lamar, born in Frederick County, Maryland, in 1755, took a prominent part in the Revolution and lived to serve gallantly in the war of 1812.[27] It is with the generation of Justice Lamar's father that the family enters the field of statesmanship as well as of planting and soldiering.

John Lamar, grandfather of the subject of this study, was a planter of wealth and culture, and one of the largest slave owners in Putnam and Lincoln counties. Shortly after 1800 he established himself some eight miles south of the little town of Eatonton, Putnam County, Georgia, upon a large plantation where, in 1804, he built for himself the finest home in the countryside.[28] Here he lies buried beside his daughter, Evalina (Mrs. Harvey), just outside the yard fence some four hundred and fifty feet from the house, under a slab upon which are inscribed the following words written by his distinguished son, Mirabeau:

In memory of John Lamar, who died August 3, 1833, aged sixty-four years. He was a man of unblemished honor, of pure and exalted benevolence, whose conduct through life was uniformly regulated by the strictest principles of probity, truth, and justice: thus leaving behind him as the best legacy to his children a noble example of consistent virtue. In his domestic relations he was greatly blessed, receiving from every member of a large family unremitting demonstrations of respect, love, and obedience.

The stream that flows not far from the house is to this day known as the Little John River, and even now the fine old Georgia Colonial mansion retains something of its ancient glory. For one hundred and thirty years there has been not a single alteration in the house, though the once beautiful shade trees have disappeared and in the past few years the building itself has been sadly in need of repairs. At present it is occupied by Mr. C. I. Humber, but several years ago the "Old Lamar Homestead," as it is still commonly known, passed into the possession of the Georgia Power Company. Something of the breadth of its original acres is to be seen in the fact that even to-day almost one thousand acres remain about the house.

Lucius Q. C. Lamar, the father of the Justice, was born in Warren County on the 15th of July, 1797, though his boyhood was chiefly spent at the homestead in Putnam. In 1816 he began the study of law with the Hon. Joel Crawford at Milledgeville, the capital of the State, and a year later enrolled in the famous law school of Judges Gould and Reeve, at Litchfield, Connecticut. In 1818 he was admitted to the bar, and opened an office in Milledgeville where, on March 10th, 1819, he married Sarah W. Bird, daughter of a prominent physician of that city.

The ancestry of Sarah Williamson Bird should be briefly noted, for it was from her that Justice Lamar must have inherited much of his mental acumen. Sarah Gilliam, her grandmother (believed to be a niece of the well known Episcopal divine, the Rev. Devereux Jarratt of Virginia) married Micajah Williamson, of Bedford County, with whom, in the year 1768, she moved to Georgia where in Wilkes County her husband exchanged sixty slaves for an extensive plantation. Williamson served throughout the Revolution in the Army of the South, and after the cessation of hostilities he quickly recouped his fortunes. When he died in 1795 he left five sons and six daughters.[29]

All of the children were prosperous and respected, but the daughters of the family were chiefly remarkable. Mary married the Hon. Duncan G. Campbell, a well known lawyer who was appointed one of the two commissioners to arrange the terms of the treaty whereby the Creeks surrendered their lands in Alabama and Georgia. To this couple was born Justice John A. Campbell, gifted member of the Supreme Court of the United States who, with the almost certain knowledge that he would have succeeded the great Taney as Chief Justice,[30] resigned in 1861 to become Confederate Assistant Secretary of War, and one of the three commissioners (the others were R. M. T. Hunter and Alexander Stephens) to confer with Lincoln and Seward in Fortress Monroe in February, 1865. Another daughter, Mrs. Griffin, was twice married, each time to a judge, the second of whom, Hon. Charles Tait, served twelve years in the United States Senate. Nancy married General John Clarke, subsequently governor of the State, while Susan, the grandmother of Justice Lamar, married Dr. Thompson Bird (usually spelled "Byrd") of the prominent Maryland and Virginia family of that name. The latter was educated in the best schools of his day, having been graduated from the College of William and Mary, and from Jefferson Medical College in Philadelphia.

Lucius Q. C. Lamar, the father of the most distinguished member of the family, was to have a brilliant but short career at the Georgia bar, after his admission in 1818. Returning to Georgia from the Litchfield law school he entered into a partnership with Judge Crawford and, after the first period of becoming established, quickly built up a practice which, for that day, made him unusually affluent. But, though Georgia had always been noted for the strength of her bar, he found the technical aspects of the law in deplorable condition. In the first place, the State had never provided for a Supreme Court, though the functions of that body were exercised by several circuit courts which were not superseded until 1848 when such a body was expressly created by the legislature. Hence the commonly accepted statement that the elder Lamar sat upon the Supreme Court of the State is not technically correct.[31] Moreover, there was no digest of the laws and no rules of practice, for which reason "a lawyer was often at a loss as to how to conduct his pleadings or prepare his interrogatories. The consequence of this was that hardly half of the litigated cases were tried on their merits."[32] It was natural that the brilliant young lawyer, who had evinced decidedly scholarly interests at the celebrated Litchfield law school, should take an interest in supplying some of the deficiencies in the arrangement of the body of the law. This interest was quickly recognized for its value, and before he was twenty-three years of age he was chosen by the legislature to compile the Laws of Georgia (Reports) from 1810 to 1820. This work was accepted with commendation by Governor Clark in 1821, and was published in a quarto volume of thirteen hundred pages. Standing as the first scientifically arranged digest of Georgia laws, it is of historic importance and until late years was recognized as Volume III of the "Georgia Statutes." Subsequently he increased his fame by revising and enlarging Clayton's *Georgia Justice*.[33]

Before the elder Lamar was thirty years of age, it was commonly said that he was material for the highest court in the State. The public demand for his services in the judiciary, his own scholarly inclinations, and the fact that he had already secured a financial competence, made his selection almost inevitable. He might have had the place when he was thirty-two years of age had he not retired in favor of, and thrown his support to, United States Senator Thomas W. Cobb, whose warm friend he was and whose recent disfavor with a large element in the State had aroused his sympathy and loyalty.[34] A year later, however, the way opened, and on the 4th of November, 1830, he accepted the judgeship of the Ocmulgee circuit, this before his thirty-fourth birthday—the youngest man ever to hold that office in Georgia.

The importance of this judgeship is attested by one who, having practiced in the courts of that time, later set down his impressions: "The superior courts of the several circuits constituted, then, the highest law tribunal in the State, and a Judge of this court was a person of very great consequence, charged with responsibilities and onerous duties, as they appear chronicled in the old records, almost too great for belief."[35] According to the sketch in Miller's *Bench and Bar of Georgia*, the young Lamar "presided with great dignity, and was most effective in the dispatch of business. No one who knew the man ever ventured on an act of rudeness or disrespect to his court. Yet every person whose deportment was worthy of it had unfailing assurances of his kindness. His lectures of instruction to the grand juries, at the opening of a term, were delivered in admirable style; and his charges to special and petit juries in the trial of difficult and much litigated cases might well serve as models to any bench."[36]

So good a judge as Hon. Joseph Henry Lumpkin, referring to two of his decisions that appear in *Dudley's Reports:* Brewster *vs.* Hardeman, and Kendrick *vs.* the Central Bank, said that they "'may be placed on a level with the best productions of the American or English bench.'" Perhaps he was too enthusiastic in his other statement that Judge Lamar's "active genius...and profound erudition would have given éclat to any name. There is no instance in England or America where a judge so rapidly gained public favor. In less than four years from his succession to the bench he was commonly known as 'the great Judge Lamar,' and was its brightest luminary. He could not have been displaced; there was no desire felt by his political opponents to give his office to another; and it was his singular merit, his crowning glory, that both Union and State rights men would equally have renewed his commission."[37] Carson, in his *History of the Supreme Court of the United States*, recognizes the exceptional talents of the elder Lamar when he refers to him as "an eminent jurist, a judge of the Supreme Court [sic] of Georgia and an eloquent speaker."[38]

Fortune, apparently, was smiling upon the young judge and his attractive family, and it was freely predicted that he was destined to fill a large place on the national stage. Without any apparent cause, so far as contemporary or family records show, his mental health began to fail, and he sank into a profound melancholia. Surrounded by a loving family and a solicitous and sympathetic following throughout the State, he continued to exercise the functions of his office. Though the passage of a few months made it necessary for him entirely to give over the holding of court, the bar, hoping for his recovery, insisted that he not resign. Then on July 4th, 1834, at the age of thirty-seven, he took his life in a moment of temporary aberration.[39] That morning, upon returning from a public function, he kissed his wife and children and, walking into the garden, shot himself.

Fortunately, the young widow, only thirty-two years of age, was left in comfortable circumstances. Henceforth, until her marriage seventeen years later to Colonel Hiram B. Trout-man of Vineville, near Macon, Georgia, she devoted herself to the education and rearing of her three sons and two daughters (three other children having died in infancy). To all of them she gave exceptional educational advantages. Lucius Q. C. and Thompson Bird attended Emory College at Oxford, Georgia, the latter being subsequently graduated from Jefferson Medical College. Jefferson Mirabeau, the youngest of the sons, was educated at the University of Mississippi, while the two daughters—Susan Rebecca and Mary Ann—were placed in the best boarding schools available (the younger in the newly founded Wesleyan College at Macon, perhaps the only school for women that at that time made any pretense of offering a course of study comparable to that given in the better men's colleges).

Within the family circle it was generally believed that the youngest of the sons, Jefferson Mirabeau, was the ablest. In September, 1862, as Lieutenant Colonel, he was to die leading his command as it stormed the breastworks at Crampton's Gap. Two years later, the second son, Thompson Bird, Colonel of the Fifth Florida, fell mortally wounded near Petersburg. Only Lucius, the eldest (but the fourth of the eight children),[40] lived to fulfill the promise of his brilliant young manhood.

III

BOYHOOD AND EMORY COLLEGE

THE EARLIEST, perhaps the happiest, memories of Lucius Quintus Cincinnatus Lamar—the future member of the Supreme Court of the United States—entwined about the old Lamar homestead situated outside of Eatonton, in Putnam County, where he was born on the 17th of September, 1825.[1] Many of the stories that in later years made Henry Adams call him the incomparable *raconteur* were associated with his early life here. Often his memories were to revert to the handsome old two-story Georgia Colonial mansion which stood in the midst of extensive holdings, with the lawn shaded by gigantic and immemorial oaks. At the rear the land sloped gently to the Little River, scene of many of his boyish exploits in hunting and fishing. The house, too, was one of the most prominent in the countryside, and as such was a regular stopping point for the stage coach which each day drew up at the door with a flourish of horns to the tremendous delight of the smiling blacks who crowded about.[2]

Important, too, was the fact that the old homestead acted as a rallying point for the whole Lamar connection in the Southeast. Here he heard his uncle, President Mirabeau Buonaparte Lamar, of the Republic of Texas, relate the story of the cavalry charge which he led to break the Mexican lines at San Jacinto.[3] Always there were floating back from South America romantic tales of his distant cousin, José Lamar, soldier of fortune. Fighting with Spain against France, the latter had been made a general by Ferdinand VII, and after taking a leading part in the founding of the Peruvian Republic, had been rewarded for a short time with its presidency.[4] Occasionally there were visits from his relative, Gazaway B. Lamar who, born and reared in Georgia, had moved to New York

City where he had attained the presidency of the Bank of the Republic and become one of the leading financiers of the nation.[5] Nor could the youthful Lamar have been insensible to the loyalty with which he still held his allegiance to the State of Georgia—a loyalty which a few years later was to cause him to throw in his lot with the Confederacy, for which he acted as the financial agent in the manufacture and sale of bonds and notes and the purchase of military supplies, after the war to be imprisoned but eventually freed by Andrew Johnson. For weeks at a time, when Congress was not in session, his cousin, Henry Graybill Lamar (later to sit in the Supreme Court of the State) would remain at the homestead where he would regale the children with stories of Washington City;[6] while another cousin (and uncle by marriage), Absalom Harris Chappell—soon to enter Congress to fill the vacancy caused by the resignation of Representative-elect John G. Lamar—was a frequent visitor.[7]

Particularly was "Lushe" (as Lamar's youthful acquaintances called him) attached to John Basil Lamar, a first cousin. But twelve years his senior and even then widely known as a writer, the latter had established himself as a leading planter and by 1850 was to have become one of the half-dozen largest slaveholders in the entire South. Elected to Congress in 1843, he resigned because of the responsibilities involved in the care of his extensive holdings in land and slaves (by the middle of the century he owned almost one thousand blacks). He was to become an officer on the staff of his brother-in-law, General Howell Cobb, and on September 14th, 1862, was to fall at Crampton's Gap beside L. Q. C. Lamar's own brother, Jefferson Mirabeau.[8]

But Lamar was not lacking for boon companions among his contemporaries. Besides his own brothers and the boys from neighboring plantations, there were a number of his cousins who, nearer his own age, spent much of their time at the old homestead. Among these, Charles A. L. Lamar was to become a Confederate colonel and was to fall near Columbus, Georgia, a week after Lee's surrender;[9] and Richard F. Lyon was to serve in the Supreme Court of the State.[10] Perhaps of all his cousins his closest associate in his early boyhood was Jabez Lamar Monroe Curry, whose parents removed with him to Alabama in 1838, but who returned to graduate from the State University at Athens. Later, their intimacy was to be renewed in the national House, and both were to serve in high place in the councils of the Confederacy.[11]

One does not wonder at Lamar's fame as a *raconteur* when one considers that much of his childhood and boyhood was spent on a plantation near to that where a few years later Joel Chandler Harris was to grow up and to collect his immortal tales of Uncle Remus and Brer Rabbit. It was on the Turner plantation, outside of Eatonton and close to the old Lamar homestead, that the young Harris began his literary career on the *Countryman*.[12] All his life the future Justice retained and cherished vivid recollections of the tales narrated by his old black mammy, folk stories to which a few years later Harris was to give immortality.

After the death of Judge Lamar in 1834 the widowed mother moved with her family to the little town of Covington, only a short distance from the Georgia-Conference Manual-Labor School, for the purpose of educating her sons. Speaking of this period of study, conducted largely under the guidance of his mother, Lucius was to say, many years after: "Books? I was surrounded with books. My father's library was unusually large and varied for those times. The first book I remember having had put into my hands by my mother, after juvenile books, was Franklin's *Autobiography*. The next was Rollin's *History*. Then came Plutarch's *Lives*, which I keenly enjoyed. Then Mrs. Hemans' innocent poems were intrusted to me, and Young's *Night Thoughts*. As an antidote, or at least a foil, for these, came Byron, which I devoured with eagerness. It was not till later years that I discovered that I had read an expurgated edition—'Don Juan' had been carefully cut out. After this was Robinson's *America*, Marshall's *Life of Washington*,

Brown's *Lectures on the Intellect,* and, after a while, Cousin's *Psychology.*" [13]

Mention has been made of the Methodist Manual-Labor School, just outside of Covington, where Lamar received his formal preparatory education. In the early part of the century this type of institution had become a great vogue throughout the nation. Everywhere they were being established. By 1832 the Reverend Mr. Sherwood had set up such a school at Eatonton, and in 1835 the Methodists had instituted a like beginning near Covington. [14] In a very real sense the whole movement was a fad, despite some very solid elements in the theory that underlay it. The idea had gotten abroad that the correct way to develop a sound mind in a healthy body was in a school where the students, regardless of their affluence, must alternate between physical labor and their studies. Such institutions were in no sense "technical" as the term is understood today, for the chief studies were Greek, Latin, history, and the like, with a smattering of the natural sciences. Under the presidency of Dr. Alexander Means, the Methodist Manual-Labor School at Covington had prospered greatly, and it had become necessary to restrict the enrollment so as to bar the several hundred boys who, in the course of a few years, had applied for entrance from other States.

Lamar was an apt pupil, though he always disliked greatly the physical labor entailed by the system. Even in his early teens he showed something of that remarkable aptitude for public speaking that in after life was to stand him in such good stead. A fixed element of the school curriculum was declamation before the student body in the chapel, and these periods were customarily times of great "amusement and hilarity" at the expense of the younger and more timid boys. But Lucius, with his perfect poise and complete freedom from self-consciousness, "was never their sport." [15]

Probably the most significant influence in the molding of the character and talents of Lamar was his entrance, in 1841, in the Freshman class of Emory College, at Oxford, Georgia, situated some two and a half miles from the town of Covington.

In 1838, soon after the founding of the institution, Mrs. Lamar had taken her children to the new college town where she had erected a comfortable two-story residence. Important, too, was the fact that just prior to Lamar's matriculation the presidency had fallen to a strong man, Judge Augustus Baldwin Longstreet, who took office in January, 1840, at the commencement of the second session.[16]

The selection of Judge Longstreet was a fortunate circumstance for the college. Born at Augusta, Georgia, on the 22nd of September, 1790, he had done his preparatory work at Waddell's famous school in South Carolina where he had become closely intimate with John C. Calhoun, a former graduate, whose political disciple he became. He had made an excellent record at Yale where he was graduated in 1813, and afterward he had followed in the footsteps of so many other eminent Georgians in attending the law school at Litchfield, Connecticut. Admitted to the bar in 1815, at an early age he had occupied a seat in the highest judicial body in the State, holding the judgeship of the Ocmulgee Circuit, the position afterwards filled by the elder L. Q. C. Lamar. As a result of personal bereavement at the death of a beloved son, he had turned to the Methodist ministry, and then into a notable college administrator, serving as President of Emory College, Centenary College of Louisiana, the University of Mississippi, and finally the University of South Carolina. In his early manhood he had begun the writing of those humorous bits of local color known as the *Georgia Scenes*, considered to this day as unexcelled examples of realistic writing, and as the earliest of such portrayals in American Literature.

Entering upon his administrative career at Emory College, Longstreet delivered his inaugural address on February 10th, 1840. The college property at this time consisted of four brick buildings which were combination dormitories and classrooms, a steward's hall, and the small wooden chapel, all situated on a campus from which the streets of the town of Oxford spread out like the stays of a fan.[17] The new president found a faculty of but four men: Mitchell, Professor of Moral Science and Literature; Lane, of Ancient Languages; Means, of Natural Science; and Myers, of Mathematics. Soon he instituted a chair of modern languages to which he called Professor Haderman, a graduate of Leipsic and of Paris.[18] Because of the slight demand for French and German, this was shortly discontinued, but not before the young Lamar—who had been attracted to these courses—had laid the foundation for a knowledge and a love of the continental literatures. With the almost immediate expansion of the student body, Longstreet increased his faculty by the addition of a number of instructors whom he recruited from the ranks of recent graduates of the college.

In a short time he was justified in saying that he had built up the college to the point where it was "the rival of the State University in reputation and patronage,"[19] and by 1844 Emory was graduating as many students each year as did the State University which was more than forty years its senior. And there was solid basis for the growth. As the little town of Oxford had its being because of the college, and since there were many families that had moved there for the education of their children, Longstreet turned all of the dormitory space into classrooms and arranged for the students to board out in the village. Hence Mrs. Lamar was never without a few boarders to help defray the expense of educating five children from the modest competency that her husband had left her. Fifty dollars a year would secure tuition, room-rent, and fuel; and board, including "eating, room, and washing," cost from nine to twelve dollars a month.[20]

Lamar entered Emory with the freshman class of 1841, and took his degree at the July commencement of 1845. As a student he was not particularly distinguished, though his standing was always an honorable one, and he attained real distinction in the classics—his favorite studies. He was, however, especially prominent in the literary societies, notably as the champion debater of Phi Gamma. Never throughout his college career, in fact, was he without a place on the debating teams which represented it in the annual debates.[21]

Naturally a dreamer and a mystic, Lamar's student life at

Emory College left a profound impress upon his religious views. A member of a family rooted in the Methodist faith and daily sitting at the feet of the leaders of the church, it was to be expected that he would always feel kindly toward that denomination. But despite his deep religious convictions he could not entirely satisfy himself as to certain tenets of the church, and he was profoundly distrustful of his own religious life. Hence, it was not for many years, until a visit to Macon, Georgia, during the Civil War, that he could gain his consent definitely to take the vows of the denomination.

Judge Longstreet, whose sheer force of character and ability had done so much for the college, seemed a great man to his students to whom, having lost confidence in the current political leaders, he looked as the future saviors of the country. Many years later, in 1873, Lamar was to write to General Walthall, his best-loved friend: "I don't know what I would give for old Judge Longstreet's faith and courage." [22]

Always, Emory College held a warm place in Lamar's heart, and periodically throughout his life he revisited its halls and addressed its student body. Here he had first met the girl who was to become his wife, and here he had formed friendships which lasted through the years. At a later day it was with regret that he was forced to refuse a professorship in his Alma Mater. In a commencement address delivered there in July 1870, he recalled many of the events of his college days, which he described as "bright and happy," saying: "No spot on earth has so helped to form and make me what I am as this town of Oxford." Both of his brothers, he recalled, and many of the classmates with whom he was most intimate, had since gone to soldier's graves on the red clay hills of Virginia and Georgia. [23]

The years have flown, and Emory College, grown fifty-fold in wealth, has been moved away to the city. The old brick buildings at Oxford stand reminiscent of an honorable past and a frustrate future. But in the university of today the memories of her greatest son have not perished, but take on immortality in the school of law which bears his name.

Oxford's character as a college town was unmistakable, for its population apparently contained no elements other than boys, church people, and families affluent enough to remove to Oxford to educate their sons. Even in Lamar's day it must have been a place of surpassing charm. The writer can remember more than one of his old professors who, on the new campus of the greater Emory, felt that the best part had been left behind and who could never reconcile themselves to the change. Illuminating is the comment of a visitor to the commencement of 1842 : "Imagine to yourself a dense forest with only enough trees [cut out] to make room for the dwellings which have rapidly sprung up since the place was started—with here and there a fine mansion, or beautiful cottage, embowered in a grove of forest oaks, adorned in front with a tastefully arranged flower garden, and you may have some notion of the place. The college buildings are at the extreme end of the village, and arranged more for convenience than show.... Of the citizens I have never fallen among a people more after my own heart." [24]

The town is situated in a section which was, at that time, perhaps the most prosperous in the State. Around it stretched the great plantations upon many of which each child in the family had his own slave and where only the blacks performed any semblance of manual labor. In the State as a whole, the general level of culture was perhaps the highest in the entire South with the exception of Virginia and in many respects the latter did not make so good a showing. Schools and colleges (such as they were) were appearing everywhere. Of the several woman's colleges, at least one, Wesleyan, was offering a course of study that might be called "liberal" in somewhat the real sense of the word. According to the census of 1850, Georgia, with no more than a half-million white population, possessed thirteen colleges with approximately 1500 students and with many thousands of volumes in their libraries. Liberal and enlightened thinking at the University of Georgia was preparing two boys, the LeConte brothers, who one day were to be among the foremost scientists of the nation. There were twenty-two publications—scientific, literary, and miscellaneous —with a total circulation of approximately 40,000, and there were almost forty non-private public libraries with an aggregate of considerably more than 30,000 volumes. All in all the record of no other Southern State was so impressive.[25]

Again, no other Southern State possessed so many prominent men who were strongly union and nationalistic in their hopes and aspirations. Of these, Alexander Stephens and "Bob" Toombs were perhaps the most influential in the years immediately preceding the Civil War. And the sentiment of the people as a whole was so pro-union that the Democratic party had never attained a position of commanding influence. Nevertheless, Judge Longstreet—despite his Yale education—was a radical States' Rights man, and he lost no opportunity to inculcate his political and social beliefs in his speeches to the student body of Emory College. This was perhaps to be expected from one who had followed Calhoun at Waddell's school in South Carolina, and had ever since worshiped at the shrine of that statesman. The teachings of the old Judge were to bear fruit in the large number of Emory men, including Lamar, who took leading parts in the Civil War.

Moreover, Emory—the most important Methodist college in the South—was at the heart of the social and political ideas which resulted in the split within that Church, and which culminated in the secession of the Southern States. President Longstreet, it was, who on June 5th, 1844, at the General Conference that met in New York City, had presented the memorial which resulted in the division of the Church. Shortly thereafter he had returned to Oxford where he continued to teach States' Rights to his students and to turn out numerous tracts, pamphlets, and articles presenting the Southern and slaveholding side of the questions at issue. Little Oxford became all the more a center for the dissemination of secession propaganda.

IV

THE LAUNCHING OF A CAREER

LAMAR was graduated from Emory College in 1845 and soon thereafter entered upon the study of law in the office of his relative, Hon. A. H. Chappell, in the city of Macon. At his admission to the bar two years later, so brilliant was his examination that the presiding judge, Christopher B. Strong, publicly congratulated him and recalled the exceptional legal abilities of his father.[1] As one of the youngest members of the local bar, Lamar for a time practiced with Mr. Chappell; but soon he moved to Covington where he had spent his preparatory school days, and here he offered for practice.

On the 15th of July, 1847, he was wedded to Miss Virginia Longstreet, the daughter of President Longstreet of Emory College. Born in June, 1826, Virginia Longstreet, as well as her sister, had attended Wesleyan College. Vivacious and with "rare powers of mimicry to which she occasionally gave rein in the retirement of her own home," she was a charming young lady.[2] She was to bring great happiness into Lamar's life; but in ways other than this the alliance had an important bearing upon his subsequent career, for from henceforth he was to be intimately associated with Judge Longstreet who had already wielded a powerful influence in the molding of his views and character. The close bond that linked the two is evident in a letter written by Lamar in 1859 after he had become an influential member of Congress: "I am indebted to you for ennobling influences from my boyhood up to middle age. I have doubtless often pained you, but for many years I have loved you as few sons love a father. And many a time in moments of temptation your influence, the desire of your love and approbation, have served me when my virtue might have failed. No applause of the public delights me so much as your declaration that I am unspeakably dear to you."[3]

His mother-in-law, too, was a remarkable woman. Of her he was to write years later, when she was dead and he had become a figure of national importance: "Mrs. Longstreet was the mother of my wife; and she was in love, tenderness, and goodness *my* mother. It is, therefore, hardly possible for me either to think or speak of her as if in the perspective.... The war did not subdue her spirit. She came from its desolations undismayed by the poverty which it entailed upon herself and the dear ones of her own family. She visited the homes of the poor and turned her own into a hospital, and did not hesitate to bathe her gentle hands in blood that she might bind the wounds of the dying.

"The gentleness of her manners, the grace of her motion, the reserve of her dignity, only served the better to set off the brightness that shone in her conversation and to disclose an intelligence that threw a charm over the modesty of her nature. Full of warmth and tenderness and depth of feeling, confiding, trustworthy, a lover of home, a true wife and mother, her hand touched and sanctified all domestic relations."

That Lamar's home life was singularly beautiful is the testimony of all contemporary records including the large part of his private correspondence that has survived. The pervading influence of his association with the beautiful Virginia Longstreet will be seen to the very last chapter in his life's history. When she died on December 30th, 1884, a vacancy came that could never be filled. After his death, in a small notebook kept during his Cabinet days, were found the following words which must have been a summation of his views of the beneficent influence of all the good women who had influenced his life: "It is to the influence of woman that all man's greatness or his viciousness may be traced. No man (or history is false), no man has ever won the world's applause for noble deeds, for self-sacrificing efforts, around whose infant brow a mother's hands have not placed the chaplet of virtue and honor, or upon whose heart her love or the affections of a sister or the attachment of a wife have not impressed the indelible lineaments of true greatness." [4]

In September, 1849, Judge Longstreet left Georgia for Oxford, Mississippi, to take over the presidency of the State University. So impressed was he with the promise of his new location that he persuaded Lamar to follow him in November to begin the practice of law in that city, the latter making the journey in a carriage with his wife and infant daughter, followed by wagons which transported the slaves and household effects. Oxford, at this time, was a rapidly growing town and was the county seat of one of the most fertile sections of the State. Lamar's situation in his new surroundings is well pictured in a letter of May 14th, 1850, addressed to Mr. Chappell, a cousin who had married his youngest and favorite aunt, and with whom he had studied and begun the practice of the law. "This," he said, "is a magnificent country for planters. There are men here who left Newton County [Georgia] poor and in debt eight and ten years ago, who now have a good plantation and fifteen to twenty hands, and are buying more every year.... There will be, a month or two hence, an election of two additional tutors for this university; and as the duties of one of them will not be so onerous as to draw my attention from my profession, I shall apply for it. My motive for this step is to provide myself with ready money until I get a practice, but more particularly to extricate my mother from some pecuniary embarrassments in which she has become involved, rather by untoward circumstances than by her own mismanagement.... It is my duty, and it will be my pleasure, to avail myself of this opportunity to relieve a mother whose whole widowhood has been a history of self-sacrifices for her children." [5]

Oxford in Mississippi had much in common with Oxford, Georgia. Essentially a university town, it had a high grade of citizenry, among whom were several of the trustees of the institution, including the President of the Board, Hon. Jacob Thompson, subsequently the Secretary of the Interior in Buchanan's Cabinet. Moreover, the Branhams (Mrs. Branham was Longstreet's other daughter) had moved to Lafayette County, in which Oxford was situated, early in 1850, and the whole family connection was very happy together. President Longstreet was a most excellent business man and always he made considerable money over and above his salary as executive of the universities over which he presided. Indeed, after the devastation of the Civil War with all of the economic loss that it entailed, Judge Longstreet, at his death in 1870 had so far recouped his fortunes that he left an estate appraised at considerably over fifty thousand dollars, half of which was in cash. In their new environment never was there a more harmonious family circle, and according to all accounts they were forever finding some excuse for being together in the same house.[6]

For several months before Judge Longstreet's arrival, the University of Mississippi had been getting into a more and more deplorable state, due to the fact that it had been without an administrative head, the former president having resigned on account of ill health. All discipline, apparently, had disappeared and, as one of the professors who himself was subsequently president, later wrote, "infidelity [sic] had amazingly increased."[7] Mr. Edward Mayes, also at one time president of the institution, doubted that there had ever been a student body so disorderly and turbulent; in morals and intellectual development, said he, the students were idle, uncultivated, and ungovernable. Their favorite sport, if one may judge by contemporary accounts, was the imbibing of an excess of liquor bought from the cotton wagons that rolled toward Memphis.[8] All of this Judge Longstreet, with the young and popular Lamar as his chief lieutenant, soon remedied, and he had been at Oxford only a short time before the size of the student body was tripled. The physical plant and equipment he had found upon his arrival to be excellent, perhaps the best in the far South at that time.

It is certain, however, that during this first period of residence in Mississippi Lamar was never quite satisfied. A series of letters recently discovered in the walls of the old dwelling in Covington, Georgia, owned at this time by his college chum, Mr. Robert G. Harper (later to be occupied for a short period by Lamar himself) are illuminating because of the frankness and intimacy of their writing. Under date of December 20th, 1850, he was writing of his teaching at the University.[9] Mathematics, he felt sure, would never supplant his love for the law, and as a subject it left much to be desired: "All that is required for its complete mastery is close, *minute* and sustained study; and this *any one* can give. I have very serious doubts about the beneficial effects upon the mind which its advocates claim for it. It gives the mind *habits* of close and consecutive study, it is true, but I doubt very much whether the *kind* of study for which it prepares the mind will avail on anything outside of mathematical problems. It is said that this science gives habits of connected and methodical reasoning. It may be a great accomplishment, that of putting truths all in a row 'each holding to the skirts of the other'—but in my opinion if Newton's *thoughts* had been compelled to go through the process which is now employed in the *demonstration* of his binomial theorem the world would never have heard of its discovery."

This letter is illuminating, too, as explanatory of the frequency with which throughout Lamar's life one encounters references to the taste and neatness of his dress. "Having relieved myself of the peril of losing your friendship [Harper had threatened this if he allowed mathematics to crowd out his interest in the law] I must express my delight at your conversion to my views of dress. I do 'wear good clothes' and keep them good—my linen always pure white—my boots spotless and my coat and pants strangers either to lint or motes of dust. The importance of clothes has not been appreciated. Upon this subject I could write you a full sheet....If you wish to pursue the subject, I advise you to read *Sartor Resartus* by Carlyle. It may not interest you as much as *Chitty on Pleading*, but you will nevertheless find it an entertaining volume. You will learn that there are more things in clothes than have been dreamt of in your philosophy. The grand proposition of the

work is that 'Man's earthly interests are all hooked and buttoned together, and held up by clothes'—that 'Society is founded
upon cloth.' Do not be disgusted with his style. Read on...
and you will be delighted with Carlyle, notwithstanding 'the
dislocated joints of his spavined sentences.'" Incidentally this
letter reveals Lamar as a disciple of Carlyle at a time when,
even among professedly literary men, he was hardly more
than a name in America.

There is significant mention, too, of "our little scheme" (a
previously discussed plan for Lamar to return with his family to
Georgia where he and Harper might form a partnership in the
law at Covington). Harper, so they had planned, was to push
to successful conclusion his suit for the hand of a certain young
lady, and both couples would reside, at least for a time, in the
same house (the one which—recently torn down—yielded from
its walls the correspondence which is being quoted). Harper,
however, had grown despondent concerning the success of his
suit. "Now my last and strongest argument," wrote Lamar—
"Stand firm in your tracks lest ye be upset at the first shout:
If you will get her in love with you and marry her, I *promise*
as soon as you inform me of the engagement *to return to
Georgia and practice law with you for the balance of my life!*"
Henceforth, a great part of each of the long letters that passed
between the two was devoted to plans for their future legal
partnership, and in a letter of March 8th, 1851, Lamar was
assuring his friend that "my return to Georgia you may now
regard as a *fixed fact*." [10] He asked, too, that Harper recommend a number of legal books for purchase, remarking that he
had one hundred dollars immediately available for such a purpose and that he desired to have the books sent direct to Covington to escape the wear and tear incident to transporting them
from Mississippi.

It would be almost eighteen months, however, before Lamar's
dream of a return to Georgia could be realized. In the meantime
his hands were full with his duties as Adjunct Professor of
Mathematics and with his growing legal practice outside the

academic walls. And all unexpectedly, in the autumn of 1851, the opportunity presented which started him on the road to fame—this when he was called upon, almost impromptu, to defend the States' Rights principle against that able politician, United States Senator Foote.

The circumstances leading up to the debate should be briefly recalled. The immediate occasion was the matter of the admission of the State of California with an anti-slavery constitution and, as the representatives of the South claimed, in a highly irregular and dishonest manner. From the inception of the Federal Government the jealousies and rivalries between the North and the South had been extremely bitter. This natural rivalry was kept alive and augmented through the years of the early nineteenth century by the question of the formation of new States and their provisions relative to slavery. In the first place, the mere admission of a State, North or South, necessarily increased the power of the section to which it was added; hence it had long been an accepted principle that States should be formed and admitted in pairs for the sake of a balance of power and influence in the Federal Government.

In April, 1849, General Bennett Riley, exercising with the authority of the President his prerogatives as Military Governor of the newly acquired province of California, called a convention for the purpose of framing a constitution. This was put into effect and on the 13th of October the constitution was adopted, with a drastic anti-slavery provision, and was subsequently ratified by a vote of the people. When in December the government had been formed in accordance with the requirements of the constitution, and application was made for admission as a State, the question inevitably arose as to the Missouri Compromise which provided that all territory should be slave below the parallel of 36 degrees and 30 minutes. The measure introduced before the Senate to the effect that this line should continue to the Pacific was defeated by a vote of thirty-two to twenty-four, the votes being cast strictly along sectional lines except that two Senators—one from Missouri and the other from Kentucky—voted with the "nays" from the North.

As is commonly known, the North—through superior numbers—had always controlled the House of Representatives, while in the Senate, through the custom of admitting states in pairs, there had been preserved a balance of strength between the two sections. The Southerners realized that the admission of California as a Free State would give the North control of both Houses and virtually turn over to their opponents the government of the United States. Moreover, Southern leaders did not believe that there were legal grounds for the admission of California. They freely admitted that any new State had the unquestioned right to determine the nature of the constitution under which its citizens were to live, and hence to determine whether their commonwealth should be free or slave. They held, however, that there were not enough citizens of the United States in the proposed State to fulfill the requirements for admission, and they claimed that the population, such as it was, was largely composed of Mexicans and Spaniards who had not been enfranchised. Again, they believed that the federal troops, which since the Mexican War had remained in the territory, had taken an unlawful and unconstitutional interest in the formation of the new government. Outgrowths of the controversy were the "Compromise Measures of 1850" which provided that California was to be admitted as a Free State; in the remainder of the territories the matter of slavery was to be determined by a vote of the settlers themselves; considerable land should be purchased from Texas and added to New Mexico; the domestic slave trade (though not the possession of slaves) in the District of Columbia was to cease, with the promise that nowhere else would there be any interference with the established institution of domestic slavery; and, as a decided concession to the South, a fugitive slave law more stringent than the one of 1793 was enacted. However, as the preceding fugitive slave law had been practically nullified by the legislatures of the Northern States, the South had no confidence in the new law, and felt that the

Compromise of 1850 had been, as a whole, greatly to the harm of their section.

On March 5th, 1850, the legislature of the State of Mississippi adopted a series of resolutions to the effect that the government, in its action relative to California, had espoused the cause of the abolitionists, and that the admission of California, under the circumstances, was a fraud and a wrong to the Southern people. Moreover, the resolutions directed that the Representatives and Senators from Mississippi exert their full power and exhaust all constitutional means to defeat the admission of the State.[11]

Senator Foote, although he had joined with Senator Davis and the four Representatives from Mississippi in asking instructions from the legislature, disregarded the resolutions and, influenced by the Compromise of 1850, voted for the admission of California. As a result an extra session of the legislature was called, at which the action of Mr. Davis and the Representatives was approved, but it was declared that "this legislature does not consider the interests of the State of Mississippi committed to his [Senator Foote's] charge safe in his keeping."[12] He, however, stood his ground, and, refusing to resign, gathered about himself the Union party in the State, this composed largely of the old Whigs augmented by a considerable body of Democrats. Senator Foote was put forward as their candidate for governor, opposing ex-Governor Quitman as the representative of the States' Rights party. In the election of delegates to a convention which had been called for November, 1851, to consider the problems confronting the State, particularly in reference to Congressional legislation, the Union party was victorious, as a result of which Mr. Quitman withdrew his candidacy, and Mr. Davis was prevailed upon to resign his seat in the Senate to run in the gubernatorial election in his stead. He, however, was able to make only a limited canvass, due to the serious condition of his health, and was defeated in the ensuing election by a majority of less than one thousand.

It was during this campaign that Lamar met Senator Foote in joint debate. A committee of States' Rights Democrats had waited upon the young professor, whose gifts as a speaker were coming to be remarked upon outside of academic circles, and requested that he answer Mr. Foote when the latter came to Oxford. Only twenty-six years of age, untried and new to the political life of his day, and given only a few hours to prepare himself for the encounter, Lamar accepted the invitation only because the party was without a champion, and he felt that he must take up the standard at the solicitation of his friends. That he could sustain himself in the face of Senator Foote's brilliant forensic ability that had driven John A. Quitman from the canvass, was hardly to be expected; but the University community knew its man and was solidly behind him in his support of Jefferson Davis.[13] On the appointed day the little town of Oxford was jammed with several thousands of Foote men and Whigs who openly proclaimed that the eloquence and wit of their champion would humble the young professor who had not even passed his middle twenties. When Lamar arose to answer the eloquent Foote, who had dwelt with patriotic fervor on the benefits that the South would derive from the Compromise of 1850, there was a subdued note of apprehension even among his closest associates. This, however, was soon dispelled, for Lamar's magnificent presence and his self-confident, modest, and dignified bearing, inspired confidence.

This speech it was, preserved to us only in a few pages of manuscript, that laid the foundation for his fame as an orator and started him upon his political career. Speaking for the most part extemporaneously, he deprecated his own ability and felt his incompetency to meet a tried and able foe who had proved his mettle in numerous campaigns before the people of the State and before the Senate of the United States. But "the gentleman came not only equipped with his own great abilities, native and acquired, but also panoplied in the armor furnished to him by his Northern allies in the battle against the South recently fought at the capital and now renewed before his constituents." Nevertheless, the speaker "did not consider himself at liberty to consult his own reputation or interests. The State was entitled to all that he was, be it little or much; and have it she should, whether her summons is to the lecture room, the hustings, the field, or the gibbet, if it be treason to obey her call against the Senator's particular friends, Clay, Cass, and Webster—*par nobile fratrum*." Ably reviewing the history of the controversy Lamar continued with an exposition of the South's claims as predicated upon the Constitution of the nation.[14]

There is no reason to question contemporary records which picture the debate as a remarkable triumph for the young orator, for his forensic ability had been notable in his college days, and subsequently—when he had come to loom in the national picture—he was without a superior in a period conspicuous for the eloquence of its public men. With the termination of the contest, the University "students bore him away upon their shoulders," and the populace of Oxford realized that in their midst was a figure destined for a brilliant career. Judge C. P. Smith, of the High Court of Errors and Appeals, heard the debate and the next day he was relating in Jackson, to a somewhat incredulous audience, the story of Lamar's triumph.[15]

It is one of the paradoxes of Lamar's life that the debate under discussion had as its central point the question of the authority of legislative instructions. So far as the records show he never again met Mr. Foote on the platform. The latter was facing the crisis of a distinguished career, and thereafter his influence was to fade until he dropped from the picture even in State politics. Some thirty years later Lamar was to face precisely the same question at the flood-tide of his own political fortunes. How he met that crisis, and its influence upon his own subsequent career and the course of history, is today a part of the nation's record.

FROM LEGISLATURE TO CONGRESS

MEANWHILE Lamar had in no sense given over his plans to return to Georgia. "I have not heard from the Board of Trustees yet," he wrote to his friend Harper in a letter dated early in February, 1852.[1] "You cannot be more anxious than I am that my return to Georgia should be a speedy one, for I fully appreciate the importance of my being at once in the profession; and I lament that I am not master of my own actions. In going to Georgia, I shall have quite a painful duty to perform. The contemplated separation of my wife from her parents even now begins to wring all their hearts. But my wife is resolute, now that she has given her consent to return with me to Georgia. I shall leave some pleasant acquaintances here who have treated me with great cordiality and respect; and I shall leave no enemies that I know of. I shall return to Covington where I have (I hope) some warm friends, *and some enemies also, equally warm.*"

One paragraph in this letter is especially interesting in view of the close association of Lamar's subsequent career with the history of Mississippi. "I could get rich out here at what I am doing," he wrote, "but I don't care about it. The truth is I have no Mississippi ambition. It would not be hard to get to Congress from this district, but all my patriotism and ambition (these are synonymous words now, are they not?) is in Georgia. It is not only my native State but it is the home of most all that is dear to my heart. There is one circumstance which alone is sufficient to endear me to Georgia above all other places: in her bosom rests the sacred dust of my honored father whose blood, whose name, whose very temperament, whose everything (save his shining virtues and surprising genius) I have inherited. Such things have a greater influence on my actions than on those of most men. I am very forcibly struck, in reading the history of England, with the first question which William, Prince of Orange, asked of the ambassador sent from his own dear native Holland to congratulate him upon his glorious elevation to the throne of England. 'Well,' said he, 'and what do our friends at home say now?' My heart has often had the feeling which prompted that question. When I deliver a speech that elicits applause and praise, my first thought is: 'What of it, what good does it do? Bob will not hear of it, my *mother* knows nothing about it, none of my *Georgia friends* will know of it.' Often when I write anything, the thought arises in my mind: 'Bob would like this idea, or Bob would be pleased with this expression.' All that is good in me is for Georgia and my friends in Georgia. So long have I felt identified with you in all my aims and efforts that I cannot shake off the habits of thinking and writing and speaking with reference to what I suppose would please you. So you see, my friend, I can hardly do without you."

Too, the intensely sectional character of Lamar's views during the period of his young manhood are strikingly revealed in this letter. "Well," he inquired of Harper who was a Constitutional-Unionist, "how do you stand upon the question of your party sending delegates to the Democratic convention at Baltimore? Against it, I hope.... It is high time for your party to show its Southern spirit by standing aloof from all conventions with free-soilers, anti-slavery men, and enemies of the South.... My party has quit its principles and is begging to get admission into a National party which we denounced as thoroughly corrupted on the slavery question. I cannot leave it; but I will leave politics if *your* party will make amends for its past misconduct by repudiating all parties that will not repudiate free-soilers."

In the intimacy of Lamar's correspondence with Harper, the ordinary affairs of his life seem vividly realistic. "I am somewhat embarrassed as to what disposition I shall make of my negroes," he wrote of one of his problems. "I have fifteen and will have no place for them when I get to Georgia. A great many of them are young, too. Some lawyers get rich out here in this way. A firm invests all its surplus in negroes and hires a farm till they can buy one; and all they make goes to stocking their farm. Old Roger Barton told me that many fortunes are made in this way. He says it gives them a nest egg and makes them economical and industrious and is a source of enjoyment and recreation. He says, however, that 'lawyers make damn poor farmers though,' but the property is there at least supporting itself, and accumulating."

Six months after the writing of this letter, in the summer of 1852, Lamar—having wrung from the trustees of the University a grudging acceptance of his resignation—returned with his family to Georgia and entered upon the practice of law in partnership with Harper at Covington.

His short stay in Mississippi, however, had been fruitful of a number of influences that were to be lifelong with him. Probably the most notable of the friendships begun at this time was with the Hon. Jacob Thompson, then a member of Congress as well as a trustee of the University. Some thirty-five years later, at the death of Mr. Thompson, Lamar was to write: "He was one of the few men whose presence in this world invested my own life with much of its own interest. I first met him in 1849. I was then a youth of twenty-four years of age, while he was near the zenith of his high honors and intellectual powers. I had then, as I am now aware, many faults of high temper and impatient aspirations; but he was on all occasions kind, considerate, and reserved. My first nomination to Congress was due largely to Mr. Thompson's influence, openly exerted in my behalf against very distinguished and powerful men in the district. From that time to the day of his death our friendship, personal and political, has been unbroken." [2]

In the practice of law at Covington Lamar was from the first successful. Within hardly more than a year after he had established residence there, he had become so well known that, while in Newton County the Whigs held a large majority and were in the habit of controlling the election, he was elected to the legislature as a Democrat. Here he quickly came to the front. A contemporary gives a vivid account of his first speech in the

43

assembly.[3] It seems that the Whigs had mustered enough votes to defeat the motion to suspend the rules in order that the immediate election of a United States Senator might take place. "The next day, on a motion to reconsider," says Mr. W. B. Hill, an eyewitness, "Mr. Lamar made his first speech. He was then young, not more than twenty-seven, with a handsome face, a full head of dark hair, brilliant eyes, in figure rather below the medium of height, handsomely dressed, with fine musical voice. He at once attracted the attention of the House. In a short speech of not more than thirty minutes he captured the whole assembly. I remember how he scathed the motives of those who would thus seek to defeat an election that under the law and constitution had devolved upon the General Assembly.

"Such an excitement as was produced by his speech I never saw in that body. When he finished no one sought to reply. A vote was taken, and a large majority reconsidered the action of the House of the preceding day, and the resolution passed with almost a unanimous vote. His speech was a remarkable exhibition of the power of the orator and logician, and his appeal to his opponents to step manfully and patriotically forward to discharge their duty was so overwhelming that all party spirit was subdued, even in the breast of the most bitter partisan, and none even ventured a reply."

"Lucius Lamar," in the florid words of another contemporary, "is of over-endowed brain and nerve power, is charged as if by a galvanic battery in all his physical and mental composition when called forth to make intellectual effort....Disappointment may await, but its augurs have no terror for the brave heart and buoyant hopes of this young man, eloquent, who comes heralded by parental greatness and powerful family prestige." [4]

Lamar's letters of this period (these chiefly to Harper when one or the other was away on business or in Milledgeville, the State capital, serving in the legislature) are mainly concerned with the routine affairs of legal cases and State politics.[5] Then in the fall of 1853, when the professional outlook for the budding legal firm seemed most assured, Harper (who had just received the nomination of his party for promotion from the House to the Senate) was stricken with tuberculosis and was forced to surrender—permanently, it seemed probable—the practice of law. With the severing of the tie that had been the determining factor in his move to Covington, and realizing that that little town offered small scope for a distinguished legal career, Lamar was faced with the necessity of making other plans for his future.

A letter of December 3rd, and addressed to Harper from the hall of the House of Representatives, shows something of the problems with which he was faced.[6] "My own designs for the future are unformed," he wrote, "and I am positively ignorant of what I shall do. Mr. Chappell [Lamar's uncle by marriage, it will be recalled, and a prominent attorney of Macon] still urges his proposition but there are some difficulties in the way of that. I have also had a proposition from Thornton of Columbus. He is a fine fellow and a rising man, but I am pretty certain that I shall decline his offer....I am more favorable to the Texas trip than I have ever been before [President Mirabeau Lamar had been urging that he throw in his lot with the Lone Star State]. But I cannot tell; I am surrounded with difficulties on every side, not the least of which is the absence and approaching confinement of my wife....Can you not come to Milledgeville this winter? I would rather see you than any *man* in the world—mind, I say *man*; there is a little lady and girl [Fannie, Lamar's eldest daughter] in Mississippi that I want to see fully as much."

There were minute directions, too, in respect to his house and other property which he wished Harper to look after if his health permitted, and there was considerable gossip about affairs at the capital. "I have made some very pleasant acquaintances here—Ward and Anderson of Chatham are splendid men," he wrote. "Old Latham is here and has 'let off' on one or two occasions. He is emphatically *Vox et nihil praeterea*. Tom Hardeman has made some *mean, very* mean speeches. Jim Lyons never opens his mouth. I gave [Alexander] Stephens your letter. He is a great friend of yours, says he never formed a

45

stronger attachment for a man than he did for you. He is a
very courteous and talented gentleman. In consequence of our
being...on different sides in politics we have not been much
together but we are perfectly friendly; and I have heard of his
paying a very high compliment to a speech that I made....I
have made very few speeches—and they were extempore....
Since I wrote the last line I have stopped and made a *rip-snorting*
speech. If I had you here I would distinguish myself—but without my partner I never can do anything." "I write this amid
noise and confusion," he added in an amusing postscript. "The
new counties are running over everything. I have tried to
strangle them in committee, but I shall have to fight them in the
House."

Eventually, Lamar made his decision and in the summer of
1854 he moved to the larger city of Macon where he quickly
built up a respectable practice in the law. He was, however,
finding it difficult to care for and profitably employ his slaves
while he was himself busied with his professional duties; hence
he began a correspondence with Judge Longstreet that led to
his making a hurried journey out to Mississippi where he left his
slaves under the care and direction of the Judge who, in addition to his presidency of the University, had acquired extensive
land holdings. Inevitably, upon his return, he seemed to drift
toward public life. He had hardly become settled in his practice
when he was importuned to run for Congress as a Democrat
from the third Congressional district, wherein Macon was
situated, on the assumption that Mr. Bailey, the incumbent,
would not care to offer himself another time.

The Whigs, formerly powerful in Georgia, had begun to
disintegrate at the death of Henry Clay and by 1854 the Know-
Nothings had become dominant there as in New York and
several other States. When it became evident that Mr. Bailey
would offer himself for nomination again, Lamar—in the interest of party harmony—published an open letter withdrawing
his candidacy and requesting all of his friends to support the
party selection. They, however, refused to cease their efforts,
and when the convention assembled at Forsyth on the 22nd

of May, a bitter fight, led in his behalf by Edward D. Tracey of Bibb county, ensued. The two-thirds rule was adopted, and on the eleventh ballot Lamar received eighteen votes to Bailey's nine, and his supporters claimed that he was nominated. The chair, however, and properly it would seem, ruled that a candidate must secure two-thirds of the convention and not merely of those present and voting. This ruling was supported by a majority vote. As a compromise candidate, James M. Smith was eventually nominated, but lost in the ensuing election. Lamar, however, had swallowed any feelings that he might naturally have had at the outcome of the nominating convention, and had campaigned powerfully in his behalf and against the Know-Nothing party.

In October, 1855, Lamar returned to Mississippi—this time finally—and henceforth his name is as intimately associated with the history of that State as is Calhoun's with South Carolina. Many considerations conspired to cause this final move. In the first place he was a Democrat from principle, and he probably saw no opportunity for a successful public life in a State so largely dominated by other parties. Moreover, there was the natural desire for a reunited family—for he considered the Longstreets as his own—and he was possessed of numerous slaves for whom, as we have seen, he could find no adequate employment in Macon. But he had begun to make for himself a prominent place in the councils of his native .State, and his departure was viewed with chagrin by a number of his friends and political acquaintances. "Your friends," wrote one of his correspondents from Covington, "seem to regret much your resolution again to leave the State, and some of them express this feeling and their surprise in language more forcible than elegant." [7]

Upon his return to Mississippi, Lamar purchased a plantation where, until he was caught in the swirl of political life, he spent two of his happiest years. His land consisted of some eleven hundred acres lying in the bend of the Tallahatchee River, less than a mile from the railroad (now the Illinois Central) which was at the time being put through that section of the State.

The soil was fertile, there was a variety of excellent timber, while the dwelling itself was ample and the servant quarters and outbuildings requisite to plantation life were in good condition. Here Lamar lived the life of the typical Southern gentleman of that period, with either the Branhams or the Longstreets, or both, spending most of the time with him. His crops were excellent and his lands rapidly appreciated in value. Indeed, his fortunes prospered to the extent that he found it possible to build what was in the deep South of that day somewhat of a rarity—an ice-house, the contents of which were shipped in from the North.

"The family," says Lamar's son-in-law, Edward Mayes, "have many traditions about the stay at 'Solitude' [as he called his plantation]. Surrounded by his slaves, to whom he was at once master, guardian, and friend, loved and petted by his women folk and his children, visited by cultivated and attractive friends for days and even weeks, and visiting them in turn; the summers were devoted to the growing of cotton and corn, while the winters were occupied in killing hogs, curing bacon sides and delicious hams, making sausages, and trying out snowy lard."[8]

For Lamar himself, to whom (unlike his first cousin, John Basil Lamar, by this time one of the half dozen largest slave owners in the South) planting was rather an avocation than a career, it was a period of little physical exertion and much study. "Solitude" was a place well adapted for meditation, and at the office set off under the trees some little way from the house he spent a large part of the time in study. Here he kept his extensive library of books of law, history, politics, philosophy, and mathematics. In later years he was often to say that the most rigid and most valuable study of his life took place during this plantation interim, this despite the fact that—as in all of the "first" homes of the day—much of the time was given over to long visits to and from relatives and friends, and to the very considerable social life that existed among the families of the planters.

Despite Lamar's duties on the plantation, and the rigorous course of mental discipline to which he was subjecting himself, he had by no means surrendered the practice of law. Soon after his arrival in Mississippi he had formed a partnership with James L. Autrey and Christopher H. Mott, with whom he had taken offices in the nearby town of Holly Springs. Both of these gentlemen were men of culture and the best education that the South of that period afforded. Mott, with whom he was particularly friendly, was a native of Livingston County, Kentucky, where he was born on June 22nd, 1826. His preparatory education was received at St. Thomas' Hall in Holly Springs, to which town his parents had moved, and he had completed his education at Transylvania University, in Lexington, Kentucky. Shortly after graduation he had followed Colonel Jefferson Davis to the Mexican War as an officer in the First Mississippi Regiment. Autrey, born in 1830 in Jackson, Tennessee, was also educated at St. Thomas' Hall, son of one of that group who gave their lives at the Alamo in the cause of Texan independence.

The firm of Lamar, Mott & Autrey was not dissolved until the outbreak of the Civil War, in which both Mott and Autrey, as well as Lamar's brothers, gave their lives to the cause of the South. Who can deny that much of the South's lack of leadership in the period since Appomattox has derived from the fact that so large a part of her best blood and talent fell in defense of a cause that, once her all too meager armies had been ground away, dissolved like the baseless and unsubstantial fabric of a cloud? Mott was to fall leading his troops at Williamsburg; Autrey at the bloody battle of Murfreesboro, and sometime thereafter the sign of Lamar, Mott, & Autrey, wrenched by the hands of the invader from its fastenings on the door of the office in little Holly Springs, was to be picked up in the Mississippi River as it floated toward the broad bosom of the Gulf.[9]

Meanwhile Robert Harper—his health greatly improved—was corresponding with Lamar in respect to the possibilities offered for a legal career by the rapidly growing city of Memphis, Tennessee, where the latter was frequently called on business. A letter from Lamar, written under date of March 21st, 1857, from Oxford, Mississippi, whence he had gone to appear in federal court, has many points of interest.[10] "Memphis," he wrote Harper, "will probably never equal either Saint Louis or Chicago," but "is nevertheless a great city in every respect and especially in our profession. Until within a few months past, there has been a great demand for good and reliable lawyers there; those which they had being dissipated, gambling, and rather prodigal of client's money." Recently, however, "members of the profession have congregated there from all parts of Tennessee and Mississippi," though "the character of this accession is yet unknown. But no great jurist has made his appearance yet.

"I do not think, however, I can go there to practice my profession," he informed Harper who had suggested a renewal of their partnership in that city. "I do not look to be more than a village lawyer or a country gentleman. I have relinquished all my high hopes of imperishable fame; and I have lost much of the energy and animation of character which I had when with you. When I get through here with business in which I am engaged for a friend [he wrote in semi-humorous vein] I shall return to the Tallahatchee bottom—there to dwell and to wilt in the shadow of my life's failure—and though there is desolation in the thought there is *peace*."

But the peace of "Solitude," begun in 1855, was not long to continue. First the family circle was broken late in 1857 when Judge Longstreet, who had resigned the chancellorship of the University of Mississippi in 1856, was called to the presidency of the University of South Carolina. In his place was chosen Dr. F. A. P. Barnard, subsequently to be the long time president of Columbia College and the father of Columbia University, who was later to say that it was Lamar's influence that had forced his call to the chancellorship and his coöperation that had done most to stamp out the spirit of disorder rampant in the University, and to place that institution on a sound financial basis. Likewise, in the year that Judge Longstreet departed, a movement was started by the influential *Memphis Appeal* (still important as the *Commercial-Appeal*) which had a wide following in Mississippi, to send Lamar to Congress. At the same time he was being pressed to return to the faculty of the University of Mississippi, as professor of metaphysics, at a salary which, for the time, was extremely attractive and under circumstances the most pleasant. But for the present the dream of a return to the academic life did not materialize, for destiny had laid hold of his career. The situation which led to his entrance in the House of Representatives was as follows.

The Whig Know-Nothing coalition had, for the campaign of 1857, chosen the prominent lawyer and orator, James L. Alcorn of Coahoma County, as its candidate from the district. Although still a comparatively young man, he had gained prominence by his services as one of the founders of the State levee system, and he had great popularity among the Delta planters.[11] Because of Alcorn's proven ability and popularity the Democrats had almost lost hope of putting forth a candidate who would have the slightest chance of success. In their quandary a meeting was called at the beautiful home of Jacob Thompson, at Oxford, at that time a popular gathering place for prominent representatives of the Democracy, of which Mr. Thompson, who had earned his position because of his eminent career in Congress and in Buchanan's Cabinet, was the leader in the State. Every prospect for the nomination was canvassed, and since no one with a prospect of winning was found, deep gloom settled upon the gathering. "We must have a man endowed by genius and culture with the qualities that make a politician and a statesman," remarked Thompson, according to the florid account of a contemporary. "He must be gifted with eloquence and of scholarly attainments, he must have no political or moral sins to answer for, he must be ready to meet any question that may arise in an exciting campaign and be able to win the masses over such an adversary as Alcorn."

"Judge Howry," continues the account, "asked 'if we have such a man.' To which Mr. Thompson replied, 'Yes, fill your glasses, gentlemen, and drink to his success when I name him.' The glasses were filled; on every face were gleams of hope shaded with lines of anxiety. Mr. Thompson lifted his glass and threw back his head as he said, 'Here's to L. Q. C. Lamar, our next congressman.' For a moment there was a hush as if every heart had ceased to beat; then, as with one voice, arose the cry, 'Lamar!' 'Lamar!' " [12]

At the time that Lamar was proposed as a candidate for Congress on the Democratic ticket, a number of serious problems were agitating the nation, these chiefly having to do with slavery and the admission of new States. Something of the contemporary political situation must be noted as having important and direct bearing upon his public course.

When the Congress of 1853-54 convened, Stephen A. Douglas had introduced a bill to erect a tremendous block of ungoverned land into the Territory of Nebraska. Immediately, however, he had become aware that the measure could not possibly pass. Consequently he hit upon the idea of separating the territory into two divisions, Kansas and Nebraska (apparently believing that one would affiliate with the Slave States and one with the Free), the dividing line between them to be the fortieth parallel. The revised bill provided that "the said Territory, or any portion of the same, shall be received into the Union with or without slavery, as their constitution may prescribe at the time of their admission," this copied verbatim from the New Mexico and Utah bills of 1850. [13] That there might be no misunderstanding, a further section of the Act stated explicitly that it was the true intent of the law "not to legislate slavery into the Territory or State, nor to exclude it therefrom, but to leave the people thereof perfectly free to form and regulate their domestic institutions in their own way, subject only to the Constitution of the United States." [14]

This bill, written by Stephen A. Douglas and favorably reported by the Committee on Territories of which he was the chairman, left no room for misunderstanding of its provisions. Direct reference was made to the Compromise Measures of 1850 (which, after abolishing the slave trade in the District of Columbia, pledged among other things, that elsewhere there would be no interference with slavery or the internal slave traffic) with the statement that "those measures were intended to have a far more comprehensive and enduring effect than the mere adjustment of the difficulties arising out of the recent acquisition of Mexican territory. They were designed to establish certain great principles which would not only furnish adequate remedies for existing evils, but, in all time to come, avoid the perils of a similar agitation by withdrawing the question of slavery from the halls of Congress and the political arena, and committing it to the arbitrament of those who are immediately interested in it, and alone responsible for its consequences." [15]

We have seen that at the time that the Compromise of 1850 was proposed, it had the bitter opposition of Lamar and many of the Southern leaders who opposed the admission of California as a Free State, and believed that the concessions tendered the South substituted the shadow for the substance. But the election of 1851, fought with the Compromise as the chief issue, had indicated that the majority of the Southern people favored it. Hence the Southern leaders, Lamar among them, had acquiesced, and, accepting its provisions in good faith, had set about carrying out its measures as the settled public policy.

The supporters of the Douglas measure—which had been predicated upon the 1850 Compromise—contended that the latter was intended to apply to all other territories as well as to those acquired from Mexico, whereas the extremely vocal anti-slavery group held that the extension of the Compromise to the land acquired in the Louisiana Purchase was an instance of bad faith on the part of their opponents, chiefly Southern Democrats. When the Douglas bill was introduced for consideration in the Senate, it passed overwhelmingly by a strictly non-sectional vote, only seven States voting against it with three divided. Since at this time the question of the organization of the Kansas territory had arisen, the measure was amended so as to apply to both and henceforth became known as the Kansas-Nebraska bill.

In the interpretation of his measure Douglas, the leader of the Northern Democracy, set forth his doctrine of "squatter sovereignty," to the effect that the settlers in a given territory might, through their elected representatives, determine the status of slavery and, before organization as a State, say whether the territory in question was to be free or slave. He denied the duty, or even the right, of Congress to protect persons or their property (slaves) in a territory against the will of a majority therein, and he held, in effect, that a territorial legislature was stronger than Congress itself and could determine the policy of a territory before it was ready to frame its constitution for statehood.[16] Any such position the representatives of the South bitterly opposed. They claimed that the right to carry their property into the territories was accorded to citizens by the Constitution and consequently they denied that even Congress could interfere with this right. As a result, Douglas and his following of Northern Democrats refused to coöperate with the Southern wing of the party, and, though the Democracy had a majority in both houses of Congress, the attempt to admit Kansas under the provisions of the Lecompton Constitution (which, drawn up at a convention dominated by Southern men, had provided for slavery) failed. Up to this time Douglas had had a considerable following in the South, but henceforth he was to be anathema to a large element in that section.[17] Such a situation made inevitable the division of the party in 1860, with the resultant election of Mr. Lincoln.

The controversy over Kansas was the paramount issue in the election in which Lamar was a candidate for Congress. He was a kinsman, as we have already seen, of Howell Cobb, of Georgia, who was the most influential member of Mr. Buchanan's Cabinet and whose opinion was commonly known to have great weight with the President. Although as Speaker of the House Cobb had been influential in the adoption of the Compromise Measures of 1850, he had afterwards been elected Governor of his State on the Union ticket, and many of the Democrats in the far South, particularly in South Carolina and Mississippi, had come to feel that he was not entirely sympathetic with what were commonly denominated "Southern aims." Lamar was known to be one of Cobb's warm admirers and his personal friend, and since it was believed by many that the latter as well as the President was committed to the support of Walker, the anti-slavery governor of Kansas, it was feared in some quarters in Mississippi that Lamar might espouse the supposed views of the administration and hence not fairly represent the position of his constituents on the questions involved.[18]

As a matter of fact there was no occasion for the people of Mississippi to become exercised, for Lamar himself felt that Governor Walker had exceeded his authority and in actively espousing the cause of the abolitionists had destroyed his usefulness. Moreover, Mr. Buchanan had shown the utmost consideration for the views of the South, and as the year wore on he probably leaned to their position more than common fairness should have allowed—this in view of the fact that the anti-slavery forces in Kansas had definitely succeeded in establishing an ascendancy in numbers. Cobb, too, had been entirely fair to the South and should not have met the bitter opposition that was accorded him by a considerable element in his own section. On the other hand, there is no basis in fact for the contention of Rhodes and some other historians that there was an organized plot, engineered by Secretary of the Interior Thompson and Howell Cobb, to use the influence of the administration in an underhand fashion to turn over, illegally, the government of the state of Kansas to a Southern, pro-slavery minority.[19] These latter are as much in error as were the Mississippians who held that Cobb was conspiring against their interests.

Despite this opposition the candidacy of Lamar advanced unimpeded. In June, 1857, at a meeting in Oxford of the Democrats of Lafayette County, he introduced resolutions condemning Walker's abolitionist affiliations and his course in Kansas, and delivered what was described as a powerful speech in support of his resolutions. These were adopted, and Lamar received the nomination from his district for the Lower House of the State legislature. He was never to serve in this body, however, for when the Democratic Congressional nominating convention assembled in Holly Spring in July of the same year, his name, along with a number of others, was placed before the convention, and on the sixteenth ballot he received the nomination by acclamation.

It is recalled that Lamar's plantation, "Solitude," was near Holly Springs where he had his law offices and where the nominating convention had been held. He was to have a very real fondness for the little town. Years later, in 1879, on the occasion of a visit to the place, he said that the first political speech he "ever made which attracted general public attention in Mississippi" he made there. "Near twenty years ago," he remarked, "I was nominated as a candidate for Congress by a convention assembled here, and I attribute that result largely to the manifestation of local attachment by the people here. What I said upon that occasion has long since passed from my memory, but the kindness and support which I then received and have ever since received from you I never can forget." [20]

Lamar was no sooner nominated than he set about arranging a speaking tour of all of the communities in the district from which he was to run. He seems to have made an excellent impression wherever he appeared. "I must write you what I have heard at Jackson," wrote Mr. Thomas Walton on the 25th of September. "I only heard what convinced me that you have much to do to sustain your reputation. Every man was asking about you, every man remarking that Mr. Alcorn...would be most egregiously disappointed if he expected an easy passage through this campaign, for that you were going to prove a more unmanageable character than any other he could have found in the State." Moreover, "they all talk of what you are going to do for the credit of the State when you reach Washington," and it is clear that "you have more reputation than any other man in the State, considering that you have never been here and that it is all built on hearsay." [21]

Under the date of August 17th, the month following his nomination as the Democratic candidate for Congress, Lamar received from his brother, Thompson Bird Lamar, a letter that is remarkable for the fairness of its views on national questions and for the sageness of its advice. In reading this letter from a young man hardly thirty years of age, one is again impressed with the loss that the South was to suffer in the Civil War which swept him away as it did many others as able. "I am afraid," he wrote among other things, "that if you are elected this time you will not be able to hold your seat—that is, if Jeff [Lamar's youngest brother] writes that which is correct. He says that you will probably assume an attitude of hostility to the administration on account of Governor Walker's position. I shall be sorry if it proves to be the case. Opposition to the administration will necessarily drive you into a sectional party. The Northern Democrats will sustain it and will act with those at the South who do. You will be defeated whenever you have a national Democrat for a competitor."

The question of slavery had already been settled, he thought, in favor of Kansas as a free State, for "all reliable accounts agree in stating that the pro-slavery party are vastly in the minority." Mr. Buchanan was right in refusing to remove Governor Walker who had been too dictatorial, to be sure, but "who had advocated the claims of each and all of the citizens of Kansas to take part in forming the government under which they were to live." [22] It must be admitted that the facts and their interpretation as set forth in this letter are as much better grounded than those of L. Q. C. Lamar at this period as the political views commonly held in Georgia were broader and better balanced than those in Mississippi.

Despite all misgivings Lamar was triumphantly elected and on the 1st of December, 1857, he took his seat in the Thirty-fifth Congress. His first appearance on the floor of the House came on the 13th of January, when he delivered a speech concerned chiefly with the Kansas question. [23] This, his first address, established his importance in the House and gave him, as Mr. S. S. Cox said, a reputation for eloquence, "impetuous, scholarly, and defiant." The press of Mississippi and of the entire South was unanimous in hailing him as a new and eloquent champion. In this speech we find exemplified the first stage in Lamar's political development when his views and sympathies were narrowly and even unpleasantly sectional: "Any proposition which has for its object the advancement and progress of Southern institutions, by equitable means, will always commend itself to my cordial approval. Others may boast of their widely extended patriotism, and their enlarged and comprehensive love of this Union. With me, I confess that the promotion of Southern interests is second in importance only to the preservation of Southern honor." Not only was his outlook strictly sectional, but it was aggressively so: "If I could do so consistently with the honor of my country, I would plant American liberty, with Southern institutions, upon every inch of American soil. [It was many years later that Lamar was to tell Henry Adams "that he never entertained a doubt of the soundness of the Southern system until he found that slavery could not stand a war."] [24]

"Before I consent to any new schemes of territorial acquisition," said Lamar in reference to Republican imperialistic tendencies, "I desire the question of the South's right to extend her institutions into territory already within the Union practically and satisfactorily settled by the legislation of Congress." There was true eloquence in his statement that "these territorial acquisitions, so far, have been to the South like the far-famed fruit which grows upon the shores of the accursed sea: beautiful to sight, but dust and ashes to the lips."

Turning to the constitutional question at the bottom of the Kansas-Nebraska controversy, he discarded the narrowly sectional viewpoint of the earlier part of his speech, and gave a closely reasoned exposition that foreshadowed his later eminence as perhaps the most learned authority of the post Civil War period on the subject of constitutional law.

It has been intimated that Lamar's extreme States' Rights position and his limited sectional interest was strongly influenced by the opinions of his father-in-law, Judge Longstreet. The latter had long since lost all hope of "justice" within the Union and had for his dream the ideal of a separate nation composed of the Southern tier of States. Lamar's own attitude toward the controversy between North and South is nowhere more clearly seen than in a letter which he wrote at this time to Mr. B. S.

Rozell, a prominent citizen of his district. He said, among other things, that he had "never been one of those who run ahead of the issue, who create evils in order that they may destroy them. I have preferred always a peaceable settlement of political questions. But I hold to the old motto: 'In peace prepare for war.' I can see too plainly the clouds that are hanging over us. I can hear and interpret too well the mutterings of an approaching storm. I have measured the extent of that danger which we must, sooner or later, look resistantly in the face." [25]

Already he perceived what many leaders, North and South, did not understand, even in 1861—namely, that the Union would never be dissolved peaceably. "I believe with you," he said, "and with what I trust will soon be the unanimous South, that the refusal of Congress to admit any territory into this Union merely because that territory should present a pro-slavery constitution would be at once and forever an abrogation of political equality. Should that time come, I may deprecate, but would not prevent, the fearful consequences. *Dissolution cannot take place quietly; the vast and complicated machinery of this government cannot be divided without general tumult and, it may be, ruin. When the sun of the Union sets it will go down in blood.*" [26]

On the night of February 5th, or rather at one o'clock on the morning of the next day, occurred an incident in the House that had its amusing as well as its serious aspects. The reference is to the Keitt-Grow fight which took place while the House was deadlocked over whether the President's message on the Lecompton Constitution should be referred for consideration to the standing Democratic committee or to a specially constituted committee of fifteen. As the all-night session wore on, Mr. Grow, a Republican from Pennsylvania, crossed over to the Democratic side to confer with Mr. S. S. Cox. While he was at the desk of the latter, Mr. Quitman of Mississippi requested permission of the House to make an explanation, to which Mr. Grow strenuously objected. This incensed Mr. Keitt of South Carolina who asked him why he did not return to his own side of the House if he wished to object perversely to a reasonable request.

What followed, despite its serious aspects, was most ludicrous. "Mr. Grow replied that it was a free hall, and that he would object from any point in it which he pleased," reported the correspondent of the *New Orleans Picayune*. "The parties exchanged angry words—Keitt calling Grow a black Republican puppy, and the latter retorting that he would not allow any nigger driver to crack whips around his ears....Mr. Keitt caught Grow by the throat, but they were separated by Mr. Reuben Davis, of Mississippi, who had followed Keitt for the purpose of restraining him and keeping the peace. Immediately afterwards, however, he broke loose and again seized Mr. Grow, when the latter (as he himself says) struck him a severe blow, which felled him to the floor. Mr. Keitt denied that he fell from the effects of a blow, but asserts that he stumbled. By this time quite a number of gentlemen (among them were Barksdale of Mississippi, Craige of North Carolina, and others) rushed forward, some probably for the purpose of getting a better sight of 'the ring,' and others to separate the contestants.

"This all occurred on the Democratic side of the chamber; but when the Republicans saw so many rushing toward Grow they thought he was to be badly handled, and quick as thought started *en masse* for the scene of conflict. Potter of Wisconsin, a stout fellow with a fist like an ox, was foremost, and bounded into the fray like a maddened tiger. Just then Barksdale had hold of Grow, with a view of leading him out of the *mêlée*. Potter, mistaking his purpose, planted a 'sockdolager' between Barksdale's eyes, which only had the effect of rousing his grit. ...It was a jolly row, and no bones broken. The Speaker cried in vain for order....It was evident that nobody, unless Keitt, intended to fight in the beginning; but even Lamar of Mississippi, and Parson Owen Lovejoy had a little set-to in the course of the passing gust....Nobody was hurt much, and they had nothing to do but apologize. Gentlemen who got acquainted for the first time in the midst of the 'shindy' shook hands over the mutual assurance that they went into the fight only to prevent a fight, and in half an hour the house was quieter than ever." [27]

That Lamar was not considered as one of the bullies of the House is clear from this notice which says that *even* Lamar entered the fray. The sane and leading position that he had taken upon entrance to the National Legislature is seen in an article of January 25, 1893, published in the *North American Review*: "As a member of the House prior to the Civil War he won considerable notice as a conservative Southern man, eloquent in debate, and a power when fully aroused.... He was always on the alert and fully cognizant of the stirring scenes almost daily enacted in the House. Much of the wrangling disgusted him as puerile and without object. He was a peacemaker oftener than a peacebreaker. As jealous of the rights and claims of the South as other and more boisterous members, his methods were free from much that rendered the more fiery representatives of the oligarchy offensive both as respected manners and language."

During his first session in Congress Lamar was appointed to a number of important committees and, without particular effort on his part, at once assumed the position of a leader. In the Vallandigham-Campbell contest over the seat in the House from the Third District of Ohio he took a prominent part, and it was his aggressiveness as a member of the Committee on Elections (he had drawn up the minority report and secured its acceptance), and his speech before the House on May 22nd, that were chiefly responsible for the seating of the former.[28] Two other of his speeches delivered during his first term in Congress attracted particular attention. The first of these, on the 17th of January, 1859, during the short session of the Thirty-fifth Congress, was in memory of Hon. T. L. Harris of Illinois, deceased.[29] Commonly referred to as "*the* speech of the day," it was widely printed as was no other delivered on that occasion. On the 21st of the next month, in answer to Mr. Stanton, of Ohio, who was demanding a more excessive tariff law which would embody serious discriminations against the less industrialized sections of the country, he demonstrated his scholarly aptitude for presenting the results of the serious research which he had expended on the subject.[30] But it was

61

noteworthy that as compared with most of the Congressional leaders he seldom took the floor, and then only on important occasions.

Citizens throughout Mississippi had hailed with delight Lamar's quick rise to prominence during his first session in Congress. On November 3rd, 1858, appeared a notice in the Jackson *Weekly Mississippi Gazette* to the effect that "the whole State has witnessed with pride the successful Congressional début of this rising young statesman, and a general desire is expressed to hear his views upon the important topics of the day." On that evening he spoke before a joint assembly of both Houses of the State legislature, having come before them at their invitation "irrespective of party." Introduced by the Chief Justice of the Supreme Court he delivered an address which the *Gazette* fulsomely characterized as one "which, in all its parts, we have never heard excelled in earnestness of eloquence, richness of diction, brilliant antithesis, and all the elements which make up a powerful production."

Though Mr. and Mrs. Lamar were without any particular desire to figure prominently in Washington society, their social gifts made them greatly in demand. Years later, Henry Adams was to comment on Lamar's social charm that made him sought after in Washington, London, and Paris society,[31] while Jennie Longstreet had from girlhood been noted for her grace and her wit. The center of the social life of the Southern contingent in Congress was at Brown's Hotel where the Lamars lived, as did their cousin, Representative J. L. M. Curry, of Alabama, and his wife. In the same building, or within a stone's throw, wrote Mrs. Clement C. Clay, wife of the Senator from Alabama, lived, among others, Senators Bell, Slidell, Butler, Benjamin, Mason, and Goode.[32] At the same "mess" with the Lamars, the Currys, and the Clays, she wrote, were "Orr, Shorter, Dowdell, Sandidge and Taylor, of Louisiana, with the young Senator Pugh and his bride, Governor Fitzpatrick and wife,...David Clopton, ...and General and Mrs. Chesnut." "It is safe to say," Mrs. Clay recorded, "that no member of our pleasant circle was more generally valued than that most lovable of men, Lucius

Q. C. Lamar, 'Moody Lamar,' as he was sometimes called; for he was then, as he was always to be, full of dreams and ideals and big warm impulses, with a capacity for the most enduring and strongest of friendships, and a tenderness rarely displayed by men so strong as was he. Mr. Lamar was full of quaint and caressing ways even with his fellow-men, which frank utterance of his own feelings was irresistibly engaging." He was, she thought, the most "affectionately held" of any of the Southerners.[33]

But it is certain that Lamar often yearned for a quieter and more studious life. Essentially a scholar and thinker, the distractions of public life often palled upon him. "Washington is now a most beautiful place," he wrote to his mother-in-law, Mrs. Longstreet, in a letter of May 4th, "and the Capitol Hill is the most splendid and picturesque scene my eye ever rested upon. But I am ready and willing to leave the city forever. The center of my enjoyments is the home where are my wife and children, and I have no wish to wander out from that home in pursuit of any pleasures that the world presents."[34] Moreover, to his wife, in the same letter, he wrote that he had not "made up his mind what to do about running a second time."

The academic life of a professor at the State University held many charms for Lamar who was at this time in active correspondence with the Chancellor, Dr. F. A. P. Barnard, relative to the Professorship of Mental and Moral Philosophy. Most of his friends, however, thought that he would desert his field of greatest usefulness if he quitted public life. Illuminating is a letter from Chancellor Barnard, dated March 25th, 1858. "I had been led, by outgivings of your friends," he wrote, "to believe that you would not persevere in your choice to leave the more conspicuous position in which you are placed for our dull obscurity; and while I felt that the change of your previously understood purpose would be, to myself personally, a severe misfortune, and to the University of Mississippi no slight calamity, yet I could not find it in my conscience to disapprove the determination to which, as I understood the matter, you were likely to come. I have said to you before, and I say to you again, that I believe the country has need of such men as you in precisely such positions as that which you hold, and those to which, in the course of time, I should expect to see you advanced." [35]

Chancellor Barnard, himself a Northern man, was despondent in the face of the problems that faced the nation: "The future is all dark before me, and the spirit of prophecy fails. But the thing which I do know is that...it is a social necessity that we should have a government; and it is a matter of the deepest interest to us all that our government should be in able and honest hands.... Now while I believe that, among the admirers of your genius and intellectual strength, no one of all your friends can take precedence of me, it is not so much that the country might profit by your talents, as that it might reap the benefit of your inflexible rectitude of purpose, that I should delight to see you permanently devoted to public life." [36] He wished Lamar to understand, however, "that the university would be delighted to have his services," and that if he decided to accept the professorship it would be considered a decisive step toward building this institution "into the great university of the Southwest." As it turned out, however, Lamar was not at this time to accept the place that had been proffered him, for in June, 1859, he was unanimously renominated as the Democratic candidate for Congress, and in October was elected without opposition.

On the 11th of November, 1859, Lamar was again requested by the legislature of the State of Mississippi to deliver an address before the joint session of the House and the Senate on the subject of the State's relationship to the nation. Of this address it was reported by the *Vicksburg Whig*, the organ of the opposing party, that it was "the ablest speech, as we have heard stated on all hands, delivered in that hall for years, in defense of Democratic men and Democratic principles."

With the opening of Congress a few weeks later came a bitter struggle over the speakership of the Republican controlled House. The controversy arose in the following manner: In the same year as the Dred Scott decision, a book was published by one, Hinton Rowan Helper, who was born in upland North Carolina but who had spent most of his life in Missouri and California. This pamphlet, entitled *The Impending Crisis of the South; How to Meet It*, was compounded of many elements with the chief ingredient derived from the abolitionist viewpoint. The "facts" (sociological and economic) which it cited were almost all erroneous, as has been pointed out by Channing.[37] It must be said for Helper, however, that he seems sincerely to have believed that slavery was a millstone about the neck of the South. His father had himself owned a few slaves in the little North Carolina mountain town where he lived, but the son evinced the common dislike of the hill people for the wealthy slave-owners of the lowlands, as well as for the Negroes themselves, and this bias seems largely responsible for the most objectionable features of the pamphlet.[38]

A circular that advertised and recommended this indictment of the Southern System had been signed by a number of congressmen, including Mr. Sherman, who was now proposed by the Republicans for the speakership. On the 6th of December, however, Mr. Sherman arose to admit that his name was appended to the circular but to deny that he had any recollection of having signed it. Certainly, said he, he had never read the book, and nothing was further from his purpose than the intention to oppose the rights of Southern citizens. But the Southerners were relentless and eventually they forced the selection of Pennington, of New Jersey, an able man who was a representative of the People's party.

It was on the occasion of this controversy that Lamar made a truly eloquent speech which was vociferously applauded both from the floor and from the galleries, and that solidified his position of influence throughout the South where, already, he had come to be recognized as more than a mere spokesman for Mississippi.[39] After analyzing something of the contents of the Helper pamphlet, and linking its propaganda with John Brown's raid in Virginia, he gave clear expression to what may be termed his pre-Civil War attitude toward the Union: "All

65

that I desire to say, Mr. Clerk, is that, for one, I am no disunionist *per se*. I am devoted to the constitution of this Union; and so long as this Republic is a great tolerant republic, throwing its loving arms around both sections of the country, I, for one, will bestow every talent which God has given me for its promotion and its glory. Sir, if there is one idea touching merely human affairs which gives me more of mental exaltation than another, it is the conception of this grand Republic, this great Union of sovereign States, holding millions of brave, resolute men in peace and order, not by brute force, not by standing armies, indeed by no visible embodiment of law, but by the silent omnipotence of one grand, glorious, thought—the Constitution of the United States. That constitution is the life and soul of this great government. Put out that light, and where is 'that promethean heat which can its light relume'? That is our platform. We stand upon it. We intend to abide by it and maintain it, and we will submit to no persistent violation of its provisions. I do not say it for any purpose of menace, but for the purpose of defining my own position. When it is violated, persistently violated, when its spirit is no longer observed upon this floor, I war upon your government, I am against it. I raise then the banner of secession, and I will fight under it as long as the blood flows and ebbs in my veins."

In passing, Lamar lunged at Thaddeus Stevens, the abolitionist radical who had been particularly obnoxious in his very real malignity toward the South. Calling him out, Lamar pilloried him with the devastating irony that on occasion and at a later day was to make Hoar, Blaine, and Conkling wince. "Great laughter and applause," reads the House record at the point where Lamar concluded his brief remarks upon Mr. Stevens who—as able as any man in Congress and universally feared for his whip-lash tongue—discreetly and unprecedentedly decided to suffer in silence.

With the attention that he was receiving from the Eastern and Northern press, Lamar could not fail to realize the importance on the national scene with which he was coming to be regarded. To Judge Longstreet, at this time president of the

University of South Carolina, he wrote on March 15th: "My position here is a far higher one than I ever expected to attain. The praises which I receive are so extravagant that I sometimes feel it is flattery. The President has sent for me two or three times to consult with me upon his message which he contemplates sending in." Lamar was now, as always, on the very closest terms of love and affection with the old Judge. "I do assure you, though," he wrote, "that *your* opinion of my speech, and your gratification at my success, is the richest and dearest reward of my public life. You never have known how deeply your approval of anything I do sinks into my heart and sweetens my life. I have hardly a hope or a fear that does not connect itself with you. No son ever loved a father more, and no one (except your wife) ever loved, honored, and *tried* to obey you more faithfully." [40]

THE APPROACH OF THE CONFLICT

THE CRISIS that led to the firing on Fort Sumter was rapidly approaching, and the course of events, like a river approaching its rapids, was relentlessly accelerating.

On the 23rd of April, 1860, the national Democratic convention assembled at Charleston, South Carolina, with Lamar as one of the delegates. It was a solemn affair, an assemblage of able men who realized that history was being made and that all boisterousness would be out of place.[1] At first it appeared that the West, with sixty-six votes, would act solidly with Douglas while the South, with fifty-one, would have none of him. At the first testing of strength, however, it was seen that while the Douglas men had a majority of the delegates, California and Oregon would act with the South, thus giving the anti-Douglas men seventeen out of thirty-three States. Almost to a man the Southern delegates felt that Douglas, in his enunciation of his principle of squatter sovereignty, had rendered himself unavailable as the candidate of the Democracy.

On Saturday the convention was unable to agree on matters of policy, and as a consequence adjourned until Monday. On that day the Committee on Platform brought in a majority report which declared, among other things, "that the Government of a Territory by an act of Congress is provisional and temporary; and that during its existence all citizens of the United States have an equal right to settle with all their property in the Territory without their rights, either of person or property, being destroyed or impaired by Congressional or territorial legislation." This resolution differed from the platform of 1856 in that the words, "or territorial legislation" were included and were obviously aimed at Douglas' doctrine of squatter sovereignty. In the bitter fight that ensued, the Douglas platform, or minority report, was adopted by a vote of 165-138, with the balloting strictly along sectional lines.[2]

No sooner had the Douglas platform been declared adopted than the chairman of the Alabama delegation arose and after formally protesting the action of the convention, announced the withdrawal of the delegation from his State. In quick succession Mississippi, Louisiana, South Carolina, Florida, Texas, and Arkansas followed suit. Before the convention assembled on the following day, Georgia had thrown in her lot with the other States of the deep South, and the delegates who had withdrawn had organized themselves and called for another convention to assemble in Richmond on the second Monday in June. With the withdrawal of so many of the delegates, the Charleston Convention made no further attempt to transact business, but dispersed with the understanding that it would reassemble on the 18th of June in Baltimore, requesting, meanwhile, that the various States elect delegates to fill the places of those that had withdrawn.

Just how serious the split was regarded by conservative statesmen is seen in the conversation of Alexander Stephens with a friend shortly after the adjournment of the convention. "Men will be cutting one another's throats in a little while," he said. "In less than twelve months we shall be in a war, and that the bloodiest of history. Men seem to be utterly blinded to the future." "Do you not think that matters may yet be adjusted at Baltimore?" he was asked. "Not the slightest chance of it," was the reply. "The party is split forever. Douglas will not retire from the stand he has taken.... The only hope was at Charleston. If the party could have agreed there, we might carry the election.... If the party would be satisfied with the Cincinnati platform and would cordially nominate Douglas, we should carry the election; but I repeat to you that is impossible." "But why must we have civil war, even if the Republican candidate should be elected?" Stephens was asked. "Because," he replied, "there are not virtue and patriotism and sense enough left in the country to avoid it. Mark me, when I repeat that in less than twelve months we shall be in the midst of a bloody war. What is to become of us then God only knows. The Union will certainly be disrupted." [3]

Lamar had been one of the more conservative of the Southern men at the Charleston convention (where his brother, Thompson Bird, had also been a delegate), and had made a strong speech in favor of a conservative stand; nevertheless, he had withdrawn with the others with whom he had considerable sympathy. Shortly after, he joined with Mr. Davis and a number of other prominent Mississippians in an "Address to the Public," in which it was urged that the bolting delegates forego their proposed meeting in Richmond, and join with the others at Baltimore. His attitude toward these stirring events is to be seen in a letter of May 29th, 1860, to his partner, C. H. Mott. "You will have seen ere this," he said, "that I signed with Jeff Davis the address which advises the return of the delegates to Baltimore. Davis has signed it, and I was determined that his name should not go unsupported by any of the delegation. It was in obedience to his wish that I went to Charleston." That his sympathy, if not his judgment, was with the extreme Southern group is clear: "Their position (whatever may have been the policy of it) is certainly based upon high grounds, and was prompted by the purest devotion to the rights of the South. It deserves the indorsement and approval of the people of Mississippi. I have linked my future with it, for weal or for woe." [4]

Intense as was Lamar's sympathy with the Southern wing of the Democracy, he knew only too well the gravity of the crisis that faced the nation, and he was not without the most intense misgivings. That he quickly came to feel that the actions of the Charleston seceders had been too precipitate and ill-advised is to be inferred from a letter from his cousin, Mr. Justice John A. Campbell, of the Supreme Court of the United States. "I received," said the latter, "your penitential letter of the 7th inst. yesterday. If I had the powers of a Turkish Cadi, I should condemn all the Southern actors in that scene to wear veils for four years. Their faces should not be seen among Democrats. I am not sure but what my sentence would comprise certain bastinadoes for all those from whom something better should have come. In that case, you and your friends, Cable and Jackson, would have carried sore feet for a long time."

Eventually, both wings of the party met in Baltimore on the same date, June 18th. Though the interim had afforded time for reflection, the animosity between the Charleston seceders and the Douglas men flamed brightly as ever. As a result, Virginia led another withdrawal, carrying with her most of the delegates from North Carolina, Tennessee, Kentucky, and Maryland, almost all of them joining with those who had withdrawn from the Charleston Convention and, adopting a platform embodying Southern views, nominated Breckinridge of Kentucky for President and Lane of Oregon for Vice-President.[5] After this second withdrawal, Douglas was nominated for President by the Northern Democracy, and when Senator Fitzpatrick of Alabama refused the second place on the ticket, it went to Herschel V. Johnson, of Georgia. Further to complicate matters, and to assure the election of a Republican President, the remnant of the old-line Whigs and Americans, on the 9th of May, had assembled in Baltimore and choosing for their motto "The Constitution of the country, the union of the States, and the enforcement of the laws," had nominated Bell of Tennessee for President and Everett of Massachusetts for Vice-President.[6]

Meanwhile Lamar was more strongly than ever meditating a retirement from public life to the academic quiet of Oxford. When the trustees of the University, late in June, offered him the chair of ethics and metaphysics, he accepted at once. In the crisis, however, he was not willing to desert his friends; hence he planned to finish the term of Congress for which he had been elected. "Hon. L. Q. C. Lamar, of this county, who takes the chair of Ethics and Metaphysics," said the *Oxford Intelligencer*, in announcing his appointment, "is too well and widely and favorably known, abroad as well as at home, to justify us in pronouncing upon him the eulogium he deserves. It is agreed on all hands that he possesses a peculiar fitness for

71

his chair....Prof. Lamar will serve out his full term as a member of Congress, but this will involve his absence from the University only for the period of three months during the next session." Even those who were nominally his political enemies spoke of his services in terms of strongest commendation, none more so than the *Vicksburg Whig*, the leading opposition paper of the State. "We see it stated," reported that organ, "that Col. Lamar intends resigning his seat in Congress, to accept a position in the University of Mississippi. We sincerely trust that this report is not true.... In our judgment Mr. Lamar is the ablest man in either branch of Congress from this State, and far ahead of the generality of Congressmen from the Southwest. There is hardly a question of governmental policy on which we do not differ materially with him; but, if his side is to have the Congressmen, we at least feel a sort of State pride that such a man as L. Q. C. Lamar is made the recipient of the honors of his party." But he had been caught in the whirlpool and could not withdraw, and many years would pass, and much history would be written before he would again enjoy the quiet of Oxford town.

As the momentous year of 1860 wore through, it became evident that no man from Mississippi, with the possible exception of Jefferson Davis, had laid hold so powerfully upon the affections of the State. "We have just had the largest mass meeting in Columbus ever known in this State," wrote Colonel Young of Waverly, on October 26th, to Judge Longstreet in South Carolina. "Davis spoke in the forenoon. Pettus was to follow in the afternoon, but the country people were so importunate for Lamar that he was forced up immediately after dinner.... The universal opinion was that it was the most statesmanlike speech which had been heard. Pettus spoke at night; then Barksdale, of Jackson. And yet, when so late, the cry burst forth for Lamar; and for one hour and thirty minutes he transported his audience, and covered himself with glory. The Bell men followed and serenaded him. His appeal to them subdued all hearts, and made patriots of partisans.... Saturday we take him to Aberdeen, to speak there. They sent for him to go to Mobile....Lamar is carried away with Columbus, where he was feasted and lionized not a little." [7]

With the election of Mr. Lincoln, the majority of the people of the South were convinced that both Houses of Congress, as well as the executive branch of the government, would be in the hands of their opponents, and they had long since lost hope of a peaceful solution of their problems within the Union. Probably the latter conclusion was correct; certainly the adamantine determination of Lincoln not to yield in the slightest to the desires of the South for an extension of slave territory, and the active desire of many Southern leaders for secession, made futile any hope of compromise. But from this distance it seems clear that at least for two more years the Southerners might have gone on controlling the country, for all estimates agree that the representatives of the South, taken with their active sympathizers among the leaders of other sections, would have had a majority in both Houses of the 37th Congress. [8]

Lamar, it is certain, had become convinced that the only hope for the South and for the preservation of Southern institutions lay in secession from the United States, and the forming of a Southern union. Many years later, in a letter written in 1883 to Mr. William A. West, Lamar set forth the political philosophy that had actuated him at that time. It was not, he pointed out, a conspiracy of individuals. "On the contrary, it was the culmination of a great dynastical struggle, an 'irrepressible conflict' between two antagonistic societies, a culmination which had been foreseen and predicted by the wisest statesmen of the nation....This culmination was a result of the operation of political forces which it was not within the power of any individual man or set of men to prevent or postpone." [9]

It is not to be thought that Lamar espoused the cause of secession against his will and from force of environmental necessity. True, he loved the Union even though his life had been spent largely in the far South at the very center of the disunionist movement. But by 1860 he seems to have lost all hope of what he considered justice within the United States. There is absolutely no basis for the statement of Mr. Blaine, who at another place does Lamar better justice, that "His reason, his faith, his hope, all led him to believe in the necessity of preserving the union of the States; but he persuaded himself that fidelity to a constituency which had honored him, personal ties with friends from whom he could not part, the maintenance of an institution which he was pledged to defend, called upon him to stand with the secession leaders in the revolt of 1861." [10] As a matter of fact, Lamar was bound to his section by the strongest ties of blood and affection, but he had come to feel that the South must inevitably choose between two courses: either she must weakly submit to a denial, within the Union, of the rights that she felt to be guaranteed by the Constitution; or she must withdraw, peaceably if possible, from an association into which the States had entered of their own free will, but membership in which had become no longer practicable.

Meanwhile, Lamar was keeping up a correspondence with his father-in-law, Judge Longstreet, who was finding life very congenial at the University of South Carolina where at last he was situated in an environment where his extreme States' Rights views were commonly applauded. Moreover, in the decade preceding the Civil War, South Carolina demanded that the President of its State University live in what might be termed real magnificence. He was furnished an imposing house, and his salary, together with the income from his already considerable wealth, made it possible for him to do so without embarrassment. In his home, moreover, was evidence that the young Congressman, Lamar, had prospered during the years when he had been practicing law, teaching at the University of Mississippi, and latterly sitting in Congress, for at Mrs. Longstreet's parlor windows hung curtains that originally had been made in Germany for President Buchanan's use in the White House but which, the President having refused them because of their costliness, had been bought by the young Lamar as a present for his mother-in-law.[11]

On the 13th of November, 1860, Lamar wrote to the Judge that "the election of Lincoln had diffused a general feeling of dissatisfaction throughout the State." No longer did he have any hope of a peaceful settlement of the sectional controversies that were agitating the nation. "If South Carolina will only have the courage to go out," he thought, "all will be well. We will have a Southern Republic, or an amended Federal Constitution that will place our institutions beyond all attack in the future." [12]

On the 22nd of November, at the invitation of Governor Pettus, the Mississippi Representatives and Senators, with the exception of Mr. McRae, met in Jackson to consider the proper course to pursue in the emergency, and to discuss the forthcoming Governor's message. Throughout the conference Lamar, despite his belief in the hopelessness of any effective compromise, exerted the full force of his influence for conservative action. The chief question to be decided was whether Mississippi should encourage South Carolina to withdraw immediately from the Union, and herself secede without regard to the actions of the other Southern States, or whether there should be delay with the view to possible steps toward conciliation with the North.

A resolution was framed by Congressman Reuben Davis (the account of the meeting is his), to the effect that "the Governor insert in his message to the Legislature a recommendation that they call a convention for the purpose of seceding the State of Mississippi by separate State action." A vote was taken upon this resolution, "Singleton, Barksdale, and R. Davis voting for, and Jeff Davis, Brown, and Lamar against it. Governor Pettus gave the casting vote in favor of the resolution, and it was adopted, the vote being made unanimous." Next a telegram was read from the Governor of South Carolina requesting advice as to whether the State should pass an ordinance of secession, this to take effect at once, or whether the ordinance, if passed, should become effective on the 4th of March. "A resolution was then introduced by Reuben Davis," as he records, "to the effect that Gov. Pettus should advise the Governor of South Carolina to cause the ordinance to take effect from and after its passage. This resolution was opposed by Jeff Davis, Brown, and Lamar, and supported by Singleton, Barksdale, and R. Davis, Governor Pettus again giving the casting vote in favor of the Resolution." [13]

Thus it is clear the Lamar's counsel and his votes were all for moderation. But when the die had been cast, no one was more eloquent or insistent in advising instant and vigorous action. The day after the conference in Jackson, Lamar delivered an address in the town of Brandon. "His speech was an earnest, dispassionate appeal to the people of the South to arouse from their lethargy, and arm for resisting Black Republican domination," as a local paper reported. "He declared that secession was the only remedy now left for the Southern people to save themselves from a doom similar to that of the former white people of San Domingo. He submitted a plan by which the Southern States, or so many of them as may choose to do so, might secede from the Union in a few days' time, and resume all the functions of government." The plan was for them to "adopt the old constitution, without the crossing of a 't' or the dotting of an 'i'; adopt the present Federal laws; elect new electors, to choose a President and Vice President; and, in short, to readopt for the United States South all the laws, rules, and regulations now prevailing for the United States. This could all be done in a very few days, and there would be no anarchy, no bloodshed, or anything extraordinary to disturb the peace and quiet of the people." [14]

When the legislature assembled in special session, Governor Pettus addressed to that body a message calling for secession. The response was a call for a convention to assemble on the 7th of January following, and the passage of a resolution to the effect that "secession by the aggrieved States, for their grievances, is the remedy."

On the 3rd of December assembled the eventful Thirty-sixth Congress with all of the Representatives and Senators

Congressman Lucius Q. C. Lamar

from Mississippi present. Every attempt at arbitration was fruitless, and the individuals and delegations from the Southern States
began to withdraw. A contemporary who was himself a member of Congress from the North, in describing the withdrawal
of the Southerners, wrote of Lamar's "rare oratorical and dia-
lectical skill," and remarked that "for impetuous debate, there
was Lamar, of Mississippi, scholarly and defiant." [15] The description of Lamar's abilities in debate was just and accurate,
but as a matter of fact he resigned his seat without taking the
floor. Mr. Blaine, who was certainly not prejudiced in favor of
any Southerner, does Lamar and his fellow Representatives
from Mississippi fine justice in respect to the mode of their
retirement. "There was no defiance, no indulgence in bravado,"
he wrote. "The members from Mississippi 'regretted the necessity' which impelled their State to the course adopted, but
declared that it met 'their unqualified approval.' The card was
no doubt written by Mr. L. Q. C. Lamar, and accurately described his emotions. He stood firmly by his State in accordance with the political creed in which he had been reared,
but looked back with regret to the Union whose destiny he
had wished to share and under the protection of whose broader
nationality he had hoped to live and die." [16]

The motives for Lamar's action have been indicated by quotations from his letters and speeches. The reasons that impelled
all of the Southern leaders to go with their States had much
in common, and for no one of them are the motives hard to
discover. The position taken by Thomas R. R. Cobb, Lamar's
kinsman, is comprehensible as he related it in a meeting of the
legislature of the State of Georgia on November 12, 1860.
On the night of November 6th, said he, "I called my wife
and little ones together around my family altar, and together
we prayed to God to stay the wrath of our oppressors, and
preserve the Union of our fathers.... And when the telegraph
announced to me that the voice of the North proclaimed at
the ballot-box that I should be a slave, I heard in the same
sound the voice of my God speaking through His Providence,
and saying to His child, 'Be free. Be free.'" It is not difficult

to understand Lee's motive for action, as he stated it in a letter to his cousin, Lieutenant Robert Jones, of the United States Army: "I have been unable to make up my mind to raise my hand against my native State, my relatives, my children & my home," reasons which caused him to surrender his commission in the army of the United States rather than accept the chief command of the forces destined to coerce Virginia back into the Union. [17]

Lamar left Washington on the 12th for the purpose of canvassing the State in the interest of the coming secession convention. His state of mind is revealed in a letter written to Judge Longstreet on the day before he left Washington: "We are living in eventful times, and the only pleasure that I have among the tremendous responsibilities upon me is the thought of those I love.... I send you a letter of mine by to-day's mail. You will doubtless deem it too subdued in tone. What I know will happen has taken all the 'highfaluting' out of me. God bless you, my darling old father." [18]

The letter to which Lamar refers was one dated December 10th, addressed to Hon. P. F. Liddell, of Carrollton, Mississippi, and widely published. In it is outlined in detail the plan (to which brief reference has already been made) for a Southern Union. Of it, the *Vicksburg Whig*, one of the leading papers of the State, said: "Mr. Lamar advances a plan for the formation of a Southern Confederacy. It is the first which has yet been promulgated having the least spark of practicability about it." Nothing is more evident than that Lamar, after hesitatingly reaching the conclusion that there could be no peace within the Union, had sorrowfully set himself the task of constructively helping to build what he hoped would be a new nation.

Just before he left the Capital, Lamar was the witness of a dramatic incident that he was never to forget. To it he often referred in his later speeches, notably in an address before the United States Senate on January 24th, 1878. [19] "I remember," he said, "hearing on this floor the then distinguished Senator from New York (Mr. Seward) declare that the power had departed from the South; that the scepter was now taken from her hand; and that henceforth the great North, stronger in population and in the roll of sovereign States, would grasp the power of government and become responsible for its administration. I am aware that I listened to him with impatience, and, perhaps, with prejudice. For it seemed to me that he spoke in a spirit of exultation that scarcely realized the magnitude of the task about to devolve upon him and his associates. It struck me that he spoke in a spirit far removed from that sadness and solemnity which I think always weighs upon the mind and heart of a truly great man in the presence of a grave crisis of national life.

"I remember the answer that was made to him by a South Carolina Senator, Governor Hammond....He was surrounded by a circle of Southern statesmen whom no future generation will see surpassed in ability or purity, be the glory of our growth, as I trust it will be, unrivaled in the history of nations. ...Among these...the Senator from South Carolina...addressed to his Northern associates on this floor the words which I have never seen in print from that day to this, but which I can never forget; and which, if the Senate will permit me, I will here repeat: 'Sir, what the Senator says is true. The power has passed from our hands into yours; but do not forget it, it cannot be forgotten, it is written upon the brightest page of history, that we, the slaveholders of the South, took our country in her infancy, and, after ruling her for near sixty out of the seventy years of her existence, we return her to you without a spot upon her honor, matchless in her splendor, incalculable in her power, the pride and admiration of the world. Time will show what you will do with her, but no time can dim our glory or diminish your responsibility."

Back in Mississippi, Lamar was elected as one of the two delegates from Lafayette County to sit in the State convention that had been called for the 7th of January, 1861. How he, a young man but thirty-five years of age, was regarded by the other members of the convention, which contained all of the ablest men of the State, is to be seen in the words of Thomas

H. Woods, who himself served in that body. Among others, he said, there was Lamar, "towering amid his fellows in all positions." [20] At the assembling of the convention, William S. Barry, of Lowndes County, was formally elected President and an organization was immediately effected. Thereupon Lamar offered a resolution calling for the appointment by President Barry of a committee of fifteen "with the instructions to prepare and report as speedily as possible an ordinance providing for the withdrawal of the State of Mississippi from the present Federal Union, with a view to the establishment of a new Confederacy to be composed of the seceding States." The resolution was adopted and Lamar was appointed chairman of the committee. Serving with him were the most influential men of the State, including J. L. Alcorn and J. Z. George, both of whom were subsequently to serve in the United States Senate.

On the 9th the committee reported, Lamar, who had himself drafted the ordinance, presenting it to the convention, as follows:

An ordinance to dissolve the union between the State of Mississippi and other States united with her under the compact entitled "The Constitution of the United States of America."

The people of Mississippi, in convention assembled, do ordain and declare, and it is hereby ordained and declared, as follows, to wit:

Section 1. That all the laws and ordinances by which the said State of Mississippi became a member of the Federal Union of the United States of America be, and the same are hereby, repealed, and that all obligations on the part of said State, or the people thereof, be withdrawn, and that the said State doth hereby resume all the rights, functions, and powers which, by any of said laws and ordinances, were conveyed to the Government of the said United States, and is absolved from all the obligations, restraints, and duties incurred to the said Federal Union, and shall henceforth be a free, sovereign, and independent State.

Section 2. That so much of the first section of the Seventh Article of the Constitution of this State as requires members of the Legislature and all officers, both legislative and judicial, to take an oath to support the Constitution of the United States be, and the same is hereby abrogated and annulled.

Section 3. That all rights acquired and vested under the Constitution of the United States, or under any act of Congress passed in pursuance thereof, or under any law of this State, and not incompatible with this ordinance, shall remain in force and have the same effect as if the ordinance had not been passed.

Section 4. That the people of the State of Mississippi hereby consent to form a Federal Union with such of the States as have seceded or may secede from the Union of the United States of America, upon the basis of the present Constitution of the United States, except such parts thereof as embrace other portions than such seceding States.[21]

The ordinance was to be called up for consideration and final passage on the afternoon of the 9th. At that time a number of amendments were proposed, all of which were voted down overwhelmingly. With the galleries of the hall packed, the vote was finally begun upon the ordinance itself. Immediately it was apparent that the result would be almost unanimously in favor of secession, and a stillness as of death fell upon the assemblage.[22]

That night there was a firing of cannon and a ringing of bells, but withal a hushed note of sadness. In the minds of most was the thought that they had of necessity severed ties long standing and dear, and that they were witnessing the birth of a new nation. But "within three years the torches of Grant's and Sherman's armies had so laid the city in ashes that it became known, partly in derision and partly in wrath, as 'Chimney-ville.' "[23]

VII

WAR AND DIPLOMACY

LAMAR's plan that the organization of the State government should be disrupted as little as possible by the withdrawal from the Union was carried out in respect to the Senators and Representatives that were appointed on the 26th of January to take their seats in the Congress of the Confederate States. A resolution was adopted directing that the same legislators who had served at Washington be continued in office in the new Confederacy, thus designating Messrs. Davis and Brown for the Senate, and Messrs. Lamar, Singleton, Reuben Davis, McRae, and Barksdale for the House. As it turned out, this delegation was never to be seated, for on February 4th a convention of the seceding States met at Montgomery, where the delegates drew up a provisional government with Mr. Davis at the head, meanwhile resolving itself into a Provisional Congress to legislate for the Confederacy.

It became immediately evident that the Confederate Government would have a unified army that would take precedence over the State militias. Mott, who had been appointed a brigadier-general in the army of Mississippi, set to work with the coöperation of Lamar to recruit a regiment for service "during the war." The quota of men was quickly raised; indeed, so fast did volunteers pour in—particularly after the gray dawn of April 12th heard the booming of the first cannon of the war at Sumter—that soon no more could be accepted. Mott was elected colonel while Lamar took the lieutenant-colonelcy. Of necessity he resigned his professorship at the University, and by the middle of May was in Montgomery offering his regiment to the Confederate Government for service. This regiment, the Nineteenth of Mississippi, as it was designated, was the first from the State raised for service "during the war." [1]

Mott and Lamar at once began desperate efforts to complete the equipment for their hastily mustered troops. In the meantime the Provisional Confederate Congress had, by the resolution of May 21st, moved the seat of government to Richmond, to which city Lamar went directly instead of returning to Mississippi, leading his troops with him. On the night of June 1st he was at the Spottswood Hotel with Mr. Davis when the later was serenaded by a tremendous crowd of citizens to whom he made a speech from the balcony. There were several other addresses, after which Lamar was called upon for the final speech. His words were a ringing challenge for a united and determined policy of resistance. "The time has arrived," he said, "when...the deliverance of this fair State depends not upon argument, not upon eloquence, not upon statesmanship; but upon the fighting manhood of the people of this country [cheers], upon the courage which dares strike a braver blow for the right than the enemy dare strike for the wrong....

"...This very night I look forward to the day when this beloved country of ours—for, thank God! we have a country at last—will be a country to live for, to pray for, to fight for, and if necessary, to die for. [A voice: 'Yes, I am willing to die for it a hundred times over!']." [2] Lamar's speech was highly regarded, and for some time was much commented upon. Mrs. Mary Chesnut (wife of Senator James Chesnut of South Carolina), shortly after its delivery, noted in her diary that his speech was rather generally known by heart. [3]

Lamar now went into camp for the purpose of drilling and preparing his regiment. Though he carried out his duties with meticulous care, he was not happy in a military environment. Primarily a thinker and social philosopher, he was greatly irked by the divorcement from books, cultured society, and the scholarly contacts that had come to mean so much to him. But his personal courage and his great devotion to the cause in which he was enlisted, was recognized by his men with whom he was extremely popular.

However, he could not—like so many leaders North and South—delude himself into thinking that the war would be either short or comparatively bloodless. "Mr. Lamar," noted Mrs. Chesnut in her diary under date of June 27th, 1861, "says the young men are light-hearted because there is a fight on hand, but those few who look ahead, the clear heads, they see all the risk, the loss of land, limb, and life, home, wife, and children. As in 'the brave days of old,' they take to it for their country's sake. They are ready and willing, come what may. But not so light-hearted as the *jeunesse dorée*," who had not yet come to realize that many of their sweethearts and husbands would never return to them. Likewise, Mrs. Chesnut confided to her diary that of all the men in high office at the Confederate capital, "Lamar [is] the most original, and the cleverest." [4]

During the period of this encampment at Richmond, Lamar suffered the first of a series of apoplectic attacks which were thenceforth periodically to impair his physical vigor and ultimately to take his life. "It was a violent vertigo," says his son-in-law, Edward Mayes, "something like an apoplexy, accompanied by unconsciousness more or less prolonged, and followed by more or less of paralysis of one side. Sometimes even his speech was affected." [5] "Poor Mr. Lamar has been brought from his camp—paralysis or some sort of shock," Mrs. Chesnut entered in her diary on June 29th, 1861. "Every woman in the house is ready to rush into the Florence Nightingale business. . . . Lamar will not die this time. Will men flatter and make eyes, until their eyes close in death, at the ministering angels? He was the same old Lamar of the drawing-room." [6] This attack, which occurred about the 1st of July, made it impossible for him to accompany his regiment to the front. No one, including Lamar himself, fully realized the seriousness of his trouble. We find Colonel Mott, on the 12th of July, writing to him that "our regiment seems to be ready and eager for the conflict, but I trust it will not be forced upon us till we can have your assistance. We need that sort of *vim* and *propelling power* which you possess in a greater degree than any man I ever saw, and which the Major and I are very deficient in." [7]

"Lamar is out on crutches," recorded Mrs. Chesnut on July 13th. "His father-in-law [Judge Longstreet]...bore him off to-day....Mrs. Lamar and her daughter were here." [8] By slow stages they carried him home to Oxford where he might recuperate under the ministrations of his family. Here he remained for three and a half months, eating out his heart at the enforced inactivity and bothered with numerous "slight rushes of blood to the head." Before August had passed, he could stand it no longer, and by the 1st of November he reached Richmond, though with one leg practically useless. His first thought was to secure further supplies—particularly overcoats—for his ill-equipped troops. On the 22nd of November he was writing his wife that with his regiment he would "probably start next Monday for General Johnston's headquarters....There is some ill feeling between the Potomac generals and the President. I fear that cousin James Longstreet is taking sides against the administration. He will certainly commit a grave error if he does." Again we see his mind reverting to the time when peace would have returned: "If I were well enough off, I should give up public life and devote myself to social duties; but as it is not possible to do that yet, I will do all I can to improve the condition of my family. I have now no other earthly object in life." [9]

Shortly after Christmas of 1861, while in winter quarters around Centerville, General Johnston proposed to Lamar that he be recommended for advancement to the rank of brigadier general.[10] He, however, refused on the plea that he would never accept promotion over the head of Colonel Mott, to whom he requested that the promotion be given. This suggestion was accepted, but the untimely death of Mott was to come before he could be commissioned.

In April, near Yorktown, Lamar had his first taste of battle. The Confederate General, Magruder, whose command contained the Nineteenth Mississippi regiment, had about sixteen thousand men, while McClellan at first possessed six times that number,[11] and up to April 11th there was no time when the Federal army did not outnumber the Confederates at least three to one.[12] The authorities at Washington had requested McClellan to attack as soon as possible, and with the meager Confederate force stretched along a line thirteen miles in length, it is almost inconceivable that he could have failed to find a weak spot in their defense. But the Union leader spent his time in erecting siege works and planting heavy parrot guns and mortars against the Confederate fortifications, meanwhile writing bitterly to Lincoln and to his admiring wife that he was not receiving sufficient support from Washington. At length, when the elaborate preparations were completed and he was ready to attack, he found that the Confederates, timing nicely the operations of their opponents, had withdrawn and were making off toward Williamsburg and Richmond.[13]

It was the night of May 3rd that the Confederates had begun their withdrawal. Their movements were soon observed, and McClellan gave orders that the pursuit be immediately and hotly pushed; hence, about two miles east of Williamsburg, a part of the Confederate forces under Longstreet threw up fortifications in an attempt to beat off their pursuers, commanded by Hooker. The Southern strategy was this: instead of waiting for an attack, General Anderson was to organize an assault, using as the "spear head" of his attack the brigades of A. P. Hill supported by those of Pickett and Wilcox.[14]

At the appointed time the Confederates charged over their breastworks and the line of battle broadened out until the brigades of Pryor, Jenkins, Early, and Colston were drawn into the conflict. The brigade of Wilcox, including the regiment of Lamar, opened the attack with their objective the capturing of the forest in which the Federal troops were concealed. They had barely entered the wood when they were subjected to a heavy fire from the enemy, who, some two hundred yards away, were fortified behind a rail fence, augmented by felled trees. Here Lamar momentarily encountered his warm friend, General Pryor, who had believed that secession would not result in war, and whom he had not seen since the Charleston convention. "Oh, Pryor," he called (so the General subsequently told his wife) as the shot and shell crashed through the branches, "what do you think of the right of peaceable secession?"[15] With Pryor's brigade of seven hundred men forming the right wing, the order to charge the fortifications was given. There was a momentary repulse as the Tenth Alabama—caught in a cross fire and thrown back with some confusion—was rallied by the appearance of General A. P. Hill. The combat continued without intermission until darkness closed upon the scene, with the result that the Union forces were defeated with heavy losses.

The Nineteenth Mississippi, forming the center of the attacking force, had charged to the base of the fence which had been made impregnable with logs and dirt. Within thirty yards of the barrier, Colonel Mott was shot down as he led one wing of the Confederate onslaught, but his men continued the assault and swarmed over the fortifications to put to flight those of the enemy who had not drawn back and taken refuge in the fallen timber. With the death of Mott in the first desperate advance, the command of the regiment devolved upon Lieutenant Colonel Lamar, who had led the attack of the other wing of the regiment. How well he bore himself is to be seen in the official report of General Wilcox: "The Nineteenth Mississippi, after the fall of its highly esteemed and brave colonel, was commanded during the remainder of the day by its lieutenant colonel, L. Q. C. Lamar. This officer, suddenly called to the command of his regiment, acquitted himself creditably throughout this long and stubbornly contested musketry fight, proving himself in all respects a competent, daring, and skilful officer."[16]

Something of the nature of the attack, and Lamar's personal experiences, is to be found in the following excerpt from his own detailed report to brigade headquarters: "At about 8.30 A.M., Col. C. H. Mott, then commanding our regiment, was ordered by Gen. Wilcox to make a sortie from the second redoubt, on the right of Fort Magruder, through a field into the forest supposed to be occupied by the enemy in large force.

...In consequence of the dense undergrowth and uneven ground, Col. Mott placed the right wing of the regiment under my command, and directed me to operate with it according to my own discretion. At the command of our colonel the men advanced with great spirit and steadiness. A destructive fire was at once opened upon us by the enemy. In the first volley, as I was afterwards informed, Col. Mott fell, shot through the body while cheering on his men. The fight became at once general along our whole line. The men under my command pressed on to the attack with the utmost eagerness, and yet with perfect coolness, keeping our line as unbroken as the nature of the ground would allow, and firing with deliberation and telling effect. The enemy, partially protected by the fence behind which they were posted, contested the ground most stubbornly. The opposing lines could not have been more than thirty yards apart, and for a time I expected a hand to hand conflict with the bayonet; but at last, wavering before the impetuosity and undaunted resolution of our men, the enemy began to yield the ground, continuing to fire as they retired. ...From the time the order to advance was given until the conflict terminated this regiment was under fire, and through it all both officers and men bore themselves with an intrepidity which merits the highest commendation." [17]

The battle, however, had sadly decimated the ranks of Lamar's command. As they stormed over the Union fortifications, three color bearers in succession had been shot down; but the fourth, Lieutenant Jones, had planted the flag of Lamar's regiment among the Federal cannon. When, at the end of the day, he checked the roll of his command, he found that the casualties amounted to one-fifth of his men.

In addition to the flattering official mention by General Wilcox, Lamar was cited for gallantry under fire and for effective leadership by three other generals, A. P. Hill,[18] Pryor,[19] and Longstreet,[20] while to the regiment itself, General Johnston granted the honor of inscribing "Williamsburg" upon its battle flag. Lamar, however, never exhibited pride in his military record, for his ambitions and aims in life were entirely of another nature. In the post-war days in Washington some of his most popular stories were humorous burlesques on the part that he played at Williamsburg, and the transitory nature of military glory.

Suddenly, though not without warning, Lamar's military days were over. While reviewing his regiment about the middle of May, he suffered a severe stroke of apoplexy, and "fell as if he had been shot." He was placed upon a litter, covered with the regimental flag and carried to his tent where he was given medical attention, and when he had recovered sufficiently to permit moving, he was carried on to Richmond by ambulance. By June he was able to stand the travel to Mississippi, from whence he was carried to Macon, Georgia, where his mother and sister assisted his wife and daughter in nursing him back to some semblance of health.

But for the Lamars, as for so many Southern homes, the autumn tints were already appearing in the Southern cause. On September 4th of the same year in which L. Q. C. Lamar was stricken, his youngest brother, Jefferson M., the lieutenant colonel of Cobb's Georgia Legion, was mortally wounded while leading a charge at Crampton's Gap, in Maryland.[21] In this battle, one of the most desperate and bloody of the war, considering the number of troops involved, he had been ordered to hold a position at the right of the field. Finding this occupied, and the enemy entrenched behind a stone fence, he had ordered a charge. As his horse cleared the stone barrier, the animal was shot from under the rider who, leaping to his feet and calling to his men to follow, was pierced by a number of shots before he could take a step. Himself wounded to death, he rallied his men who died almost to a man, the few remaining being taken prisoner. In the same battle, Colonel John Basil Lamar, whom we have already had occasion to mention as L. Q. C.'s close intimate, was also mortally wounded. Indeed, before four years had passed, the South had poured out much of her best blood for a cause in whose very theory of States' Sovereignty was sown the seeds of dissolution and death. Perhaps the Lamars suffered no more severely than other representative Southern families, but of the thirteen who bore that name—all of them related and descendants of Thomas the emigrant—and who served in the Civil War with rank as high or higher than lieutenant colonel, more than half were to perish on the field of battle.[22]

Among those who were to survive was young Lucius Mirabeau Lamar, cousin of L. Q. C. and likewise named for the latter's father, who marched away at the outbreak of war with the famous Oglethorpe Light Infantry, from Savannah, under the brilliant Francis S. Bartow.[23] This body of troops had formed the nucleus of the 8th Georgia regiment of the Army of Virginia, with Bartow as its commander. In the first great battle of the war, at Bull Run, young Lamar had seen Colonel Bartow and his mount go down in the mêlée. Thinking that only the horse had been killed, "young Lamar," says a contemporary, "dashed across the field amid a hail of bullets to procure another mount for his colonel. Suddenly Lamar was seen to fall with his horse. Extricating himself, and perceiving that his horse was shot, he started to proceed on foot; the wounded animal tried to rise and follow. Our men saw Lamar turn in that deadly fire, stoop down, and pat the poor horse on the neck. Another volley of bullets ended the noble animal's life, and Lamar returned just in time to bear Bartow's body from the field."[24] Lamar succeeded to Bartow's command as colonel of the 8th Georgia Regiment, and lived through four years of bloody warfare to become an important factor in the rebuilding of his State at the end of the conflict.

Colonel Albert R. Lamar, too, was to survive. He had been elected secretary of the Georgia Secession Convention, and had played an important part in the deliberations of that body. After serving throughout the war, he was to become the editor of the *Macon Telegraph*, and in the post-war years to act as a leading and liberalizing force in the intellectual life of Georgia and the South.

By the fall of 1862 it had become evident to Lamar that his health would forever preclude a return to active military duty; hence it devolved upon him to seek another way that he might serve the cause to which he had devoted himself. In October he resigned his colonelcy, though the officers and men in general assembly suggested that he retain his command in absence with the expectation that he might some day resume his leadership of the regiment. He, however, feeling that such a course would work an injustice upon the other officers, declined the suggestion. N. H. Harris, his successor in the colonelcy, afterwards a brigadier general, later wrote that "the soldiers of the regiment regarded him as a heroic leader and felt deep sorrow at his resignation; that great and lasting mutual affection existed between the men and himself." [25]

Meanwhile, the letters that he was receiving from his father-in-law (who, after the closing of the University of South Carolina, had returned to Mississippi) were not reassuring. In November, 1862, Judge Longstreet was writing that the Northern armies were laying waste the countryside, and that "your plantation will soon be a battlefield.... Mac is ready to move off the hands, but where to, he knows not, and I know not how to advise him.... Your plantation... will have neither stock nor provisions in the spring. Of course, Oxford falls into the hands of the Yankees...." [26] In less than thirty days General Grant had led his troops into the town and had taken up his headquarters in the buildings of the University. Much of the residential as well as business section was burned, and Judge Longstreet's home was itself fired with a torch composed of his treasured private papers representing the correspondence of a lifetime. [27]

Lamar's resignation from the colonelcy of his regiment transferred, but did not end, his efforts in the cause of the Confederacy, for on the 19th of November, 1862, he was appointed Special Commissioner of the Confederate States to the Empire of Russia, succeeding the distinguished scientist, Matthew Fontaine Maury. He was to journey, however, by way of London and Paris, where he was to come in contact with the most brilliant diplomatic and social life of the European capitals. In his portfolio he carried a communication from

President Davis to the Czar, a letter from the Secretary of State to the Russian Minister of Foreign Affairs, copies of the letters of instructions already given to Messrs. Mason and Slidell, and his personal letters of instruction from Secretary of State Judah P. Benjamin.[28]

Secretary Benjamin's letter of instructions laid down the motives actuating the War Between the States, it outlined the international situation and the failure, thus far, of the great governments of Europe to recognize the Confederacy as a sovereign nation. It was suggested to Lamar that in opening negotiations for Southern recognition on the part of Russia, "it is not deemed necessary that you resort to argument to maintain the right of these States to secede from the United States any further than may be embraced in the statement above given of the reasons which have caused delay in approaching that government on the subject. You will, of course, not refuse any explanations on this point which may seem to be invited, but we now place our demand for recognition and admission into the family of nations on the result of the tests to which Europe, by common understanding, submitted our rights. We have conquered our position by the sword. We are ready and able to maintain it against the utmost efforts of our enemies in the future, as we have already done in the past. We were independent States before secession; we have been independent ever since...

"If your efforts to open negotiations with the Russian Cabinet on the basis of our recognition shall prove successful, you will be expected to continue your residence near that court as Envoy Extraordinary and Minister Plenipotentiary, and to that end you will receive herewith your commission as such, together with letters of credence to his Imperial Majesty."[29]

Near the 1st of December, Lamar started upon his mission, going by way of Mexico instead of Mobile where he had at first planned to sail on the warship "Florida." The uncertainty as to when the latter would weigh anchor, and the high probability of capture in any event, made this change desirable. After five days spent in Vicksburg, he reached Alexandria,

Louisiana, on the 19th, and on the 24th of December was in Niblett's Bluff, whence he wrote to his wife that the little settlement was "on the Sabine River, one hundred and twenty-five miles from Houston, Tex. We got to Alexandria last Saturday. It took us three and a half days to get here in a hack. The country we have come through is one long stretch of pine barrens interspersed with patches of prairie. The settlers are not in ten miles of each other, and so far as I can judge, have no means of support. I shall leave to-night on the boat for Houston." [30]

Leaving San Antonio on the 3rd of January, 1863, and stopping briefly at Matamoros, Havana, and Saint Thomas in the Virgin Islands, he reached London on the night of the 1st of March, accompanied by young Longstreet, his wife's nephew, who had been intrusted to his care. "I reached London on the night of the 1st of March, and have been much occupied ever since in receiving company and going to dinners," he wrote Mrs. Lamar from the Burlington Hotel on the 19th. "I have...witnessed the grandest pageant, I presume, that has appeared in London for many years [in honor of the marriage of the Prince of Wales, which took place on the 10th of March, 1863]....I have been with Mr. Mason a good deal. He is very popular here. Mr. Adams, the United States Minister, has complained that he was only treated with civility, while Mr. Mason was treated with cordiality....I dine Tuesday next with Hon. Mr. and Mrs. Pococke (parliamentary folks). I expect to meet some of the rulers there, as the invitation was very ceremonious. The dress of a gentleman at these dinners is a full suit of black, white kid gloves, and white cravat." [31]

Lamar soon discovered that, for various reasons, there was small probability of recognition by any of the great European powers. The diplomatic situation, as he found it, is succinctly outlined in a letter of March 20th to Secretary Benjamin. Among other things, he wrote, "though I have been in London but a little more than two weeks, I have had, through the kindness of Mr. Mason, unexpected opportunities of obtaining information in regard to the state of public opinon here and throughout Europe touching American affairs. In this country the leading contestants for power in both parties, Conservatives and Whigs, supported by the great body of their respective adherents, are favorable to the success of the South. Many causes, however, operate to prevent this partiality from yielding any practical results." Among the considerations that he mentions as operating against the recognition by England of the Confederacy, was the fear of war with the United States, for, he writes, "they seem to consider that a war with that country would be the greatest calamity that could befall Great Britain; and they have the impression that the United States would not regret the occurrence of a contingency which would justify them in declaring war." Again, he pointed out that the radicals, "under Bright and others" hold the balance of power between the Conservatives and Whigs, and these Radicals "are the warm partisans of the United States, and have of late made a series of striking demonstrations by public meetings, speeches, etc. I do not see any causes now at work to change this state of things." Finally, he urged that commissioners be sent to the governments of Austria and Prussia, and outlined something of the international complications in Europe which, he says, take precedence in the public mind over the situation in America.[32]

Lamar, in addition to being commissioned Minister to Russia, was special envoy to England and to the Court of France. Much of his time he spent in Paris and at the French Court, where he became a great favorite. A recent biographer of Mr. Slidell says that it was soon evident that "Lamar was really an able man," and not just another eccentric with a Roman prenomen. He "struck Paris as an imposing, even picturesque personality, and in his broad-brimmed hat, tight buttoned coat, and hirsute luxuriance he cut a striking figure on the boulevards."[33] Mr. Slidell honored him at a dinner party which was attended by several representatives from the Court, and soon Lamar was on intimate terms with a number of the most influential personages at the French capital, where his social gifts made him in great demand. He was the only diplomat at the French Court, remarked a celebrated French beauty, "who fully recognized, and endeavored to utilize, the power of the women there." [34] Especially did he enjoy his associations with the poet Lamartine (a distant, but blood relative), who entertained him and introduced him into the most cultured circle of Paris. Nowhere were his brilliant social gifts more appreciated and more useful in the service of the cause which he represented.

There had been time, too, for personal enrichment: short periods when he tore himself from his strenuous diplomatic and social duties to bury himself in the historic past of which all his life he had been a student. When his period of European service was ended, he had stood upon the summit of Mont-Saint-Michel with its eleventh century Norman Church and looked out over the Northern sea that for eight centuries had lain beneath its brooding shadows. He had paused briefly—his itinerary shows—in a number of the cathedral towns of Northern France where the twelfth and thirteenth centuries still lived in architectural monuments that breathed a rich medievalism. In the little Norman city of Mantes, he had stood at the spot near the church of Gassicourt upon which William the Conqueror, Norman like the blood that flowed in Lamar's own veins, had died in 1087; and in the legendary tales of Western Europe he had bathed his luminous and imaginative mind—walked with Arthur and Launcelot, and reread the immortal stories of Tristram and Iseult, of Roland, and of Abélard and Héloïse. Philosophically, he had communed with Saint Francis Assisi, Albertus Magnus, and Saint Thomas Aquinas.

But nothing that he encountered in Europe impressed him, he was frequently to say in after years, as did the twelfth century Cathedral to the Virgin at Chartres, that most perfect example of Medieval architecture and perhaps the world's finest architectural monument. Here, it seemed to Lamar, he had found the perfect expression of an age which appealed powerfully to his mind and imagination. Esthetically, he was never to see anything, he thought, so perfect as the "old tower," the foundation for which had been laid before the first crusade, with its vertical lines, its height and reach that seemed to strive toward heaven itself; to express man's noblest aspirations in a period when his concepts and aspirations were the highest; to lay hold on the infinite, and to emulate the intelligence and energy of God. Himself of a mystical and religious bent, he saw—in this cathedral raised in honor of the Virgin Mother of God—a Christ of infinite love, and mercy, and salvation; and not of judgment, justice, and suffering.[35]

Because of many factors beyond his control, however—and satisfactory as were the personal aspects of his foreign residence—the diplomatic affairs which claimed Lamar's attention in France were not prospering. Almost a quarter of a century later, in 1887, he gave an interview to the noted correspondent, Donn Piatt, in which he outlined the views held by the French Government at this time in respect to the American struggle. "I knew very well," he said, "that Louis Napoleon was not only in favor of interfering in our behalf, but warmly so. He received me kindly, and spoke with the utmost frankness upon the subject. There were two obstacles in his way. One was the fact of our slaveholding, that would make intervention in our behalf unpopular among the masses of the French people. The other was the need of a naval power like England or Russia to join in the movement. The Count de Morny, the emperor's confidential adviser, opened his mind to me yet more freely, and gave assurances that made us hope with reason for the intervention of the Imperial Government of France. On one occasion I was shown a note from the emperor, in which he gave a positive order that, had it not been revoked, would have brought on the intervention which we so earnestly sought.... The motive for this course on the part of the emperor was not altogether a sentiment. In the blockade of the Southern ports France suffered as England suffered, only in a less degree, from a cotton famine." [36]

Perhaps no incident during Lamar's stay in Europe impressed him so vividly as a scene he once witnessed in the House of Commons. Years after, in a formal address, he told of the occurrence. Some time before, "a young member who had never claimed the attention of the House before arose to address them...his voice was drowned by groans and hoots, hisses and tumultuous cries of 'Down! sit down!' from every part of the floor...he seized upon a momentary lull to exclaim:...'I yield to you now; I relinquish the floor, but mark my words: the time shall come when this House *shall* hear me.' Years afterwards, in 1863," Lamar said, "one of those weighty questions which constitute epochs in the political history of England arose....I was present when the great debate occurred. Again was England faced by an almost unsupported man; but this man was the herald and the champion, not the victim of a new order of things;...this was the hissed and derided speaker of many years before. He had studied the temper and measured the mind of that peculiar body. He had reformed his type of expression....He concluded, and the shout that arose from the reeling hall swept over the tumult of London like a pæan of old Rome. He had plucked his laurels from the grasp of an opposing nation, and with them had bound, in a brotherhood of immortal renown, the might of an unconquerable resolution and the name of Benjamin Disraeli." [37]

Of all of the enduring and valued friendships made by Lamar while in England, none was quite so cherished as that with Mr. Thackeray, the novelist, whom he often encountered at semi-official dinners and with whom he became very intimate. Lamar, who was greatly impressed by the eloquence of the Baptist minister, Spurgeon, was on one occasion telling of a sermon that he had heard from the divine. With that peculiarly retentive memory which all his life was to be a marvel to his associates, he narrated portions of the sermon with his usual fidelity to the original. Finally, Mr. Thackeray, who had never heard Mr. Spurgeon and who expressed skepticism as to his eloquence, remarked, "but, Mr. Lamar, that is your sermon, and not Spurgeon's. I believe that you can beat him preaching." [38]

Certain comments of Henry Watterson throw interesting sidelights upon Lamar's personality and character, and upon his intimacy with Thackeray. "It was Schurz, as I have said, who brought Lamar and me together," remarked Watterson. "The Mississippian had been a Secession Member of Congress when I was a Unionist scribe in the reporters' gallery.... I later learned that he was very many-sided and accomplished, the most interesting and lovable of men. He and Schurz 'froze together,' as, brought together by Schurz, he and I 'froze together.' On one side he was a sentimentalist and on the other a philosopher, but on all sides a fighter.

"They called him a dreamer. He sprang from a race of chevaliers and scholars. Oddly enough, albeit in his moods a recluse, he was a man of the world; a favorite in society; very much at home in European courts, especially in that of England; the friend of Thackeray, at whose home, when in London, he made his abode. Lady Ritchie—Anne Thackeray— told me many amusing stories of his whimsies. He was a man among brainy men and a lion among clever women.... We had already come to be good friends and constant comrades when the whirligig of time threw us together for a little while in the lower house of Congress....

"I rather think that Lamar was the biggest brained of all the men I have met in Washington. He possessed the courage of his convictions. A doctrinaire, there was nothing of the typical doctrinaire, or theorist, about him. He really believed that cotton was king and would compel England to espouse the cause of the South.

"He once told me a good story about his friend Thackeray. The two were driving to a banquet of the Literary Fund, where Dickens was to preside. 'Lamar,' said Thackeray, 'they say I can't speak. But if I want to I can speak. I can speak every bit as good as Dickens, and I am going to show you to-night that I can speak almost as good as you.' When the moment arrived Thackeray said never a word. Returning in the cab, both silent, Thackeray suddenly broke forth. 'Lamar,' he exclaimed, 'don't you think you have heard the greatest speech to-night that was never delivered?' " [39]

Years later, Mr. Leroy F. Youmans, before the bar of the

Supreme Court of the United States, analyzed some of the exceptional qualities which made Lamar a favorite in the most exclusive social circles of two continents. "This profound thinker, this master of abstract thought," he said, "was in social life genial and full of humor, loving and making pleasantry with the merriest in the circle. Who can forget his wonderful powers as a *raconteur*, or his merriment over those of others? Like so many other men of large achievement in the affairs of the world, the capacity which fitted him for these was allied to that which made him the lover of jest, and of playfulness with childhood, when relaxation made it proper and right. He could wield the battle-ax of Richard and the scimitar of Saladin, but could cheer the social circle with his anecdotes and play games for the delight of infancy." [40]

Henry Adams, perhaps the greatest of our social commentators and historians, had much to say of Lamar in his celebrated *Education*,[41] particularly of Lamar's diplomatic service. "No one," he said, "understood why Jefferson Davis chose Mr. Mason as his agent for London at the same time that he made so good a choice as Mr. Slidell for Paris. The Confederacy had plenty of excellent men to send to London, but few who were less fitted than Mason. Possibly Mason had a certain amount of common sense, but he seemed to have nothing else, and in London society he counted merely as one eccentric more.... Yet at the same time with Mason, President Davis sent out Slidell to France and Mr. Lamar to Russia. Some twenty years later, in the shifting search for the education he never found, Adams became closely intimate at Washington with Lamar, then Senator from Mississippi, who had grown to be one of the calmest, most reasonable and most amiable Union men in the United States, and quite unusual in social charm. Above all,... he had tact and humor; and perhaps this was a reason why Mr. Davis sent him abroad with the others, on a futile mission to St. Petersburg. He would have done better in London, in place of Mason. London society would have delighted in him; his stories would have won success; his manners would have made him loved; his oratory would have swept every audience; even Monckton Milnes could never have resisted the temptation of having him to breakfast between Lord Shaftesbury and the Bishop of Oxford.

"Lamar," said Adams, "liked to talk of his brief career in diplomacy, but he never spoke of Mason. He never alluded to Confederate management or criticized Jefferson Davis's administration. The subject that amused him was his English allies. At that moment—the early summer of 1863—the rebel party in England were full of confidence, and felt strong enough to challenge the American Legation to a show of power....

"With Roebuck's [the Southern spokesman in Parliament] doings, the private secretary [Henry Adams, himself, secretary to his father, Charles Francis Adams, United States Minister to England] had no concern except that the Minister sent him down to the House of Commons on June 30, 1863, to report the result of Roebuck's motion to recognize the Southern Confederacy. The Legation felt no anxiety, having Vicksburg already in its pocket, and Bright and Forster to say so; but the private secretary went down and was admitted under the gallery on the left, to listen, with great content, while John Bright, with astonishing force, caught and shook and tossed Roebuck, as a big mastiff shakes a wiry, ill-conditioned, toothless, bad-tempered Yorkshire terrier....

"All the more sharply he was excited, near the year 1879, in Washington, by hearing Lamar begin a story after dinner, which, little by little, became dramatic, recalling the scene in the House of Commons. The story, as well as one remembered, began with Lamar's failure to reach St. Petersburg at all, and his subsequent detention in Paris waiting instructions. The motion to recognize the Confederacy was about to be made, and, in prospect of the debate, Mr. Lindsay collected a party at his villa on the Thames to bring the rebel agents into relations with Roebuck. Lamar was sent for, and came. After much conversation of a general sort, such as is the usual object or resource of the English Sunday, finding himself alone with Roebuck, Lamar, by way of showing interest, bethought himself of John Bright and asked Roebuck whether he expected Bright to take part in the debate: 'No, sir!' said Roebuck sententiously; 'Bright and I have met before. It was the old story—the story of the sword-fish and the whale! No, sir! Mr. Bright will not cross swords with me again!'

"Thus assured, Lamar went with the more confidence to the House on the appointed evening, and was placed under the gallery, on the right, where he listened to Roebuck and followed the debate with such enjoyment as an experienced debater feels in these contests, until, as he said, he became aware that a man, with a singularly rich voice and imposing manner, had taken the floor, and was giving Roebuck the most deliberate and tremendous pounding he ever witnessed, 'until at last,' concluded Lamar, 'it dawned on my mind that the sword-fish was getting the worst of it.'"

Another amusing incident of Lamar's diplomatic career was narrated by Mr. John A. Cockerill, in the *New York Advertiser*, shortly after Lamar's death. Said he, "I recall with interest an hour's conversation held with Mr. Lamar in Washington in 1877. He was then a Senator from Mississippi. At a reception given by Mr. Hutchinson (whom I had aided in founding the *Daily Post*) to Senator Thurman and some of his colleagues, quite a crowd of Washington flaneurs gathered." Mr. Lamar, who "was one of the honored guests,...came and dropped himself on the sofa beside me, languidly and apparently much bored." He "told one or two amusing stories of backwoods life which he had picked up when a young lawyer practicing in Georgia and Mississippi. He had a Southern dialect which he brought to the relation, as quaint as that which had made Proctor Knott famous as a *raconteur*.

"Mr. Lamar, on this occasion, related an amusing journalistic experience which came to him during the period when he was begging alternately at the doors of St. Cloud and St. James for aid for his Southern cause. He said that he was anxious to win the friendship of the London press. He prepared one day a careful article gently leading up to the point of interesting the English Government in the struggle for Southern independence. He called upon Mr. Delane of the *London Times*, and submitted it. After a careful reading the editor accepted it, and said that he would use it as a leader in the *Times*. 'I waited for days,' said Mr. Lamar, 'for the appearance of that article, which I fondly hoped would open the way for others more direct and forcible. Time rolled on, and the article did not appear. I was anxious, for our cause could not well wait. I had kept a copy of the article. Concluding that Mr. Delane had decided on reflection not to use the article, I carried it to the editor of the *Telegraph*. He accepted it. Two days after, he printed it as a leading editorial, and, by a most singular coincidence, it came out as an original article in the *Times* of the same morning, word for word. I was never so mortified in my life. I could not explain. I never saw either editor afterwards, and I have never been able to estimate just what the Confederacy lost by that *faux pas*. I know that it stopped my writing for the London press.''

In the early summer of 1863, Lamar delivered perhaps the most important address of his European sojourn before a distinguished group, including several members of Parliament, in London.[42] The South, he said, was fighting a battle for constitutional government, and the outcome was fraught with serious consequences for other peoples whose institutions might be likewise threatened if the citadel in America should fall. He would not, he said, evade the issue of slavery which he knew to operate against the formal recognition of the Confederacy by the European powers, particularly England and France. Severe indictments could be brought against the institution of slavery, but it had been the university that had taken an uncivilized and barbaric race and brought it forward in the scale of human culture more rapidly than had ever before occurred in the history of mankind. This was no small achievement, he felt, when it was considered that the blacks had never shown the ability to build an indigenous civilization of their own, and that they represented—so science taught—probably the least capable branch of the human family. The culture and civilization of the South faced an apparently insoluble problem in the settling of the racial question, but the world might be assured that, when the Negro had advanced to a certain point, the South would accord him his freedom; indeed, when the black race had shown an aptitude for the ways of civilized man, the "whites could not, if they would, withhold the boon" of freedom.

The question naturally arises as to Lamar's personal, pre-Civil War beliefs in regard to the institution of slavery. Two things can be stated with certainty: that he felt that the Negroes had profited more than their white masters by the relationship; and that, as conducted in the South, the practice was not morally wrong.[43] Certainly he came to believe after the Civil War that emancipation of the blacks had been a great boon to the white race. The evidence, indeed, is incontrovertible that, while in the pre-war South he felt that the only workable relationship between whites and blacks was that of master and slave, he was not wedded to the institution of slavery *per se*. His intimate friend, Mrs. Chesnut, expressed the belief in her diary, under date of June 27th, 1861, that Lamar was no more in favor of slavery than Sumner himself.[44]

We do know that Lamar came to believe, shortly after his arrival on his diplomatic mission to Europe, that slavery was the one insurmountable stumbling block between the Confederacy and recognition on the part of England and France. This issue he recognized clearly, and he did not hesitate to lay before President Davis and Secretary Benjamin the situation as he saw it. The authorities at Richmond might take time by the forelock, he said, and, by freeing the slaves, greatly enhance the possibility of recognition of the Confederacy. Without such action, the diplomatic situation was well nigh hopeless. His views on this subject he never saw occasion to change. "I firmly believe," he wrote many years later, "that if, after the reports of its Commissioners in Europe and the evidence of public reprehension in England and France, the Confederate junta in Richmond had thrown over slavery and had announced emancipation by purchase, both the French and English governments would have recognized the Southern Confederacy and she would have taken her place amongst the nations of the earth."[45]

In July, 1863, the foreign policy of the Confederacy was extremely muddled. A contributing element to the unsatisfactory condition was the discord that existed between various purchasing agents representing the Southern States abroad. Lamar and Slidell did effective work in harmonizing the conflicting elements,[46] but it is hardly too much to say that none of the agents were friendly among themselves. More serious, however, were the activities of the British Consuls in various Southern cities such as Richmond, New Orleans, and Mobile. These representatives claimed that they were responsible to the Legation at Washington and they made themselves extremely obnoxious by continual communication with the British Ambassador there, and by studiedly ignoring the Confederate Government at Richmond. Soon, however, they were to feel the iron hand of Secretary of State Benjamin. George Moore, at Richmond, and Cridland, at Mobile, he expelled from the country along with some of the smaller fry, and the balance were effectively silenced. But the resentment against Europe, and especially against the discourtesies lately shown Mason in England, grew to such dimensions that the Senate began to consider withdrawing all of the Confederate envoys.

As a result of this feeling, the Senate refused to ratify the nomination of Lamar as Commissioner to Russia, Benjamin assuring him that the action was in no sense personal but that it was the result of "a deep-seated feeling of irritation at what is considered to be [the] unjust and unfair conduct of neutral powers towards this Confederacy [which] prevails among our people. The feeling is not unnatural and has been reflected in this action of the Senate," which, wrote Benjamin, President Davis much regretted. "If the objection of the Senate had existed only to a mission to Russia, he would have been happy to have availed himself of the services of yourself and Mr. Fearn [Lamar's private secretary] at some other European Court; but their objection is known to be a general one, and he is thus left with no alternative." [47]

"I have the honor to acknowledge the receipt of your dispatch No. 2," Lamar wrote in reply to Benjamin's notice of recall, "advising me that, the Senate having failed to ratify my nomination as Commissioner to Russia, the President desires that I consider the official information of the fact as terminating my mission. I have to thank you for the regrets you express, on the part of the President and yourself, at this decision of the Senate; but, while I cannot free myself altogether from a feeling of disappointment in the expectation of finding a career of usefulness, it is my duty to state that the reasons which you inform me actuated the Senate are fully confirmed by my own observations of the conditions of European politics." Complications, which he details in his letter, induced him "after frequent consultation with Messrs. Mason and Slidell, to delay my departure for my post; and, as latterly the prospect of a restoration of cordial relations became more remote, I had almost reached the determination of recommending to you that I should be released from my duties, or, at least, that they should be directed to another field." [48]

Lamar's stay in Europe, chiefly in Paris and London, had been a period of mental culture and broadening that was to bear significant fruit in his brilliant later career. New vistas had opened before him, and his already broad culture and deep scholarship had taken on a riper tone. Again, he had made good progress in bettering his knowledge of French, the literature of which language he had, since his college days, enjoyed in the original. Moreover, though far from well, his health had greatly improved and he had become an adept at fencing—an accomplishment which was to come as a shock in later years to at least one acquaintance who had challenged him to a friendly skirmish with the idea that he would be easily vanquished.

"Beneath Mr. Lamar's quiet and dreamy exterior one would recognize the fact that he was a man of passionate nature, and that at one period of his life he was much devoted to athletic sports," according to an account published after his death. "He was always happy to take up the foils with any one who pretended to be skilled in fencing, and at one time he was possessed of wonderful physical strength.... Those who have only considered him as dreamy and scholarly would have been surprised if they could have seen Mr. Lamar behind a foil. He had great ability and vigilance, and he often crossed swords with professional teachers of fencing, and rarely could one of them touch him with the button." One day a government official, who kept a pair of foils in the room of the Committee on Public Lands and who prided himself upon being an expert swords-man, invited Lamar—of whose knowledge of fencing he was unaware—to practice with him. He would be careful, he promised, not to injure his guest. At first the latter acted on the defensive, reported the official, "but when I got through amusing him, that room was full of sword cuts. He hit me ten times a second, and I might just as well have had a straw to defend myself with. He came under and over, and I have an indistinct recollection of seeing the finest constellations that man ever looked on. When I got my breath, which I did while he was putting on his coat, with that grim smile still on his face, there were thirty chalk marks on me, five of which were right over my heart. I was blue for a week afterwards. While I was putting up the foils he went out, stopping at the door to say: 'I thought I had forgotten how to use them, and I sadly needed practice.' " [49]

With one leg still partially disabled by paralysis, Lamar would have derived great benefit from a longer stay in Europe under expert medical care, and with the supervised exercise that he had been instructed to take. But he begrudged every moment lost from the cause which he had espoused, and he at once began laying plans for a return to the Southern States. "If you were here," he wrote to his wife on the 1st of August, "I would remain much longer, as it is necessary for my health. But I sup-pose it is my duty to go home and help the fighting. I only wish that our people knew how they are admired all over Europe. It would nerve their souls to go through with the increasing troubles that threaten them.... If I should be cap-tured by the Federals, do not be alarmed. They will only place me in confinement, if they do that. Well, I can stand anything that they can inflict. *They can't break my spirit*, and I will be restored to you sometime or other." [50]

In returning home, Lamar mapped out a course different from the one by which he had come. Sailing from Liverpool to Halifax by the "Asia," he went on to Hamilton, in Bermuda, from whence he took the "Ceres" into Wilmington, North Carolina, through the federal blockade. With him were his cousin, Charles A. L. Lamar (come home to die in a gallant charge at Columbus, Georgia), and his former private secretary, Mr. Walker Fearn. The running of the blockade was an exciting experience, for they were sighted and closely pursued by an enemy vessel, and their ship was badly wrecked. The crew and passengers escaped by taking to the boats, but Lamar lost practically all his effects, and the few remembrances that he was bringing to his family. Once safely ashore he set out for Richmond to make his personal report.

Mrs. Clement C. Clay, in whose home Lamar visited while in Richmond, recorded that he was not optimistic in respect to the recognition of the Confederacy by the European powers. William L. Yancey had returned some time before, she said, and had been unable to hold out encouragement in regard to the situation abroad. "By a singular coincidence, almost under the same circumstances but some months later, a similar conference took place in our rooms, but Mr. Lamar was now the returning diplomat. But recently home from an unfinished mission to Russia, our long-time friend talked, as had Mr. Yancey, with a conviction that our cause was hopeless. Mr. Lamar had proceeded only so far as London and Paris, when, observing the drift of public feeling abroad, he took ship again, arriving, as did many of our returned foreign emissaries, on the top of a friendly [sic] wave." [51]

"Lamar," noted Mrs. Chestnut, in her diary under date of January 18th, 1864, "was asked to dinner here yesterday; so he came to-day. We had our wild turkey cooked for him yesterday, and I dressed myself within an inch of my life with the best of my four-year-old finery. Two of us, my husband and I, did not damage the wild turkey seriously. So Lamar enjoyed the *réchauffé*, and commended the art with which Molly had hid the slight loss we had inflicted upon its mighty breast. She had piled fried oysters over the turkey so skillfully, that unless we had told about it, no one would ever have known that the huge bird was making his second appearance on the board. Lamar," she remarked, "was more absent-minded and distrait than ever." [52]

In the course of the dinner the subject of conversation shifted to the literary work of George Eliot and George Lewes. The conversation, as jotted down that night by the hostess, is a remarkable commentary upon Lamar's breadth of mind and depth of understanding. He had just finished reading *Romola*, a book of which Mrs. Chesnut had a poor opinion because of its (she thought) dubious morality. She was, too, shocked at George Eliot's unconventional life with Lewes. "She had an elective affinity," replied Lamar, "which was responded to, by George Lewes, and so she lives with Lewes. I do not know that she caused the separation between Lewes and his legal wife. They are living in a villa on some Swiss lake, and Mrs. Lewes, of the hour, is a charitable, estimable, agreeable, sympathetic woman of genius."

"Lamar," despite his own exemplary life, said Mrs. Chesnut, "seemed without prejudices on the subject; at least, he expressed neither surprise nor disapprobation. He said something of 'genius being above law,' but I was not very clear as to what he said on that point.... 'You know that Lewes is a writer,' said he. 'Some people say the man she lives with is a noble man.' 'They say she is kind and good—if a fallen woman.'" [53]

Meanwhile, the situation in the Confederacy had been rendered increasingly difficult by the attitude of a number of the South's own civil leaders in opposing the policies of President Davis. In Georgia, where Davis was bitterly and ably attacked by the redoubtable Toombs, as well as by the Vice-President, Mr. Stephens, and Governor Brown, the situation was particularly serious. Hence the administration decided to send Lamar to Georgia, his native State, in an effort to counteract the influence of the opposition. It is an interesting fact that in his efforts there he worked in harmony with Ben Hill, the brilliant Georgia statesman and orator, with whom he was to be associated in more than one hard fight in the United States Senate in the years after the war had become but a bloody memory.

His first speech, on "The State of the Country," was delivered in Milledgeville, the capital of the State, on the 15th of March.[54] Opening with a review of the diplomatic situation, he passed on to a consideration of the controversial questions in which the administration was involved. As a war measure the government had suspended the writ of *habeas corpus*, an action which had been bitterly assailed by Governor Brown in his message to the State legislature. Lamar, in an address which was widely quoted throughout the Confederacy, upheld the President's act as an emergency measure, and called for a unified front to the enemy. Of his speech a contemporary Milledgeville newspaper said: "There was something peculiarly impressive in the circumstances under which this distinguished son of Georgia appeared, to address these burning words of counsel to our people. He was near the spot of his birth, and stood in the very spot where his honored father had received the highest judicial functions known to our laws. These influences seemed to give inspiration to his powers, and he held his large auditory spellbound for nearly two hours."

Again he spoke at Columbus, Georgia, on about the 20th of March, and afterwards at Atlanta where he answered a speech of Vice-President Stephens who had supported Governor Brown in opposition to the Administration.[55] The latter address was delivered on the 25th of March to a tremendous gathering. After discussing the position of the Confederacy in the society of nations, he turned to the question of the *habeas corpus*. "The efforts," said he, "to excite opposition and dissatisfaction among the people with the measures of the last Congress are certainly to be lamented for the effect which will be produced abroad, and upon our enemies, who will not understand their spirit and purpose; but of the effect upon our own people I have no apprehension." He passed to a discussion of the fallacies in the Governor's message to the State Senate, and speaking simply and without rhetorical adornment he presented an impressive argument, based upon his knowledge of the evolution of the law and his mastery of questions of constitutional government. In that part of the address in which he specifically replied to Mr. Stephens, the writer thinks that no unbiased student can fail to admit that Lamar had much the better of the argument.

In conclusion, he made a ringing appeal for the submergence of individual differences in the interest of the common cause: "O my countrymen, cease your repinings; and when you bend your knee to God thank him for giving you such a country and your children such a heritage. If you love that country, do not complain because she cannot in this mortal struggle to give you liberty, give you also ease and luxury and gold...."

The success of the Atlanta speech was at once apparent. Said a local paper: "We predict that new luster has been added to the historic name of Lamar by the grand effort spoken of. The speech was one of the ablest and most effective we have ever heard, and never have we seen an audience carried so irresistibly with every conclusion of the speaker, as was the case on this occasion."[56] The *Columbus* (Ga.) *Enquirer* of the 25th, in an editorial typical of many other press notices, remarked that it had "long been the fashion of our public speakers in this country to devote themselves in their harangues as much to the amusement of fools as to the edification of men of sense. The first office is that of a demagogue; the last, that of the statesman; and the Hon. L. Q. C. Lamar is certainly no demagogue." The same paper asserted that "with thorough and perfect success," he had "undermined Mr. Stephens' ingenious defense of Governor Brown's position," and that he did it, too, "in such a manner that we are left in doubt whether most to admire the massive power of his argument or the excellent temper in which it is set forth."

With his health still extremely infirm, Lamar spent most of the time from April through November, 1864, between Macon and Oxford in Georgia, serving the cause as best he might in a civil capacity. "I send you my speech," he wrote in June from his sickbed in Oxford, to Mrs. Clement C. Clay, who resided with her husband in Richmond.[57] The address in question, like others that he delivered as his strength permitted, dealt with various phases of the diplomatic situation, and presented the administration viewpoint on subjects of current interest.

But for the South the shadows were lengthening, and for Lamar the days were dark. Many of his relatives and warmest friends had died in battle. Both of his law partners and his youngest brother, Jefferson M., were long since dead, and now Thompson Bird Lamar, his other brother and colonel of the Fifth Florida, was killed in battle just outside of Petersburg.[58] As a captain in the First Florida, the latter had been severely wounded at Antietam while rescuing the colors of his regiment, after which he had served on the staff of General Joseph E. Johnston, and finally had been elevated to the colonelcy of the Fifth.

Many of Lamar's letters reflect his intense grief at the loss of his brothers and friends who were dear to him. Too, one aspect of his life and character—his deeply religious nature and the doubts and spiritual struggles which were the natural expression of a complex mind that was at once mathematical, mystical, and speculative—is frequently in evidence, throughout the period with which we are concerned, in the voluminous and intimate correspondence with his wife. "I have nothing to write about this morning," he had said in a letter of December, 1858, postmarked at Washington, when he was just entering upon his Congressional career. "I regret to say this, for I would be glad to lay before you the record of holy thoughts and fervent aspirations and prayers. I want to be a Christian, but I fear that as long as I am in public life my mind will be too much bound up in the affairs of this world." [59] Again, from Richmond in 1861 : "I often unite you in my broken and humble petitions, and pray that ours may be a household of faith." [60] "May God grant me the privilege of once more meeting my family," he wrote from the battlefield a few weeks later, "and of gathering them around the domestic altar to send up to his throne thanks for his mercies and prayers for his favor and grace!" [61] En route to his diplomatic post in Europe he was writing that the reverses suffered by the Confederacy and the prospect of leaving her (his wife) had made him seem despondent at his departure, but that recently he had "been more prayerful. I read the Scriptures more every day.... Now I feel more hopeful, and trust implicitly in God." [62] And from Richmond (where, his health somewhat improved, he had arrived on December 1st, 1864, to be commissioned Judge Advocate of the military court in the Third Army Corps—commanded by A. P. Hill—with the rank of colonel of cavalry), under date of December 15th he was expressing dissatisfaction with his own spiritual life. "Pray to God, my darling," he wrote tenderly to his wife in this letter, "that we may all be his children." [63]

About the middle of January, 1865, he was issued a special invitation to address Harris' Brigade, which included the regiment that he had once commanded. Standing upon a stump, with the foot-sore and ragged veterans of Lee's army crowded about him, he spoke to them simply from the heart. Bullets whizzed dangerously near, even splintering the stump upon which he stood, until finally the fire grew so heavy that he was forced to desist. Years after the close of the war, General Harris wrote that never would he "forget that scene; the earnest faces and torn and tattered uniforms of officers and men as shown by the flickering torchlights, the rattle of the musketry on the skirmish line, the heavy detonation of the enemy's constant artillery fire, the eloquent and burning words of the speaker, and the wild cheers of the auditors, stirred to the innermost depths of their hearts by his patriotic words." [64]

But the end had come. On the evening of April 8th, 1865, the worn soldiers of Lee pitched camp at Appomattox Court House to rest for the next day's march. Morning came, and with it a view of dismounted Union cavalrymen holding the elevated land that overlooked the road to Lynchburg. Gallantly the shattered Army of Northern Virginia, not a brigade in condition for battle, drew into formation and advanced against the enemy, only to have them drawn aside to expose the multiplied thousands of Grant's infantry. [65] By the middle of the afternoon the Union commander had extended generous terms for the surrender of the Confederate Army, and Lee had accepted.

On the morning of April 12th, the shattered remnant of the Army of Northern Virginia marched to the appointed place to stack arms for the last time. In front rode General Gordon, and behind him marched the gray column "with the old swinging route step and swaying battle flags." As they reached the front of the first Federal division, a bugle sounded and the entire Union army, regiment by regiment, saluted by shifting from "order" to "carry arms." "As Gordon heard the sound of shifting arms, he looked up and, quickly realizing what it meant, dropped the point of his sword...." Facing his own men, he "gave word for his brigades to pass with arms 'at the carry,'— honor answering honor. There was an awed silence 'as if it were the passing of the dead,'" [66] as, in truth, it was, for the cause of Lee, and of Jackson, and of Davis, and of a host of men who had bled and died had passed into nothingness.

VIII

RETIREMENT AND PREPARATION

AFTER Appomattox many of the leaders of the Confederacy were meditating the question of whether they should leave the country, or remain among the ruins of their hopes. When the question was put to Lamar, he said with tears in his eyes: "I shall stay with my people, and share their fate. I feel it to be my duty to devote my life to the alleviation, so far as in my power lies, of the sufferings this day's disaster will entail upon them." [1] Such was the advice of those other two beloved Southern leaders, Wade Hampton and Robert E. Lee. The former could understand the common desire to leave a section that had been "reduced to so deplorable a condition," and he found the sentiment to be as "widespread as it was natural." But he advised his followers to "devote their whole energies to the restoration of law and order, the reëstablishment of agriculture and commerce, the promotion of education and the rebuilding of our cities and dwellings which have been laid in ashes." [2] For all who sought Lee's advice he had the same words. If they had already left the country, he was sorry, and if they contemplated doing so he advised against it. All true Southerners, he felt, should remain to "share the fate of their respective States." "The thought," he said, "of abandoning the country and all that must be left in it is abhorrent to my feelings, ... I prefer to struggle for its restoration.... The South requires the aid of her sons now more than at any period of her history." [3]

On the 20th of May, 1865, when Lamar started home from Richmond, the last gun of the war had been fired. Indeed, for all practical purposes it had been ended at Appomattox; but on the 26th of April General Johnston surrendered to Sherman at Raleigh, and on the 4th of May, General Dick Taylor stacked his arms before Canby at Citronelle, Alabama. It was, in its very nature, a sad journey that Lamar undertook back to Mississippi, but he was by no means hopeless. Moreover, for a large part of the distance he had as his companion General E. C. Walthall, with whom there ripened a mutual regard and intimacy that was to become historic in Mississippi. Walthall, a native of Richmond, Virginia, had, when very young, been brought out to Mississippi where he had attended St. Thomas' Hall, at Holly Springs, the same school attended by Mott and Autrey, law partners of Lamar. Throughout the Civil War he served brilliantly, and in 1864 had been promoted to a major generalship in the Army of the West, serving with particular renown at Missionary Ridge and at Franklin where with Forrest he formed and protected the rear guard of the army after its bloody defeat. By appointment in 1885 he was to succeed Lamar in the United States Senate, and in 1886 was to be elected to the seat that he had held. He was to be reëlected in 1888, this time unanimously, and in 1892 was to return to the Senate without even being a candidate. He was regarded by Lamar, after the Civil War, as the strongest man in Mississippi.

After remaining a few months at Oxford with the Longstreets, Lamar set about the planning of his future. The prospect was not encouraging. Mississippi had been ravaged during the war, and the conservative ruling class that had once dominated the politics of the commonwealth was now all but disfranchised, those who had taken a leading part in the war actually so. Moreover, he was anxious to identify himself with a locality where there would be an adequate future. For awhile he toyed with the idea of settling in the rapidly growing city of Memphis, Tennessee. But the roots of his life had been set too deep in Mississippi soil, and early in September, 1865, he arranged a partnership in the law with General Walthall for the purpose of practicing in Coffeeville, and moved his family thence almost immediately.

For a year Lamar quietly practiced his profession, convinced that his days of public activity were finished. But in the very nature of things he was deeply concerned over the impending fate of the South. In a very real sense he felt that he was responsible for many of the woes of his people. True, he had from the first counseled moderation in the dealings with the North. But when the issue seemed inevitable, he had gone with his people and nerved them to the uttermost in their attempt to create a new nation. Now he felt that he was discredited—a leader who had carried his people into the wilderness from which there had been no return.

Near the end of 1870, when the period of Lamar's retirement had lengthened into five years, it seemed inevitable that he would be drawn back into public life. In the sketch of a speech which it seemed that he must unavoidably deliver in that year, he explained the considerations that had led him to abjure all activity in regard to the State government. Whenever a leader of the Lost Cause "might take his stand, suspicion and distrust would spring up around him and choke him. Feared by all, any party with which he might seek to array himself would exclaim, 'save us from our friend!' and such an affiliation as would alone enable him to accomplish his purpose would be impossible. Hence it is that for five or six years past I have deemed every duty to which man is subject—duty to himself, duty to family, duty to country—to dictate to such men silence; and by this I mean not to censure those whose convictions and acts are different from mine. I have thought, and still think, that all such a one can do, or should do, is not to uphold or approve, but quietly to acquiesce in, the result of the wager of battle. This have I sought to do, and happy am I if my example has inspired in a single breast the desire which animates mine: the wish to be a peaceable law-abiding citizen." [4]

Despite his own disfranchisement, and his complete withdrawal from public life, Lamar was keenly alive to all of the political movements about him. Particularly was he concerned for Mr. Davis, languishing in a Northern prison, and for Burton N. Harrison, Mr. Davis' private secretary who had been an assistant professor at the University of Mississippi and, appointed to the secretaryship at Lamar's suggestion, was suffering a like fate. [5] Moreover, he could not fail to suffer with his intimate friend, Hon. Clement C. Clay, of Alabama. The latter had been a United States Senator, noted for his culture and eloquence. During the war he had been one of Mr. Davis' most loyal supporters in the Confederate Senate, and toward the end of the conflict had been dispatched on a secret mission to Canada. With the fall of the Confederate Government, and the murder of Mr. Lincoln, he had voluntarily surrendered, though accused of complicity in the President's taking off. Subjected for a time to harsh treatment as a prisoner in Fortress Monroe, he was eventually to be acquitted.

"I have not time to write now," wrote Lamar when he heard that Clay had been released, "except to beg you to come right here and make your abode with me. We have a large house.... I would share the last dollar I have with you. Come, my friend, and *live with me*, and let us henceforth be inseparable." [6] Under date of March 15th, 1866, Mr. Clay replied: "Your fraternal letter only reached me on yesterday....If my means were adequate to my will, I would fly to you, my dear friend, ere a month passed over us. But there are insuperable difficulties in my way....I confess to you that my interest and my inclination both incline me to go elsewhere; but as I feel in some measure responsible for the sufferings of the people of this State, and as I have been honored by them beyond my deserts, I am persuaded that it is my duty to share their fate." [7] Such seems to have been the sentiment of almost all of the most trusted leaders of the Confederacy.

Of the imprisonment of Jefferson Davis, Mr. Clay wrote in the same letter: "I left our friend and chief in delicate, not bad, health. His beard is snowy white, his step not as firm and elastic as formerly, and his voice is stridulous. Guarded and goaded as he is, he cannot long survive. I trust that the guard will be removed from his prison before long; it is kept there, not for his security, but, I fear, to torture him. There is scarcely an officer in the Fortress besides the commandant (a Massachusetts Radical and *protégé* of Wilson's), who does not regard his treatment as cruel and unmagnanimous and mean." Truly the leaders of the Old South had fallen on evil days! [8]

Many years later, in December, 1880, the mistreatment of

Mr. Davis at the hands of Commandant Miles had its equal.
On the 15th of that month, Jefferson Davis wrote to Lamar (by
this time Senator from Mississippi), saying that Miles, who had
ordered the shackles riveted upon his legs and who had visited
upon him every privation and indignity until an aroused public
opinion had caused a cessation of his torture, had been nominated for promotion by the President. He wished Lamar to use
his influence to prevent confirmation, not only for his unkind
acts but because, as Davis pungently said, he was an "ignorant
vulgarian." Unfortunately, Lamar had been detained in Mississippi by the illness of his wife, and as a result did not reach
Washington until after the confirmation had taken place, when
he found the letter from Mr. Davis awaiting him. Answering
the communication on the 1st of January he said that had he
been in Washington he would have opposed the appointment
to the limit of his influence.

"While the circumstances connected with your barbarous
treatment at Fortress Monroe," Lamar remarked, "are fresh in
the memories of all who shared the destinies of the Confederacy,
the names of those whose cowardly deeds made the story of
your incarceration infamous, were forgotten; and I very much
doubt whether there was a single man among all the Southern
Senators who thought for an instant, when consenting to or
failing to oppose the nomination sent in by President Hayes,
that he was elevating the creature who had insulted our whole
people in his mistreatment of their Chief Magistrate. I have not
expressed myself accurately when I used the word *doubt;* I
am *absolutely confident* that no one of those Senators would
by his action, positive or negative, have been consciously a
party to the condoning of one of the most dastardly and cowardly crimes of the century." [9]

Although both the Lamar and the Longstreet connections had
suffered severe losses by the War, the devastation and impov-
erishment among them was by no means so complete as among
many of the leading families of the South. Brigadier General N.
H. Harris, of the brigade to which Lamar's old regiment be-

longed, writes that "we are hard at it now. When our senior returned he found his home shattered in pieces.... Our office furniture consisted of one desk, two chairs, and one book: the Code of 1857. This was our start. We have a neatly furnished office, some two or three hundred books, and are little more than paying expenses." [10] Thus did the manhood of the South set about rebuilding their lives on the wreckage of the old.

A letter to Lamar from his mother, Mrs. Troutman, dated March 23rd, 1866, and written from Macon, Georgia, shows to what straits the people of that city had been reduced. "Our people here are very despondent," she said. "The Federals are seizing all the cotton they can get hold of, upon the plea of its being subscribed to the Confederate Government. Georgia is anxious to be at peace. The people are yielding, and submit as well as they may to compulsion. Everything is quiet and still. The people earnestly desire to do right, and are well pleased with President Johnson. There is great destitution among many of our people; those who have been accustomed to even the luxuries of life. In Calhoun, where I went with your sister two weeks ago, there were such striking evidences of poverty as to make it painful to imagine.... The village is in a ruinous condition. Many of the houses burned, and no repairs going on. I was told that persons who had been rich have now barely the necessaries of life. It was a sad thing to witness.... Write soon, dear son, and tell me you have courage to meet all the trials of life with cheerfulness, and that you are contented to commence life again with renewed hope and confidence in your final success. May God aid you in all your efforts." [11]

Such was the courage of a mother who, with one son left to her, had yet given both her two younger to the cause of the South. In another letter, this written on September 4th, 1865, she wrote concerning his spiritual life: "If we could truly realize this [God's love], how many of the sorrows and afflictions of life would lose their poignancy, and a sweet feeling of implicit trust and love would fill our hearts with happiness. I trust, dearest Lucius, that, in some degree, you feel this blessed assurance, and can trust God for the future. Be encouraged.

God opens your way before you, and when an avenue of use-fulness is closed he leads you gently on, his redeemed child, into ways you have not known. And thus he will ever do; only put your unfaltering trust in him." [12]

The mention, in the letter of the 23rd, of the stealing of cotton by Federal agents on the plea that it had been subscribed to the Confederate Government, calls attention to an abuse that was only too widespread. Treasury agents swarmed over the whole tier of Southern States confiscating all the cotton that they could find, hardly a fraction of it being turned over to the Government of the United States. [13] Occasionally the civil authorities would have the temerity to arrest the thieves, but when they were caught red-handed they were merely released by the army of occupation, often Negro troops that drove the whites to a frenzy, though they were powerless to resist. [14] Since the burden of proof was always upon the planter, and nothing that he could do or say would have any effect, the stealing was unusually good, as when one Union agent in Alabama stole eighty thousand dollars' worth of cotton in a single month. [15]

Throughout the entire South, in the months since Appomattox, a ragged stream of crippled and half-starved men in gray had struggled back to their desolate and ravaged homes. "They are so worn out," said one observer, "that they fall down on the sidewalks and sleep." [16] There is "a degree of destitution," wrote a Northern correspondent, "that would draw pity from a stone," [17] and a lady traveling between Chester and Camden, South Carolina, could hardly restrain her tears when she found no sign of previous habitation other than the blackened chimneys over which rambler roses had already begun to climb. [18]

A man who was formerly one of the wealthiest planters of Mississippi returned to find upon his broad and desolate acres only a single cow and a few mules. [19] Every house, barn, and fence had been destroyed, and he had not a dollar with which to rebuild. Moreover, there seemed no possibility of raising a crop unless the blacks were willing to cultivate the land on shares. Happily, many of the former slaves went about their work "very quiet and serious and more obedient and kind than they had ever been known to be." [20] With fine delicacy old slaves would leave fruit and game and turkeys on the doorstep of their former masters, and slip away without being observed. But all this was soon to end, for the carpetbagger —together with the soldiers that had been stationed throughout the South—strove to turn the blacks against their former masters; and soon in every Southern town was to be heard the statement that "de bottom rail done got on top," as the Negroes, drunk with their own importance, sunned themselves on every corner.

All might have worked out but for the unfortunate presence of the soldiers who made the Negroes believe that in their new estate it was unnecessary to work. According to the diary of Mrs. Chesnut, "Negroes were seen in the fields plowing and hoeing corn," and a few weeks later she records that "the negroes have flocked to the Yankee squad." [21] Wave after wave of religious emotionalism swept the blacks into frenzies, and after a particularly exhilarating revival service the countryside would be pillaged of poultry and vegetables on the basis of the preacher's declaration that the Lord would provide. [22] "The negro girls for miles around," said one commentator in reference to the influence of the Northern soldiery in the neighborhood, "are gathered to the camps and debauched.... It surely is not the aim of those persons who aim at the equality of colors to begin the experiment with a whole race of whores." [23]

The Southern men deplored the presence of the soldiers throughout the land, but they treated them courteously and, accepting the result of the war in good faith, asked only that they be allowed to work out the salvation of their section in peace. Not so the ladies, who ostracized the officers and men and often crossed the street to keep from meeting them; and, indeed, in many cases there were considerations of safety that made it wise for them to avoid particularly depraved characters. But when the Federal Government stationed Negro troops throughout the section (to the indignation, even, of a great many people in the North), these often marching four abreast and jostling the whites from the pavement, the seeds of revolution had been sown among the oppressed people.

Meanwhile, Carl Schurz, in the early and radical phase of his career, had come South through the subsidization of Sumner and some of his associates, and was recording every word or look that he might use as an argument for keeping the soldiers quartered among the stricken people; and Salmon P. Chase, the radical, political Chief Justice of the Supreme Court of the United States, was attending a Negro fair in the once beautiful home of Pierre Soule and watching the blacks selling ice-cream, gambling, and throwing about the books in the Soule library.[24] The Negro women, reported one of Chase's companions, were quite "as handsome, as elegantly dressed, and in many respects almost as brilliant" as any white women that Soule had probably ever invited into his house.[25]

In these trying days Lamar was quietly going about the task of building up his law practice and attempting to provide for his family. An intimate glimpse of the household is to be had in a letter of February 16th, 1866, written by Mrs. Lamar to her mother, Mrs. Longstreet, shortly after they had taken up their residence in Coffeeville: "Perhaps it will all turn out right in the end. I try to take this view of everything which happens, and be thankful for the portion of this world's goods which is left to us. True, the times are very much changed, but they might be worse. We keep no man servant now about the lot. Lucius has been working about the fences and gates and locks to his outhouses. He feeds his cows and helps cut the wood and does a great deal of work. If he can only have good health, I feel as if we would be happy under almost any circumstances."[26]

With large responsibilities beyond those of his immediate family, and with a few debts incurred before the war that in his impoverished condition now became most onerous, Lamar had need of all the courage that he could command. Resolutely he set about the meeting of his obligations, which in the end he discharged to the last penny. In the years immediately succeeding the war, however, he was forced to part with most of the family silver and with many treasured heirlooms in his efforts to meet the situation in which he found himself.

Life with Lamar was still in a state of flux. In June of 1866 he was reëlected to the chair of ethics and metaphysics in the State University, the same professorship which he had held for a short time in 1860-61. The board of trustees informed him, moreover, that he was at liberty to accept such cases at law as came his way. Consequently, he moved with his family to Oxford where he quickly became absorbed in his work. His labors were intensified because during the session of 1866-67 he was called upon to discharge, *ad interim*, the duties of professor of law. Relieved of a part of his own work, he was still expected to conduct classes in psychology, in logic, and in law. However, the extreme pressure was lifted in January when he was unanimously elected to the chair of law and relieved of all other duties in the University.

As a professor of law, Lamar's work was notable and in some respects historic. In 1867, three years before Christopher Langdell had entered upon his career as Dane Professor of Law at Harvard, Lamar had introduced and established a method of teaching from adjudicated cases that was in essence the very same as the Case System, developed by Langdell and today used in every recognized law school in the nation.[27] Lamar predicated his instruction on the belief that the mastery of the law was to be attained through analysis of the actual legal reports, and through a study of every phase of adjudicated cases, rather than by text books which gave second hand information about the law. He set up well defined standards for graduation and instituted a regular system of written examinations upon the body of the material that had been assigned or discussed. In doing so he broke definitely with the contemporary methods of teaching which customarily involved a study of certain texts with class quizzes and comments from the instructor.

Because so much of the body of the law was at that time poorly organized, the labors entailed by Lamar's methods of instruction were arduous in the extreme. Without the elaborate system of indexes and digests at hand today, he of course could not refer his students to volumes that contained references to all cases involving certain points of law, but was forced laboriously to assemble much of the material himself. Never, however, did he lose sight of the fact that beyond any amount of formal memory work, the important thing was the mastery of legal principles attained by working out their application to concrete cases. It was Lamar's destiny to live at a time when the press of a great social upheaval made it impossible for him to devote his life permanently and solely to scholarly pursuits. But the work which he had begun was not to die, for Langdell, upon his own invention and initiative, was to carry it to a high degree of development at Harvard, an institution which was one day to confer upon Lamar its highest honor in recognition of his distinguished work as an educator and statesman. By 1900 Stanford had set up a school along the lines and upon principles evolved by Lamar and Langdell, and by 1902 Beale had carried the gospel to the growing University of Chicago; then, in rapid succession, Michigan, Columbia, Yale, and all of the recognized law schools of the nation accepted and instituted the Case System of teaching.

Of Lamar's teaching and his influence in the University, a close associate who was subsequently to be the Chancellor of the institution, says: "There was but one voice from those who came in contact with him in regard to Prof. Lamar's efficiency. ... As a member of the faculty he was always wise and prompt in counsel, temperate and considerate, although firm when occasion arose." [28] Furthermore, he was devoted to the interests of his students: "He felt that, for the time, he was the representative of the true principles of the science which he taught, and that he was individually responsible for his teaching. He possessed in a wonderful degree the faculty of infusing his own spirit into all who sat under his instruction."

His own deep scholarship and research in the principles of English and Roman law bore particular fruit in his teaching. Said the author of the above statement: "To a knowledge of the law coextensive with its range, he united a power of analysis, generalization, and elucidation which nearly divested it of all obscurity. His lectures upon the most intricate and obscure branches, such as conditions and limitations in deeds, executory devises, contingent remainders, and the exact boundaries between the law and equity, presented those troublesome subjects in entirely new lights, and gave to them a symmetry, consistency, and perspicuity equally admirable and unexpected.... Cases for trial were devised by the Professor, which were brought and defended by students appointed for the purpose, with all of the formalities and details." [29]

Of the prominent men of Mississippi and the South who left their impress between 1866 and 1900, particularly those eminent in the legal profession, a surprising number had sat at the feet of Lamar at Oxford. The hold which he had upon the minds and imaginations of his students is well seen in a memorial address delivered by a former student, Hon. C. E. Hooker, shortly after Lamar's death: "The love and affection which he aroused in the hearts of young men was wonderful.... You will not find a graduate of that institution who was educated there during the period that Mr. Lamar acted as professor that does not feel for him, and has not borne for him in all the changing stages of life, that perfect affection and profound admiration that he inspired in the hearts of all young men who came in contact with him." [30]

"I knew him first," said Bishop Charles B. Galloway, "in my boyhood at the University, where he occupied a professor's chair, and there learned to love and admire him. He was the Gamaliel at whose feet I sat and from whose lips I received instruction. The thrill of that flashing eye, the tone of that magic voice, the strange magnetism of that magnificent presence, filling as he did the broad heavens of our imaginations, and the loftiest ideal of my young ambition, have lingered and inspired me for more than half a jubilee of years. He stirred many a noble impulse and set on fire many a laudable ambition." [31]

A recent biographer of the late Senator Joe Bailey, of Texas, has much to say of the enduring influence of Lamar even after he had quitted the university and become a national figure: "Lucius Quintus Cincinnatus Lamar was soon to become the leader in one of the most courageous and desperate rebellions in the history of any people. One of the lasting folk heroes of the Southern people, this statesman and jurist was indirectly to influence Bailey greatly at a time when he was passing from boyhood to manhood." [32] At seventeen, Bailey had enrolled at the University of Mississippi. "Although he could afford any cut of clothes he desired, it was soon noted that he did not follow the immediate fashion for undergraduates. At the time he was one of a group of students who sought out and rather reverently called on Lamar at such times as he was at home in Oxford between sessions of Congress. By now Lamar had been made United States Senator, and his home, at such times as he was there, was a sort of shrine to the young Mississippians who had come from distant parts of the State.... The influence of Lamar, and all he stood and fought for, was infinitely greater [than any other] though, on the young visitor. It was from Lamar that the young man, whose ideas already looked beyond a legal career to active politics, was able to orient his ideas of classical Southern politics to the renewed national outlook. From the example of Lamar he saw that the South was not done for as a factor in the Federal Union; that, without making apologies for the war, and without foreswearing the political ideals of the major prophets such as Jefferson and John C. Calhoun, the New South had much yet to contribute to the nation." [33]

One other incident in connection with Lamar's teaching at the university should be noted—his association with the Sigma Alpha Epsilon fraternity. In his regiment during the campaign around Williamsburg had been a number of young college men who had left their studies in various institutions to fight for the Southern cause. At the termination of the war, when the Colonel had become a professor at the University of Mississippi, two or three of these young men, influenced by the desire to study under their former leader, matriculated at Oxford for the purpose of completing their training. Under the leadership of Thomas B. Manlove (himself an ex-soldier but not a former member of Lamar's regiment), who had been initiated into Sigma Alpha Epsilon before the war at the old University of Nashville, this group set about the organization of a new chapter of that fraternity. Under the circumstances, it was natural that the young men should invite their favorite and most celebrated professor to membership. Lamar, as was to be expected, accepted the invitation and was regularly initiated with the others.

The fraternity has never allowed his memory to fade. In the library of the beautiful Gothic temple, dedicated by the fraternity on December 28th, 1930, to the memory of its war dead, of all the wars since its founding, hangs a splendid portrait of Justice Lamar, painted by Johannes Waller of Munich, and in the Chapel, one of the most beautiful stained glass windows in the nation commemorates his services to the country.[34]

Unforeseen conditions, however, were about to put a final end to Lamar's association with the University—at least an end to his active participation in its affairs. In 1870 the State Government, which had been deplorable enough under the military régime, was turned over entirely to the carpetbaggers. This had been effected by the election which, occurring in the fall of 1869, was dominated by the armed forces of the Federal Government, and which placed in control James L. Alcorn, a radical governor who, though not personally dishonest, turned over the legislature to the most depraved element—white and black—in the State. The Governor, who was *ex officio* President of the board of the University, and who had been opposed by Lamar, changed the personnel of the governing body of the institution, and Lamar recognized that his period of usefulness on the faculty was over. Accordingly, he resigned and on June 27th, 1870, delivered his valedictory in the form of the annual address to the literary societies of the University. Of his address, the *Weekly Clarion* said that "it was one of his ablest and most eloquent efforts," and that "for one hour he held his vast audience as delighted listeners."

Lamar now devoted his entire time to the practice of law,

particularly in the federal court at Oxford. For a while he toyed with the idea of returning to Macon, Georgia, where it had been suggested that he associate himself with the prominent law firm of Nisbets & Jackson. This suggestion appealed to him because the social and political situation in Mississippi had become almost intolerable. Evidently he was much depressed in his letter of May 30th, to Judge James Jackson. "The lawyers here," he said, "are deeply discontented with the shock which Alcorn and his Legislature have given to their interests, and many of the leading men have gone to New Orleans and Memphis. The wound is an incurable one, and the state of things is permanent. The negroes have a large and increasing majority. I must take my property and family from the State." That he had not lost his love of teaching is seen in his statement that, if he should leave Mississippi, he "would so much like to move" ...his "law school to Macon and have you all in it, the Judge [Longstreet] to be the Chancellor." [35] But indissoluble bonds of affection and interest had come to bind him fast to Mississippi, and eventually he discarded all idea of leaving her.

Lamar's eloquence made it almost impossible for him to retire from the public gaze without constant and urgent requests that he enter the forum on public questions. As far as he could do so, however, he refused to be drawn into political discussions. A widely quoted speech of real practical value he delivered before the Agricultural and Mechanical Association of Carrol and Choctaw counties in the fall of 1869. He advised his listeners to make use of the latest mechanical and scientific inventions in the cultivation of their lands, and he urged them to plant a smaller acreage of cotton and to institute a wider diversification of crops. The more intense cultivation of a smaller acreage, with rotation, he pointed out, would stave off exhaustion of the land and would make farming less expensive. Again, he discussed the evils of class legislation, of excessive and unwarranted taxation, and the unfairness to agricultural communities of the existing tariff laws.[36] It is clear that Lamar, believing that the future held nothing for him in the nature of

political preferment, had turned his mind resolutely to bettering the economic situation of his people.

A letter that he wrote during this period, on December 5th,
1870, attracted wide notice.[37] The occasion was the recent death
of General Lee, whose birthday was to be commemorated with
memorial exercises at Vicksburg. Lamar had been invited to
deliver the chief address but when the pressure of business made
it impossible for him to attend, he wrote the long and frequently quoted letter. His words are notable in that he was
writing shortly after Lee's death and at a time when his relative
and close friend, General Longstreet, was becoming peculiarly
offensive in certain of his remarks concerning the Southern
leader. Lamar had had occasion more than once in the course of
the war to bring his personal influence to bear upon Longstreet
when the latter was not fully coöperating, he thought, with
the Confederate Government.

His discriminating estimate of Lee's character and ability—
among other things he characterized him the greatest of America's military geniuses—is as valid today as it was when it was
written, though the South is now willing (as soon Lamar himself was) to have him viewed as a great national figure rather
than as the peculiar heritage of the section to which he had
devoted his talents.

The greater part of Lamar's time, however, was taken up
with the prosaic task of winning a livelihood for his family.
While going about his labors in the courts, there occurred an
incident,[38] on the 22nd of June, 1871, which gives an indica-
tion of the tense state of affairs that existed under the reconstruction government. The situation was as follows: The little
city of Oxford had become the center of the United States
Government drive against the Ku Klux Klan, and in the federal
court there had been instituted proceedings against a number
of citizens from all sections of the State. There was an air of
suppressed excitement, and the neighborhood was filled with
strangers (witnesses, prisoners, soldiers, and the lawless element
of drifters and carpetbaggers that was to be found all over the

South). On the 22nd of June, as Colonel Lamar went to his
office, which was located in the same passage as the federal
courtroom, he observed that one of the government witnesses,
Whistler (sometimes spelled "Wissler") by name, a rough and
disreputable character, was abusing and severely beating an old
man, who, under the influence of liquor, was entirely helpless.

The confusion continued so long and so loud that the federal court was forced, for the time being, to adjourn, and the
judge ordered that those creating the disturbance be arrested.
Meanwhile, the old man, who was being savagely beaten, called
upon Lamar to intervene. Before the latter had ever spoken,
Whistler began to curse him. Lamar stepped to the nearby
door of the Mayor's office and, requesting that the offender
be put under arrest, passed on. As it happened the Mayor
was too much intimidated by the soldiers to carry out the
arrest which had been legally requested and which he had the
authority to perform. Eventually a deputy marshal for the court
reached the scene at the very moment that Whistler had drawn
a pistol and was apparently about to shoot the old man. The
deputy carried both of them before the Mayor, where Whistler
continued to flourish his pistol until a gentleman, Roberts by
name, took it from him. Meanwhile, federal soldiers espoused
Whistler's cause and carried him away before the Mayor, who
had police powers, could sentence him. The civil law was
entirely powerless to cope with the situation.

At the afternoon session of the court, several of the alleged
Ku Klux cases were scheduled to be taken up, and Lamar, as
well as many citizens of Oxford, was present. Seeing the deputy
who had taken Whistler in charge that morning, he asked
what had been done with him. The former explained that he
had carried the desperado before the Mayor, but that he had
insolently walked off before the executive's face, in company
with some soldiers. When the deputy assured Lamar that he
would arrest him again, and turn him over to the town marshal,
he was told that that would be useless, but that he, Lamar, would
himself speak to the presiding judge in reference to the matter.

At this juncture, Whistler, who—it turned out—was to appear as a paid government witness that afternoon, walked into the court. Lamar immediately arose and, after stating his reasons, requested that the judge have Whistler placed under arrest. The latter drew a huge pistol from its holster, and approached Lamar, who held his ground, meanwhile saying to the judge: "I ask your Honor to make this man take his seat and keep it until I finish my statement." When the judge hesitated, Lamar picked up a chair with the remark: "If the court won't make you, I will." Whistler leaped backward, and Lamar put down the chair. Meanwhile several of the officials had begun to cry, "Arrest Colonel Lamar!" while one of them said to several soldiers who were guarding the prisoners, "By virtue of the authority of the United States I order you to arrest that man," all the while pointing to the Colonel. The only response made by the soldiers was to the effect that they were not under the speaker's orders.

When the court deputy approached Lamar, the latter stated that he had broken no law, and waved the officer aside. At this point United States Marshal Pierce came running up, and laid his hands on both Lamar and Whistler. Afterwards it was discovered that he had come in merely in the rôle of a peacemaker, but as he had his face turned toward Whistler, Lamar did not recognize him and struck him such a blow that he was knocked over several benches and across the courtroom with his jaw severely bruised and dislocated. While the United States Attorney cried for Lamar's arrest, the foreman of the grand jury rushed out and called in another squad of soldiers who entered to the click of the hammers on their muskets. Lamar, however, was not without support, for two lawyers who were present, Major Thomas Walton, a Republican who was afterwards United States Attorney, and E. O. Sykes, a former student at the University, drew their pistols and stood at his side.

Lamar himself had become greatly incensed at the dilatory tactics of the presiding judge. Raising his arms above his head, he denounced the lax enforcement of the laws that allowed such outrages as that perpetrated by Whistler, and the parading of

United States soldiers in the courts of the land. As the troops faced him with their cocked guns, Lamar clenched his fist and warned the officers of the court that if he were placed in jail the streets of the town would "swim in blood." At length General Featherston and Colonel Manning, both prominent citizens and friends of Lamar, intervened, and when the passions of all concerned had somewhat subsided, the latter apologized to the court for the part that he had taken in the disturbance. When Lamar discovered that it was the marshal, bent on friendly advice, whom he had struck so severely, he expressed the keenest regrets which were immediately accepted. As the sergeant in charge of the company of soldiers said to a citizen later: "We didn't want to hurt him; we never saw a better fight or heard a better speech. He hadn't broken any law."

Meanwhile, no attention was paid to Whistler, who slunk off. Certain very illuminating facts have been uncovered concerning this unsavory character.[39] Arriving from the North immediately after the war he had been appointed a carpetbag magistrate at Macon, Mississippi, from which place he was forced to flee after he had been indicted for embezzling the funds of the court. He set out across the country with an acquaintance but was accused and narrowly escaped conviction on a charge of robbing his companion, and, having rendered him unconscious, setting him on fire with the oil from a lamp, this according to the man's dying testimony. At the time of the courtroom incident he was employed by the Federal Government as a guard over Ku Klux Klan prisoners and as a paid witness who was in attendance wherever the trials were being held. Before his arrival in the South he had been an Ohio "bounty jumper" and had had a long criminal and penal record as a counterfeiter. Shortly after the incident at Oxford he was killed in a drunken brawl. Such were many of the adventurers who, with the blacks, were set to rule the South after the war.

Certain testimony subsequently given before the federal investigating committee was in the main correct and sheds interesting light upon the occurrence from the viewpoint of eye-witnesses.[40] Colonel R. O. Reynolds testified that "Colonel Lamar arose and commenced to address the court, stating... that he desired the court to bind over a man who was there before the court because he had been threatening him, dogging him on the streets of Oxford, as he believed, for the purpose of provoking a disturbance. My recollection of the remark is: 'I ask your honor to protect me from the cowardly assassin.' When he made the remark Wissler jumped up and threw his hand behind him."

The story is continued by General Gholson, another witness: "Lamar ordered Wissler to sit down. He did not do so. Lamar caught up a chair and told him if he did not sit down he would make him do so. The judge seemed to be a little excited, got up and ordered silence, and somebody pulled down the chair that Lamar had in his hands. Colonel Reynolds said pretty loudly to the prisoners: 'You Monroe men sit down.' About that time soldiers came to the door. Lamar was still demanding his right to speak. The marshal came up to him and spoke. What he said I do not know. Lamar struck him a pretty hard lick on the face and sent him reeling. That increased the excitement. Lamar went on speaking."

The further testimony of Colonel Reynolds completes the picture: "My attention was then directed to the federal soldiers, and I heard the click of their guns. As soon as I heard that I said to General Featherston, 'General, let us not let these soldiers fire.' We went up to them and told them there was no use in interfering, and they brought their guns from a 'ready' to an 'order.' Everything became quiet. Colonel Lamar [was] still on the floor. Judge Hill ordered him to sit down. He said he would not do it, that he claimed his constitutional right to be heard and said something else which was handsome. Finally General Featherston and other friends led Colonel Lamar into another room. Everything quieted down and, as General Gholson said, 'we went on with our case.'"

Since his apologies had been accepted by the judge, and the incident had ostensibly been closed, Lamar thought that he would hear no more of it. On the next day great was his surprise when the following order was entered upon the court record:

Whereas a most unfortunate and much to be regretted difficulty occurred in the presence of the court on yesterday, in which Col. L. Q. C. Lamar, a member of the bar of this court, was a party; and whereas soon thereafter the said Lamar made an apology to the court which was satisfactory to the judge of the court as an individual, yet, being the judicial representative of the United States for the time being, the judge of the court deems it necessary for the vindication of the court and the government that the name of said L. Q. C. Lamar be stricken from the roll of attorneys thereof, and that he be prohibited from practicing as an attorney and counselor therein.[41]

Lamar's disbarment was denounced widely throughout the State, particularly in the conservative press. The members of the local bar prepared a memorial to the court, but upon Lamar's insistence that he would neither petition nor supplicate for reinstatement—that he had merely defended himself from a murderous assault and from illegal arrest—they agreed to drop their protest. Within a few days the district attorney himself moved that the judge rescind this action, as was promptly done. The radical press of the North, however, distorted the facts and attempted to make it appear that Lamar was in league with the Klan prisoners, that he had fomented a disturbance into which he had drawn the University students, who, they said, had swarmed into the courtroom and intimidated the judge.

Lamar was to hear repercussions of this affair for many years. At one time, in the Senate, he had had reason to expect that Blaine would bring up the matter, and in consequence he had planned to clear himself once and for all. When Blaine failed to project the subject into the debate, he was disappointed, for he was prepared to vindicate himself completely. When Cleveland appointed him to the Secretaryship of the Interior, those who opposed him revived the discussion; and when he was nominated for the Supreme Court of the United States, the *New York Tribune* made it the text of a savage assault.

As a matter of fact, these attacks merely discredited those who uttered them and the intelligent people of the nation evaluated them for what they were worth. No case could have stood against Lamar—had it been necessary for him to present a defense—in the face of the facts set forth by Colonel Pierce, the marshal whom Lamar had unwittingly struck, to the effect that "our relations, officially and personally, were always most pleasant, as also were his with the other officers of the court. I had known that it was mainly due to his efforts and personal influence that a riot was averted in Oxford, at an election held during November, 1869; and from intercourse with him I knew him to be conservative, law-abiding, and considerate of the views of other men. Knowing his great ability, his extensive knowledge of our institutions, and his conservative tendencies, and believing that he could best represent the people of that district, I favored his election to Congress, and voted for him." Judge Hill, who presided at the time that the incident occurred, wrote to Lamar, in a letter of July 5th, 1887, that a mutual friend had shown him "a copy of the *Tribune*, in which there is an allusion to a difficulty which occurred in the court at Oxford, regretted by no one more than yourself, the allusion to which is regretted by no one more than myself. I trust that it will not be alluded to again. If so, and it becomes necessary, I will do all in my power to render it harmless to you, as well as to myself. It occurred under most extraordinary circumstances, its disposition was at the time satisfactory to all concerned, and it ought to be buried in the sea of forgetfulness." [42]

The period under discussion had seen changes in the family life of Lamar. In the month of November, 1868, came the death of his mother-in-law, Mrs. Longstreet, to whom he had been greatly attached, and in the following July Judge Longstreet, in his eightieth year, passed away surrounded by the members of his family circle. The death of the latter made a profound impression upon Lamar, who was at his bedside. Lamar was an intellectual, albeit a deeply spiritual man, and was not given to fancies, religious or otherwise, yet he could never quite free himself from the impression that the eyes of the saintly old gentleman, in the instant of death, had caught a glimpse of another and a better world.[43] Shortly afterwards, on the occasion when he delivered the commencement address at his Alma Mater, where he had first known Judge Longstreet as the President, he spoke impressively of the death scene, and commended the life of the deceased for emulation by those to whom he spoke. Incidentally, on the occasion of this address at Emory, he was tendered the professorship of Belles Lettres and History. This he declined, for he had finally determined to link his destiny with that of his adopted State.

In May of this same year, 1869, came the marriage of Lamar's oldest child to Mr. Edward Mayes, a young Confederate veteran who was subsequently Chancellor of the University of Mississippi and one of the most brilliant lawyers and enlightened and liberal thinkers in the State. Still a young man himself, Lamar must have been reminded that time was passing, and that he was barred by circumstances, apparently, from the fulfillment of the rich promise of his youth. However, his practice in the law had greatly prospered and according to his own statement it was "very large," judged by the standards of the South of that time. Having discharged the debts and heavy obligations with which the Civil War had left him encumbered, he now set about the building of a permanent home in the northern part of the town of Oxford—the first of his own since he left "Solitude" in 1857. The site selected was large, about thirty acres, and by April of 1870 he had erected upon it a very comfortable residence.

On May 28th of this same year, writing from Memphis whence his legal practice had taken him, Lamar resumed his correspondence with A. T. Bledsoe, his former chief in the department of mathematics at the University of Mississippi and now editing the *Southern Review* in Baltimore. "I have never, since our separation in England [during Lamar's service as diplomatic agent of the Confederacy], in feeling, thought, or outward deed swerved or wavered in the sentiment which a loyal friend always feels for his loyal friend," he wrote in explaining that the struggles of the five post-war years had brought about a lapse in his entire correspondence.[44] He had been asked, he said, to advise Dr. Bledsoe in certain financial matters connected with the *Review*. "I told them that if there was anything from me that you would be likely to disregard or laugh at, it would be my advice about business—that you did not think me overstocked with common sense (the only mistake I have ever caught you in) but that I would write to you and recommend you to consider the matter before you took any final step." The two men were never, henceforth, to lose contact until Dr. Bledsoe's death, and the latter was always fond of saying that he "taught Lucius how to think," a statement which, when repeated to Lamar during the Senate years, he smilingly admitted not to be without some elements of truth.[45]

But the period of exile was drawing to a close. The plight of Mississippi, as we shall see in the next chapter, was pitiable, and no longer could the former leaders of the State see their people endure the Black Republican and carpetbag rule. It was only natural that they should turn first of all to Lamar, who, but forty-five years of age, was at the height of his mental and physical powers (though always threatened by the dread shadow of paralysis and apoplexy). His reëntrance into the arena was signalized by the debate in which he engaged with Governor Alcorn, on the 9th of October, 1871.[46] When General Lowry, the Democratic candidate for the governor's chair, was taken sick just before his scheduled debate with Alcorn, Lamar, who chanced to be in town on business and was present in the audience, was requested to present the Democratic viewpoint extemporaneously.

According to contemporary newspaper accounts, he acquitted himself in notable fashion. Mr. Clarke, his junior law partner, wrote under date of October 13th that "with the general approbation that your speech has elicited, the complimentary things that Alcorn said of you, and the opportunity that you had of being a little magnanimous toward him, I think that it was altogether a field day for you." [47] "Imagine my consternation," wrote Lamar a few days later. "I had not made a political speech in ten years, and was almost ignorant of the current campaign politics....While I did not meet the natural anticipations of what the occasion required, my speech answered more to the hidden thought and to the hearts of my audience than if I had followed the established lines. It certainly disconcerted Alcorn so much that he was unable to get along in his reply, though usually a most irrepressible 'slangwhanger.'" [48]

IX

THE RETURN TO THE NATIONAL ARENA

THE horrors of reconstruction during the period of Lamar's retirement—so ably narrated by a host of recent commentators who have recreated its stirring drama—it is useless to retell. Generally speaking, the Thirteenth Amendment had long since enfranchised the blacks, and the Fourteenth and Fifteenth had more recently given them the power (with their carpetbag associates) to control the State governments while barring from public life the leading citizens of character and property. Trumbull's Civil Rights Bill and other acts of the radical-controlled Congress had set up the machinery for an attempted regulation of the minute details of the social relationship of the two races; Johnson, bravely fighting, had been crushed; and the Congressional scheme of reconstruction and the inauguration of General Grant had destroyed the last vestige of local self-government in ten States of the Union, and had established the "black and tan" governments firmly in the saddle.

In the period from the close of the war to 1871, Lamar, as has been pointed out, studiedly refrained from reëntering public life, or even expressing himself freely on the contemporary policies of the Federal Government. He was, he felt, in a sense responsible for the dire suffering that had come upon his people, and, as one of their former leaders, he thought it most fitting that he hold his counsel.

But popular demand had made it impossible for him to hold without exception to the rule that he had set for himself. In June, 1866, for instance, when he presented medals to the successful declaimers of the sophomore class at the University, he seemed less optimistic concerning the future of the country than the orator who had preceded him. In an extemporaneous speech that the local press termed "eloquent and impressive," he expressed the belief that no vestige of States' Rights was left; that the way in the future was extremely dark; and that he could see no liberty when a political line was drawn with right on one side and power entirely on the other. Although he had used all of his personal influence toward the defeat of the radicals in the election of 1869 (he delivered, however, no speeches in the campaign) and as a result of their victory resigned his chair in the University, we hear from him no further utterance on the questions of the day until 1871.[1]

It was a period, however, when Lamar was spiritually and intellectually ripening for his great work. With his personal finances in reasonably satisfactory condition, he was yet weighed down with the griefs that had engulfed his people.

Near the end of North Street (now known as North Lamar), on the eastern side, stood the attractive six room cottage that Lamar had recently built. The house itself, situated some two hundred yards from the road, was almost hidden from view by the dense tangle of cedars and fruit trees, and the yard was dotted with beautiful magnolias and an occasional forest oak. Some of the beauty of the location is still evident in the house that stands to-day just as it was when Lamar built it; in the great old magnolias that have lasted through the years; and in the remnant of the two rows of cedars that bordered the road from North Street to the house.

"At this period," it has been recorded by the late Edward Mayes, "upon almost any clement evening, late, if one should follow the plank walk until the white picket fence which marked the premises of Col. Lamar should be reached, there he would be found; clad in a drab study-gown, somewhat frayed and stained with ink; his face long, massive, and sallow; bareheaded, with his long brown hair stirred by the breeze; his deep mysterious eyes fixed upon the yellowing western sky, or watching dreamily the waving limbs of the avenue of water oaks across the way; abstracted, recognizing the salutations of the passers-by with a nod half courteous, half surly, and yet obviously unconscious of all identities; a countenance solemn, and enigmatical," as brooding upon the hopeless future of his stricken State, he watched his neighbors crowded from the pavement by the newly enfranchised blacks. "There were loving eyes which watched him narrowly then—eyes which seeing, yet seemed not to see—and loving hands diligently wove bonds of silk to draw him away from the perilous verge upon which he stood; for more than one anxious heart interpreted those volcanic moods, and trembled lest in some weaker hour a dreadful deed, born of fury and despair, should spring like a tiger from its lair, and ruin all." [2]

Lamar, as we have already seen, came near the brink of desperate action in the Oxford court incident when he was threatened with arrest merely for asking the indictment of a desperado who had assaulted an aged man of the town. His was a strangely passionate nature, but he had disciplined himself until throughout life he was known, in the words of Henry Adams, as the "gentlest" of men. But it was not without the bounds of possibility that he (despite his profound respect for the observance of the laws, and a humanity and catholicity of outlook that caused him involuntarily to look for virtues and redeeming traits even in those whom he most cordially disliked) might have been goaded by the wrongs of his section into leading a forlorn and bloody revolt against the intolerable conditions.

As it was, he was to return to public life from his voluntary retirement with a nature deepened and enriched by suffering. He had had the time to think profoundly upon the nature of human conduct and man's social institutions, and his already philosophical mind had taken on a richness which was often to be remarked upon in his later career. All those things with which his life had been most closely associated had turned to ashes, and he faced a new world. In pre-war days we have seen that he was a sectionalist, though a sectionalist with the kindest regards for the rights of the whole people of the United States. When he emerged from his Gethsemane, he was a nationalist who saw that the future happiness of the country could only lie in a spirit of mutual confidence and coöperation between all sections and all States, and in his subsequent rôle of the Great Pacificator, he was to leave his mark upon a quarter of a century of American life.

Before 1870 there was a large and responsible element within the Republican party who had come to see that Grant's administration and the party machinery had come under the control of audacious, cunning, and evil men who were plundering the nation. Moreover, they recognized that the reconstruction measures of 1867 had been conceived in hate and fostered by the radical element in Congress for political and financial purposes. As a result had come the liberal Republican movement in Missouri that in 1870 had sent Carl Schurz to the Senate and had made B. Gratz Brown the Governor of the State.[3] This movement, the immediate inception of which had been the result of a party split in Missouri over the question of the removal of political disabilities from Confederate sympathizers, soon spread widely, and throughout the North and East, liberals (who also demanded tariff and civil service reform) began to appear within the Republican party. Above them all in effectiveness stood Carl Schurz who, with great forensic talent and fine general ability, was denouncing Grant's maladministration and proclaiming the principles of the new movement.

In May, 1872, the adherents of the liberal Republican bloc gathered in Cincinnati where, having adopted a platform largely Democratic, they set about the nomination of candidates for the Presidency and Vice-Presidency. The best element among those assembled was for Charles Francis Adams, perhaps the purest and ablest man on the national stage at that time. At the beginning of the balloting, Adams (who had been virtually described by Schurz in his speech accepting the chairmanship of the convention) held a clear lead, but in the end the editor of the *New York Tribune*, Horace Greeley, was given the first place on the ticket and Gratz Brown of Missouri received the nomination for the Vice-Presidency. Nothing could have been more ridiculous than the nomination of the erratic old abolitionist, and quickly the most respectable element among the liberals began to turn away in disgust. However, even the incorruptible Bayard, who rather despised Greeley, felt that as against Grant he would have to vote for him once his party had accepted him as its nominee. The *New York World*, which before the Democratic convention at Baltimore had denounced the possibility of Greeley's nomination as "preposterous," [4] was driven at last to support him, though, as *Harper's Weekly* remarked, much "as a man supports an aching head." [5]

Lamar had small respect either for Greeley's attainments or his character, and he thought that from the standpoint of practical politics his nomination by the liberal Republicans was abominable. Indeed, it was such a ticket as no real Democrat could view with enthusiasm, though the platform which had been drawn up chiefly embodied Democratic principles. On May 6th, 1872, shortly after the Cincinnati convention, we find Lamar writing to his Ohio friend, Mr. Reemelin, that "there is not much enthusiasm for Greeley and Brown. It will require a great deal of eloquence on the part of their advocates to get it up. Carl Schurz is the only genuinely popular man in the country. The people think him patriotic, disinterested, and intellectual....Mr. Schurz has somehow touched their hearts." [6]

On July 9th the Democratic convention assembled in Baltimore where, by a vote of 670-62, they accepted the Cincinnati platform and then moved to take Greeley and Brown as their candidates. *The Nation*, impelled by the current distaste for Greeley's candidacy, added a new expression to our vocabulary when editorially it said that "Mr. Greeley appears to be 'boiled crow' to more of his fellow-citizens than any other candidate for office in this or any other age of which we have record." [7]

On July 15th, within a week of Greeley's acceptance by the Democratic convention, Lamar was expressing his distaste in a lengthy letter to Mr. Reemelin: "Your objections to Greeley are incontrovertible. His election, if it should by possibility occur, will not *per se* be the triumph of a single great constitutional principle. He has ever been the living embodiment and concentration of all that we of the South and of the Democracy are accustomed to regard as unsound and pestilent in politics." His campaign biography, perhaps, would not be devoid of interests and perhaps value, for it would be the record of forty years of "active and feverish intellectual life." [8]

Much as he disliked the idea of Greeley for President, Lamar felt that nothing could be worse for the South than the situation under the Grant administration: "Its grim despotism glares upon us at every point. Spies and secret detectives swarm through the country, dogging the footsteps of our best citizens, noting and perverting every chance word, following up with arrests, arbitrary searches, indefinite and unexplained imprisonments, trials before vindictive and partisan juries packed for the purpose of insuring convictions, and ending, of course, in verdicts of 'guilty' and sentences of transportation to Northern prisons. Tortured to madness, the friends of the victims have sometimes, not often, resorted to secret conspiracies and bloody retaliations; which latter bring down upon our defenseless heads still more terrible bolts of Congressional wrath. I fear, if this agony is prolonged without hope or relief at some period, the Southern people will feel that death is better than life; and then despair and nemesis will rule the hour."

The South, he said further, is interested only in ridding herself of her oppressors and plunderers. She believes "that there is a large majority of the Northern people" who "are disposed to treat the South...with gentleness and justice, and even with magnanimity.... She was neither embittered nor humiliated by the result of the late war. Though vanquished, she was conscious that she had well attested the sincerity of her convictions by grand battles, numerous victories, and heroic sacrifices. With a sentiment of increased respect for the martial spirit and military power developed by the North in her vindication at the cannon's mouth of the integrity of the Union, the Southerners yielded in good faith and without any mental reservations. They laid down their arms. They submitted to the authority of the constitution with the North's interpretation of it. They abrogated the right of secession and wrote the abnegation in their fundamental laws. They acknowledged the extinction of slavery and also the political and civil equality of their late slaves with themselves. They *will never disturb the Union again*. Since the formal surrender of their armies there has not been a single instance within the Southern States of an insurrection against the authority of the government, although a part of the time the people have been without civil magistrates, and nearly all the time have been writhing under oppression, injustice, and violence. Yet," said Lamar, "the administration of President Grant, regarding them as only vile traitors to be repressed by the strong hand, has never ceased to treat them with contemptuous distrust, severity, and vengeance."

It is natural, he points out to Mr. Reemelin, for the masses of the Southern people "to clasp hands across the bloody chasm" even though the offer of fraternalism and assistance comes from a strange quarter. Many of the more intelligent among the Southerners, however, possess "a hopeless skepticism of anything sound or valuable in Mr. Greeley, a dislike of his character, and a determined adherence to their own political principles." As for himself, Lamar stated that he had taken no part in the movement for Greeley, for "the time has passed with me for looking to political parties, Democratic or Republican, as a means of improving public affairs." Despairing of any political alleviation for the Southern people, he had no advice to give them, he said, other than *"to go to work* in restoring their material prosperity and establishing their institutions of education."

Attention has already been directed to Lamar's feeling that the leaders in the secession movement should quietly refrain from reëntering the national political arena. He makes his position very clear in his letter to Mr. Reemelin: "It has seemed to me that wisdom, as well as self-respect, should restrain those of us who aspired to statesmanship before the Southern overthrow from obtruding our counsels and views upon a crisis which we failed to control by arms.... There is a strong movement in my district to send me to Washington." He had, he said, discouraged this movement as best he could, for, since he had been accustomed to regard his "political principles with profound and even awful respect," he did not care to accept political advancement on any basis other than that in which he sincerely believed. The principles to which he had committed himself were now "down and under the ban." Moreover, he had "a practice growing every day more lucrative," and he was loath to give it up.

The movement to send Lamar to Congress was rapidly gaining momentum despite his refusal to encourage it, and the State press, except the extreme radical, helped it along mightily. The hitch came in the fact that under the terms of the Fourteenth Amendment, Lamar was disqualified from holding office. Despite this handicap the nominating convention of the first Congressional district met at Tupelo on the twenty-first of August, 1872, with the leaders bent upon the reorganization of the party and Lamar's selection as their leader. After extended balloting he received the unanimous vote of the convention. In writing to Mr. Reemelin on August 2nd, not quite three weeks before his nomination, Lamar had remarked that "in the struggles of my intellect after the truth, 'I have trod the winepress alone.'... I know the Anglican character, even the German and French, better than I do the Northern.... I also wanted your advice as to whether I should go back and get my mind saturated again with politics. I have a good practice, my family are happy as possible, and I have disciplined myself to bear final exclusion from official functions and holdings with a serene and self-sustaining mind. Do I really owe it to the South and Mississippi (excuse the limits; I have not yet learned to expand my sense of political duty) to get into public employment?"

Having at last decided in the affirmative and hesitantly accepted the nomination, Lamar set about arranging for an aggressive canvass of his district, the first, in which he was opposed by R. M. Brown, an independent in politics, who was the owner and editor of a paper, the *Central*, published in Water

Valley, and by Colonel R. W. Flournoy, candidate of the administration radicals. Lamar, however, was very dubious concerning his proper course because of his political disabilities under the Fourteenth Amendment. The independent candidate used it as an argument against his candidacy, and he himself had some apprehension lest Congress refuse to remove his disabilities. In that event the operation of Section 15, Article 13, of the "Buzzard Eggleston Constitution," which the blacks and carpetbaggers had imposed upon the State, would probably operate to seat the minority candidate. All praise, however, must be accorded Colonel Flournoy, the radical nominee, who acted in an exceptionally fair and gentlemanly manner. Among Lamar's papers his executor found a crumpled note in which Flournoy had written: "Col. Lamar, I wish to be understood distinctly as saying I will not claim a seat should you resign." [9]

Early in the campaign it developed that despite Lamar's unchallenged Southern sympathies and his opposition to the carpetbag rule, he would poll a tremendous nonpartisan vote. Indeed, his support within the Republican party was quite as enthusiastic, if not as widespread, as in his own. His courtesy in the joint debates and his unfailing brilliance and moderation won him respect and admiration from the opposition. Moreover, his personal following in both parties was very large. Even Colonel Pierce, the United States Marshal whose jaw he had come near breaking in the courtroom at Oxford when he was threatened with false arrest, supported him against Colonel Flournoy and voted for him. It is significant that "his application for the removal of his disabilities received the cordial support of the Republican Governor, Powers, who, of his own motion, prepared a memorial to Congress in that behalf, which was signed by all of the Federal officers at Oxford and Holly Springs, besides Republican judges and chancellors. The three Republican judges of the Supreme Court presented a similar document; and his cause was supported by Auditor Musgrove, by James Hill, the colored Secretary of State, and by O. C. French, the Chairman of the Republican State Committee. A letter from Judge R. A. Hill, of date December 1st, says: 'I have not met with any leading Republican in the northern part of the State who was not in favor of your relief specially.'" [10]

Lamar's victory over Flournoy by a majority of five thousand votes, Brown having withdrawn from the race, was widely heralded throughout the South, and the general tenor of press notices seemed to express the viewpoint that here at last was a representative capable of moderately but ably presenting the case for his section. Writing to Mr. Reemelin on the 4th of November, the day before the balloting, Lamar had expressed the belief that he "would probably be elected to-morrow.... You are aware that I am under disabilities, and that it will require a vote of two-thirds to remove them before I can get my seat....I think the Republicans of the State will favor the bill for my relief....You may be assured of one thing: I am a patriot—that is, my heart beats with more fidelity to the interest and happiness of the American people, and to the principles of public and individual freedom, than it does to my own tranquillity." [11] Another remark in the same letter foreshadows his striving for civil service reforms and for purity and integrity of government that were to make his service as Secretary of the Interior so notable: "If elected to-morrow and sent to Congress, I will be in *one* sense a Representative according to the standard established in the purer days of the republic. Not a dollar will be spent, except for the printing of tickets, in my district. Such a thing as a *fund* or a committee to raise money for electioneering purposes is unknown within its limits. There will not be a vote bribed, either directly or indirectly; and no *personal influence* will, so far as I know, be brought to bear upon anybody. No money drawn from any source is applied to the purpose. What do you think of that?"

In December, 1872, Lamar went on to Washington to present his credentials, and on the 5th his petition for relief, together with the memorial of Governor Powers, was placed before the House by Mr. Dawes, of Massachusetts. Immediately it was turned over to the Judiciary Committee for consideration. On the 9th Mr. Bingham, of Ohio, called attention to the fact that the petition had the favorable endorsement of "most of the United States officials in the State of Mississippi," and advised that the committee had given it its hearty approval. Under a suspension of the rules, the bill for Lamar's relief was at once passed by a vote of 111 to 13, and on the 11th it was given the unanimous consent of the Senate.

Just before his petition for relief was approved, Lamar, in a letter to Judge Peyton, of the State Supreme Court, had indicated the attitude which would dictate his policy upon his return to the national stage: "Should I be permitted to take my seat in Congress, my course will be marked by moderation and reserve. If I say or do anything it will be to give the North the assurance it wants that the South comprehends its own great necessities, and wishes to be no longer the agitating and agitated pendulum of American politics." [12]

No sooner had Lamar been admitted to the national House than he suffered a recurrence of the apoplexy that was to shadow his whole life and eventually cause his death. He was removed to Baltimore, which even by the early seventies was known as something of a medical center, and at the home of the former head of the Department of Mathematics at the University of Mississippi, Dr. Bledsoe, he slowly pulled back from the brink. His rugged constitution finally prevailed, and shortly thereafter he was able to return home where he recuperated.

An examination of Lamar's correspondence for the year 1873 shows that he was chiefly meditating the course that he was to take upon his entrance to Congress that fall. Already he had caught a vision of the great mission of reconciling the North and South, and the tenor of his correspondence with Northern conservatives, such as Hon. M. C. Kerr (one of the purest men in national life at that time and subsequently Speaker of the House) was a seeking for the viewpoints of the best informed men of sections other than his own. Moreover, in June was reopened a correspondence with Dr. Barnard, by now President of Columbia College, New York City, who wrote: "I have never ceased to think of you with affection, as one of the noblest of men and the most valued friend I ever knew."

It is necessary for an understanding of Lamar's relation to the future course of events in Mississippi to have in mind the sequence of events from the installation of James L. Alcorn as Governor in 1869 up to the election of 1873 when Ames was elevated to that office (which, it will be remembered, he had once held by appointment of the military administrator of the district). Alcorn, one recalls, was a man of personal integrity who, a former slaveowner and a member of the Mississippi Secession Convention, had after the war gone over to the Republicans and aligned himself with the Negroes and carpetbaggers. Some of his appointments, especially in the judiciary, were worthy, but the great majority of his selections for office were from the ranks of the carpetbaggers and blacks. The situation under his "reign" was made particularly serious because the State legislature was a disreputable body composed of thirty-six Negroes (most of whom could neither read nor write), with a number of whites whom the historian Rhodes calls "the dregs of the constituencies [that] had risen to the surface."[18] The county which contained Jackson, the State Capital, sent three Negroes to the legislature; Adams, known for "its ancient aristocracy, its wealth and culture," of which the largest town was Natchez, was represented by four blacks, as was the county which contained Vicksburg. Altogether, the cities of Vicksburg, Natchez, and Meridian were being pillaged by Northern adventurers and their colored allies; and a carpet-bagger, Dr. Franklin, sat in the Speaker's chair at Jackson. The old ruling class, mostly barred from participation in their own government, endured in silence and near hopelessness.

Property had become as much a liability as in the neigh-boring State of Louisiana, for the people were systematically robbed by excessive taxation and the money disappeared among a multitude of unnecessary and lucrative offices and through the most bald-faced embezzlement. There is no record that

Alcorn himself was venal, but the men with whom he associated were adept at plundering the public treasury. When he was advanced to the United States Senate, he was succeeded by R. C. Powers, an ex-Union soldier. On the whole, the responsible citizens were sorry to see Alcorn leave the State, for, despite the evil conditions under which they lived, they feared that his office might fall to one of the prominent carpetbaggers who were gnawing at the vitals of the Commonwealth.

The year 1873 saw the power of the carpetbaggers in Mississippi even more firmly entrenched. The Africanization of the State, moreover, had gone on rapidly, and whereas in the legislature of 1869 there had been but 36 Negroes, in that of 1873 there were 64, approaching one-half of the total. However, the ancient proverb that the darkest hour is just before the dawn was in this case literally true. In the first place, the Negroes and radical Republicans, having secured all the power and having the State at their mercy, began to quarrel among themselves for the spoils; and, secondly, conditions were rapidly becoming so bad that two years later the whites would rise in a revolution that would sweep away forever their Negro and carpetbag rulers. The split within the Republican ranks became open as a result of the quarrel between Senators Alcorn and Ames, the latter a carpetbag native of Maine whose lack of identity with the interests of Mississippi was indicated by his statement that if he were not an officeholder he would not live within the State should he be presented with the whole of it. [14]

Ames, as military governor shortly after the war, had so conducted himself that his name was a byword throughout the State. There was fitness and irony in the fact that he was the son-in-law of the notorious Ben Butler. Alcorn, who had come to tend more and more toward the conservatives, had denounced him on the floor of the Senate, and had not hesitated to brand some of his nefarious proposals with their true character. As a result, Ames resigned from the Senate and both men returned to Mississippi to run for the governorship with the idea of trying their case before the people (or rather before the radical Republicans and blacks who controlled the balloting at almost every precinct). Ames, who possessed a really marvelous influence with the Negroes, succeeded in securing the regular Republican nomination, whereas Alcorn ran as an independent with the backing of the conservative Republicans and the Democrats, who, at their convention in September, had decided to present no candidate of their own, but to support Alcorn as the one most likely to deal moderately and honestly with the State.

Lamar's position in regard to the election is made clear in a letter of the 14th of October to his warm friend and one time law partner, E. D. Clarke, of Vicksburg. "This is one of the most important elections, perhaps *the* most important, that we have had since reconstruction," he wrote. "I am for Alcorn, and perhaps it will surprise you to learn that I am as warmly in his favor at this time as I have been in times past opposed to him." He explains, however, that this support of Alcorn does not involve any shift in his own stand on public questions, and, incidentally, he gives some important insight into his own political philosophy. "If I could talk to you," he says, "I think I could show that I am consistent in *purpose* and *principle*, though I have changed my relative position as to men and measures. This is true patriotism and statesmanship in my opinion. Consistency in your *end* and *aim*; variety, change, and adaptability in the use of your means." Lamar's end and aim had been the obtaining of "restitution of federal relations and freedom from military rule," but he had never been willing to buy this by aligning himself with, or submitting to, the coalition which the radicals and carpetbaggers had formed with the Grant administration. Now, however, Alcorn had taken the position that the future of the State required the expulsion of Ames and the radicals, and Lamar was willing and glad to support him with those objects in view.[15].

Two factors, however, conspired to Ames's election: the radical Republicans had control of most of the election machinery with the Negro militia at their command; and, even more important, the hatreds and prejudices engendered by Alcorn's former association with the oppressors of the South were too fresh in the minds of the masses of the Democrats to make them willing to support him enthusiastically. As a result, many of the Democrats stayed away from the polls, and, since the radicals within the Republican party outnumbered the conservatives, Ames was elected and with him three Negroes. Cardozo, at this time under indictment in New York for larceny (the indictment signed by District Attorney Benjamin F. Tracey, later a member of Harrison's Cabinet) [16] was placed at the head of the public schools of the State, and two other blacks held the offices of lieutenant governor and secretary of state. Certainly Mississippi's darkest day had come; but the Republicans had gone too far, and the hour of her deliverance was approaching.

Despite the apparent hopelessness of their situation the people of Mississippi did not waver in their loyalty to the United States. As in the other parts of the late Confederacy, they struggled on in silence and abided in good faith the results of the war. They were back in the house of their fathers, though perhaps as step-children, and they intended to stay.

When the Forty-third Congress assembled in December, 1873, Lamar returned to the body from which he had resigned at the outbreak of the Civil War. But his situation was sadly altered. Sectional animosities, he found, were extremely bitter, and almost daily he was forced to listen to tirades against his people, and to the introduction of measures which appeared hostile and destructive of the rights and interests of the State which he represented. In connection with one of these incendiary "bloody shirt" tirades occurred an incident which touched Lamar deeply. The first of the famous *Georgia Scenes* in the 1835 collection published by his father-in-law, Judge Longstreet, was "Georgia Theatrics." This little sketch relates how a man, riding through the Georgia countryside, hears what is apparently the noise from a fight, and from certain exclamations he judges that one of the combatants has gouged out his opponent's eyes. Although "gouging" was currently accounted a fair mode of warfare on the Georgia frontier, the traveler presumed to interfere and severely reprimand the victor, when, to his amazement, he found that only one man had been engaged. The fellow had stopped his plowing to rehearse a fight, and his exclamation had come, not as he gouged his fingers into his opponent's eyes, but into the soft earth where the two holes made by his thumbs were visible. This story, read before the House at the appropriate moment, had the most wholesome effect of stilling the tirade. Lamar could hardly restrain his tears as he wished that the old Judge, now dead, might have known how his little story had, momentarily at least, brought confusion to the enemies of the South that he had loved and served so devotedly.[17]

Upon Lamar's entrance in the Forty-third Congress he was immediately accorded a prominent part in the proceedings. He was appointed, among others, to the committee on elections, and his speech, soon after his seating, on a contested election in West Virginia received wide and favorable comment.[18] "The little speech I made," he wrote his family, "attracted far more attention than it deserves. Its only merit consisted in presenting the truth of the case disengaged from the irrelevant points with which it had been confused."

A letter to his friend, Hon. T. J. Wharton, of Jackson, Mississippi, dated December 25, 1873, shows much of what was in Lamar's mind, and some of the things that he was planning to accomplish. "There will be very little opportunity for me to say anything that will strike my own people impressively," he remarked of his work in the House. "I am on a hard-working committee, where I can be of some use, though not in an imposing way. It is well understood here that I have already contributed effective aid to our friends in defeating the project of putting in the Republicans from West Virginia. I think, too, that I have won the confidence and respect of the members of my committee. The chairman of it told me that he would rather agree with me in action upon the case than all the others. Probably this was flattery, but it shows a desire to secure my coöperation rather than to provoke antagonisms."[19]

Lamar's account of his first interview with President Grant is interesting in that it gives a good picture of the executive as observed by an intelligent and penetrating contemporary. Accompanied by Alexander Stephens, former Vice-President of the Confederacy, he was ushered into a reception room and informed that the President would appear shortly. "Very soon," wrote Lamar, "another person came in, whom I took to be one of the upper servants.... I had seen his pictures, and had heard A. G. Brown describe him, but I was taken by surprise. He is, at first sight, the most ordinary man I ever saw in prominent position.... After *scanning him closely* you see before you a very strong, self-contained man, full of purpose, resolute even to obstinacy, and of infinite *sang-froid*. He talked freely in a voice not very deep, but with a slight rasp in it, such as you sometimes observe in men who drink a great deal. He is by no means deficient in conversational power.... I judge him to be a man of rather narrow range of ideas, but of clear perception within the range of his mental vision, close observation, and accustomed to forming very decided opinions about men and things. He does not look at you when he converses. There is nothing furtive in his manner. He simply looks straight *by* you. Once he turned and looked at me very steadily and sharply all over, and then turned his eyes from me and began to talk very freely."

Lamar discussed with Grant many subjects of domestic policy as well as certain phases of the foreign relations of the country. Grant, he thought, was a man of exceptional dynamic force, but one who was dangerous because of his inordinate love of power: "I take him to be the most ambitious man that we have ever had. His schemes are startling. With the machinery of the Civil Rights Bill transferring to the Federal Courts jurisdiction, civil and criminal, over the protection of persons, property, and liberty, in every State, against injuries committed on account of race; with the control of telegraph lines and railroads, which he is seeking to get; and with all the emissaries, spies, employees, and tools that his patronage gives him, there will be no limit to the despotic power which he is ever ready to use relentlessly and fearlessly for his own purposes: which purposes are the most arbitrary that have ever yet been cherished by a federal Executive."

In this same letter to T. J. Wharton is again evident Lamar's desire to say something which would alleviate the sufferings of his people and conciliate all sections of the nation. "I have an idea, as yet vague, of making a speech on the relation of the Southern people (the original citizens) to the reconstruction policy of the government," he wrote. "It is a very delicate subject, and it is very difficult to determine what *not* to say."

He did not have long to wait, for on the 11th of March, 1874, Mr. Sumner died, and on the 28th, Lamar, upon invitation from the Massachusetts delegation in Congress, delivered his famous speech on Sumner in the presence of the House of Representatives, with the galleries packed with the diplomatic corps from the leading nations of the world, together with distinguished men from all parts of the United States. The dramatic setting of the tribute to Sumner, and its tremendous effect upon those assembled as well as upon the country at large, have already been discussed, but one is better able to understand the remarkable nature of the address when one bears in mind the afflictions under which the South was suffering at the time that it was delivered. The opportunity for which we have found him so often wishing had come, and he was equal to the occasion.

It is generally believed that no speech ever delivered by a member of the House so quickly attracted the attention of the whole nation. It alone, of all the eulogies of Sumner, was reproduced in its entirety throughout the press of the country. Representative of the sentiment of the nation was the exclamation in the *Memphis Appeal*: "How suddenly L. Q. C. Lamar has become famous—famous above all American orators and statesmen! His funeral eulogium upon Charles Sumner has been printed in every newspaper in America, and has now gone into the 'patent outside,' and passes thence into the school reader." [20]

Nowhere was the speech more widely praised than in the

East. Said the *Springfield* (Mass.) *Republican:* "When such a Southerner of the Southerners as Mr. Lamar, of Mississippi, stands up in the House of Representatives to pronounce such a generous and tender eulogy upon Charles Sumner as this which the wires bring us this morning, it must begin to dawn upon even the most inveterate rebel haters in Congress, and the press, that the war is indeed over, and that universal amnesty is in order." [21] The Boston press was unanimous in its commendation. "Of the eulogies of Senator Sumner pronounced in Congress, Monday," remarked the *Boston Daily Advertiser* (Republican), "none will give more gratification to the people of New England than that of the Hon. Lucius Q. C. Lamar, of Mississippi.... The manner of the act comported with its magnanimous spirit.... There is no sentence in Mr. Lamar's speech that breathes of any motive inconsistent with chivalrous honor. The pathos is in its sincerity. It contains no lament for the irrevocable past. It is instinct with the patriot's pride and faith. In the remarkable passage concerning Senator Sumner's battle flag resolution he exhibits a charity and nobleness which we shall not justly appreciate unless we can imagine ourselves in the position of the vanquished. It is no disparagement to any one to say that Mr. Lamar's speech is the most significant and hopeful utterance that has been heard from the South since the war." [22]

"As an evidence of the real restoration of the Union in the South," editorialized the *Boston Globe*, "this speech must certainly attract much attention in Europe, and wherever our institutions are studied.... The appreciation by a leader of the vanquished, so soon after our great strife, not only of the identity of interest between the sections, but of the motives of the most determined assailant of slavery, is something to excite gratification and wonder; the more so as it is accompanied by a reiteration of a belief in the justice of the Southern cause." [23]

Representative of almost all the more influential papers of his own section was the statement in the *Richmond Enquirer:* "It was a bold, brave, eloquent appeal to the old fraternal feelings between the Northern and Southern people.... And after that speech the Northern man who says that the South is opposed to reconciliation must admit that he denies and defies the facts that confront him." [24] The *Memphis Daily Avalanche* felt that "as Mr. Sumner, in pleading that the battle-flags should bear no evidence of strife between fellow-citizens, rose above the fiercer elements of his own party, so has Mr. Lamar risen above the same classes in the South. Without abating a jot or tittle of his political convictions; without uttering aught involving an inconsistency, he has done that which the intelligence and patriotism of the South, of the country and of the world, will honor, but which will be condemned by every one unable to discover anything but infamy in a political opponent; every one to whom a national sentiment is a crime." [25]

Lamar's speech was delivered in no spirit of self-seeking either for himself or for the section that he represented in Congress. It was born out of a sincere desire to heal the wounds of the fratricidal war—wounds that had grown only the more painful as the sad days of reconstruction progressed. It is commonly conceded that its deliverance marked the birth of a new era in national good will. As the first truly reconstructed statesman either North or South, it was given to him to allay the suspicions on both sides and to usher in the day when sectionalism should be merged in a common interest in the great republic.

It is evident, from a study of Lamar's letters, that the ideas embodied in the Sumner speech had been ripening in his mind and heart for a long time. In retirement from public life after the War, teaching at the University of Mississippi and rebuilding his law practice, he had thought deeply upon the problems confronting the South and the nation. Searching earnestly for a means to free his section from the degradation into which it had been forced by the policies of Congressional reconstruction, and desiring to reunite the nation, he had at length found the way which, reëntering public life, he at once pro-

PEACE WINDOW IN SIGMA ALPHA EPSILON TEMPLE
INSPIRED BY LAMAR'S SUMNER ORATION

ceeded to put into operation. In a letter of July 15th to Mr. Reemelin, he had said:

"In my opinion the two sections are estranged simply because each is ignorant of the inner mind of the other, and it is the policy of the party in power to keep up and exaggerate the mutual misunderstanding. When, for instance, Morton proclaims in the Senate, 'That these men are cast in the mold of rebellion and cannot bend,' the South, taking it as the sentiment of that party and of the people it represents, are embittered, and grow reckless and defiant. The North, seeing only the effect and accepting it as confirmation of the truth of Morton's allegations, allows Congress to go on in its mad career of ruthless legislation.

"But is not this an appalling spectacle? On the one hand a brave, impulsive, but too sensitive people full of potent life and patriotic fire, ready—aye, eager—to abide with knightly honor the award of the bloody arbitrament to which they appealed; and yet, as if dumb, unable to speak intelligibly their thought and purpose. On the other hand a great and powerful section (I came near saying nation), flushed with victory and success, but full of generous and magnanimous feeling toward their vanquished brethren; and they too, as if under some malign spell, speaking only words of bitterness, hate, and threatenings.

"He indeed would be a patriot and benefactor who could awake them from their profound egotism, and say to them with effectual command: 'My countrymen, *know* one another.' For then nature herself with her mighty voice would exclaim: 'Love one another.' " [26]

That he had succeeded materially in presenting the case for the South and had forcibly brought home to the North the hardships under which that section had suffered and was at the time suffering, is to be seen in many of the editorial comments. Said the *Boston Transcript:* "The tone and spirit ... of the remarks of the ex-Confederate officer ... indicate the mistakes made by party politicians in some of the features of the adopted plans for reconstruction, in which they lost sight of principles, in their eagerness to secure immediate pacification and power, at the expense of permanent and prosperous quiet. Too late to change the past it may be ; but it is not too late for public men to return, in their policy for the future, to the recognition of the sound philosophical views of government that will stand the test of time." [27] The *Boston Herald* thought that Lamar had taught "us all a lesson in reconstruction. John A. Andrew advocated the reconstruction of the Southern States by and through the ruling class in that section : the men of intelligence and character, the men who had been faithful to their opinions with their lives and fortunes. But counsels less wise prevailed, and the Southern States governments were thrown into the hands of 'scalawags' and 'carpetbaggers.' Even Sumner was not wise in time." [28]

Characteristic of the sentiment of the New York papers was the expression in the *Commercial Advertiser* : "Yesterday the full glory of a generous Southern manhood shone forth upon Congress and the nation, when Mr. Lamar ... exclaimed— 'My countrymen ! *know* one another, and you will love one another.' Mr. Lamar's speech was grave and tender ; but it rose to impassioned earnestness at the close, and swept the House in a tumult of applause," while the *Philadelphia Press* exclaimed : "What a manly speech Mr. Lamar of Mississippi pronounced on Charles Sumner last Monday !" [29]

Lamar was to engage in many bitter parliamentary struggles in the House and Senate during the years to come, but the respect in which he was held by his political opponents was never to wane. Two weeks after the Sumner eulogy, Carl Schurz was to rise before ten thousand citizens of Boston and hail Lamar as the eloquent prophet of a new day. Through the years to come, this liberal Republican was to be one of the Southerner's most ardent advocates. The lasting influence of the speech was never more forcibly demonstrated than four-teen years later, on the 7th of January, 1888, when Senator Stewart, a Republican from Nevada, in an open letter to his constituents, explained that he would vote against his party in support of Lamar's confirmation as Associate Justice of the Supreme Court of the United States, and said of the Sumner

Eulogy: "When a member of the Senate in the year 1874 my attention, with that of many other Senators, was attracted to Mr. Lamar by his eulogy on Charles Sumner, its exalted sentiments, and its appeals for the restoration of that lofty and enlarged patriotism which embraces both sections of the country. Those who were most enthusiastic in the praise of that speech were then the most ardent of Republicans, and I distinctly call to mind a tribute paid by Hon. George F. Hoar, then member of the House of Representatives and now Senator from Massachusetts. I have it before me.... It is as follows: 'The eloquent words of Mr. Lamar, of Mississippi, so touched the hearts of the people of the North that they may fairly be said to have been of themselves an important influence in mitigating the estrangements of a generation.'"[30]

"It was a mark of positive genius in a Southern representative to pronounce a fervid and discriminating eulogy upon Mr. Sumner, and skillfully to interweave with it a defense of that which Mr. Sumner like John Wesley believed to be the sum of all villainies," said Mr. Blaine a decade later. "Only a man of Mr. Lamar's peculiar mental type could have accomplished the task. He pleased the radical anti-slavery sentiment of New England. He did not displease the radical pro-slavery sentiment of the South.... There is a certain Orientalism in the mind of Mr. Lamar, strangely admixed with typical Americanism. He is full of reflection; seemingly careless, yet closely observant; apparently dreamy, yet altogether practical. It is the possession of these contradictory qualities which accounts for Mr. Lamar's political course...."[31] Such was Blaine's somewhat cynical statement of after years, when his political ambition had made it seem expedient to wave the bloody shirt with the fiercest; but under the power and impact of Lamar's wonderful speech, he had wept with the others.

Never again was Lamar to be without an attentive audience. After his death in 1893, the *Illustrated American*, commenting upon his services to the nation, said of the Sumner speech: "The House listened entranced. The country read with awe and admiration a tribute so earnest, so graceful, so truthful, so imbued with fraternal appreciation, so tinctured with lofty sentiment that, insensibly, the soul of the man lost seemed to be found in the man that perpetuated his memory. The 'bloody shirt' became a byword of scorn. The warriors of peace that had traded upon the agonies of the war were discredited forever. Lamar had closed the gaping chasm of the civil war.

"Never in the history of civil convulsions was the single voice of honor so potent; never was the magnanimous impulse of manhood so generously accepted, so universally understood. From the hour of the Sumner eulogy until the hour of his death Lamar meant to the South the voice that had stilled faction, restored constitutional right; to the North the intellect that had penetrated the darkness of Northern doubt. This surely was a great rôle to play: to bring distrusting, self-destroying millions together; to make the mulctuary covenant of the Appomattox apple tree the broad charter of a reunited people. Lamar's single speech did that, for, though the powers of partisan darkness held sway a little longer, the heart of the North had been deeply touched; and in 1874 the miscreant régime of carpetbag anarchy in the South began to topple, and fell with a crash in 1876.

"It is, therefore, as the inspired pacificator that Lamar will stand out unique, almost incomprehensible, to other times than those that knew the incredible baseness of the policies that followed the war." [32]

It had been customary, since the return of the Southern Representatives after the Civil War, for many of the Northern members of Congress to act with studied insolence when their colleagues from the South arose to speak. Their actions usually took the form of deserting the hall or reading or writing throughout the duration of the address. The stand taken by Lamar in his first term after returning to Congress, and particularly his speech on Sumner, gave him a reputation so commanding that never thereafter was he without an attentive audience. His power in debate was the more felt in that he seldom spoke at length and then only upon matters of serious import.

Probably no man who ever sat in Congress was a more brilliant extemporaneous speaker than Lamar. The rapier thrusts of his flashing wit made him the ideal debater on those occasions when opportunity was not presented for formal preparation of arguments, and his colleagues came to rely upon him in those emergencies which, arising often in Congress, call for immediate analysis and answer. In a letter written at this time to Mr. John C. Butler, a cousin who resided in Macon, Lamar made some interesting comments upon his habits of speaking. "I am now forty-eight years old, and have not done such a thing [commit a speech to memory] but once or twice (on literary occasions) since I was twenty-one. *I cannot write a speech.* The pen is an extinguisher upon my mind and a torture to my nerves. I am the most habitual extemporaneous speaker that I have ever known. Whenever I get the opportunity I prepare my argument with great labor of thought.... But my friends all tell me that my off hand speeches are by far more vivid than my prepared efforts." [33] And it can be safely affirmed that those among Lamar's speeches which are today the most impressive in retrospect are the ones called forth by emergencies when he spoke passionately and without specific preparation out of his wide and varied experience.

X

THE LOUISIANA ELECTION CONTROVERSY

LAMAR had not long to wait after the Sumner address until the way opened for him to present the cause of the South, and the wrongs that she had endured since Appomattox, more fully than they had up to that time been set forth. On June 8th, he delivered his speech dealing with the contested Louisiana election and the deplorable situation in that State. His subject, however, served as a text about which he constructed a forcible indictment of misrule in the Southern States as a whole.[1]

For an understanding of this address, as well as of the course of Lamar's subsequent career, it is necessary that one comprehend something of the situation as it existed in Louisiana—a State which suffered as severely as any other from the abuses of the reconstruction period. New Orleans was, for that day, a tremendously wealthy city, situated in a region that produced most of the cotton, sugar, and rice for the entire nation; and, drawing its patronage from a whole tier of States, it was the natural location wherein the vultures of the post-war period should flock. No phase of corruption or crime failed to be perpetrated upon the unfortunate city and State. The entire government had for years been in the hands of the carpetbaggers and blacks, upon whom there rested no restraining influence.

In 1872 there were but two tickets in the field—the radical Republican, allied with the Negro, Pinchback, offering as its candidate for Governor the notorious William Pitt Kellogg, carpetbagger from Vermont and Illinois, who with Casey (brother-in-law of President Grant), headed the Custom House Ring; and the Democratic which, fusing with the reform Republicans, put out for Governor John McEnery, a native of the State, an able lawyer, and an ex-Confederate officer of unimpeachable character and bravery. At the general election in November, it was evident that the coalition ticket headed by McEnery had won a substantial victory. This, however, the radicals—sure of Grant's support—refused to admit, and they at once set about gaining the day by fraud.

It was charged, probably correctly, that Grant had prepared a message recognizing the McEnery government, but that Morton, in glowering mood, had forbidden its transmission on the grounds that it would cost the party eighty thousand votes.[2] There is no inherent improbability in the story, for Morton was much the stronger man, and Foulke, his biographer, after a careful examination of the evidence, accepts it as true. In any event, Kellogg, the radical nominee for Governor of Louisiana, was given Presidential recognition, and Pinchback, the Negro Lieutenant Governor, was given the tacit, if not enthusiastic, backing of the federal administration in his fight for a seat in the United States Senate.

The first step of the radical conspirators was to corrupt Judge E. H. Durell of the United States Circuit Court, and to persuade him to assume jurisdiction over the controversy in order to give a color of legality to their attempt to set up the Kellogg government. Durell was kept under close surveillance, and his cellar was kept well stocked with the choicest wines.[3] His first move was the appointment of one of the conspirators to the position of General Assignee in Bankruptcy. As a large per cent of the property of the State, particularly in New Orleans, was being sold for taxes and its owners being forced into bankruptcy, there were rich pickings in this office. Meanwhile, Kellogg was helping along the cause by calling in certain of Durell's closest associates and informing them that he had assurance that Grant and the Attorney General desired the judge to intervene in favor of the Custom House Gang, and assuring him that the administration would support his interference.[4] To make doubly sure that Durell would act, Kellogg called in one, Billings, who had great influence with the judge and, pointing out that Durell was old and would soon be forced to retire, he guaranteed that he, Billings, would be appointed as his successor. Thus was everything arranged with the weak and corrupt judge.

That the whole procedure was carefully planned and executed with flawless precision and with the knowledge of President Grant, there can be not the slightest doubt. On the 3rd of December, the Attorney General of the United States telegraphed to the United States marshal in Louisiana ordering him to enforce all decrees and mandates of the federal courts, no matter who resisted, and instructing that General Emory, in control of the federal troops, should give him assistance in any plans that he might lay. This dispatch was undoubtedly shown to Judge Durell in anticipation of his order. The official record of the Senatorial Investigating Committee shows that on the night of December 5th, Judge Durell closeted himself shortly after midnight with the United States marshal and with Kellogg's attorneys and dictated an order directing the federal soldiers to take possession of the State House and to permit no one to enter except certain persons specified in the order, all of them members of the Custom House Gang. The action of Judge Durell, afterwards declared the Senatorial Investigating Committee, "is without parallel, and it is hoped it will remain so in judicial proceedings." At two o'clock that morning the State House was seized by federal troops and batteries were set up about it to make sure the installation of Kellogg as Governor, and the seating of the radical group that claimed to have been elected to the legislature. When the duly elected coalition legislature, backed by the conservative and property-owning citizenry of the State, appealed to Grant against the military rape of the highest offices in the State, he at once showed his hand by openly aligning the administration behind the Custom House Ring.

The majority report of the Republican-controlled Senatorial investigating committee stated that either in or out of court the judge would have had no such authority as he had assumed. Furthermore, "it is impossible to conceive of a more irregular, illegal, and in every way inexcusable act on the part of a judge. Conceding the power of the court to make such an order, the judge, out of court, had no more authority to make it than had the marshal. It has not even the form of judicial process. It was not sealed, nor was it signed by the clerk, and had no more legal effect than an order issued by any private citizen." Again: "But for the interference of Judge Durell in the matter of this State election, a matter wholly beyond his jurisdiction, the McEnery government would to-day have been the *de facto* government of the State. Judge Durell interposed the Army of the United States between the people of Louisiana and the only government which has the semblance of regularity, and the result of this has been to establish the Kellogg government, so far as that State now has any government. For the United States to interfere in a State election, and, by the employment of troops, set up a Governor and Legislature without a shadow of right, and then to refuse redress of the wrong, upon the ground that to grant relief would be interfering with the rights of the State, is a proposition difficult to utter with a grave countenance." But that the Republicans, although recognizing the wrong that had been done in Louisiana, would not embarass themselves by throwing their support to McEnery is evident from a remark by Senator Matt Carpenter of the investigating committee: "We *can't* recognize the Kellogg usurpation and we *won't* recognize the McEnery Government." [5]

In order to support the usurpers, the Congressional radicals set up an extra-legal commission of their own, this commonly known as the "Lynch Board" which gave a decision in favor of the Kellogg faction. But the victory of McEnery and the coalition ticket was so clear that in the three official canvasses of the election results, none of them in control of the McEnery group and one of them by a Senatorial committee upon which there was but one Democrat, all declared that the coalition ticket headed by McEnery had been elected by a majority of from nine to fifteen thousand. That the radical Congressional extra-legal committee had based its findings upon the examination of not a single officially certified ballot, and that the board itself had no foundation in law or color of authority, was demonstrated by Senator Matt Carpenter, of Wisconsin, who, as has been justly said, was not disposed to be prejudiced in favor of the South. "There is nothing," said he for the investigating committee, "in all the comedy of blunders and frauds under consideration more indefensible than the pretended canvass of this [radical] board."[6]

The Packard-Kellogg legislature met in the Capitol on the 9th of December, 1872, despite the provision in the constitution of the State to the effect that the 1st of January was the appointed time. The Negro, Pinchback was installed as President of the Senate, and in a farce setting Governor Warmoth (who had latterly aligned himself with the conservative element) was impeached for "high crimes and misdemeanors," after which Pinchback seized the gubernatorial office. Meanwhile, so patently had Judge Durell prostituted his office at the order of the Washington Administration that the national House, despite its acquiescence in the results of the election fraud, instituted impeachment proceedings against him. No sooner had the charges been filed than he resigned. Evidently, those who had connived in his unlawful actions did not care to have the spotlight of an investigation turned upon their deeds. The trail too clearly led to the White House.

Against the foregoing lightly sketched background, Lamar's speech on the situation in Louisiana and the South can be better understood. The immediate occasion was the question as to whether the Negro, Pinchback, who had figured so nefariously in the contested election, should be seated in the Senate over the protest of G. A. Sheridan (not to be confused, of course, with General P. H. Sheridan) who, Lamar believed, had been elected. Having applied himself to a demonstration that Sheridan was elected by a majority of 10,614 votes, Lamar, as was his purpose, turned to a discussion of reconstruction abuses within the Southern States (not, however, before he had made out an indictment so powerful that Pinchback's aspirations to a seat were destroyed once and for all). Reviewing the history of the disgraceful proceedings under which the Kellogg-Packard-Pinchback faction was fraudulently given control of the State of Louisiana, he advanced the theory that the Republicans had tolerated these abuses because they feared that the seating of the McEnery officials would give power "to that class in the South which was engaged in the attempt to overturn the government, and among which yet lingers the spirit of disunion and slavery; that its accession to power means the supremacy of the white race and the oppression, or at least the subordination and subjection, in some form, of the black race.

"I desire," he said, "to remove these impediments to a decision of this case upon its merits. I do not believe that the interests of the Republican party are identified with the maintenance of that so-called government now fixed upon the people of Louisiana, or of the governments of a kindred nature in the Southern States. No party supported by the moral sentiment of the American people can long bear the responsibility of the infamy and disgrace which these grotesque caricatures of government have brought upon the very name of Republicanism. . . ."

From the foregoing he passed to an exposition of the two constitutional theories that had clashed, and, in the clashing, had produced the Civil War, pointing out that "with defeat for the South and victory for the North, the controversy was closed. . . . But, sir, the North was not satisfied with these results. Holding that, having plucked the black race from the shelter as well as the restraints of existing institutions, protection to the race was an imperative duty, and holding that they were further bound to fortify the results of the war against further disturbance or reaction into the organic law of the Republic, they adopted the Thirteenth Amendment, which was followed in quick succession by the Fourteenth and Fifteenth Amendments, for a stricter enforcement of which were added your reconstruction measures, whose pitiless provisions sunk the iron deep into the soul of the Southern people."

Perhaps the most significant part of the address dealt with the finality of the outcome of the war in once and for all destroying the institution of slavery within the borders of the United States, and with the definite acceptance by the Southern people of the principles of government established by the appeal to arms: "Sir, the Southern people...fully recognize the fact that every claim to the right of secession from this Union is extinguished and eliminated from the American system, and no longer constitutes a part of the apparatus of the American Government. They believe that the institution of slavery, with all its incidents and affinities, is dead, extinguished, sunk into a sea that gives not up its dead. They cherish no aspirations or schemes for its resuscitation.... They would not, if they could, again identify their destiny as a people with an institution that stands antagonized so utterly by all the sentiments and living forces of modern civilization. In a word, they regard the new amendments to the constitution which secure to the black race freedom, citizenship, and suffrage, to be not less sacred and inevitable than the original charter as it came from the hands of the fathers. They own allegiance to the latter; they have pledged their parole of honor to keep the former, and it is the parole of honor of a soldier race."

Continuing his remarks, Lamar was interrupted when the hammer fell with the intimation that he had taken as much time as the rules of the House allowed. On unanimous request of the Representatives of both parties, however, this suggested by Mr. Garfield, he agreed to continue. The citizenry of the "reconstructed" States, he said—after discussing the situation under the carpetbag régime—could do nothing to end their oppressions because their rulers were appointed as dictators and were not subject to the will of the governed. "That constituency [to which those who govern the South are responsible] is here in Washington; its heart pulsates in the White House. There is its intelligence and there is its iron will," he said. "I do not exaggerate when I say that every one of these governments depends every moment of its existence upon the will of the President. That will makes and unmakes them. A short proclamation backed by one company determines who is to be the Governor of Arkansas; a telegram settles the civil magistracy of Texas; a brief order to a general in New Orleans wrests a State government from the people of Louisiana and vests its control in the creatures of the administration. Sir, even conceding that the decision in one or two of these cases accorded with the rights of the people, there stands the startling fact that all the rights, peace, and security of those people hang upon the precarious tenure of one man's will or caprice. Is it wonderful that beneath the chill shadow of such a colossal despotism the hope and enterprise and freedom of that people wither and die?

"Mr. Speaker, my heart has on more than one occasion thrilled under the tributes of applause paid by Northern members, who were Federal officers in the war, to the valor of Southern troops and the fortitude of Southern people during the war. Sir, if the conquest over self is the greatest of all victories, then that people deserve a still higher meed of praise for their conduct in peace; for, sir, they have borne unprecedented indignities, wrongs, oppressions, and tortures, with unexampled patience and dignity."

In conclusion Lamar laid upon the pages of the *Congressional Record* the official government correspondence involved in the disgraceful prostitution of the judiciary in Louisiana which had led to the seating of the radical ticket. Involving as it did communications to the President himself, and answers obviously dictated by Grant and signed by the Attorney General and others high in administration circles, its evidence was conclusive and damning. That it convicted Grant of the most shadowy and illegal dealings, no competent historian has ever denied. As the distinguished Beck of Kentucky wrote to the editor of the *Kentucky Yeoman*, published in the issue of October 8th, 1874, "Though listened to by all the Republican leaders, they were neither answered nor contradicted and could not be, because the facts were indisputable."

This speech on the wrongs of the South received immediate and national acclaim. Not an important newspaper in the country failed to carry more or less extensive quotations with editorial comment. In many instances it was printed entire, and the sensation that it created was comparable to that succeeding the Sumner oration. "Mr. Lamar, of Mississippi, made in the House, Monday, another of those stirring and eloquent speeches which are sure to strike a sympathetic chord in the hearts of all generous people," said the *Boston Advertiser.* "The generous temper, the nobility of sentiment, and the moving eloquence of the present representative from Mississippi are doing more than anything else could to dispel the unpleasant feeling,... and to promote good offices between sections of the Union no longer divided."[7] Even the bitterly radical *New York Tribune* remarked that "Mr. Lamar, of Mississippi, made another great speech in the House to-day, which will, not less for its noble tone and sentiments than for its eloquence and sincerity, no doubt receive as much praise and attention as his former speech on the character of Charles Sumner," and the *New York World* thought that he "again distinguished himself...as an able and eloquent representative of the South, and a real states- man, by delivering a prepared speech on the present political condition of the South. It was the first full and fair statement of the attitude of the white people of the South toward the general government, and also the State governments of the South, that has been made upon the floor of Congress....The speech was a sequel to Mr. Lamar's oration on Sumner, and was listened to by every member of the House present." Par- ticularly discriminating was the appreciation that appeared in the *New York Herald.* "Lamar's speech," said that paper, "at- tracted general attention for its earnestness and its allusions to the Civil War and its results. He was peculiarly happy in ac- cepting the political situation made for the South by the amend- ments to the constitution. His exordium and peroration were alike characterized by pithy and pertinent illustrations."[8] The *Syracuse Journal,* in its statement that he would "be looked after as a candidate for the second place on the Presidential ticket two years hence," seems to have been the first paper to make a suggestion that was to be urged upon Lamar at the approach of every Presidential election for the next decade and a half.

The press of the South was unanimously of the opinion that her case had been, for the first time since the war, fully and competently presented. Said the *Louisville Courier-Journal,* "This is the first time since the war that the case of the South has been adequately presented by one of her own sons, and it was done to-day in a style to which even Northern Republicans could take no exceptions." The same paper is authority for the statement that it was commonly accepted as the "ablest and most statesmanlike speech of the session. Nearly the whole House gathered around him at the close." [9] To the *Anderson* (S. C.) *Intelligencer* it seemed that he had "won greater reputation in a short time than any Southern Congressman since the war....Last week he made a speech upon the Louisiana troubles which attracted much attention for its earnestness and its frank allusions to the results of the Civil War. The members crowded around him during the delivery of his pithy and pertinent defense of the South, and listened with absorbing interest to his graphic illustrations of the gross caricatures upon republican government now existing in this section of the Union," and the *Jackson* (Miss.) *Clarion* thought "it a most triumphant vindication of a wronged people, executed in a style so knightly as to disarm opposition and compel attention and respect." And, remarked this paper, "all bear witness to the invaluable service he has rendered." [10]

The radicals were blind enough, however, not to understand that the masses of the Northern people were losing all patience with bayonet rule in the South, and that they might easily overplay their hand. "The national heart," says one commentator, "had been profoundly stirred by Lamar's incomparable and immortal Sumner address. It is not too much to say that no other oration in all our history ever produced such a deep and abiding impression, or one so widespread. It touched the long dormant chords of sympathy and kinship in all, except the most obdurate radical partisans," and having won their attention he followed on June 6th with a speech, the "spell and force" of which no man could equal, on the evils of Southern rule, particularly in Louisiana. [11] But the whole story of race distrust and radical implacability was illustrated on the night after Lamar's Louisiana speech, with his Sumner eulogy still ringing in the nation's ears, when the Negro leader, Fred Douglas, arose to speak before a Republican Congressional caucus. "There can be no reconciliation between the negroes and their old masters," cried the black, in urging the obnoxious Civil Rights Bill. "The former would not believe that slavery was beyond revival. They would not trust a white man with their liberties. They could pardon fraud or corruption in a Republican and would sooner vote for one like Moses, of South Carolina [a most disreputable character], than Lamar." [12]

On June 16th Lamar wrote to his sister, Mary Ann, now Mrs. Ross, that he had worked hard but unobtrusively during the session. "My speech," he said, "was listened to attentively and respectfully by the Northern members. It would never have been heard or read by the North had I not made the Sumner speech." It is not to be thought, however, that Lamar had spoken with any idea of personal aggrandizement or currying favor with his opponents. His purpose in all his speeches he stated clearly in a letter of this period to his cousin, Mr. John C. Butler, of Macon, Georgia: "My recent speeches have not been prompted by self-seeking motives. It was necessary that some Southern man should say and do what I said and did. I knew that if I did it I would run the risk of losing the confidence of the Southern people, and that if that confidence were once lost it could never be fully recovered. Keenly as I would feel such a loss (and no man would feel it more keenly), yet I loved my people more than I did their approval. I saw a chance to convert their enemies into friends, and to change bitter animosities into sympathy and regard. If I had let the opportunity pass without doing what I have, I would never have got over the feeling of self-reproach. If the people of the South could only have seen my heart when I made my Sumner speech, they would have seen that love for them, and anxiety for their fate, throbbed in every sentence that my lips uttered." [13]

But his State and the South as a whole were indeed proud of him. Henceforth he was to hold Mississippi—even when he disobeyed his instructions from the legislature—as powerfully as ever Calhoun held South Carolina. The intelligent men of his constituency came to grasp the fact that they were represented not by a time-server but by a statesman of the first order.

Typical of the comments, even of the opposition press throughout the State, was that of the *Hernando Press*, written upon the
adjournment of Congress: "The first session of the Forty-third
Congress has closed. To Mississippians it is chiefly remarkable
as being the first Congress in which they have been represented
since 1861. Certainly we have reason to be proud of this, our
first representative in thirteen years.... With singular skill and
good judgment he made the contested election case from
Louisiana the occasion of a somewhat elaborate inquiry into,
and exposure of, the ills that affect the Southern States. It is by
far the ablest, most philosophical, and statesmanlike presentation of our unhappy section that has been given to the world
since the surrender.... Of Mr. Lamar's speech in eulogy of
Charles Sumner, it is not too much to say that it is the most
notable speech delivered in the American Congress since Lee's
surrender. It attracted a wider, more instantaneous, and universal applause than any single speech within our memory....

"Mr. Lamar possesses, in an eminent degree, two qualities
not often combined, and which, when they meet, must always
produce a first-class orator: he has great beauty and power of
expression, and a mind deeply philosophical and analytical....
Certainly the South has had no such promise of a great statesman in very many years...."

It is significant of Lamar's commanding ability that long before the end of the first session that he served in the House,
after an absence of thirteen years, he had come to be recognized
as one of the leaders. The average Congressman of good ability
may serve for the better part of a lifetime and still be practically
unknown outside his own district and of no importance at all,
other than his vote, nationally. A man of outstanding ability,
who belongs to the minority party, commonly has little or no
opportunity to distinguish himself and only becomes widely
known when his party chances to organize the House. Indeed,
the usual road to prominence is through the slow workings
of the rule of seniority, where longevity plays a determining
part in elevating a man to the chairmanship of an important
committee. But it was not so with Lamar. He was a master of

men who made his impress instantaneously upon any group with which he came to be associated. Naturally of a retiring nature, and one who never strove for advancement, he was a born leader whom ordinary mortals delighted to follow. "He was a very interesting and very remarkable and noble character," wrote Senator George F. Hoar after Lamar's death. "The late Matthew Arnold used to say that American public men lacked what he called 'distinction.' Nobody would have said that of Mr. Lamar. He would have been a conspicuous personality anywhere, with a character and quality all his own." [14]

XI

THE FIGHT AGAINST RADICALISM

MEANWHILE, the explosive potentialities of the Louisiana situation had become more and more serious. Throughout the summer of 1874 it seemed that every steamboat brought shipments of guns for distribution to the Black Leagues.[1] The spark that ignited the conflagration came when federal officers began systematically to disarm the whites, refusing them their constitutional right of possessing arms, and enforcing their edicts with Negro deputies and Negro troops. On the night of September 13th, 1874, a call was sounded for the able-bodied citizens to assemble in mass meeting at the Clay monument on Canal Street in New Orleans. "Speak," said a widely circulated bulletin, "in tones loud enough to be heard the length and breadth of this land," and declare "...that you are, and of right ought to be, and mean to be free."[2]

Early the next morning a body of three thousand citizens assembled on Canal Street where they adopted resolutions reciting their wrongs, and demanding Kellogg's immediate abdication. It was a popular uprising in the truest sense of the word, and Nordhoff was correct when he reported that among the better class of business and professional men there existed an almost universal hatred of the notorious rulers of the State. A committee of five was appointed to wait upon the Governor with the demand, but he insolently refused to see them, and through a subordinate refused to comply with their resolutions. McEnery was out of the city, but Penn, who had been elected lieutenant governor on the same ticket, proclaimed himself acting governor and issued a proclamation directing that all men of military age, "without regard to color or previous condition," arm and assemble "for the purpose of driving the usurpers from power."[3] Soon the indignant citizens had barricaded not only Canal Street but many of the other thorough-fares. That afternoon, about four o'clock, five hundred metropolitan police under the command of ex-Confederate General Longstreet (now aligned with the South's oppressors) appeared, armed with artillery, near the river on Canal Street where they deployed and opened fire as the insurgents charged them with the old rebel yell. When Longstreet saw among the embattled citizens a number of his old "boys" and heard the familiar rebel yell, reported a spectator, he paused and his face went pale as death while his Negro troops broke and fled in wild confusion.[4] Some thirty on both sides were killed and many were wounded, but the determined citizens won the day (shortly, however, to have Grant place their oppressors even more firmly in the saddle).

When Lamar, some time later, wrote to his wife of the friends who had aligned themselves with the oppressors of the South, he almost certainly had in mind General Longstreet who had gone over bag and baggage to the conquerors. The latter, writing to General Lee who was spending the twilight of his life as President of little Washington College, had asked his blessings on the course that he had adopted. "I cannot think," wrote Lee, "that the course pursued by the dominant party the best for the interests of the country, and therefore cannot say so, ... This is the reason why I could not comply with the request in your letter."[5]

During the months of October and November, while conditions were becoming increasingly serious both in Mississippi and Louisiana, Lamar visited all parts of his district speaking frequently, particularly in the larger towns. It was in no sense a campaign for reëlection, for the legislature had that year passed an act fixing the time for the election of Congressmen in 1775 and thereafter every two years. But there were numerous questions of intense interest agitating the minds of the people, and the tour of the district gave him an opportunity intelligently to mold the opinions of his constituents, and to discuss his own acts in Congress. Particularly did he pay attention to the troubles in Louisiana and to the cause and effects of his Sumner speech.

Then came November 3rd with the news that the House had gone Democratic by a tremendous majority. At last, the people felt, they would be freed from the tyranny of the radicals who had not yet loosed their hold upon a large section of the lower South. The danger, as Lamar saw it, was that the Southern people might be unable to bear the return of prosperity as they had borne their deep adversity. He pointed out and reiterated to his constituents that, although the Democratic platform had carried an indictment of the Republican party on the count of "Southern wrongs," it was the duty of the Southern people so to demean themselves as to hold the confidence of the conservative element throughout the nation. The victory in the election had not been gained, he thought, entirely upon the issue of Republican misrule in the formerly seceded States. It merely indicated that the tide was turning, and that the Southern spokesmen would at last have a hearing in the national arena.[6]

The contemporary Mississippi press was burdened with flattering notices of the success of Lamar's speeches wherever he appeared. Always, it seems, he urged his hearers to accept in good faith the results of the war, particularly that they support the new amendments to the Constitution even where he, and they, had opposed their enactment in the first place. "They are fixed in the constitution as immovably as are those provisions which guarantee to each State an equal representation in the Senate," he would say in standing for the validity of all of the amendments. "Now is the time of the South's probation and her trial. Her trial will be within the limits of the constitution as it *now* stands. Her patriotism and intelligence are invited to aid in working out a most difficult problem affecting the whole country."[7]

When Lamar returned to Washington at the opening of Congress in December, he found the Democratic party about to take over the control of the lower House (they would actually organize that body early in March), and himself, as one of the leaders consequently advanced in national importance. Writing to his wife on the 11th he remarked that "nearly all the papers in New England have come out for me as Speaker, but there is nothing in this beyond the expression of kind feeling. The party does not want a Southern man, nor should a Southern man permit himself to want this office.

"I am very often spoken of, or rather spoken to, about the Vice-Presidency. That would be comfortable, would it not? It would give four years of rest and a good income, and Gussie and Jennie a fine time. I found myself thinking this way about it, and then I considered that in these thoughts I was considering my own advancement and happiness, and that there was no thought of what benefit it would be to our poor people in Mississippi. So I have given up all further thoughts about it." [8]

The radicals, meanwhile, with the knowledge that their power to control the government would soon cease, redoubled their efforts to fix their policies irrevocably upon the nation. Their plan was to force the passage of a number of laws that the Democrats would not have the necessary two-thirds of Congress to rescind (for, obviously, such action would have to be taken over the executive's veto), and to confer upon the President extraordinary powers that he might exert irrespective of the will of Congress.

That much of the radical bloody shirt waving and incendiarism had its inception in the high councils of the Republican organization was proven when an authentic letter, sent to all the editors of administration papers in Indiana, was found and published. "I desire to call your attention to the horrible scenes of violence and bloodshed transpiring throughout the South and suggest that you give them as great prominence as possible in your paper from this time until after the election," [9] it read. Signed by Thomas J. Brady, Republican State Chairman of Indiana, it was charged and generally believed that the author was Senator Morton, the leader of the administration forces in the Senate. That the public was becoming wearied with such propaganda, however, was evident in the election which turned the national House over to the Democracy, and in the chorus of criticism evoked by Grant's mismanagement in Louisiana.

To Lamar, the prospect for national unity and constitutional government was coming to appear more and more hopeless. On February 15th he was writing to his wife that the future of Mississippi was very dark. Ames, he feared, would become so oppressive and his negro troops so insolent that the people would arise and destroy them all; "then Grant will take possession for him. May God help us!"[10] He was aware that it was no time for forensic pyrotechnics, and he held to his determination to indulge in no useless declamation. On the contrary, though letting his position be known on every important subject, he worked constantly and unobtrusively for harmony and better understanding between the sections. Typical were his remarks on the 3rd of February, 1875,[11] in respect to the Civil Rights Bill, a sublimation of Sumner's bill, the intent of which was to force association between blacks and whites, and to secure to the former equal access to inns, public conveyances, theaters, and other public places. "Mr. Speaker," said Lamar, "I have no hope that any argument of mine will avail to prevent the passage of this bill or one similar to it in its essential provisions. It is evident that in the opinion of this House no light can be thrown upon the subject which will control its action. This chamber is empty. Were I to speak, I would have to address vacant chairs.... But, sir, as a representative of a portion of the people on whom this proposed legislation is to operate, I feel it my duty to protest against this measure in any of its forms, as not only violative of the constitution, but irretrievably disastrous to the peace, prosperity, and happiness of that people."

Many people in the South, not understanding the conditions faced by their representatives in Washington, must have had feelings in common with that of one of Lamar's constituents who, among other things, wrote in a long and insistent letter that "it is the privilege of our representatives in Congress, few though they be, to denounce and expose the villainy and corruption of our rulers, and, in the name of the constitution of our country, solemnly to protest against these outrages upon our liberties.... It is feared by some of your friends that you are almost too slow in availing yourself of the opportunity and occasion, that you are inclined to temporize too much. Your past course in Congress has established the impression with our oppressors that you are not an extremist, or radical, fire-eating disloyalist; now, then, take the benefit of it to expose their villainy, and publish the unprecedented wrongs of our people to the world." [12]

"I do not think you fully understand the situation here, or what I am doing," Lamar wrote in answer to this letter. Federal interference in the South, he points out, has a twofold aspect: first, the prosperity and self-government of the Southern people, concerning which there is comparatively little interest in the North. "They would be gratified to see the South prosperous; but they would not take the trouble to put Grant or any other Republican out, and to put a Democrat in as President, to accomplish this object." The other aspect of the situation "involves the existence of liberty and constitutional government at the North; and the demonstrations by the Northern people, in view of this danger to their own free institutions, give me more hope of ultimate justice to our people than I have had for some weeks past."

The Civil Rights Bill had not, he wrote, been introduced into the House for debate. When this is done, the representatives of the South, he hopes, will have the opportunity to be heard. "Their protests should be firm and manly; their exposure of the corruptions and wrongs which the governments of those States have been guilty of must be unsparing. But their animadversions upon the President of the United States should be marked by dignified moderation. The Northern people have more pride in General Grant than they have in any living man. ...They will tolerate no abuse of him in Southern representatives. The radical party would raise a purse of fifty thousand dollars to pay prominent Southern men to denounce him in the style which you suggest as the proper course for me. I could not please these enemies better, or help them more, than by calling General Grant a 'besotted tyrant.'"

In respect to his correspondent's remark that "I know that you are fully capable of taking care of yourself," Lamar thinks that he is, though he writes that he is "not attempting that just now. While events of such magnitude are passing before his eyes, a man who did not forget himself would deserve to be forgotten. I have thought of nothing but the situation of my country. At any rate, I have not sought *éclat* at home by attempting imposing displays of passionate invective against a party which has even yet the power to inflict upon our defenseless people any suffering or oppression which awakened resentments may invent. The strength and energy and will of Southern radicals are underestimated. The program which they are attempting to force upon their party is as bloody and vigorous as that of the French Jacobins, and they are backed by Grant. A few inflammatory speeches from our side would do their work for them. Never was there a more critical period in our history than the present. The only course I, in common with other Southern representatives, have to follow, is to do what we can to allay excitement between the sections, and to bring about peace and reconciliation. That will be the foundation upon which we may establish a constitutional government for the whole country, and local self-government for the South." [13]

It was this entire absence of any tendency to "play to the galleries" or even to speak extendedly where there was no apparent gain to be had that dictated Lamar's course throughout this trying and eventful period. That his position was evaluated for its statesmanlike qualities is evident from an editorial, among many others, in the *New York World*. "Hon. L. Q. C. Lamar," it remarks, "is winning for himself the respect of both sides of the House. His speeches hitherto during this term have been distinguished by their pertinency. There is no more valuable reputation for a legislator to have, and none more sure to command 'the ear of the House,' than the reputation of never speaking except when he has something to say. This Mr. Lamar has fairly earned. His speeches on the new rule and on the Civil Rights Bill have been true, timely, and pointed.... In the hot

debates of the last three days he has done more to vindicate the
Southern people from the imputations recklessly put upon them
than almost any other member of Congress. The Southern people could do themselves no greater service than by sending
more such men as Mr. Lamar to represent them."

In this year, 1874, Arkansas, Alabama, Mississippi, Louisiana,
Florida, South Carolina, and North Carolina still writhed in the
grasp of radical governments, but the spirit of the South had
suffered all that it would stand. The spirit aflame throughout
all the oppressed States was that expressed in a bitter editorial
in the *Atlanta News.* "We have submitted long enough to indignities, and it is time to meet brute-force with brute-force,"
it read.[14] The organization of the Black Leagues under radical
Republican direction had created the race issue and regimented
the Negroes in opposition to the Southern whites. In reply, the
Southern Democracy of every town and county would organize to free itself from the black and tan governments. Let
a white man support the pernicious Civil Rights Bill or align
himself with the black Republicans and he would find himself
completely ostracized and dropped into a well of silence by his
neighbors. That year, the people of Alabama defied all attempts at intimidation and, sweeping the election, placed Houston in the governor's chair with a Democratic legislature at
his back. In that State the day of the carpetbagger and the
scalawag had forever ended and Alabama had taken her place
with the already redeemed States of Virginia, Georgia, Tennessee, and Texas.[15]

In the 1874-75 session of Congress Lamar performed one of
his greatest services to the South in being chiefly responsible
for the defeat of the Force Bill. The situation was this: The
November elections had determined, as we have seen, that the
House which assembled in the spring would be controlled by
the Democratic party for the first time since the Civil War.
Hence the Republican "Lame Ducks," with the connivance
of Grant, were determined to pass certain measures which
would perpetuate their authority after the new members had

been seated. For this purpose the chief instrument was to be the Force Bill which, as *The Nation* pungently said, converted the President into "a sort of tawdry Cæsar."[16] The purpose of this proposed legislation was baldly and brutally set forth in large type on February 26th, in the *National Republican*: "THE PASSAGE OF THE BILL IS REQUIRED TO PRE-SERVE TO THE REPUBLICAN PARTY THE ELEC-TORAL VOTES OF THE SOUTHERN STATES. REMEMBER THAT IF THE DEMOCRATS CARRY ALL THE SOUTHERN STATES, AS THEY WILL IF THE WHITE LEAGUE USURPATION IN SOME OF THEM IS NOT SUPPRESSED, IT WILL REQUIRE ONLY FIFTY DEMOCRATIC ELECTORAL VOTES FROM THE NORTHERN STATES TO ELECT A DEMO-CRATIC PRESIDENT. THIS IS A LIBERAL ESTIMATE." This notice, printed in the Presidential mouthpiece in Washington, was merely the open admission of the purpose of the measure which was everywhere commonly understood.

The passage of the Force Bill would have turned over to the President the election machinery in four Southern States where he would have been an absolute dictator, for it provided that he might, in Arkansas, Mississippi, Louisiana, and Alabama suspend the privilege of the writ of *habeas corpus* for "two years and from thence until the end of the next session of Congress thereafter."[17] This bill had not passed the party caucus without denunciation of its tyrannical measures, for Speaker Blaine, Poland, Garfield, and Hawley had unavailingly tried to block its acceptance as a party measure. A Republican Representative from Massachusetts, Henry L. Pierce, pointed out and denounced the motive behind its proposed passage. "We are told by high authority," he said, "that one hundred and thirty-eight electoral votes of the reconstructed States rightfully belong to the Republican party; and that if the bill now pending in the House becomes a law it will secure these votes to that party, and otherwise they will be lost."

The Democrats were aware that unless extraordinary measures were resorted to the bill was certain of passage because of the powerful influence wielded by the President and the whip-lash methods of Ben Butler who would hold most of the weaker Republican Representatives in line. The Democratic strategy, however, was to block its passage in the House for such a period that there would not be time left for the Senate to consider it. However, since the bill was to be taken up on the 24th of February, there would be only seven working days remaining before the lapse of time would force an adjournment. The conclusion was inevitable that only by a filibuster of re-markable proportions could its passage be defeated. Under the astute leadership of Mr. Randall, the Democrats put into effect probably the most extraordinary example of such tactics that the national House has ever seen. Every parliamentary device that would slow up procedure was resorted to: motions to ad-journ were made with startling frequency; the matter of a quorum had to be decided, often at intervals of no more than a few minutes; questions of preference on the floor were argued *ad infinitum*; every question had to be decided by a complete roll call where such a procedure was manifestly unnecessary, and almost every decision of the chair was appealed. In such manner were Wednesday and Thursday successfully "killed."

Only five days remained for the consideration of the bill, but its opponents had exhausted their resources and it was evi-dent that, with the Friday assembly of the House, there would be nothing to hinder the Republicans from forcing its passage. The Democrats, particularly the Representatives from the South, were in despair. It was at this point that Lamar did what no other member of the House could have accomplished and which he himself could not have effected except for the high and statesmanlike position that he had attained in the eyes of the leaders of both parties. He had taken no part in the fili-bustering tactics of his colleagues and hence had not become engaged in the acrimonious discussions that had bred so much ill-will. When the House adjourned on Thursday, with the prospect of the passage of the Force Bill on the following morning, Lamar, late that night, visited the Speaker, Mr. Blaine, at his residence. Bringing to bear his remarkable analytical and persuasive powers he convinced Blaine that the passage of the measure would well nigh destroy the lower South and hence would result in serious repercussions in other sections of the country. The Speaker, after some consideration, suggested to Lamar that if the Clerk, in reading the minutes of the preceding day, were forced to read the names of all the "yea" and "nay" votes of every roll call, hours would be consumed before any business could be transacted.[18]

At the assembling of the House at eleven o'clock on Friday, the Clerk began to read the minutes of the preceding session. Lamar, in accordance with Blaine's suggestion, had instructed Mr. Storm, Democratic Representative from Pennsylvania, to raise the point of order that the Clerk was not reading the negative and affirmative of the votes on the forty roll calls of the preceding day. To read them, it was obvious, would consume most of the day. "Does the gentleman insist on their being read?" Replied Mr. Storm, "I do." In view of the important legislation to be disposed of, there was nothing for the Republicans to do except to agree for the discussion of the Force Bill to be put off until the night session, with the agreement that it would be debated but not brought to a vote that night. The issue was settled, for when the House finally passed the measure at midnight on Saturday, February 27th, it could only go to the Senate on Monday which, under the rules of that body, was too late for it to be acted upon before adjournment on March 4th. Its defeat remains as a milestone in our national history.

As time passed, Blaine was to enact the part, on various occasions and for political effect, of one of the most radical of the bloody shirt wavers, but Lamar could never forget his services to the South in her hour of extreme need. Often he recurred to it, and when in the Presidential campaign of 1884 the former—all too vulnerable—was subjected to the most humiliating disclosures and abuse, Lamar, while vigorously campaigning for the Democratic ticket, refused to attack him personally.

As a matter of fact, though the party caucus determined the

vote of the Republican Representatives, many of them were glad when the obnoxious measure failed. Nevertheless, that there was a large element in the East that was in no sense kindly disposed toward the Southern States became painfully evident in the Congressional debate on the bill. "We are undertaking to coax the devil out of the miserable whelps down South when nothing but cannon and strychnine ought to be used," cried the Rev. J. B. Ives of Boston, whose words before an assembly of ministers were read in Congress. "The more I hate the rebels of the South the more I love God." [19] But throughout the nation— North as well as South—the Republican Congressmen who opposed the Force Bill were generally applauded. Even the radical *New York Tribune* remarked that "outside of Washington only one or two journals have been so blinded by partisanship as to support the nefarious force bill."

Ben Butler was the evil genius behind the measure, and he conducted himself so offensively that he antagonized many members of his own party, a bitter altercation ensuing between the "Beast" and Mr. Poland, an aged Republican Representative from Vermont, and one of the most respected and influential men in the House:

"You have no right to say that," said Judge Poland [in respect to one of Butler's highly questionable statements about the South]. "What evidence have you?"

General Butler: "None, perhaps, but I believe it."

Judge Poland: "I believe you are a damned liar."

General Butler: "My courage, sir, has never been impeached. I am quite able to resent an accusation like that. You had better be careful."

Judge Poland: "I don't think I have great courage, but I have quite enough for this occasion. Not much is needed."

As the two men parted and as Judge Poland turned around, Mr. Lamar of Mississippi, who stood at his elbow, remarked that he thought Judge Poland might have needed some assistance, and intimated that he was ready to render it. Mr. Poland thanked Mr. Lamar cordially, but remarked in a dignified way: "I am a fighting man myself, sir." [20]

However, another coercive measure—the long pending Civil Rights Bill—had been finally put through Congress toward the close of this session. This measure, intended to force social intercourse and break down barriers between the races where it was utterly repugnant, was an inheritance from Charles Sumner, who, on his deathbed a year before, had begged his radical associates to "take care of the Civil Rights Bill." Thus bequeathed, it, also, had descended to the management, in the House, of the notorious Ben Butler, who had forced it through under the party lash. In the form in which it finally passed the Senate, it had been greatly modified, against the bitter opposition of the extremists. Much to the disgust of the latter, the schoolhouse and the graveyard were stricken from the list of places where it had been originally declared that the races must mingle indiscriminately.

In the course of one of Butler's harangues in support of this Civil Rights Bill, he had referred to the Southern whites, who were struggling against Negro and carpetbag rule, as "murderers," "lawless men," "banditti," and "horse-thieves," and had regretted that he had not hung more of the rebels while he was stationed in New Orleans. On February 4th, John Young Brown, of Kentucky, had taken the floor and had characterized the proposed measure as the "culminating, crowning, iniquity of radicalism.... The people of the country do not favor these radical schemes," he had pointed out among other things. "They have repudiated their originators. You men who propose to pass them have been weighed in the balance and found wanting. Judgment has been passed upon your political record, and nearly two-thirds of that side of the House returned to private life. And your conduct now in this and other matters, Mr. Speaker, reminds me of a passage in Junius where he describes a bad tenant, having received notice to quit, breaking the furniture, putting the premises in disorder, and doing all he could to vex the landlord." [21]

At this point his address had taken a more personal turn: "Now again that accusation [against the Southern whites]... has come from one who is outlawed in his own home from respectable society; whose name is synonymous with falsehood; who is the champion, and has been on all occasions, of fraud; who is the apologist of thieves; who is such a prodigy of vice and meanness that to describe him would sicken imagination and exhaust invective." To every member of the House, including Ben Butler himself, it was clear who was being described. But, since the Kentuckian had as yet called no name and, when challenged by the Speaker, Mr. Blaine, denied the right of the latter to make an identification of the subject of his discourse, there seemed no way to stop his remarks. "In Scotland years ago," he continued, "there was a man whose trade was murder, and who earned his livelihood by selling the bodies of his victims for gold. He linked his name to the crime, and to-day it is known as 'Burking.' If I wished to describe all that was pusillanimous in war, inhuman in peace, forbidden in morals, and infamous in politics, I should call it 'Butlerism.'"

As his last word rang through the House, that body was thrown into a tumult with many of the Republicans on their feet, led by Mr. Hale and Mr. Dawes, demanding either a formal vote of censure or his expulsion on the grounds that he had prevaricated to the Speaker (though, in fact, he had not), and had indulged in conduct unworthy of his office.

When it seemed that they might, in truth, use their temporary majority to expel Brown, Lamar took the floor.[22] It was a mistake, he said frankly, for his Democratic friend and colleague to have spoken so bitterly or in a manner so little suited to the body in which he sat. But the provocation had been great. His retort to Butler had been no more unparliamentary than the remarks that had elicited it. Moreover, "this is the first instance where, men using against each other the weapons of sarcasm and invective, the House comes in and by main strength seeks to put down one of the antagonists who proves himself the hardest hitter."

But if the Kentuckian was to be expelled for his admittedly unwise and unparliamentary remarks, said Lamar, what were the precedents in the case? Had not Butler, in the not distant past, accused one of his colleagues in the House (Mr. Bingham) of a "judicial murder," and did not the latter respond that such language was unworthy of the dignity of this House and could only emanate from a man who "lived in a bottle and was fed with a spoon"? (This a sly dig at Butler of whom Grant had said that with a large body of troops facing an inferior force he had been "as completely shut off from further operations against Richmond as if he had been in a bottle strongly corked," and who was commonly accused of having pillaged silver spoons from the inhabitants of New Orleans during the period of his military dictatorship.) As Lamar continued to read from the *Record* various personal remarks that had been made about one another by the Republicans, those urging the expulsion of the Kentuckian became increasingly uncomfortable. Even the Speaker, Mr. Blaine, appealed to the House for protection lest his particularly vitriolic attack upon Mr. (now Senator) Conkling be recited.

Eventually the attempt at expulsion was abandoned, but the motion to censure was passed by a strictly party vote. The incident had an epilogue some months after, on May 2nd, 1876, when, with the fires of partisanship somewhat cooled, every leader in the move to punish John Young Brown (except, of course, Mr. Butler) united in support of a motion, submitted by Lamar, to rescind the too hasty imputation that Brown had prevaricated to the Speaker in the course of his dissertation on "Butlerism." [23]

A decade later, when Lamar was serving in Mr. Cleveland's Cabinet, the newspapers carried an amusing story concerning himself and Butler. One recalls that when stationed in New Orleans, General ("Beast") Butler had issued an order that any lady of the city who did not pay proper respect to the federal soldiery should be treated as a prostitute. His memory then, as now, was loathed in the South. As the story goes, "one of Secretary Lamar's characteristics is sympathy for inebriates. This kind of philanthropy, however, has its drawbacks. The other day an individual tottered into a street car where the Secretary was riding. The first thing that he did was to throw a dollar through the opening in the front door. By and by the driver passed back the change done up in a little package. The drunken man shoved it into his pocket. Pretty soon the driver opened the door and called sharply: 'Put in your fare!' The drunken man stared, but didn't move. People began to titter. 'Never mind,' said Mr. Lamar, looking benevolently at the befogged passenger; 'I'll fix it for you.' And he stepped up and put a nickel in the box. The situation was still misty, but the drunken man recognized that in some way the Secretary had done him a friendly act. He extended his hand, and Mr. Lamar shook it, saying: 'That's all right.'

"The drunken man gazed steadily and earnestly at his bene-factor for nearly five minutes. Then a broad grin spread over his face as he reached out his hand and said: 'How d'ye do, General Butler? I thought I know'd yer; fit with yer at New Orleans.'

"Mr. Lamar accepted the hand again, but with less suavity. 'I know'd yer,' continued the drunken man; and he kept on grinning, while the people began to snicker. 'You don't think he takes me for Ben Butler, do you?' asked Mr. Lamar, rather painfully, of a friend who sat beside him. The Secretary wasn't left long in doubt, for, after another hard look, the drunken man delightedly pointed to his left optic, and broke out with: 'Got yer eye fixed sence we was at New Orleans, hain't yer?' [Butler was blind in one eye.]

"Mr. Lamar dropped out on the next corner, with an effort to look responsive to the smiles which followed him." [24]

Throughout the controversies resulting from the considera-tion of the Force Bill and the Civil Rights Bill, the press had made frequent reference to an article that Lamar had written for the *New York Herald* of January 9th, 1875. In answer to the question: "What socially and politically would be the result in your State if the Federal Government should at once and entirely cease to interfere in the affairs of your State, and leave Mississippi to govern itself and its people to manage their own local affairs just as the people of New York or Pennsyl-vania manage their own?" he replied, among other things, that "the rights of personal security and of property would be under the changed circumstances referred to as secure as they are in any community on earth. The disturbances there now are purely of a political nature. Public opinion in that State regards any white man as ignoble and cowardly who would cheat a negro or take advantage of him in a trade or who would wantonly do him a personal injury. A jury, if it should incline in its sympathies either way, would favor the weaker man in an appeal to the laws." The suffrage and other political rights, he thought, would—with occasional disturbances for a short period—be quickly secured to the freedmen.

Lamar pointed out that the Federal Government, by its interference, had separated the Negroes and the whites into different political parties. Furthermore, "the white man is made by the direct action of the Federal Government the political antithesis of the black, and is pointed out to the latter as the common enemy.... By constituting itself as the negro's sole protector in the State it drives him to trust only its agents and partisans, often men of the vilest character, and rarely men who have any material relation to the State or to society among us. The negro is thus isolated from the white people among whom he lives, and the federal power thus makes him an alien in our society.... Here is the true cause of the disturbances of which you in the North have greatly exaggerated accounts. Withdraw the disturbing force, leave our population to the responsibility of local self-government and to the natural operation of social and industrial forces, and all that is now deranged and disorderly will certainly and permanently arrange itself...."

This letter provoked wide discussion, and in Mississippi precipitated an extended argument between the Democratic and Republican press, the former led by the *Jackson Clarion* and the latter by the *Jackson Pilot* which, as the organ of the Republican party, attempted to wrest Lamar's expression of a "purely political nature" from its context and to give it a sinister connotation.

With Congress adjourned, Lamar had intended to return to Mississippi for a time. But at the urgent request of the Democratic State Executive Committee of New Hampshire, he, with Senator Gordon of Georgia, consented to campaign that State in the interest of the Democratic nominees for office in the election to be held on the 9th of March. At Nashua he presented possibly his most notable speech of the canvass which was reprinted in full in most of the Eastern metropolitan papers. Among other things, the *Boston Advertiser* of March 7th, in a discussion and résumé of the speech some five thousand words in length, remarked that "Representative Lamar, of Mississippi, spoke to the citizens of Nashua last evening on the condition of his people at the South. Though the hall was engaged by the Democratic Committee, and he was invited to speak, it was by no means a party gathering that assembled. Republicans and Democrats, attracted by the reputation which he bears for eloquence, ability, and worth, crowded the large hall till they filled it to overflowing. His address was exactly suited to the mixed character of his audience. It was remarkably non-partisan, consisting merely of a statement of facts braced by the reports of Congressional investigations and a logical tracing of the causes which have led to whatever turbulence and disquietude exist; containing scarcely an allusion to either of the two political parties, and none whatever to the approaching election. He spoke for about two hours, not concluding till nearly eleven o'clock, and retained the closest attention to the last; and then, as several times before, there were loud calls for him to continue. The address was earnest and forcible, and made a deep impression upon those who listened to it."

"I have come," said Lamar in this address, "under the persuasion that the citizens of this State, as indeed the people all over this country, desire that the era of sectional discord and alienation and strife from which the country has been so long suffering shall be brought to a close; and that a new one shall be inaugurated which shall be illustrious as an era of cordial reunion between the sections, of harmonious fraternity between the people." The only obstacle, he thought, was the apprehension in the minds of many honest people that "such is the condition of affairs in the Southern states, such the temper of the Southern people, that local self-government in that section will not give the guarantee of personal security, of personal liberty, of prosperity, and of political rights to which American citizens of all classes and of all races are entitled." He was sorry that he was appearing before them on the occasion of a political canvass, for "if there were in my heart a glancing thought of party profit or party advantage at any approaching election, I should feel that I was trifling with sacred interests." Through misrepresentation, he pointed out, the North and the East had been led to believe "that upon the part of the native white population of the South there is a determined scheme to obtain supremacy and control, if necessary by organized fraud, violence, murder, for the purpose of subjecting the newly enfranchised race of that section to a servitude something akin to their former bondage, and to defeat the results which you have achieved by the war that you closed in 1865." He would satisfy his hearers that no such purpose existed.

The South, he made clear, had accepted the new amendments to the Constitution in good faith, and the occasional disorders in that section had no origin in dissatisfaction with the provisions that had, in a sense, been forced upon them. Rather the ills from which his section of the country suffered were largely to be charged to the interference of the Federal Government which had driven from public life the most intelligent and honorable element of the people. From this point he passed to a graphic description of the abuses under which the Southern people were struggling. He pictured the "sway of corruption, cupidity and graft, peculation and embezzlement, intimidation of voters, bribery, waste of public treasure, loss of public credit, false Returning Boards, fraudulent balloting, intimidation by the federal military, taxation in all its grinding and diversified forms." The remainder of the speech represents a detailed analysis of the evidence furnished by Congressional investigations that had been conducted in various of the Southern States. "I assure you," he said in closing, "that there is no antagonism to the Union in that Southern country. If you were to attempt to confer a separate nationality upon them, they would not accept it as a boon. They all believe and feel, in their shattered condition, that their hope and the hope of the American people is the preservation of the Union. ... They are ready to rally around your old flag, which for the last ten years has been to them not an emblem of protection but an emblem of force. Just vouchsafe to them the benefits of government as you enjoy them yourselves; give them the right of local self-government; that is all they ask, and they will teach their children to lisp, 'Liberty and union, now and forever, one and inseparable.'"

Purposely, Lamar and Gordon had been requested to help in a district where the Republican majority was normally the largest. On the whole, the results of the election brought little satisfaction to the Democrats, but there was some consolation in the fact that they gained one Congressman. In commenting on the outcome, the *Philadelphia Times* remarked that "wherever Gens. Gordon and Lamar spoke the Democrats made unprecedented gains." The *Springfield* (Mass.) *Republican* thought that the greatest value of their Northern "invasion" was not political but social, in that they had done much to remove the false impressions relative to the South which had been built up by agitators. Said the Democratic *Washington City Herald:* "If the sincere and eloquent words of these honest and earnest men, pleading for peace and good will between the sections, could have been listened to by every voter in the Granite State, the result might have been, as we firmly believe, an overwhelming conservative triumph. In the district where their addresses were made, a Democratic Congressman was chosen, although it has hitherto been represented by a Republican."

On his way back to Mississippi, Lamar addressed a notable gathering in Boston. Stopping in that city for a few hours, he and Gordon were dined by the Marshfield Club at the Somerset Clubhouse on Beacon Street.[25] President Harvey proposed the toast, which was always given at meetings of the Club, to "the memory of Daniel Webster, the defender and expounder of the constitution." In Lamar's response to the toast to his health he remarked that "he was glad to be the guest of men who aimed to follow the precepts taught by the immortal Webster. In his boyhood he had imbibed the doctrines of John C. Calhoun; but now that the war had settled the issues upon which Calhoun and Webster most disagreed, he could see that upon all points bearing upon the questions which agitate the country to-day the views of Webster and Calhoun were substantially the same. Each, in his day, was considered the defender and expounder of the constitution. They simply differed as to its interpretation. Were they alive now, they would stand, hand in hand and shoulder to shoulder, in opposition to the usurpations and violations of the constitutional rights of the States that had been practiced during the later years. All the teachings of both these men were opposed to the idea of executive interference with the domestic concerns of the States. They were opposed to everything that bore a semblance of absolutism in government. They did not believe that the constitution was a thing that could be lightly set aside...." Brief addresses in response to the speeches of the Southerners were made by ex-Governor Gardner, and the Hon. Leverett Saltonstall, and Henry W. Paine.

Passing from Washington through Atlanta on the way home, Lamar was interviewed for the *Atlanta Herald* by the youthful Henry W. Grady. It was the intimate friendship of the older man that was to do most to mold the political and social philosophy of the young orator (though Lamar—unlike his gifted disciple—always retained a thoroughgoing skepticism concerning the desirability of an ultra-industrialized social order) of whom it was said that "when he died he was literally loving a nation into peace." Incidentally, it detracts nothing from Grady's most famous speech, the "New South," to observe that the influence of Lamar's ideas, particularly of his oration over the dead Sumner, is to be seen in every line. And it is noteworthy that, except for certain of Lamar's other addresses, there was an interval of twelve years between these two great orations when no other such liberal voices were heard from the South or, for that matter, from the nation.

The lengthy interview, as published in the *Atlanta Herald*, was prefaced by a discriminating editorial in which Grady pointed out Lamar's services to the South and to the nation.[26] "The very high character for statesmanship and patriotic devotion to the South which Mr. Lamar has borne through a long career of public life," said Grady, "should give his utterances more than ordinary significance. There are few men in the country to whom the appellation of 'Statesman' can be more justly applied, and none to whom the much-abused adjective of 'eloquent' more properly belongs...." The country, Grady felt, was approaching a grave crisis and constitutional government could only be accomplished and preserved under the leadership of such men as Lamar.

His picture of the latter is worth preserving: "Mr. Lamar has all the physical characteristics of his knightly and illustrious family—that peculiar swarthy complexion, pale but clear; the splendid gray eyes; the high cheek bones; the dark brown hair; the firm and fixed mouth; the face thoroughly haughty and reserved when in repose, and yet full of snap and fire and magnetism; all those were there. Added to these was that indefinable something which all great men carry about them, and which hangs about even small men who have been for a time in very high position." Grady thought it apparent at a glance that Mr. Lamar was no ordinary Congressman, and that there was nothing accidental or fortuitous in the national reputation which he has achieved. "His record is truly a brilliant one. What Gordon is in the Senate, Lamar is in the House. And these two Southerners stand ahead, in the spirit of nobility, at least, of all their colleagues. Lamar is a finer talker than Gordon. If I am not mistaken, he is a better scholar than Gordon: by this I mean of more classical aptness and of broader culture."

The interview itself dealt chiefly with the approaching presidential campaign. Lamar thought the tidal wave of the preceding year, that had turned over the House of Representatives to the Democrats, was not mainly a party victory; rather he felt that it was an anti-administration revolt which brought over many liberals to the Democratic party. He believed that the Democracy, by aligning itself with the Republican liberals, could win the Presidency by nominating Charles Francis Adams, United States Ambassador to Great Britain during the Civil War, or Judge Davis of the Supreme Court. "These gentlemen," he said, "have the entire confidence of the Democracy of this country. Either of them would develop its full strength. If they can carry the liberals, there would be no doubt of it." Grant, he felt, was already a candidate for renomination. "An immense effort will be made to defeat him in the nominating convention, but this I have no idea can be done."

A large part of the interview was given over to an appreciation of those Republicans who had dared their party's displeasure and stood for the South in her hour of greatest need. "...We must not," Lamar said, "by trotting out dead issues, drive off our allies. I want you to understand...that I have a thorough and genuine appreciation of the liberal Republicans who have rebelled against the power of party in behalf of my people. Take the case of old man Poland, the man who saved Arkansas. He absolutely put behind him a lifelong ambition when he made his protest against Grant's interference. He had all his life cherished the hope that he might get a certain judgeship. Just before he made his report on Arkansas affairs he became aware that his ambition was about to be realized. He knew that if he made that anti-administration report it would crush his hopes forever. It was his pride and his ambition against his convictions. I shall never forget how the gray-haired old hero rose and spoke that which unspoken would have realized the proudest dream of his life. He was just leaving public life, and knew that he was destroying his last hope. Yet, with a stern and unfaltering hand, he buried his hope and saved a State."

Lamar's remarks about the unfaltering principle and courage of Luke P. Poland are strictly true. In 1874 the Democracy of Arkansas, under the leadership of the able lawyer, Augustus H. Garland, had secured control of their own government.

The radicals immediately turned to the administration and to Congress with the plea that they be supported in power by the Federal Government. As a result, a select Congressional committee of five, under the chairmanship of Poland, was appointed to investigate the situation in the State. A long line of disreputable characters passed in review before the committee, among them the corrupt Chief Justice McClure who appeared shortly before General Sheridan had sent to Grant his notorious suggestion that the leading citizens of Louisiana and Arkansas be declared bandits. When it became know that Poland's report would be against the radicals and in favor of non-intervention by the Federal Government, the whole weight of the administration's influence was brought to bear upon him. But neither threats nor promises would move him and on February 6th, 1875, he submitted his report.[27] His conclusions were so obviously fair that against the bitter opposition of President Grant, the report was accepted and Arkansas was free.

Lamar reached home the latter part of March, and was at once faced with two insistent problems: that of leading his people in the struggle to free themselves from radical domination; and secondly the securing of his own renomination to Congress. But he, essentially the scholar and the dreamer, was often wearied of the turmoil of public life and longed for the privacy of the ordinary citizen. "I have gained in influence and reputation," he was writing to his wife just before the close of the Forty-third Congress, "but it is all vanity, vanity. Would that I could live in peace and obscurity the rest of my life with my dear wife and children."[28]

That Lamar be returned to the House was peculiarly necessary from the standpoint of the entire South. He had faced on broad statesmanlike grounds every issue that had arisen during his previous incumbency, and he had held out the olive branch to the North and had striven to place the case for the South in its truest light. As has been seen, he had purposely held to a moderate course in his speeches because he knew that in such manner he would gain increasing influence that he could exert for the salvation of his people from carpetbag and radical rule, and already a large element in the Northern press had come to take his loyal and moderate expressions as typical of the feelings of the better element in the South. Should the people of Mississippi refuse to sanction his course by returning him to Washington, they would, by their action, repudiate the stand for national amity and good will that he had taken. On the other hand, his renomination and reëlection would be an assurance to the North that the principles for which he stood and the ideas that he had expressed truly represented the people of his section.

That Lamar's return to Congress was felt to be a matter of national moment is shown by the editorial notices that at this time appeared in the press of every part of the country, all of them laudatory. The *Milwaukee Sentinel* asserted that "he is in every respect, at least in appearance, the gentle, quiet, firm, and uncompromising statesman, and is really reflecting more credit upon the extreme Southern locality from which he comes than any other member." [29] To the *Augusta* (Ga.) *Chronicle and Sentinel* he seemed the "foremost statesman of the South in Public Life," while the *Alta Californian* thought that "the example set in Congress by Mr. Lamar, of Mississippi, who behaves like a true gentleman toward other members of the House," could well be emulated by his colleagues of both parties. "He has made friends of both sides of the House, not by pandering to or flattering the vanity of either, but by exhibiting a spirit of fairness on all occasions, an independence of thought truly statesmanlike, but at the same time not leaving his own political preferences at all in doubt. Such men are an honor to the country." [30]

His increasing stature in the public eye was attested when on the 22nd of May, the United States Commission, which had in charge the preparation for the Centennial Exposition to be held in Philadelphia in the following year, selected him with Charles Francis Adams as the orators of the national celebration. As it turned out, the urgency of other duties made it necessary for Lamar to decline the honor, but his selection was a notable tribute to his national importance, particularly his recognition as the most important statesman of the South, and to the powers of his oratory.

The Democratic press of Mississippi was for him without exception. Even the radical Republican organs were accustomed to pay him the highest praises, with the added statement that he could not be considered a typical member of his party. "The enclosed brief article contains my real sentiments," said an open letter from ex-Senator A. G. Brown which appeared in the *Clarion* of March 26th. "I feel more inclined to express them, inasmuch as I did not at first fully approve of Lamar's speech over the dead Sumner. But, having witnessed its good effects, I recant. It is now, I think, on every account our policy to make him our *recognized* leader. We thereby, amongst many other advantages, get the benefit of his conservative statements so often and so boldly expressed. By making him our leader we make these expressions our own, and thus disarm our northern slanderers." The very next issue of the *Clarion* called for Lamar's nomination and election with an appeal to the members of all parties to align themselves under his banner. It pointed out that the principles for which he stood were greater than any party, and that the welfare of all citizens required his return to Washington.

Long before the meeting of the Democratic Congressional Convention it was apparent to all that no one would enter the field against him. The *Clarion* of April 14th stated that "in the First District no man is thought of except the present peerless representative, Hon. L. Q. C. Lamar, in whose return the whole State (may we not say the whole country?) is interested, who will be reëlected almost by acclamation to the place he has honored." Before the convention met, every county in the District had held mass meetings in which Lamar was indorsed "first, last, and always," and when the convention assembled in Corinth, on the 22nd of July, he was renominated by acclamation. When the State convention assembled at Jackson on the 3rd of August, the resolution was adopted that "this convention cordially approves the course of Hon. L. Q. C.

Lamar in the Congress of the United States, and holds in the highest estimation his great services in the cause of reconciliation, peace, and good government."

To the other sections of the nation, the renomination of Lamar came as a warrant that the people of his section were in sympathy with the conciliatory and moderate course that he had espoused. "The unanimous nomination of Congressman Lamar by the Democrats of the First Mississippi District is sufficient evidence that the genuine citizenship of that State is competent to look out for itself if left alone," asserted the *Boston Post*. Furthermore, "he has risen to the full requirements of a statesman, and has exerted an influence felt for good throughout the whole nation. Regeneration in politics, reconciliation, and all the immediate needs of our new Union, he has devoted himself to with all the enthusiasm and brilliant, even vivid, eloquence that he possesses. His influence could not well be spared from the forces that in the next few years are to bring this republic up to a higher plane of honor and prosperity." [31] The arch-Republican *New York Tribune* characterized him as "one of the ablest and most deservedly popular men in Congress," while the *Detroit Free Press* thought it "no disparagement to other Southern Representatives to say that he more ably and successfully than any other, laid the views, hopes, and feelings of the South before Congress and the people of the country."

Once he had been nominated, Lamar carried forward a militant campaign throughout his district, greatly assisted by Senator Gordon whom he had invited to come from Georgia. Denouncing the white men, mostly adventurers from the North and East, who had preyed upon the credulity of the Negroes, he pleaded for a better racial understanding and for the confidence of the blacks themselves. [32] The present situation, he pointed out, was unfortunate for both races. The Negroes were not to be blamed for being misled by their pretended friends, but they should no longer allow themselves to be used as the excuse for the pillaging carried on by men who had interest neither in them nor in the State. The white people of the South would always, he felt, hold in grateful remembrance the loyalty and the services of the blacks in the long years before reconstruction.

XII

MISSISSIPPI REDEEMED

As HAS been seen, Lamar was intensely concerned with the sad condition of the State of Louisiana under carpetbag rule. As a matter of fact, the fortunes of Louisiana and of Mississippi were inextricably interwoven, for New Orleans was the financial, commercial, and cultural center of a region that embraced both States, and both were under the dictatorship of General Sheridan who, more than once, had sent soldiers to Mississippi to maintain the corrupt black and tan government. Moreover, the newspapers of New Orleans, together with those of Memphis, Tennessee, held a wide circulation throughout the State and were of commanding importance in the molding of public opinion.

Lamar was now (coincidentally with his campaign for and reëlection to Congress) to take a leading part in a cause even closer to his heart than any that he had previously espoused— the final rescue of Mississippi from black Republican and carpetbag rule, an accomplishment which renders the year 1875 as perhaps the most important in the history of the State.

Under the administration of Governor Ames, the Maine carpetbagger, the affairs of Mississippi had gone from bad to worse. Against the opposition of the liberal Republicans, the Democrats, and the Independent Conservatives, he had been elected in 1873 through skillful marshaling of the tremendous Negro vote and through outright fraud, and in January, 1874, he was installed. As Military Governor his course had been evil; his administration as Civil Governor was now worse, for a dull man himself, he appointed and supported ignorant and corrupt public officials, mostly Negroes and carpetbaggers from the North and East. Apparently, nothing could be done about it all, for he made good his purposes through threats of military force, federal and State, and the people sank further into despondency because of the burden of taxes. The courts were of no avail, for Ames constantly appointed his henchmen to judicial positions and dictated their decisions.[1]

In Mississippi the Negroes outnumbered the whites by 61,000 and Ames proposed to honor their demands for adequate recognition among the higher State offices. Among these were the lieutenant governorship, the secretaryship of state, the speakership of the house, the superintendency of education, and the commissionership of immigration. During the summer Ames would go North and turn over the administration of affairs entirely to the plunderers. The Lieutenant Governor had a considerable income from the sale of pardons and commutations, and the State Superintendent of Education, under indictment for larceny at Brooklyn, New York, and for malfeasance as circuit clerk of Warren County, Mississippi, made away with a large part of the school funds.[2] Blanche K. Bruce, by far the most intelligent and the ablest representative of the Negro race in Mississippi public life, had been sent to the United States Senate.

Jobs were made for all carpetbaggers who were not cared for by the Federal Government and in some counties where white Republicans were scarce, the same individual would hold several positions.[3] Of all offices the most to be desired, of a modest nature, was that of sheriff, for the opportunity for excessive fees and for all types of graft was here unparalleled. All such places were held by Northern white men or Negroes. The tax rate ran as high in certain localities as 5%, and in 1874 landowners who could not pay their taxes forfeited more than 6,000,000 acres of land, considerably more, as Rhodes points out, than was contained in Massachusetts and Rhode Island together.[4]

But the people of the State were no longer willing silently to bear their oppressions. On the 4th of January, 1875, a convention representing the taxpayers and organized without respect to color or party, met in the city of Jackson. In an orderly fashion they discussed the ills under which they suffered and drew up certain suggestions for consideration by the legislature. These had to do with a more economical administration of the government of the State. Among other things, it was pointed out that "in 1869 the State levy was ten cents on the hundred dollars of assessed value of lands. For the year 1871 it was *four times* as great; for 1872 it was *eight and a half times* as great; for the year 1873 it was *twelve and a half times* as great; and for the year 1874 it was *fourteen times* as great as it was in 1869. The tax levy of 1874 was the largest State tax ever levied in Mississippi, and to-day the people are poorer than ever before." When the memorial was presented to the legislature, it was studiedly ignored, and that same night Governor Ames, in testifying before a Congressional committee, spoke contemptuously of those "who were howling about taxes." [5]

Particularly unfortunate was Vicksburg, a city of 12,443 inhabitants, more than half of them Negroes. By 1874 the blacks, who had been drilled and furnished with arms by Ames and the carpetbaggers, were strong enough to throw out their white co-conspirators and take entire charge of the local government. In 1869 the entire debt of the city and county combined had been but $13,000, but by 1874 this had been increased for the city alone to $1,400,000, and the debt of both was being rapidly increased by the Negro ring which was in control, this composed of the sheriff, the chancery clerk (who was also the clerk of the county supervisors) and the four blacks who dominated the latter body of five.[6]

In Vicksburg, as the municipal election of August 4th approached, the Negroes became increasingly arrogant. The ticket which they put up in the name of the Republican party was even worse than that already in power, if that were possible. A notoriously corrupt white man, Martin Keary, was nominated for Mayor, and seven of eight selected for aldermen, six of eight for school trustees, the city marshal, the cotton weigher, the wharf and harbor master, were blacks. From such a slate all but the most inveterate Republicans turned away. Meanwhile a company of Negro militia was constantly paraded up and down the main business street with muskets loaded and bayonets fixed, while talk of bloodshed and slaughter of the whites on election day was common and open. Throughout the county and just across the river in Madison Parish the companies of Negro militia were being raised and drilled to march on Vicksburg, as one of the black leaders declared, "ready to shoot every damned white man." [7]

Then on July 9th the local Negro "boss," the corrupt chancery clerk, gave a statement for publication in the city papers: "The time was not far distant when miscegenated marriages would occur daily. He would go further and say that there were many thousands of Southern women, many of the most respectable families in Vicksburg, who would marry negroes to-day were they not afraid. But these things would change, barriers would be broken down; for the white women now see that the negro is the coming man, that they have the control of the State and city governments. If he were not a married man he could get the daughter of one of the best families in Vicksburg, and were he in the matrimonial market he would buckle on a brace of pistols and meet the woman's father or brothers who would dare interfere in his love affairs; to prevent daughters and sisters from their choice in the selection of husbands whom they were anxious to have among the colored men." [8]

With the knowledge that the whites would probably carry the election by the solidarity of their voting, Ames called upon President Grant to detail federal troops to "supervise" the Vicksburg municipal election, but his request was refused and the conservatives won a sweeping victory. Mississippi historians are unanimous in attributing Grant's unprecedented failure to coerce the election in favor of the radicals and blacks to the public sentiment throughout the North and East which had been aroused shortly before by Lamar's speeches in New England, particularly the one delivered at Nashua, New Hampshire, in which he had pointed out the abuses in the use of the federal army in controlling elections in the South, and in supporting those who were pillaging the Southern States. This address, as has been seen, was given wide circulation by the conservative press, and it had come just at the opportune moment to aid in the redemption of Mississippi.[9]

But despite the victory within the municipality of Vicksburg, the corrupt county and State officials were still in office and their power to collect taxes left the city at their mercy. In December, 1874, Crosby, the sheriff (who was ex officio tax collector) was about to collect some $160,000 in county and States taxes, this representing more than 5% of the total valuation of the property. His bonds were dateless and otherwise defective and his sureties were all propertyless and illiterate blacks with the exception of one married woman whose signature was legally not binding. The Republican district attorney, disgusted with the farcical nature of the sheriff's pretensions, pointed out that the surety which the sheriff presented was worthless on account of the way the bonds were drawn up; that the bondsmen were without character or property; and that in any event the surety, if accepted at its purported value, was entirely insufficient. In answer Crosby published a notice in which he declared that he had no intention of improving his surety, and arrogantly stated that he would collect every penny of the exorbitant taxes.[10]

The nature of the county government was further revealed when in August it was discovered that a large number of forged witness certificates had been issued by the Circuit Clerk, A. W. Dorsey, and his predecessor, T. W. Cardozo, both of them unprincipled Negroes, and the latter (by now Superintendent of Education) under indictment in New York State for grand larceny. The same investigation revealed that the chancery clerk, a black named Davenport, had made free to alter the county records to hide his stealing, and that he had not given bond—in fact, could not have secured bond, so well was his character known. Some, even, of the carpetbaggers were up in arms, and the Republican district attorney, at the November term of court and before a grand jury composed of ten blacks and seven whites, succeeded in finding a number of indictments against Davenport, Dorsey, and Cardozo. It would have been just as easy, he subsequently stated, to have secured five hundred indictments. Shortly before the day of the trial, the conspirators, assisted by the sheriff, stole all of the records from the courthouse and hid them under Davenport's residence where they were afterwards discovered.

Naturally, all confidence in the officials was destroyed, and the citizenry was determined to go any lengths before it would pay more taxes, merely to have the money stolen. Life had become intolerable in the face of such conditions, and the taxpayers set up a committee, composed both of Democrats and Republicans and representing both races, with the instructions that it wait upon the county officials and demand their immediate resignations. Only Crosby and Davenport could be found, but these two promised that within thirty minutes they would give definite answers to the demands of the committee. Instead, both crawled out the back way and slunk off. Thwarted for the moment, several hundred taxpayers repaired to the courthouse where they discovered Crosby and received his resignation, after which they placed a Republican, Captain Baird (a former Union officer) in temporary charge of the records of the sheriff's office. Davenport had fled.

Meanwhile, the deposed sheriff had hurried to Jackson to enlist the support of Governor Ames, who straightway advised him to return to Vicksburg and resume his office, with the assistance, if necessary, of the black militia. Ames further ordered General A. G. Packer to start the militia towards Vicksburg where he might be on hand in case troops were needed. The North, Ames told a group of already inflamed blacks, had endured bloodshed in their cause. If they were unwilling to do likewise, they were unworthy of their freedom. Then, in a proclamation intended primarily for Northern consumption, he issued an incendiary statement in which he ordered the riotous and disorderly persons, who were depriving the Negroes of their rights merely because they were black, to retire to their homes. On Sunday the disreputable Negro Superintendent of Public Education, Cardozo, was writing Crosby not "to make any compromise with those fellows. The

Governor is at your back." But the revolution had begun and was being everywhere justified by the Northern press. "My God!" exclaimed Colonel Gordon Adams, as quoted in the *Cincinnati Commercial.* "The whites have borne and borne until forbearance ceased to be a virtue, and almost became crime." [11]

On Monday the sheriff, Crosby, would be called upon to perform certain important functions of the Circuit Court which was in session—that is, if he were to be considered still an officer of the county. In preparation he decided upon a revolutionary move. Having supervised the printing of handbills calling upon all Negro men to arm themselves and appear in Vicksburg at the opening of court, he sent the circulars about the county by means of fifteen colored horsemen who rode throughout Saturday and Sunday. Negro ministers further spread the news from their pulpits. When on Sunday afternoon the action of Crosby became known, General Packer at once made a vain attempt to keep the blacks from assembling, and early the next morning it became known that a band of several hundred armed blacks were advancing upon the city of Vicksburg. The situation was further complicated in that it was feared that there would be a rising of the town Negroes who constituted more than half of the population, and among whom was the Negro militia organized and equipped with the most modern army rifles, the Negro captain of which had been ordered by the Governor, on Friday, to coöperate with Crosby.

The streets of Vicksburg were filled with terrified and weeping women and children, while the white men armed themselves as best they could and prepared to meet the invaders at the edge of the town. The blacks, about seven hundred in all, appeared from three directions, armed and bent on serious mischief. The whites afterwards said, and impartial historians have verified their statements as true, that the Negroes began to fire as soon as they came in sight.[12] In the pitched battle that ensued the Negroes were driven off with the loss of fifteen or more killed and many wounded, while one white man lost his life.

In this banding together for protection all party lines were, of course, obscured, and Republicans took perhaps a more important part than did the Democrats. Afterwards, before a Congressional investigating committee, Brigadier General Furlong, a distinguished ex-Union officer, said that "every ex-soldier of the federal army in Vicksburg was out in arms, the same as the other citizens, that day.... I reckon about one hundred. All of them joined, and I think took an even more conspicuous part than the ex-Confederates." [13] General Packer informed the same committee that in his opinion the citizens were justified in their actions, and that it was a great mercy to the women and children that the blacks were kept from entering the city.

A few days later, on the 11th of December, Lamar was writing to Judge Wiley P. Harris, of Jackson, asking if the taxpayers had any available legal recourse against the collection of the enormous levies and the subsequent almost certain stealing of the money by the courthouse ring. "The truth is (I speak from sad experience)," declared Judge Harris, "that under our government, as it now exists, there is no remedy for the peculations of public officers. We are fleeced and robbed on all sides, and we are powerless to prevent it, either by law or the force of public opinion." Moreover, "whilst I have labored to come to an opposite conclusion, I am satisfied that the experiment of trying to make self-governing people out of the negroes will fail—in fact, has already failed. Let any Northern man who thinks the negro is capable of self-government imagine the condition of Mississippi, or any other State, at the end of twelve months from the day when the last white man has left it, and there remains no obstacle to the full development and free exercise of African statesmanship."

In regard to the Vicksburg affair, concerning which Lamar had especially inquired, Judge Harris regretted that "our Vicksburg friends resorted to anything that even looked like force. I know that their action will be misconstrued, and it will be made the occasion of giving another turn to the screw. But when I look at the condition of affairs here—the constant and daily sources of irritation, the rapid decline in all values, the almost hopeless task of getting subsistence even, after the demands of the tax-gatherer have been satisfied—I am astonished at the moderation of our people." [14]

The apprehension that the "battle" of Vicksburg would be misunderstood outside the South was well founded, for the radicals made a great outcry and an investigating committee was constituted by Congress. As a matter of fact, the citizens of the State were only too glad to have the opportunity of vindicating themselves, and the *Clarion* of December 17th welcomed the investigation with the words: "Let the facts go to the country." Lamar himself felt that any fairly conducted investigation would be to the interest of the South. "The citizens of Vicksburg," he told the House of Representatives, "do not shrink from that investigation; they court it, and are only anxious that all the facts connected with that transaction, as well as the causes which produced it, shall be fully exposed to the country." [15]

On the Congressional committee that was constituted were Messrs. Hurlbut of Illinois, Conger of Michigan, and Williams of Wisconsin, Republicans; with Speer of Pennsylvania, and O'Brien of Maryland, Democrats. On the 28th of February they presented their findings consisting of majority and minority reports covering, in all, five hundred and sixty pages. Of this even the radical *New York Tribune* was moved to say that "the Mississippi investigation, like that in Alabama, has brought forth two reports, each strongly colored with the political opinions of its signers. Indeed, that of the majority [the Republican] has so strong a partisan tincture that it will have no weight whatever with any one outside of the administration party. Some of its statements seem entirely without foundation in the testimony given to the press from day to day during the progress of the investigation."

Meanwhile, a special session of the legislature had convened on the 17th of December at the call of Governor Ames. In his message he denounced in unmeasured terms the whites who had protested against the taxes and he reported that the State was in a "fortunate financial condition." The citizens of Vicksburg, who had protected themselves against the Negroes, he

denounced as insurrectionary, and requested that the legislature take steps to bring about order in Warren County. Not
one word of condemnation did he have for the Negro and
carpetbag officials who had embezzled the public funds and
bankrupted the State. The current reaction in Mississippi to
the Governor's course may be inferred from an open letter
written and published by Joshua S. Morris, a Republican who
had been a long-time attorney general of the State: "Either
the orders [given by Ames to certain troops where later he
denied there were any] were officially false, or the message
is officially false. In either case the Governor is an official *liar;*
and in either case, as a veteran Republican, I feel that I am
sold." [16]

The message of the Governor was followed by a session of
the legislature that was remarkable for the violence of the
speeches of the Negro leaders who forced through both Houses
a resolution calling upon the President of the United States
to send the federal army to Mississippi. The white minority,
having lost all confidence in President Grant, decided to address an appeal direct to the American people. This lengthy
document was signed by forty-six members, representative of
both branches of the legislature. "The people of Mississippi,"
it was said among other things, "are utterly powerless to defend
themselves against their constituted rulers, unless we shall have
the sympathy and good will, not of any particular party, but
of our fellow-citizens throughout the Union. We are too much
concerned here to save ourselves from local misgovernment and
oppression, to participate in any partisan contests which agitate
other parts of the Union." [17]

Matters continued to develop with increasing rapidity. On
January 5th, 1875, the legislature assembled again after a twelve-
day recess. Although there was no semblance of disorder
throughout the State, Governor Ames, on the 5th, had telegraphed Grant for troops to maintain the law. On the precise
day that the Mississippi legislature convened, General de Trobriand was breaking up and reconstituting the legislature of
the neighboring State of Louisiana. On the 5th, moreover,

General Sheridan wired Ames that he had taken command of the Department of the Gulf and was sending troops to Vicksburg. Condemning the defenders of the city as "banditti" and requesting that they be arrested and tried before a military tribunal, Sheridan allowed the ex-sheriff, Crosby, and his criminal associates to return to power in Vicksburg. Coincidentally, Ames started a movement to have Lafayette County transferred to another district where a black majority might retire Lamar (who was the recognized leader of the Mississippi Democracy) from Congress. Moreover, the legislature, at Ames's dictation, enacted a bill that would, in effect, allow him to organize a small standing army to be composed entirely of blacks, and to be used for the domination of Warren County of which Vicksburg was the largest town. Too, he was empowered to dissolve the State militia, withdrawing all commissions and recalling all arms under penalty of criminal prosecution if any were not immediately delivered to the quartermaster general. The Governor was then to reorganize the militia after his own taste, and was empowered to buy a number of Gatling guns. Incidentally, it was commonly understood that a white company would not be acceptable to Ames even if it were raised. This legislation was popularly known as "An Act to Rob and Murder the White People of Mississippi," and, in truth, that was precisely what it amounted to.

Perhaps the most serious consequence of the carpetbag control of the Negroes was the organization and grouping of the blacks into a party of opposition to the whites, with the division made strictly on racial lines. They were taught that their former masters were their enemies who were only waiting for an opportunity to reënslave them. The white adventurers made particularly effective use of the schools and the churches which were employed as headquarters for the dissemination of incendiary propaganda, and for secret meetings, often held at midnight, where loyal leagues were organized and drilled. Charles Nordhoff, reporting for the *New York Herald* under date of May 21st from Montgomery, Alabama, said that "the division of political parties on the race or color line has been a great calamity to the Southern States.... But it is the federal interference under the Enforcement Acts, and that alone, which enables unscrupulous politicians to mass the negro vote upon one side and to use it for their own aggrandizement.... Gov. Ames in Mississippi refuses to stir to prevent a riot in Vicksburg till after the riot, after forty or fifty blacks have been killed; and when the negroes are demoralized and feel utterly helpless sends for federal troops which come at his command and reassure the blacks. Such manifestations of power strike the imaginations of the negroes, as they would an ignorant population, and they follow very rapidly and blindly its possessor. Some colored witnesses in Alabama, being asked why they all voted against Sheats for Congress, replied: 'Because Perrin told them to.' Being asked if they would have voted the Democratic ticket if Perrin had told them to, they answered unhesitatingly: 'Yes.' ''

Furthermore, Nordhoff found that the leaders of the Negroes appeal only and continually to the Negroes' fears and to their sense of obligation to the federal power. In Alabama they were told that the bacon, sent as a flood-relief measure, was from General Grant, and that its receipt obliged them to vote a "straight Republican ticket." In Louisiana he found that the blacks were commonly called to political meetings by order of "General Butler," and that in at least one instance "a candidate for a county office circulated a printed 'general order' commanding all colored men to vote for him, and signed 'U. S. Grant, President'; and he received the solid colored vote." Nordhoff, in his dispatch of June 22nd, thought it "an evidence of the good nature of the mass of the whites that in the main they conduct themselves towards the blacks kindly and justly. They concentrate their dislike upon the men who have misled and now misuse the black vote, and this I cannot call unjust. It is commonly said: 'The negroes are not to blame; they do not know any better.' ''

After the conflict at Vicksburg, Mississippi was apparently saddled heavier than before with the reign of corruption. But as time wore on, hope began to return to the people, along with the conviction that the only way to offset the organized voting of the Negroes was to revive the old Democracy and constitute it strictly as a white man's party. With the reorganization of the party in the State Lamar was heartily in sympathy, but he was opposed to the drawing of the color line. He recognized, of course, that the majority of the blacks, in fact almost all of them, had already been regimented in opposition to the whites and that as a whole they would adhere to the Republican standard, but he felt that the isolation of the races into separate parties was fraught with great danger for the future of the whole South. This position he was to maintain throughout his career.

For some time, as has been seen, the disbanded Democracy had felt that it could work effectively in conjunction with the so-called "Conservative Independents" and with the liberal Republicans. This had not been a success, and in consequence of the rising sentiment for the resurgence of the State Democracy and in view of the victories of the party in the North, the Democratic members of the legislature assembled in caucus on the 3rd of March, 1875. Out of this caucus came a committee composed of Democrats and Conservatives which was to lay plans for the reorganization of the Democratic-Conservative party. They in turn issued a call for a meeting to be held on the 17th of May in Jackson, and issued a public invitation to "such friends of our cause as are willing to give us counsel and support."

At the convention which assembled in Jackson on May 17th, 1875, Lamar, for the committee on memorials, drew up a list of grievances to be broadcast to the country. In essence it was an appeal to the nation for protection against the federal administration.[18] Among other things it was shown that in the five years since the carpetbaggers and blacks secured complete control, the State tax levy had increased *fourteen fold,* and in the single month in which the taxpayers had met, half a million acres and four-fifths of the town of Greenville had been put up for sale because of taxation.[19] In addition, Lamar submitted plans, which were accepted, for a delegate convention to meet at the same place on the 3rd of August for the purpose of drawing up a platform and selecting a slate of candidates for the ensuing November election.

Hope began to spring in the breasts of the people of Mississippi, and in every county mass meetings were held, and the newspapers dealt predominantly with the all-important topic of the August meeting. Lamar was everywhere in demand for speeches, and he well nigh exhausted himself. Throughout the State the local organizations adopted the following resolutions that had been formulated by Lamar:

Resolved, That we are in favor of a vigorous and aggressive canvass in the contest now approaching in Mississippi, and we appeal to our fellow-citizens throughout the State to unite with us in our endeavors by legitimate means to regain control of our public affairs, and thus secure to all classes, white and black, the blessings of a just and honest government.

Resolved, That we favor low taxes and an immediate reduction of all public expenditures.

Resolved, That honesty and capacity are the only proper tests of official fitness.

Resolved, That all men are equal before the law, and are endowed by their creator with certain inalienable rights, amongst which is *not* the right to hold office unless the aspirant possesses the integrity and other qualifications necessary to its execution.[20]

At the meeting of July 12th in Pontotoc County, at the inspiration of Lamar who was the orator of the occasion and copied by almost all of the meetings which were subsequently held elsewhere, a fourth resolution was added:

Resolved, That we hereby freely and cordially invite all persons, of whatever race, color, or previous affiliations, to unite in securing for all a good, economical, and honest government in lieu of the oppressive, extravagant, and corrupt one we now have.

In this fourth article we see embodied Lamar's belief that party lines should in no sense be based upon color or race. So strongly did he feel in this respect that, at the convention which renominated him for Congress, he drew up and submitted the following resolution which was adopted at the conclusion of his speech:

Resolved, That we are opposed to the formation of parties among the people of this State founded upon differences of race or color, and we cordially invoke the union of good citizens of every race and color in patriotic efforts to defeat at the next election the present State administration and its supporters, and to secure to all the blessings of an honest and capable government.

When the Democratic State convention assembled in Jackson on August 3rd, Lamar (one of the delegates from Lafayette County and the recognized leader in the movement) delivered, as had been previously arranged, the main address. His lengthy speech was thought by the *Clarion* of the 4th to be "the ablest that has been pronounced in the Capital since the war. It was massive in argument, irresistible in logic, statesmanlike in the policy it advocated, and eloquent. A great deal was expected, but the highest expectation indulged by the public was more than realized." Even the *Pilot,* generally considered the personal organ of Governor Ames, praised the speech quite as highly and its analysis of Lamar's discussion was even more discriminating. Immediately following the address, letters of greeting and encouragement were read from Benjamin H. Hill, Allen G. Thurman, and Thomas A. Hendricks.

The platform which was adopted by the convention represented a concise statement of the main points of Lamar's speech.[21] It recognized the civil and political equality of all men as established by the Constitution of the United States and the amendments thereto; it called for the education of all of the children of the State without regard to color (but with separate schools); the selection of honest, faithful, and competent men for all the offices, from the highest to the lowest; economy in every department of the government; the selection of an able and competent judiciary, and the confining of the activities of judges to judicial functions purely; and the encouragement of agriculture and manufactures. Again, the platform denounced the building up of partisan newspapers by legislation, the arming of the militia in time of peace, the unconstitutional attempt to take from the people the election of tax collectors, the corruption of the judiciary by the use of executive patronage, and the unconstitutional authority constantly assumed by Governor Ames, the Republican executive. Finally, under the influence of Lamar, were invited "the voters of all the people of both races to unite vigorously with us in the approaching canvass, in a determined effort to give success to the foregoing principles, and thus to secure to ourselves and our posterity the blessings of an honest, economical government, administered by able, efficient, and competent public officers."

Lamar, in his speech before the convention, had devoted considerable attention to the proposal that the Democracy bar all members of the colored race from its ranks. We have seen that he believed such a course to be fraught with great evils for the State and for the South. The Republican *Pilot* thought that the "speech of Col. Lamar knocked the *Herald's* and the *Monitor's* color line arrangement higher than a kite." Lamar's efforts toward understanding and mutual kindliness between the races had been an important factor in saving the State from even more serious bloodshed after the Vicksburg affair. Shortly after the convention just discussed, in a letter of August 25th to Mr. Reemelin, he was writing: "I have just emerged from a struggle to keep our people from a race conflict. I am not sure yet that we are safe, for the *black* line is still maintained by the agents of the federal Government. The negro race, which has no idea of a principle of government or of society beyond that of obedience to the mandate of a master, sees in these agents the only embodiment of authority (mastership) in the country, and their obedience is not a whit less slavish than it was formerly to their masters. We could, by forming the 'color line,' and bringing to bear those agencies which intellect, pluck, and will always give, overcome the stolid, inert, and illiterate majority; but such a victory will bring about conflicts and race passions and collisions with federal power. Our only deliverance is in a change of federal policy toward us."[22]

In all previous State conventions there had been the restriction of party lines. That of 1875 represented the united manhood of the native whites of Mississippi who had come together to free themselves from intolerable conditions. The chasm that separated the people from their despotic rulers was evident in an incident that occurred just before the assembling of the convention, when the delegates, about 500 in number, were gathered in the front yard of the capitol. "At about half-past ten in the morning," said the *Natchez Democrat*, "when this crowd in the court was large enough to fill it, the governor [Adalbert Ames] was seen to come from the mansion, proceeding to the executive office. He passed through the groups, obliged to elbow his way very slowly from the court entrance to the front door of the capitol. And from the first to the last, in all this assembly from every portion of the State, not one man turned to him to say, 'Good Morning, Governor'— not one gave him a glance of recognition—and he, the governor of the State, passed through the body representative of its worth, property, and intelligence with downcast look like an alien and an outcast, a telling commentary upon radicalism in Mississippi!"[23] It was against such domination that the citizenry of the State had risen. "The contest is rather a revolution than a political campaign," said the *Aberdeen Examiner;* "it is the rebellion, if you see fit to apply that term, of a downtrodden people against an absolutism imposed by their own hirelings, and by the grace of God we will cast it off."[24]

Lamar, as well as his ally, General J. Z. George who was to have active management of the revolution at the polls, had determined to win the November election, but they wished to do so in such a fashion that they would hold the sympathy and respect of the rest of the country. At the Democratic convention Lamar had said that "if any one thing is true, the people of Mississippi have pledged themselves to maintain the three amendments to the Constitution [XIII, XIV, XV] and

have no power or desire to change them," and he had pleaded
that the sacred rights of "the newly enfranchised race" be not
violated. The chief danger, as Lamar, George, and the other
leaders saw it, was in conflicts between the races that would
cause Grant to interfere with the federal troops and thus nullify
all attempts of the whites to gain freedom through a revolution at the ballot. In this work of restraining their followers,
General George, as chairman of the Democratic State Executive
Committee, and having the work actively in hand, showed
marked ability.

But despite all efforts by the leaders of the Democracy,
so tense was the atmosphere that several outbreaks occurred.
In September it seemed that race trouble would irreparably
wreck the Democratic plan. At Yazoo City there was trouble
when the sheriff, a depraved ex-Union soldier who was living
with a mulatto woman, was interrupted in an incendiary speech
to a large gathering of Negroes. Worse was the affair at the
little town of Clinton, home of Mississippi College. Here (at
Moss Hill, a quarter of a mile from the depot) the Republicans,
who were holding a barbecue, had agreed to a joint debate
with the Democrats, Judge Amos R. Johnston to speak for
the latter. The judge had managed to finish his address (an
appeal for coöperation between the native whites and the
blacks) despite the cries of certain of the Negroes: "Damn it,
what do we want to hear a Democratic speech for?" [25] After
the Republican orator, Captain H. T. Fisher, had spoken for
about thirty minutes, a disturbance—its exact nature has never
been determined—occurred in a glade about seventy-five yards
away, and a shot was suddenly fired, by whom is not known.
The blacks, most of whom were armed, raised the cry of "Kill
the white men!" and began firing into the little group of eleven
who retreated in a body telling the blacks to keep their distance. A flank movement on the part of the blacks, however,
cut off their escape and two of them (Martin Sivley and Frank
Thompson) were shot down and disemboweled by the frenzied
mob of savages, one of whom paused at the body of Sivley
long enough to cut off the one finger that bore a ring. [26] As the

blacks pursued the whites toward the town a short distance away, they passed the home of a respected gentleman, Charles Chilton, who stood with his wife and children in the yard. Opening fire at sight they murdered him before the eyes of his family. By this time the firing had aroused the citizens of the town and a race riot ensued in which many Negroes were killed before the citizen soldiery could get the situation in hand. However, despite the misrepresentation in the radical press, the true nature of this deplorable incident was too evident to serve as an excuse for the declaring of martial law by Grant, who would have liked nothing better than an excuse for doing so.

Meanwhile the white citizenry was holding meetings at every crossroads and hamlet, and Lamar, often delivering as many as two or three speeches in a single day, was arousing enthusiasm to a high pitch. In every speech he denounced the color line and attempted to show the blacks that their real interest was with the native whites rather than the carpet-baggers who were merely office seekers with no personal interest in the State. Without inflammatory appeals, and never striking a demagogic note, he urged the Democracy to stand firm, and he hurled philippics at the scalawags and carpetbaggers.

Ames, seeing the handwriting on the wall and realizing that his only hope lay in interference by President Grant, telegraphed the latter on September 7th. "Domestic violence, in its most aggravated form," he said, "exists in certain parts of this State," and he cried for troops under the terms of the presidential proclamation of December 21st.[27] When Grant refused with the statement that the whole country was weary of these repeated calls for federal interference, Ames requested protection under Article IV, Section 4 of the Constitution. Undoubtedly, Grant would have liked to comply as he had done so often before under like circumstances, but the conscience of the North had been awakened, especially in respect to Mississippi. This had been largely brought about through the impact of Lamar's Sumner speech and also by his recent addresses in New Hampshire where he had fully presented the case of his people and had indicted their oppressors. On the

precise day that Ames was making his second request that Grant
send him federal troops to coerce the ensuing election, George
William Curtis, one of Lamar's warmest friends and admirers,
was presiding over the Republican State convention of New
York, a body which declared for "a just, generous, forbearing
national policy in the Southern States and a firm refusal to use
military power except for purposes clearly defined in the Constitution." [28] Moreover, Grant was now having to deal with an
aroused public sentiment as well as with a new Attorney General, Edwards Pierrepont, who protested vigorously against
complying with Ames's requests. "The whole public," Grant
replied to Ames in a dispatch that showed his awareness of
popular sentiment, "are tired out with these annual autumnal
outbreaks in the South and the great majority are ready now
to condemn any interference on the part of the government." [29]

The dull Ames, refused federal troops, immediately set about
the organizing of armed forces of his own from among the
blacks. "The blood of twenty-five or thirty negroes," he told
General Harris, the Republican Attorney General of the State
who had protested the danger of raising Negro troops, "would
benefit the party in the State." [30] Ames called upon William
Gray, a debauched and drunken Negro senator and preacher,
and requested him to direct the calling and organizing of a
large body of black militia. At the head of the newly raised
troops Gray arrogantly dominated Ames himself as well as his
carpetbag supporters. When he wrote threateningly to the
Governor that he was of a mind to slap his face, Ames answered humbly and subserviently.[31] Then Gray proclaimed
in a number of speeches that his troops would be well equipped
and that he would carry the election if he found it necessary
to kill every white man, woman, and child in his county, which
was predominantly black.

The great problem now confronting the leaders of the Democracy was to insure that the whites would not become so
incensed that they would attack the black militia that Ames
was marching and counter-marching throughout the State. Such
an eventuality was just what Ames most desired, for it would

furnish the administration radicals at Washington the pretext
for taking over the conduct of the elections and dictating the
selection of State officials. With the rising tide of public indignation and the fact that some 10,000 Spencer rifles had been
imported into the State during the year, it became evident
that something would have to be done. The Democrats under
General George informed Ames that they disclaimed all responsibility for the actions of the outraged citizenry unless
the Negro militia was at once disbanded. On the other hand,
they guaranteed that, once Ames had dispersed his black co-
horts, they would themselves be responsible for order throughout the State. The compact was made and there is no doubt
that both sides fully observed their promises, Ames from necessity and George, Lamar, Barksdale, and the other leading
Democrats because they had pledged their honor and had the
welfare of the State at heart.[32]

The election took place on November 2nd. That there was
fraud on both sides no one can doubt. Rhodes thinks that from
the disreputable character of the Republican officials, who were
largely in control of the election machinery, it might be inferred that they were better fitted to play the game than their
opponents.[33] However, although the balloting was largely in
control of their enemies, the Democracy was by no means
helpless, their chief weapon being the intimidation of the blacks,
this carried on against the advice and consent of Lamar and
George. The mildest form that this took was to threaten to
discharge the black hands if they voted the Republican ticket.
By nature, moreover, the credulous blacks were easily imposed
upon. Cannon were dragged through the streets and fired about
the countryside; and often when the carpetbaggers and Negroes
were holding a "speaking" the Democrats would appear and
insist upon a division of time. On the night before the election
the whites gathered at the fords of the Tombigbee River and
turned back the blacks who were coming to vote at Columbus.[34] It had always been customary for the Negroes to flock
to the polls early in the morning and to hang about laughing
and playing until the time to vote. Taking advantage of this

situation, several white men with ropes coiled about the pummels of their saddles, would ride up to a voting place and ask the officials how soon the polls would be opened. "Not for about fifteen minutes," would be the reply. "Well," the spokesman would answer, "then the *hanging* will not begin for about fifteen minutes." "Not a word was spoken to the blacks, but before the fifteen minutes were up not a negro could be seen." [35]

In those counties where the Negroes and carpetbaggers greatly outnumbered the native whites, the latter let it be understood that they would carry the election at whatever cost. If the Republican officials fraudulently handled the balloting, they were told that first the scalawags would be killed, then the carpetbaggers, and last of all the blacks. This was probably no idle threat, for the oppressed people of the State were determined to win their freedom, and had they not been able to do so at the polls, it is almost certain that there would have been a bloody revolution. Fortunately, the Democrats carried the State by more than thirty thousand votes, with intimidation practically confined to ten counties out of seventy-three, those where the carpetbaggers had most obnoxiously organized the blacks. [36] But despite fraud on both sides, impartial historians have generally agreed that had the kindly and enlightened policy of Lamar and George been followed to the letter throughout the campaign, the Democrats would still have carried the State and gained control of the legislature. [37] In any event, the Democrats were successful in carrying both Houses with a majority of 93 in the lower, they placed their men in office in almost every county of the State, and chose four of the six members of Congress, one of whom was Lamar. Of the other two, one was an anti-Ames Republican who had the active support of the Democracy, while the single Negro was the mulatto, John R. Lynch, who survived for two more years as a reminder of carpetbag rule.

Undoubtedly, many Negroes, thousands of them, had begun to rebel against governmental abuses and voted the Democratic ticket. This was made easier by Lamar's fight against the color line, and his success in securing in the Democratic platform an appeal to the black race to ally itself with the native whites. The more intelligent among the Negroes had lost all confidence in the carpetbaggers, and colored men like ex-Senator Revels (who had indicted Ames and the radicals in a letter to the President) and Ham Carter had come out openly on the side of the Democracy. An enlightened Negro minister of Holly Springs, J. G. Johnson, published a letter in the *Jackson Clarion* of September 22nd, 1875, in which he urged his race to "join hands with the white people in redeeming from the spoiler our common country." In June, 1876, ex-Senator Revels was to be subjected to an inquisition by the Republican majority of the Boutwell Senatorial committee, but he would stand by the letter that he had written to the President on the preceding November 6th, and would amplify the grounds for the conservative stand that he had taken.[38] Five hundred blacks, it was shown, took part in a Democratic procession in Raymond, and a like number in Jackson, and everywhere they turned out by the hundreds to hear Lamar and the other Democratic speakers plead for a common front to the enemies of the State.[39]

Sometimes this return of the blacks to their old masters had amusing consequences. Jeff Walker, a colored leader who had affiliated with the native whites and was speaking at Prairie Station, Monroe County, actively supported the Democratic position that hog stealing should be made a penitentiary offense. One of the blacks in the audience accused him of being a hog thief himself during the past year. "Yes," he replied, "dat is so, but den I wuz a Publican and it wuz part of our 'ligion to steal hogs from de white folks." [40]

How the political situation was viewed by the more enlightened blacks is to be seen in the previously mentioned letter that was written to Grant on November 6th by the prominent Negro, ex-Senator Revels. "The masses of my people," he said, "have been, as it were, enslaved in mind by unprincipled adventurers" who urge them to vote for candidates "notoriously corrupt and dishonest," and browbeat them into voting a straight Republican ticket. "To defeat this policy, at the late election, men, irrespective of race, color, or party affiliation united and

voted together against men known to be incompetent and dishonest." As Grant read this letter he received a communication
from the Republican Attorney General of Mississippi laying
the blame for the troubles in the State directly upon the shoulders of Governor Ames.[41] That same summer, Charles Nordhoff, traveling in Mississippi, wrote of Ames that "his personal
adherents are among the worst public thieves....He has corrupted the courts, has protected criminals, and has played even
with the lives of the blacks in a manner that, if this fall a
good legislature should be elected, ought to procure his impeachment and removal."[42]

Ames knew that his days of power had ended. With the
assembling of the legislature in January, 1876, immediate steps
were taken for his removal and for that of Lieutenant Governor
Davis and Superintendent of Education Cardozo. Davis was
quickly convicted of bribery and removed from office, while
Cardozo resigned rather than face a trial in which his deeds
would have been aired with the certainty of conviction. On
the 22nd of February, the investigating committee of the legislature presented damning evidence against the Governor and
called for his impeachment on twenty-three counts. Meanwhile, Lamar was writing to General Walthall in a letter of
February 23rd that the Northern radicals were very fearful
that the impeachment of Ames would bring them further into
disrepute; that Ben Butler had promised that, if the charges
against Ames were withdrawn, he (Butler) would personally
guarantee that Ames would resign his office and leave the
State.[43] On the 2nd of March the articles of impeachment were
reported to the House, and the Senate set the date of the trial
for the 29th. On the 28th Ames let it be known through a
letter to his counsel, Messrs. Durant and Pryor, that he would
be glad to surrender his office but for the fact that the charges
had been placed against him.[44] On the day of the trial, the 29th,
before the members of the House went to the Senate chamber,
manager Featherston read Ames's letter and presented a resolution that the charges against him be dismissed. This was
done; Ames immediately resigned and hastened from the State;

and the government of Mississippi had at last been returned to the hands of its own citizens.

In all of this Lamar had been the moving spirit, and to him Mississippi chiefly owes her redemption. That he was the "head and front of that great movement," all historians agree, for it was his appeal for racial understanding, for the honesty of the ballot, and his denunciation of violence that, despite the actions of some lawless characters, made the election pass off without bloodshed.[45] It was, moreover, the moderate stand that he had taken in Congress and the speeches that he had delivered in the North that had made Grant afraid to put a further strain upon an aroused public opinion by sending federal troops to coerce the election that had given Mississippi her freedom.

But the dishonesty and hypocrisy of the federal administration was not to go unrebuked, for in the elections of 1875, as has been seen, a tidal wave swept into office the first Democratic House since the Civil War, and the Republican majority in the Senate was greatly reduced.

XIII

PARLIAMENTARY ENCOUNTERS IN
THE HOUSE

EVIDENCE that a new day had come was to be seen in the
Forty-fourth Congress which assembled on the 6th of December, 1875.[1] In the Senate, Andrew Johnson of Tennessee had
returned to hurl a final philippic at Grant and the dishonest
men with whom he was surrounded. From Georgia came the
gallant John B. Gordon who had led the gray hosts of Lee
as footsore and worn they stacked their arms for the last time
at Appomattox. Texas was to be represented by General Samuel B. Maxey, a graduate of West Point who had gone with
his State, and from Missouri, in place of Schurz, appeared General Cockrell, late of the Confederate Army.

James G. Blaine, after eight years as Speaker of the House
of Representatives, was to more than meet his match in the
rough and tumble debate on the floor of that body at the hands
of Lamar of Mississippi, and Benjamin H. Hill of Georgia.
From the latter State came another—small, weighing about
eighty-eight pounds, with twisted body which bore an over-
sized head from which burned great lustrous eyes—Alexander
H. Stephens, it was, Vice-President of the Confederacy and
former federal prisoner in Fort Warren. There were, too, other
Representatives who had been high in the councils of the Con-
federacy: Postmaster General John H. Reagan and Colonels
David B. Culberson, and Roger Q. Mills of Texas; General
Eppa Hunton, John Randolph Tucker, Major Beverley B.
Douglas, Colonel George C. Cabell, and John Goode, Jr., of
Virginia; General Robert B. Vance, brother of Zebulon,
Thomas S. Ashe, of the Confederate Congress, Colonel A. M.
Waddell, and Major Jesse J. Yeates from North Carolina; and
General Randall Lee Gibson, prominent from among several

230

ex-Confederates from Louisiana. That the South was not yet entirely "redeemed" was evident from the presence of that most able product of the Negro race, Blanche K. Bruce, sent to the Senate by a former Republican legislature of Mississippi, and from the seven blacks who still sat in the House of Representatives.[2]

By all odds it was the ablest Congress that had sat in Washington since the Civil War.[3] On the Saturday before it assembled on the 6th of December, the Democrats in the House held their first caucus. Lamar's commanding position among his associates was shown by his election as permanent chairman of the caucus, being so selected with the common consent of the three candidates most commonly mentioned for the speakership: Messrs. Kerr, Cox, and Randall, after he had eliminated himself for consideration for that office, against the urgent persuasion of perhaps the most important bloc in the House. "His leadership," says Carson in the *History of the Supreme Court,* "was masterly, and fixed the gaze of the nation."[4]

Lamar had declined to allow his name to be put forward for the speakership because, he frankly told his friends, he feared that his former prominence in the secession movement would prove an embarrassment to the party at this period so soon after the war. That he would be the unanimous choice for the permanent chairmanship of the caucus was evident, and in the preparation of his inaugural address he had given long and deep thought to the problems which confronted the party and the nation. Assuming the chair after the election, he delivered an address which was to become, with slight modifications, the program of the party not only throughout the present Congress but in the coming national election.[5] "There has been for some time in the public mind a conviction, profound and all-pervading," he said, among other things, "that the civil service of this country has not been directed from considerations of public good, but from those of party profit, and for corrupt, selfish, and unpatriotic designs. The people demand that a vigilant examination be made into the administration of the public revenue of the country, both in its collection and

its disbursement; that all the public accounts shall be scru-
tinized by us, as it is the solemn privilege and duty of the
House to do; and that corruption be ferreted out, and wrong-
doers, no matter how high or low, shall be fearlessly arraigned
and fully exposed and punished." He suggested a statesmanlike
program which reviewed the needs of every department of the
government for which the House had to legislate, and he
pleaded for coöperation and a better understanding between all
races and all sections of the nation.

Demanding that the nation return to the governmental principles upon which it was founded, he declared that the noblest
"aspiration of the Democratic party is, and its crowning glory
will be, to restore the constitution to its pristine strength and
authority, and to make it the protector of every section and of
every State in the Union and of every human being of every
race, color, and condition in the land." The South was proud
of her membership in this great nation, and "the people of
whom I speak (of whom I am one) are here to honor any
draft which the American people may draw upon their patriotism or their faith in the glory and the beneficent destiny of
American institutions." He demanded that the party legislate
upon no partisan lines, and reminded his hearers "that the great
victory of last fall, which brought us here, and which gives
us these opportunities and great responsibilities, was achieved,
not alone by Democratic votes, but with the coöperative efforts
of patriotic and unselfish men of all parties, who, wearied and
alarmed by the unceasing evils resulting from corruption and
maladministration, chose to call us to the duty of checking
these evils and clearing away these corruptions. If we are wise,
we shall so rule ourselves and so serve our country as to retain
the confidence of these voters."

The speech won wide acclaim from both parties and from
all sections. The press was unanimous in the encomiums that
were heaped upon the speaker, the *Chicago Courier* proclaiming Lamar's "a national voice which rings upon the air in
Washington; the voice of a man whose fealty to party binds
him in no sectional harness; a brave and able man, worthy of

the best days of the republic." [6] The *New York Evening Post* thought that "a more genuine, conservative, comprehensive, sound, politico-economic, and above all, Union speech could not have been made by Thomas Jefferson himself, had he appeared in the flesh and moved to address the people he loved so well"; while the *Philadelphia Times* regarded Lamar's speech as "a careful, conservative, and statesmanlike utterance, which will increase the esteem in which this able representative of the South is held in all sections of the country." [7] To the *Albany* (N. Y.) *Argus* it seemed "worthy of the ablest statesmen of any period of our history."

Among the praises heaped upon Lamar's address by the entire press of the country there was an insistent demand that he be immediately elevated to the Senate. It was commonly said that his remarkable talents demanded a wider field of service for the nation. The *San Francisco Chronicle* asked: "If the spirit of Lamar's address fairly represents the feeling of the Southern Democrats, will not Mississippi now show that Lamar did so represent the feelings and sentiments of the South by electing him to the Senate?" [8] The *Memphis Appeal* asserted that "he has contributed more than any one man in all the broad Union toward securing the present Democratic majority in the House of Representatives, and there is a universal desire among Democrats outside of Mississippi to see the great talents, statesmanship, and patriotism of L. Q. C. Lamar transferred to the United States Senate."

Not until the reorganization of the Mississippi Democracy in 1875 was the matter of a Senator from that party of more than academic interest. But with the resurgence of the native white element into active control there arose the burning question as to who should succeed James L. Alcorn, the Republican whose term was to expire on the 4th of March, 1877. The election must be held considerably before that time. Early in April, 1875, the *Holly Springs South* was calling for his nomination to the Senate, and after the Democratic victory in November the matter of the Senatorial succession became a live question with Lamar figuring most prominently among those mentioned for the office. Others frequently mentioned were the generals George, Featherston, and Lowry. On the other hand, Lamar was faced with considerable opposition from those who opposed his course in reference to the new constitutional amendments which he had declared binding with the same force as the other parts of the Constitution, and from those who, though professing to admire extravagantly his course in Congress, felt that he was peculiarly needed in the place which he held, and that it would be more valuable to the State to keep him there and to send another strong man to the Senate.

The tides of destiny, however, had laid hold of Lamar and the demand that he be sent to the Senate was becoming irresistible. Early in December Judge Harris was writing in the *Clarion* that "the great office of Senator is a trust, and not a prerequisite. It is to be bestowed upon consideration of public good, and not of personal liking, or even of personal services; though upon this score none can exceed those of Colonel Lamar. Mississippi has many fine lawyers, gallant soldiers, able jurists, and worthy citizens; she has but one distinguished statesman.... The day that Colonel Lamar takes his seat in the Senate he ranks at once with Thurman and Bayard, and when he rises to make his first speech the whole nation will listen." [9] Likewise, the *Memphis Appeal* remarked that "to Colonel Lamar, more than to any other one Southern man, is due the dawn and development of that kindly Northern feeling for the people of the South which President Grant was afraid to defy when Ames called upon him for troops with which to control the elections.... His defeat now, in the hour of victory, would be construed by our enemies and deplored by our friends in the North as a partial lowering, at least, of that high tone of restored nationality upon which the canvass was made." [10] To the *New Orleans Picayune* it seemed that "the interests and cause of Lamar in this election ... are the interests and cause of the South, and of the Democracy at large.... He seems to be almost, if not quite, the only Southern man who has won a hearing for his people before the tribunal of Northern opinion," and the *New York Herald*, calling him "one of the ablest and most statesmanlike of the Democrats," thought that "his defeat would be a calamity to Mississippi, and would be regretted by the country."[11]

One other great Mississippian, and a warm friend of Lamar, General J. Z. George, might conceivably have had an equally valid claim to consideration for the Senate, and certain of his friends urged his selection. However, there was an almost universal feeling that, since the triumph of 1875 was due more to Lamar than to any other, he should have the first reward.[12] On the night of January 6th, when the Democratic-Conservative caucus was held, the sentiment for Lamar was so strong that before the taking of a single ballot the names of all other candidates, including that of General George, were withdrawn, after which Lamar was nominated by acclamation and without a dissenting voice. On the next evening, by special invitation, he addressed a joint session of the legislature in a speech which was mainly a plea for the broadest nationalism and the death of racial and sectional animosities. Indeed it was the widespread conviction held irrespective of party that Lamar's "broad statesmanship, wonderful eloquence and national standing as an advocate of fraternalism between the North and the South,"[13] made him the logical choice.

On the 19th, Lamar was elected United States Senator on the first ballot by the almost unanimous vote of a joint session of the two Houses. Even the papers that had opposed him joined in a chorus of approval once the election was over. The *Meridian Mercury*, which had constantly assailed him on the score of his Sumner speech, said that his election was a "result of deliberation and judgment upon the platform of his record and national reputation, with design to further peace and reconciliation between the lately belligerent sections.... 'Peace hath its victories no less renowned than war'; and Lamar's achievements already accomplished in the direction of a peaceful conquest of peace are more glorious, if not more brilliant, than his high daring and deeds in the bloody fray."[14] Such was the general tenor of the comments even in those papers which had not at first looked with favor upon his candidacy.

The intervening period before Lamar was to take his seat in the Senate on March 6th, 1877, however, was to be an eventful one, particularly in the House where he was one of the directing forces. Peace seemed to have settled upon Congress and the nation, but in less than two weeks after Congress assembled from the Christmas recess of 1875, there was to occur a most acrimonious quarrel.

The controversy arose in the following manner: James G. Blaine had lately—in his last term as Speaker of the House—increased the respect in which he was held throughout the nation by his fairness toward the stricken South. It has been seen that in order to defeat the iniquitous Force Bill he had secretly outlined to Lamar a plan whereby he, as Speaker, would coöperate with the Democrats to this end. But the tendency toward opportunism and lack of moral stability that was ultimately to wreck Blaine's career became evident when in January, 1876, he deliberately precipitated a debate with the aim of stirring up the passions of the war, and hence enhancing his own political fortunes and those of the party that he represented. On December 15th, Mr. Randall, the Democratic floor leader, had introduced a measure that would extend universal amnesty to all ex-Confederates. There was every reason to believe that it would pass, for it embodied only the features that Grant himself had advocated in his message of December, 1873, and which had been subsequently included in a bill that passed the House but failed to gain the assent of the Senate. At that time Blaine had sanctioned the measure, but now he saw the opportunity, by waving the bloody shirt, to furnish campaign ammunition for the weakening Republican party, and to enhance his own position of influence in the North and East. When the amnesty bill was introduced on December 15th he had asked time for consideration, and now, on January 10th, he was prepared for his assault upon the South.

After a few remarks concerning Toombs, he passed to Davis

whom he denounced as "knowingly, deliberately, guiltily, and willfully," responsible for "the gigantic murders and crimes at Andersonville." To a noisy house and a disorderly gallery he painted in highly colored terms the alleged "atrocities visited by the Confederates upon the Union captives." "I now assert deliberately before God, as my judge," he cried, "knowing the full measure and import of my words that the cruelties of the Duke of Alva in the Low Countries, the massacre of St. Bartholomew, and the screws and tortures of the Spanish Inquisition did not approach in cruelty the atrocity of Andersonville."[15] Proposing an amendment to bar Jefferson Davis from the amnesty, he exerted every effort to make the Southern Representatives lose their self-control. As the witty Sunset Cox said, the dead enemy smelt well in Blaine's nostrils, and he found "musk and amber" in revenge. His obvious aim was "to re-inspire wrath and capture the ear of his willing partisans." He might live a thousand years, said one Democrat, but he would never enter the White House by any such means.[16]

That Blaine's purpose was to arouse animosities and to goad the Representatives of the Southern States into rash words that would furnish campaign material in the ensuing Presidential election, is generally admitted, even by his apologists. At the same time, most of the cooler heads on the Democratic side of the House recognized his unworthy purpose and felt that any notice whatsoever of such attacks would merely serve to throw them into the power of the enemy. Among these was Lamar who—absent at the time of the controversy—believed, as he stated later, that the country would have recognized the false nature of Blaine's statements, and felt that for the sake of amity and conciliation his words should have been entirely ignored that they might fall of their own weight. Unfortunately, Lamar was in Mississippi and Benjamin H. Hill, less circumspect, felt that Blaine's charges and strictures must not go unanswered. Taking the floor at the end of the day, against the advice of every Southern leader in the House, he made known his purpose of answering Blaine on the following morning.[17]

With the Senate deserted and the House galleries packed,

Hill began his speech by calling the assembled Representatives to witness that nothing was further from his purpose than the reopening of the wounds of the war.[18] "The gentleman from Maine" had maliciously and "for obvious partisan purpose," brought about "a bitter sectional discussion," which he hoped would redound to his own advantage and that of his party. Weighing the evidence from impartial sources, he showed that conditions were much the same in both Northern and Southern prisons, and that Blaine had introduced as evidence merely a notorious *ex parte* report of a House Committee made shortly after the war when passions were at fever heat. True, Northern soldiers in prison camps had suffered, but they had been served the same rations (all too pitiful) that had been given to Southern soldiers, and there would have been no high mortality had not the North relentlessly refused to exchange prisoners. Serving notice that the representatives of the South would no longer allow such unsupported calumnies to pass unchallenged, he begged that the passions of the war be allowed to die. Asserting that he cherished no desire for revenge and harbored no enmity, he declared that it was "unworthy of statesmanship" to put obstacles in the way of pacification. "Sir," he said in closing, "my position is this: There are no Confederates in this house; there are no Confederates anywhere; there are no Confederate schemes, ambitions, hopes, desires or purposes here. But the South is here and here she proposes to remain.... We are here: we are in the house of our fathers, our brothers are our companions, and we are at home to stay, thank God!"

Many papers the nation over, and most of those in the South, felt that Hill, for all the brilliance of his speech, had played into the hands of the radicals and furnished the Republicans some much needed campaign material. The *Jackson* (Miss.) *Clarion* thought that the debate "was a chapter of blunders from beginning to end," and wondered what could have prompted Mr. Randall (for surely he knew that the Republicans "had nothing under heaven on which to build a hope of defeating the Democratic party in the Presidential election except a revival of sectional issues") to thrust the sub-

"As he went on, discriminating with analytical grasp the constitutional aspects of the question involved, the attention which he excited because of his peculiar position was changed into absorbed interest. In vigorous crystallization of law, logic, and reason, by which his faith was justified, he appealed only to reason. There was no claptrap invoked. Blaine had been heard with glistening eyes, clenched hands, and grinding teeth; with repugnance, indignation and incredulity; but this man, nursing almost the same themes, asked only the rational judgment of his hearers, and resorted to no surprises in argument or tricks in expression to recommend his reasoning to the House.... The Republicans listened in stupefaction.... Here was a man who had battled for the cause now grounding arms and showing unanswerable cause for the civil as well as the military surrender. Ready, audacious, self-reliant, his piercing eyes fixed upon men who opposed his arguments, he poured out an exposition of nationalism and constitutionalism which equaled in effect one of Webster's masterpieces.

"Remembering this man's place, the real leader of the South politically and the successor of Davis in the Senate, the scene was in every respect the most surprising recently witnessed in this House of revolutions and surprises. He went square to the root of the States' Rights argument.... 'Not a nation?' he asked, throwing his fine head back and raising his arms; 'a people who repelled again and again foreign invasion, who equipped navies, who accoutered the most tremendous armies the world ever saw, who conducted four years of civil war and who recovered from it—not a nation? Can any man read the record and deny the majestic sovereignty of our nationality?' The House, which followed line and precept with immovable attention, burst into prolonged applause....

"It was the testimony of jurists present that as an argument the constitutional part of the speech was the most clearly put and the most coherent recently delivered in either House. While the keenest attention of the House was still fastened upon him, and the weight of his argument had visibly taken its intended effect, Lamar passed to another theme. He singled out Townsend, who made such a capital speech last week, to deliver a word of reproach. That gentleman, conscious of what was coming, began to laugh complacently as Lamar alluded to his jocose comments on the personal appearances of ex-Confederates; but his laugh died out and chagrin took its place as the speaker, with measured, almost pathetic, accents, reminded him of the mischievous results of his Preston Brooks allusions. It was not friendly. It was not patriotic. It was not decent. The noble American who suffered wrong at the hands of Brooks left his sentiments on record, and these sentiments should shame those who seek to perpetuate discords and enmities that were buried ten years ago.

"No conception of the real effectiveness of Lamar's utterances can be given by the cold language of comment. Blaine, tightly squeezed between both hands until nothing but hair, nose and mouth was discernible, colored visibly, dropped his eyes before Lamar's gaze, and moved restlessly in his seat. Townsend, whose face is naturally a flame, coughed irresolutely, turned in his seat, and looked the very picture of discomfort. Judged by its effect on the House and the comment of the town, the speech was the most masterful in moderation, exhaustive in argument, and captivating in method so far delivered. It told on every soul."

"It is my desire to see the pacification of these sections," said Lamar in closing as continuous rounds of applause punctuated his every statement, "to see my people of the South restored to the proud position of dignity and equality in this Union to which, under the constitution, they are entitled; and to do that it is necessary that these Representatives of the North, and if not they, then their constituencies, the people of the North, should become satisfied of the longing and desire of our people to live with them in peace and perpetuity in a restored and fraternal Union. Before that cherished purpose and inspiration all others with me sink into insignificance....

"I seize the opportunity to make the equal rights of all secure through peace and reconciliation; but this infinite boon you would postpone. Seven years have passed since we laid aside our arms; but unhappily during all this period there has been a hostile spirit toward each other, while the rights of our colored fellow-citizens have been in perpetual question. Seven years mark a natural period of human life. Should not the spirit be changed with the body? Can we not, after seven years, commence new life, especially when those once our foes repeat the saying: 'Thy people shall be my people, and thy God my God'? ...

"I know, sir, that this sentiment, this aspiration, has not found full expression and development here in this hall. It has been kept under and stifled by the strong network of an intolerant political organization, and its voice unheeded amid the clamors of impassioned partisans. But in the political as well as in the natural world the agencies which are the most powerful are not the noisiest. Violence, passion, fanaticism, and animosity, can always find voice and rend the air with their factious clamors; while deep and earnest conviction lies unspoken in the heart of a people. The currents of passion and of feeling may flow hither and thither under extraneous influences and forces, like the dash and roar of waves lashed to fury by the storm, while the great sea, the unsounded depths of a common humanity, a common hope, a common interest, and a common patriotism, lies voiceless but almighty beneath." [24]

The press was everywhere laudatory. According to the *Vicksburg Herald*, "Senator Lamar's speech on the Centennial has electrified the nation," and the *Clarion* felt that "on Col. Lamar, more than any man, or all others combined, the hopes of the people who have suffered from the proscriptive rule of a vindictive party are centered." The *Cincinnati Commercial* was anxious to discover how the speech would be received in the South: "Will it be welcomed and praised as Ben Hill's was? That is doubtful. Hill's speech was carefully measured and adapted to prejudices and passions which he wished to please. Lamar's is rather designed to soften and remove them, and to substitute for them the higher idea of nationality and a conviction that the day for the indulgence in the worship of State sovereignty and sectional vanities is over. This sort of doctrine has not been popular in the South, but with men of the force and eloquence of Lamar to proclaim it there is a hope that in time it may become so." [25] The *New York Tribune* proclaimed him "in the front rank as a debater on constitutional questions," while the *New York Herald* believed that the speech would "add to his own fame, and be received at the North as an expression of good feeling on the part of the South, to be reciprocated by many kindly words and acts."

The *Louisville Courier-Journal* ranked Lamar with the great statesmen of the heroic age of the nation, and stated that "the one man from the South in public life who has seen and recognized the truth in all its bearings, and who, without stultifying his convictions or compromising his personality, had followed its counsels, is Lamar.... The latest exploit of this singularly fortunate and rarely gifted man was his far-seeing, right-hearted, patriotic, and courageous support of the Centennial appropriation. It is admitted that he saved the bill." [26] "He literally captivated and captured the country—more completely even than in the famous Sumner ovation of the previous year," says another commentator. "It is not too much to say that no speech in the whole history of the country ever won greater applause. Certainly no other of that discordant period appealed so powerfully to the spirit of nationalism or against the sectionalism under which the South was groaning." [27]

One of the important articles in the program laid out for the Democratic House by Lamar in his speech of acceptance of the permanent chairmanship of the caucus was an investigation of all expenditures by the government, and a stopping of the fraud and malfeasance that, under Grant, was robbing the nation of a large part of its revenue. Fresh in men's minds was the notorious Crédit Mobilier of Grant's first term, in connection with the construction of the Union Pacific Railroad. In the course of a Congressional investigation, fifteen members of the administration had been shown more or less involved: the Vice-President of the United States, the Secretary of the Treasury, two Senators, two ex-Senators, the Speaker and six other members of the House together with one ex-Representative and one no longer living, of all of whom no more than four could give convincing proof of innocence. Bribery of high officials in connection with this speculative development was wholesale, and almost every "key" man in the administration had apparently received stock or money in payment for his votes or his influence, or both. Colfax, ex-Speaker of the House and by now Vice-President, and Mr. Garfield were not only demonstrated to have been guilty, but each, in attempts to save himself, was caught when testifying under oath in palpable falsehoods.[28]

The House now proposed to examine the accounts of the expenditures of all departments in order to determine whether there was injustice, dishonesty, or extravagance. The first thing to which it applied its activity was the whisky tax frauds, the investigation of which had been inaugurated by Secretary of the Treasury Bristow, a man of unyielding honesty who was soon to find his position in Grant's Cabinet untenable, and who was to be dismissed when he pushed his investigations too close to certain of the President's intimates.[29] Inaugurating his investigations immediately upon taking office in 1874, he was now ready to take final action in the face of the open opposition of Grant and with the support of the Democratic House—an investigation which would demonstrate that millions were being stolen monthly from the government; that the President had acquiesced in the frauds that he knew were being perpetrated; and that would send a number of men to prison. Other investigation was to show numerous "frauds and wrongs committed against the Indians" by the "heartless scoundrels" who had been appointed to the Indian service, the President's brother, Orvil L. Grant, being inextricably involved, as was the Secretary of the Interior, Columbus Delano, who hastily tendered his resignation which was accepted by President Grant when the investigation was becoming uncomfortable.[30] Malfeasance, bribery, and fraud involving tens of millions of dollars were shown in the awarding of navy contracts, in the conduct of the Soldiers' Pension Bureau, and in the administration of the postal service and the Freedmen's Bank.

The plan for these investigations had been laid down by Lamar in his inaugural speech as chairman of the Democratic Caucus preceding the opening of Congress. In the most dramatic of all of the exposures, he was to play a leading part and was again to demonstrate his ability as the peer of any man in the House in "rough and tumble" debate.

On the 29th of February, the Committee on Expenditures, of which Clymer was chairman, began the investigation of charges to the effect that W. W. Belknap, the Secretary of War, had accepted bribes for the appointment of a post-tradership. Witnesses had been called, including Caleb P. Marsh, and damaging evidence had been taken that involved Mrs. Belknap as well as her husband. Briefly the story was this: The first Mrs. Belknap had been taken sick in New York, some six years before, and the Marshes had been very kind to her. Probably with the view of rewarding their kindnesses, Mrs. Belknap one day suggested to Marsh that he apply for one of the post-traderships. She knew that he would get the place, and she wished him to remember her out of the profits that he would make in his trading with the Indians. The appointment was straightway made, and Mrs. Belknap began receiving periodic remittances. Soon, however, Mrs. Belknap died, leaving an infant to the care of her sister, whom the Secretary of War soon married. The second Mrs. Belknap hastened to assure Marsh that her sister had told her on her deathbed that money would be coming in from the post-tradership for the infant, and had requested her to keep it in trust. From this time on large sums of money were sent to Belknap with the understanding that they were to be turned over to his second wife to be held in trust for the child. As a matter of fact, it was disclosed that all of the money was squandered in forwarding Mrs. Belknap's social ambitions.[31]

Early the morning after the investigation had been instituted, Belknap, his swollen and bloodshot eyes bespeaking a sleepless night, appeared at the White House. So distraught that he could not tell his story coherently, he offered his resignation and begged that it be accepted without delay. Shortly after, Grant was to say to a Congressman: "I understand that he was expecting an investigation that he would avoid by resigning; that the facts, if exposed, would not damage him so much as his wife. He spoke of his dead wife, too.... So I wrote him a letter accepting the resignation." [32]

The entire Capital was stunned at the scandal that had involved the social queen of the city as well as one of the most prominent members of the President's Cabinet.

Despite Grant's precipitate acceptance of the Secretary's resignation, Chairman Clymer of the investigating committee rose before a tense House to propose the impeachment of the man who had been his Princeton chum and roommate. The election was near, and certain of the Republicans, notably Hoar, of Massachusetts, strove to block action, their main contention being that after the President's acceptance of the resignation, it was legally impossible for impeachment proceedings to go forward. Blackburn of Kentucky, whose wife had been a girlhood friend of Mrs. Belknap and who was suffering deeply over the situation, denounced this casuistic position. "The action of the President in accepting the Secretary's resignation under the circumstances was unprecedented," he declared, "and this is the first instance in the history of the country where any man claiming manhood and holding an exalted station has sought to shelter himself from legitimate investigation by interposing the dishonor of his wife." Obviously there was nothing to do except to vote the impeachment. The resolutions to that effect, presented by the Committee on Expenditures, were unanimously adopted and the testimony was ordered printed in the *Congressional Record*. At a little past noon on the following day the Committee of Five from the House appeared before the Bar of the Senate and discharged its mission of calling for the trial of the Secretary of War, after which the Senate approved the motion that it would take "proper order thereon."

The administration found itself in an extremely precarious position. Some action had to be taken, it seemed, to stop the exposures, for the man chiefly involved was a member of the President's official family and one of his trusted advisers. On the 6th the form that the attempt to block the investigation would take was made clear when the Congressional committee was summoned before the Supreme Court of the District of Columbia, in criminal session, by a subpœna that directed it to turn over all books and papers in its possession that bore upon the charges against Belknap.

The next day Chairman Clymer of the committee arose before the House and protested the summons of the court, declaring that such a procedure would seal the mouths of witnesses and would impinge upon the prerogatives of the House which had instituted the proceedings. Mr. Robbins of North Carolina, a member of the committee, put the matter succinctly: "I say to you, Mr. Speaker, and to this House, that the inevitable effect of our being required to testify as to what transpires in the sessions of our committee before a grand jury or anywhere else will be, as the gentleman from Pennsylvania [Mr. Clymer] has stated, to intimidate witnesses, to stop their mouths, and throttle all further investigations. I say here that if it is not the design it certainly will be the result of the course now being taken by certain officials of this district, under the promptings of the head of the government, to break down investigations by shutting the mouths of witnesses. If that is not the purpose, it is the effect, unless this House takes the matter in hand and provides for the protection (not of us; we need no protection; we have nothing to withhold or conceal as committeemen) —the protection of the *witnesses* who shall come before us." As was to be expected the administration forces in the House, led by Blaine, defended the actions of the court and the President.

Lamar was disgusted at the whole debate which had dragged a non-partisan matter into the realm of politics, especially was he disgusted with Blaine who had done all in his power to obscure the issues and who had zealously stirred up the embers of sectional discord. Lamar, with his fine legal perceptions, saw that the only matter involved was the constitutional right of

248

the local court to demand the records of a Congressional committee before that committee had completed its work, and he had refused to take part in the acrimonious arguments over totally extraneous matters. Finally, when the issue had become so confused that it seemed likely to be entirely forgotten he took the floor in one of his memorable appearances.[33] "All this debate, with all the passion that has been flung in here," he said after proposing a resolution that the order of the court be disregarded and that the committee await the orders of the House, "is irrelevant, and simply tends to convert a pure question of constitutional and parliamentary law into an idle logomachy, a war of words and of passion which can but obscure the issue. ...I came forward with a resolution which states all the circumstances and then simply asserts the jurisdiction of this House over the subject-matter, over the person, over the papers in this great impeachment trial,...in the presence of which these passions, these thoughts about Presidential succession [a thrust at Blaine] and party triumph, actually, sir, fatigue my contempt."

Lamar's ensuing debate with Blaine, in which the latter was humiliated as have been few figures in our public life, came about in this manner: After Chairman Clymer had risen to a question of privilege in protesting the summons of his Committee on Expenditures before the district court, Lamar arose to propose a resolution ordering the committee to ignore the summons and to await the orders of the House. Before reading the resolution he desired to make certain prefatory remarks. Said he, among other things:

...The question is one purely of parliamentary privilege, whether or not the members of this House and of the committees of this House are amenable to the processes of the criminal court for the purpose of testifying and bringing the papers and the records that are in the various committee rooms before the courts for investigation and for revision.

Mr. BLAINE: Nobody says they are.

Mr. LAMAR: "Nobody says they are," says the gentleman from Maine [Mr. Blaine]. Then if nobody says they are, ought not this

House to take some measures to protect the privileges which have been invaded by this summons?

MR. BLAINE: It is no violation of privilege.

MR. LAMAR: No violation to issue a summons to a member of this House commanding him to bring all the records of this body before that court, and to command him there to remain and not depart until the court or the district attorney shall allow him to do so! Suppose that a member of this House should waive his privileges; suppose he should go there and take these papers. How long would it be before the district court, if it should choose to do so, would relieve us of the power, and forever deprive our committees of the opportunity to investigate?

When Lamar, after extended argument, had relentlessly forced Blaine to admit that the court had, in fact, unconstitutionally interrupted the proceedings of the committee, the latter attempted to hide his own discomfiture by "daring" the Democratic side of the House to withhold the evidence. Lamar patiently showed that at the proper time and at the proper place the evidence would be presented to the criminal court, but that the question at issue was a constitutional matter of jurisdiction. He made it clear that once the House surrendered its prerogatives as an investigating body, it would be possible for the judiciary to interfere at any time and halt proceedings against an offending official. Further: "There can be no question about the right of the criminal courts to carry on their prosecution of an offender at the same time that we prosecute him by impeachment; but they have not the right to invade the precincts of this House—this House which can impeach the judge himself. Suppose, sir, that in the prosecution of this 'safe burglary' case, matter should come up which would touch the honesty and integrity of the court, and he should at once issue his mandate upon the committee sitting here investigating that matter, and as soon as the witnesses were dismissed order that committee to come before him and to bring all their papers, all telegrams, all testimony, all receipts, everything that any witness had said before them; would the gentleman from Maine get up then, and, in that way which is characteristic only of himself, cry out: 'I dare you to withhold the information'? Sir, this House, I presume, dares to do what is right, dares to do what is honest, dares to maintain its constitutional privileges, and to continue the prosecution of this investigation."

Lamar then called for the reading of his resolution, which he discussed in detail, and showed that its only purpose was "simply to assert the authority of this House. What else? To tell those members not to regard that summons until its further order. Gentlemen say that it is suppression of the prosecution and of the testimony. No, sir; it is simply to protect the jurisdiction to which we are entitled and which, I undertake to say, has been invaded by the court. If a precedent is established, if it is allowable for members of our committees to be detailed without coming and seeking the instructions of this House to go before the court, you may at once dismiss all your investigating committees.... The House does not refuse the testimony. It does not refuse to allow testimony, but it does call upon members of that committee that the summons shall be disregarded until it orders otherwise."

When he had completed his analysis of the resolution, Lamar shifted to another phase of the discussion: "Now another point. William W. Belknap is in the custody of this House, sir. He is undergoing trial.

MR. BLAINE: I hope the gentleman——

MR. LAMAR: Wait until I get through my sentence.

THE SPEAKER *pro tem.*: The gentleman from Mississippi declines to be interrupted, and the gentleman from Maine will observe the fact.

MR. LAMAR: I repeat, sir, he is in the legal custody of this House, under its constitutional control. If the gentleman from Maine means to say that we have not the bodily possession of him by arrest, so be it; but we have got control of him.

MR. BLAINE: We never intended to arrest him.

MR. LAMAR: We may arrest him [Belknap, in fact, was put under arrest in a few hours], and will do it if it is necessary, and can do it. Do you deny our competency?

Mr. Blaine: Undoubtedly in an impeachment; I deny it, and say that it is perfectly absurd.

Mr. Lamar: You also said that it was absurd to say there was anything punishable in an impeachment; and when my friend from Tennessee [Mr. Bright], the distinguished gentleman from that State, spoke of two concurring jurisdictions, one having already acquired it by initiating the proceedings it could not be ousted, the gentleman inflicted upon him that most terrible of all punishments, the forfeiture of his respect for him as an attorney. [Laughter] I trust that the gentleman will survive; and, in view of that penalty myself, I assert, sir, that it is true, and that an impeachment is a penal trial; that there is judgment, conviction, and, in the very words which the gentleman used, "punitive punishment."

Mr. Blaine: Then the gentleman takes the ground that the man could be twice punished for the same offense? I say that impeachment is protective, and that the criminal jurisdiction is punitive. That is what I say, and I go on to say further that there never has been an impeachment in the United States in which there was any attempt to possess the body because of the impeachment. The possession of the body is of no account in impeachment. The judgment which deprives the man of the right to hold office is just as effective if the man were absent as in the case of his being present; and there never was an arrest of a man for impeachment in this country.

Mr. Lamar: Are you sure of that?

Mr. Blaine: Yes, sir.

Mr. Lamar: Then let us form this issue, plain and complete. The gentleman says that there cannot be two punishments inflicted on an individual for the same offense. The same offense. Here is the constitution, which says that the officer shall not only be removed from office on impeachment and disqualified to hold office thereafter, but that he shall be subject to indictment, conviction, and punishment by a jury, besides.

Now, sir, there is the constitution. That answers the question of the gentleman; and I am afraid that the gentleman will lose his respect for the constitution when it responds to his question by saying that a man guilty of an impeachable offense shall be punished not only by removal from office, not only by disqualification to hold office, but also by indictment, conviction, and punishment.

Mr. Blaine: Read it. Read it from the constitution.

MR. LAMAR: Here it is, sir: "Judgment"——

MR. BLAINE: "Judgment," not "punishment." Go on. [Laughter on the Democratic (sic) side of the House.]

MR. LAMAR: The gentleman's oracular wisdom calls forth a laugh. Before we are through the laughter will be at him, instead of with him. The gentleman says "judgment," and wishes me to explain the word "judgment." "Judgment in cases of impeachment shall not extend further than to removal from office and disqualification to hold and enjoy any office of honor, trust, or profit under the United States." Is not that one punishment?

MR. BLAINE: Punishment is not mentioned there. Now, read on.

MR. LAMAR: You say that is not a punishment?

MR. BLAINE: Go on.

MR. LAMAR: I put the question to the gentleman because of his interruption. Is not removal from office and disqualification to hold office a punishment?

MR. BLAINE: If the gentleman speaks of its being a moral punishment——

MR. LAMAR: No, sir.

MR. BLAINE: If he speaks of its being a moral punishment, he may be right; but a legal punishment it is not.

MR. LAMAR: I ask the gentleman, not whether it is a moral punishment or not, but is it not a legal punishment?

MR. BLAINE: It is not.

MR. LAMAR: Then the gentleman says that a removal from office, a disqualification to hold office, while a moral retribution or something of that kind, is not, in the contemplation of the law and the constitution, a penalty, a legal punishment. Very well.

MR. BLAINE: Now read the next part.

MR. LAMAR: I am coming to the next part. That is one thing. Then this provision of the constitution goes on to say: "But the party convicted"— What, sir? "The party convicted? It is not "judgment" this time; it is conviction. And what is conviction, sir, but the judgment in a penal trial? Very well. I will carry you further directly: "But the party convicted shall nevertheless be liable and subject to indictment, trial, judgment, and punishment according to law."

Now notice this language again. Perhaps I can convince the gentleman: "Judgment in cases of impeachment shall not extend further than to removal from office and disqualification to hold any office of honor, trust, or profit under the United States."

Very well. Now, sir, the gentleman says that that is no punishment, and that the only punishment in the eye of the law is that which this provision speaks of in the second clause. I have too much respect for him as a lawyer to tell him that he is under a mistake on that point, but there are men who hold a different opinion on that. May I have the attention of the gentleman and of his admiring acclaimers and applauders to the authority which is almost as high upon questions of constitutional law as himself? I read from *Wallace's Supreme Court Reports*. Now notice. The court is speaking of certain constitutional disabilities imposed, and uses this language: "The deprivation of any rights, civil or political, previously enjoyed, may be punishment."

Mr. BLAINE: "May be."

Mr. LAMAR: Well, you are nearly run to ground. The gentleman has got to the "may be." Well, I suppose his position is this: that the removal from office and perpetual disqualification from office thereafter "may be" a punishment. But whether it may be or not, the officer impeached shall "nevertheless" be liable to indictment, conviction, and punishment according to law. I have got him to the "may be" now. He said a moment ago that it was not so. Now he injects an interruption, and says "it may be a punishment." That is promising. Perhaps I can lead him on a little further. [Applause] "Disqualification from office may be punishment as in cases"— I have a great mind, sir, to let my friend off. What do you say, gentlemen? Shall I go on? [Cries of "Go on!" "Punish him!"] *"Disqualification from office may be punishment as in cases of conviction upon impeachment."*

Blaine was completely floored and humiliated. Characteristically he sought refuge in the waving of the bloody shirt, in an attempt to divert attention from his own suffering: "Let me state what I mean," he cried. "The gentleman read the opinion of the Supreme Court, which said that disability may be punishment. Well, that is just as gentlemen take it. The gentleman from Mississippi did take it as a punishment, but another gentleman from Mississippi, Jeff. Davis, regards it as no punishment. [Cries of 'O!' 'O!' on the Democratic side of the House.]"

Ignoring Blaine's weak struggles to escape, Lamar amplified upon the constitutional aspects of the matter, and requested the chair to put the question. His motion was carried and Blaine's rout was complete.

This episode has been discussed in detail with extensive quotation from the *Congressional Record* not only because of the intrinsic importance and interest of the debate, but because it is a typical example of Lamar's brilliancy in extemporaneous argument; of the analytical quality of his thinking; and of his mastery of questions of constitutional law. It was this tremendous psychic energy coupled with a marvelous eloquence and fluency that carried him through many years of rough and tumble debate in House and Senate without ever being crushed by an opponent. Again, the episode under discussion is illuminating in that something of that lack of mental and moral integrity that was to shadow Blaine's later life and thwart his desire for the highest honor in the gift of the nation is significantly present. "I am not surprised, sir," said the brilliant Blackburn of Kentucky, a member of the Congressional committee that was charged with conducting the impeachment proceedings, "at the uneasiness manifested and the nervousness displayed by the gentleman from Maine [Mr. Blaine], who seeks to inject his speeches into every man's utterances on this side of the House. Did I hold the same questionable position in this matter as gentlemen on the other side by reason of the complicity of their prominent officials, I at least would be disposed to sympathize with him and share his apprehensions.

"I do not like to charge that it is the purpose of the Executive of this country to intimidate witnesses, to throttle investigation, and to afford immunity from punishment to publicly convicted criminals. But I do say this: that this is the result, and unless this gag process is stopped the country will believe, and I will believe, that such is the purpose." [Cries of "O!" "O!" from the Republican side of the House.]

Nevertheless, despite this and other sharp clashes upon questions of law and of public policy, the personal relations between Lamar and Blaine were always friendly. Senator Hoar, writing after the turn of the century and at a time when both had long since died, was to comment that Blaine was more interested in maintaining "friendly personal relations" with Lamar than with any other Southerner.[34]

Papers of all sections, irrespective of political affiliations, acclaimed the brilliance of Lamar's exposition of constitutional law, and the completeness with which he had overwhelmed Blaine. Representative was one of several like editorials in the *Cincinnati Enquirer*: "For the first time in his congressional career, Blaine was to-day completely flattened out and squelched. He had arranged a program for defending the action of the President and the Attorney General in trying to get the Belknap case out of the hands of the House.... Mr. Hoar offered this program as an amendment to the resolution of the Democrats, which was presented by Mr. Lamar. Then the battle began. At the proper moment, after several of the 'small fry' had made their cut-and-dried speeches, Blaine took the floor, and, in his customary bullying, insolent style, attempted to overwhelm all opposition, and scare the Democrats into concessions of Hoar's amendment. Blaine's design was to call out some indiscreet remarks from the Democratic side, and then throw the House into a barroom mêlée, as he did in the Andersonville debate; but when he had finished, Lamar rose. Lamar is the coolest man on the Democratic side. No taunts can annoy him; no bullying or insolence disturbs his equanimity. In reply to Blaine's frantic bullying, he coolly began to read the law governing such cases, together with several decisions and precedents. He made no comment by way of preface, except to say that he would show Mr. Blaine to be utterly ignorant of the law and utterly unmindful of the precedents in regard to the matter, and that before he (Lamar) got through he would subject him (Blaine) to the ridicule of his opponents and the pity of his friends. The result was admirably managed by the Democrats, and Mr. Lamar deserved great credit for the masterly way in which he led the fray. The expression among the Democrats to-night is universal that Lamar is the safest and most adroit leader that could be selected. He is the only man who has succeeded in flooring Blaine."

"Mr. S. S. Cox has recently published a bright and amusing book, called 'Why We Laugh,'" reported one editorial entitled *The Fall of Blaine*, in a New York paper, "in which he has gathered together a bright and amusing number of good political stories, not without a purpose. But nothing in his book gives so satisfactory an answer to the question asked by its title as the last week's simple history of the decline and fall of that great Republican emperor, Blaine, of Maine.... If any of a dozen Republican members of Congress who might be named had put himself in the way of getting so severe a trouncing as Mr. Lamar was forced to administer in the impeachment of Belknap, his Republican colleagues might have been secretly amused; but they would probably have been able to suppress their mirth out of a fellow-feeling with the victim. But when Mr. Lamar, calmly, coolly, almost sweetly, led the unhappy Blaine steadily onward from blunder to blunder until, with Wallace's *Supreme Court Reports* in hand, he daintily but decisively turned him over suddenly, and once for all, on his back, and laid him floundering in a mess of adjectives on the floor, the bonds of party sympathy itself gave way like wisps of straw, and the Republicans joined as heartily as the Democrats in the Homeric laughter which followed.

"Mr. Lamar's treatment of Blaine on that occasion has been compared by some of the picturesque correspondents of the press to the playing of a cat with a mouse. So far as the image expresses the intellectual superiority of the victor over the victim, it is correct enough; but the cat which worries a mouse undoubtedly takes pleasure in the worrying.... Mr. Lamar was obviously sorry, on the contrary, to find himself compelled to worry Blaine." This editorial notes that Lamar purposely gave his victim "a dozen chances to escape," and that even after Blaine's persistence had placed him in such a position that neither he nor any one else could rescue him, Lamar was ready to let him off: "It was only when the House, either nobly eager to see a petulant bully made an end of, or merely hot with the fierce instincts which the spectacle of a sharp contest always excites, cried out as with one voice, 'Go on! go on! punish him!' that the sword of the Mississippian descended, and his helpless antagonist fell 'all of a heap' together at his feet. In our Congressional annals this scene will long live for an example and a warning: an example, as showing how much more effective, even in so heterogeneous a body as the House of Representatives, are the belligerent methods of a well-equipped and well-bred nature than those of a hasty and violent one."[35]

Incidentally, hardly a month had passed until, on April 24th, 1876, Blaine himself was to rise in the House to deny the current rumors that for large sums of money he had sold his influence and services to the Union Pacific Company; and shortly he was to become so involved in a tissue of lies and half-truths that upon the records of impartial history his guilt has been inexorably and ineradicably fixed.[36]

Lamar's next notable speech before the House was on the subject of the recent race "war" at Hamburg, South Carolina. On the 7th of July a pitched battle had occurred here between a company of Negro militia on the one hand and a number of residents of Hamburg who were reënforced by citizens of Augusta, Georgia. The situation was this: Across the river from Augusta, the little town of Hamburg was being terrorized by a company of eighty blacks who were heavily armed and under the leadership of a Negro who openly boasted of his hatred for the whites. The crowding of white women into the road and the arresting and fining of white men on trumped up charges had become commonplace. The inevitable explosion was touched off when the black militia drew across the main thoroughfare and refused passage to two white youths who were traveling that road. Finally the latter had been allowed to pass through after the Negro captain had cursed and threatened them.

When the father of one of the youths had the black leader arrested and carried before the court for obstructing the highway, he (the captain) acted in such an insolent manner that the Negro justice who presided had him arrested for contempt. As the day set for the trial approached, there were open threats among the members of the black militia against the lives of the two boys who were to testify. As a matter of fact, there was nothing that the whites desired so much as the disbanding of the Negro company, and the prosecutor, General M. C. Butler, proposed that the case be dropped on condition that the blacks surrender their arms to some responsible person who would see that they were shipped to the Adjutant-General. The answer to this compromise proposal was the bold declaration that the blacks, who retired to a small brick building from which they yelled and fired at all within sight, would welcome a battle. There was a moment of quietness until one of the bullets from the brick house struck a white man, killing him instantly; then the fate of the ringleaders among the Negroes was sealed. A cannon was brought from Augusta and the blacks were driven from their fortification, five of their leaders being captured and immediately shot.

Chamberlain, the carpetbag Governor of South Carolina, prepared a biased and distorted account of the occurrence for his radical friends in the Senate, giving to the affair a political significance that it did not possess; they, in turn, gave the rankly partisan account to the press. There was no motive, he declared in a letter to Grant, save "the fact that the militia company was composed of negroes...and members of the Republican Party." The men who had demanded that the blacks disband and return their arms to the Adjutant-General "were white men...and members of the Democratic Party." The real aim of his letter, however, was to be discerned when he appealed to Grant to take vigorous measures to "repress violence ...*during the present political campaign.*" [37] The President was only too glad of the opportunity for manufacturing campaign ammunition by stirring the fires of sectional discord, and he quickly framed a document in the form of a letter in which he took occasion to refer to the Democratic victory in Mississippi as gained by "force and fraud such as would scarcely be credited to savages, much less to Christian people." The partisan and vindictive nature of the letter was so patent, however, that it bore little weight even in the North.

On the 15th a discussion of the matter was precipitated in the House in connection with a resolution for the protection of the Texas frontier, on the lower Rio Grande, from the depredations of Mexican banditti. Mr. Smalls, the Negro Representative from the Hamburg District in South Carolina, offered an amendment providing that "no troops for the purposes named in this section shall be drawn from the State of South Carolina so long as the militia of that State, peaceably assembled, are assaulted, disarmed, and taken prisoner, and then massacred in cold blood by lawless bands of men invading that State from the State of Georgia." In the course of the ensuing debate, Smalls produced a purported letter (from which the signature —if there had ever been one—had been removed) which contained a highly sensational and inaccurate account of the riot. Requested to name the author he retorted: "I will say to the gentleman that if he is desirous that the name shall be given in order to have another negro killed, he will not get it from me." His answer received great applause from the radicals.

Lamar did not enter the discussion on the first day, but on the 18th, when the debate was resumed, he felt called upon, in view of his membership on the Committee of the Texan Frontier Trouble, to make his position clear.[38] He was opposed to mob law regardless of any justification that might be offered, and he had no desire to excuse or to palliate the "terrible and disgraceful affair at Hamburg." He did not think, however, that Mr. Garfield had "given a fair and impartial statement of the circumstances in which it originated." He declared that "we of the South have a lawless class, precisely as you of the North have lawless classes. As a consequence we have riots in which human life is lost precisely as you have such riots, with this difference: ours, without preconcert, flame up in different localities, and are confined to short periods of time; while yours, in more than one instance, have held several counties in terror, have extended over months of time, and have involved a large loss of human life, defying the authorities of your States."

The blame, Lamar felt, lay with the falsely called "Republican" governments of the Southern States, which had, he said, "no identification or sympathy with the views and purposes that have inspired the following of the great Republican party of this country. And, sir, those State governments have invariably encouraged these disorders and these murders by their inefficiency, by their imbecility, by their cowardice, and by their connivance; for they have in every instance not only failed to punish these murderers, not only failed to administer justice, not only failed to execute the laws, but they have used the occurrences as occasions to appeal to Congress and to the North for help in maintaining the power which they are so ruthlessly exercising." The federal administration, moreover, must bear the responsibility for quartering armed and irresponsible Negro troops upon the South.

The sending of federal troops, he pointed out, never helped in such a situation. Invariably they had merely aggravated the seriousness of the wounds with which the local governments had been suffering. Moreover, "a riot like this in the streets of a town or village is not a thing for the Federal Government to intervene about, for it violates no federal law; it does not conflict with national authority; it has no relation to the exercise of the right of suffrage. This was a riot like the riots which occurred in the State of Pennsylvania, in the mining region; or in Indiana, where, on the day of the last election, three or four colored men were killed; or like that which occurred the other day in New Jersey, where seven men were killed, two of them put to death by stoning. Why do you not apply the same remedy there? Why confine your federal intervention to prevent murder and riot to one section alone?"

As a remedy for the situation at Hamburg Lamar demanded that the Governors of South Carolina and Georgia exert themselves to bring the criminals, white and black, to justice. "He [the Governor of South Carolina] cannot," said Lamar, "use measures too vigorous or too summary to bring the men who

shot down these prisoners in cold blood to a swift retribution."
If he does this, he will receive the praises of all "good citizens
of South Carolina; but if, instead of doing that, he is rushing
to Washington to invoke once more the demon of discord and
sectionalism, to drag their material of passion through this
chamber, he will not be doing that which will prevent disorders
in that State.... I repeat, it is not the fault of the people whose
property interests and business investments and industrial arrangements depend upon peace and order, and are utterly
ruined by such disorders, but of governments either too in-
efficient to put down crime, or so much interested in producing
it that they furnish further provocation to it.

"Why, sir, the other day Gov. Kellogg, of Louisiana, appointed as a tax collector to a parish in that State (so I read
in the press) a man who was a captain of a band of murderers
and robbers. If he had sent his police to hunt him down and
shoot him like a wolf, him and his marauding band, he would
have done his duty. But, instead of that, he legalizes robbery
and theft by making the robber a public officer; and when riots
and disturbances grow out of such actions as these, he comes
here to Washington and calls on this government to bring about
order. Sir, these occurrences are ruinous to the South; they are
unnatural and morbific elements, and disappear whenever this
type of man is eliminated from political and social control in
the South, and the management of affairs falls into the hands
of her own people."

The thinking element in the population, both North and
South, hailed this forthright speech with enthusiastic approval.
Some there were in his own State who did not agree with the
sentiments that he had expressed, but the letters and telegrams
that he received from his constituency indicated that he had
the overwhelming backing of those most vitally interested in
his course. The radical press, however, saw that Lamar's temperate words were undoing much of their incendiary work of
arousing sectional distrust, and he was at once subjected to a
vicious attack from those who claimed that the sentiments that
he expressed in Washington did not correspond with those

which he uttered in Mississippi.[39] Such charges were given neither a serious nor a wide hearing, but on the 25th of July he exposed their falsity before the House in such a way that they were not revived.[40] This attempt to destroy Lamar's influence was widely remarked upon, and was generally evaluated for what it was really worth. "Nothing seems more to irritate the average radical," said the *San Francisco Examiner*, "than a contemplation of the distinguished position of respect and influence in Congress and before the country won for himself by the Hon. L. Q. C. Lamar. The more senseless and unreasonable of this class, finding in his course and conduct nothing they can misrepresent to his disadvantage, and nothing upon which they can with justice hang a tirade of abuse, like silly schoolboys, find their only satisfaction in sitting back and pouting or making faces at him."

For some time Lamar had been contemplating the delivering of a speech which, he hoped, would further arouse the nation to the evils of the administration policy in the Southern States, and on August 2nd the occasion was presented in connection with Mr. Pierce's suggestion that a constitutional change limiting the President to one term might put an end to many of the evils apparent in the administration of the Federal Government. The scope of this address,[41] probably the most scholarly and statesmanlike yet delivered by Lamar in Congress, makes any attempt at detailed analysis impracticable. As a matter of fact, he was in this speech formally laying down one more plank in the platform upon which the Democracy would make its next fight for the Presidency, but it was not strongly partisan in tone despite the powerful arraignment of the Republican administration in its dealings with the South.

The fear with which the Republicans regarded the possible effect of this speech was evidenced when their Congressional leaders called a caucus at which Mr. Garfield was selected to answer Lamar's attack. "Yesterday, Mr. Lamar made a speech of nearly two hours in length on general politics, making a very able and what is considered a dangerous attack upon the Republican party," wrote Garfield to his wife on August 3rd, in apologizing for his delay in writing home. "It was delivered with great effect. I hurried away this morning to make preparations to reply.... I find myself settling down into the despondent feeling that...I shall not succeed." As a matter of fact, his rebuttal of the 4th was commonly considered a failure in that he ignored all of the issues raised by Lamar, and was content to make a general denunciation of the Democratic party as unfit to control the nation.

In commenting upon the debate, Mr. Smith, Garfield's biographer, says: "The strength of his [Lamar's] speech lay not in vituperation or in its 'sectionalism,' for Lamar took good care to abstain from either of these, but in its use of undeniable patent facts to support a thesis, calmly argued...it is obvious that Garfield did well in not attempting to answer it—it was not open to answer." Let Mr. Smith, who lauds Garfield for what he calls his excellent "stump speech," remember that no one has ever yet evolved a formula whereby one can concede the weight and force of the arguments of one's opponent and yet—by ignoring every issue and indulging, instead, in generalizations and denunciation—win an argument.[42]

"The Representative from Mississippi was undeniably cast in a statesman's mould," remarked the *Boston Post* in a typical press notice of Lamar's speech. "Everything about his mind is large, fair, open, and comprehensive. The ordinary small devices of the political pettifogger are not for him. No more is the furnace door of passion open within his nature for the stuffing in of combustibles by stoker opponents. He is at all times in complete self-command, and from the height of view to which that fact raises him he is able to survey the whole situation without letting a single feature of it escape him; and for like reasons he is able to make its summary a harmonious and consistent one. The need of more such men in the National Legislature, from both sections, was never more apparent than now. When one does make his appearance, by an unerring law of nature he draws to himself the attention and confidence of all, without respect to party."[43]

XIV

HAYES-TILDEN CONTROVERSY AND THE SENATE

THE YEAR 1876 arrived, and with it the first election since the Civil War in which Mississippi would participate with a Democratic Presidential candidate in the field and without having to contend with federal interference at the polls. Making their last stand in the hope of regaining a position of dominance in the State, the radicals had organized and regimented the Negro vote. Obviously it would be a bitter and hotly contested campaign. There had been insistent calls from the North and East that Lamar arrange a speaking tour of those sections, but General George, the Chairman of the State Committee, insisted that the situation in Mississippi was too precarious for him to be spared. Consequently, though suffering with a threatened return of his paralytic ailment, he took a leading part in the campaign and stumped the State for the Democratic ticket, local and national.

It would be a year, the Republicans feared, of retribution for the misgovernment of the past decade; and they set about making unprecedented efforts with the waving of the bloody shirt as the main dependence. "A bloody shirt campaign and plenty of money," wrote General J. Kirkpatrick from Indianapolis to Hayes, "and Indiana is safe; a financial campaign and no money and we are beaten."[1] Hayes himself became extremely apprehensive when in October Indiana and West Virginia went into the ranks of the Democracy, and his own State of Ohio remained within the Republican fold only by a narrow margin. To the National Committee of his party he wrote somewhat hysterically that "we must look after North and South Carolina, Florida, Mississippi, and Louisiana." He might have saved himself his pains in North Carolina and Mississippi where the more intelligent blacks had already rallied to the Democratic standard in their desire to escape from carpetbag rule. All was not well with the administration party in South Carolina and Florida, and in Louisiana the Democratic candidate for Governor was receiving ovations wherever he appeared; moreover, "it was a noticeable feature...that the negroes came arm in arm, side by side with the white men, not merely out of curiosity, but bearing a banner blazoned with the names of Tilden and Hendricks." [2] Too, the people seemed uncomfortably aware of the stealing that had been going on under Grant, and even Mark Twain, who was to make just one campaign speech, had sounded the wrong note and had been gently requested to cease his political activities. Of a Republican candidate, General Hawley (the president of the Centennial Commission), he had said that he furnished "the most astounding performance of this decade,...impossible, perhaps, in any other public official in the nation." He had "taken in as high as $121,000.00 gate money at the Centennial in a single day and never stole a cent of it!" [3]

The result of the election showed that the day of the carpetbagger and radical had ended in Mississippi, for the electoral vote of the State was cast for Tilden and Hendricks by a tremendous majority, and the Democrats elected all six of the Congressmen. On the other hand, the outcome of the Presidential race was fraught with problems that brought the nation face to face with a crisis that, in its potentialities, was as severe as that of 1860. The election itself had been unusually honest for the times: No State seems to have been carried by buying votes, though the Republicans had, as in the Grant campaigns, used large sums of money which had been given by the great business interests of the nation or had been assessed against the army of federal office holders.[4] Feelings had run high, with the old soldiers of the North believing that they were voting against the "rebellion" while the Democrats grimly hoped to win in order that they might end the fraud that had been rampant in every department of the government, and that they might force the removal of the last federal soldier from the South. Hayes was known to be a man of good character and of respectable ability, though Tilden was as upright and was admittedly the abler of the two. On the night of the election, November 7th, the people of the South watched with tears in their eyes and prayers on their lips as the wires brought the first returns, these indicating that Tilden would carry New York, Connecticut, New Jersey, Indiana, and possibly even Hayes's own State of Ohio. All over the nation the Democracy rejoiced at their "great victory." Almost all metropolitan papers had conceded Tilden's election, and in the first edition of November 8th, even the arch-Republican *New York Tribune* announced the Democratic win as authentic.

But tactical errors on the part of the Democratic leaders were to give the Republicans the opportunity to formulate the plot which was to seat Hayes and to make fraud responsible, for the first time in American history, for the election of a President. Throughout the campaign, the *New York Times*, then a Republican sheet, had been Tilden's most virulent opponent. This organ now refused to concede Hayes's defeat. In the night of November 7th, 1876, Abram S. Hewitt, National Democratic Chairman, requested the *Times* to state what majority it conceded Tilden. "None!" was the immediate reply of John C. Reid, the managing editor.[5] From Senator Barnum of Connecticut, chairman of the Democratic finance committee, came another request asking the paper's figures on South Carolina, Florida, and Louisiana;[6] and at about 2:45 on the morning of the 8th the paper received from Democratic headquarters the dispatch: "Please give your estimate of electoral votes secured for Tilden. Answer at once."[7] Certainly nothing more was needed to indicate that the Democrats had not themselves received final returns, and that prompt action might save all for the Republican party, albeit fraudulently. As a matter of fact there is good evidence that the Republican managers in Louisiana and Florida had already conceded those States to Tilden and that the telegrams were suppressed with the connivance of the Western Union Telegraph which was at that time under the control of the Republican administration.[8]

In the early hours of the morning, Reid set out for Republican headquarters. This he found vacant, for the members of the Republican National Committee, believing their party defeated, had dispersed. No time was to be lost. On the way to find Zach Chandler—notorious for his dealings with Jay Cooke—he encountered W. E. Chandler into whose ears he poured his information that the Democrats had not themselves gotten final returns from South Carolina, Louisiana, and Florida, and that quick action could cause the canvassing boards of the States in question, these composed entirely of Republicans, to produce any majority that might be desired. Together they pulled Zach Chandler from his bed, and after a hasty consultation their plans were laid. Telegrams were hastily dispatched, to South Carolina: "Hayes is elected if we have carried South Carolina, Florida, and Louisiana. Can you hold your State?"; to Florida: "Hayes defeated without Florida. Do not be cheated in returns"; and to Louisiana: "The Presidential election depends on the vote of Louisiana, and the Democrats will try and wrest it from you. Watch, and hasten returns." The implication was clear, and not a carpetbagger or scalawag on the returning boards of the three States failed to understand what they were supposed to do. On November 8th, the day after the election, Zach Chandler, under the direction of Reid, sent out over the wires his iniquitous message: "Hayes has 185 electoral votes and is elected." Such action took brazen effrontery and unscrupulousness but little courage, for those involved in the plot knew that behind them was Grant with the army, the ex-soldiers and their dependents, big business, the bloody shirt, and the Senate; while the Democrats had only the House of Representatives and the conviction of a large part of the American people.

The conspirators had claimed for Hayes one hundred and eighty-five electoral votes, precisely the number that it would take to elect a President. On the other hand, there appeared for the first time the "solid South" casting its entire electoral vote for the Democratic candidate, and the States of Connecticut, Delaware, New York, New Jersey, and Indiana as well. Thus it appeared that Tilden would have two hundred and three votes, or eighteen more than what was required for election. Moreover, the Democrats might lose all three of the contested Southern States and still put Tilden in office if their claim to one vote from Oregon were sustained.

It was reasonable to believe that the corrupt Republican returning boards from the three Southern States would—under promptings from Washington—declare in favor of Hayes, but Grant was to take no chances. He openly threatened the canvassing boards with troops, and he instructed Don Cameron, Secretary of War, hastily to dispatch armed forces to Florida. The disreputable Zach Chandler hurried to that State coincidentally with the troops. But despite the Republican canvassing board and the threatening presence of troops, the Democratic margin of victory in Florida had been so large that when the count was complete there still remained a majority in favor of Tilden, this despite the lavish spending of money and the fraudulent work of the Republicans who had hurried into the State. Something obviously had to be done about it, and that immediately. Through trickery and the forgery of affidavits, 228 of which were in the same handwriting, enough Democratic votes were thrown out to give Hayes and Wheeler the decision. Rhodes, never biased in favor of the Democracy, concludes that after the count, "had these been Northern States the dispute would have ceased forthwith. These two States [Florida and Louisiana] would have been conceded to Tilden, and his election secured; but under the carpetbag negro régime, the canvassing boards of Florida and Louisiana had the power to throw out votes on the ground of intimidation or fraud, and these boards were under the control of the Republicans." [9]

The tidal wave of the Democracy had in reality been so overwhelming in Florida that in addition to going for Tilden and Hendricks, the Democrats had secured a large majority in the legislature and had elected their candidate for governor. These, when they had been installed, refused to recognize the fraudulent action of the carpetbag canvassing board, and passed a law which required a reëxamination of the popular vote. This last canvass resulted in a declaration in favor of the Democratic Presidential electors, and the Governor sent to Washington a certificate to the effect that the vote of Florida had been cast for Tilden and Hendricks.

In Louisiana the Democratic victory had been as decisive as in Florida, for the returns had given Tilden a majority of between six and eight thousand. When it became clear that the radical canvassing board might fraudulently certify the vote, Henry Watterson suggested to Tilden that he invite Hayes to proceed with him to Louisiana to see that justice was done. The Western Union Telegraph, at that time, as has been pointed out, subservient to the Republican party, notified its leaders of the message and the information was at once relayed to President Grant who, to forestall Tilden's move, hastily invited certain "visiting statesmen" to hasten to New Orleans. Among these were John A. Logan, Garfield, Lew Wallace, Matt Quay, Pig Iron Kelley, John A. Kasson, and Stanley Matthews. Tilden followed suit in selecting representatives from the Democratic ranks, among them three men who had wrecked their political fortunes because of devotion to duty: George W. Julian, Lyman Trumbull, and A. G. Curtin.[10] Others were W. G. Sumner, the economist, W. R. Morrison, John M. Palmer, Henry Watterson, ex-Senator Doolittle, L. Q. C. Lamar, and Joseph E. McDonald.

The proceedings started with Grant's troops stationed close by. Moreover, upon the canvassing board of which J. Madison Wells was president (composed in addition to himself of a scalawag and two Negroes) was not a single man who had not previously been involved in criminal proceedings, and there was no representative of the Democratic party.[11] The attitude which the Republican "visiting statesmen" brought to their work is to be seen in a note written by one of them to Hayes: "Counting the ballots as cast [he said] would be in my judgment as great an infamy as was ever perpetrated." Obviously there was no intention of seeking an honest canvass. The proceedings were a farce, for the ballots of each parish were counted in a private room by five clerks all of whom were notorious characters and at that very time under indictment for various crimes in the courts of Louisiana.[12] In order to give the vote to Hayes, more than 13,000 Democratic votes were cast out. Three days before the completion of the count, the United States Marshal in New Orleans was telegraphing Senator West in Washington: "Have seen Wells who says, 'Board will return Hayes sure. Have no fear.'" Meanwhile, the corrupt returning board was seeking a buyer and was urging Tilden's representatives to take the Presidency at a price of $200,000.[13] To Henry Watterson was made the definite offer that the electoral vote would be thrown to Tilden if the latter's friends would get together $250,000: "One hundred thousand each for Wells and Anderson," he was told, "and twenty-five thousand apiece for the niggers."[14]

In South Carolina, where the case for Tilden could not be so definitely made out, the vote was also cast for Hayes. Even here, however, most scholars agree that Tilden actually won by a respectable margin. When, in addition to the votes of the three Southern States, the contested electoral vote in Oregon was cast for the Republican candidate, the latter was apparently elected by a majority of one. Thus Tilden with a clear majority in the electoral college and with a popular majority of more than a quarter of a million, was fraudulently "counted out" of the Presidency. To what lengths the fraud had been carried is evident when it is considered that the decision of any one of these four contests in favor of the Democrats would have seated Tilden while, on the other hand, the Republicans would have to win all of the questionable votes in order to seat Hayes.

On December 6th, 1876, the very day that Congress assembled, the Republican electors met and declared Hayes to have been elected. By this time the controversy had become extremely heated, the Republicans claiming that the Democratic majorities in the Southern States had been gotten by force, and the Democrats, on the other hand, denouncing the Republican claims in the three Southern States as a fraudulent reversal of the popular will. Congress assembled with the possibility of civil war in the offing, the Republicans determined not to surrender the government which they had so long controlled, and the Democrats as determined to reap the harvest from the victory which they felt sure that they had won. Meanwhile Grant paraded soldiers close to the halls of Congress as a warning that the mailed hand would, if necessary, be felt, and the ex-Union soldiers everywhere brought pressure to bear upon Northern members of Congress.[15] At the same time the Northern Democracy talked of war if it were cheated, and Henry Watterson threatened to march on Washington with a hundred thousand men to seat Tilden. But among the Southern Democrats there was little comfort given to those who talked of an appeal to arms, for they knew the meaning of civil war, and indeed, were more interested in freeing the South of the last federal soldier than in the success of the party nationally.

With Congress rested the ultimate decision, and that body was in the anomalous position of having the Senate Republican and the House Democratic. The Constitution provided that "the President of the Senate shall, in the presence of the Senate and the House of Representatives open all the certificates, and the vote shall then be counted." This, however, was highly indefinite: it provided no answers to the perplexing questions as to who should *count* the votes; who should determine, in the event of conflicting certificates, which should be accepted; what, indeed, were the precise functions of the two Houses of Congress? If the acquiescence of both was necessary for the President of the Senate to count the votes, then must both unite in any objection to a given decision by him, or would the objection of either be sufficient to check his activities?

The committee from the two Houses, after prolonged discussion, agreed upon a bill for the appointment of an Electoral Commission, and on the 18th of January reported their findings. It was arranged that the commission should be composed of fifteen members: five Senators, to be chosen by the Senate; five Representatives, to be chosen by the House; and five Justices, to be selected from the Supreme Court; and it was agreed that the two Houses should select their representatives in such a manner that there would be a majority of Republican Senators and a similar majority of Democratic Representatives. Two of the Justices were to belong to each party, and the fifth, it was

understood, was to be Judge Davis who was commonly considered an independent.

In both Houses the chief opposition to the bill came from
the Republicans. Hayes himself opposed the submission of the
controversy to a tribunal, as did staunch Republicans almost
universally, and in this they had the active support of the *New
York Times* and the *New York Tribune*. Although Tilden himself did not favor the Commission, its chief support came from
the Democrats in both the House and the Senate. On January
25th, after an all night session, the Senate gave its approval with
sixteen Republicans and only one Democrat voting in the negative. Whereas in the upper branch the opposition had been led
by Morton and Sherman, in the House it was headed by Garfield who interposed a number of objections to its constitutionality.

It was to be expected, in view of Lamar's reputation as an
authority on the organic law and his favoring of the bill creating the commission, that he should be selected by his colleagues
to present the chief argument for the measure. On the 26th
he responded in an extended speech in which he analyzed the
measure in all its aspects, and in the course of which he was
repeatedly interrupted by sustained applause.[16] Stating that in
his opinion the bill was constitutional, he declared as his first
reason for supporting it "that it furnishes a provision which
secures our government against what has been considered by
all our wisest statesmen as the weakest and therefore the most
dangerous point in our system. They have feared that the election of President, in which nearly all the honors and emoluments of government are staked as prizes to be contended for,
would soon degenerate into a struggle and contest for these
honors and emoluments, in which party ascendency and party
triumph will be objects of far greater solicitude than the prosperity and good of the country." Moreover, he felt that "this
measure, unanimously recommended by men representing both
political parties" was "certain proof that in this Congress devotion to party is not stronger than devotion to the country,
and that the promotion of the prosperity and interest of the

country is an object of deeper and more intense solicitude than all the honors and emoluments which may be reaped as the rewards and spoils of a Presidential triumph. Its enactment into a law will be a...triumph of patriotism, nationality, harmony, and zeal for the public good, over faction, selfishness, and the struggle for party ascendancy. For this reason alone I would give my support to this bill."

Lamar then showed that the Constitution was not clear upon the question at issue, and that all parties could not be satisfied except by an agreement as to the rules by which the controversy would be decided. Showing that both Houses could delegate their authority to an impartial commission, the results of whose investigation could be accepted in good faith as final, he called up the alternative of one faction forcibly attempting to seat its candidates with resistance on the part of the other: "As to the alternative of resistance, there is no necessity to pretend to ignore it; for we all know that a good deal has been said about it, both by those who would scorn to think it possible and those who (I am sorry to say) would be glad to hear it threatened. Now, sir, the man who says that he despises such indications, who feels a contempt for the menace of civil war, no matter from what quarter it comes, permits himself to overlook one of the most important features in the problem of the government: the contentment, the harmony, and the repose and security of the society for which he legislates; and he forgets the first lesson in the elementary book of practical politics."

Lamar discountenanced all thought of civil war; yet he had not the authority to say that—in case the electoral commission failed to become a reality—the alternative of submission would be "adopted, and that resistance would not be made, at least by the Democratic party." He took note of the assertion that had recently appeared in the Southern press to the effect that the Northern Democracy had failed the South at the outbreak of the Civil War, after promising succor, and that she would fail the South again. This, said Lamar, was useless and incendiary talk: "The sorrowful lesson we have to teach our children is all our own. It is that we undertook a great political movement which time and the fortunes of war disclosed that we had not the strength and resources to carry on to successful consummation. Our vindication—and a generous victor will not deny us that—lies in our solemn conviction that we were defending the institutions and the principles of constitutional liberty, the heritage of the fathers of the Republic. It was this sentiment which inspired the courage of our soldiers in battle, and now renders our section all the more precious to us in defeat, giving her, to our eyes at least, dignity in her desolation and beauty and majesty even in her ruin and woe."

Immediately after Lamar had closed the argument for the commission, on the 26th, the vote was taken and the measure was approved by a vote of 191 to 86, with the Democrats casting all except 30 of the favorable votes.

On the 25th, the day before the passage of the measure, a complication had arisen when Judge Davis, who had been counted upon to make the fifteenth member of the commission, was unexpectedly elected to the United States Senate. But it was too late for the Democrats to turn back, even if such had been their desire, and the bill was, as we have seen, pressed through the House, with Grant signing it on January 29th. On the 31st came the organization of the tribunal with Judge Bradley of the Supreme Court selected to take the place which Judge Davis was to have filled. Although the composition of the body gave the Republicans eight of the fifteen members, there was a widespread belief that the distinguished men selected would act with justice and impartiality.

But such was not to be the case. On Thursday, the 1st of February, 1877, the two Houses met in joint session, in accordance with the terms of the measure establishing the Electoral Commission. The roll of the States was called and the electoral votes recorded without protest until Florida, the first of the disputed States, was reached. When objection was heard to the returns, the controversy was immediately referred to the commission which was sitting nearby in the chamber of the Supreme Court. Then on February 9th, by a vote of 8 to 7, cast strictly along party lines, the commission decided in favor of casting the electoral vote of that State for Hayes and Wheeler.[17]

Next was taken up the dispute as to the returns from Louisiana, where again the vote, strictly along party lines, was 8 to 7 in favor of the Republican electors. In this case the fraudulency of the returns certified by the carpetbag returning board was so patent that the question of accepting its count would not down. In order to record the votes for Hayes it was necessary for the commission to dodge the question of fraud by denying its own power, under the Constitution, to go behind the returns of the State canvassing board. Here was partisan action in favor of the Republicans and in the face of open and admitted fraud. But in their attempt to gain a temporary advantage, the Republicans overstepped themselves, for their action established a precedent which would never again allow their party, under the guise of an "investigation" to take over the ballot in a Southern State and throw out votes indiscriminately as had so often been done in the years since the Civil War.

The common belief, after the decision of the commission in the case of Florida, that every issue would be arbitrarily decided in favor of the Republicans, became a certainty when the ruling on the Louisiana contest became known. With the House tense with excitement, it was suggested that the Democrats filibuster until after the time for the installation of the President on March 4th (actually the 5th, for this year the 4th fell on Sunday), with the idea that the election would thus be thrown into the House which, according to the Constitution, might then proceed to elect a President. There was delay, but Speaker Randall, with the backing of the more influential and level headed Southern Democrats, sternly repressed the filibustering tactics that the orderly business might proceed and that on inaugural day the country might not be without a President. As was to be expected, in the case of every contested return, the decision was given in favor of Hayes and Wheeler, and at five minutes past four o'clock on the morning of March 2nd, the President of the Senate announced that he was ready to state the results to a joint meeting of the two Houses. Hayes and Wheeler, it appeared, had been awarded 185 electoral votes, while Tilden and Hendricks had received 184, with the Republican candidates consequently elected President and Vice-President respectively.

Lamar's feeling in regard to the operations of the commission is to be seen in a short address that he had prepared in explanation of his vote in the House upon the acceptance of the decision in the case of Louisiana. Undelivered for some reason, the brief outline was found, after his death, by his literary executor. "I rise with profound regret," he proposed to say, "to record my vote against the acceptance of the decision of the Electoral Commission" (it had been agreed that a concurrent vote of the two Houses would negative a decision of that body).

"When I voted for the creation of that commission, I was prepared to accept a decision contrary to my own desires and convictions, if such decision should be rendered; and I have no factious opposition to make against a result which I disapprove and which it was impossible for me to anticipate....

"With this protest my duty is discharged. I do not regret voting for the act; I would do it again. I would readily submit the question, whether Mr. Tilden was elected President, to any fifteen competent citizens of any party in this country, if they would decide the question submitted to them upon the evidence; and the decision of this commission is the warrant of my confidence. They have not ventured to say that he was not; they have simply declared that they are technically disabled from examining if he was.

"Sir, by the decision of this commission I intend to abide. To that my faith and the faith of the South, so far as I could represent it, have been pledged; and that faith will be kept ...false we never have been, and never will be.[18]...

Seeking for a legal and peaceful solution of the matter, Lamar had thrown the weight of his influence and his eloquence behind the movement for an Electoral Commission. Himself of a judicial temperament and with a high respect for the integrity of others, he had believed that men of such character and attainments as those to be selected would serve the nation without fear and without bias. He had pledged himself, and had urged others, to accept the decision of the commission as final, as indeed, it should have been accepted in the interest of peace and the welfare of the nation. When the members of the commission showed themselves to be utterly partisan and unprincipled in their decisions, he was as astounded and as disappointed as any one else. But, though he believed that the Democratic party and Mr. Tilden had been defrauded, he saw clearly that only a resort to armed force could prevent the Republicans from inaugurating Hayes in March. He had seen the ravages of one civil war, and he was unwilling to subject his people to the horrors of another; and having pledged himself to abide the result of the commission's findings, he proposed to keep his word.

Openly and frankly, before the House and in his private correspondence, he made it clear that he would accept the arbitrament that had been made rather than plunge the nation into a period of chaos perhaps more terrible than the one before. But he would salvage something from the wreck. Hayes, he felt, must give definitive promises as to his future course in regard to local self-government in the South, and he must pledge himself to remove the last federal soldier from Southern soil (they were still quartered in South Carolina and Louisiana).

The report of the commission had been rendered on Friday, March the 2nd, and at noon on the 4th Grant's term would expire. That it would have been possible for the Democrats, by filibustering to delay proceedings to such an extent that the election would be thrown into the House, was obvious. That this did not occur was due to the "bargain" that has become perhaps the most discussed incident in all American history. To understand the situation, and the part that Lamar played in it, it will be necessary to trace the growth of the feeling among certain Southern leaders to the effect that the controversy must, for the sake of their section which was still scarred by the late war, be settled peaceably.

Hayes records in his diary, under date of December 4th, 1876, a statement that "Colonel Roberts of [the] *New Orleans Times* wanted an interview with me. Had lunch at Comly's. After lunch he said he called on me to give the views of Lamar, of Mississippi, Walthall, ditto, Wade Hampton, of South Carolina, and probably General Gordon, of Georgia. 'You will be President,' he said. 'We will not make trouble. We want peace. We want the color line abolished. We will not oppose an administration which will favor an honest administration and honest officers in the South.'"[19] Again, shortly after the controversy had arisen, Murat Halstead was informing Hayes that L. Q. C. Lamar and other Southerners seemed anxious to avoid trouble and suggested some sort of guarantee.[20] At the same time Garfield was writing him that "the leading Southern Democrats in Congress, especially those who were old Whigs, are saying that they have seen war enough and don't care to follow the lead of their Northern associates."[21]

On December 12th Garfield wrote more explicitly to Hayes: "Several of our most thoughtful Republicans there have said to me during the last three days that they believe it possible to make an inroad into the Democratic camp, which should at least divide them on their policy of violence and resistance.... Just what sort of assurance the South wants is not quite clear, for they are a little vague in their expressions, but I have no doubt it would be possible to adopt a line of conduct which would be of great help to them.... It would be a great help if in some discreet way these Southern men, who are dissatisfied with Tilden and his violent followers, could know that the South is going to be treated with kind consideration by you."[22] Later in the same month Hayes notes in his diary that he has received a letter from Hampton presenting his "views of duty in case of armed resistance by the Democrats."

When after the decision in the Louisiana case the Democrats saw that they had been cheated, one group, as we have seen, composed largely of the Northern wing of the party (and led by Springer of Illinois, Cox of New York, O'Brien of Maryland, Mills of Texas, and Blackburn of Kentucky) wished to delay the count until after the time set for the inauguration. Another bloc, with Lamar the leader and John B. Gordon and Benjamin H. Hill his chief lieutenants, was convinced that any attempt forcibly to seat Tilden would bring irreparable harm to the South and to the nation. Hence they would abide in good faith the decision of the commission, but they would salvage what they could from the wreckage: the federal soldiers must be removed from those Southern States in which they were still quartered and the South must be left unhampered to work out her own destiny.

A series of conferences took place in which the details of the agreement were worked out.[23] Conferences had begun as early as February 16th, just after the Louisiana decision when Stanley Matthews (brother-in-law of Mr. Hayes and uncle of Henry Watterson) had a conversation with Major E. A. Burke, of Louisiana; and Bishop Wilmer (also of that State), after interviewing Grant in Washington and Hayes in Columbus, had telegraphed home: "Peace not to be disturbed in Louisiana." Then on February 26th came three more conferences, culminating in that at the Wormley Hotel in Washington where the agreement was drawn up and signed. Throughout these negotiations the chief spokesmen for Hayes were James A. Garfield, John Sherman, Stanley Matthews, Charles Foster, and Governor Dennison; and for the Democrats, Lamar of Mississippi, Gordon and Hill of Georgia, and Henry Watterson and John Young Brown of Kentucky. The literary remains of the principals in these transactions, and particularly the testimony given in the celebrated Congressional investigation of the controversy (that of the winter of 1878-79), show that it was Lamar's influence, exerted by letter and by personal interview, which persuaded the majority of the Democracy in Congress to vote against delaying the count, and that his was the final word for the South on every issue.

As the most active member of the Joint Democratic Advisory Committee of the two Houses, which had determined his party's policy throughout the whole affair, and as the chairman of the series of Democratic caucuses, he had set his face like flint against the dilatory tactics promulgated by Tilden and certain of the Northern Democrats.

There is not the slightest doubt that Hayes himself helped plan the negotiations which resulted in the "bargain," though he was not present at any of the Washington conferences. In any event, his representatives, with whom his diary shows that he was in constant communication, pledged him to correct certain abuses in the South in the event that he was allowed peaceably to take his seat. Before the matter was finally settled, he was to invite Lamar to visit him privately in Columbus, where he would give definite personal promises as to his course.

William E. Chandler, who with Reid and Zach Chandler had first formulated the plot to steal the Presidency for Hayes, gives a racy and, in the main, accurate account of the bargain in a letter of December 26th, 1877, to the New Hampshire Republicans: "Certain Democrats in the House of Representatives, seeing Hayes certain for President, thought they would save something from the wreck. They had, therefore, threatened by dilatory motions and proceedings to break up the count and then opened negotiations with such timid or too eagerly expectant Republicans as they could find ready. They had succeeded beyond their most sanguine expectations. Senator Sherman had visited Ohio and consulted Governor Hayes. Mr. Henry Watterson, a Democratic member and a nephew of Mr. Stanley Matthews, had acted as a go-between; and on the one side Messrs. Matthews, Charles Foster, John Sherman, James A. Garfield, and on the other L. Q. C. Lamar, John B. Gordon, E. J. Ellis, Randall Gibson, E. A. Burke, and John Young Brown had agreed (1) that the count should not be broken up in the House, but that Hayes should be declared and inaugurated President. (2) That upon Hayes's accession the troops should be withdrawn from protecting Governors Chamberlain and Packard, and that the new administration should recognize the government of Wade Hampton in S. C., and F. T. Nicholls in La. By certain general and indefinite letters since given to the public, by a secret writing now in the hands of E. A. Burke, and in other ways, the agreement was authenticated and President Grant was immediately requested by Governor Hayes's council on no account to recognize Packard or Chamberlain, but to leave the ultimate decision as to their fate to the incoming President....

"Before the actual declaration of his election and to secure the same, a deliberate written bargain was made in his behalf by the same Senator Sherman and his associates, by which it was agreed with Gen. Gordon and other Southern rebel Democrats that when he should be President no attempt should be made to enforce the above principles of his party, but that the South should be allowed to manage its own affairs in its own way, and in particular that he would abandon the lawful [sic] State governments to La. and S. C. and recognize in their stead the mob governments of Wade Hampton and F. H. Nicholls."

At noon, on March 2nd, 1877, Blackburn of Kentucky who had—unwisely, it seems—opposed every move for compromise, arose in the House of Representatives to deliver the concluding remarks upon the great fraud. "To-day is Friday," he said. "Upon that day the Saviour of the world suffered crucifixion between two thieves. On this Friday constitutional government, justice, honesty, fair dealing, manhood, and decency suffer crucifixion amid a number of thieves."

Lamar had seen that the way of statesmanship was to abide the results of the Electoral Commission, be those results what they might. It took moral courage and statesmanship of the highest order to pursue the course that he had laid out for himself, for the South believed, as did the Democracy of the whole country and many Republicans besides, that Tilden had been elected, and she wished to see him seated in the President's chair. Lamar's own natural inclination, backed by a temperament that was high and daring, was to push everything to that consummation. Moreover, though the electoral bill received its chief support from the Democratic leaders in Congress, there was, throughout Mississippi and the entire South, a widespread opposition to the commission.

Many Democrats in the South, as in the North, believed that the Republicans were merely bluffing, and demanded that Tilden be seated if it took a civil war (which it almost certainly would not have succeeded in doing). Everywhere the demagogues took this position which was, on its face, dramatic and exhilarating. Lamar's support of the electoral bill brought him into conflict with many of his warmest friends and most ardent supporters. Even Ethelbert Barksdale, editor and proprietor of the *Jackson Clarion*, which for years had backed Lamar and his policies, was estranged, and the alienation was not to be healed for many years—not until Lamar was seated in Cleveland's Cabinet.

Senator George F. Hoar, one of the most prominent figures in the national life at that time, was to write that the action of the Democracy in accepting the findings of the commission and in the preservation of peace "was due very largely to the influence of Mr. Lamar, of Mississippi." "Just after the count under the Electoral Commission had been completed," he said, "there was a very dangerous movement to delay action on the returns from Vermont, which would have prevented the completion of the work before the 4th of March. Mr. Lamar put forth his powerful influence and saved the peace of the country." [24]

Another aspect of the situation made Lamar's position a very difficult one : The very fact that from the first he counseled calmness and discouraged all talk of an appeal to arms gave rise, as early as the 1st of December, to rumors that he, as leader, with Ben Hill, Wade Hampton, and John B. Gordon, was plotting to make some arrangement by which the Democracy would acquiesce in the fraudulent counting of the returning boards and thus allow Hayes to be seated. Moreover, his insistence that the decision of the Electoral Commission be accepted; and his efforts (*after* he saw that Tilden could not be seated peaceably) to secure relief for his section, lent color to the assertions of those who claimed that all along he had been plotting to help deliver the Presidency to Hayes.

The rumors continued to be heard throughout December and during that month elicited from Lamar an informal denial in which the reporter represented him as saying that "so far as his name is connected with certain reports as to the views of Gov. Hayes, there is no truth in the story. Mr. Lamar has not seen Gen. Hampton since the war, nor communicated with him except by telegrams which have been published. He never saw Gov. Hayes in his life, nor ever communicated with him either directly or indirectly."[25] A little later the rumors that he had accepted the offer of a place in Hayes's Cabinet in return for his support became insistent. "Col. Lamar," according to an apparently authentic interview, "said that no such offer had been made, and if it had, he would have declined to receive it. If any proposition should be made to him from that quarter with regard to the settlement of the Presidential question, he should at once submit it to a caucus of his party."

Particularly offensive in its remarks was the *Union*, a Democratic sheet published in Washington by Montgomery Blair who, on January 5th, published a long editorial to the effect that the Southern Senators, led by Lamar, were conspiring with Hayes for the purpose of surrendering in the fight for the Presidential office. "This editorial," said the *St. Louis Republic*, "caused much excitement" in Washington. "On first impulse Mr. Lamar wrote a card to Mr. Blair which meant fight or it meant nothing, but up to this hour he has, by advice of his friends, withheld from sending it to Mr. Blair or giving it out for publication."

On the 6th of January, following a demand from Lamar, Blair published a retraction entitled "Mr. L. Q. C. Lamar— *A Correction*." "We said yesterday," read the notice, "that 'we had heard of no one of the Southern Senators, save only Mr. Lamar, who thinks it belongs to the Senate through its presiding officer to make the President.' We have learned since the publication from the best authority that we were misinformed respecting Mr. Lamar on the point in question; that from first to last he has entertained directly contrary opinions, holding that it is settled beyond controversy by the terms of the constitution and by the uniform usage under it that it belongs to Congress to count the electoral vote, and that the duty of the President of the Senate extends only to the safe-keeping of the packages and to breaking the seals in the presence of the two Houses of Congress.

"We make the correction with unfeigned pleasure, and regret very much having been misled to do Mr. Lamar injustice. We take the occasion also to say that nothing short of the positive statement by persons whom we had every reason to rely upon could have misled us. We had no distrust of Mr. Lamar, and approve entirely the liberal course by which, as much as by his great ability, he has attained his high position in the councils of the nation."

How Lamar himself viewed the situation, and the manner in which he faced the various rumors, is evident from a notation found on the back of a letter, dated March 5th, in which a friend proposed to publish an article in his defense. "As to my connection with politics," Lamar said, among other things, "I am a Democrat, shall always be a conservative Democrat, and do not expect to act with any other party. But a public man's status must be defined by his acts and course, and not by studied assurances; therefore decline to publish this letter." [26] Nor did he ever bother to explain the precise part which he played in the settlement of the issue between Hayes and Tilden, and his private correspondence bears witness to the fact that never did he bewail the abuse that for a time was heaped upon him, and the temporary estrangement from certain of his supporters.

That he had been a traitor to his party was not for a moment believed in Mississippi, even by his most uncompromising political enemies. Some there were who did not approve of his course, but no one, publicly, at least, accused him of being false to his trust. The failure to seat Tilden, however, was a depressing incident to the Democrats of Mississippi and of the nation. On the 6th of March, Mr. Goar was writing Lamar from Tupelo: "Our people are very much depressed here, cursing everybody, you with the balance. They talk like you, Gordon, and Hill could have had the thing your own way if you had tried. This will pass away after a little while, though." [27] Lamar himself gave no hint of his own suffering other than a comment to his wife in a letter of April 26th in which he mentioned the isolation of his position, his disappointment in certain of his friends, and in his own failures to achieve for his people all that he had hoped.

As we have seen, however, the South was not to lose all of the fruits of victory. Frankly, she was more preoccupied with her own sufferings than with the national issues of public debt and finance, the tariff, and civil service reform. It was felt, and rightly so, that all else paled into insignificance before the fact that soldiers were still quartered on Southern soil. No real liberty, or civic virtue, it was felt, could exist where the people lived under the shadow of federal military interference. Hayes's public statements as well as his private pledges, had aroused strong hopes of a lenient policy toward the stricken section. In the letter of July, 1876, in which he had accepted the Presidential nomination, he had taken a kindly attitude toward the problems with which the South was laboring, and in his inaugural address he reiterated the sentiments previously expressed, and pledged himself to encourage "wise, honest, and peaceful self-government" in those States. Naturally the South was exultant, but the radicals were mortally offended and in the ensuing session of Congress they made a concerted attack upon him. As was to be expected, the Southern members of Congress rallied to support him in the face of the attacks which he was suffering from within the ranks of his own party.

Hayes was fully aware of the obligation that he owed to the South for her support in the trying days immediately following his inauguration. "The chief disappointment among the influential men of the party," he entered in his diary under date of March 14th, 1877, "was with Conkling, Blaine, Cameron, Logan, and their followers. They were very bitter. The opposition [to the Cabinet appointments] was chiefly to Evarts, Key, and especially Schurz. Speeches were made in an at-

tempt to combine with the Democrats to defeat the confirmation of the nominations which only failed to be formidable
by [reason of] the resolute support of the Southern Senators
like Gordon, Lamar [who had himself been seated in the Senate only a few hours before that body received the nominations
to the Cabinet], and Hill." [28]

The Southern leaders had believed, and had had reason to
believe, that immediately upon his inauguration Hayes would
reverse Grant's policy in respect to the South. When he did
not take immediate action, a feeling of disquiet began to spread,
for it was well known that should the federal administration
but refuse its support, the Chamberlain government of South
Carolina and that of Packard in Louisiana would at once fall.
Undoubtedly, Hayes wished to live up to his pledges, but he was
seriously embarrassed by the determined opposition which he
encountered within the ranks of the Republican party. Moreover, the States governments which Hayes had promised to
renounce held their offices by virtue of the very election by
which he himself had been elevated to the Presidency. Manifestly, if he displaced them, he would, in a sense, be admitting
the presence of a shadow upon his own title to the office of
Chief Executive.

Again, the Republicans in the Senate attempted to browbeat Hayes to the extent that he would not dare to take action
in the matter. As early as the 6th of March, Thurman and
Blaine had argued heatedly as to the right of Kellogg, the
Lousiana radical, to take a seat in that body, and Blaine had
obviously come off second best. True to his habit when placed
in an embarrassing position, he had entered upon a wild
harangue in which he mentioned the rumors that had been circulated to the effect that "some arrangement had been made
by which Packard was not to be recognized and upheld, that
he was to be allowed to slide by and Nicholls was to be accepted as Governor of Louisiana." He had no authority to speak
for the administration, he said, but he would deny emphatically
the truth of the rumors. Such a course would be impossible
for a man of good sense and good character, he cried, and he

assumed that the President possessed both. Here was a plain warning to Mr. Hayes that he dare not follow a liberal course toward the South.

Under radical pressure, Hayes temporized and agreed to send a commission to the Southern States before taking action. Historians generally agree that the President had not given over his purpose of freeing the South, but that he had decided to send the investigating committee in the hope that such action would break the force of the storm that was blowing against him, after which he would carry out his pledges. Hayes's first move, in accordance with the shift in his plans, was to request Lamar himself to chairman the investigating committee.[29] This the latter flatly refused to do, and, further, he let it be known that he would not mildly accept a dilatory policy on the part of the President. Of all men Lamar was perhaps in the best position to know just how strongly Hayes had pledged himself to withdraw the military support from the Negro and carpetbag governments of South Carolina and Louisiana. Indeed, toward the end of February, when the controversy was nearing its acute stage, he had held a personal conference with the Ohio Governor and had received assurances on that score.[30]

He was, therefore, in a position to bring pressure to bear upon Hayes. On March 22nd, 1877, two weeks after the inauguration and in the face of the President's temporizing course, Lamar sent to him a courteous but firm demand that he carry out his promises.[31] And he, a man of no great decision of character but with the best intentions in the world, knew that he had pledged himself to one who would exact its fulfillment to the letter. "Lamar," Hayes had told William H. Roberts during the controversy (according to the latter's sworn statement to the Congressional investigating committee) is "cold as ice...keen as a razor," and "one of the ablest men in the South."

Lamar explained in his letter that only his illness had kept him from calling upon the President—an illness which had been augmented, he grimly remarked, by the report that the

President had decided to send a commission to Louisiana. The Southern Senators, he said, had *in solido* rallied behind Hayes because the latter, in his inaugural address, had said that he "would not consent to sustain, by unconstitutional interposition of the federal forces, States Governments which had no support in the character, the intelligence, and the material interests of the States which they had misruled. We felt that this resolution, promptly and firmly carried into effect, gave to the South that for which she had most earnestly contended. Believing this, we were willing to suppress the disappointment at the loss of a political victory which seemed so near and so precious, and to mark our sense of the justice and wisdom of such a course by giving you that cordial support which extreme partisans in your political following seemed unwilling to give. But the support, to be honorable to us and useful to you, must have a sure foundation."

In his inaugural address, said Lamar, Hayes had stated clearly that he planned to withdraw the troops from South Carolina and Louisiana, the only two States to which his language could have been applied. But he had not carried out his promise. And here Lamar came to the crux of the matter: "All that was required was an order to withdraw the troops from those States where they were a positive interference with the popular will, and in which the condition produced by their presence was a daily violation of your sense of constitutional right, and threatened still further and more mischievous complications. *Upon that subject we thought that you had made up your mind; and indeed, Mr. President, you told me that you had ...your declaration prevented a fearful crisis....You must do what you said that you would do....* I wish I could make you realize how hopefully I relied on the honesty of your purpose, the patriotism of your intention."

Having flatly demanded that Hayes fulfill his pledges, Lamar sought to strengthen the other's purpose by showing that his own carrying out of his part of the agreement had been at the expense of suffering and opposition. "I know that men who have loved me are beginning to grow cold in their affections," he said. "I know that men who have trusted me have begun to falter in their confidence. I have no thought of turning back, or even pausing; for I know my purpose, and, till now, thought I knew my means; and you must permit me to enter my solemn and sorrowful protest against a policy which I cannot support because I believe it fatal both to you and to the South." Lamar evidently decided that his flat demand that the President carry out his pledges would be more effective, for the rough draft of his letter shows this final section marked out, and the original in the Hayes papers has it omitted.

Lamar's insistence had the desired effect of strengthening Hayes's almost blunted resolve, and on the very next day he sent dispatches to Governors Hampton and Chamberlain of South Carolina, calling them to Washington for a conference. Less than two weeks later the federal troops were ordered removed from South Carolina, and then on the 24th from Louisiana. As Lamar had forcibly pointed out, all that Hayes needed to do was to withdraw the federal militia from the support of the carpetbag governments, which, having no sanction from the people themselves, would fall of their own weight. The President followed to the letter the course that Lamar had outlined in his communication and for which he had contended since his return to public life; and the disreputable State governments of South Carolina and Louisiana disappeared. As a matter of fact, the President allowed the already constituted investigating committee to proceed to Louisiana, but his removal of the federal troops had already destroyed its power for evil.

The course of Lamar and the other moderate leaders of the Democracy was fully vindicated within the first few months of Hayes's term as President. When two years later, in 1879, Lamar discussed his stand in the matter before his constituency in Mississippi,[32] there was not a voice to say that he had failed to act in a statesmanlike manner. His words, moreover, are as pertinent, as valid, and as illuminating to-day as they were when they were uttered, and the verdict of time has cast its seal upon his actions. "I believe that the most dangerous event

in our history, not excepting the war of secession," he said in
an extended analysis which yet remains the most authoritative
treatment of the controversy, "was the contest over the result
of the Presidential election of 1876. The war of secession must
have ended as it did, in the restoration of the Union or else in
the formation of two republics, based on different systems, but
equally represented by strong and civilized governments. But
if this last contest had reached no legal and peaceful solution,
if it had resulted in the establishment of the principle that a
Presidential election may be determined by force alone, there
would have been an end to constitutional government on this
continent."

If the Democratic House had insisted to the last upon the
seating of Mr. Tilden, said Lamar, he "would have been forced
to rely upon a solid and armed South against what would have
been shown to be a solid North, aroused to resist the rule of a
President set up by what was called 'a Confederate House.'"
Yet, Lamar pointed out, even if the Northern Democrats had
been willing to meet the issue in arms (and no Democratic
Northern statesman could have withstood the outbreak of popular sentiment whenever the South, "just admitted for the
first time to its full equality in the Union, and that upon probation, and under a suspicion and a misgiving, should again
plunge the nation into the horrors of a civil war"), "I would
never have consented. I know what civil war means, and you
know it.... Men may talk of courage and audacity, *but you
know and I know that the men who lead in cruel convulsions
are not alone they who pay the penalty of temerity*. If any
man thinks that it is a lack of courage not to be willing to
confront such consequences and dangers, let him pass judgment upon me for my course on that occasion....

"Of course I would have preferred to see Mr. Tilden inaugurated. I regarded him as one of the ablest of the many
able leaders of the Democratic party, and one of the best
representatives of its best ideas. I believed him elected, and
was deeply grieved at our loss of the precious fruits of that
election. When I voted for the Electoral Commission I voted

for the creation of a tribunal which I believed was as apt to decide one way as the other; but when it decided against us I felt sure of these things: that any decision was better than force and civil war; that any civil commotion would be fatal to the people and to the prospects and prosperity of the South; and that four years more of probation—if probation it could be called, with such a President as Mr. Hayes representing the Republican party, and with Congress Democratic—would, if we acted wisely, leave us stronger in ourselves, steadier in our policy, and in close and more friendly relations with the people of the whole country. And the condition of the South and of the Democratic party to-day proves that I was right."

Again, Lamar pointed out, there was one other point where the South gained an unwitting concession that would keep her institutions forever free from the meddling of the Federal Government. The Republican-controlled Electoral Commission had asserted that constitutionally the Federal Government was forced to accept the certificates from the corrupt State returning boards and that the commission was not empowered to go behind those certificates to determine whether they were fraudulent. As a matter of fact they were clearly so, but, as Lamar pointed out, the Republicans, for the sake of a temporary advantage, established a precedent that, to their sorrow, would henceforth deprive them of the opportunity of controlling election returns from the Southern States.

Important, too, was the fact that for the first time since the Civil War the setting up of the commission embodied a recognition "that an issue between the North and the South should be referred to the arbitration of reason and law, and not of force."

Let it be said, in closing, that there is no basis for the claim that the Electoral Commission was deliberately conceived by a few leading Democrats, working with influential Republicans, for the purpose of delivering the Presidency to Hayes.[33] If the present investigation has shown anything it is that the commission was conceived in good faith by those who believed that

it would render its decision on the evidence and without partisan bias. No less false is the statement of Bigelow that the
Republicans were able to steal the election because of "Northern Democratic cowardice in November and Southern Democratic treachery in February," [34] a statement quoted by Bowers [35]
with the comment that "it may be doubted whether there would
have been 'Southern treachery' had there been no 'Northern
cowardice.'" We have seen, as a matter of fact, that when
Lamar and his associates acted to salvage something from
the wreck by securing the pledge for the freeing of the South,
there was no conceivable situation that would allow the seating
of Tilden and Hendricks.

That the Republicans had in effect bought the electoral
votes of Louisiana, South Carolina, and Florida through promises of lucrative federal jobs for the members of the returning
boards and their associates became evident when, almost to a
man, the latter were rewarded—even the most corrupt—with
remunerative positions, this phase of the "dirty work" being
chiefly handled by John Sherman. [36] But in its final results it
is probably well that Hayes was seated. It was time for the
Southern States to be freed from their oppressors, and a Democratic President could not have done this without the active
opposition of powerful eastern factions, such as the Grand
Army of the Republic. There might even have resulted another
war had Tilden attempted to put into effect what was almost
immediately accomplished under Hayes. The incorruptible
George William Curtis felt that the orderly and dignified way
that the trying situation was handled through the commission
set up with the support of the conservative Democrats was
"one of the greatest triumphs of patriotism" in the history of
the nation; [37] and the writer has been able to discover no
reputable historian who does not accord to Lamar and his
associates the highest praise for their patriotism, integrity, and
statesmanship. That Lamar's own constituents, after the first
severe shock of disappointment, approved of his course is to
be seen from a letter of May 14th, 1877, written by Hon.
Jefferson Wilson of Pontotoc. "I must say to you in all candor,"

he wrote, "that your course as a public man for the last few months meets with almost universal approval. Mississippi will overwhelmingly sustain you in what you have done, and no mistake." [38]

Probably no finer tribute was ever accorded an American statesman than that paid to Lamar in 1893 by Dr. Harry Pratt Judson, then Dean of Chicago University, in connection with the settlement of the election controversy.[39] "No more dangerous crisis ever came to a nation," he wrote, and to Lamar, he thought, went much of the credit for saving the nation from civil war. Further: "Had either party insisted on a course not plainly authorized by the constitution, the other party would have resisted, and with perfect right; and for a time it seemed that physical force was the only solution. Party spirit and passion were high. The nation was apparently on the verge of a civil war more dangerous than the war of secession.

"It is entirely evident that in such an emergency arbitration is the only reasonable resort for enlightened people. But it was by no means evident at that time as to just what form of arbitration would be feasible, and under those circumstances the bill providing for the Electoral Commission was not merely a happy escape from a dangerous situation; it was more than that. It was also a triumph of patriotism and self-control, second only to the issue of the war of secession itself, as evidence that self-government is possible and enduring.... Lamar was conspicuous and influential; and he should have the respect which all sincere well-wishers for republican institutions will never fail to give to the men who settled the great dispute of 1877 by law, and not by violence. Their action vastly strengthened the cause of Democracy in all lands."

"He was an active promoter of secession," said Dr. Judson of Lamar, who had recently died. "He served in the armies of the Southern revolt [sic], and was an accredited agent in its diplomatic service. He probably never changed his conviction of the righteousness of the lost cause; certainly he never avowed any such change of sentiment. And yet this man, who with all his soul had warred against the nation, after the collapse of the South became a member of the National Legislature, one of the chosen counselors of the President of the United States, and finally a judge in the highest court in the land.... And the writer believes that if, after the war, that most knightly man, Robert E. Lee, had by any accident become President of the United States, he would have administered that high office as scrupulously, as honorably, as patriotically for the welfare of the whole land, as any Northern Union man. And if this is true of the Chief Magistracy, it is quite as true of the Supreme Bench, as is plainly evident by the course of the Justice who has just died, as high-minded a man as was General Lee.

"The men of the South who fought for their section were as honorable and sincere as any that history records. They fought for what they believed to be right and justice. They were defeated. Their cause was not merely lost; it vanished utterly away from the earth. And a large proportion of the soldiers and statesmen of the Confederacy accepted the result in good faith as a final settlement of all the matters in dispute, and set themselves resolutely to a rehabilitation of the South in the Union; and among these none was more earnest and more honest than L. Q. C. Lamar.

"Mr. Lamar was not primarily a politician; he was rather a scholar, one who dwelt in the philosophy of law and government rather than in their practice." His, said Dr. Judson, was the peculiar mission of allaying hates and fears, and he stood among that group of Southern statesmen who have exemplified the most "exalted patriotism. The nation is a nation again because of him and them."

The election controversy had no more than been settled, and Hayes inaugurated, than the time arrived for Lamar to present his credentials to the Senate. Normally it was to be expected that he would take his seat early in March, 1877; but from the day of his nomination months before, it had been a much discussed question as to whether the State of Mississippi would be allowed to seat a Democrat in the Senate of the

United States. "We say *if* he gets to the Senate," remarked the *Macon* (Ga.) *Telegraph and Messenger* of January 8th, 1876, just a few days before his election. "His election, of course, is a matter of moral certainty, but the ultras of the Senate under the lead of Morton will doubtless make a vigorous effort to set aside the election on the charge that the result was procured by intimidation. What is the probability of success to their enterprise, we are unable to say; but the letter writers generally predict a failure." Such was the editorial speculation that appeared in the press of every section of the nation.

Undoubtedly the radical Republicans would base their fight against Lamar's seating on the claim that the Democratic victory which had redeemed Mississippi was secured by intimidation. But they might have noticed the significance that was being attached over the country to the letter (which we have already had occasion to mention) written to Grant by H. R. Revels, the Negro ex-Senator from Mississippi, in explanation of the Republican defeat which had resulted in Lamar's elevation to the Senate. "Since reconstruction the masses of my people have been, as it were, enslaved in mind by unprincipled adventurers, who, caring nothing for the country, were willing to stoop to anything, no matter how infamous, to secure power to themselves and perpetuate it. My people are naturally Republicans, but as they grow older in freedom so do they in wisdom. A great portion of them have learned that they were being used as mere tools; and, as in the late election, not being able to correct the existing evil among themselves, they determined, by casting their ballots against these unprincipled adventurers, to overthrow them.

"My people have been told by these schemers, when men were placed upon the ticket who were notoriously corrupt and dishonest, that they must vote for them; that the salvation of the party depended upon it; that the man who scratched a ticket was not a Republican. This is only one of the many means these malignant demagogues have devised to perpetuate the intellectual bondage of my people. To defeat this policy at the late election, men, irrespective of race or party affiliation, united and voted together against men known to be incompetent and dishonest. I cannot recognize, nor do the masses of my people who read, recognize, the majority of the officials who have been in power for the past two years as Republicans.

"We do not believe that Republicanism means corruption, theft, and embezzlement. These three offenses have been prevalent among a great portion of our officeholders. To them must be attributed the defeat of the Republican party in the State, if defeat there was; but I, with all the light before me, look upon it as an uprising of the people, the whole people, to crush out corrupt rings and men from power. The bitterness and hate created by the late civil strife have, in my opinion, been obliterated in the State, except perhaps in some localities; and would have long since been entirely effaced were it not for some unprincipled men who would keep alive the bitterness of the past and inculcate a hatred between the races in order that they may aggrandize themselves by office and its emoluments to control my people, the effect of which is to degrade them....

"If the State administration had advanced patriotic measures, appointed only honest men to office, and sought to restore confidence between the races, bloodshed would have been unknown, peace would have prevailed, federal interference been unthought of, and harmony, friendship, and mutual confidence would have taken the place of the bayonet. In conclusion, let me say to you, and through you to the great Republican party of the North, that I deem it my duty in behalf of my people that I present these facts in order that they and the white people (their former owners) should not suffer misrepresentation, which certain demagogues seem desirous of encouraging." [40]

This statement is accurately descriptive of the situation which gave rise to the great Democratic victory in the election of 1875 in which Mississippi was delivered from carpetbag rule, and the legislature which elected Lamar was put in power. Nevertheless, the radicals had by no means lost all hope of regaining control of the State, and, as a first step, they denied

that any considerable number of Negroes had voted the Democratic ticket. Senator Morton disclosed the radical plan when,
shortly after Congress had assembled, he introduced a resolution in the Senate on December 15th, 1875, calling for the
appointment of a committee of five to proceed to Mississippi
for the purpose of investigating the Democratic victory in
the State election. Eventually the resolution passed, and the
committee, composed of Senators Boutwell (Chairman), Mc-
Millan of Minnesota, Cameron of Wisconsin, Bayard of Delaware, and McDonald of Indiana, was appointed. The two last
were Democrats; and the majority of three fell to the Republicans.

That the appointment of the Senatorial committee to interfere in the internal affairs of Mississippi was unconstitutional,
and that it was merely another political move for the purpose
of manufacturing capital for the approaching Presidential election, was commonly understood in Mississippi and the nation.
On the 7th of March Lamar was writing to General Walthall
that "a bill has been introduced in the Senate to appropriate
money to pay the expenses of the committee." It could, he
pointed out, be defeated in the House. This, however, he felt
to be unwise because it would appear that the Democrats had
something to hide, and it would be better to allow the radicals
to follow their own unconstitutional way than to give room
to the charge that there was an attempt to stifle an investigation. Boutwell, said Lamar, was a bitter and unprincipled man
who had been put as head of the committee for that very
reason. Moreover, "the investigation will be very hostile in its
spirit. It was selected, in its leadership at least, upon the principle that if you follow a buzzard you will find carrion." Again,
on the same day he wrote that there was good in Boutwell's
appointment, after all, because his association with the committee "has already deprived the investigation of much of its
moral power." If he exaggerates and is bitter and relentless,
people will believe that much of it is caused by his natural
tendency to unfairness; if he is moderate, the country will
know that he found nothing to reprehend. "But," says Lamar,

"our friends must be prepared for a relentless, incessant, indefatigable war of detraction and calumny."[41]

Meanwhile, as the Boutwell committee was nearing the completion of its work and Ames, the radical Governor, was about to be impeached by the legislature, Lamar was informed, in a letter of February 16th, 1876, from Colonel Reuben O. Reynolds, that Governor Ames had refused to give a certificate of his election to the Senate, saying that he would transact no business while the impeachment proceedings were pending.[42] But with the resignation of Ames on the 29th of March, and the immediate inauguration of Governor Stone, this difficulty was removed. Still there remained the Republican committee with its inevitable promise of a bitter and biased report on the election.

Three months before the Presidential election of 1876, the Boutwell committee reported. In the way of partisanship and vindictiveness it was all that might have been expected. It denied that the taxpayers of Mississippi had any just cause of complaint at the radical and carpetbag rule; it set forth that the Democratic victory had been won by violence and fraud; that the State legislature had no color of authority, and that Ames had been illegally forced from the Governor's chair. Finally, it recommended that Congress pass laws for the regulation of the social life and civil government of the people of the State; that States—meaning, of course, "Southern"—be denied representation in the national legislature so long as they were in anarchy; and that, unless "disorder" be ended, the offending States be reduced to the condition of territories. Unquestionably, Boutwell had fallen into the error that Lamar had predicted: he had destroyed the credibility of his report by its inherent radicalism.

The minority report, signed by Senators Bayard and McDonald, was designed to show the partisan spirit in which the investigation had been conducted, and it demonstrated that the committee had transcended the letter and spirit of the constitution in dabbling in powers "reserved to the States, and not subject to federal control." Assailing the findings of the majority, it asserted that the testimony upon which the conclusions had been reached was worthless in any court of law. "Every rule which the experience of mankind has established as essential for the regulation of evidence and the establishment of truth has been disregarded in the course of this investigation," said the minority report, "so that the great bulk of the testimony which has been taken is such as would not be received in any court of justice in this country to convict the meanest felon of the pettiest offense.... Opinion, hearsay, wild rumor, anything and all things which excitement, prejudice, hate, love, or fear can suggest, have poured in without discrimination or check. No individual, no community, can be safe against such an order of things. The usual tests of discrimination between truth and falsehood have been abandoned, the result cannot be satisfactory to any just mind."

Whether the Senate would have been able to stomach this report and act upon its biased advice will never be known, for the Presidential election of 1876 intervened, and put an entirely new face on things. Regardless of whether Tilden had been elected—and most men who were not blinded by prejudice believed that he had been—a warning had been served upon the Republican party that the nation would no longer tolerate the conditions that for ten years had been imposed upon the South. Even the radicals had come to realize that the patience of the people had been strained to the breaking point. Possibly the Boutwell committee had never been intended as anything more than a machine for the manufacturing of campaign material, for once the Presidential election was over, the entire eighteen hundred pages that constituted the report were allowed to be filed away unnoticed.

On the 5th of March, 1877, after the inauguration of Mr. Hayes, Lamar presented his credentials, upon which, under the rules of the Senate, no action could be taken until the following day. That evening a meeting of the Committee on Privileges and Elections came to the conclusion—with only one dissent—that no valid reason existed for declining to seat the gentleman from Mississippi. The radicals, however, thought to gain some advantage from the seating of Lamar by "riding in" the corrupt Kellogg as a prerequisite to his acceptance. The cases of the two men were in no sense parallel, for Kellogg was certified merely by a claimant to the governorship of Louisiana, and was elected by a legislature that had a rival body with more color to authority. Lamar's election, on the other hand, had conformed to all of the legal requirements and no flaw could be found in his credentials unless the radical report of Boutwell's committee—which condemned the whole Democratic government of Mississippi—were accepted.

In pursuance of this plan Senator Morton called a caucus of the Republican party. He laid before this group the necessity of seating Kellogg in order that the party might retain its tenuous hold upon the Senate. His plan was agreed to, either openly or tacitly, by all of the Senators and it was determined, in the words of a responsible contemporary, "that the Republican Senators would give Mr. Kellogg his seat on his *prima facie* right, and then seat Mr. Lamar at once [believing, apparently, that the Democrats would be forced to vote for the acceptance of Kellogg in order to insure the later seating of Lamar.]... Mr. Kellogg's case should be referred to the Committee on Privileges and Elections,... the committee should report back favorably in a few minutes, and Mr. Kellogg should be seated." [43]

It was at this point that Mr. Blaine, who had conceived a high regard for Lamar's character and abilities, and who possessed no great love for Morton, much less Conkling, stepped in to thwart the plan of his radical associates. It is, indeed, probable that his action resulted as much from his desire to discomfit certain members of his own party as to see that justice was done Lamar. In any event, says the account, "after the caucus was over, Senator Blaine went to Senator Morton and asked as a personal favor that he might be allowed to take charge of the Kellogg case in the Senate.... Senator Morton, seeing no objection and no trick in the request and being anxious to accommodate Mr. Blaine, if possible, consented to his request. The Democrats in the body were of course determined

to seat Mr. Lamar and to keep Mr. Kellogg out; and the vital
point for the Republicans was to bring the Kellogg case before
the Senate first.... When the proper hour on Tuesday arrived,
Mr. Morton was astounded to observe that, instead of the
Senator from Maine bringing up the Kellogg case, Mr. Wallace
from Pennsylvania was allowed to obtain the floor, and offer
a resolution that the credentials of Mr. Lamar be taken from
the table, and that he be sworn. Mr. Anthony, of Rhode Island,
seeing what had happened, at once moved that the Senate
adjourn, but this dilatory motion was voted down; and Mr.
Morton was then astonished to hear Mr. Blaine take the floor
and express the hope that the Senate would not adjourn without admitting Mr. Lamar. He proceeded to say that his election
was entirely regular; that there was no contest against him,
and that Mr. Lamar had the same right to be sworn in that
he had, and he cordially seconded the resolution of the Senator
from Pennsylvania."

The radicals exhausted every parliamentary device to delay
procedure, and Morton and Blaine became involved in an acrimonious argument in which the former charged Blaine with bad
faith. "But [reads the account] the fat was in the fire for the
Republicans, and delay was of no avail.... The result was that
Mr. Lamar was seated. The action of Mr. Blaine was, and is,
regarded by many of his associates in the chamber as a gross
infidelity to his party. He was committed to the agreement
in caucus that the Kellogg case should be taken up first. He
deliberately allowed Mr. Wallace, of Pennsylvania, who is his
friend, to bring up the Lamar case first; and it is believed by a
large number of Republican Senators that he did this in pursuance of an agreement with the Democratic party."

The seating of Lamar elicited a wide variety of comments
in the press. The radical *New York Tribune*, characterizing
him as "an exceedingly well-read man and one versed in the
ways of courtesy," presented an interesting picture of his personal appearance just prior to his entrance into the Senate:
"His face is described as one that might have come out of Van-
dyke's pictures, needing only the setting-off of wide-brimmed

plumed hat and velvet doublet to make the vraisemblance complete; strongly emphasized features, a heavy, dark mustache which is gravely romantic, a pointed beard on chin, large hazel eyes, straight hair, between brown and black, worn so long that it falls down over the coat collar; a lofty forehead; form of medium height and well shaped, save for the stooping shoulders." [44]

XV

THE FIGHT FOR SOUND MONEY

DURING the spring and summer of 1877, following his admission to the Senate, Lamar remained quietly at home recuperating from the strain of the preceding winter and fortifying himself against the paralysis which, like the sword of Damocles, always threatened his life. During this period he greatly enjoyed the stay in his home of Hon. Stewart L. Woodford, of New York, who had journeyed to Mississippi to speak at the State University. Later, in 1879, Mr. Woodford gave an interesting account of his trip to the South. He had, he said, known little or nothing of the situation in the Southern States until the summer after the inauguration of President Hayes when "I went to Missisippi to deliver an address at the University, where I met many of the leading gentlemen of the State and I was afterward the guest of Senator Lamar at his home. Then I studied the situation, and became convinced that the white people of the State were in earnest in their endeavor to conciliate the blacks and secure peace; and I determined to use all my endeavors to leave them undisturbed to work out their social problems for themselves. I believe that Senator Lamar, Wade Hampton, and most of the Southern Senators and Governors are honest in their promises, and I honor President Hayes for pledging his word to give them a fair chance. By the way, I ought to mention that while I was in Mississippi some of the members of the Republican State Committee called upon me and asked my advice as to the course that was proper for them to pursue. I frankly advised them to make no nominations for State officers, and let the coming election go by default."[1]

Lamar had planned to spend the summer of 1877 entirely in relaxation and study, and had not expected to make a single public appearance. However, the Democratic State Convention was to meet on the 1st of August, and as several very important matters were to be opened for discussion, Lamar thought that he should be in attendance. Moreover, he had been forewarned of the possibility of an attack upon his public record (which, however, did not materialize), and he was prepared to sustain and defend himself. Elected as one of the delegates from Lafayette County, he was also placed upon the platform committee.

Lamar's decision to attend the convention, however, was motivated primarily by his desire to strike a blow at the impending split within the ranks of the Democratic Party which, as we have seen, had been rejuvenated in Mississippi in 1875. This tendency showed itself in the newly suggested "Independent Party" which was being agitated within the State. In his lengthy speech, delivered the night succeeding the adjournment of the first session of the convention, Lamar warned the people that the present was no time for the disbanding of the Democracy. Nevertheless, he counseled against the drawing of the color line, for the blacks, he felt, should be welcomed within the fold of the party. Said the *Weekly Clarion* of August 1st, 1877, he "delivered an eloquent congratulatory address upon the reëstablishment of local self-government and of liberty regulated by law. He counseled harmony, and suggested several important reasons why the Democratic party should maintain a perfect organization and a united front. The Republican party had practically disbanded, but was ready and waiting to take advantage of any divisions that might appear in our ranks." A more extended account appears in the *Memphis Appeal* of the following Friday. He praised the men of all parties and both races who had helped to heal the wounds of the late war, said this account. The North, he thought, was now convinced that the South held no element of danger for the Union. At the head of those who had taken a friendly attitude toward this section, "stands the present President of the United States, who, in the discharge of his high duty as the President of the whole people, had struck a blow for the restoration of the South to her position of equality, which had vibrated to the extremities of the Union, and had carried consternation into the ranks of his own party." Lamar pleaded for a view, not sectional, but looking to the welfare of every part of the nation. Calling for the retention of party organizations as fundamental to the operation of our type of constitutional government, he deplored radical partisanship either North or South: "If the time should come (may God forbid that it ever shall!) when she shall be called upon to choose between her own local interests and the welfare of the nation at large, he believed that she [the South] would sustain her public men in subordinating the former to the latter."

The most significant subject, in relation to Lamar's subsequent career, that was discussed at the convention, was the question of the remonetization of silver. This had been taken up on the morning of the 2nd of August, by the Committee on Platform. There was considerable discussion on both sides of the question until Lamar suggested that the matter was too intricate for extemporaneous debate and settlement, and moved that no resolutions be passed. His suggestion was accepted and, as the platform was finally presented and adopted, it contained no expression on the silver question.

With the assembling of Congress in special session in November of 1877, Lamar was at his desk in the Senate chamber; and on the 30th he delivered his maiden speech, this having to do with the seating of Mr. M. C. Butler of South Carolina.[2] So high had been the recognition accorded him as a member of the House that immediately upon his entrance to the upper chamber he was given a position of the greatest influence in the deliberations of that body. During the first regular session he was to deliver a speech upon the subject of the remonetization of silver that was to be historic in the annals of our national currency and that thereafter was often to be cited as one of the greatest ever delivered before either branch of the National Legislature. It is necessary at this point briefly to trace the course of the silver question up to the point when, on January 24th, 1878, Lamar delivered his address.[3]

Between December of 1871 and the year 1873 the Congress of the United States had passed measures which had stopped the coinage of the standard silver dollar ($412\frac{1}{2}$ grains), taking away its legal tender value for amounts of more than five dollars and thus, in effect, adopting the gold dollar as the sole standard of value. During the Civil War the tremendous production of silver, particularly from the famed Comstock Lode in Nevada, had caused the metal to begin to shrink in value as compared with gold, and when in 1873 the Comstock Ledge was opened, the fall in the value of the metal became precipitate. Between 1874 and July of 1876 its value had depreciated 21% (to a ratio of 20:1), and the value in bullion of the old standard dollar of $412\frac{1}{2}$ grains was only ninety-two cents and obviously destined to further depreciation. Meanwhile the years from 1873 to 1877 had been a period of depression with suffering and unemployment widespread. As at all such times, the demagogues, the quacks, and the exponents of quick panaceas came forward with the cry for uncontrolled inflation through the printing of unlimited amounts of paper money and for the free coinage of silver. Such proposals were fraught with dire consequences and involved intricate questions of economics and finance, for the saner and more practical thinkers were aware of the axiom (none the less true because of its triteness) that bad money always drives out good money. Moreover, the government of the United States, chiefly as a result of the Civil War, had incurred immense debts in the form of bonds, certificates, and notes—these owed to foreign nations and to citizens of the Northern and Eastern sections of our own country, some of the obligations calling for payment in "coin" and some in "dollars." With the agitation for the resumption of legal tender silver coinage, there arose the obvious question as to whether the United States could honestly discharge its obligations (not only to its own citizens but to foreign governments and individuals) in silver dollars which had greatly depreciated in value below what they were worth when the debts were contracted.

We have seen that the question of the free coinage of silver had arisen at the meeting of the Mississippi State Democratic Convention of 1877, and that, due to the opposition of Lamar, the platform which had been drawn up included no statement in regard to the silver question. At that time he had taken particular pains to make clear his stand as a firm believer in the principle of "honest money," and it was as a sound currency man that he had been elected to the Senate.

It was during the extra session of Congress that convened immediately after the Mississippi State Convention that Mr. Richard P. Bland of Missouri, a free coinage zealot, introduced in the House a bill providing for the resumption of the coinage of full tender dollars of 412½ grains troy, the weight of the old standard dollar of 1837. With the rules suspended, cutting off debate, the measure was forced through by a vote of 163-34. Before the Senate could take up consideration of the bill, Secretary Sherman's report in opposition was made public and the President's message, delivered at the opening of the regular session in December, 1877, held that the use of silver currency should be encouraged, but that it should be used only at its actual market value. That it would be an act of bad faith to pay the nation's debt upon the basis of a dollar worth between eight and ten cents less than when the debt was contracted, he had no doubt. "If the United States had the undoubted right to pay its bonds in silver coin," he remarked further, "the little benefit from the process would be greatly overbalanced by the injurious effect of such payments if made or proposed against the honest convictions of the public creditors."[4]

As a matter of fact, President Hayes's message—sound in many respects and honest in all—could hardly be termed a valuable contribution to the discussion. Although it contained many pertinent and well-established facts, it consisted for a great part of personal opinion unbuttressed by a comprehensive knowledge of the subject.

By action of the Senate, the Bland Bill was transferred for consideration until the 11th of December. In the meantime, Mr. Stanley Matthews, of Ohio, introduced a concurrent resolution to the effect, among other things, "that all the bonds of the United States issued or authorized to be issued under the said acts of Congress hereinbefore recited, are payable, principal and interest, at the option of the Government of the United States, in silver dollars, of the coinage of the United States, containing 412½ grains each of standard silver, and that to restore to its coinage such silver coins as a legal tender payment of said bonds, principal and interest, is not in violation of the public faith nor in derogation of the rights of the public creditor." This Matthews resolution was called up for discussion on the 10th, the day before the Bland Bill was scheduled for consideration. When it seemed fruitful of a long debate, the Bland Bill (which, as we have seen, called for the coinage of depreciated silver dollars as legal tender) was in effect postponed until the former (which in a sense called for a repudiation of part of the national debt) should have been voted upon.

In the debate upon the question of the payment of the government's debt in terms of the "light" silver dollars, all party lines were smashed. Dawes of Massachusetts termed the proposal "a blot upon our honor," [5] and inflation in its "most insidious and dangerous form," while to Morrill of Vermont it appeared as "a fearful assault upon the public credit." [6] Voorhees, the eloquent Democrat, supported the resolution brilliantly, though in much the manner of the Bryan of a later day. Favoring the extensive coinage of silver and the payment of the national debt in that metal, he claimed that there were two classes: those who desire money to be plentiful and cheap because they work for it, and those who desire it to be scarce and dear because they already have it. Senator Randolph of New Jersey put his finger upon the issue when he pertinently asked: "If the bonds should be declared payable in a coin debased in comparison with the other, would it not be in effect repudiation? We cannot afford to rest under a suspicion of that crime." [7] The Democracy was almost universally in the silver camp, but Bayard of Delaware, faced with threats to depose him from his important committee assignments, Lamar of Mississippi, and Ben Hill of Georgia, showed that wisdom and courage and patriotism had not departed from the Democratic party.[8] So important was the subject regarded that thirty-four Senators took part in the debate.

Lamar, with the approach of the student and the thinker, had studied the subject in all of its ramifications. Having exhausted the books and pamphlets available in Washington and America, he had given detailed study, in the original, to the minutes of the Paris Conference. Judicially, he had decided that the payment of the debts in a debased currency was an ethical wrong and a practical mistake; and on the 24th of January he arose to tell his colleagues the result of his researches, and the reasons for his conclusions.[9] He would base his argument on no narrow grounds, but would approach it from the practical as well as the moral viewpoint. Senator Matthews, who introduced the resolution, had said that he viewed the subject solely from the viewpoint of the nation's "rights" and had not considered what the interests of the government and the country required. Lamar thought that the very fact that the author of the resolution had disregarded this momentous question was enough to condemn the measure as unsound.

As a matter of fact, Lamar—unlike the other opponents of the free silver bloc—was ready to affirm the constitutional right of Congress to determine (and hence to change) the value of the nation's money. With his superb knowledge of constitutional law, he could come to no other conclusion. Granting that right, however, he pointed out that the question was one primarily of sound financial policy and public morality. In his speech he struck at both the Matthews resolution and the Bland Bill, as well as the Edmunds amendment to the former. Our national credit for years to come would be embarrassed by such an action spread upon the books of the nation. The amendments and substitutes that had been offered were quite as objectionable because each of them implied a policy opposed to a *sound* remonetizing of silver (which, as he pointed out, he had always favored). There were ways, and Lamar was prepared to suggest those ways, in which silver could be coined other than in the objectionable manner being considered. Again, the effect of the proposed measure would not be bimetallism, but the consolidation of the currency of Europe upon a gold basis and the establishment of a silver monometallism in America.

The balance of his argument is too extended even to be hinted at here in its entirety, but among other things he asserted that the effect of the proposed bill would be to expel gold from the country to the extent that silver was used; that the bill was pressed not as a measure looking to the lasting prosperity of the nation, but as a temporary relief for the distress of certain classes of the population. That the people should be helped was a consummation devoutly to be wished, but the proposed method would not, he thought, work to that end. Moreover, in a few years the public debt would have to be refunded. Let her immediate obligations be paid in a debased currency, and he prophesied that, from loss of credit, the total debt could be refunded only at a prohibitive rate.

In closing Lamar touched upon a number of the broader aspects of the matter. He deprecated the distinctions made between mind workers and the toilers in manual labor. Both should be honored, and both should have the full protection of the government. He scouted the idea that all holders of bonds were, perforce, "bloated" as had been demagogically said upon the floor of the Senate. The South, he thought, should be the last section of the nation to give comfort to those who were attempting to radicalize the currency of the nation. Had not the Southerners, even when denounced as "bloated" slave-holders and *effete* aristocracy in the years gone by, been true to their allies of the Northern Democracy? Had not they been faithful to the interests of the laboring classes of the North? The speaker represented himself as holding settled convictions as "to the necessity of the laboring classes of this country being protected in all their rights and in all their interests, for when that class sinks, the entire fabric of our society must sink and crumble;" but their interests held nothing in common with free silver, fiat money, and repudiated bonds.

Lamar's speech was loudly applauded at its conclusion and widely remarked upon in the press. In every instance he himself was given high praise for his courage, though the views of the papers as to the Matthews resolution were widely divergent. "The country has great cause to thank the Democracy of Mississippi, yea, the 'shotgun,' 'rebel' Democracy of that reconstructed State, for having sent to the councils of the nation a man at once so brave, so able, and so truly patriotic as Senator Lamar," said the *Newark Daily Journal* in an editorial representative of the many that appeared in the Eastern papers. "This justly distinguished man," it said further, "had followed up Senator Randolph in a speech on the financial question, which is declared on all sides to have been the greatest effort of his Washington career and a most masterly presentment of the statesmanlike side of the debate.... What adds force, not to the speech—for it is difficult to imagine anything more forcible—but to Senator Lamar personally, is the fact that he has shown the highest type of human courage in delivering such a speech: moral courage. The Mississippi legislature, unlike the New Jersey legislature, is possessed of the silver craze, and had given evidence of its purpose to instruct Senator Lamar to vote for the Bland Silver Bill. At once Lamar resolved to disobey the mandate of his State, should it come."

Another opponent of the measure, Benjamin H. Hill, the gifted Senator from Georgia, took the same position as Lamar, though not with the decided opposition in his State legislature and not for precisely the same reasons. Concerning the course of the two Southern Senators, the *Harper's Weekly* of February 16th declared: "It is a remarkable spectacle, that of Senators Lamar and Hill, on one side, earnestly and eloquently insisting upon keeping faith and redeeming in their full spirit and intention the promise of the government, and, on the other, that of devoted supporters of the Union during the war now insisting that the government shall partially repudiate its obligations in a way which will necessarily distress industry and labor."

When the ballot on the Matthews resolution was taken on the 25th, the day after he had made his speech, Lamar cast his vote in the negative while B. K. Bruce, the colored Republican Senator from Mississippi, voted in its favor. Meanwhile the situation in Mississippi had been rapidly developing. On the

10th of January, the Hon. Benjamin King, a member of the Senate, introduced in that body a resolution instructing Senators from Mississippi, and requesting Representatives, to support the Bland Bill as well as the proposed "Resumption Act" of 1875, and on the 15th Mr. Gibson, Representative from Alcorn County, introduced a like resolution in the House. Although the latter passed, both had opposition and were delayed in the Senate.

In a letter of the 21st the Speaker of the House was writing to Lamar from Jackson that much to his disgust the House had passed the bill instructing the United States Senators how to vote. The people, he said, were under the pressure of hard times, and they were striking out blindly for anything that might give relief. Moreover, "while, without any special study of the subject (for I have been too much occupied to give it study unless it came in the line of duty), I think that an increase of currency, of the circulating exchangeable medium, would be of service to the whole country, and specially to our section; yet I regard it as a presumption for men who have given the subject, I judge, no more study than I, to undertake to instruct our Representatives, whose special duty it is to thoroughly investigate the whole subject. Especially is this so when those Representatives are men of unusual ability and unquestioned integrity." [10]

On the 30th of January a member of the lower branch of the legislature introduced the following resolution which Lamar justly felt to be a blow at himself over the shoulder of Senator Bruce:

Resolved, That Hon. B. K. Bruce, Senator of the United States from this State, in his recent vote for the resolution offered by Hon. Stanley Matthews in the Senate, favoring the remonetization of silver, has reflected the sentiment and will of his constituents; and the thanks of the Legislature of the State, now in session, are hereby tendered to him on the part of the people of Mississippi.

As passed, the resolution was amended so that after the word "constituents" it read: "and said vote is hereby indorsed and approved." Lamar's friends were disgusted at this action, which was considered in the forcible words of the Speaker of the House, Mr. Percy, as a "damned outrage."

Five days later the Senate concurred in the action of the House with the following resolution:

Whereas in the judgment of the Legislature of the State of Mississippi and the people whom we represent, the act now pending before the Congress of the United States remonetizing silver will restore public confidence and relieve the existing public distress, and will not violate the faith of the general government, nor impair the national credit; *therefore,*

(1) Be it resolved by the Senate of the State of Mississippi (the House of Representatives concurring), That our Senators be instructed, and our Representatives requested, to vote for the act remonetizing silver, and to use their efforts to secure its passage.

(2) Be it further resolved, That the Secretary of State transmit immediately a copy of that resolution to our members of Congress.

On the 28th of January the United States Senate took up the consideration of the Bland Bill. There ensued a lengthy debate which was not closed until the 15th of the following month and after significant compromises had been effected. Lamar— placed in a situation as severe as could be manufactured for a legislator—after giving the question searching study had become convinced that it was basically wrong and had determined, despite his instructions, to vote against it. "I recognize the right of a legislature to express its opinions upon questions of federal policy," he was writing to Hon. James Gordon, a member of the legislature, on February 8th, "and I think such expressions of opinion are entitled to the most respectful and patient consideration of the federal Representatives: and if there be any doubt in the mind of either a Senator or a Representative as to what his course ought to be, he should give to the sentiment of his people, as expressed by the legislature, the full benefit of that doubt, and vote in accordance with their wishes. But in that particular case their wishes are directly in conflict with the convictions of my whole life; and had I voted as the House of

Representatives directed, I should have cast my first vote against my conscience." A public man, he thought, who wishes most effectively to serve his people, must give careful study to the questions that come before Congress, but "if he allows himself to be governed by the opinions of his friends at home, however devoted he may be to them or they to him, he throws away all the rich results of a previous preparation and study, and simply becomes a commonplace exponent of those popular sentiments which may change in a few days. Without assuming to be a man of any largeness of character myself or intellect, *I do know that such a course will dwarf any man's statesmanship....* Were I to act differently from what I have, I should not be the man that I feel I now am in this country. I would be simply considered as a commonplace echo of current opinion, not the result of mature deliberations even among the masses who entertain that opinion." [11]

Lamar's disinterested and statesmanlike view of the question was challenging national attention. "What an astonishing thing that the best statesmanship, and almost the only statesmanship, we have now is furnished by the South, and that the truest friends to the Union are those who honestly tried once to get out of it!" wrote Dr. F. A. P. Barnard, President of Columbia College of New York City, in a letter of February 12th to Lamar. "That was a capital hit of Hill's where he said he tried his best to make the bondholder who purchased at sixty cents lose the sixty cents that he gave, but now he was for giving him the dollar he was promised." [12]

That Lamar had definitely decided upon his course is evident from a letter of the 14th, to his wife, wherein he wrote: "The legislature has instructed me to vote for the Silver Bill. I cannot do it; I had rather quit politics forever." [13] On the next day, just before the final balloting, Lamar rose in his place. This was the first time that he had taken the floor since his celebrated Silver Speech. "Mr. President," he said, "having already expressed my deliberate opinions at some length upon this very important measure now under consideration, I shall not trespass upon the attention of the Senate further. I have, however, one other duty to perform; a very painful one, I admit, but one which is none the less clear. I hold in my hand certain resolutions of the Legislature of Mississippi, which I ask to have read." Upon the order of the Vice-President, the chief clerk read the resolutions, already quoted, calling upon the Senators from the State of Mississippi to vote in favor of the Bland Bill.

Lamar's short explanation of why he could not follow his instructions—delivered immediately after the clerk's reading—stands as one of the classics of American oratory: *"Mr. President:* Between these resolutions and my convictions there is a great gulf. I cannot pass it. Of my love to the State of Mississippi I will not speak; my life alone can tell it. My gratitude for all the honor her people have done me no words can express. I am best proving it by doing to-day what I think their true interests and their character require me to do. During my life in that State it has been my privilege to assist in the education of more than one generation of her youth, to have given the impulse to wave after wave of the young manhood that has passed into the troubled seas of her social and political life. Upon them I have always endeavored to impress the belief that truth was better than falsehood, honesty better than policy, courage better than cowardice. To-day my lessons confront me. To-day I must be true or false, honest or cunning, faithful or unfaithful to my people. Even in this hour of their legislative displeasure and disapprobation I cannot vote as these resolutions direct. I cannot and will not shirk the responsibility which my position imposes. My duty, as I see it, I will do; and I will vote against this bill.

"When that is done my responsibility is ended. My reasons for my vote shall be given to my people. Then it will be for them to determine if adherence to my honest convictions has disqualified me from representing them; whether a difference of opinion upon a difficult and complicated subject to which I have given patient, long-continued, conscientious study, to which I have brought entire honesty and singleness of purpose, and upon which I have spent whatever ability God has given me, is now to separate us; whether this difference is to override that complete union of thought, sympathy, and hope which on all other and, as I believe, even more important subjects, binds us together. Before them I must stand or fall; but be their present decision what it may, I know that the time is not far distant when they will recognize my action to-day as wise and just; and, armed with honest convictions of my duty, I shall calmly await results, believing in the utterances of a great American who never trusted his country in vain, that 'truth is omnipotent, and public justice certain.' " [14]

The bill was passed, as Lamar knew that it would be, but he had been true to his trust and he was willing to leave the decision to history. The logic and eloquence with which he had presented his case against both the Matthews resolution and the Bland Bill were widely acclaimed, and the courage with which he fought for his convictions was commented upon in countless editorials throughout the nation. "One of the most interesting incidents in Friday's proceedings in the Senate was Senator Lamar's explanatory remarks regarding his intention to vote against the Silver Bill," said the *Washington Capital.* "Mr. Lamar arose....Every Senator immediately gave his attention, and the Chamber became as silent as the tomb....The scene was an impressive one, and as soon as Mr. Lamar sat down Senators of both sides of the Chamber crowded around him to shake his hand. Not only did several of his extremest political opponents warmly congratulate the Mississippi Senator upon his manly action, but his Southern friends who differ radically with him upon the question of finance gathered about his desk; and while they did not indorse his financial views, still they commended him for daring to do what in his mind he believed to be right. Among those who were first to grasp Mr. Lamar's hand were Senators Ransom, Morgan, Withers, Bailey, and Saulsbury." [15]

Of all men in our public life, no one ever shrunk from sensationalism more than did Lamar. Yet he had that quality of "color," "distinction," as Senator Hoar remarked, that made him a conspicuous figure in any assembly, however brilliant. Had he striven with all his powers he could have done nothing that would have created a greater sensation than his words in explanation of his vote in defiance of the instructions of the legislature of Mississippi. His mail was at once burdened with hundreds of letters from all sections of the nation: from university presidents, professors, doctors, lawyers, and all grades of the business life of the nation—all uniting in praise of his courage and his eloquence. Said Mr. William Walter Phelps, writing from New York on February 18th: "Just from Chicago, and my two days on the cars were made delightful by the generous praise I heard in every mouth of your bold and noble act. The affecting speech with which you announced your vote was read aloud in the palace car that I was in, and men and women were moved as only good deeds can move the human heart." Typical of many that he received was a note from Rev. James Otis Denniston, of Wappinger's Falls, New York, dated February 19th, 1878. "I am of a different political party from yourself," he wrote. "You have no acquaintance with me; I have no right to address you, except as each one of your countrymen is of your constituents. But I cannot resist the impulse to express to you my very hearty admiration and gratitude for the speech which you made in the Senate....My eyes were suffused with emotion while I read your words. Your act helps to bring to an end the evil results of the cruel war. It is easier for everybody in the whole land to act out the belief that 'truth is better than falsehood, honesty better than policy, courage better than cowardice.'"

Many letters arrived from the South—notably from H. C. Warmoth, reconstruction Governor of Louisiana, most of whose earlier policies Lamar had bitterly opposed, and from Benjamin H. Hill of Georgia, who wrote, "Your manly course in obeying your own convictions of duty on the passage of the Silver Bill reflects great credit upon yourself, but will soon be claimed by your people as a greater credit to the State itself." Letters there were, too, from Charles Reemelin of Ohio who characterized as profoundly important Lamar's assertion of the "principle of political science...that a matured public will must not implicitly obey an immature (inchoate) public will;" from members of the legislature that had given the instructions; and notably from his close friend (and eventual successor in the Senate), General E. C. Walthall. "When I read your speech, submitting the resolutions from Mississippi," the latter wrote on the 16th, "I said: 'he has done it, but grander even than I thought; and now his claim to greatness is permanent and fixed.' ...The victory of truth *is* sure, and your full vindication will come. The people will save you from the machine work which has been set in motion against you, and which has not been moved by their hands." Then, on the 18th of February, thirteen members of the State Senate drew up a joint letter which they sent to Lamar assuring him that he had not lost the confidence of his constituents, and that his action in disregarding the directions of the Senate would be sustained by the people of the state.

The general tendency of the criticism to which he was subjected from certain quarters in his own section is to be seen in editorial comments in the *Memphis Avalanche* (a paper at this time not disposed to be favorable to him) of the 28th: "He is consistent in his logic. He is following in the footsteps of Edmund Burke, who disregarded the instructions of his own constituents of the city of Bristol; and Lamar's defense will likely be fashioned after Burke's argument when he justified his vote contrary to instructions. The city of Bristol, however, took care that its member did not refuse twice to obey instructions. A unanimous vote for the Silver Bill was cast in the House of Representatives of the legislature of Mississippi by approving the vote of Mr. Bruce for the silver resolution of Mr. Matthews. This was a vote of censure on the other Senator (Mr. Lamar) for voting against Bruce." Again, his "solitary vote appears by the side of the solid and unanimous votes of New England and New York," and he "is the only Democratic Senator in the West who still stands upon the St. Louis platform." "Some of our Mississippi contemporaries complain of Senator Lamar's currency views," said the same paper in an editorial of the 24th. "He would not face both ways for the sake of catching votes, as most of the lesser leaders have been doing for years."

But the position he had taken, thought the *Avalanche,* was not for the best interests of the South.

Lamar's course in relation to the Bland Bill received the widest editorial discussion. Said *The Nation* concerning the leading speakers in the silver debate: "Mr. Lamar is perhaps entitled to more credit than any of them, as his vote will probably cost him his seat. He presented to the Senate on Saturday resolutions of the Mississippi Legislature instructing the United States Senators to vote for the Silver Bill, which, however, he announced his intention of disregarding, in a short speech, which, for manliness, dignity, and pathos, has never been surpassed in Congress.... At such a crisis a man of Mr. Lamar's courage serves his State best by thinking only of his country. But how absurd and quixotic his performance must seem to Blaine and Conkling!" [16] Again, he had "honored himself and the South."

"No Senator has shown himself more worthy of universal respect than Mr. Lamar," was the opinion of George William Curtis in *Harper's Weekly* of March 9th. "The Democratic Senator from Mississippi has shown the manly courage which becomes an American statesman; and his position, apart from its moral dignity, is the true position for a Senator in regard to the question of instructions." In his own State his stand had elicited various reactions, though almost the entire press took the position of the *Vicksburg Herald* which could not see its way clear "to attack a man who says that he did what he thought to be right.... All of our readers understand fully that Senator Lamar voted against the financial policy that this journal has taught for years, and we were grieved that he did so. But the future is before us. His vote never hurt his State one particle, and if he, with his great courage and eloquence, can aid Mississippi in the future, the *Herald* will not throw one straw in his way.... If Lamar is not an able, true, Southern statesman, there is no timber in this State of which to make one."

Lamar, we have seen, was led to take the position that he did from considerations of national honor and sound finance. There was yet another consideration that, while it did not determine his vote, made him feel that the course which he had laid out for himself was best for his own section and for the country at large. He felt that the entire rehabilitation of his beloved South could come only when she had fully established herself in the confidence of the whole nation. Northern men of the Morton stripe had continually said that if the South once more came into control of the nation, she would repudiate the debt that had been incurred during the war years. Thus, in the issue of the Silver Bill, Lamar had the satisfaction of knowing that his own principles and the best interests of the South went hand in hand. A remarkable editorial which appeared on February 16th, 1878, in *Harper's Weekly*, discussed the relationship of the North and the South in connection with the legislative questions that had been agitating the country:

"It has been said for a long time that there could be no really better understanding between the sections of the country that were divided by the war so long as the old party organizations continued. The dominant Southern population, it was argued, associate all the suffering that has befallen their States with the Republican party, and could have no other politics than the overthrow of that organization. It was assumed that Southern leaders in Congress would offer steady and unreasoning aid to every proposition to embarrass or discredit the national government; that they had no purpose but revenge in any way and at any cost; and that if they could embroil parties to the point of violence they would be only too glad to do so. It was this apprehension which alarmed 'the North' during the summer of 1876 with the prospect of a 'solid South'; and there were Republican leaders who relied upon this jealous fear to promote their personal advantage in the success of the party. It is but the truth to say that this apprehension has not been justified by events, and that the conduct of eminent Southern leaders in critical public situations has shown a patriotism, moderation, and wisdom with which they had not been credited.

"Since the end of the war there have been two questions of vital importance to the public welfare. One was the electoral dispute of last year, and the other is the silver scheme which is now under discussion. It is now evident that, had the Southern leaders in Congress acquiesced a year ago in the schemes of Northern Democrats...like David Dudley Field, civil commotion would probably have ensued; but they did not acquiesce. Many of them voted for the Electoral Bill, and they sustained the decisions under it, as they held that they were honorably bound to do. Their conduct was certainly not such as had been anticipated by the Northern feeling that they awaited only an opportunity of revenge, and they are entitled to all the credit of wise and patriotic action. ... Their conduct was not that of disappointed rage and vengeance. It showed that great injustice had been done to them in this part of the country. ...

"It was still less to be expected that upon a question involving the full and fair payment of the war debt some of the most conspicuous representatives of Southern opinion should have so cordially and so powerfully advocated the honorable maintenance of the nation's faith. ... The anticipation that Southern leadership, after reconstruction, would probably attempt some kind of evasion or repudiation of the debt, led to the adoption of the fourth section of the fourteenth amendment to the constitution. It was to baffle the probable action of men like Senators Lamar and Hill; yet now, when it is proposed virtually to dishonor the faith of the United States in the payment of the debt, Senators Lamar and Hill vigorously oppose, and Republican Senators like Messrs. Allison, Ferry, and Howe warmly support the proposition. Such action, with the declarations of the Charleston and New Orleans chambers of Commerce, is another great step toward better mutual understanding. It shows that mere sectional politics are becoming more and more obsolete. It shows that old party lines are disappearing, and that if good understanding was impossible so long as they were sharply drawn, another barrier is falling."

Lamar bore himself calmly throughout the storm that he had created. That he was suffering deeply, no one who reads the intimate letters to his wife can doubt, but he was never one to wear his heart upon his sleeve, and only his family and his most intimate friends were aware of his feelings. True it is that a person is more subject to hurt from one who is deeply loved than from an enemy! And so it was with Lamar and Mississippi. Misunderstanding and criticism from other sources he could bear with equanimity, but Mississippi, the State closest to his heart, could pain him deeply. "Can it be true," he wrote his wife, "that the South has not the intelligence and public virtue needed to meet the emergencies upon her? Can it be true that she will condemn the disinterested love of those who, perceiving her real interests, offer their unarmored breasts as barriers against the invasion of error? Have the spirit of her fathers, the sagacity of Jefferson, the patriotism of Washington, the virtue of Clay, departed from her? And is she to be the victim of the demagogue—blind leaders of the blind to their common destruction?" [17]

Again, he writes of his "heart almost mated to despair," [18] and in a third letter: "I have been the recipient of a good deal of praise here lately, but I take no further pleasure in it. If I thought I could do good by remaining in public life, I would care very little for either praise or blame; for my eye has long been fixed on objects far higher than any personal failures or defeats.... The only thing that depresses me (so far as I am personally concerned) is the fact that I am not in a pecuniary condition to vacate my office without doing my family great injustice." [19] On March 16th he was again writing to his wife in a like strain. "I wish that I was well off enough to quit politics," he wrote. "The South has now her destiny in her own hands; and my efforts in her behalf to promote her power and her influence, as well as the prosperity of her people, will be ineffectual unless fully and heartily responded to. I can quit public life with heart pure and hands clean, and I want to get away from it before I become so habituated to it that I can't live happily in my family." [20] The trial through which he was passing, Lamar wrote Hon. John M. Allen on March 17th, was the most severe of his life. "It is indeed," he said, "a heavy cross to lay upon the heart of a public man to have to take a stand which causes the love and confidence of the constituents to flow away from him. But the liberty of this country and its great interests will never be secure if its public men become the mere menials to do the biddings of their constituents instead of being representatives in the true sense of the word, looking to the lasting prosperity and future interests of the whole country." [21]

Lamar had said, in the midst of the controversy, that he would cast his vote in opposition to the Bland Bill, and that at the proper time he would place his case before the people of the State of Mississippi for their decision. While at home in 1879 he took occasion to present the considerations behind his vote.[22] This speech, which because of its technical aspects and its length it is possible merely to touch upon, was well received, and Lamar was able to say in closing: "I believe that the condemnation of my course has now somewhat abated. The measure became a law in spite of my vote. . . . Have the results so confidently predicted from that measure been reached? Not one. No man has been enriched, no industry fostered, no debts paid, by the light silver dollar. Since, however, the policy has been adopted, I shall do all in my power to make it successful. I believe in and shall advocate bimetallism: an honest silver dollar, and the reëstablishment of universal bimetallism by the concurrent legislation of all commercial nations."

Throughout the balance of Lamar's life the silver question was to be a stirring element in American political and financial history. "The thing to be regretted is that the South, against whom mistrust has been kept alive on this very point of its hostility to the material interests of the dominant section," he wrote in 1886 to Judge James Jackson of the Supreme Court of the State of Georgia, "confirms that mistrust, or furnishes additional ground for it in its solid opposition to the demand of the commercial and business classes of the North for a uniform standard of currency. Apart from the unstatesmanship of such a course politically, it is an unsound position financially for them to take."

Lamar took an active part in all of the proceedings of the Senate, but it was not until his speech upon the Texas Pacific

Railroad Bill, later in the same session, that he again came prominently before the nation. Since almost two decades before the Civil War there had been constant agitation for a great transcontinental railroad that would connect the Atlantic and Pacific. The South had pushed her claims from the first, arguing that the Southern route was shorter and possessed the additional advantage of crossing a terrain that presented fewer natural barriers than did the Central or Northern. The Civil War, however, had nullified any chance for the securing of the project for the South, and during the turmoil the heavily subsidized Central-Union lines were constructed. With the end of the conflict the South returned actively to the field with a demand for a competing Southern line. Lamar had been particularly active in pushing the claims of his section, and he had always felt, and said privately, that his advocacy of the measure was one of the principal causes of the savage assaults to which he was subjected in Washington in the winter of 1876-77 under the guise of opposition to him because of his advocacy of the Electoral Commission compromise.

In 1871 the Federal Government had allowed the incorporation of the Texas Pacific Railroad with a large land grant, but the depression of 1873 had sapped the resources and retarded the work of the company, which, in 1874, appeared before Congress as petitioner for a further extension of time for completing the project, and a government guarantee of the payment of the interest upon the construction bonds. This application, however, was strongly and successfully opposed by the promoters of the Southern Pacific of California, which corporation had itself laid plans for working into the Texas territory. With the organization of the Forty-fourth Congress in December, 1875, Lamar had been appointed Chairman of the standing committee on the Pacific Railroad, a position which he soon found to be extremely vexatious, for, as he wrote to Judge H. H. Chalmers, of Mississippi, on the 4th of March, 1876, "The Pacific Railroad project cannot be pushed through this Congress in consequence of the apprehension of each party that the other will make capital out of it, and the desire of each to make capital against the other." Eventually, on the 24th of January, 1877 (near the close of his service in the House) Lamar, as Chairman of the committee, presented to the House a majority report designed to eliminate the points of contention between the rival companies, and to extend substantial aid to the Texas Pacific Railroad.[23] For various reasons this measure failed to become a law.

When Lamar entered the Forty-fourth Congress as a Senator, one of his committee assignments was to that on railroads. The situation had changed but little except that the compromise that he had proposed had apparently been abandoned, and the two interests were warring against each other. On March 19th, 1878, Mr. Matthews, for the committee, reported a bill in favor of the Texas Pacific, and Lamar—whose ideas had been chiefly embodied in the measure—spoke on the 22nd in its behalf.[24] Having presented the argument for the measure in terms of its economic and financial aspects, he closed with an appeal that the representatives from the New England States lend their influence to its passage. He was led to do so because there seemed a tendency on the part of certain Senators from that section to oppose or take little interest in the proposed legislation because the Texas Pacific did not touch, and seemed of little immediate benefit to, their States. The point that he wished to emphasize was the unity and common interests of all the States, no matter how small as compared with others, or how widely separated.

"Four millions of people," he said in pointing out the political power wielded, under the Constitution, by a number of States of small area and population, particularly in New England, "have an actual affirmative force in the legislation of the nation as great as, perhaps greater than, that of fifteen millions in other States, simply by virtue of State sovereignty and State equality in this Chamber. It is a principle which is essential, in my opinion, to the preservation of liberty on the American continent; but the people in some parts of this country are growing restive under the inequality of popular representation; complaints are being made as to this great disparity...." Lamar felt that there was danger of a contest developing with the question at issue involving the equal rights of all States regardless of size. "Such a contest may be averted," he thought, "by exercising these vast powers in a spirit of correspondence with the will and interests of the whole people, and not as representatives exclusively of the local interests of their constituencies.... I would therefore invoke these Senators, when they come to act upon this question, to look in a large, liberal, and benignant spirit to the interests of the twelve millions of people who are deeply and directly concerned in its success.... Their constitutional power will thus have, sir, a large foundation in the affections and gratitude of a constituency far wider than that whose suffrages have sent them here."

Particular attention is directed to Lamar's appeal for support from New England, and his reasons for so doing, for in December he and Blaine were to clash in a memorable debate which had for its subject the constitutional right of small States to the same Senatorial representation as the larger.

XVI

SENATORIAL BATTLES

Upon the adjournment of Congress in June, 1878, Lamar returned home to recuperate from the strenuous labors of the preceding term, and with the purpose of delivering addresses at "key" points in the State in explanation of his course in the Senate. His first public appearance, at the University Commencement at Oxford, demonstrated that the affection with which he was regarded had not lessened, for as he entered the chapel he was accorded an ovation that lasted for many minutes. He had other assurances that he had not lost the affections of his people. General Reuben Davis, a candidate for Congress on the Greenback ticket, found that his audience would not allow him to finish his address until he had ceased in an attack upon Lamar; and a candidate for Congress from the third district was dismayed to find that his criticism of the Senator merely called for a spirited defense from certain of the audience who turned the meeting into a Lamar rally. So constant were the evidences of loyalty with which he was regarded that he could not doubt that his hold upon the State had not loosened, despite the independence of his course.

The appearance of the dread plague of yellow fever at New Orleans on the 22nd of July effectively ended Lamar's plans for a speaking tour of the State in the cause of the Democratic candidates for Congress and in explanation of certain of his own votes. Until the middle of November the epidemic raged, with the result that the mails were in great part suspended and public meetings of whatever nature were legally banned. Lamar, in the meantime, had taken his family into isolation upon a farm some ten miles from Oxford, and here the summer and fall passed uneventfully.

Chiefly because of the emergence of the "solid South" the

Congressional election of 1878 gave to the Democracy not only a margin of victory but a working majority in the House of Representatives and a commanding lead in the Senate. This had no sooner been ascertained than news began to emanate from Washington that President Hayes would revise his Southern policy upon the plea that promises of coöperation made by the Southern leaders had not been carried out. That Hayes did not, in reality, think any such thing is evidenced by contemporary entries in his diary, where he mentions the fidelity with which Lamar, Gordon, Hill, and others of the Southerners had supported him at critical times when his own party stalwarts deserted him. As a matter of fact, Hayes was allowing his judgment to be somewhat warped by the pressure of the Republican organization that was already making preparation for the next Presidential campaign. As usual, the *New York Tribune* was the arch offender in the waving of the bloody shirt and in doing everything possible to heighten sectional discord. That radical Republican organ said editorially that after 1880 there would be a solid North with two hundred and thirty-one electoral votes that would assume entire control of the government. "It will then be considered," said the editorial, "whether States in which free elections are not held, and the Constitution of the United States is systematically disregarded and defied, are entitled to cast electoral votes or to elect Congressmen at all. If we are to have forced upon us the unwelcome issue which a solid South invariably raises, a patient and enduring North will not be found wanting when it is settled."

About the middle of November, while on his way back to Washington, Lamar was interviewed in Cincinnati for the *Enquirer* of that city. In the course of the discussion, and when asked concerning the prospects of a third party movement in the South, Lamar was reported to have said: "Well, as to that, so long as the right of the people of the South to self-government is made an issue in the national politics the people of the South will not, and in my opinion ought not, to allow any question as to currency to divide them. The South is more solid in favor of self-preservation than divided as to national policies." With this interview as a text, the *New York Tribune* made a savage assault upon Lamar in particular, and the South and Southern leaders in general.[1] Its position, however, found little support within the Republican party, many of the leaders of which publicly disavowed the sentiments expressed. "Much indignation," said the Washington correspondent of the *New York World*, in an article dated December 1st, "has been excited here among respectable Republicans, as well as Democrats, by the atrocious attacks of the *New York Tribune* on Senator Lamar. It is considered that Senator Lamar, more than any other man, made the existence of the Hayes administration possible, while Conkling was denouncing it everywhere as 'infamous.' . . . All the summer through, Senator Lamar was at home in Mississippi with his dead and dying, while pestilence was busy in all homes. There was absolute peace throughout the State, complete acquiescence in the electoral results on the part of all, blacks as well as whites. The *Tribune* now attempts to drive the Southern people into general hostility to honest money by conspiring with Sherman and Hayes, whom Sherman now openly rules, to create a belief at the North and West of an attempt to revive sectional controversy. Senator Lamar, when interviewed in Ohio, said very truly that if the South found self-government assailed, or attempts made to overthrow order at the South by black Kearneyism, no question of currency could be listened to." The correspondent thought that the attack upon Lamar had a sinister origin in a "deliberate attempt of Jay Gould and his clique to disturb the business of the country, depress values, and weaken the influence of those Southern men who have bravely and loyally supported the keeping of public faith in the public treasury." It was in the nature, too, of a decoy designed to prevent any investigation of the operation of the existing Pacific Railway. The whole country, it was felt, should rise against such attempts to "blacken the best men in the South," and to inflame sectional hatreds.

With the assembling of Congress and the annual message of the President, it was evident that Hayes had, in fact, determined upon a less generous attitude toward the Southern States. This, however, was not entirely unexpected, for as time passed it became increasingly evident that the Republicans would have to prepare ammunition for the coming elections. In his message, Hayes claimed that the Southern Negroes were not given their rights, and that Congress should look particularly into the situation in South Carolina and Louisiana, as well as in certain Congressional districts in other States. That this was a concerted administration move was seen, too, at the first session, when Blaine introduced in the Senate resolutions calling upon the Judiciary Committee to investigate the conduct of elections in any States of the Union with the view to determining if any citizens or classes of citizens were deprived of their rights, and to consider recommending such legislation as would provide "perfect security of the right of suffrage to citizens of the United States in all of the States of the Union." This, of course, was merely a blind which concealed the determination of the radicals again to take charge of the election machinery in the South.

When, on the 11th of December, the resolutions were called up for consideration, Blaine read a carefully prepared and incendiary address in their support, this consisting in the main of a savage attack on the South. He spoke of the "frauds and outrages" which he alleged were perpetrated by the Democracy in that section during the late Congressional elections; he indicted the South on the score of the most dastardly mistreatment of the black race; and he ventured "now and here" to warn the men of that section that the North would ever stand as the defender of the rights of the blacks.

Thurman answered Blaine's denunciation in a dispassionate speech in which he suggested that the resolutions were merely the pretext upon which to hang inflammatory charges against a disarmed and defenseless section. Beneath all of the efforts to arouse sectional animosities for campaign purposes, said Senator Thurman, was to be discerned the purpose of eliminating thirty-five Representatives from the South that had been awarded that section because of the Negro population, for it was this objective which the Senator from Maine had most stressed in his speech. Rightly understood, he thought, the Blaine resolutions were to be considered as nothing more than a partisan political move.

Thurman was still speaking when the Democratic leaders in consultation decided that Lamar must close for the Democracy in an extemporaneous address which would answer any points left untouched.[2] Among other things Lamar confessed "to some regret that a Senator so distinguished, in looking upon this recently dislocated member of this great American empire, instead of regarding it with reference to those great interests that affect the whole country through the long track of coming years, should have concentrated his whole attention upon its relation to parties and party contests; that nothing should have struck the Senator's notice or engaged his thoughts except the connection of that people with the ascendancy and defeat of parties and their influence in federal elections....I cannot but feel the regret that one of such resolute energies, of such tenacious purposes, such daring ambition, and such great abilities should have so narrowed his mind as to give to party what was meant for mankind."

Blaine had contended that Southern representation should not be determined by population as in other sections of the country, but—because so many of the Negroes did not go to the polls—on the basis of votes actually cast. "Mr. President," said Lamar, "every member of the population in those States entitled to vote ought to be counted. You have no right to draw the line between the black and white, and assume that the black man, because he did not vote the Republican ticket, is therefore a suppressed voter. Is it to be assumed that in every Southern State the property and population of the State are in such necessary antagonism that no amount of local misrule can teach them the advantage of their natural alliance? What right has he to assume that whites and blacks are never to vote and act together as citizens of a common country?"

Answering Blaine's cry for reapportionment and the elimination of thirty-five Southern Representatives, Lamar said that such an arrangement, once started, might "operate further than the gentleman thinks. What is the population of the State of Maine? I believe it is 625,000. It has been diminishing within the last twenty years. I cannot now recollect, but perhaps it is 623,000. Vermont, which is also solid, has not more than 350,-000. And yet the State of Maine has as much power in this government with her 600,000 as the State of New York with her 5,000,000." Elaborating this last statement, Lamar declared that he had spoken advisedly, for "a positive equality of States, whatever be their population, in either Chamber where concurrent legislation is needed, is positive affirmative power in the passage of any law....I will speak to the people of the New England States and tell them that in my opinion the direst foe they have got on earth is the Representative or Senator, whether from their own section or any other, that will kindle this fire whose subterranean flames will liquefy the very foundations on which these proud and free commonwealths now rear their aspiring heads." This last statement called Blaine to his feet:

MR. BLAINE: I understand this to be about the residuum of Mr. Lamar's observations: that if I move an inquiry into the unconstitutional representation of Mississippi in the other House, he will move one into the constitutional representation of Maine in this branch.

MR. LAMAR: That will do pretty well for wit and pretty well for the Senator's peculiar species of perversion, but it will not do for the truth; for, sir, I protested that I not only would move no such inquiry, but that I would oppose and fight any such purpose. No, sir: the doctrine that I stated was that if the right of suffrage be invaded anywhere or any constitutional right infringed upon in any quarter or by anybody it shall be maintained and enforced, if necessary, by all the constitutional power of the government.

MR. EDMUNDS: Then we are all at one.

MR. LAMAR: Exactly so, but not upon the ground that States shall be deprived of any of their Representatives, because under the operation of the constitution, either in its original provisions or in its amendments, their political power may be not in exact proportion to their numerical power in this government. And I repeat the warning against this agitation about sectional power based on numbers: I warn Senators that in throwing their net into this troubled sea they may drag to the shore a vase like that of the fisherman in the "Arabian Nights," from which, when the seal was once broken, a demon emerged more potent than his deliverer and threatening his destruction.

The correspondent of the *New Orleans Picayune*, describing the debate, said that "Lamar's expression of regret that Blaine had not brought forward some liberal measure of education for the blacks made Blaine wince and look as if he had forgotten something.... The Republicans will not be willing to let the debate stop at this point.... They will want to mend their hold." A particularly interesting account was contributed to the *Cincinnati Enquirer* by its Washington correspondent who remarked that the floor and galleries of the Senate were packed with those who had come to see their idol, Blaine, make a brilliant display: "It was Blaine's crowd, without a doubt; but it had to see its idol son worsted by Thurman. Lamar finished the good work in an eloquent speech, which took a broad, statesmanlike view of the subject. He regretted that a man of so much ability, so wise statesmanship, and so great ambition had neglected to offer a comprehensive plan for the education of the negro at the South, which would strike at the root of the whole evil, but had prostituted his great powers by contracting himself to the narrow limits of partisanship. It was the most dignified and cutting rebuke that has been heard in the Senate for a long time.... His effort was thoroughly impromptu. In the short though sharp badinage between himself and Blaine he held his own; and his keen retort that one of Blaine's assertions would do very well for wit, but not for truth, made rather a sensation."

The prediction was correct that after their defeat the Republicans would desire to mend their hold and would at the first opportunity return to the fray. Five days later, on the 16th, Blaine reopened the controversy by referring to Lamar's previous speech.[3] In any reapportionment he claimed that the South, or at least six States in that section, stood to lose more than did New England. In the course of his remarks he attempted to distort Lamar's plain statement that the Constitution guaranteed to all States, great and small, the same representation in the upper House, and that any attempt to change this provision would be striking at the very foundation of the government. This strategy called forth an interruption from Lamar:

MR. LAMAR: Mr. President, the Senator from Maine misunderstood the position which I took with reference to the representation of States in this Senate, owing entirely, no doubt, to the want of clearness in my own statement. If I did not misapprehend the Senator from Maine on that occasion, his argument was that, under the amendments which conferred freedom and citizenship and suffrage upon the black race, the South...had obtained a representation in the House of Representatives disproportioned not to her population, but to the actual voters at the polls; and if I did not mistake him, he quoted from the Supreme Court Reports of the United States a decision that the power of Congress did not extend far enough to remedy that disproportion of representation in the other House. If I understood him, he said that that decision which denied the power of Congress to legislate so long as the laws of a State itself did not deny or abridge any of these rights to the negro population—that Congress was powerless to intervene—was indorsed by him as being true to the letter of the constitution which killeth. I understood him to say that the constitution as thus construed was a killing constitution, and that the letter of it stood up as a barrier to the enforcement of the rights conferred upon the colored citizens.

MR. BLAINE: The Senator misunderstood me.

MR. LAMAR: Owing to my own obtuseness, no doubt.

MR. BLAINE: Such might be the ruling of the courts, I said, on the letter which killeth; but I protested against the equity and justice of it. I did not at all admit that that was what in my judgment the constitution was designed to be.

MR. LAMAR: Precisely. He did not admit that it was what it was designed to be; but did I understand the Senator to say that he differs with the court in its construction of the constitution?

MR. BLAINE: I do. That may not be a great shock to the court, but nevertheless I do.

MR. LAMAR: I differ from the Senator. The court will be greatly shocked, but perhaps will survive the attack. [Laughter] Then, sir, I thought that it was not amiss to suggest that if there were remedies in the American people to prevent this disproportionate representation, and if we could so legislate as to make, not population, but actual voters at the polls to be the limit of the representation of a State; and if Congress, or the people by their amending power, should thus interpose to reform the government and to make it a government based entirely upon numbers, not that New England alone, but that the South also might apprehend that you would go further and crumble into ruin our entire system. Sir, when the gentleman tells me that the South is in the same danger that the East is, that the New England States are, he only reiterates a fact that I have attempted to impress upon both sections, and that is that the inviolability of the constitution is the only shield and safeguard of New England, as well as of the South.

Sir, the menace does not come from the weak and impotent South. When this popular movement, this effort to bring this government to the pure principle of democratic absolutism, trampling down in its relentless strides the barriers of the constitution, arises, he will find the power not in the South, but in the mighty West, whose little finger is greater and more potent than the two thighs of South and East united.

This time Blaine suffered a worse defeat than on the first day, and henceforth, in Lamar's presence, he would allow the matter to rest.

A sparkling description of the encounter appeared shortly after in the *Boston Post*, written by the Washington correspondent of that paper: "The debate in the Senate on the Blaine resolution last Monday and Tuesday was one of intense interest and excitement, not so much on account of the subject under discussion as the combatants engaged in it. It called out the best talent of the Senate, and reminded one of a war among the gods....

"In his retort Blaine roused Lamar, of Mississippi, and I suspect that he wished that he hadn't. It was like Mars letting slip the dogs of war. Horse, foot, and dragoons descended upon him. Grape and canister, shot and shell rattled about his devoted head. He attempted resistance, and spent one swift shaft at his adversary, but it was instantly returned, tipped with acrimony; and the champion who had so gallantly withstood the repeated attacks of fresh adversaries apparently concluded that this was a stroke too much for even his Samsonian [sic] strength, and so beat an orderly retreat, or at least attempted no further defense. While watching this conflict I mentally characterized Blaine as the tiger and Lamar as the lion, the closely cropped iron gray whiskers and hair, as well as expression and motion of the former, and the flowing brown hair and beard of the latter, bearing out the similitude."

An interesting epilogue to the debate in question occurred on the floor of the Senate on the following day. In the discussion on the 17th, Blaine, in caustic language, had expressed a disbelief that any considerable numbers of Negroes had anywhere in the South voted the Democratic ticket. "In the 'whiplash' district of Mississippi," he had said among other things, "where they placed in those cotton counties in the delta all the negro population that they could crowd into one district, and four to one—I do not believe I overstate it—as compared with the white men, represented at the time by one of their own race, who, I do not hesitate to say, is a man of commanding ability, considering his advantages and his birth, John R. Lynch, fitted to represent a constituency of white men, naturally and inevitably a favorite of his own color, at the very first election after this miraculous conversion, when the Democracy got hold of the State, he was beaten overwhelmingly by Gen. Chalmers. Of course the negroes saw it in a moment. They had no doubt the moment Gen. Chalmers was put up that it was their duty to support him and to vote against Lynch."

On the day after his second worsting at the hands of Lamar, Blaine recurred to this theme under amusing circumstances, as narrated by the correspondent of the *New York World*: "Lamar's merciless punishment of Blaine yesterday, which delighted even the Republicans, brought forth an amusing incident to-day. Lamar left the Senate early, and Chalmers, a Mississippi member of Congress, strolling in to hear what was going on, the House being abnormally stupid, sat innocently down in Lamar's seat. Blaine espied and recognized him; and, as Chalmers is not more than half the size of Blaine, the valiant Senator evidently thought he had a chance to apply the militant maxim dear to the schoolboy's soul: 'I cannot whip you, but I can make faces at your sister.' He accordingly made a short turn in his speech, and, fixing his eyes ferociously on the un-suspecting Chalmers, began a tremendous tirade on bulldozing in the Vicksburg District, which Chalmers represents. Of course, Chalmers could make no reply, but he is like Shakespeare's Hermia—though little, he is fierce; and sternly facing his foe, he heard him through, and to-night there is music in the air. Chalmers is hard at work packing dynamite for Blaine, and he will explode it in due time on the floor of his own House. The drollest thing of the session was to see the care with which Blaine inspected the Senate Chamber to make sure that Lamar had really gone, before he fell upon the helpless Representative seated in his chair." [4]

During this year, 1879, occurred one of the most depressing incidents of Lamar's life. This came through his old friend Jefferson Davis, with whom he had been closely associated in high official position during the Civil War. Though their paths in life had not, in the post-war years, thrown them into close association, their relationship had been uniformly pleasant. Lamar had always retained a marked loyalty to his old chief and had honored him for the cause of which he had been chosen leader. At all times it had been his custom to come to the defense of Davis when he was abused by his foes. Some-thing of the relationship between the two men is to be seen in a letter written as late as August 28th, 1878, wherein Davis had written to a mutual friend that Lamar "has in my adversity re-mained my firm friend."

Ever since his disregard of the instructions of the State legis-lature, Lamar had been the subject of sporadic attacks by certain Mississippi papers, notably the *Jackson Clarion*, once his own organ. Shocking to Lamar was the notice that ap-peared in that sheet on the 15th of January: "We are gratified to have the opportunity to publish the following letter, written by Hon. Jefferson Davis in reply to inquiries designed to elicit his opinion upon a subject of vital importance. It will be read by his countrymen with the interest which they attach to everything that emanates from its distinguished author." There followed, then, under date of December 14th, 1878, an assault by Davis upon Lamar's position in regard to legislative instructions. "To deny the responsibility of the Representative to his constituency would be to attack the foundation of our political system," wrote Davis. "If the people of a Congressional District were to assemble in mass and instruct their Representative upon any particular question, who will gainsay their right to do so, or his duty to obey?... It has been the practice of the Democracy either to obey instructions or to resign the office held from the people, so that their constituents might, if they so desired, select some one else who would more truly represent them. In opposition to the right of the constituency to instruct, I know of no argument which deserves notice, unless it be that which denies to the people the requisite amount of intelligence....

"So, sir, I end as I began, with the expression of the belief that the coexistence of liberty and power requires the direct responsibility of the Representative to his constituency.... Let me express the conviction that, unless this be maintained, and the virtue and intelligence of the people keep pace with the demand for both in the exercise of the high power they possess, we must look forward to corruption among officials, and anarchy, to be followed by despotism."

Davis' letter received wide publicity. Most papers, as the *New York Herald* of January 25th, interpreted it as a personal attack upon Lamar, and its author was treated to some particularly caustic editorial notice. Apparently the attack, if so it may be interpreted, in no wise injured Lamar, for it was disregarded by his friends, while his enemies (as Mayes remarks) needed no support in their antagonism. "I wish his letter were stronger," wrote Lamar to General Walthall in a note which indicates his reaction. "It does not present that side of the question for half its worth. I hate to see anything trashy come from him." The injury that Lamar suffered was not in his political fortunes, but in that most painful of all experiences—the feeling that he had been betrayed by an old comrade and a friend. This deep personal wound is evident in a letter to his wife, written just after the publication of Davis' attack: "My enemies [he said] have inveigled Mr. Davis into writing an article against my position on the instructions of a State legislature to a Senator.... I am surprised that I *should be surprised* at his letter. But it is not the first time that such a thing has befallen me. When the war closed I knew that there would be men whom we loved and honored who would go over to our oppressors; and yet when —— and —— did so, I could not reconcile myself to it, and could not keep from being overwhelmed with amazement. So when I went into politics I expected to be abandoned and assailed by former friends. But Jeff. Davis! I had no idea that he could do such a thing as to put such a letter into Ethel Barksdale's hands.

"His course does not shake my confidence in men at all. I know but few men in politics who would have done what he has done. To strike a man who grew up a young man under him, his friend, admirer, and unwavering supporter! If he thought I was going wrong, why did he not write to me and advise me not to carry my opposition to the extent of disregarding the instructions of the legislature? But not a word of counsel or suggestion did he give me while the question was open. It was after I had acted that he struck me. I can bear it." [5]

With the recent publication of Davis' private correspondence, new light has been thrown upon this disheartening incident. The letter to Davis from Ethelbert Barksdale, editor of the *Clarion*, shows that he gave no intimation that the subject had any bearing upon Lamar's course in the Senate.[6] Nevertheless, Mr. Davis must have understood, in view of the wide publicity given the refusal to obey instructions, that what he wrote would, in effect, represent an assault upon Lamar. However, there is reputable evidence that he was somewhat dismayed at the many criticisms which his communication evoked, and that he felt that Barksdale had used his letter in an unfitting manner, for in his correspondence appears a letter from the former the import of which seems to be summed up in the simple admission that he, Davis, had written "without knowledge of all the attending circumstances." [7] Evidently he had learned his lesson, for some time later—when Lamar alone among Southern Senators had lent his voice in favor of allowing ex-President Grant the pension of a regularly retired army officer—we find Barksdale writing Davis without success (so far as it can be determined) for a communication in opposition to the stand Lamar was taking. [8]

That Lamar would never allow Jefferson Davis to be abused in his presence has already been remarked upon. A few days after the former's gratuitous assault in the *Clarion* letter, he was again called upon to speak in defense of the man who had so lately traduced him. On the 1st of March, when the Senate had before it a resolution to extend the pension act that applied to the soldiers of the War of 1812 in such a manner that the same benefits would prevail in regard to the veterans of the War with Mexico, Senator Hoar presented the following amendment:—"*Provided further*, That no pension shall ever be paid under this act to Jefferson Davis, the late President of the so-called Confederacy." In the angry debate which followed, Lamar took no part until Hoar remarked that "the Senator from Arkansas [Mr. Garland] alluded to the courage which this gentleman had shown in battle, and I do not deny it. Two of the bravest officers of our Revolutionary War were Aaron Burr and Benedict Arnold." As Lamar rose to his feet the hall of the Senate became painfully still:

Mr. LAMAR: It is with extreme reluctance that I rise to say a word upon this subject. I must confess my surprise and regret that the Senator from Massachusetts should have wantonly, without provocation, flung this insult——

THE PRESIDING OFFICER (MR. EDMUNDS in the chair): The Senator from Mississippi is out of order. He cannot impute to any Senator either wantonness or insult.

Mr. LAMAR: I stand corrected. I suppose it is in perfect order for certain Senators to insult other Senators, but they cannot be characterized by those who receive the blow.

THE PRESIDING OFFICER : The observations of the Senator from Mississippi, in the opinion of the Chair, are not in order.

MR. LAMAR : The observations of the Senator from Mississippi, in his own opinion, are not only in order, but perfectly and absolutely true.

THE PRESIDING OFFICER : The Senator from Mississippi will take his seat until the question of order is decided.

MR. LAMAR : Yes, sir.

．　　．　　．　　．　　．　　．　　．　　．　　．

THE PRESIDING OFFICER : The judgment of the chair is reversed, and the Senate decides that the words uttered by the Senator from Mississippi are in order, and the Senator from Mississippi will proceed.

MR. LAMAR : Now, Mr. President, having been decided by my associates to have been in order, in the language I used, I desire to say that, if it is at all offensive or unacceptable to any member of this Senate, the language is withdrawn ; for it is not my purpose to offend or stab the sensibilities of any of my associates on this floor. But what I meant by that remark was this : Jefferson Davis stands in precisely the position that I stand in, that every Southern man who believed in the right of a State to secede stands.

MR. HOAR : Will the Senator from Mississippi permit me to assure him——

THE PRESIDING OFFICER : The Senator from Massachusetts will address the Chair. Does the Senator from Mississippi yield to the Senator from Massachusetts ?

MR. LAMAR : O yes.

MR. HOAR : Will the Senator from Mississippi permit me to assure him and other Senators on this floor who stand like him that, in making the motion which I made, I did not conceive that any of them stood in the same position in which I supposed Mr. Davis to stand. I should not have moved to except the gentleman from Mississippi from the pension roll.

MR. LAMAR : The only difference between myself and Jefferson Davis is that his exalted character, his preëminent talents, his well-established reputation as a statesman, as a patriot, and as a soldier, enabled him to take the lead in the cause to which I consecrated myself and to which every fiber of my heart responded. There was no distinction between insult to him and the Southern people, except that he was their chosen leader, and they his enthusiastic followers; and there has been no difference since.

Jefferson Davis, since the war, has never counseled insurrection against the authority of this government. Not one word has he uttered inconsistent with the greatness and glory of this American Republic. The Senator from Massachusetts can point to no utterance of Jefferson Davis which bids the people of the South to cherish animosities and hostilities to this Union, nor does he cherish them himself.

The Senator—it pains me to say it—not only introduced this amendment, but he coupled that honored name with treason; for, sir, he is honored among the Southern people. He did only what they sought to do; he was simply chosen to lead them in a cause which we all cherished; and his name will continue to be honored for his participation in that great movement which inspired an entire people, the people who were animated by motives as sacred and noble as ever inspired the breast of a Hampden or a Washington. *I say this as a Union man to-day*. The people of the South drank their inspiration from the fountain of devotion to liberty and to constitutional government. We believed that we were fighting for it, and the Senator cannot put his finger upon one distinction between the people of the South and the man whom the Senator has to-day selected for dishonor as the representative of the South.

Now, sir, I do not wish to make any remarks here that will engender any excitement or discussion; but I say that the Senator from Massachusetts connected that name with treason. We all know that the results of this war have attached to the people of the South the technical crime of rebellion, and we submit to it; but that was not the sense in which the gentleman used that term as applied to Mr. Davis. He intended to affix (I will not say that he intended, but the inevitable effect of it was to affix) upon this aged man, this man broken in fortune, suffering from bereavement, an epithet of odium, an imputation of moral turpitude.

Sir, it required no courage to do that; it required no magnanimity to do it; it required no courtesy. It only required hate, bitter, malignant, sectional feeling, and a sense of personal impunity. *The gentleman, I believe, takes rank among Christian statesmen. He might have learned a better lesson even from the pages of mythol-*

ogy. When Prometheus was bound to the rock, it was not an eagle, it was a vulture, that buried his beak in the tortured vitals of the victim.[9]

The effect of Lamar's rebuke to Hoar has been well described by Senator Ingalls, of Kansas, one of the South's bitterest critics: "During his eulogy and exculpation of Jefferson Davis the Northern senators sat in silence; the boldness of the performance was paralyzing; such an emergency had not been anticipated. No one was ready. The passionate and excited spectators in the galleries wondered why no champion of the North took up the glove."[10]

This episode was an immediate sensation in the press, and the debate was widely reproduced. "Lamar rose," said one much quoted news-letter. "There was a dead silence as he began to speak. Senators on both sides leaned forward expectantly. He had left his seat in the other row of desks, and taken his stand midway on the Democratic side in the front row, with Harris, of Tennessee, on one side and Wallace of Pennsylvania, on the other.... The first sentence he uttered was punctuated by the sharp quick rap of the President's gavel.... The roll was called, and by a large majority the decision of the Chair was reversed. ...There was a faint effort at applause in the galleries; but Lamar threw up his hands deprecatingly, and the President's gavel came down with a quick, sharp sound, and perfect stillness reigned. With an effort at self-restraint, and slowly and deliberately, Lamar began again. Senator Blaine, who of all men is certainly a competent critic, says he never saw a man display more tact than Lamar, under the trying circumstances in which he was placed.... In speaking of the motives that inspired Hoar's motion, Lamar used a singularly appropriate figure of speech.... As he said, 'it was not an eagle that plucked at his vitals,' the arms were thrown up, and the curving swoop of the king of birds was described in the gesture; and as he hissed out, 'it was a vulture!' the right arm straightened out, and the index finger pointed at Hoar. It was as fine and effective a piece of oratory as I have ever witnessed. Hoar felt the sting."[11]

Blaine, with a fellow feeling for Hoar that is entirely understandable, entered the debate at this point and followed his usual procedure of changing the subject by injecting a new and incendiary element. Lamar had spoken of the resolution of Hoar as being "intolerant." Blaine chose to twist his words, and charged Lamar with saying that the United States Government had been intolerant, after the war, toward the Southern people. Lamar killed this forensic trick in a very few words: "I was speaking of the intolerance involved in the legislation now proposed. But, sir, I have no disguises whatever on this subject. I do not wish to go back now and discuss the policy of the reconstruction laws nor the general policy of the Republican party. I have in the other House repeatedly given my views very fully upon each of these topics. I will say that a policy which emancipated the servile class of the South and disfranchised the Southern people, excluding them from all participation in the government maintained by force over them, was rank intolerance. I say, sir, that a harder and more ungracious system of legislation could not be devised than thus to disfranchise a whole people and put them under the domination of their slaves. I assert that it was a policy more severe in its punishment and more terrible in its consequences than if a general confiscation had been inflicted upon that people. It not only subjected them to that humiliation which is the greatest of all tortures to a proud and manly race, but it held them down by force while they were being robbed and plundered by their dishonest officers." He was careful, however, to point out that the great masses of the people of the North were not responsible for the sufferings that had been inflicted upon the prostrate South. "Many Republicans in this Senate," he continued, "and many in the other House have been always willing to remove the political disabilities imposed upon the Southern people by the proscriptive section of the fourteenth amendment, although they have inexorably required a formal petition in every instance to be made by the party relieved. I have always considered this action by Republicans, with their views in relation to the war, as magnanimous. I have felt so in my own case.

I have, therefore, no hesitation in saying that there has been in this respect much of an imposing character in the action of the victorious section in its treatment of the section that was conquered. The very fact that representatives of a people who were in insurrection against the national authority—for this is the status to which the fortunes of war have assigned us in history—are now participating in the exercise of the national authority is a great, imposing, and inspiring spectacle of the benignant power of free institutions, and it gives me pleasure to express my admiration of it."

Mr. Davis greatly appreciated Lamar's defense. "Please accept my thanks for your defense of me against the petty malignity of Hoar, Blaine, and others," he said in a letter of March 15th. "I am truly thankful for the kindness of the other Senators who spoke in my behalf; but it was needful, for my entire satisfaction, that Mississippi's Senator should be heard in my vindication." [12]

Despite the bitterness of this clash, Lamar and Hoar always held each other in high respect. "He was the last person from whom I should have expected an expression of compliment, or even of kindness in those days," the latter was to write in commenting upon the controversy. "Yet when the question of my reëlection was pending in 1883 and the correspondent of a newspaper which was among my most unrelenting and unscrupulous opponents thought he might get some material which would help him in his attacks, called upon Mr. Lamar in the Democratic cloak room, and asked him what he thought of me, Mr. Lamar replied in language...which was inspired...by his indignation at the attempt to use him for such a purpose.... The more I knew of him, the more satisfied I became of his patriotism, of his profound and far-sighted wisdom, of the deep fountain of tenderness in his affectionate and simple heart, and of his brave and chivalrous quality of soul. I was more than once indebted to him for very great kindnesses, under circumstances when I do not think he supposed it would ever come to my knowledge." [13]

In this same month (March, 1879), in the *North American*

Review, appeared a symposium on the question: "Ought the Negro to be Disfranchised? Ought he to have been Enfranchised?" Included were articles by Blaine, Lamar, Wendell Phillips, Alexander Stephens, Garfield, Hampton, Montgomery Blair, and Hendricks. Lamar's contribution is chiefly interesting because of its temperate and liberal outlook. It is a tribute to the breadth and penetration of his thought that this article can be read at the present time with the feeling that it could have been written by an enlightened social philosopher of the nineteen-thirties.

It is unlikely that anything that Grant did during his terms as President created such a lasting distrust of his character and leadership as his use of the federal troops to intimidate the Florida, Louisiana, and South Carolina canvassing boards in the election controversy of 1876, and to coerce Southern elections at other times. In the second session of the Forty-fourth Congress, measures had been introduced forbidding the use of the army and the navy to support the claims of any candidate or any State government until he or it had been duly recognized by Congress; but with the House controlled by the Democracy and the Senate not yet surrendered by the Republicans, no agreement could be reached. The leaders of the Democratic party, however, particularly those from the South, were determined upon the passage of such measures as would effectively insure that no President would hereafter assume such unwarranted and dictatorial powers as Grant had exercised in the Hayes-Tilden controversy. Consequently, the House flatly refused to make any appropriation for the War Department unless the legislation carried the express provision that none of the money voted would be used in patrolling the polls. As a consequence, the Forty-fourth Congress adjourned without providing money for that department and from July to August, 1877, the army was without lawful appropriations. Consequently, President Hayes called an extraordinary session of the Forty-fifth Congress. Under the wise leadership of Abram S. Hewitt, former Chairman of the Democratic National Committee, the Army Bill was passed without the attachment of the "rider" that had previously been insisted upon by the Democrats. In the second session of this Congress, however, the Democracy succeeded in securing a law which forbade the use of the army in the capacity of a *posse comitatus* except as expressly provided by the Constitution or by an act of Congress.

At the Democratic caucus held at the beginning of the third session of the Forty-fifth Congress, that of 1878-79, the Democrats determined to insist upon the unequivocal repeal of the statute under the provisions of which troops had been used in the South, ostensibly to preserve order at the polls, but in reality to enable the Republicans to control the elections. This provision the House attached to the Army Bill for that year, and when the Senate failed to agree, the President found it necessary again to call an extraordinary session, this time of the Forty-sixth Congress which assembled on the 18th of March, 1879, for the purpose of making an appropriation for the army. After a protracted debate, the Army Bill, the sixth section of which provided that troops might not be used "to keep the peace at the polls," received the assent of both Houses. Five days later, on April 30th, the President—for various reasons which he stated—returned it with a veto. However, on the 20th of June, House Resolution No. 2175, bearing upon the abuses in the use of the federal militia, passed both Houses and, having received the approval of the President, became a law. The heart of the measure was embodied in a clause to the effect "that no money appropriated by the act was to be expended in using the army as a police force to keep the peace at the polls at any election held within any State."

Lamar had ardently favored some such legislation, but he had felt that the Democrats were making a tactical error in pushing such measures by attaching them as riders to the various appropriation bills. However, since the matter had been determined in caucus, and since he favored the ends sought in the proposed legislation (and the principle involved, if not the method) he had voted with his party. The *Jackson Clarion*, at this time, as we have seen, unfavorably disposed toward Lamar, nevertheless well stated his position in an editorial of the issue of May 7th: "Since the question has been reduced to this complexion, we are strengthened in the opinion heretofore intimated that the proposition originally supported by Senators Bayard, Morgan, Lamar, Hill, Coke, Maxey, and others, to introduce separate appropriation and repealing bills, would have been preferable. It would not have admitted of the insane cry of 'starving the government,' and of 'revolution' which the Republican agitators have raised with damaging prospects to the Democracy in the Presidential election."

In all of these Senatorial debates, Senator Conkling, of New York, had been a conspicuous and arrogant figure and had shown more than the usual amount of that swagger and contemptuousness toward his colleagues that, despite his acknowledged ability, had made him extremely unpopular even within his own party. "If there are any two men in the country whose opposition and hatred are a certificate of good character and sound statesmanship," President Hayes entered in his diary at this time, "they are Conkling and [Ben] Butler. I enjoy the satisfaction of being fully endorsed by the hatred and opposition of both of these men." [14] Lamar, who had a notable reputation for the closeness and number of his Senatorial friendships which disregarded all boundaries of party or section, had some two years before broken off all personal relations with Conkling, who, Lamar thought, had in the course of a personal controversy treated Senator Gordon, of Georgia, badly. At the same time, Lamar professed admiration for the undoubted abilities of the other man, and when a friend had taken occasion to repeat certain words of Conkling relative to Lamar, the latter had refused to hear, on the grounds that Conkling had been treated shamefully by reason of a breach of confidence in respect to his privately expressed sentiments. To General Walthall during this same period Lamar had said that "Conkling is going to jump on me, and I wish he'd keep off. My conservative speeches and position have irritated him, and he will try to make me lose my temper and say something

349

foolish and rash. I've a dozen things laid away for him, but I'm afraid he won't come at me any of those ways." [15]

He was not mistaken in his belief that Conkling would "come at him," as indeed occurred on the occasion of the second debate of the extra session on the Army Bill. It was on the 18th of June, while the Democratic majority was pressing the acceptance of the clause prohibiting the expenditure of any of the army appropriation for the alleged purpose of keeping peace at the polls, and the Republicans, on the other hand, were filibustering to the limit of their endurance. Early in the day, before the debate on the Army Bill had begun, Lamar called up for consideration the bill to create a Mississippi River Commission, this reported from a committee of which he was chairman. The morning was spent upon consideration of the measure in question, and finally the hour arrived for which the consideration of the Army Bill had been set. Lamar asked unanimous consent for an extension of twenty minutes in order that the vote on the Mississippi River Bill, in which he was naturally tremendously interested, could be taken. After some discussion, of relatively little importance, this was granted.

At the end of the twenty minutes, the Army Bill was called for consideration and then began a prolonged siege of filibustering on the part of the Republicans. The session did not adjourn until noon of the following day, for the opponents of the measure fictitiously absented themselves and used every parliamentary means to obstruct action. In the early morning hours a controversy broke out between Senators Saulsbury and Blaine, in which the Democrat accused the latter of willfully obstructing needed legislation. This brought into the argument Senator Conkling who began speaking in his most imperious and offensive manner. He charged his opponents with every kind of bad faith, calling names and dealing in personalities, mentioning Lamar first of all and saying that when the twenty minutes extension on the Mississippi River Bill was granted the Democrats had made certain promises as to the order of business, which, Conkling asserted, had been subse-

SENATOR LUCIUS Q. C. LAMAR

quently violated. "I have endeavored," he said finally, "to show this proud and domineering majority—determined apparently to ride roughshod over the rights of the minority—that they cannot and they should not do it. But I am ready to be deemed responsible in advance for the assurance that while I remain a member of this body, and, at all events, until we have a previous question, no minority shall be gagged down or throttled or insulted by such a proceeding as this. *I say, Mr. President (and I measure my expression), that it was an act not only insulting, but an act of bad faith.* I mean that."

Mr. Lamar (interrupting Mr. Conkling) : Mr. President,... I learn for the first time that an impression exists on the mind of any Senator on this floor that further time was to be extended for the discussion of the bill,... based upon any proceedings or upon occurrences connected with the measure that I had the honor of reporting this morning, and asked unanimous consent to consider and have passed. I am not aware of anything that occurred which would produce such an impression....

I repeat, sir, that if I had imagined that any Senator had any such expectation from anything that occurred in the incidents of that proceeding, it would have been my pleasure to have made that motion. In fact, sir, I was not here. I was not aware of the fact that the Senator from Wisconsin had risen for the purpose of addressing the Senate. I came in at a later stage of these proceedings. With reference to the charge of bad faith that the Senator from New York has intimated toward those of us who have been engaged in opposing these motions to adjourn, I have only to say that if I am not superior to such attacks from such a source I have lived in vain. It is not my habit to indulge in personalities ; but I desire to say here to the Senator that in intimating anything inconsistent, as he has done, with perfect good faith, I pronounce his statement a falsehood, which I repel with all the unmitigated contempt that I feel for the author if it.

Mr. Conkling : Mr. President, I was diverted during the commencement of a remark, the culmination of which I heard from the member from Mississippi. If I understood him aright, he intended to impute, and did, in plain and unparliamentary language, impute, to me an intentional misstatement. The Senator does not disclaim that.

Mr. Lamar: I will state what I intended, so that there may be no mistake——

The Presiding Officer: The Senator from New York has the floor. Does he yield to the Senator from Mississippi?

Mr. Conkling: And I am willing to respond to the Chair. I shall respond to the Chair in due time. Whether I am willing to respond to the member from Mississippi depends entirely upon what that member intends to say, and what he did say. For the time being, I do not choose to hold any communication with him. The Chair understands me now; I will proceed.

I understood the Senator from Mississippi to state in plain and unparliamentary language that the statement of mine to which he referred was a falsehood, if I caught his word aright. Mr. President, this not being the place to measure with any man the capacity to violate decency, to violate the rules of the Senate, or to commit any of the improprieties of life, I have only to say that if the Senator—the member from Mississippi—did impute or intended to impute to me a falsehood, nothing except the fact that this is the Senate would prevent my denouncing him as a blackguard and a coward. [Applause in the galleries.] Let me be more specific, Mr. President. Should the member from Mississippi, except in the presence of the Senate, charge me, by intimation or otherwise, with falsehood, I would denounce him as a blackguard, as a coward, and a liar; and, understanding what he said as I have, the rules and the proprieties of the Senate are the only restraint upon me.

I do not think I need to say anything else, Mr. President.

Mr. Lamar: *Mr. President, I have only to say that the Senator from New York understood me correctly. I did mean to say just precisely the words, and all that they imported. I beg pardon of the Senate for the unparliamentary language. It was very harsh; it was very severe; it was such as no good man would deserve, and no brave man would wear.* [Applause on the floor and in the galleries.]

The Presiding Officer: The Senate must be in order, and there can be no cheering upon the Senate floor.

Mr. Conkling: What is the question before the Senate, Mr. President? [16]

This episode created a sensation, with the press viewing it from widely different angles, but almost without exception feeling that Conkling had received an unprecedented and richly deserved humiliation. "That Conkling's bearing was that of a bully suddenly brought to taw no Senator present doubts or questions," commented Donn Piatt in the *Washington Capital.* "In the dead silence that followed Lamar's subtle and fatal stab Conkling was to the last degree unnerved and confused. His assumed nonchalance of repose and swagger of acting both deserted him; and looking wildly about him, he stammered, hesitated, and lost control of both thought and voice. This was evident not only from his vulgar retort, after being pronounced a liar, of 'you're another!' but in committing himself to a line that he has not since had the courage to carry out. He served notice on Lamar that some other time and at some other place he would attend to the insult. We all know what this means. It is either a duel under the code or an assault on the street, and there is no getting away from the cruel conclusion: either Conkling did not know what he was saying, or he lacked the nerve to carry out what he had said.

"The point in the whole affair, however, is the fact that the terrible thrust came from the coolest, politest, and most self-controlled member of the Senate. Lamar, of Mississippi, has been noted for his courteous bearing in both public and private life.... All who know him united in saying that his character and life gave more point to his assault than the deadly words in which it was uttered. Exit Conkling."

Said the correspondent of the *New York Star:* "Mr. Blaine hugely enjoyed the spectacle of Lamar's torture of Conkling and the latter's towering rage in the Senate last Wednesday. While the Maine Senator was descending the steps of the capitol, shortly after the affair, he encountered one of the members of the House from Massachusetts, who questioned him in relation to it.

"'O, it was exceedingly rich!' exclaimed Blaine; 'I don't think I ever saw Conkling's wattles quite so red.'"

Even such an arch Republican and radical organ as the *Chicago Tribune* expressed little sympathy with Conkling, whose "extraordinary statements startled the Senate," it reported.

"There was breathless silence in the chamber when Lamar arose and remarked: 'I have only to say that the Senator from New York understood me correctly. I beg pardon of the Senate for the unparliamentary language. It was very harsh; it was very severe; it was such as no good man would deserve and no brave man would wear.'

"The silence that followed was broken by a sharp clap of the hands from Vance, of North Carolina, who had seated himself near Lamar, and was noticed to make suggestions to him. The excitement overcame the temporary presiding officer (Cockrell, of Missouri), who seemed to try to regain his equanimity by raps of the gavel. This ended at 1 o'clock A.M. The Democratic Senators immediately commenced telegraphing to all their paired colleagues to return.

"On the floor Senators are talking of nothing else. Southern Senators unanimously sustain Lamar, and have overwhelmed him with congratulations. One Senator, who is Lamar's most intimate friend, and who, in the event of a challenge, expects to act as his second, says: 'I don't think that Conkling will fight. I don't regard him as a man of courage. Lamar will only be delighted to have Conkling challenge him. Of course, everything rests with Conkling, as he is the insulted party. Of one thing you may be assured: no effort will be made to fix up the matter, as was the case when Conkling had his difficulty with Gordon. There is no power on earth that will induce Lamar to withdraw his words.'...

"On the Republican side great regret is expressed; but all agree that Lamar was the aggressor, and made his attack on Conkling without requisite provocation. No idea is entertained by the Republicans that Conkling will send a challenge, but some think it possible that he may call Lamar to account at the first opportunity outside the Senate Chamber. The Republicans were too much startled to call Lamar to order."

No better description of Lamar's reply to Conkling has survived than that of Senator Ingalls: "For the first time in the six years that I had known him, Conkling was, figuratively speaking, 'knocked out.' Accustomed to obsequious adulation which had swollen to the point of tumefaction, his habitual attitude was that of supercilious disdain. That this Alcibiades of Republicanism should be called a liar and denounced as an object of unmitigated contempt in the forum of his most imposing triumphs, before crowded galleries and by a 'Confederate Brigadier,' was an indignity that seemed incredible. Had a dynamite bomb exploded in the gangway of the brilliantly lighted chamber, the consternation could hardly have been more bewildering.

"Instantaneous silence fell. The gasping spectators held their breath. Mr. Conkling acted like one stunned. He became pallid and then flushed again. His disconcertion was extreme. He hesitated and floundered pitiably. He pretended at first not to have heard the insult, and asked Lamar, in effect, to repeat it. . . .

"Mr. Conkling never seemed quite the same afterward. His prestige was gone. His enemies—and they were many—exulted in his discomfiture. Two years later he resigned his seat in the Senate, and his life afterward was a prolonged monologue of despair." [17]

Lamar's own reaction to the incident is seen in a letter, dated the 20th, to his old friend, General Walthall: "Conkling has been building up this trouble for some time," he wrote. "He has noticed my silence—a disciplined silence—through all the extra session. He knows that it is giving me some moral power, which may be of some use hereafter for the South, and he had determined to make me take part in the silly and unwise discussions that our party has been carrying on. My success in the morning, in getting the Mississippi River Bill through by an unprecedented majority, a large number of Eastern men voting for it (avowedly on my account), stung him very deeply. It was all a lie about my appealing *to him*, except so far as asking unanimous consent made it an application to each Senator. I have not spoken to him, privately or personally, for two years. I have no purpose of making any call upon him. The Southern Senators were delighted at the affair, and showed their exultation too much. There was a general coming in, yes-

355

terday morning, of Southern Representatives to see me and congratulate me...for once in my life I feel that I am *right*, even in the most extreme alternative." [18]

For days after the passage-at-arms with Conkling, Lamar's mail was filled with letters, and he received an almost unbelievable number of telegrams. The great body of the communications was in commendation, many people begging that in case of a duel, they be allowed to act as his second. These messages came from all sections of the nation, but chiefly from the South where his course was approved, apparently without dissent. Lamar's final retort was "an answer perfect in its temper, tone, and tact," observed the *New Orleans Daily Democrat* of June 22nd. "It was final, absolute, conclusive. The preparation of a lifetime could not improve on it. It has all the Toledo's keen glitter and elastic swiftness, with the ice-brook's temper. Mr. Conkling was silent, of course. The thrust was through the heart. The only sound heard was that of the shell against his breast, as the deadly blade was driven home."

"No gentleman would have spoken of a great political party, his superiors in numbers and influence, as 'sneaks and frauds,'" continues the same editorial. "None but a man of low instincts and mean habits of thought would have charged upon a rival advocating a cause of transcendent importance to his people that he was acting in bad faith. If he did not lie when he asked what the member said, implying that he did not hear or understand him, his duty was to have waited for Mr. Lamar's answer....Like the bully that he is, he turned his back upon his man and broke out into a wild tirade of abuse, in language such as only vile men use. From the safe security of his place in the Senate he vapored about what he would say or do if not restrained by a sense of decency which he utterly outraged.

"And Mr. Conkling contents himself, like Horace's bargeman, with a *tu quoque*."

The *Louisville Courier-Journal* regretted the "angry passage," and thought that "reading the naked report of the proceedings, both Senators appear to have been hasty." Nevertheless, "Mr.

Conkling had made an insulting general assertion in coarse words. They touched Mr. Lamar more nearly than any one else....He retorted impulsively: 'If the gentleman says that I acted in bad faith, he says what is untrue.' Mr. Conkling might very well have explained or qualified his offensive language. Instead of doing so, he advanced in a menacing way, and flowered out in a tirade of vulgar epithets, worthy only of a stable yard or a fish market. Mr. Lamar, by this time quite himself, answered with perfect decorum that he had applied to Mr. Conkling that 'which no good man deserves and no brave man will wear.'"

No one, says this editorial, could understand the "true inwardness of the occurrence" who did not understand that nothing short of the insolence and bullying of Conkling could have made Lamar speak so caustically: "No man in America has a sweeter, gentler, more womanish nature than Lamar. He is a dreamer, a poet. His life has been passed among books. Just enough of active, practical experience as a soldier and as a traveler he has had to give him somewhat of the knowledge of a politician and a man of the world...; he is a statesman and a philosopher, a man of profound convictions, and owes his place in popular esteem to his genius, sustained by his physical and moral courage of so high an order that his enemies respect him. All men who know him at all know him to be incapable of premeditated discourtesy or offense. Known to be a fearless man, he never had a difficulty or altercation in his life; and nothing short of the intolerable insolence of Mr. Conkling could have stung him into the kind of rejoinder which he made."

Many Republicans, who in the heat of the moment had tended to side with Conkling, decided, in retrospect, that he had gotten from Lamar just the chastisement that he deserved. The Washington correspondent of the *St. Louis Globe-Democrat*, in his "Special" of June 23rd, reported it "evident from the conversation of the Republican Senators that they are not entirely in sympathy with Mr. Conkling. Several of them, recounting some of the former controversies of a similar character in which the Senator from New York has been a conspicuous and an aggressive party, recalled the time of his parliamentary tilt with Blaine on April 30th, 1866," when the two men, in vitriolic attacks upon each other, developed an open breach that was never healed.

There is no evidence that Lamar in the least lost prestige or influence among his senatorial colleagues of either party. On the other hand, the acclaim that he received in Mississippi was phenomenal. Already he was commonly recognized as the greatest living statesman from the South; from henceforth he was destined to grow into a character almost legendary for the regard in which he was held in his own State. "You will remember," wrote S. A. Jonas on July 1st, "that I assured you on the night—or rather morning—of that memorable encounter with the burly braggart of New York that its effect would be to crystallize public sentiment in our beloved State and rally your people in solid phalanx to you; but I had no conception of the strength of the sentiment until I reached home, and no idea that the enthusiasms which I believed would pervade the hearts of all political allies would be shared alike by friends and foes in politics; but so I found it. Greenbackers and Republicans were as ready as Democrats to indorse your action; and the timely rebuke administered to the man who 'measured his words' when he sought to insult, but paused to *measure his antagonist* when the insult was hurled back compounded beyond the forbearance of any brave man, was regarded as a vindication of Mississippi upon the floor of the Senate, and, as such, entitling you to the thanks of Mississippians without regard to race, color, or political affiliation." [19]

Lamar was not the man to feed his anger, once the incident had passed, and he made no attempt to capitalize the situation. Never an admirer of Conkling, he always extended to him the same courtesies that he paid to the other members of the Senate, and gave him full credit for his great abilities. The controversy had placed the New York Senator in a bad light before his constituency and before the nation at large, and it represented a major step in his declining prestige which led to his retirement from public life two years later. "Mr. Conkling does not need to hold official place to wield vast influence in the United States," Lamar was quoted in 1881 as saying to a correspondent of the *Vicksburg Herald*. "He towers above a vast majority of office holders; and a vast number of the American people have confidence in his ability, his statesmanship, and his incorruptibility. As the people esteemed and honored Clay, Calhoun, and Webster in their day, and as they honor Seymour now, they honor Conkling. This, of course, is not spoken in any party sense. Mr. Conkling is a great orator, a bold leader; and any man in his own party or the opposition who does not take him into the account in making up the political calculation will be largely at fault....It is a mistake to imagine that a man of such power over men must hold a Senatorial position to accomplish great political purposes." And Conkling, despite his and Lamar's incompatibility, held the latter in high regard. "The two great men of the Democracy are Thurman and Lamar," he said in an interview at the time when speculation was rife as to the composition of Cleveland's first Cabinet.[20]

It is indeed paradoxical that a man of Lamar's gentleness and broad sympathies should have been, upon occasion, the master of wit and invective as corrosive as any that American history records, with the possible exception of that of John Randolph of Roanoke. Henry Watterson, who admired him exceedingly, records an interesting episode in which Bob Toombs was involved. Toombs had shortly before taken occasion when in Washington to pay a visit to President Grant (whom, incidentally, he had rendered temporarily inarticulate by his casual remark that he never visited a foreign country without paying his respects to its ruler). "Not long after this at the hospitable board of a Confederate general, then an American senator," said Watterson, "Toombs began to prod Lamar about his speech in the House upon the occasion of the death of Charles Sumner. Lamar was not quick to quarrel, though when aroused a man of devilish temper and courage. The subject had become distasteful to him. He was growing obviously restive under Toombs's banter. The ladies of the household, apprehending what was coming, left the table.

"Then Lamar broke forth. He put Toombs's visit to Grant, 'crawling at the seat of power,' against his eulogy of a dead enemy. I have never heard such a scoring from one man to another. It was magisterial in its dignity, deadly in its diction. Nothing short of a duel could have settled it in the olden time." [21]

That Marse Henry was not merely drawing upon his imagination for the episode is proven by the following denial, published in the Washington press and copied throughout the country: "A report that the Hon. Robert Toombs of Georgia, and Hon. L. Q. C. Lamar of Mississippi, had a personal altercation at a dinner given in Washington by General Gordon recently, growing out of Mr. Toombs's criticism of Mr. Lamar's eulogy of Sumner, is authoritatively denied. They are intimate personal friends and were never friendlier than on the occasion referred to, though the public need not be told that the strong national sentiments in Mr. Lamar's eulogy are utterly repugnant to the erratic Toombs, who boasts that he is the great 'rebel,' as if there were some special merit in the fact. Toombs is wild and windy. His vagaries create no sensation in the South, and we hope nobody North will sit up o' nights to guard against attempts on his part to establish an empire. It is only between 'the sherry and the champagne' that such visions are seen." [22] Certainly there would have been no occasion for this obviously inspired notice had no such incident occurred. Let it be said, however, that the affair had no lasting influence upon the warm friendship which, for fifty years before and after, existed between Toombs and Lamar.

That Lamar, in the parlance of the time, was a "fighting man" it is useless to deny. "Reared in a community where, and at a period when, every person who aspired to be regarded as a 'man' was expected to be prepared to fight on just provocation; when and where the only questions were whether the provocation was adequate and the fight made was manly, he never rid himself of the inclination to belligerency," says his son-in-law, Edward Mayes, "nor ever sought to do so."[23] He was, however, in no sense a bully or a braggart, and never boasted of "what he would do." Instinctively men knew that here was an individual who would not stand for aggression and who, if aroused, would be fierce in his anger. Never, though, did he carry a deadly weapon except upon certain occasions when he had been threatened with an attack.

It has been seen that Lamar acquired great fame in Washington as a *raconteur*. Some of his best stories were humorous accounts of the "scrimmages" of his youth, in Georgia and Mississippi, particularly those in which he was worsted. "No man could have been more indignant and outraged than I was at the ruffianly assault made upon you; and had I been present, I would have knocked that fellow down," he wrote on the 15th of May to a prominent friend who had been assaulted. "I may do it yet if he struts and talks around me any. But... the truth is, my dear ——, my own dear bought experience in the varying fortunes of such scrimmages has perhaps caused me to look upon them in a different light, and to think that you attach too much importance to it. Frank Nelms knocked me down in the courthouse in Covington, Georgia, and I have to this day a vivid recollection of the stunning effect. Frank was a big, six-foot country fellow, whose long arm, when it fell upon me, made me think of an elephant's snout. Three days after that, I had it over again in Dick Burns' grocery; was knocked down by Newt. Skelton, and was beaten until I think I should have 'hollered' if my Democratic friends had not 'took him off.' The next night (in the dark) in the courthouse square I whipped Newt. like a sack....

"A short time before I was elected to Congress (since the war) I had the misfortune to have to knock down the United States Marshal and dislocate his jaw right in the presence of the court. So you see these affairs will happen to the most prudent. My dear friend, you must not be morbid. Avoid brooding over such things. Your friends admire you and love you as much as ever."[24]

Never in his exciting and dramatic life did Lamar fight a

duel, though he was not, theoretically, opposed to the practice. He had accepted and lived by the "code of honor" to its minutest detail, and from time to time had acted as a referee in such affairs. In every such case he had managed to settle the issues involved and prevent a fight. Always, however, he refused to act as a "second." He never attempted to force upon others an acceptance of the code, and he frankly acknowledged that any man, especially if he were a Christian, had a right to repudiate it. Writing, while in the Senate, to a young friend who anticipated an assault, he said: "If that misfortune should visit you, stand by your higher convictions. Every Christian man—every true man, even if he be not a Christian—has a right to live his own life and to stand upon his own principle of action. No just or truly brave man will now respect him the less for doing so. The sentiment of the world has changed in that respect, even here in the South.... Never say that you look down on the code of honor.... Say only that your aspirations and your hopes lie in other directions."

In the Senate, several years after the Conkling episode (according to a widely publicized newspaper account), Senator Conger, the Michigan radical, took occasion to snarl some innuendo at Lamar about his fighting proclivities; but the Mississippian paid no attention to it until the next day, when he stepped to Conger's desk and remarked: "'Conger, you are always talking about fighting, but never fight; that's where you and I are a good deal unlike. I don't talk about fighting, but I am ready for it any time.' Then he made his way back to his seat in the coolest possible manner. It was some time before Conger heard the last about his 'duel,' and his Republican colleagues tried their best to egg him on to a fight with Lamar."[25] Henceforth, the transactions of the Senate show, Conger (despite his peculiar predilection for personalities) treated Lamar with marked civility in the debates on controversial subjects.

By the time of the Conkling episode, Lamar had become a figure of intense interest to the whole nation. There was something about the man that, without the least intention on his part, lent a touch of drama to almost everything that he did, and naturally the curiosity of the public was piqued. An interesting sketch, and one that shows him as he was in these Senate years, was published by William Preston Johnston in January, 1879, and was widely copied in the press. "Among Southern Senators," reads the account, "the man who most interests, puzzles, and influences the Northern mind is Lucius Quintus Cincinnatus Lamar, of Mississippi. He is by all odds, 'to the mind's eye,' the most picturesque figure in the Senate. The popular imagination, dwelling on some phases of character not commonplace, has converted him into a political sphinx. A few plain, intelligible passages from his life and some outline touches of character will solve the riddle which people have chosen to make for themselves.

"The Lamars are Huguenot in origin.... The fatal dowery of genius was on that house. All that came forth from it felt its touch, its inspiration, its triumphs, and some share of its wretchedness. Mirabeau B. Lamar [the uncle of L. Q. C.] is known as the second President of the Republic of Texas; as the soul of chivalry...; impassioned orator;... gifted, lamented son of the South."

The post-war years, Johnston points out, constituted a period of suffering and desolation for the South unparalleled in modern history. "It was to face this reign of terror that Col. Lamar returned to his home.... When he entered the House it was still the correct rôle for the radical patriot to perform on the floor of the House the melodrama of 'The Rebellion Crushed,' with immense applause.... Lamar, it will be remembered, administered some of the most effective rebukes received by this spurious patriotism. At the same time he has conceded to the national sentiment as much as it was possible for any Southern man to do. He has, in fact, taken a position which any man would have failed [in] who lacked either the courage of his convictions or the confidence of his constituents. He has maintained it because of the Southern estimate of his statesmanship and integrity...."

Johnston directs attention to the important legislation that had already come to bear Lamar's name: measures, among others, for the internal improvement of the South, particularly in the way of levees and flood control of the Mississippi, and in the building of the Texas Pacific Railroad. He pictures him, moreover, as "of the straightest sect of the hard money men," but with "a Democracy as unimpeachable as that of Andrew Jackson."

"An eminent physician of Northern birth," wrote Johnston in illustrating from incidents known to him personally the widespread interest in Lamar, "said to a Southern surgeon of the first rank, on a steamer returning from Brazil, that the man he most desired to see in America was Senator Lamar. Again, lately, a Boston gentleman, who, if named, would be at once recognized as of national reputation in his profession, said to a friend that, on being presented to Lamar, he was speechless from emotion, and that when he turned away he could not restrain his tears at the thought of that man's sacrifices for reconciliation."

Particularly effective is the description of Lamar's personal appearance as portrayed in this contemporary sketch: "Lamar is about five feet nine inches in height, heavy set, long barreled, with handsome feet and hands. His profile is regular, his features regular, but rather massive, with brown hair and pointed beard, and heavy eyebrows over clear, gray, brilliant eyes...the voice and flashing eyes and ever present evidence of tremendous intellectual activity seem to derive an additional force from what is seemingly the expressive force of the will controlling the countenance.

"As Lamar walks the streets, cold and impassive in aspect, often abstracted and far away in realms of thought outside the living, moving world around him, the casual acquaintance might believe him hedged by a barrier of unsympathetic reserve and egotism; but let the circumstances alter a little; let even accidental companionship open up some natural avenue of communication, throw open some postern gate and admit him within the walls, and he discovers a realm such as when

'In Xanadu did Kubla Khan
A stately pleasure-dome decree,'

with its splendors in Oriental profusion all at his behest. He
is astonished to find out for his private behoof and benefit
floods of thought and feeling beside which the studied efforts
of the orator seem pale and cold. He treads upon the lava and
feels beneath the heat of a volcanic soul. Lamar is at once
ardent and sagacious; tender, sentimental, and romantic; or
metaphysical, analytical, and laborious, as the mood sways him.
In that face which, submitted to final tests, exhibits an antique
French type, you imagine that you can read, as under a mask,
Abelard looking from the luminous eyes, and speaking in the
full sonorous tones; and again, when images of the Gallic breed
rise from the historic pages to confront you, with a full armory
of poetry and eloquence and epigram. Lamar is a man constant
in friendship; and, however much his absence of mind may
ruffle an acquaintance or friend, such is the power of his generous and genuine contribution that he has rarely lost a friend
or alienated an ally. He is eminently a public man. In him all
private feelings are subordinated to a broad philosophy which
makes the destiny of the nation its daily food. The lesser matters of life concern him very little. Success has sought him
out. May it continue to attend him!"

No man had better reason to know whereof he was writing
than Senator Hoar of Massachusetts who said of him: "He was
a very interesting and very remarkable and noble character.
The late Matthew Arnold used to say that American public
men lack what he called 'distinction.' Nobody could have said
that of Mr. Lamar. He would have been a conspicuous personality anywhere, with a character and quality all his own." [26]
Henry Adams, writing on November 28th, 1878, to Charles
Milnes Gaskell concerning a recent dinner party at which he
had entertained a number of distinguished guests, made particular mention of "Mr. Senator Lucius Quintus Cincinnatus
Lamar of Mississippi, the most genial and sympathetic of all
Senators and universally respected and admired." [27]

XVII

REËLECTION AND NATIONAL LEADERSHIP

As soon as Congress had adjourned and the Conkling affair had been disposed of, Lamar returned to Mississippi where, on the 24th of June, he delivered the commencement address at Whitworth College, at Brookhaven. Immediately thereafter he went to his home at Oxford where he planned to spend the summer. When it seemed probable that there would be a repetition of the previous year's plague of yellow fever, he took his family to Virginia for the summer and himself returned to Washington. But the epidemic failed to materialize, and Lamar began to receive numerous letters from Mississippi to the effect that party matters were demanding his presence. As a result, he returned about the middle of September and began a series of addresses over the State—the first of these being delivered in Oxford on September 29th.

A glance must be taken at the situation that confronted him in Mississippi. First, there were certain matters in connection with his own course in the Senate that he wished to present directly to the people. Chief among these were his advocacy of the Electoral Commission in the Hayes-Tilden controversy, and his votes upon the Matthews Resolution and the Bland Silver Bill, for which, in disregard of the instructions of the State legislature, he had refused to vote. In the second place, the Democracy of the State was faced with a crisis. Revived in 1875 out of somewhat inharmonious factions, it now threatened (once the carpetbag rule had been destroyed) to resolve itself into its original elements.

Within the Democratic party in the State, there were a number of men who had ambitions for high place. Lamar himself was so clearly the ablest public man that none openly challenged his right to leadership, but there were others whose aspirations led them to espouse any tendencies toward faction-alism within the party. Again, there were the so-called "Bour-bon" Democrats who boasted that they were "unreconstructed." These felt that Lamar had perhaps gone too far in his attempts to still factionalism between the various sections of the country. Lastly, there was the "Greenback Party" which had come into being immediately following and as a result of the panic of 1873 and which was in favor of fiat money issued in a prac-tically unlimited quantity upon the "resources of the coun-try."

Lamar was of the opinion that the presence of two strong parties in any State was, generally speaking, a necessity for a healthy condition of public affairs. But he felt, as did the sanest of the other leaders of the State's Democracy, that the time was not ripe for the disbanding or splitting of the party. Too recently had the State been delivered from radical rule, and those unprincipled men who had dominated the Negroes and debased the government were, in a great measure, still present and ready at the first opportunity to seize the reins of the local government.

These considerations were set forth clearly by Lamar in a letter of February 21st, 1879, to Mr. C. E. Wright, of Mis-sissippi. "Especially have I been unwilling," he wrote, "to in-spire or to request friendly newspaper articles. I have always preferred a support which should be entirely voluntary, self-suggested, and spontaneous, with perfect freedom of dissent at any time. The able support that you and others have given me has been much more highly prized than if I had sought it, because it resulted from the accord and sympathy created by independent observation of my public career.... It will be a sad day for the politics of Mississippi when they degenerate into a mere personal conflict of Senatorial aspirants. With my views of public duty, I should be guilty of little less than a crime were I to seek so to obtrude myself. I need not point out to you the extent to which the politics of the State would suffer if permitted to degenerate into such a conflict.

"Your suggestion of the probability of a split in the Democratic organization in Mississippi gives me great concern, for it is the prophecy of unnumbered woes to the people." It would "lead logically to radical ascendancy in the State...we must not think of secession from the organization, or doubt our ability to win such an overwhelming victory within the party as shall put at rest the clamor and demagogism that now disturbs its unity. Should we surrender the organization into the hands of the Bourbons, who unwisely invite upon themselves and the State a restoration of the evils from which, since Democratic supremacy was established, we have been slowly recovering by means of conservatism and moderation, we shall yield them much advantage in prestige.... The safety of Mississippi lies in the maintenance of the Democratic organization and in its wise direction by conservative leaders who will not forfeit the confidence of the country." [1]

Lamar's speeches, the first of which was delivered at Oxford on the 29th of September (and succeeding ones at Coffeeville, Jackson, Vicksburg, Meridian, and Columbus), dealt with all of these questions, but particularly did he face the issue of the authority of the legislature to command a Senator to vote according to its dictation. On this subject he did not quibble, for he believed that the duty and privilege of a Senator to act in accordance with his conscience and his judgment was fundamental to American Republican institutions, and he did not propose to have his position misunderstood. In a suggested resolution that he had previously drawn up at the request of General Walthall is found the essence of his belief:

Resolved, That we believe in the right of the legislature of a State to instruct the United States Senators for such State on any question of public policy; that such instructions are addressed to the patriotism and sense of duty of Senators, and to the respect due from the Senators to the expression of any opinion by the legislature of the State which they represent; and that no Senator should depart in his votes from an opinion thus expressed or given, *unless in case of a clear and conscientious conviction that in following such instructions he would be violating the constitution or injuring the interests of the whole country.*

In the twentieth century the question of legislative instructions is of less importance because Senators are now elected directly by the people. Hence we shall not, here, follow in detail the close constitutional argument presented by Lamar in justification of his position. To understand that it is not even now a "dead" issue, however, one has but to recall that within the past four years a legislature has attempted to instruct its national representatives as to their votes, and the positions and arguments advanced by Lamar have been referred to and widely cited as precedents.

Speaking to assemblages of thousands of people throughout the State, Lamar appealed to reason rather than to sentiment. Granting that the majority of Democrats of his day believed in the right of binding legislative instructions, he reiterated the constitutional and judicial basis of his position that the demands of the State legislature were not, in certain instances and under certain conditions, obligatory. The details of his citations from the records of the Supreme Court, Congress, and the lower judiciary are elsewhere available in full. It is enough to say that he was justified in his stand, for not only did his constituents in Mississippi accept and sustain his position, but no serious student of our democratic institutions to-day contends that he was wrong. "I have always thought that the first duty of a public man in a Republic founded upon the sovereignty of the people as a legitimate source of power is a frank and sincere expression of his opinion to his constituents," he was accustomed to say in closing his discourses on the subject. "I prize the confidence of the people of Mississippi, but I never made popularity the standard of my action. I profoundly respect public opinion, but I believe that there is in conscious rectitude of purpose a sustaining power which will support a man of ordinary firmness under any circumstances whatever." [2]

It has been observed that in public questions of an intricate nature Lamar customarily discarded all appeal to the emotions. But on occasion he was an impassioned speaker, though never, in his maturity, a verbose or "flowery" one. Our public life has probably never seen a man with more power to sway an audience. This statement is not to be discounted, for Lamar won his laurels at a time when American oratory was in one of its flowering periods, and he won them in the national arena. Henry Adams, looking back over a long life spent in close contact with the public men of this and other nations, thought —let it be recalled—that had Mr. Davis sent Lamar rather than Mason as envoy to England, "his oratory would have swept every audience." [3]

"While his orations in the Senate Chamber were models of diction, rhetoric, and resistless logic," said a noted contemporary, "yet it was on the hustings before the people that he was most powerful and superb. I doubt if any man ever lived who excelled him in the power to touch the heart, stir the emotions, and sway the judgment of such an audience. I have seen assembled thousands hang breathless upon his words, laughing, crying, elated or serious by turns, as he ... played with their emotions and subdued their judgments. It was not so much by beauty of speech or logical sequence of statement that he did this, for in these respects many, perhaps, have equaled him; but there was peculiar to him a passion, an intensity, a charm that spoke less from his tongue than from his soul-lighted and changeful countenance, as he himself was dominated by his masterful emotions." [4]

Throughout the course of his canvass of Mississippi, the press of the State united in paying glowing tributes to his speeches. "The speech delivered by Senator Lamar Thursday night was one of remarkable power, "editorialized the *Vicksburg Herald* of October 24th." The whole address, which was something near three hours duration, was remarkable for its elevated tone, its lofty patriotism, and its pure morality. There was not a single appeal to the selfishness, the prejudices, or the passions of his audience.... It was evident that Col. Lamar's purpose was not so much self-vindication as the vindication of the *principles* upon which he has acted, and to recall his constituents to a just and accurate perception of the *political* attitude which the South occupies toward the North, and to the essential conditions upon which she can hope to enjoy her full share in the councils, benefits, and advantages of the Union.... We believe that if the people of the South would put their destinies in the hands of such men as Senator Lamar it would be but a short time before all sectional issues would disappear from American politics.... The judgment and discrimination, as well as the enthusiasm, with which his remarks were applauded were, we think, something unusual in a popular assemblage. It is not often that such an audience will applaud mere logical and philosophical deductions, but this was done Thursday night repeatedly and with great animation. On one occasion the manifestations of approval were so loud and continuous as to remind one of the enthusiastic encores of a dramatic performance."

"Whenever Lamar touched upon his own political course and action," said the *Grenada Sentinel* of his Coffeeville speech, "cheer after cheer rang out from his auditors," while the most prominent Greenbacker of the State, the position of whose party on finance Lamar had characterized as "boundless, bottomless, and brainless," said amid the acclaim with which Lamar passed from the platform: "That was the speech of a statesman; only a noble and patriotic man could have made it."

In his return to Mississippi, Lamar had accomplished all for which he had hoped: he had succeeded in welding together the Democracy of the State, and the people themselves had shown overwhelming approval of his course in the Senate, including his disregard of the legislative instructions. General Walthall, in a letter of December 5th, attested to his success: "You ought to be more than satisfied with the results of your canvass in the State. You worked a complete revolution wherever you went, which has had a wonderful effect in all parts of the State. If your speech had been published in full and generally distributed, the work would have been complete in all quarters." [5]

One of the most important matters before the people of Mississippi was the succession to the Senatorial seat of Mr.

Blanche K. Bruce, the Negro Senator from Mississippi, whose term was to expire the following year. Lamar was extremely desirous that General Walthall, who had championed his silver position in the State and whom he considered the strongest man among all his acquaintances, should have the place. To support his candidacy Lamar remained in Mississippi after the opening of Congress, and went to Jackson that he might be close at hand during the caucus of the Democracy. When the vote, after thirty-four fruitless ballots, seemed hopelessly dead-locked between Messrs. Barksdale, Singleton, and Walthall, the latter withdrew and threw his influence to Chief Justice James Z. George, who was declared elected at the end of nine more ballots. Lamar would have preferred General Walthall as his colleague, but Judge George belonged to the same party, he was a warm personal friend, and he had been put forward as a compromise candidate by the Lamar-Walthall group.

While all this was occurring, Lamar himself was not without sickness and sorrow. On the 31st of October, at Macon, Georgia, his mother, to his great sorrow, had died. Then, in the midst of the deadlock in the vote on the new Senator, he was himself stricken with an apoplectic attack, this time more severe than those immediately preceding. His illness was heard with sadness in Washington, and he received many communications from his friends there, as elsewhere. "I doubt if the political and journalistic community of Washington has ever mourned more sincerely over the sickness of any public man," wrote Mr. Frank Alfriend in a letter of January 27th; while Mr. S. A. Jonas, editor of the *Aberdeen Examiner* and at this time resid-ing in Washington, assured him in a letter of January 20th that every one here "rejoices to hear of your improvement, and it would almost have compensated you for the suffering that you have endured to have heard the many kind things said of you by even those of your stalwart political opponents who have no compliments to pay or kind words to speak when you are in your chair." [6]

Early in February Lamar's strength had so far improved that he was able to return to his official duties. He was not yet well, however, and was still walking with the assistance of crutches. "I took my seat in the Senate yesterday," he wrote to his wife under date of February 17th, 1880, "and received many cordial hand pressures. Conkling was not among those who welcomed me. He stood aloof and eyed me gloomily. My own health is good. I am easily fatigued, and writing makes my head swim. My arm is heavy and weak; but I have thrown aside my crutches, and walk with a stick," and again on March 1st he wrote that Blaine had welcomed him "with the utmost cordiality," and in the course of their conversation had questioned him as to the possibility of Grant's winning a Southern State if he should succeed in again securing the Republican nomination. Blaine's real opinion of the Republican course toward the South came out in a moment of frankness when he remarked that Grant's nomination would justify the South in voting solidly Democratic.[7]

Lamar's first speech to attract general attention in this session was in relation to the so-called Negro "exodus" from the South that had first begun to assume decided proportions in the winter and spring of 1879.[8] In the four or five years preceding, race relations had greatly improved, and except at times of political excitement, less and less was being heard of the "Negro question." That a great many blacks at this time left the Southern States cannot be doubted, and, though the radical remnant in the North attempted to make it appear that they were fleeing from persecution, an examination of the facts indicates that the migration had its inception in a variety of causes: there were political aspects to the situation; agitation, subsidized by certain philanthropists, was being carried on by ministers of the Negro race itself; and, despite the agreement of all authentic reports in respect to the unhealthfulness of the Liberian climate and the total failure of the Liberian experiment (which had for its purpose the founding of a black republic), the directors of the American Colonization Society continued their futile agitation.

Particularly were the land speculators, agents of the railways, and even Governor John P. St. John of Kansas active in advertising the advantages of Kansas as a State for prospective Negro colonization. There was no reason, the agitators felt, why the blacks might not become actively useful Republican voters in the Northern States. Coincidently with the mass of handbills and papers which painted glowing pictures of the promised land, appeared the locust swarm of swindlers. The eyes of the blacks glittered as they listened to tales of trees which rained dollars at the slightest agitation.[9] The old forty acres and a mule were made to do service again, and thousands of Negroes from the lower South lined the banks of the Mississippi because they had been led to believe that once they reached "de ribber" they would receive money and free passage northward to the land of milk and honey. A grandson of John C. Calhoun, owner of a large plantation in Arkansas, had eighty of his hands throw down their implements and start for the boat landing after they had bought for $2 from two wandering gentlemen of fortune pieces of cardboard bearing the picture of a farm that President Grant had bought for them and bearing the printed words: "Good for one trip to Kansas."

In preparation for the ensuing Presidential election, the Republicans had consumed the session of Congress in attempting to make it appear that the Negroes were fleeing from the South because of cruelty and oppression visited upon them by the whites. On the other hand, the Democrats, as well as many of the liberal Republicans, held, and rightly, that in the main the emigration was artificially induced by Republican campaign propaganda with the old cry of Southern "outrages," and with the end in view of reducing the Southern and increasing the Northern representation in both the electoral college and Congress under the new apportionment of the approaching census.

Writing on March 24th, 1880, to Colonel W. B. Montgomery, of Starkville, Mississippi, Lamar had given his own reaction to the alleged exodus. Their leaving would mean, he thought, "the dawn of a new and grand era for the South. I believe it would be an auspicious event for both races, white and black—I mean the two *races* as contradistinguished from the *individuals* who may be immediately affected." It would cause some bankruptcies among the large planters, and some suffering among the

Negroes, "but these would be the incidents of all great social transformations. It would be the beginning of a veritable reconstruction of the South." The Negro could be elevated quicker, he believed, in a section where he had never been closely associated with the institution of slavery, and, he felt, "they need an isothermal shock (if you will permit the phrase) to infuse into them the qualities which do not show themselves in the present conditions. The only mode by which they can ever get rid of their characteristics as a *parasite race* (sticking on a civilization without partaking of its nature and identity) is to move it from the structure to which it is attached." From the standpoint of his own race, Lamar believed that the emigration of the Negro held "no terrors." He would hail it as the beginning of a "glorious Southern renaissance." [10]

On the 15th of December, 1879, Mr. Voorhees had introduced a motion in the Senate for the appointment of a Senatorial commission for the examination of the causes of the so-called exodus. Aware that his own State of Indiana was being overrun by indigent Negroes and believing that the movement was fostered by the Republicans for political purposes, he felt that the only way to expose the roots of the trouble was by an impartial investigation. Consequently he introduced the following resolution:

Whereas large numbers of negroes from the Southern States, and especially from the State of North Carolina, are emigrating to the Northern States, and especially to the State of Indiana; *and*

Whereas, it is currently alleged that they are induced to do so by the unjust and cruel conduct of their white fellow-citizens toward them in the South; therefore be it

Resolved, That a committee of five members of this body be appointed by its presiding officer, whose duty it shall be to investigate the causes which have led to the aforesaid emigration, and report the same to the Senate; and the said committee shall have power to send for persons and papers, compel the attendance of witnesses, and to sit at any time.

Upon the adoption of the resolution a committee was appointed, constituted of Senator Voorhees of Indiana as Chairman; Pendleton, of Ohio; Vance of North Carolina; Blair of New Hampshire; and Windom, of Minnesota. When the committee completed its work on June 1st, 1880, Senators Voorhees, Pendleton, and Vance brought in a majority report which presented a vindication of the South and gave the true causes of the exodus, and Senators Windom and Blair a minority report embodying all of the stock charges of "outrages" committed by Southerners. Throughout the spring the authors of the minority findings had remained in Washington interviewing the stream of Negroes that passed through the city on their way to Missouri, Indiana, and Kansas, or who sunned themselves on every corner in the capital city. Always they were bulldozing the witnesses, building up testimony of outrages, and preparing their thunder for the ensuing election. At the close of Senator Windom's incendiary address which accompanied the minority report, Lamar took the floor and delivered his celebrated speech on race relations in the South.[11]

Lamar's address attracted great attention for its moderation of tone, and the fairness of its presentation. Refuting unjust indictments of the South, but admitting that conditions were by no means ideal, he presented elaborate evidence to show that in comfort and fair treatment, Southern labor was in as good or better condition than that of the Northern mill towns. Many papers throughout the nation reproduced his entire speech, but almost without exception they gave his final words: "The truth is, all these statements, so far as they represent the condition of things in the South, are unjust and deceiving. The South is no such country as is represented. I do not deny that there has been violence there. I deplore it; I condemn it. Respecting these cases of violence, you will find when you get down to the bottom facts that they are generally precipitated by unscrupulous political demagogues and tricksters, who inflame the prejudices and passions of the races for their own political purposes. But these cases of violence no longer occur to any appreciable extent.

"The great trouble has been that the investigating committees which have been sent to the South, and have brought hither their reports, went with purposes hostile to the character of that people. Accordingly, their entire social and political system has been uncovered to hostile eyes. Every evil, every fault, has been searched out as with a microscope, and dragged pitilessly into view; all that is good has been utterly ignored. Sir, no society on earth can undergo such a process of investigation as that to which the South has been subjected without becoming a spectacle of shame.

"Sir, you may distort the most perfect specimen of human beauty by searching only for its blemishes and defects and looking at these through a magnifying and refracting glass, into a hideous deformity.

"Sir, the enemies of the South have pursued this course. Every act of violence, every murder, every uprising of an angry mob, which has neither the head to think nor the heart to feel; every instance, every incident, which can bring reproach upon a community, has been hunted out and magnified and multiplied and grouped together and presented to the world as the portrait of the South. . . .

"And, sir, I say to-day, with all the emphasis of truth, that if, in the history of the last ten years, the coming of peace has been delayed; if in that time the good have been disheartened and the base encouraged; if the two races have not moved forward with the progress which was expected toward a common prosperity, it is because the Senators and public men who wielded the powers of this great government, and had the confidence of the mighty constituencies behind them, have not risen to the level of their duty and opportunity to bring, as they should have done, rest and quiet and love and universal patriotism over a troubled land."

"The great event of the late session of Congress," wrote one Washington correspondent, "was the masterly speech by Colonel Lamar in reply to Windom and in vindication of the South, and more particularly Mississippi. . . . It has been apparent to the Senate for weeks that the Minnesota aspirant for 'dark horse' honors was preparing an elaborate speech in reply to Mr. Voorhees [who had presented the majority report in vindi-

cation of the South], for he was continually writing at his desk
during the session, and for days could be seen referring, at
frequent intervals, to the printed volume of testimony taken
before the 'Exodus Committee'; and it leaked out through his
admirers that the larger portion of the remarks was to be devoted to our State. Learning this, Mr. Voorhees called upon
Colonel Lamar to reply, a demand which was readily assented
to, with the understanding that no mention should be made
of the matter, as Colonel Lamar was fearful that he might not
be well enough to take the floor when the time arrived. Probably
there were not a dozen persons who knew of this agreement;
but somehow or other Windom happened to be one of them,
and, with the prudence that usually characterizes those who
anticipate crossing swords with the great Southern statesman
and orator, he abandoned four-fifths of his carefully prepared
speech (in fact, dispensed with every allusion to Mississippi that
could be eliminated from his manuscript), and when he took
the floor, on the 14th inst., confined himself in great measure
to the stale and 'oft told tales' of outrages alleged to have occurred in Louisiana years ago, and, to the surprise of every
one, yielded the floor at a very early hour."[12]

Lamar, according to the same account, was apparently placed
at a great disadvantage for he had not expected to speak until
the following day when he would have had the opportunity of
studying Windom's speech in the *Record* and preparing an
answer. But because the session of Congress was so near its
close, it seemed a case of "now or never" and he took the floor
without special preparation. "The result may best be described
in the language of Senator Hoar, of Massachusetts, who, walking over to the lounge where Bruce [the Negro Senator from
Mississippi, who would soon be succeeded by General George]
sat listening with delight to what he pronounced 'the fairest
exposition of the Southern situation that ever fell from the lips
of man,' exclaimed: 'Brother Bruce, that is a great speech, sir;
the greatest speech of the session, sir. It's the very best speech
that could possibly be made on that side of the question. Your
colleague is a very able man, sir; a great statesman and orator.'

This is the universal opinion expressed of the speech by all men of all parties; and it is generally conceded that, if it shall be largely circulated and read in the North, it will have the effect to eliminate at once [and] forever the 'bloody shirt' from politics and place the South and her people of both races in a new light before the reading and reasoning world.

"The influence wielded in Congress by Colonel Lamar is peculiar and wonderful, and it is fair to say that no man's utterances are so attentively regarded and considered by the members of all parties in both Houses; while in the North and East he always has an audience, and commands a degree of respect and confidence that has not been accorded to any other Southern man of this generation. If it is known that he is to speak, the galleries are crowded to their greatest capacity; every official of the capitol deserts his office for the Senate Chamber; while all the members of the House of Representatives who can get away from their own hall are found on the floor of the Senate. It is also noticeable that when Lamar speaks it is always to a full Senate and to a quiet and attentive Senate. There are no calls to order after he takes the floor; no pause at the request of the presiding officer to 'enable honorable Senators to take their seats or get through with their private conversation'; no reading of newspapers, as is usually the case when other men are speaking; but the 'ambassadors of States' gather as closely around as possible, listening attentively, each man feeling that, in the remarks that are falling from the lips of the distinguished Mississippian, his peculiar political faith or belief is receiving the strongest possible support, or is being entirely undermined and crushed.

"At the conclusion of the great speech referred to, Senator McMillan, of Minnesota, walked across to Lamar's seat to thank him for the handsome tribute he had paid to the statutes of his State, and to compliment him otherwise. Colonel Lamar shook hands with him, and said he was very much prostrated. 'Yes, I know you are,' replied the Minnesota Senator, 'but you are not half so badly prostrated as my colleague is.'"

At the adjournment of the 46th Congress, Lamar, at the earnest solicitation of his warm friend, Senator Bayard, attended the Democratic National Convention which assembled in Cincinnati on June 22nd, 1880. As an influential member of the committee on platform, he took an active part in the proceedings, and his eloquent speech in seconding the nomination of General Hancock was enthusiastically received. The Democracy, it seemed, had picked strong men to head its ticket. General Hancock had served in distinguished fashion with the Union army, particularly at Gettysburg, while William H. English, of Indiana, nominated for the Vice-Presidency, was a Union man who held views similar to Lamar's upon economic issues, particularly the tariff and the currency. Hancock had endeared himself to the Southern people by the liberal course that he had pursued in Louisiana, where at the order of President Johnson, he had supplanted the tactless Sheridan. But despite strong candidates (though Hancock was not always fortunate in his public statements) and an admirable platform, the Democracy would be forced to wait four years before placing its candidate in the chair of the chief executive.

Once the convention was over, Lamar returned directly to his home at Oxford where he spent the summer of 1880 in recuperating his depleted energies. That he fully understood the precariousness of his health is seen in a speech which he delivered at Lafayette Springs about the middle of September, in which he spoke of the possible and probable sudden end to his life, and mentioned the threatened apoplexy and paralysis as the sword of Damocles suspended above his head by a hair. He had promised that early in October he would deliver an address at Holly Springs, and writing on the 1st of October to Hon. J. W. C. Watson he regretted that he had accepted the invitation. "I am," he said, "so liable to attacks of vertigo that I cannot prepare a detailed speech. I cannot study documents without a painful swimming in the head, nor bend over to write without a rush of blood to the brain." [13]

In the same letter he wrote of the failing health of his wife. "I have," he remarked, "been in the room of my invalid wife for twenty-one days, scarcely an hour of which she has spent in freedom from pain. She is indeed seriously ill; suffers from constantly recurrent fevers.... She also has a cough that grows worse and more settled.... What my own feelings are I need not state. You, who have been blessed with a good and beloved wife, can understand how impossible it is for a man in the shadow of such an affliction to think about public matters or to discuss political topics." That his wife was in truth afflicted with a mortal illness was verified that same day, when a consultation of physicians resulted in the verdict of an advanced case of tuberculosis. This came as a great shock to Lamar, for his home, and above all his wife, had been a refuge during those thirty years of his married life which had seen him play a leading part in the most troubled period of the nation's history. Through a lingering illness of four years, until the end came in December, 1884, he was to devote a large part of his time to the personal care of his dying wife.

The promised speech was delivered, according to the arrangement, on the 4th of October. The *Holly Springs South*, an organ that had consistently opposed Lamar's policies, characterized it as a "really great one, of the most patriotic character and worthy of himself," while the dominant paper of the entire section, the *Memphis Appeal*, gave it enthusiastic notice. According to this paper the Negroes were very largely represented and were as interested as the whites. Moreover, the "speech was one of the ablest efforts of his life, being logical in style, comprehensive in scope, replete with data, admirably delivered, and thoroughly unanswerable."

Following this address, Lamar conducted an active canvass which took him to Macon, Meridian, West Point, and to numerous other points along the Mobile and Ohio railroad. While the national Democratic ticket, headed by Hancock and English, was defeated in the ensuing election, Lamar had solidified his own position throughout the State, for never was it more evident that his constituency would follow wherever he led. They felt, too, a great pride in his achievements as a national figure. "The whole South feels a pride in Senator Lamar, and the radical North confesses that in him its theory of government finds a foeman who can parry its heaviest attacks and rebut its strongest arguments," editorialized the *West Point News* in voicing the sentiment that had become a commonplace in the papers of the South. "He stands a great, central, conservative power in himself, able to repel force with force when the attack is directed against his people, able to restrain impolitic impetuosity when his own people rush to the attack. In heart, in interest, in high commission, a Mississippian, he is a great national conservator of the peace, whose sphere and influence are almost limitless."

In December Lamar accompanied his wife (with her sister as companion) to New Orleans where she might spend the cold winter months, himself returning to Washington to resume his official duties. On the 25th of January, 1881, in support of the motion of Senator Logan, of Illinois, which provided that General Grant be placed on the retired list as a general of the army, Lamar made the previously mentioned notable speech.[14] His was the only voice among the Southern Democratic Senators raised in support of the motion. He pointed out that "had General Grant at any time when he was General desired to be retired from the command of the army, no one would have objected to the liberal provision proposed in this bill." It was only a just provision, he thought, that when its generals, its admirals, and its judges had spent a lifetime in the public service, the country should secure them, in return, adequate and honorable independence. Moreover, the people of the United States did not give General Grant the opportunity to retire; rather, "they summoned him to abandon his place of professional eminence in order to become President." Without caring to pass judgment upon Grant's career as soldier or President, Lamar did not think "that his consent to the expressed wish of his country ought to deprive him of the provision which is secured to those who served in the army with him and after him."

"I would with great pleasure," said Lamar, "vote for a law by which every President, upon closing his administration, should be placed upon the retired list with such allowances as are fitting for the rank of Commander in Chief of the Army and Navy given him by the constitution. Nor do I see any sectional feature in this measure. It threatens danger to no Southern interest; it does not impair any Southern right; it ought not to be considered as wounding any Southern sentiment....I am in favor, as was done with those who had completed their service under the Roman eagles, of writing opposite the name of General Ulysses S. Grant, *Emeritus*."

Again Lamar was attacked by certain Southern and Mississippi papers for his vote, but he had come to expect this from the extreme "fire-eating" element, and felt no concern over the matter. This time Ethelbert Barksdale was unable to elicit from Jefferson Davis a criticism of Lamar's course.

The assembling of Congress on March 4th, 1881, indicated that the elections of the preceding year had increased the power of the Republican party. Garfield was President, though the change of 6,601 votes in Indiana and 11,000 in New York would have given the Democrats the victory by 190-179 electoral votes. Nevertheless, besides winning in the race for the chief executive, the Republicans, by a small majority, had gained control of the House for the first time since 1875; and the new Senate was evenly divided with thirty-seven Republicans and thirty-seven Democrats, while Senators Mahone of Virginia and David Davis of Illinois had aligned themselves with neither party. However, both were in a sense Democrats, as Davis had been elected by a coalition of Democrats and Independents, while the demagogue, Mahone, had been elevated by the "readjuster" wing of the Virginia Democracy and would on occasion act with the Republicans.

A brief explanation is necessary in regard to the situation in Virginia. That State, before the Civil War, incurred a debt of approximately $31,000,000 which had increased by 1871 to about $45,000,000. Meanwhile, West Virginia had been created from its parent by a cæsarean operation. In 1871 it was arranged that Virginia bear approximately two-thirds of the indebtedness and West Virginia was to be regarded as responsible for about

383

$15,000,000; but a large element in the parent State felt that she had been called upon to assume an unnecessarily large share of the debt, and argued, as a consequence, that all of the interest and indebtedness that had been added on by the war and during the period of reconstruction be again readjusted so that the principle would not exceed $20,000,000 in all. On the other hand, the more conservative element in the Democracy held that Virginia's honor demanded that the full share of her indebtedness be funded and paid as soon as the State was in a position to do so. This controversy gave rise to the two factions within the Democracy known as the "Funders" and the "Readjusters," General Mahone being sent to the Senate as the representative of the latter element.

Each party held its Senatorial caucus with Davis and Mahone attending neither. As the Democrats had more Senators present in Washington, they proceeded to organize the upper House and to give the Republicans minority representation on the committees. This the latter refused to accept. The Democratic list of standing committees was submitted on the 10th, and on the next day Senator Davis announced that he would give his support to that party. But the Republicans, holding that they would have a majority when the places of three Senators who had been appointed to the Cabinet had been filled, determined to fight the Democratic organization.

Thus the affiliation of Senator Mahone became a matter of paramount importance, and Conkling, in his peculiarly offensive fashion, tauntingly informed the Democrats that they were "attempting to do on Friday what they would not be able to do on the following morning." Whether the Republicans could fulfill their boasts, Mr. Pendleton replied on the 14th, he did not know, but he had heard (referring to General Mahone) of mysterious, "unusual, and extraordinary visits to the other end of the avenue," on the part of a certain distinguished Senator; that this Senator has been promised federal patronage at "conferences in the capitol in which champagne and satisfaction were equally enjoyed." Further, Senator Pendleton expressed the belief that it was the duty of the Democratic majority to effect immediate organization for the transaction of the nation's business.

Senator Conkling made another incendiary address, and then Benjamin H. Hill took the floor. Having replied to Conkling, he then proceeded to put pressure on Mahone himself. Hill's speech showed the brilliance that might have been expected, but unfortunately it possessed elements that aroused antagonisms and thus complicated the situation. "The Senator from New York," he cried, "has repeated over and over again, in language too plain to be misunderstood, that within a few days the Republicans will control a majority of the Senate, and that that constitutional majority will have it in its power to select the committees.... I have believed that when every seat shall be filled the Senate will be Democratic, precisely as it is now.

"I have a list of the Senators before me chosen by the legislatures of the several States to the Forty-seventh Congress, except the few the Senator mentioned who have not yet arrived. I assume what I believe is true, that every Senator yet to arrive will be a Republican; I believe all the seats vacated will be filled by Republicans; but when full how will the Senate stand? That is the question. I have the list before me. I state what every man knows, that the Senate, when full, consists of seventy-six members. Thirty-eight members of the body now in the hearing of my voice were sent here commissioned to sit here as Democrats. Let that fact go to the country.... They hold no commission that was not given to them as Democrats and by Democrats. That thirty-eight amounts to precisely half the Senate. One member of the Senate, the distinguished Senator from Illinois (Mr. Davis), was not sent here as a Democrat. He was sent here by Democratic votes, and in words of high and lofty patriotism and fidelity to trust, worthy of the very best days of this Republic, he announced on Friday that he would be true to the trust that sent him here and which he agreed to fulfill....

"This being true, I challenge contradiction to the statement I make when I say there are thirty-nine members of the Senate now sitting here commissioned by Democrats, elected by Democratic votes. Thirty-nine constitute a majority of this body when full.... Sir, who is it that has changed? Whom of these thirty-eight does the Senator [Mr. Conkling] rely upon to vote with the Republicans? That one has not notified us; he has not notified his constituency. Therefore I say it is not true, and I cannot sit here quietly and allow a gentleman on the other side of the Chamber, however distinguished, to get up here and assume and asseverate over and over that somebody elected as a Democrat is faithless to his trust, and not repel it.... Who is ambitious to do what no man in the history of this country has ever done, to be the first man to stand up in this high presence, after this country has reached fifty million people, and proclaim from this proud eminence that he disgraces the commission he holds?..."

An angry debate ensued in which the actors were chiefly Senators Hill, Hoar, Mahone, Logan, and Brown of Georgia, in which Mr. Hoar saw fit to characterize the Southern Democracy as "slave drivers," and to accuse Senator Brown of treason because he said that the Democrats would never yield what they considered their rights even if the controversy continued until the end of the session. Particularly brilliant were Hill's remarks, and no one can doubt, who reads the account in the *Congressional Record*, that he carried off the honors, such as they were.

Weeks passed, but still the filibustering continued. In his speech of March 31st, Senator Cameron gave away the secret of the peculiar eagerness of the Republicans when he exclaimed: "There is something higher than and above all this, something the great importance of which has not escaped the attention of our opponents here. It is the coming political contest in Virginia." If Mahone could be drawn in with the Republicans, remarked Senator Cameron, the solid South would be "a thing of the past; and this is the true meaning of the present struggle."

Up to this point Lamar had refrained from entering the argument. Now, with the only sane voice among the leaders of the Senate, he was able to bring to bear the full weight of his influence in a highly effective argument.[15] Perhaps his most effective stroke in this debate was his undermining the position of the whole Republican contingent, by showing that *they were affiliating with the "Readjuster" group of Virginians who were committed to repudiating the State debts owed to their Northern constituents.* This fact was immediately broadcast throughout the Northern and Eastern sections, and instantly pressure from "back home" was exerted upon the recalcitrant Republican Senators.

That the "solid South" held any danger for the nation Lamar denied. That the local governments of that section had improved, and that corruption in high places in the Federal Government had diminished since the resurgence of Democratic influence, he held to be evident. And no one arose to question his facts. "There is one point," he said, "and one only, upon which they are solid, on which they will remain solid; and neither federal bayonets nor federal honors will dissolve that solidity. They are solid in defense of and for the protection of their own civilization, their own society, their own religion, against the rule of the incompetent, the servile, the ignorant, and the vicious. . . .

"I have said nothing to-day that was intended to stir up any feeling of animosity between individuals or sections," began his remarkably beautiful peroration. "I belong to that class of public men who were secessionists. Every throb of my heart was for the disunion of these States. If that deducts from the force of the statements that I have made to-day, it is due to candor and to you to admit it. I confess that I believed in the right of secession, and that I believed in the propriety of its exercise. I will say, further, that it was a cherished conception of my mind—that of two great, free Republics on this continent, each pursuing its own destiny and the destiny of its people and their happiness according to its own will.

"But, sir, that conception is gone; it is sunk out of sight. Another one has come in its place; and, by the way, it is my first love. The elements of it were planted in my heart by my father; they were taught by my mother; and they were nourished and developed by my own subsequent reflection. May I tell you what it is, sir? It stands before me now, simple in its majesty and sublime in its beauty. It is that of one grand, mighty, indivisible Republic upon this continent, throwing its loving arms around all sections; omnipotent for protection, powerless for oppression, cursing none, blessing all." [Applause in the galleries.]

In Lamar's speech there had been no hint of discourtesy, and in tone there was no element of incendiarism. But his arguments had been powerful and unanswerable, and he had accomplished his purpose through driving a wedge between many of the Northern Senators and their constituents, and through his appeal to the broadest patriotism. The Republicans capitulated and on the 4th of May the Senate was allowed to go into executive session.[16]

The year 1881 had arrived, and with it the general State election wherein was to be chosen the legislature which would determine Lamar's successor in the Senate. There was an element in the Democratic party that, pretending from force of public opinion to support Lamar, yet continually disseminated propaganda designed to do him political injury. The old and worn charges relating to the Silver Bill, the Electoral Commission, the pension for General Grant, and others, were drawn out and paraded before the people. No opposition was, in fact, open, except that which appeared in the *Brandon Republican* and in the *Vicksburg Commercial*, but these two organs were not nearly so dangerous to his reëlection as certain others which, protesting their friendship and admiration, yet did all in their power to lower his prestige.

Again, there were attempts to complicate the issue by involving Lamar's candidacy with that of the various aspirants for the Governorship, the *Grenada Sentinel* saying in June that "the way a portion of the State press now figure up the slate is: Lamar for Senator, [Ethelbert] Barksdale for Governor. ...In other words, if Lamar is elected to the Senate he needn't expect to see one of his friends head the State ticket." But the sentiment for Lamar continued to gain momentum and by June 1st, the majority of papers in the State had decided that they would consider only him for the Senate, and would support only one of his followers for the governor's chair. Papers all over the South took up the matter. The *Memphis Avalanche* felt that "a concentration of the Mississippi Democratic mind on Lamar may save the party, and it can safely be said that nothing else will save it."[17] The *Memphis Appeal* concurred in the feeling of the *Mobile Register* that Lamar's return to the Senate was important to the South and the nation as well as to his constituency in Mississippi, while the *Augusta* (Ga.) *Constitutionalist* pronounced him "one of the most prominent of American statesmen, and one of the strongest individually. ...He is the Master of his own soul, and sad indeed will it be for the State of Mississippi when his voice is no longer heard in her councils and his seat is vacant in the Senate."[18] The most respected representatives of the Mississippi press joined with the *Vicksburg Herald* of May 6th, 1881, in the feeling that "Lamar is a safe, wise man, and the people should sustain him with greater confidence than ever before."

No sooner had the returns from the county nominating conventions begun to come in, in July, than it was evident that the tide for Lamar had set in irresistibly. Before the 1st of August, almost every county in the State had indorsed him enthusiastically, and in many of the conventions as in that of Monroe, without a single dissenting voice. During this month, Colonel J. F. H. Claiborne, prominent historian and politician of Mississippi, was writing him: "Your wise, just, and liberal course on all questions and your conservative views and the support you have given the Executive to enable him to carry on the government, command, in my opinion, the approbation of two-thirds of our people. We are tired of perpetual party warfare and an indiscriminate opposition to the government."[19]

The result of the State Democratic Convention of the 3rd of August was the nomination of a "dark horse," General Robert Lowry, of Rankin County, for Governor. Lamar had not espoused the cause of any of the candidates, though his preference was for the reëlection of Governor Stone, who was, however, handicapped by his third term candidacy. The votes of the Lamar supporters had been scattered to Barksdale and other candidates as well, but that it was in a sense a personal setback could not be denied, especially in view of the fact that Barksdale's friends insisted that since he had been defeated for the governorship he should be given Lamar's seat in the Senate. "The result of the action at Jackson is not a favorable one for me," Lamar wrote his friend E. D. Clarke soon after the convention, "but it is less unfavorable than the preëxisting conditions were capable of working out....I must begin to work, but I am greatly at a loss what to speak about. There is a lull in national politics, and it is not easy to attack a party whose chieftain [President Garfield] lies dying, amid the sympathies of the whole people." [20]

Lamar had not long to wait for a topic for discussion, for a large element in the local Republican party joined with the Greenbackers and placed in the field a fusion ticket headed by Benjamin King, an ex-Democrat of Copiah, for the governorship. That this combination, formed of what Lamar considered the worst elements in the State, had the potentiality for boundless evil for the Commonwealth, he had no doubt. In a letter to the *Brookhaven Ledger* he set forth clearly his ideas. Among other things he characterized the coalition as "simply *negro government*, to be reëstablished by carpetbaggers and a few ambitious natives, taking the rôle of the scalawags under the names of Greenbackers and Independents....I believe that life will be unbearable in Mississippi if it succeeds."

On September 5th, he began his speeches of the fall campaign at DeKalb, the county seat of Kemper County. According to the *Kemper Herald*, he denounced "the recent coalition of the Greenback and radical parties of this State"; and he warned the citizenry of the danger of the radical domination of the Negro vote, though he disclaimed any adherence to the drawing of the color line which would forbid Negroes to vote the Democratic ticket and virtually shut them out of participation in local government; and he earnestly called for the election of General Lowry regardless of the attitude of the latter toward his own Senatorial aspirations. He explained, too, his own votes on the important questions that had arisen during his preceding six years in the Senate of the United States. "Every reference to his votes was received with demonstrations of enthusiastic applause," recorded the *Kemper Herald*, "and we can safely say that there are not ten men in this county who do not feel that Colonel Lamar's course was dictated by broad, liberal, and conservative views, which, in our opinion, are fully in line with those of the people of this State. ... Amid the wildest applause he closed one of the grandest speeches we ever listened to in our lives, and which instructed and at the same time aroused the people, and convinced them that the duty enjoined upon them of maintaining good government was imperative."

Of his next address, delivered at Canton, the *New Orleans Times* said that particularly he "discountenanced all plans of influencing the election through any irregular methods; either violence, intimidation, direct or indirect, or any unfairness; saying that these means would defeat themselves in the end and be an element of disintegration in the party." Here again he warned against radical-Negro domination of the State, expressing the hope that by fairness and education the blacks might be made to see that their best future lay with the law-abiding white element. He was unalterably opposed to a State government based upon the color line; but, said he, "If the government necessarily falls into the control of the white race, it is a less evil than the one which we are seeking to prevent, especially if we so carry on the government as to make its action fair and just and protective to both races."

His Yazoo City speech, delivered on the 12th of September, the *Sentinel* characterized as a "masterpiece of eloquence, wisdom, and logic." "Colonel Lamar," it remarked, "spoke for three hours and thirty-five minutes, and during the whole time the large audience appeared not in the least fatigued, and he was frequently and heartily applauded." Yazoo County, incidentally the family seat of the Barksdale connection, was considered as especially strong territory for Lamar's opponents. A partisan of Barksdale had arranged to ask him certain questions in the expectation that he would be embarrassed. In his replies, the *Yazoo City Herald* reported, "he rose to the 'height of great argument' in explanation of his course as one of the Senators from Mississippi," and the enthusiasm that greeted his discussion indicated that most of his opponents were now as strongly for him as they had been against him previously. The same paper thought that "the colored people, many of whom were present, could not but feel that in Senator Lamar they had a friend who would gladly see them enjoy for long days to come...the rights guaranteed them by the constitution, which it is every man's duty to respect," while "his peroration was a splendid piece of eloquence." All in all, Lamar was striking "a note in our State campaign which will ring beyond our own borders."

After the Yazoo City speech, Lamar delivered some eight more addresses closing at Raymond on the 30th of September. Meanwhile, he was appraised that in a number of counties the citizens were refusing to vote for certain candidates for the legislature unless they promised, in advance, to support him for the Senatorship. "I do not hesitate to say that I neither indorse, nor acquiesce in, the purpose which you tell me has been publicly announced in your county, to subordinate the election of the members of the legislature and county officers to the return of myself to the Senate," he wrote on the 21st to one of his most influential supporters, Hon. J. R. McIntosh, of Chickasaw County. "...First for the reason that they are the chosen nominees of the party for their respective offices, and I am not (as yet at least) their chosen nominee for United States Senator; second, I deem the choice of a United States Senator, between Democrats, as of less importance than the defeat of this new attempt to band the negroes of this State together for the purpose of restoring Republican misrule."[21]

Due to a called session of Congress, Lamar was forced to suspend his campaign after his speech at Raymond on the 30th of September. But the extraordinary session adjourned earlier than had been anticipated (on the 29th of October), and leaving a day or two early, he was back in the State by the end of the month prosecuting his canvass. Particularly did his speech of November 7th, at Hazelhurst, attract attention, for here, said the correspondent of the *New Orleans Democrat*, he was most effective in his denunciation of "Kukluxism, ballot box frauds, bulldozing, and violence of every character."

That there was general recognition of the high plane upon which he had placed his campaign was evidenced in the multitude of editorial notices throughout the entire country. Moreover, a large element in the nation's press, Republican as well as Democratic, saw in his candidacy a test of whether the South had in reality accepted the enlightened and progressive views that he had so often reiterated on the floors of the House and the Senate. "Nothing more hurtful to Democratic interests at large could happen in the South than the defeat of this eminent person by his own party," said the *Louisville Courier-Journal* of October 3rd. "Mr. Lamar stands as the foremost representative of all that is liberal, progressive, and genial in the South. In type essentially Southern, he is known to the country not merely as the eloquent pleader and brilliant politician, but by its best intelligence he is recognized as a thoughtful and enlightened statesman, capable of assimilating ideas and events and of deducing out of the chaos of things current the philosophy of political action and the exigencies and ethics of party policy. A refusal on the part of the Mississippi Democrats to return him would be a declaration of war upon the principles of the new era. It would announce a reaction in the South."

The Republican *Illinois State Journal* for September thought that "it would be a great misfortune to Mississippi and the whole South if some Bourbon of mediocre abilities should be elected to succeed Mr. Lamar," and characterized him as "a man of talent, of pure life, of tried statesmanship, and of commanding influence in the nation," while the *Memphis Appeal* believed that "but for the ostracism of the South, on account of the war and sectional hatreds, Senator Lamar would now be as formidable a candidate for the Presidency as he is for United States Senator." "With, perhaps, the exception of John Q.

Adams and James A. Garfield," said the same paper, "no man in Congress was ever such a lover of books as L. Q. C. Lamar," while it is universally acknowledged that "no man in the Union has contributed so much to the obliteration of sectional hatreds" as he. Such were the representative editorial notices throughout the nation.

In the face of the swelling tide of public sentiment, the last vestige of opposition to Lamar's candidacy disappeared. It seemed that wherever he went he converted his opponents into loyal disciples. For instance, in Yazoo County—the home of Barksdale and the citadel of his opposition—by a rising vote the county convention instructed its representatives in the House and Senate "to vote for him and work for him, first, last, and all the time, as the choice of this people for United States Senator." [22] The impression that he made upon mature listeners is evident in the comments of two of the Mississippi Congressmen, Catchings and Hooker, who recorded their opinion of his campaign. "His exposition of the relations existing between a United States Senator and the legislature of his State could not have been excelled in power and logic by John Marshall himself," thought the former, while Hooker was convinced that "no more powerful orator has ever lived." [23]

The Mississippi legislature assembled in January, 1882, with one of its most important pieces of business the election in which Lamar's seat in the Senate was at stake. Even the formality of a caucus was dispensed with, and in each House he received, on the first ballot, the unanimous vote of the Democracy. Among those who supported him was Mr. J. A. Shorter, the Negro Republican Representative, who, in explaining his vote, said that since it would in no sense injure his party, he wished to cast his ballot for "the eminent statesman," who, he believed, was "the choice of a very large majority of the intelligent and substantial citizens of my county and of the State." "To have secured such a triumph by bravely following your own convictions in the most trying moments, relying upon the sober judgment of your constituents for vindication, must fill the measure of your ambition," [24] wrote ex-Senator

Eustis of Louisiana in a congratulatory message that was typical of a great number that he received.

However, the year 1882, though one of political triumphs for Lamar, was saddened by the continued failing health of his wife. In April she had begun to weaken appreciably, as a result of which he had practically surrendered all other duties and for months had devoted himself to cheering and attempting to nurse her back to health. "A death of hope and happiness has fallen upon me," he wrote his sister, Mrs. Ross, during this period. "But, though it has crushed all ambition and desire for the pleasures of life out of me, it has left in me an unabated sense of the duties of life; and I think I shall arouse to full activity in the discharge of them." [25] By December, her health seemed improved, and Lamar was able to arrive in Washington at the assembling of Congress. "A very sad domestic affliction," he explained to a friend, "has for many months withdrawn my attention from my public duties, and I resume them under many disadvantages. I fear that I shall need indulgent consideration in order to escape unfavorable criticism, but shall not murmur if it comes." [26]

Under these conditions, on February 7th, 1883, he delivered his widely-reviewed speech on the tariff, to what amounted to a joint assembly of the two Houses, for when it became known that he would speak the Representatives *en masse* found seats in the galleries or on the floor of the Senate. [27] The question of the tariff had lately come in for a great amount of discussion even for that controversial subject, for, through the operation of prohibitive duties, a considerable surplus had piled up in the national treasury with the result that much of the money was being squandered in various questionable enterprises, while the balance remained as a standing challenge to the cupidity and dishonesty of unscrupulous public officials. Lamar, with Henry Watterson, had drawn up and placed in the platform of the preceding national Democratic convention the demand for "a tariff for revenue only" (so phrased—it seems—for the first time), and those who shared with them a belief in this economic principle looked with disfavor upon a protective system which increased the federal revenues beyond what was needed and thus took money from those who struggled for the necessities of life. Even President Arthur (Garfield had died at the hands of an assassin), himself a protectionist, recognized in his message to Congress that the condition must be corrected and cautiously advised revision of the more unreasonable duties.[28]

Meanwhile, the high tariff men, chiefly Eastern Republicans, were maintaining headquarters in Philadelphia where, with the hearty backing of certain large manufacturing interests, they were flooding the country with pamphlets tending to show that any reduction in the excessive duties would wreck the industrial life of the nation and reduce the economic status of American labor to that of the Southern European nations. It was hoped that the commission appointed to investigate the tariff—this authorized by Congress on May 15th, 1882—might be fruitful of much good; but its membership was packed with the advocates of excessive duties, and throughout the summer and autumn of the year it succeeded only in squandering a great deal of money in futile traveling and in collecting such data as would support the preconceived opinions of the majority.[29]

The length and many technical aspects of Lamar's speech preclude the possibility of any detailed analysis of it here. Generally speaking, he traced the history of the tariff controversy from its inception in the early days of the Republic; he discussed the theory of protection in its broader economic aspects; and he made a detailed analysis of its actual working out in relation to each of the important American industries.

The address made a profound impression, for despite its great length (considerably more than twenty thousand words as it appears in the *Congressional Record*) it was reproduced in almost every representative of the metropolitan press, Republican as well as Democratic. The New York Free Trade Club passed resolutions of commendation and thanks, and ordered thousands of copies for general distribution, while the *New York Herald* characterized it as "the most masterly speech yet

made in Congress on the tariff question." Most of the important
Republican organs expressed the belief that it was the finest
possible statement of the Democratic position. The arch-
Republican *New York Tribune* felt that the very brilliance of
its exposition might overpersuade many people to take the
"wrong" side of the question. It is, said this mouthpiece of the
high tariff exponents, "a misfortune for Mr. Lamar, and not
for Mr. Lamar only, that his brilliant rhetoric and impressive
oratory have not always been employed for the public welfare.
When a man of such gifts makes a mistake [as in his position
on the tariff] and gives his aid to the wrong side, the fact is
sure to be remembered." [30] The *Washington Evening Star*,
remarking that "he was listened to with marked attention by
the Senators of both sides of the Chamber," and that "many
members of the House occupied seats on the floor," thought the
address "the feature of the Senate proceedings."

"Two ideas in particular," it seemed to the *New York Evening Post*, "he set forth with peculiar force: one is that this
is probably the only country in the world whose people were
severely and superfluously taxed for a series of years only
because their rulers were unable to devise a mode of reducing
that taxation, and this only because taxes were not imposed
for the only legitimate purpose of raising revenue, but for the
purpose of paying bounties to certain business interests.... The
other leading thought in Mr. Lamar's speech is that the protective system had brought forth a vast organization of capital
and labor which professes itself to be dependent for existence,
not upon the natural development of resources and the natural
growth of industries, but upon taxation by the government." As
a student of the tariff, and of American institutions, and as the
leading Southern statesman, the *Post* thought that Lamar was
peculiarly well adapted to speak on a subject which, because of
the rapid industrialization of the South, was coming increasingly into the consciousness of that section.

It was fitting that the last extensive speech that Lamar delivered before the Senate—shortly before he was advanced to
even higher honors—should have dealt with the extension of

federal aid to public education throughout the States. Himself a distinguished ex-Professor of the University of Mississippi, he had followed the course of secondary and higher education, and had often expressed the belief that the solution to many of the South's and the nation's most vexing problems lay in the general education of the people and in a trained leadership.

Public education and the development of the colleges and universities had gone forward faster in the North than in the South, the latter still impoverished by the late war. Perhaps one must not take too literally the words of Henry Grady before the New England society at Delmonico's when he said that the South had "planted the school house on the hill top and made it free to white and black"; but each of the Southern States had made, since the close of reconstruction, decided increases in its appropriations to public education. Moreover, a number of wealthy men, notably George Peabody of Massachusetts and John F. Slater of Connecticut, had set aside munificent gifts under excellent administration for the benefit of Southern education. The former, contributing in all $3,500,000, had selected as his chief administrative agent Dr. Barnas Sears who resigned the presidency of Brown University to accept the position. He was to be succeeded by the brilliant and enlightened cousin of Lamar, J. L. M. Curry, ex-United States Congressman and member of the Confederate Congress, who was born in Putnam County, Georgia, and had often played about the old Lamar homestead outside of Eatonton.

It will be recalled that in answering the incendiary speech of Mr. Blaine, in December, 1878, Lamar had condemned the latter for his sensational resolutions in respect to the race problem in the South when he might have brought forward "some well-devised scheme of public education by which this newly enfranchised race may be fitted to exercise their great duties as freemen and citizens and as the participants in the sovereignty of Commonwealths." Lamar's speech on the development of the educational facilities of the nation was delivered on March 28th, 1884, on the Senate Bill No. 398, which proposed, under certain conditions, the establishment and temporary aid to common schools by the Federal Government.[31] From the standpoint of the constitutionality of the bill, he did not believe that valid objections could be raised, and he thought "that this measure [was] fraught with almost unspeakable benefits to the entire population of the South, white and black," and that it was "the first step and the most important step that the government has ever taken in the direction of the solution of what is called the 'race problem.'" Too, he believed that it would provide the needed stimulus to public school education in the South. "It is true," he said, "that before the war the common school system did not flourish in the South. We had an education there, and an educated people whose culture was as high as that of any people on earth. They were a people—one-fourth of them at least, perhaps—who had all the function and discipline and intellectual development that the finest education could give, not only from their own colleges at home, but from the best universities in America and Europe."

Nevertheless, because of the sparseness of the population and what has been called the "aristocratic tradition" in American education, the common school did not thrive. "But," said he, "the result of the war overthrew the conditions of society; and colleges, schools, and academies shared in the general crash and desolation. In that section the educated classes suffered more than all others." The South was now struggling heroically to better her system of secondary education, as well as to rebuild her colleges and universities, and the provisions of the measure under discussion would furnish just the needed impetus for the building of a sound structure at the basis of the educational pyramid.

The year 1884 was memorable as that of the presidential nomination and election. Lamar had been favorable to the selection of Mr. Bayard as the standard bearer of the Democracy, but in the nomination of Cleveland and Hendricks he acquiesced, and behind their candidacy had thrown the full weight of his influence and oratory.

Representative of his speeches during this campaign, and

perhaps the most notable, was that delivered at Holly Springs, on October 6th. He was unable, he remarked, to say anything to the people of Marshall County that he had not already, and perhaps better, said before. He deplored all racial antagonisms, and all chicanery at the polls, and he called upon the citizenry to see that justice and fairness were accorded to all without respect to color or station. The population of Mississippi, he realized, was almost evenly divided between the white and black races, and serious practical problems made it necessary that the white population take an active interest in their government and see to it that only capable and honest officials be put in office. While the Negroes should always be welcomed into the Democratic fold, the crux of the situation which faced Mississippians could be put in one sentence: "*We white people ought to keep united.* So much of our highest interest, of our truest prosperity, and of our best hope depends upon this union, that brethren of the same blood must not allow themselves to divide between contending parties or over the claims of party candidates; for here in Mississippi unity of purpose and concert of action (and very vigorous action at that) are not a policy, not a sentiment, not a principle, but a supreme necessity of self-preservation, an only refuge from ruin and woe.

"Let me read some words from the border of eternity," he said. "A short time before the death of Senator Ben Hill,...I received this letter from a friend of Georgia:

"*My Dear Cousin Lucius:* A few days since, in company with a friend, I called upon Senator Hill. I had not seen him since the early days of the Hancock campaign, at a time when his grievous affliction had just begun to excite apprehension....We were warned that we could but pass into his room and shake his hand, as his strength was fast going with the deepening shadows of the summer day. In a comfortable sitting room, near a window, sat the great Georgian in an invalid's chair....There was nothing left of Ben Hill but the great gaunt form, and those luminous eyes which, made large by suffering, seemed to be surcharged with soul and almost capable of speech. With his collar thrown open at the neck, his hands lying listlessly upon the arms of the chair, and his head slightly inclined downward and forward, he reminded me of the Dying Napoleon as illustrated in the celebrated statue in the Corcoran Art Gallery ; while his eyes followed one with a sad and questioning power, like those of Charlotte Corday peering through the bars of her prison window. Motioning us to chairs near his own, he grasped our hands and sat for many moments in silence, gazing fixedly into my face as if to read my thoughts. Alas ! he read but too plainly that thought, which was : 'The hand of death is upon him.' He suddenly raised himself, and fronting us fully, with a mighty effort, as if in direct response to my un-uttered thought, he said : 'I had desired to live for two reasons. The chief one was that I might make one more speech to the people of the whole country, which I have partly prepared, upon the relations between the white man and the black man. I am in favor of giving the negro equal and exact justice ; nothing less and nothing more. My friend, we cannot have good government or stable so-ciety when one party seeks to dominate the other by the use of the negro vote.' His voice had grown stronger and more distinct as he spoke ; and then came the old flash to his eye, the familiar poise of his head, and his remarkable gesticulation. ..."

Passing from the race question, Lamar dealt with "the uni- versal and deep disapproval of the then existing administration of federal affairs manifested all over the country, and the causes of that disapproval; the extravagance of the public ex-penditures and the burdensome taxation, including the vicious-ness of the tariff." He called attention to the abuses in the dispensation of patronage, the "spoils system" as it operated under the Republican administration, and the dishonesty and fraud that had been uncovered. This was a "reform" election in the real meaning of the word, for Mr. Cleveland had been nominated above the claims of "leaders beloved and honored in the party," because the people of the nation, irrespective of party or race or section, had desired such reforms in the na-tional government as Cleveland had already instituted as chief executive of New York State.

To such liberal Republicans as Charles Francis Adams and Carl Schurz, who had led thousands of their fellows into in-dependency because they could not serve a party whose leaders were doing nothing to eliminate the abuses in government, including the frauds that had robbed the national treasury of millions of dollars, and who had turned over to special interests far more of the public lands than the area included in the original thirteen colonies, he gave the highest praise. On the other hand, the "history of each successive [Republican] administration is a history of disappointed hopes and violated pledges. The Crédit Mobilier in one administration, embezzling Cabinet officers under another, gigantic Star Route frauds under a third,... the shameless purchase of a State publicly boasted of, open interference in popular elections by federal officers, systematic assessments upon salaries drawn from the public treasury to influence and control elections, have convinced them that only by ejecting the Republican party from power can the people realize a pure, economical administration of the government. They feel that they cannot support such a party, and have declared their purpose to vote for Cleveland and Hendricks." [32]

Parts or all of this speech were used as campaign material throughout the country, and it elicited considerable notice in the North and East. The *Memphis Appeal*, devoting three editorials to it, said—probably too enthusiastically—that it was "more likely to make a deep impression than anything which was ever before presented from this great statesman.... Lamar's tribute to the Independent Republicans will electrify the whole country. The speech will be generally read and attract the attention of the nation, for no public speaker now in political life in the United States so closely rivets the attention of the public as the brilliant Senator from Mississippi. In the Senate of the United States [and here there is no exaggeration in the account] he has repeated again and again the triumphs of parliamentary eloquence which used to illustrate the era of Clay and Webster and Calhoun; and this last great speech will attract as much attention as the utterances of this triumvirate upon the hustings."

When the November elections arrived, Lamar was in the university town of Oxford, ill at the home of his son-in-law,

Edward Mayes (himself a brilliant lawyer who was shortly to become president of the University). Two days had passed, and since no definite news had been received, the citizens had despondently decided that the Democrats had suffered another defeat. A young man came running to the Mayes home on the outskirts of the village bringing a telegram to the "Colonel" from General Gordon, Senator from Georgia. Its message was brief: "Thank God! Cleveland is elected. Turn the rascals out!" At first Lamar could not believe it. "Gordon is too impulsive," he remarked. But, a little later, when additional confirmation quickly arrived, "he sat up in bed, and, without the least sign of exultation, but looking very serious, exclaimed: 'It is a terrible responsibility!' and fell into a long and deep reverie, one of those phases in which those who knew him rightly knew that he was engaged in earnest thought.... The labors of his later life were about to be crowned in the success of his party, and the dead past had buried its dead; but the current of his feelings was too deep and strong to break out into the sparkle and bubble of jubilation in the sunshine. He took no part in the merry-making, for the spell of the future was upon him." [33]

All over the South the election of Cleveland aroused the greatest enthusiasm. When the telegraph wires carried to Atlanta the definitive news of his election, a column—headed by Henry Grady—formed and moved swiftly toward the capitol where the new legislature was sitting. As they poured into the Hall of the House of Representatives, Grady, bearing aloft an American flag, brushed past the sergeant-at-arms and marched down the aisle and up to the Speaker's desk. Seizing the gavel from the hand of Lucius M. Lamar (Senator Lamar's kinsman and Speaker *pro tem.*) he rapped for silence and in the name of Grover Cleveland, President-elect of the United States, declared the House adjourned.

Shortly after the election of Mr. Cleveland, the *New York Tribune* took as the text of one of its periodic assaults upon Lamar his alleged statement that "the South simply recognizes in the result of the election the placing in power, for the first time since the war, of an administration not hostile" to her. "If Republican administration since the war had been hostile, or even without being positively hostile, had been just without being merciful, Lamar instead of being to-day in the U. S. Senate, the peer of loyal men, would be a political outcast, debarred from voting and from holding office, a man without a country," screamed that radical organ. "And yet this Rebel Colonel who, not content with taking up arms against the Union, went beyond the seas with the design of poisoning foreign sentiment, actually complains that the Republican party has been 'hostile' to the South.... His fellow-traitors have also been restored to all the rights and privileges which they enjoyed before the war—Jefferson Davis, even, has not been hanged on a sour apple tree or any other sort of an extemporized gallows." And this in the face of the proscriptive "reconstruction" régimes under which the Southern States had groaned for so many years: "Republican administration has been characterized by mercy and forgiveness; by the olive branch and not by the club!" [34]

Lamar had returned to Washington and had taken up his duties in the Senate when, on the 28th of December, he received a telegram to the effect that his wife was failing rapidly. On the night of the 30th, before he could reach her bedside, she peacefully slipped away. Silently and sorrowfully he stood by the lifeless form of the woman who for thirty-seven years had shared the triumphs and disappointments of his eventful career. The sweetest chapter in his life's history had closed, though the next decade was to see him attain an even more distinguished eminence in the councils of the nation.

Of the letters of sympathy which he received, many were from his bitterest political opponents. "I have learned from the morning papers of your affliction, and I feel that I must intrude on your sadness to tell you of my deep sympathy," wrote the supposedly cold and cynical Senator George F. Edmunds. "I know, alas! too well—how little friends and friendly feeling can do for the hearts that ache and souls that taste the bitterness of such occasions; but still every true heart feels that it must express itself to those who suffer, in words of consolation and encouragement. May the good Father of us all give you and yours in this hour of trial every blessing!" Again, in reply to Lamar's acknowledgment of the 4th of January, he was writing: "Do not grope. There *is* a hereafter; there must be. Every rule of logic, even, leads to this result. . . . Up those shining stairways some that you love and some that I love have gone to rest and happiness. Let us work bravely on till we join them." [35]

Lamar was a reserved man who never wore his heart upon his sleeve, but the death of his wife fell upon him with crushing impact. "Jennie Longstreet's pure and gentle soul has left me and gone to heaven," he wrote on the 4th of January to an old friend who resided in Macon, Georgia. "There are now not many people living that you and I knew before we knew her. Ever since she became my betrothed wife she first liked and then loved you. Our memories were all the same, and our married life was full of happiness even in the midst of sorrow. I can't tell you why I think of you in the midst of this black darkness. But I do, and if I were able to accept relief from any source, I feel that it would give me some to know that you realize the awful thing that has fallen upon me, and that you are sorry for it. Doc. Flewellen's face also comes up before me. My wife was very fond of him, and so am I. Do you know where he is? If you do, send him this note; or, if you prefer, keep it and send him a copy, and tell him I cherish for him a warm affection.

> Your old friend,
> LUSHE LAMAR.[36]

With Lamar's return to Washington shortly before the middle of January, he was immediately drawn into the last debate in which he participated upon the floor of the Senate—his own part a short and effective defense of President Davis from an attack by General Sherman.[37] The controversy had arisen in this manner: General Sherman, in a speech of the previous October before the Frank P. Blair Post, No. 1, of the Grand

Army of the Republic, in St. Louis, had charged that he had seen unpublished letters that had been written by Jefferson Davis to a Confederate, now a member of the United States Senate, which proved "the rebellion to be more than a mere secession: it was a conspiracy most dire." These letters proved, according to Sherman, that Davis "was not a secessionist." His object was to start a rebellion and to involve his own section of the country in such a manner that he could use it to attack the remainder of the United States. According to the account in the *St. Louis Republican*, General Sherman expressed the belief that "had the rebellion succeeded,...the people of the North would all have been slaves." The *Globe-Democrat* quoted him to the effect that he had seen a signed statement by Jefferson Davis in which the latter had said that he planned to "turn Lee's army against any State that might attempt to secede from the Southern Confederacy."

Davis replied in a dispatch to the *St. Louis Republican*, under date of November 6th, in which he characterized Sherman's statements as unqualifiedly false, and remarked that "this public assault, under the covert plea that it is based upon information which regard for a United States Senator does not permit him to present, will, to honorable minds, suggest the idea of irresponsible slander.... If Gen. Sherman has access to any letters purporting to have been written by me which will sustain his accusation, let him produce them, or wear the brand of a base slanderer."

As a matter of fact, Sherman had spoken without his facts, and he was placed in a very embarrassing position. First he announced that he would reply to Mr. Davis' letter through the files of the War Department. Meanwhile, Senator Vance, who had been Governor of North Carolina during the war, and to whom—it was understood—General Sherman was referring, produced a letter from Davis that contained just the opposite statement from that vouched for by General Sherman. Next, the latter sent a statement to the War Department, asking that it be made a part of the Civil War Records, in which he inserted a letter from Alexander Stephens, Vice-President of the Confederacy, written toward the end of the war to Herschel V. Johnson, in which Stephens voiced suspicions as to Mr. Davis' motives. This obviously had no bearing upon the question at issue, and since many papers had taken up the discussion, General Sherman was placed in an even more awkward position.

The matter was brought forcibly to the attention of the Senate when Senator Hawley, of Connecticut, proposed a resolution to the effect that the President should be requested to communicate to the Senate General Sherman's statement before the Grand Army post. This was clearly a move on the part of certain of the more radical Republicans, led by Senators Hawley, Conger, Ingalls, and Sherman to bolster the weak case of the General by placing behind it Presidential sanction; hence the resolution was bitterly opposed by Senators Isham G. Harris of Tennessee, Morgan of Alabama, Vest of Missouri, and others, who claimed that it was merely a personal controversy between General Sherman and President Davis, and that, in any event, it was no concern of the Senate.

Particularly venomous were the remarks of Senators Ingalls of Kansas and John Sherman of Ohio, who claimed that the matter was not a personal controversy but was of vital importance to the nation. The latter (zealous in defense of his brother) closed his speech by calling Mr. Davis a traitor and a conspirator, and likening him to Benedict Arnold. "I must stand, as I have always stood," he said in closing, "upon the firm conviction that it was a causeless rebellion, made with bad motives, and that all the men who led in that movement were traitors to their country."

Lamar had entered the hall of the Senate just in time to hear Sherman's diatribe, at the conclusion of which he took the floor. "That speech, sir," he pointed out, "is marked by flagrant inaccuracies in his statement of the issue between General Sherman and Mr. Davis. The issue between those two distinguished gentlemen is not the issue which the Senator from Ohio represents, and the issue which does exist between them he has not brought to the attention of the Senate."

The question as to whether the secession of the Southern

States "was a conspiracy of a few ambitious individuals, or whether it was the uprising of a whole people, to preserve, as they thought, their autonomy and their institutions," said Lamar, "is one which I am willing shall be remitted to the verdict of posterity. . . . I wish here to say," he remarked in deftly pointing out the question at issue and cutting the ground from beneath his opponent, "that there is no man on this floor who personally has kinder feelings for General Sherman than myself; no Senator here entertains a higher admiration for his military sagacity and genius. But General Sherman was betrayed by his feelings and by misinformation into an allegation and charge against Jefferson Davis that he cannot sustain, and which is not the truth; and that is that he saw a letter from Jefferson Davis asserting that if a Southern State should secede from the Confederacy he would put that down by military coercion of the Confederate Government. That is the statement which General Sherman made. There is no question of historical fact in relation to the character of that movement between General Sherman and Mr. Davis. It is outside of the record, and when he says there is no personal controversy between these two distinguished gentlemen, his statement comes in direct conflict with the assertion of General Sherman himself; for when he was interviewed by the press of St. Louis as to Mr. Davis' denial, he refused to make a statement, and said: 'This is not for the press of the country; it is a personal matter between me and Mr. Davis.' The personality of it is made by General Sherman himself.

"And, sir, the discussion which is brought out here can throw no light whatever on that naked, bald issue of fact, whether or not General Sherman saw a letter written by Jefferson Davis to a Senator now in the United States Senate, saying that he would coerce a Southern State if it should secede from the Confederacy. I assert that no such letter is in existence; and, in my opinion, no such letter was ever written; and, in saying that, sir, I wish to disclaim here any reflection whatever upon the veracity of General Sherman. That is not my purpose. What I do mean to say is that he has been misled, and misinformed. . . ."

Remarking that during the war he had been closely associated with Mr. Davis, though not more so than many other men, Lamar said that from personal knowledge he could vouch that if Mr. Davis "varied one hair's-breadth from the beginning of that controversy to its close, as to the importance of maintaining that government upon the consent of the people engaged in it, and not upon any force to be brought upon them, his most intimate friends were ignorant of any such revolution of sentiment. No man stood more firmly by the doctrine that it should be a government based upon consent, and not upon force, through all the eventful scenes of the struggle, than Mr. Davis did; and General Sherman was simply mistaken; he was misinformed. No such letter was written by Mr. Davis, for no such letter could have been written, entertaining the views that he did."

In closing, Lamar remarked upon the unexpected nature of his participation in the debate, for, said he, "I was not aware that the simple issue of fact, whether or not General Sherman saw such a letter, was to be remitted to the arena of the United States Senate." Though the South had accepted the results of the war as conclusive, though she had cast in the balance her most cherished political beliefs and lost, "No man," said Lamar, "shall in my presence call Jefferson Davis a traitor without my responding with a stern and emphatic denial." Thus he finished his senatorial career, carrying the fight to the opposition with all the brilliance of his analytical and forensic powers.

As a matter of fact, whatever may be said of General Sherman—and he was possibly the ablest military leader produced by the North—it is not to be denied that his standards of personal veracity were not of the highest. "In my official report of this conflagration," he had said of the burning of Columbia, South Carolina, "I distinctly charged it to General Wade Hampton, and confess I did so pointedly, to shake the faith of his people in him, for he was in my opinion boastful and professed to be the special champion of South Carolina." "In other words," comments James Truslow Adams, "Sherman lied,... There is nothing further to be said about a man who lies in an official report deliberately, and the...general has written himself down as not realizing what honor means to a gentleman." [38]

The years of Lamar's senatorship had coincided with the period in all his mature life when he was least threatened with apoplexy and during which he was possessed of his greatest bodily vigor, though for another five years one finds no diminution in the energy with which he executed the difficult tasks with which he was confronted. Hence it is that many of his most enduring achievements fell within the Senate and succeeding Cabinet years—not because he was naturally better fitted for these (perhaps, indeed, not so well) than for the Supreme Court, but because the latter honor was to come to him when the fires of his physical being had almost burned out, though his mind remained scintillant as ever.

Perhaps the best testimony, outside the record of his actual achievements, as to his stature as a Senator, is to be found in the statements of competent contemporaries. His voice, said one of these in commenting upon the compelling power of his oratory, "thrilled with an eloquence almost divine," [39] while Matt Carpenter remarked to another Senator, after listening to one of his great speeches: "He never touches a subject that he does not exhaust." [40] A prominent member of the contemporary American Bar thought that "in a temple dedicated to American oratory his image would appropriately appear among those of Patrick Henry and Fisher Ames and William Pinkney and William Wirt and George McDuffie and S. S. Prentiss and Henry Clay and Ben Hill and James G. Blaine and the Olympian thunderer, Daniel Webster." [41] "Not for a generation or more," said Bishop Galloway, the eminent divine, "has there been a man among us who could, like him, sway and compose vast audiences at will, and by the authority of his imperial eloquence compel the people to adopt his principles and enthusiastically follow his policy. At times he had the classic diction of Edward Everett, and again he could rival the peerless periods of Edmund Burke. He could on occasion pursue an argument with the analytical precision and remorseless logic of John C.

Calhoun; and then, if need be, kindle enthusiasm as with the magic word of Henry Clay." [42]

Moreover, "he was of a philosophic cast of mind. He dwelt in the higher realms of thought. This gave him the loneliness and sometimes the moodiness of genius. He studied and mastered great principles; beneath surface facts he saw their philosophies and discovered their unerring trend." [43] "His record," said the editor of the *New Orleans Times-Democrat,* "will compare favorably in point of ability with those of the greatest statesmen that the country has ever produced," [44] while Senator Walthall felt that "of all the spheres of usefulness in which he served the public, the United States Senate was so much the best adapted to his talents and his taste that his State was reluctant to see him leave that high arena, and the strongest protests against his retirement came from the closest of his friends.... There is not one of his published speeches upon any of the grave questions to which the late war gave rise—questions such as never confronted the illustrious statesmen who went before him—that would not have established the reputation of a public speaker previously unknown; and the greatest of all his efforts was made before the people of his own State, which, to the world's great loss, must be transmitted only by tradition." [45]

XVIII

THE CABINET

No sooner had the election of Mr. Cleveland been conceded than public curiosity turned to speculation as to the probable composition of his Cabinet. On February 8th, 1885, Henry Adams was writing to Monckton Milnes: "The Foreign Department is the only one with which I have to be intimate, and I am waiting with curiosity to see who is to take charge of it. With Bayard, Pendleton, or Lamar, I shall be well satisfied, and these are now the most talked about."[1] Generally it was conceded that at least two Southern men would be among those selected, and as early as December the name of Senator Lamar had come to be among those most prominently mentioned.

Personally, Lamar would have preferred to stay in the Senate, and he offered no encouragement to the agitation in his favor. He would not, he said, volunteer assistance or suggestion to the President-elect, in the selection of his official family, but if Mr. Cleveland called upon him, he would exert his full influence toward the appointment of General Walthall, whom he regarded as the ablest of the public men within his acquaintance. A letter from Lamar to a friend (evidently sent by the latter to Mr. Cleveland), dated December 18th, 1884, and extant among the Cleveland Papers, shows how thoroughly Lamar believed that public office should seek the man. He would be highly gratified, he said, to see General Walthall selected, but he had "no talent whatever for getting up influences and agencies to subserve the advancement of any man."[2] Always he had applied himself "to operating on masses and not on single individuals." In any event, he was not "in connection with the lines of communication with the President-elect," and he would not proffer advice before it was sought. If and when the President suggested

412

a conference, he would, he remarked, press Walthall's claims to the utmost. This, when the opportunity presented, he did.

As a matter of fact it was soon evident that Cleveland had determined upon Lamar as one of his two or three most trusted advisers, and when shortly after Christmas Horace White had an interview with the President-elect, the latter informed him "that he had not made a pledge to any human being for a place in the Cabinet, or any other place, and that he should not do so until he had consulted certain party leaders, among whom he mentioned Carlisle and Lamar." [3] His commanding influence with the incoming President was early recognized by Carl Schurz and his fellow Independents who hastened to lay before him their recommendations for certain Cabinet officers and high appointive government officials, with the plea that he exert his influence in their behalf. [4]

That Cleveland was not unmindful that his elevation to the Presidency was chiefly due to the support of the South was evidenced in the kindly consideration which he evinced for the former leaders in the Confederacy who—once the war had closed—had striven to build a united nation. Dramatic was his advising with the aged John A. Campbell, Lamar's cousin, who had resigned his position of commanding influence upon the Supreme Bench of the United States to go with his section in 1861. "Mr. Lamar concurs with me," wrote Thomas F. Bayard on December 10th, 1884, to the old man, "in considering it highly important that your counsel and opinions should be freely given to Mr. Cleveland at this important juncture, and respectfully and earnestly I trust you will concur in our judgment in the matter." [5]

In less than a week after the election of Cleveland, under date of November 10th, Garland of Arkansas—never backward in urging his own cause—had written to Lamar to ask that he exert his influence in behalf of his appointment to the attorney generalship. The latter, in his reply of the 15th, expressed the conviction that he, Garland, was admirably fitted for the office and informed him that personally he would be highly pleased at the appointment. He explained, however, that "an active support of one friend [General Walthall] on such occasions as this is apt to involve an ungracious disservice to another friend. I may not feel entirely free to contribute to your appointment; but you may be assured that your being a member of Mr. Cleveland's Cabinet will be a source of unmixed pleasure to me, and will greatly increase my sympathy with his administration, and intensify my purpose to support it."[6] Again, on January 1st, at Garland's solicitation, he was writing to Cleveland to assure him that certain criticisms of his (Garland's) views on the Constitution—and opposition to his appointment—were unwarranted, and did not represent the best-informed sentiment of Mississippi and the South.[7]

Without the least desire to enter the Cabinet himself, Lamar was only anxious that the President-elect surround himself with the ablest men, particularly that those chosen from the South be highly competent. At Albany, on February 5th, he canvassed with Mr. Cleveland the entire slate of those who had been proposed for Cabinet office. "When you referred yesterday to a gentleman from Georgia who had been recommended as a member of your Cabinet," he wrote on February 6th from New York City whence he had gone from Albany, "it was my purpose to refer to another gentleman, from the same State, whose name had been mentioned in the same connection. That gentleman is General John B. Gordon. I know him well, and have full confidence in his intellect and integrity. He is full of ardor, *vim* and energy; and his abilities are fully equal to the responsibilities of a Cabinet position. As a General in the Southern army he exhibited rare genius not only on the field of battle, but in the organization of his splendid corps. He was one of the bosom friends of General Lee and commanded his entire confidence....I have not a shadow of doubt about his purity of character in every respect."[8]

But it was General Walthall who first, and above all others, he desired to see Cleveland call to national service. "In my opinion, General Walthall, in the highest qualities of a Cabinet officer, excels any man of my acquaintance in the Democratic party, either north or south," reads Lamar's letter of December

18th, extant in the Cleveland collection. "He is a man of unusual intellect and of truthfulness and integrity of character beyond any man I have ever known in a long and somewhat eventful public career. His courage, both moral and personal, is perfect. His industry, habits of detail, accuracy, and power of organization are wonderful. There is one feature of his character that I find it hard to define. Whilst he is absolutely independent, his convictions and actions always going together, his loyalty to his chief is undeviating and unfaltering. Besides this he has a charm of personal presence, a happy facility of intercourse with men, that make him popular and influential.... If Mr. Cleveland will put Walthall in his Cabinet, he would link me to his administration by a band as strong as steel and as soft as silk." [9]

Eventually it became clear that Cleveland had determined to have Lamar himself in his Cabinet, and that he would take no refusal. "From some hints thrown out by two or three friends of Mr. Cleveland," he wrote to General Walthall on February 3rd, "I am led to think that he desires me to share in the management of his administration. It has given me a great surprise, for I have put my foot upon every movement to recommend me to him. If, therefore, he asks me to go into his Cabinet, it will be the result of his own felt need of my influence, etc., and not of any management." Mr. Cleveland had sent for him, Lamar remarked, but he had not been able to make up his mind to accept the appointment which was apparently forthcoming. "Whilst I think that I might serve him better in the Senate," he wrote in explanation of one consideration which lent weight to the possibility of his acceptance, "I am apprehensive of inferior and obscure men being imposed upon the President.... If they get in, the whole thing will be a farce; and get in they will unless some of us take hold. Cleveland, I am told, realizes the importance of having the best men in the party in his Cabinet....

"My present purpose is to talk freely with the President-elect on every subject that he sees fit to broach. I shall certainly tell him that he can get a man my superior in every respect, and better fitted for a Cabinet office than any man in the Democratic party, North or South. If, however, he presses me to become a member of his Cabinet, I shall not give him a definite answer at once, but will take time to consider it.

"I know all *I* give up if I leave the Senate," he said of his personal feelings in the matter. "I close my career in Congress, and will go into private life at the close of four years, perhaps sooner. If my present feelings are any test of what my feelings will be four years hence, I shall be perfectly willing to quit. I have thought much about it. I really think that my public career has been one of honorable usefulness and great benefit to my people. I know that it has been honest and true, without one element of disregard for the welfare of my people. I can see some mistakes in it. I am inclined to think that I ought to have retired when I saw the South restored to her constitutional position in the Union. Now that she will have her just representation in the Executive Department as well as in the Legislature, with some prospect for the same in the Judiciary, I feel as if my time for making my bow has come. I have always thought that it was a serious blemish, or, rather, defect in our American statesmen, that they always cling to office too long, and beyond their period of usefulness and popularity. One chief ambition with me has been, after exercising the power intrusted to me to the best of my ability, *voluntarily* and with *perfect disinterestedness* to lay it down." [10]

Revealing glimpses into Lamar's mind and heart frequently appear in his private correspondence of this period. "Yes, the praises of me are, *just now*, gorgeous," he wrote to his daughter, Mrs. Gussie Lamar Heiskell, of Memphis, Tennessee; "but wait; and if I should accept a Cabinet position (it has not yet been tendered to me), soon after I get in, the irate clamors of disappointed office seekers will be a story compared to which the fuss on the Silver Bill was an April shower.

"The man at Albany is in a critical position, beset with difficulty; but that is no reason for my backing out if he thinks he needs my help.... Just now we need to develop Democratic *administration* more than Democratic speechmaking," was his comment upon the advice of the many people who felt that he could be of most help to the Democracy and the nation by retaining his position of tremendous influence in the Senate. "It does not make much difference what becomes of one man if, while he lives, he can advance the good work of establishing a government of justice and constitutional law." [11]

Despite his eminence in the national scene, Lamar was suffering mentally and spiritually as is evident in his letter of February 14th, to his sister, Mrs. Ross: "The present is a dark period of my life. The pale face of my wife is ever before me, and my grief seems to have fixed itself in my heart." Again, in the same letter: "The newspapers are fuller than usual of praises of me; virtues which I do not possess, and talents which I know do not belong to me. I should feel humiliated did I not know that in a very short time they will teem with criticism and censures and jeers, with no more of justice in their dispraise than in their present laudations." [12]

Just how earnestly Lamar hoped that Cleveland would take General Walthall for the Cabinet, and how little he himself desired the place from any consideration of personal glory, is evident in a letter from his friend and one time *protégé*, Burton N. Harrison, who—at Lamar's solicitation—had seen the President-elect in furtherance of Walthall's claims. "It is evident," wrote Harrison, "that he specially desires *you personally* to be a member of the Cabinet, and that, though I have had his attention drawn again to our friend who is your choice for the place, it was not wise for *me* in my own name to attempt *at this juncture* to divert his desires. . . . Nobody has produced on Cleveland the impression you did, . . ." [13]

When Cleveland, at Albany on February 5th and in his letter of the 19th, urged upon Lamar his acceptance as a public duty, the latter could no longer refuse his assent. "I esteem it both a pleasure and a duty to place at your disposal any services which I can, in your opinion, render to you and the country," he wrote on February 21st. "In accepting this important trust, allow me to thank you personally for the honor you have done me, and to express even more warmly my grateful sense of the obligation you have conferred upon the South in giving one of its representatives an opportunity of showing how loyally and faithfully it desires to serve the interests of a common country." [14]

It is interesting to speculate as to the causes of Cleveland's determination to have Lamar in his official family, for they had never been thrown together in public life and Lamar had championed the nomination of Bayard at the time that Cleveland had been selected to lead the Democracy. Rhodes is undoubtedly correct when he says that Cleveland's desire to have about him the ablest men in the party, coupled with the high position that Lamar had taken in courageously voting against the free silver bill (this against the instructions of the Mississippi legislature), together with his interest in Civil Service, must have led to his selection. [15]

"I hope that the step I am about to take will meet your approval," [16] Lamar wrote to Jefferson Davis on February 28th. "It certainly proceeds from no motive of ambition; but when pressed by my friends in the Senate and in the House, and through the country, and by those nearest to the President-elect, to take a position in his Cabinet, I have hardly felt at liberty to decline. If, by conducting the affairs of the executive department prudently and honestly and fairly to all sections, I may serve the interests of a common country, I may do more good than I have ever yet been able to accomplish. Recent events have crushed out all ambition in my heart, and I now have no other desire connected with public affairs except to serve to the best the interests that our people have intrusted to me so often."

Thus Lamar had made his decision. But when the time came for him to leave the legislative branch of the government he had seen almost healed—and largely through his efforts—the wounds of the fratricidal war; and the irreconcilables of both sections were dwindling into an insignificant minority. Near the close of Lamar's Senatorial career, Joel Chandler Harris wrote for the *Atlanta Constitution* an editorial which evidences the extent to which the Mississippian had become the voice of the New South. "In the North," wrote Harris, "there is a handful of men—a handful compared with the great mass that refuses to train with them—who call themselves *stalwarts*. They have been pursuing the South for years with a ferocity that is intended to represent a public sentiment which no longer exists.... In the South, *the stalwarts* have been well matched by a few politicians and editors, so that upon both sides of the line we have had a tremendous burlesque going on—at the North a few men strutting and swaggering and declaring that the Confederates were still warring upon the nation, and at the South, a few men strutting and swaggering and inviting the entire Yankee nation to tread upon their coat-tails. The Southern strutters were quite as bitter and as proscriptive as the Northern stalwarts.

"When Senator L. Q. C. Lamar, whose views have become the views of the Southern people, delivered his remarkable eulogy upon Charles Sumner, the Southern strutters were ready to tear him limb from limb. They attacked him on all sides and made a great outcry, protesting vehemently upon the representative character of his deliverances. Not the least remarkable feature of Senator Lamar's career since the war is the fact that he has utterly refused to cater to the views of the strutters who made him the object of their commonplace vindictiveness. He is as liberal and progressive now as he was when he made the Sumner speech, and he has lived up to his highest ideal of American statesmanship, which means love for the whole country...." [17]

Mr. Cleveland was inaugurated on the 4th of March, 1885, with the Senate scheduled to assemble in executive session for the purpose of considering Cabinet nominations on the 5th. "Three hours before the time fixed for the opening of to-day's session of the Senate people began occupying the seats in the visitor's galleries," according to the interesting account of the correspondent of the *New York Times*. "An hour before noon every seat was taken, and the outside corridors were thronged with men and women who grumbled because they had come so late. The Senators began to gather on the floor soon after 11 o'clock.... Mr. Pruden... presented Mr. Cleveland's first message to the Senate.... Everybody knew that this message contained the nominations of the men selected by the President for his Cabinet, and the visitors leaned forward as if they expected to hear the names read. Instead of this, they heard Mr. Sherman move that the Senate proceed to the consideration of executive business, and a moment later the Sergeant-at-arms was instructed to clear the galleries.[18]...After every outsider had been driven out from the place, and all the doors carefully locked, the big envelope was torn open, and the Executive Clerk read the names of the gentlemen whom President Cleveland had selected as his chief advisers, as follows—Secretary of State: Thomas F. Bayard, of Delaware; Secretary of the Treasury: Daniel Manning, of New York; Secretary of War: William C. Endicott, of Massachusetts; Secretary of the Navy, William C. Whitney, of New York; Secretary of the Interior: L. Q. C. Lamar, of Mississippi; Postmaster-General: William F. Vilas, of Wisconsin; Attorney-General: Augustus H. Garland, of Arkansas.

"Then began a very lively scene, which ended with an adjournment twenty-five minutes later without any of the seven nominations having been confirmed. It is the traditional custom of the Senate to confirm without delay any one of its members who has been chosen by the President for any other office. When, therefore, Mr. Cockrell moved that the nominations of Messrs. Bayard, Garland, and Lamar be confirmed, the Senators were nettled at hearing Mr. Riddleberger object to the present consideration of Mr. Bayard's name. Senators from both sides of the Chamber crowded around him and begged him to withdraw his objection. He refused, and listened with stolid indifference while sharp remarks about his conduct were made by Mr. Edmunds, Mr. Ingalls, Mr. Harris, Mr. Ransom, and others. Mr. Riddleberger told them to go on and confirm Messrs. Lamar and Garland and all the rest if they wished, but he should continue to object to placing the foreign policy of the government in the hands of a man who had more sympathy with England than with the United States. The Senators had no intention of confirming two of their number and not the third, and they pointed out to the Virginian the awkward position in which they would be placed if they accepted his proposition."

Upon Riddleberger's insistence, and since by the rules of the Senate a single objection holds a nomination over for a day, the Senate finally adjourned with the understanding that on the morrow all of the appointees would be confirmed regardless of protests, for the Republicans even more than the Democrats were disgusted with his attitude. But by the next day (the 6th) Riddleberger had been prevailed upon to withdraw his objections, and the whole slate of Cabinet nominations was unanimously confirmed.[19]

A critical and sensationalized sketch of Lamar, published in the *New York Tribune* of the 6th, evidences in its willful misstatements the depravity to which that yellow journal had attained, though Lamar would not have objected to the characterization (which to the *Tribune* seemed so damaging) had it been true. Every statement in the following excerpt, the reader will recognize, is false: "He achieved [according to this account] military distinction at the battle of James Island, or Secessionville, near Charleston, S. C., June 16, 1862. According to the *Charleston Mercury* he directed the opening fire of the rebels in defense of the works, and 'to his cool courage and energy in the early part of the action is due the preservation of the position. His brave example and personal efforts greatly inspired his command.' He was finally wounded by a rifle-bullet and carried from the field." The purported quotation from the *Charleston Mercury* is sheer fabrication.

Among the almost unanimously favorable expressions elicited in Washington by Lamar's selection was the statement that the new Secretary is "a Gentleman and a scholar,... with perhaps the apparent indolence of many great thinkers. He adds to solid attainments a fervid eloquence that surpasses that of the once famous William L. Yancey, in as much as it possesses the dramatic power and feeling of the latter, and a deep and tender poetry." The high regard in which he is universally held "softens to a degree the disappointments of other States than Mississippi that their favorite sons were not called, while his more substantial equipment renders him an ornament to the executive councils." [20]

According to one authoritative account, as Lamar "was leaving with the portfolio of the Interior in his breast pocket, so to speak [after his first interview with the President-elect], Mr. Cleveland remarked, 'Senator, I warm to you more than to any statesman yet met. How will it do to put in [the Cabinet] four real big men and fill up with young fellows who will polish up?" [21] The arch-Republican *Cincinnati Commercial Gazette*—consistently unable to see anything worthwhile in the personnel and plans of the incoming Democratic administration—aroused one of its readers, who, on the 6th of March, wrote forcefully if somewhat extravagantly: "Mr. Lamar is one of the ablest men in this world. He is a thinker, and one of the purest men I know of, and Mr. Cleveland has made no mistake in putting him into the Interior Department, where there is the largest field for stealing." [22] The new Secretary, it seemed to the protester, was by far the strongest member of the Cabinet.

The young Theodore Roosevelt, after declaring his disgust with the Republican platform as well as the Presidential nominee had, in a typical shift of position, found it expedient to return from the West in time to proclaim the period of Republican reconstruction as the "golden age of the nation" and (after the Democratic victory) the Cabinet selected by Mr. Cleveland as the "apotheosis of the unknown." But the general nonpartisan opinion was (and is) that "the new Cabinet was one against which no reasonable criticism could be brought. More than that, it was a very remarkable body of administrators. For personal distinction it has had few, if any, superiors in the whole history of the government." [23] A note of February 24th by Carl Schurz, the leader of the Republican Independents who had rallied to Cleveland, throws interesting light upon the composition of the Cabinet. "I have been thinking over the names you mentioned to me yesterday in connection with the Cabinet," he wrote to the President-elect, "and it has occurred to me that while the three Southern men among them [Lamar, Bayard, and Garland] are all United States Senators of renown and experience, the Northern men named are all new men, nationally speaking, that is, men without experience and established standing in national affairs." [24] It was desirable, he thought, to balance the Southerners with as strong a selection as possible from the other sections of the country.

Likewise, George F. Parker, Cleveland's personal friend and closely associated with both of his administrations, recorded that the "question of the attitude of Mr. Cleveland's administration towards the South was the matter most often under discussion...the new President took the bold step of drawing Messrs. Bayard, Garland, and Lamar from the United States Senate for Cabinet advisers. They had long experience in public life, and unquestioned character and ability. They had conquered the respect of the whole country by these qualities and by the exhibition of courage and patriotism in trying times. No man of equal prominence or political standing to any of these was taken from the North. *It would not have been possible to find such men*, and yet the charge of undue influence could not be laid against the South, nor, outside of the lowest partisan quarters, was this ever alleged. Once more, the distinctions of section, so long potent, had been demolished, never again to be established on the old lines." [25]

As a matter of fact, every member of Cleveland's first Cabinet was well above the average of Cabinet officers (except— possibly—Norman J. Colman, Secretary of Agriculture, whose office was not created until 1889), but history has recorded the verdict that Lamar and Bayard were the statesmen of the group, while Garland, as Attorney General, failed to enhance the distinguished record that he had made as lawyer, Governor, and United States Senator.

Thus Lamar entered upon what was for him a new and totally untried field; and, as the best known member of the Cabinet (with the possible exception of Mr. Bayard) and as the chief of the department where the need for reform was most crying, he was to work in a continuous blaze of publicity. "I enter upon my new field of activity with great diffidence," [26] he wrote to a friend. Among those who had been most intimately associated with him, none doubted that he would shed luster upon his office, but there were many in the North, and some in Mississippi, who viewed him as a "scholastic dreamer and moody idler—one who was absent, abstracted, contemptuous of detail and drudgery, inert, except when at rare intervals aroused to the tremendous energy of which he was capable." General Walthall, however, expressed the prevailing feeling among Lamar's friends and followers when on the 5th of March he wrote that "everybody in Mississippi is proud that you were *called* to the Cabinet,"[27] although every one regretted that it meant the surrender of his seat in the Senate. He, on the other hand, was to see one of his most cherished ambitions come to fruition in the appointment of General Walthall to fill the vacancy created by his resignation from the Senate. As we have seen, it had long been Lamar's desire to see the latter transferred from the comparative obscurity of his private law practice into the broader field of public service.

"If I were to select the one man of all others with whom I have served in the Senate, who seems to me the most perfect example of the quality and character of the American Senator," said Mr. George F. Hoar in a statement which substantiates Lamar's estimate of Walthall and justifies the former's almost dictation of his successor, "I think it would be Edward C. Walthall of Mississippi.... He rarely took part in debate. He was a very modest man. He left to his associates the duty of advocating his and their opinions, unless he was absolutely compelled by some special reason to do it himself. When he did speak the Senate listened to a man of great ability, eloquence and dignity. I once heard him encounter William M. Evarts in debate. Evarts made a prepared speech upon a measure which he had in charge. Walthall's reply must have been unpremeditated and wholly unexpected to him. I think Evarts was in the right and Walthall in the wrong. But the Mississippian certainly got the better of the encounter."[28] So powerful was the hold that Walthall gained upon the affections of his State that only death could have removed him as its representative.

Perhaps the *New York Times,* in an editorial of March 6th, best exemplified the reaction of the nation to Lamar's appointment. "Mr. Lamar, of Mississippi," said this paper, "has been rightly judged by the President from the first. His original and thoughtful mind, conservative habit, and sobriety of judgment, left upon Mr. Cleveland at their first meeting a marked and most favorable impression. In him the President secures a good adviser and an administrative officer whose deep-rooted aversion to such doubtful and devious ways as have of late caused the Interior Department to be made the subject of unfavorable comment cannot fail to have a wholesome effect upon the service of the department from the moment of his accession to office. It has been said that Mr. Lamar has a distaste for confining, routine work; and, so far as this is true, it would be a defect in his equipment for a place demanding so much steady, hard work as that to which he has been appointed. But it is known that he has a liking for doing well anything he undertakes, and he is not without that enthusiasm which lends interest to even the driest details of man's daily toil. We do not believe that Mr. Lamar will be inattentive to the needs of his department. The criticism which calls in question the propriety of appointing an ex-officer of the Confederate Army to a post giving him charge of the bureau through which Union soldiers receive their pensions is one to which we attach no great importance. This objecton would be waived, we imagine, if some brave veteran of the Union Army were appointed Pension Agent."

As Lamar had pointed out in his campaign speeches, the nomination of Cleveland was distinctly a reform movement, and his powerful support by the Independent Republicans was the result of the belief that many of the abuses in the government would be corrected under his leadership. Because Lamar had always lent his influence to the reform element in both parties, such Civil Service enthusiasts as Schurz were most insistent that he be given a Cabinet post. In pursuance of his own convictions in respect to the Civil Service, Lamar did not, in so far as he could possibly avoid it, disturb or discharge the subordinate officials and clerks in the Department of the Interior during their term of appointment. But one very sound principle he insisted upon: namely, that the heads of all bureaus be men of tried Democratic principles whose loyalty to the administration he could absolutely trust. Thus it was that on the day that he entered office he called for the resignation of the chief of every bureau and set about finding capable men to fill their positions. "Secretary Lamar threw in his scythe among the heads of the Interior Department to-day, and cut a stalwart swath," reported the Washington correspondent of the *New Orleans Times-Democrat*. "There was nothing dreamy or absent-minded in the manner of his doing it, either. What Secretary Lamar did was to ask the resignation of every chief of bureau in the department under his dispensation. Nine important and prominent offices will be vacated.... The affair has created something of a sensation, though chiefly on account of its sudden and sweeping character.

"Of course this will give a fresh impetus to applications for office, though no impetus seems to be needed, since a trifle over one thousand telegrams were received to-day from patriots willing to sacrifice themselves for a salary.... Public opinion has taken a reef in apropos to Mr. Lamar. It appears that he is not so slipshod and visionary as was supposed, but can exert a fine nervous energy on occasion."

Shortly after entering office, Lamar and Attorney General Garland made another change, slight in itself, that elicited much favorable comment: they ordered the numerous horses and carriages that had been kept for their departments at the public expense, and had been driven by government "clerks," to be sold and the proceeds—slightly more than $10,000—to be turned into the public treasury. This they had not done for political effect, but because retrenchment and the economical administration of the government had been, together with Civil Service Reform, the most important principles and pledges of the campaign. Their action received wide and favorable notice as indicative of the attitude of the new administration toward the squandering of public funds. Lamar's own method of conveyance, it should be noted, was a modest one-horse carriage which he bought and maintained at his private expense.

During the administrations previous to that of Mr. Cleveland the public had come to feel, and with justice as was subsequently shown, that the Land Offices (under the jurisdiction of the Interior Department) were fraudulently and illegally allowing the most desirable portions of the public domain to fall into the hands of speculators and railroads that had in no sense earned their grants. One of Lamar's first acts was the selection, with the approval of the President, of the best man that he could find for the position of Land Commissioner, Mr. W. A. J. (Andrew Jackson) Sparks, instructing him that the evils be corrected, and that with the help of the Attorney General as much of the public lands as had been fraudulently taken from the government be recovered. Such measures were vigorously prosecuted and with great success, as we shall presently see.

One of the first investigations that Lamar personally conducted was in respect to the large land grant to the New Orleans, Baton Rouge, and Vicksburg Railway which, up to the day before Cleveland took office, had laid out for itself sections of land to the amount of 1,015,993.76 acres. These, however, were not legally patented. On the Friday preceding Cleveland's inauguration, Secretary Teller—at the request of the railroad company, and over a number of protests that the terms of the grant had not been complied with—set a large force of clerks to work issuing patents for the land. The clerical force labored throughout Sunday, and on March 3rd Secretary Teller certified patents for 679,287.64 acres. It was clear that an effort was being made to transfer this immense tract before the new administration came into power.

Lamar investigated the situation, and on the 10th he ordered that the transfer of the land be halted. When the press got wind of the affair there was a great outcry. Ex-Secretary Teller, who had just been seated in the Senate from Colorado, heard himself denounced by Senator Van Wyck, of Nebraska, a Republican, who called for an investigation. Gould and Huntington,

427

the latter claimed, were responsible for the scheme to get possession of the land grant. He further stated that, though no representative of the settlers who had built homes upon the land was present, a Cabinet meeting was called for the legalization of Secretary Teller's act, and that in this case, as in many others, the Land Bureau of the Interior Department had merely acted at the command of the financiers. It is only fair to say of ex-Secretary Teller, however, that while Lamar questioned the wisdom and propriety of his actions, he did not believe him guilty of any intentional dishonesty and was careful to make this clear in his first annual report to the President.

Lamar's decisive action received equal praise from the Republican and Democratic press, but the *Jacksonville* (Fla.) *Journal* feared that the action of the Interior Department was coming "too late to recover the interest which a long maladministration of the Land Department has betrayed and wasted. It is a well established fact that for years that department has been thronged with agents of States, corporations, and individual speculators, who either through the Commissioner or his subordinates, have been able to consummate the most stupendous frauds in nearly every State of the Union where there was a large unoccupied domain. And so strong and well organized was this combination that any attempt on the part of any citizen, or even a member of Congress, to protect the public interest would only result in accusation and crimination, until the party would be compelled either to join in the villainy or acquiesce and hold his peace through fear of personal injury." [29]

"The new Commissioner of the General Land Office, Mr. Sparks, has evidently entered upon his work with the intention of protecting the government from the rapacity of land grabbers, aliens, and speculative cattle dealers," commented the *Philadelphia Press*, in an editorial which indicates something of the scope of the immediate steps taken to conserve the public domain. "He has suspended the issue of warrants in certain sections of Dakota, Nebraska, and Kansas, and in the whole of Colorado, with the declared intention of investigating all the entries with such care as shall protect the government from plunder." The real settlers, pointed out the editorial, had been kept out by the cattle men who had fenced off large tracts of land. Moreover, in every State west of the Missouri, fraudulent entries had been responsible for the dissipation of much of the public domain. Stating that never before had the Land Office exerted itself in the interest of the people, the editorial commended Lamar and the new Commissioner for "that strict watchfulness without which the public lands will soon be diverted from the purpose intended by the law."[30]

Throughout the nation there was marked approbation of the way that Lamar was conducting the affairs of the Interior Department. The political commentator of the *Washington Post* remarked that those who thought of Secretary Lamar as preoccupied with metaphysics and philosophical speculation to the hurt of his "onerous duties" were "never more mistaken in their lives." Apparently, he is always the first to appear in the morning, even before the official opening of the office, and "depend upon it, when this judge gives out his *ipse dixit*, the boomers, cattle men, and Indians may rest assured that it will be just, fair, and final.... The conclusion of the whole matter is that the new Mississippi Secretary is not only the brainiest, most logical, and clear-headed man this department has ever had at its helm, but the most laborious and practical.... Were his physical strength commensurate with his mental caliber, it would be of iron."[31]

To the *Augusta* (Ga.) *Constitutionalist*, Secretary Lamar seemed "not only the most fascinating member of the Cabinet, but the most active, hard working, and industrious. So far he has completely put to the sword all predictions that he would be a scholastic dreamer and moody idler.... As a Senator, Mr. Lamar was apparently conspicuous for inertness, when not, at long and rare intervals, roused to tremendous activity by some occasional thrust from Conkling or Hoar.... All attempts at industrious effort were eschewed or carefully concealed. He appeared only on great occasions, and bore himself like a Jupiter Tonans." Some people, says this paper, have been unable to account for the remarkable drive and energy that he had put into his Cabinet post, when to understand properly they should view "Mr. Lamar as a man of genius," and, hence, necessarily "a man of surprises; for he is not so essentially a philosopher that profound dramatic calculation does not give method to much of his action or inaction." One should understand that "Mr. Lamar, the Senator, knew the value of silence as well as of speech; that he understood how to secure the drudgery of others, so that his mind might dwell in serene and thought-breeding altitudes; that he attained a greater reputation for himself by two or three famous speeches than commonplace men have made in two or three hundred harangues.... He cannot, therefore, be judged by ordinary methods, because he is an extraordinary man. The men of Rome who took Brutus to be a fool have descendants in this country who believe Lamar to be only a coruscating visionary." [32]

The turn given to the customary criticism in the *New York Tribune*, however, was highly amusing. Admitting that Lamar "has a well-trained and scholarly mind," and that "his legal acumen is of the sharpest," it said that in the Interior Department "the chiefs of bureaus are either old men, whose toothless malignity has covered Mr. L's administration with ridicule, or young men whose talents, if they ever had any, were exercised in fields entirely different from those to which political preferment and the caprice of party leaders have now called them." [33] This criticism, however, was mild compared to that heaped upon other governmental departments in the same article.

It will be recalled that in one of his letters Lamar had predicted that the chorus of praise elicited by his suggestion for a Cabinet post would, with as little reason, soon turn to abuse. On March 24th, less than three weeks after he had been installed as Secretary of the Interior, came the death of ex Secretary Jacob Thompson who had served as head of the Interior Department under President Buchanan. On the next day Lamar ordered that on the day of the funeral, the 26th, the flag over the Interior Building be flown at half-mast, and that its bureaus be closed out of respect to the former head of the department. Immediately the Republican press recalled the secession sympathies of the departed, and almost without exception they broke into vituperation of the conventional courtesy that Lamar had shown to the dead.

The new Secretary had foreseen no criticism of an action that was customary in every department of the government irrespective of the personality of the deceased, and in any event he would have disregarded it and acted as he did. "On the walls of the office of the Secretary of the Interior are displayed portraits in oil or crayon of every Secretary who has filled the office since its creation by Congress in 1837," wrote the correspondent of the *New York Herald* on the 27th. "No exception has ever been taken to the fact that the portrait of Secretary Zach Chandler has been a companion piece with that of Secretary Thompson, whose funeral took place yesterday; nor have any of the Republican Secretaries of the Interior complained of Secretary Thompson's picture in the group adorning the office." The correspondent pertinently remarked that if such intense partisans as the late Secretary Chandler and Mr. Kirkwood could serve under the shadow of Mr. Thompson's picture, it was not to be expected that Mr. Lamar should except him from the "usual mark of respect when a former head of the department dies."

"It really begins to look as if the Confederates have captured the capital," screamed the incendiary *New York Tribune*. "The maimed veterans of the war must wait for their pensions while the officers and clerks of the Interior Department take a holiday to honor the memory of a conspirator and traitor who gloried in breaking his oath of office and divulged Cabinet secrets to the South Carolina rebels." "Still, there are some persons who are disappointed," editorialized the same paper. "They are the creatures who professed to believe that the Democratic party had become transformed, that loyalty had become its ruling spirit.... The people who believed that sort of thing have only themselves to thank if the conduct of affairs does not suit them."

Many papers, however, recognized the criticism and agitation for what it was worth. The *New York Herald*, already quoted, was quick in its defense of Lamar's action, while the *New York Sun* characterized it as an attempt of the Republicans "to revive against Mr. Cleveland's administration the passions and animosities of the Civil War," and the celebrated correspondent, Donn Piatt, sent to the *Cincinnati Commercial-Gazette* a spirited defense that was copied widely throughout the nation. To this paper, which had been peculiarly fierce in its assault on Lamar, Piatt suggested the elimination of some of its political bias and the substitution of an open-minded consideration of the matter. "Lamar was the first to rebel and the last to surrender," he said, "and in both he exhibited the same manhood that has won for him the respect of his enemies and the love of friends. . . . It was his duty to lower that flag on the death of a predecessor, not in honor of the man, but the official. . . . It was an official ceremony, and no discretionary power is given the living official. He complies with the law and the custom. Let me illustrate: When the former Secretary of War, Belknap, comes to depart this life, his successor in office will droop the flag and drape the doors with mourning. Can such successor say: 'No, this can't be done; the man disgraced his office, and the building must not mourn?' To those knowing Secretary Lamar—and he is getting rather well known—the charge of disloyalty, for this is what it amounts to, cannot be sustained. The man who stood up in his place to eulogize Charles Sumner—whose breadth of intellect marks the statesman, while his generous impulses make him lovable as a man—is not one whose official acts are likely to hurt him or the cause he represents." [34]

Many other editorials there were espousing each side of the controversy, and Lamar was the recipient of numerous telegrams and letters in reference to his action. For himself he had only this to say publicly: "that he was surprised at the tumult that had arisen over an official act, and that he had no apology to make for his orders." [35]

It has been said that Lamar was an advocate of the principles behind the movement for Civil Service Reform in so far as those principles could be given practical application. Believing as he did, the importunities of the great swarm of office seekers that had descended upon Washington even before the inauguration of Mr. Cleveland, many of whom were seeking appointments in the Department of the Interior, were a severe trial to him. As some one pertinently remarked, "the great throng of Democrats who were anxious to grasp Mr. Cleveland's hand on that occasion were also anxious, in the vast majority of instances, to grasp also the spoils of victory." [36] "Tennesseans turn up at every street corner," remarked a commentator from that State, "and are found in most unexpected localities and on all sorts of expeditions. Some come for the fun of the thing, but most of them for office. It is safe to say that there are from 10 to 25 men for every office in the State." [37]

That there would be no indiscriminate turn-out of the employees of the Interior Department was evident when Lamar, immediately upon taking office, reinstated Mr. Hanna as private secretary, a position which he had held under both Schurz and Teller. Though he had replaced the heads of all bureaus with men whose loyalty to the administration could not be questioned, and though as a general rule he appointed competent Democrats when a given Republican had served out the period for which he had been appointed, his attitude was in all cases kind and considerate, this extending even to the most lowly colored menials. Blanche K. Bruce, the Negro ex-Senator, stated that Lamar never failed to do justice to any Negro whose job was in question, and that he was always glad to use his influence with his fellow Cabinet members in a worthy cause. Once, said Bruce, when he had reported to the Secretary that a Negro charwoman, who had for some reason been discharged, was in dire need, he was told that it would be impossible to reinstate her over the orders of the head of the bureau for which she had worked, but that he (Lamar) would see that she received the modest sum that she had always been paid for her work. It was years later that Bruce discovered that Lamar, throughout his tenure of office, had sent her the money out of his comparatively modest salary.[38] And this was not the only instance, recorded the Negro ex-Senator, when Lamar had

433

been generous far beyond his means. Generally speaking, little or no dependence can be placed in the writings of the Mississippi Negro ex-Congressman, John R. Lynch. But there was no reason for him to pervert the facts (as he did in all cases that suited his purpose and in some where falsifying apparently brought him no advantage) when he said that except in cases of open immorality Lamar removed none of the Negroes with whom he (Lynch) was acquainted during the period for which they had been appointed.[39]

"I eat my breakfast and dinner and supper always in the company of some two or three eager and hungry applicants for office," Lamar was writing to his relatives and closest friends shortly after taking office. Again: "I have to be in my office, generally, at nine o'clock; and if not there am kept by the visitors who call on me before I rise in the morning and stick to me until I start. It is rarely the case that I get to bed before twelve o'clock, so constant are the demands upon my time and attention;...I am nearly drowned in an inundation of ink, made up of streams from all parts of the country."[40]

"The pressure upon me for the lowest offices in the department is absolutely greater and more distressing than that for the higher positions," he was writing to a friend in a letter of February 5th, 1887. "Refined and intelligent women from the South tell me that they do not know where they will get their next meal; that they have children, a poor mother, or a consumptive sister; and they are willing to go into the paste room or to scour the floor, or to take any position that will give them from twenty to twenty-five dollars per month; and all that I can give them is something that they do not want, and this is my keenest sympathy. This, however, is not appreciated, and no one believes but that I am able to find some position somewhere if I choose to do so....The helplessness with which I contemplate all this suffering, and listen to these complaining importunities, is making existence wretched."[41]

At least three million men, Lamar believed, voted in hopes of directly or indirectly being benefited by federal patronage. "The thirst for a general 'turn out' all over the country," he said, "was almost fearful." Moreover, he could not escape the personal conviction that the majority of those who sought to dwell in Washington in the employ of the government were parasites upon the body politic. Continually he urged his friends and acquaintances to find employment at home unless they could come to the capital as the accredited representatives of their people. Writing to one Georgia lady who had solicited a position, and explaining the hardships of unremunerative clerical work, he told her: "I have had some Southern women here with me. I had one very nice lady from ——, and she refused the very first day to climb up a ladder and pull down some papers which my Democratic chief of division had ordered her to bring.... I have come to the conclusion that it is no act of friendship, no act of real good service, but a veritable injury, to appoint any lady from the South to office in any of the departments of government." [42]

"He hated the drudgery of the place less than he did the importunities of his party for office," editorialized the *New York Times* of January 25th, 1893. "It seemed to him that the principal part of his office duty was to listen to and refuse (because it was impossible to grant them) the requests of the crowd that constantly filled his rooms.

"One day a gentleman who was not a caller for office was shown into Mr. Lamar's inner apartment. In the outer room were several prominent Democrats, including a high judicial officer, several Senators, and any number of members of the House. Mr. Lamar waved his visitor to a chair without saying a word. He was evidently too much exhausted to speak. By and by his visitor said that he would go away and return at some other time, as he feared that he was keeping the people outside.

" 'Pray sit still,' requested Mr. Lamar. 'You rest me. I can look at you, and you do not ask me for anything; and you keep those people out as long as you stay in. I can have them at any time I choose to send for them. I can't get you. Please do not go away.' "

Another painful yet amusing aspect of the situation was his

experience in respect to recommendations. He found, his letters show, that from at least one State it was practically impossible to appoint any one to office because the Democratic leaders were so critical among themselves that they found it impossible to agree upon any one whom they could back. Further: "It is the same with every office that I touch—on one side, eulogies of the applicant that would make George Washington blush if pronounced upon him to his face; and, on the other, denunciations that would make even a felon tremble for his reputation. Thus, in several instances, *whomsoever* I appoint, there will be on record in my office charges of his own party associates against him greater than those filed against the Republican incumbent whose removal is urged." [43]

It was well that Lamar had expected, as his letters indicate, to reap criticism and abuse as unwarranted as had been (he felt) so much of the praise that had been heaped upon him. Two months had not passed before he was inundated with letters, telegrams, and personal visits for the purpose of warning him of the dire evils that would come to the party if he did not displace more Republicans and show greater favor to the Democrats. On the other hand, the Republicans had been in power for many years and had become used to the rich spoils of the nefarious system that had grown up since the days of Andrew Jackson. Their cries and criticisms were as raucous as those of the disappointed Democratic office seekers. That this situation was not peculiar to the Interior Department is, of course, to be understood. President Cleveland bears witness to the fact that his ability to act for the welfare of the nation was well-nigh stopped by the importunities of the many thousands who wished to enter the employment of the federal bureaucracy.

The Cleveland Democrats had gone to the country with a Civil Service plank which declared that a great proportion of the offices should be filled on the basis of examination given under the supervision of a commission, and that appointees should, on good behavior, hold office until the end of their terms, regardless of any change in the administration. "Every day I meet the President I am more deeply impressed with his patriotism, his self-oblivious devotion to duty, and his determination to carry out the principles of reform to which he has pledged his administration," Lamar wrote on July 1st, 1885 to Major General Pennypacker, of Philadelphia, in a letter which shows his loyalty to his chief and the principles which he had enunciated. "It may be the Democracy of this country will not sustain him. That, however, will not cause him to falter one moment in his steady, unfearful, and undoubting march to the object before him. The thirst for a general 'turn out' all over the country is fearful.... If, however, it is yielded to; if the opportunity is lost under this administration of establishing the great principle that the offices and honors of this government are not the mere rewards and spoils of party victories, but great public trusts to be administered for the benefit and the highest and best interests of the country, I believe American liberty will be lost with it." [44]

How President Cleveland himself viewed the matter of appointments and removals is evident in a letter which he wrote on August 25th, 1885—while on his vacation at Saranac Lake, in the Adirondacks—and which, having been sent to Lamar for approval and suggestions, was subsequently unmailed. "Nothing, it seems to me, could be more distinct than the promise I made to the people during the campaign, and since its close," he wrote to a prominent politician of the Northwest in explanation of his refusal to replace certain Republicans with members of his own party, "that officers whose duties are purely executive should not be displaced during the continuance of their terms merely and solely to make way for those who are in affiliation with the party to which I belong.... I fully share in the sentiments to which I have referred, and sincerely believe that a change of administration should not be the signal for an entire change in the servants who are employed to do the people's work.

"It follows that honor, good faith, and my conviction of what is right and just, all combine to cause me to remain firm and steadfast in the line of conduct which has been marked out for the guidance of the present administration. All officers connected with the furtherance of the political policy of the government should be of the same political creed and party as the administration, but faithful and honest officers not thus related, and whose removal is not deemed necessary to the proper consummation of needed reforms, and having fixed terms, will not be removed merely upon the allegation that such officers belong to the party lately defeated at the polls....

"It can only be those who suppose that, under a code of morals peculiar to political affairs, promises can be made when the people's suffrages are solicited and easily forgotten afterwards, who can find fault with the course which I have determined to pursue." [45]

Cleveland himself, as well as the members of his official family, were not without sympathy for, and understanding of, the feeling within the Democracy that since the Republicans had for so many years enjoyed preferment, it was but fair that the Democrats should have their turn. Secretary of State Bayard was acting as a practical but honest public servant when he replied when questioned in regard to certain of his consular appointments: "I am prepared to give no other than the same reasons which have controlled the nominations of diplomatic officers—in order that the foreign service may be in more perfect political harmony of opinion and policies of action with the administration which is now responsible for their action." [46] According to Bayard, the principle laid down by Cleveland was that those officials who had served their full term of four years should as a rule be replaced by competent men from within the ranks of the Democracy. Government employees might for due cause be removed at any time, and resignations from among the Republican office-holders were always welcome. [47]

But the President became increasingly exasperated by what he termed "the damned everlasting clatter for offices," [48] and continually he was wounded by former friends who, disappointed because they had not been appointed to remunerative offices, went over to his enemies. "Oh, Dr. Keen, those office seekers! Those office seekers! They haunt me in my dreams,"[49] he was to cry during his second administration (when the pressure was less severe than in the first) just before he was placed under the influence of ether preparatory to a serious operation upon his throat. "My Civil Service friends," he remarked caustically of Schurz and some of the latter's associates who failed to show any proper appreciation of his struggles for reform, "have sometimes seemed to think that the government was to be conducted merely for the purpose of promoting Civil Service reforms."

It must be said to the credit of the Cleveland administration, which was the first wherein the Civil Service was extended by executive action, that in its larger aspects the course which the President had mapped out was conscientiously followed. A precedent was established which so appealed to the nation that when four years later the Republicans resumed control, they were forced to concede the point and not remove employees, except for due cause, until the end of their appointed terms.

Lamar, himself possessed of the "clan spirit" to a high degree and with an extensive family connection, refused to appoint members of his own family in the Department of the Interior. A firm believer in the evils of nepotism, relationship with him constituted an insurmountable barrier to appointment. "The charge is a public one, and the offices to be disposed of are public trusts," he wrote in explanation of his refusal to make an appointment. "If I could give them out according to my own wishes, not only Mr. ——, but some very poor members of my own family, would be provided for. They have my heartfelt sympathies, but the limitations upon me as a public man are such as to prevent my giving them help through public offices....

"I confess to you a reluctance toward appointing my own relatives to office. It is proper to state here that the applications from this source are numerous and distressing to me. There is no personal sacrifice that I would not make for my own kin, except that of using the patronage which is in my hands as a public trust for the purpose of advancing the private interests of relatives and friends." [50]

Of all of the Civil Service reformers, Carl Schurz was the most progressive and the most persistent. Indeed, his interests along this line amounted almost to a monomania, as he later admitted. He had bolted the Republican party to support Cleveland, and once the latter was inaugurated he felt privileged to call upon him continually, in person as well as by letter, in the interest of his own pet projects. Moreover, he seemed incapable of understanding how impossible it was to realize a Utopian idealism, and his persistence became one of the major annoyances of Mr. Cleveland's administration. At length, out of considerations of self-defense and the necessity of giving his time to the public service, Cleveland was forced to refuse to communicate with him, either in person or by letter.

Schurz was a sincere admirer of Lamar, had corresponded with him regularly upon questions of public moment, and had been delighted when he was appointed to the Cabinet. But his persistence became almost as burdensome to Lamar as to the President. Schurz would presume to advise and to criticize by letter and through the press when he was totally unacquainted with the details of the case in question.[51] "I am to-day surrounded with men of the opposite party, with whom I have no relations except those that are purely official, and have retained them against the protest of my personal and political friends, who believe that they are bitter political enemies, not only of the party to which I belong, but of my own success as the chief administrator of this department," Lamar replied on the 2nd of October, 1886, to a communication from Schurz. "Nothing is needed to defeat the purpose and the operation of the Civil Service law except bad faith; and the fact that the great body of the clerical force is still Republican is due not so much to the compulsory power of the law as to a sincere coöperation with its intent and purpose." [52]

This letter, moreover, is illuminating in that it gives an intimate glimpse of the President from the viewpoint of one who was closely associated with him. "I am very glad to find that you think that the President has done many good things," Lamar wrote. "Let me communicate to you one fact about the President, in the perfect freedom of private and personal confidence. A man's life is twofold: one, internal, which is his real nature—the life of thought, feeling, intention, and purpose; the other, external and public, which is very often a hindered and imperfect embodiment of the former. I have been in close contact with the President, and I have never seen, in moments of the most unrestrained familiarity and unconscious disclosures of himself, a thought, word, or deed inconsistent with his ideal of a pure Civil Service." Whatever aberrations might occur during the administration from the course marked out must be charged to the failing of subordinate agents, said Lamar, and not to Mr. Cleveland, for "I do not believe that the President would swerve one inch from his policy." Schurz, in his reply of the 9th, agreed "with you in all you say of the President,... the sincerity of his professions and his integrity of purpose," after which protestations he launched into an extended discussion of certain removals and appointments concerning which his information was most inaccurate.[53]

Meanwhile, Lamar's time was chiefly consumed by the routine of his arduous duties. "I send these lines to you, Colonel, instead of the President," he wrote to Mr. Lamont (Cleveland's secretary) in a lengthy executive communication of November 20th, "because I know how vexing it must be to have these matters thrust upon one who is engaged in the preparation of a state paper.... I have had to leave Washington for a few days, otherwise my report will never be completed. I swear that I cannot finish *one sentence* without being interrupted. You can reach me by mail, or by a special messenger at College Station, on the B. & O. Railroad, Maryland. You would enjoy yourself by a short run over here. Or, if the President would like a few days of quiet to compose any part of his message, my cousin I know would be glad to have him under his roof." In any event, Lamar wrote, he would on

Monday send Cleveland "something that perhaps may save him some work on the Indians, the public lands, and other matters pertaining to my Department." For the President's consideration, too, he drew up a brief memorandum on the tariff,[54] a subject which he thought of little public interest at the moment and which might well be treated with brevity in the message to Congress.

During this first year of his secretaryship, Lamar had applied himself untiringly to a survey of every activity and every bureau under the control of his department. As a result, in an extensive annual report (that of 1885) embodied in five volumes of more than twelve hundred pages each (with an eighty-seven page introduction written by himself) he laid before the President a survey of the accomplishments, plans, and needs of the department.[55]

So comprehensive and constructive was this report that it immediately attracted wide attention. "Great industry, great conscientiousness, and great good sense, as well as uncommon length, distinguish Secretary Lamar's report," remarked the *New York Sun* of the section written specifically by the Secretary himself. "It is one of the longest documents of the sort, if not the longest, ever submitted to a President by a Cabinet officer.... This happens not because Mr. Lamar has wasted many words, but because he has been so diligent in informing himself as to the conditions and needs of the multifarious interests under the supervision of the Secretary of the Interior, and so anxious that Congress shall have, to the fullest extent, the benefit of his investigations and conclusions.

"It is proper to say that this document is as far as possible from being the production of a dreamer who goes around with his head in the clouds. It is the work of a practical intelligence, able to express itself in excellent English. Few State papers in the rapidly accumulating literature of the Cleveland administration are so well written." [56]

According to a dispatch in the *Chicago Inter-Ocean* of December 12th, "The Report of Mr. Lamar is considered the best that has come from the Cabinet, not only as a literary work, but for its comprehensive, statesmanlike review of public questions," an opinion commonly voiced throughout the press. This paper wondered, however, whether Lamar did not often long to be back in the Senate, away from the importunities of office-seekers and the exactions of arduous routine work. In any event, he applies "his ideas of justice and law with a vigor that fills the building with electricity."

A number of papers remarked contritely upon their earlier predictions that Lamar was too much the dreamer to be fitted for the exactions of a Cabinet post. "Rarely does a department report receive as much favorable mention from the press of the country as has been accorded to that of Secretary Lamar," commented one widely copied editorial. "Notwithstanding the misgivings expressed at the time of his appointment, the idea is now very generally entertained that he is the right man in the right place." [57] Meanwhile the Minister in far-off Switzerland, under date of December 28th, was characterizing the report as "a perfect model" that furnishes "a combination of philosophy, thought, and the highest culture, with ability for details and practical affairs."

It is necessary to look in some detail at the contents of this first annual report, for here we find the inception of many reforms which Lamar put into full effect during the balance of his term in office.[58]

The first section dealt with the situation in respect to the Indians, all of whom were under the direction of the Interior Department. Their problems he found to be rooted in the ignorance and brutality of the Indian agents, their own tendencies toward shiftlessness and cruelty, and the frequent invasion of the rights of the tribes by the great "cattle kings" who claimed to have obtained leases from them. As a matter of fact, under the preceding administrations many of the cattle barons had secured leases to millions of acres for a payment of an average of not more than two cents annually, and often the Indian agents had played corrupt parts in the letting of the contracts. Such leases, said Lamar, had not been open to public competition; the Indians had been allowed to make contracts without government supervision and protection; and the Department of the Interior had *permitted* but not *sanctioned* the execution of the pretended leases. An example of what had been allowed under the preceding Secretary, Mr. Teller, is seen in a "deal" consummated in 1883 whereby the Cherokees leased to one cattle company a tract of 6,000,000 acres (an area larger than that contained in several of the States) for a term of five years at an annual rental of $100,000, while this company had sublet the tract for $500,000 a year with a total profit during the period of $2,000,000 or 400%. High government officials defended their actions on the grounds that the great cattle companies would take the land anyway; hence it was best to secure whatever tribute was possible from them.

Lamar had instituted legal proceedings by which he had dispossessed these unlawful invaders of millions of acres of land. The *Omaha Herald* of September 29th said that Lamar was "making a close study of the needs of the Indians, and also of the character of the men who are to have charge of their interests. This is equally true in respect to appointments to the land offices in that and other States. The philosopher-statesman of Mississippi may be a 'dreamer,' as he is sometimes called by the politicians; but it might better be understood now than at a later time that he is a dreamer of very practical dreams."

Further, he presented a careful analysis of the conditions that had caused great discontent among the Indians, and had been at the bottom of their uprisings, and he made technical proposals as to the allotment of lands; the disposition of the Indian trust funds; and the administration and curriculum of the Indian schools. Particularly did he call for action by the Attorney General in the case of the leases of extensive tracts of land that had been executed since January, 1883, and without public competition and at ridiculous rentals. "From all the facts developed on the subject," he said, "I am convinced that the assistance rendered by the respective Indian agents in the making of these alleged leases was directed more for the interest of the cattle men than that of the Indians placed under their care and supervision...in many instances I fear that they have shared in the profits of these speculative transactions." Lamar ruled that no contracts made by or for the Indians were valid unless they conformed to laws passed by Congress and unless they were executed with the supervision of the Federal Government, and he urged immediate action by the Attorney General. This was immediately forthcoming, and it was held by the courts that the leases that had been made without conforming to these conditions were invalid and without a shadow of authority in law. Moreover, it was found that they had been at the root of much of the friction and complaint in the Arapahoe and Cheyenne Reservations.

Again, Lamar indicted the common practice of building fences and holding by force the historic cattle trails through the territories, and he called for an examination of the right of way of certain railroads that had proposed to lay tracks through the reservations. He explained, too, the motive behind his reversal of the policy of the preceding administration which had thrown open to white settlement the reservations that had long before been set aside for the Crows, the Creeks, and the Winnebagos. He had, he said, acted upon his own initiative in removing all settlers who had preëmpted lands in these reservations.

Having concluded his analysis of the Indian situation, he proposed definite reforms. "It is evident that the Indian race has reached a crisis in its history," he said in summary. The practice of moving him "to more distant reservations can be continued no longer. He must make his final stand for existence where he is now....I recommend," he said among other things, "that a portion of every reservation be divided up into separate tracts of suitable size for farms, to be allotted to each individual as his sole and separate estate. Provision should be made against the power (until after a time limit) of selling or mortgaging the same, or even leasing it to any except Indians living within the same reservation. Without legislation of this kind, all efforts to make the Indian support himself by his own labor will prove fruitless and unavailing. To overcome his natural aversion to labor there must be the incentive, given alone by a sure guarantee that the fruits of his labor shall be enjoyed in security. No man will clear forests, inclose fields and cultivate them, and rear houses and barns, when at any moment he may be removed and carried off against his will to some distant and unknown region. The ownership of land, freeholding, tends to inspire individual independence, pride of character, personal industry, and the development of the domestic virtues. Provision should be made that the Indian accepting a patent for his land shall not thereby forfeit any of his rights as a member of his tribe, nor the protection and benefit which the laws of the United States extend to the Indians generally...." All of these recommendations Lamar was to see enacted into law and, by the time that he resigned his office, working better than he had dared to hope.

In closing this section of his report, Lamar dealt with the situation in Oklahoma—particularly with the illegal settling of Indian lands by the "boomers" who had disregarded all executive and judicial orders.[59] From the late seventies until the beginning of the Cleveland era, every effort to control the "land grabbers" had been futile. One adventurer, "Oklahoma" Payne, had formed "land companies" for settlement in the Indian territories and, issuing bogus certificates at $2.50 each, he was reported to have cleared some $100,000 by 1884. Lamar conceded that there was a "vast surplusage" of land contained in the territory, and he presented a plan for consolidating the Indians upon an adequate stretch of the best territory, but he held, with the support of the President, that the hand of the administration could not be forced by "rapacity and lawlessness." The government would act in due time for the best interests of all, but such adventurers as the boomers were not to think that they could "ride roughshod into possession of the lands of the Indian reservations." Hence he had, he showed, used military force to displace these unlawful invaders, and he felt that it should be the policy of the government "to show to such transgressors that the way is hard, and that nothing would render the Indian occupation more permanent, or postpone the change in the use of the lands longer, than the attempts to invade and by force to obtain possession and enjoyment of them."

Next in line of consideration was the subject of those Public Lands not specifically belonging to the Indian territories. Lamar carefully detailed the acreage that had been disposed of during the current year, and indicated the method of disposition. Exclusive of Alaska there remained, he showed, 600,722,654.41 acres, and he recommended that steps be taken to arrest the preëmpting of large areas by corporations that excluded the acquisition of property by the poorer settlers. Further, he recommended the passage of laws barring the presentation of land claims based upon alleged Mexican grants before the Southwest territory was acquired by the United States.

Under Lamar's direction and with the intelligent coöperation of Commissioner Sparks, the cattle kings and the "transatlantic companies" that were "parceling out the country among themselves" were indicted and actively prosecuted. Putting up fences and hiring armed riders, they had illegally "taken the best lands and practically all the waters," paying in most cases no taxes and owning no allegiance to the government. "The effect of illegal fencing is detrimental to the best interests of the State," commented this first annual report. "The *bona fide* settlers naturally avoid conflict with the large and powerful corporations which are already in forced possession of the choicest of the public lands, and they do not dare to invite the hostility of these companies by going within their inclosures in order to make settlements. Consequently, thousands of settlers are practically prevented from obtaining homes. The effect of such a policy is necessarily to shut off immigration and to delay and hamper the development of the resources of the country."

From Colorado to Kansas millions of acres had been unlawfully fenced, and sometimes *whole counties*. Lamar declared that "substantially the entire grazing country west of the 100th meridian" had been fenced by the Cattle Kings. Jones County, Texas, the cattle men had completely inclosed with a fence that had but two gates in its circuit, and it required the combined power of the Governor of the State, the legislature, and the Federal Government to free the little town that contained the courthouse. One cattle baron had built a fence of 250 miles in length, beginning at the headwaters of the Red River.[60] It extended from the eastern boundary of the Indian territory on down into New Mexico, and was designed to keep out the cattle of the Kansas ranchers. During the first year of Secretary Lamar's administration more than a million acres were restored to the open country.[61]

"Good government," said Lamar in this first annual report, "seeks to secure to the citizens the undisturbed enjoyment of his natural rights. Among these is the enjoyment of his lawful acquisitions. Land, lawfully acquired, is among the most important of his possessions. Its security depends upon the certainty of its title; uncertainty, litigation, and contention depreciate its value, disturb the peace, waste the means, and mar the prosperity of a community or nation. To insure certainty of title, the land laws should be simple, few, and, as far as practicable, general in their character. Special and local laws, known to but few, diminish the merchantable value of land; for titles acquired under such laws are not widely known, and the range of competition on their sale is diminished and limited. Laws which in their administration are liable to abuses which exceed their probable utility subject the government to suspicion, and often make it the instrument of knavery. Laws exist on the statute books which violate these principles, and are objectionable." Hence he recommended the repeal of the Desert Land Acts, of the Railroad Grant Relinquishment Act of June 22nd, 1874, of the Timber Culture laws, of certain of the measures pertaining to surveying, and he urged modification of the act of June 3rd, 1878, whereby certain companies and individuals were allowed to conduct lumbering enterprises that netted millions of dollars without recompensing the government.

He showed, moreover, that upon the suspension of the patents that had been issued to the New Orleans Pacific Railroad, the company had dropped its claims to sixty-eight miles of the

448

line. The remainder, he felt, had been built in good faith and according to supposed legal right; therefore he recommended that Congress waive technicalities and claims to that part of the development. Other phases of the Public Lands situation he discussed, but the main topics have been indicated.

The next section of the report, highly technical, has to do with the railroads that had been sponsored by the government. Each of them he discussed in turn, outlining its financial condition and stage of development. "To secure a good system of national highways for the use of *all* the people," Lamar felt, "was the primary object of the governmental grants, subsidies, and loans of credit to the several Western Railroads. Direct pecuniary profit to the government was little contemplated; still less was it intended that the system should be appropriated to the enriching of the few at the expense of the many." The problem of later governmental regulation of the railroads (in which Lamar was to have an important part) is anticipated, and it is to be noted that the occasion of such regulation is the sound one that public utilities should be conducted for the good of all of the people rather than for the aggrandizement of the few: "The field of future investigation might well include how the great franchises granted by the nation are conducted with reference to the convenience, wants, and necessities of the people whose interests they were intended to promote."

Almost the sole objection that had been urged against Lamar's appointment to the Interior Department, even by the Northern Republican press, was the contention that, as an ex-Confederate officer, he would not be sympathetic toward the pensioning of Union soldiers—the entire pension system of the Federal Government being under the control of the department for which he was suggested. "As a Union soldier," wrote one fearful citizen when he heard that Lamar's name was under consideration, "I beg to remind the President-elect that the Pension Bureau, with its three hundred thousand pension claims of Union soldiers still unsettled, is in this department, and I can imagine what will be said all through the North and at every Grand Army Post over such a selection." [62] Doubtless, Cleveland could imagine what would be said, but he had no intention of allowing criticism to interfere with the selection of the most competent executives that he could command. It was typical of Lamar's tact and fine judgment that—at his own suggestion and with the President's hearty approval—among his first official acts he telegraphed an offer of the responsible post of Pension Commissioner to the Democratic Union General, John C. Black. The offer was accepted, and the acumen and loyalty exhibited by the appointee was a tribute to the wisdom of the selection.

No part of the government, with the possible exception of the Land Office with its even greater opportunities for fraud, had been so abused as the Pension Bureau. Each year since 1879, when the measure was passed that dated the pension payments back to the time of death or disability, the nation had been literally defrauded of millions of dollars. Once the act had become a law, the business of forging claims became an activity in which thousands were engaged, for the rewards were tremendous.[63] Indeed, within a month the cases presented to the bureau had increased some sixfold. An extreme instance of the business of securing pensions was the conduct of the Washington office of a man named Lemon who openly advertised for clients and with 70 clerks had at one time 150,000 claims in process of submission.[64]

Records were freely falsified, and the whole conduct of the pension office had become a national scandal.[65] Under Colonel Dudley, who had headed the bureau during the preceding administration, conditions had become intolerable. In less than three years he had increased the expenses of his office from $5,000,000 to $30,000,000 a year, and he used his position chiefly to advance the interests of the Republican party. Employing 1,680 persons, he in one year received more than 75,000 letters from Representatives and Senators pushing the claims of "veterans" in their districts and States, this besides innumerable personal calls. During the campaign of 1884, he had left his office, though continuing to draw his salary, and by threats and promises to ex-Union soldiers, he had organized the soldier vote through a large section of the Middle West for Blaine.[66]

It was a delicate task that Lamar and his appointee, General Black, faced in handling this situation. Because of their Democracy, and because of Lamar's once prominent position in the Confederacy, they were already under suspicion of unfaithfulness to Northern interests, and must walk circumspectly as they attempted to purge the bureau of fraud and dishonesty. First, the rolls were closely examined for fraudulent claims. By the time that the first annual report was presented, Lamar pointed out, more than a thousand names had been stricken from the pension list of only two agencies.[67] The Secretary saw no reason why the fact that he himself was an ex-Confederate should in any way influence his decisions in regard to the validity of the claims of Union soldiers. "I know of no burden of government that is more cheerfully borne than that of the pension system," he said. "I concur fully in all efforts to demonstrate that it is universally regarded as a noble beneficence and in the view that *when well and cleanly administered* it is noble in its purpose and good in its results, diffusing with a liberal and just hand the wealth of a wealthy people among those who suffer from the strokes of war, and who have become impoverished by its misfortunes."

Nevertheless, he was rigid in his demand that every application be meritorious, and mere sympathy never caused him to be careless with the nation's money. When certain individuals protested at his purging of the rolls of thousands of names that had no claim to the beneficences of the government, he explained unanswerably that every real Union ex-soldier should lend his full support to the effort to keep the pension money from being squandered among those whose applications were fictitious or lacking in merit. The *Toledo Journal* of December 13th, 1885, reminded its readers that "Secretary of the Interior Lamar is called a Rebel Brigadier, and a yell was set up against him in certain quarters, fearing that he might be hostile to pensions to Union soldiers. We are glad to know that the Secretary is not hostile to liberal pensions. His report shows him to be keenly alive to the broadest instincts of patriotism.... Every veteran soldier of the Republic should thank Secretary Lamar for his splendid contribution to patriotism and valor." Such, and far more enthusiastic, notices of this section of the annual report appeared in the press of all parts of the nation.

The *Louisville Courier-Journal* took pains to quote Lamar's theory of pensions and to call to the attention of the radical Republican press, particularly the *New York Tribune* and the *Cincinnati Commercial-Gazette*, the fact that their dire predictions had not been realized. "These patriotic sentiments are from the first annual report of L. Q. C. Lamar, the Democratic Secretary of the Interior, a Southern man in all that the term implies," said the editorial in question; "a man who is great and honest and just, and who shames by his manly utterances the blatant shriekers who cried out in simulated alarm when he took office that 'the South is in the saddle; the Union in danger; that the Democratic party having come into power, the results of the war would be reversed; the soldier and the soldier's widow robbed of their pensions, while the Confederates devastated the land they had failed to destroy by war.'" [68]

It is possible here merely to mention a number of the topics with which the annual report of 1885 was concerned. It reviewed the operation of the Geological Survey, the Patent Office, the Bureau of Labor, government hospitalization, government printing, the national park system, and the recently completed tenth census. Finally, there is a consideration of the situation in the territories of Alaska, Arizona, Dakota, Idaho, Montana, New Mexico, and Utah, with special recommendations to provide for the needs of each.

It was characteristic of Lamar that in closing he should have placed particular emphasis upon education. Praising the efforts of the Commissioner of that bureau, he recommended that the office be abolished unless the government were willing to broaden the scope of its activities, and give it more extended authority with sufficient financial backing to enable it to function adequately. He reviewed the history of the proposal for a national university which had been fostered by Washington, Adams, Jefferson, and Madison, and observed that "in these latter years the idea... constitutes no part of the plans of statesmen, and seems to have been lost sight of by the people." A coördination, he thought, of the scientific bureaus that "have grown up one by one under the government, with observatories, laboratories, museums, and libraries" might furnish the basis for a university that "would be without rival in any country." This dream of Lamar's has not yet been realized, but it is not without the bounds of possibility that the day will come when a national university comparable to the Sorbonne will be situated in Washington.

No discussion of the second annual report,[69] submitted on the 1st of November, 1886, will be attempted, for enough has been said of that of 1885 to indicate the nature of Lamar's achievements. Comprehensive in its scope, it is interesting in that it shows the working out in actual operation of many of the reforms that the Secretary had instituted during his first year in office, and which he had completed or was carrying to completion.

Meanwhile, as the Lamar-Cleveland correspondence shows, the respect in which the two men held each other had deepened into a warm personal friendship and intimacy. By 1886 the President had acquired the habit of inviting the Mississippian to frequent meals in the privacy of the immediate White House family circle. These were delightful occasions for Lamar who, since the death of his wife, had maintained modest bachelor quarters in Washington. "I send you a bass caught to-day at 2 o'clock at the dam near Woodmont," Lamar wrote to the President in an undated note of this year. "It is (so they say) the largest bass ever caught out of the Potomac. I would carry it to you in person, but I am *hors-de-combat* with hay fever or something else that is very worrying." "This fish," he remarks in an amusing postscript, "weights 6 lbs 3 oz dry—and no 'Washington's hatchet' about it."[70]

Then, too, there was always a warm welcome to be found with Henry Adams, when he was in the city, with the Walthalls, the Bayards, the Vilases, the Georges, and at the homes of a number of others who had been among his former colleagues in the Senate.

Meanwhile, Lamar had become increasingly the darling of a large section of the Washington correspondents and the press in general. Long before he entered Mr. Cleveland's Cabinet, the stories associated with him had grown to the proportion of a saga in Washington society and official life, and during his secretaryship many of them found their way into public print. All of them were of a kindly nature, and most of them throw light upon his complex and attractive personality. "During all this time the searching gaze of curious, as well as anxious and just, scrutiny, was full upon him," commented Hon. T. C. Catchings, shortly after Lamar's death. "There was a subtle and indefinable influence emanating from, rather than exerted by, him that made him an object of interest, even in the quietest moments of his private life. In public life it attracted to him an eagerness of attention that within all my observation was without parallel. It made him not merely the central figure in every event with which he was connected, but so unique and imposing that public curiosity regarding him was never satisfied, his peculiarities of manner, in fact, anything and everything pertaining to him, directly or remotely, were constant topics of conversation among those who knew him." Indeed, he had become a legendary figure to multitudes who had never seen him.

Cabinet members at that time received a salary of $8,000. One of the stories related that after Lamar had been transplanted from the Senate to the Cabinet, "he wanted to rent a residence. Mrs. Dahlgren, widow of the late Admiral Dahlgren, had just completed an elegant house...which she wished to let. Secretary Lamar called upon her, was ushered into the parlor, and made known his business. The lady replied that the house was for rent, the rental being $7,500 per annum. The Secretary sat perfectly quiet, his eyes bent upon the carpet, apparently absorbed in profound thought. This was kept up so long that Mrs. Dahlgren finally inquired if he were ill.

"'No, madam,' replied the Secretary; 'I was only wondering what I could do with the rest of my salary.'"[71]

"Mr. Lamar," according to another story which seems not to have been entirely a fabrication, "has been one of the most picturesque characters in Washington society. He was eccentric and peculiar in many respects. He was frequently the victim of many ludicrous occurrences. There are many stories now recalled illustrating this and other peculiar features of his character. Although he was a most scholarly man, particularly well read in diplomacy and legal lore, he was passionately fond of light literature. Going to and from the capitol when he was a Senator, and between his home and the Interior Department when he was in Mr. Cleveland's Cabinet, he rarely spoke to any one that he met, but sat in the street car or his private carriage, as the case might be, with his nose buried in a book.

"One day, when he went to attend a Cabinet meeting at the White House, an embarrassing incident occurred. He had just descended from his carriage in front of the White House, bearing under his arm his portfolio, an official-looking leather receptacle. As he descended from the carriage a group of correspondents saluted him. In returning their greeting, Mr. Lamar's portfolio fell to the ground. A half-dozen well known 'seaside' novels tumbled out of it. They were scattered in every direction and the correspondents, with exaggerated politeness, helped the distinguished Cabinet officer to gather them together. Mr. Lamar thanked them greatly for their assistance, and, stuffing the books back into his portfolio, he walked with dignified step into the White House."[72]

The warmth and number of Lamar's friendships has often been commented upon in the course of this narrative. He "was naturally a very courteous man, but when he became absentminded he often saluted his best friends with a stony stare, and answered questions at random," according to an account vouched for by his son-in-law, Edward Mayes. "One day, as Mr. Ellis, of Louisiana, was sitting in his committee room at the capitol in Washington, Mr. Lamar walked in, and, seating himself, said in his grave gentle way:

"'Ellis, I don't believe you like me.'

"'No,' said Mr. Ellis, 'I don't. Lately you have hardly spoken to me. I pass you, and you don't look at me; and such conduct has offended me.'

"'But Ellis,' said the Senator, 'you know it's my way.'

"'I don't care," said Ellis, 'it's a damned bad way.'

"'My dear fellow,' replied Mr. Lamar, throwing his arms around Mr. Ellis' neck, 'the next time you see me in that damned bad way just come up and punch me in the ribs. Now, promise me, and let's be friends.'

"Mr. Ellis promised, and punched also." [73]

The third annual report, submitted to the President in November, 1887, was even more extensive than its predecessors, for it embodied some phases of work inaugurated by Lamar and never before undertaken by the government.[74] Moreover, enough time had passed for his plans to have come to bear definite fruit. Partly through his influence (for as a member of the Committee on Railroads in both the House and the Senate he had battled against severe opposition for federal supervision) had been established the increasingly important Interstate Commerce Commission, created by the act of February 4th, 1887, and effectively regulating the carriers along lines that he had laid down in his first annual report.[75] With the sanction and collaboration of the President, he selected the personnel of the Commission and directed its initial operation. Having observed the functioning of the new body, which was bringing fresh opportunities to millions of small shippers, he recommended that it be responsible directly to the President rather than to the Secretary of the Interior, and that it employ its own officials and clerical force with authority to draw upon the treasury for its expenses. Again, he had shown his progressivism in the development of the Bureau of Labor (of little immediate importance but subsequently to have its director elevated to a Cabinet post), for the creation of which he had exerted his powerful influence in Congress and which as Secretary he had organized; and he reported upon its work as upon that of the Interstate Commerce Commission.[76]

"Perhaps," said Lamar in this report, "the most difficult and important duty with which this department is charged is the administration of the public land system." Since he entered office on the 4th of March, 1885, there had already been recovered and restored to the public domain, he showed, more than forty-five million acres, an area equal to that contained in all of the six States of New England plus Maryland and Delaware, and that a large part of this had been taken from the government initially by willfully fraudulent and illegal practices. Moreover, action was pending within the department for the recovery of almost ten million acres additional. The present administration of the Interior Department had worked with the view, so far as practicable, said Lamar, of saving the public domain for the settlement of "independent small land owners living upon their own freeholds." In the application of the principles which he had laid down, and in the attainment of the ends which he sought, remarked Carson, some of Lamar's decisions in respect to property rights and the public domain made legal history.[77]

On April 28th, of this year, Cleveland—at Lamar's instance —performed a memorable service for the homesteader. The situation was this: In 1878, one, Guilford Miller, had homesteaded on a piece of land in Washington Territory and after improving it considerably had belatedly filed a claim to it toward the end of 1884. No sooner had he done this than the Northern Pacific Railroad stepped in with the claim that in the previous year, 1883, the company had—under the terms of its grant —selected a tract including this land as part of its indemnity grant (in other words, it was claimed that the land had been marked off as compensation for part of its original land-grant that had been found unavailable). This was merely one of many instances, Lamar found, where, with the acquiescence of the Republican Interior officials, the great subsidized railroads had passed by available vacant lands and in making their selections of "indemnity" had willfully and knowingly chosen improved farms, these in many cases occupied by settlers who had come in years before the railroad itself. And to complicate matters, Attorney General Garland was sincerely of the opinion that legally there was no relief for the settlers. With the way apparently barred, Lamar suggested to the President that he call for the complete files bearing upon the Miller case and that, after due study, he issue an executive order embodying the equity of the matter and so phrased as to bring relief to the thousands of poor homesteaders who were like situated. This Cleveland did in his celebrated and much quoted letter of April 28th.[78]

The *New York Tribune,* in a typical reaction, could see nothing praiseworthy in this solicitude for the rights of the small settlers. "Oh, it's clearly a political move designed to help Cleveland in certain quarters," explained that organ of entrenched privilege. "It is the hand of Lamar and the voice of Cleveland." [79]

This third report, which covered every subject treated in the first and second as well as the work of the newly established bureaus and commissions, also showed in detail the progress that had been made in the care of the Indians. Much of what Lamar had recommended during his first year had been put into effect by the general allotment law of February 8th, 1887. "By this law," he commented, "every Indian, of whatever age, may secure title to a farm, enjoy the protection and benefits of the law, both civil and criminal, of the State or Territory in which he may reside, and be subject to the restraints of those laws. It goes still further. Under it the Indian, in accepting the patent for his individual holding of land, takes with it the title to a higher estate: that of a citizen of the United States, entitled to all the privileges and immunities of such citizenship, and yet invested with all the lawful responsibilities of that position."

On December 6th, 1887, shortly after Lamar had submitted this third annual report, President Cleveland sent his name to the Senate for confirmation to the place in the Supreme Court of the United States left vacant by the death on May 14th of the Hon. William B. Woods, Associate Justice. When there arose considerable protest from certain Republicans who felt that no Southerner—certainly not an ex-Confederate officer— should be allowed to sit upon the highest tribunal in the land, and it became evident that there would be some delay in confirmation, Lamar, on January 8th, 1888, requested the President to accept his resignation as Secretary of the Interior. This step he took from two important considerations: because the retention of his executive position might seem to give him undue power to coerce certain Senators; and because he wished to relieve the administration of any embarrassment that might be incident to attacks aimed at him by the radical Republicans. Hence, for the first time in many years, and for only a relatively short interval, he retired again to the position of a private citizen.

Before passing to a discussion of the situation that developed in connection with Lamar's nomination to the Supreme Court, what shall be said of the measure of his success during the three years that he sat in Mr. Cleveland's Cabinet? So broad were his duties and so many his accomplishments that in this account it has been possible little more than to indicate the nature of his efforts. That his success was notable cannot be questioned, for it is commonly stated by competent historians that he instituted more permanent reforms and furnished the initiative for more important legislation than any Secretary of the Interior before or since.[80] Much of the success of his administration was due to his years of service in both Houses of Congress where he had built up a large following and tremendous prestige. It has been seen that his recommendations, beginning with his first annual report, were extensive. Many of the reforms which he instituted required appropriate legislative action that he was able to secure where the ordinary Cabinet member could only wait and hope. "His influence upon Congressional legislation by no means ceased with his retiring from the Senate to accept his high executive office," later remarked an influential member of the House. "His advice and counsel were frequently solicited by his friends, and they never left empty-handed." [81]

Perhaps it is correct to say that Lamar showed administrative acumen of as high order as legislative, but that the former— like the Supreme Court—failed to exercise one of his finest talents: his remarkable powers in debate, extemporaneous and otherwise, which had been an important factor in giving him his place of Senatorial dominance. Sargent S. Prentiss, Stephen A. Douglas, Allen G. Thurman, Blaine, Ben Hill, Edmunds, and Beck occasionally made speeches unworthy of themselves, wrote Savoyard in commenting upon the advantage that Lamar's powers as orator and logician had given him, but "L. Q. C. Lamar was an exception. Master of the most exquisite style of any man who sat in the United States Senate the last half of the last century..., he rarely spoke, but, when he did speak, it was as Jupiter would have spoken had Jupiter talked English. Nobody ever believed that Lamar ever did his best. It was impossible to fix a limit to that splendid and exquisite diction." [82]

Just how highly his services as Secretary of the Interior were regarded was evidenced in the flood of notices carried by the press at the time of his resignation. And, significantly, there was not one voice of dissent in respect to the high plane of efficiency upon which he had conducted the business of his department. Moreover, in all of the clamor connected with his appointment to the Supreme Court, not one insinuation was made, even by his most vigorous opponents, as to any taint of dishonesty in the conduct of financial affairs and the administration of the public lands and mineral rights involving hundreds of millions of dollars. His work had been the more remarkable, too, in that when he entered upon his duties the Interior Department was in a demoralized condition and was faced with problems in connection with the Indians and the public domain such as it has never, before or since, confronted.

"At the time of his appointment the air was full of rumors of apoplexy and absentmindedness," commented the *Kansas City Star* of January 24th, 1893, in an interesting albeit somewhat humorous account. "Stories were told of how the noted

Mississippian dreamed away his working hours, of how he paid double fare in the street cars, and of how he forgot his friends when he most wished to remember them. It was said that he had no capacity for details, and that his training and nature were those of the scholar rather than of the practical man." The employees of the Interior Department, according to this editorial, came late to work on the day that he took office and expected, generally, a period of leisure and millennial peace. "They continued this thought about two days, and then awoke to the fact that the new man meant business.

"Mr. Lamar reorganized the department. He formed a system by which he could see what each bureau and division was doing; and, what is more, he demanded an analytical report as to their deeds each week.... When he left the Interior Department to become an Associate Justice of the Supreme Court,... its affairs were in commendable condition....

"Justice Lamar from his youth was distinguished as a hard worker. He found his most trying times as a member of President Cleveland's Cabinet. Work piled up in sufficient quantity to drive an ordinary man to distraction, but Lamar would simply gorge himself with the work as an anaconda gorges itself with a carcass; and when he was full, when he couldn't swallow another atom, he would go to bed, sleep like a baby for ten or twelve hours, and awake as fresh as a daisy. He sometimes worked for twenty hours at a stretch. He was a very rapid worker, and always became greatly absorbed in his work. He thought much faster than he could write, and he could not do the manual work of writing to his satisfaction.... He was at home, however, with a stenographer, and he kept from one to three stenographers busy all the time. He talked off his letters and his opinions in the choicest Anglo-Saxon, and put as much emphasis into his language as though he were speaking in the Senate. He became absorbed in every piece of dictation that he did; and, while he might be dictating the quieter passages upon a lounge, he would rise to his feet when he came to an important sentence and mouth his words like the players in the 'Midsummer Night's Dream.'"

"Mr. Lamar's unobtrusive management of the Interior Department is a subject of general comment," said the *Emporia* (Kan.) *Saturday Evening News* of July 24th, 1886, after Lamar had held the office for slightly more than a year. "Let those who think of him as dreaming or sleeping, however, try some scheme with him on that basis and see where they will come out. Politicians have sought, by blandishments and subterfuges, to get on his 'blind side' for personal ends, but they have generally quit work where they began." The *Memphis Appeal* of November 7th, 1886, rated him as "one of the American statesmen who will never live too long. He makes no mistakes; he is equal to every emergency, and the longer he lives the greater will be his influence; for the whole country has confidence in his wisdom, patriotism, and statesmanship."

Perhaps no Cabinet member was ever more loved by the officials and employees under his direction. Their regard was strikingly shown on the day that he surrendered his post. "Mr. Lamar was unquestionably the most popular Secretary that ever held the Interior portfolio," remarked the *New York World*. "His manner toward his subordinates was the very essence of kindness, and the young people of the department looked upon him with a respect that was almost filial. There were many touching scenes on Tuesday, when he bade farewell to his associates and took his formal leave of the department. It was a rainy disagreeable day; but the employees of the bureaus that are located outside the main building did not mind the weather. With umbrellas and waterproofs they marched to the department to shake the hand of their chief, many of them perhaps for the last time."[83] It was a touching scene, according to the *Winona* (Miss.) *Advance*, as hundreds of employees with "sincere expressions of regret," and "misty and sorrowful countenances" bade him farewell.[84] "Those nearest in his labors only understand and have compassion for him, to try to save him all we can," Mr. E. V. D. Miller had written late in 1885 to the wife of ex-Senator Clement C. Clay of Alabama. "He would take us *all* in his arms, and confer the greatest benefits on us if he could; and a more tender, appreciative, industrious, kind-hearted man I have never been associated with, to say nothing of his giant intellect and cultivated brain and taste. I never knew him until I came to this office with him and saw him in all these entangling relations. I used to get angry and avoid him because I thought he neglected my requests and was so indifferent that there seemed to be a lack of respect; but a closer knowledge of the demands upon him has disarmed me entirely." [85]

The *Nashville* (Tenn.) *Daily Union*, after reciting his success in recovering for the people lands worth millions of dollars and in instituting reforms of a permanent nature, said that "the completeness of a fully rounded character gives him the undisputed place among the first statesmen of the age." "That Secretary Lamar possesses in as high a degree as any of our men the attributes of oratory, philosophy, and statesmanship, has long been conceded," said the same paper; "that he had the courage of his convictions, and without fear marched in the advance guard of public sentiment, has been demonstrated in every stage of his life; that his integrity and honor were without impeachment, even the most prejudiced of his political opponents never questioned." [86] And the voice of detraction, predicting that the habits of the scholar and the dreamer would unfit him for an executive position, had been forced to admit him within the select group of the really great Secretaries in the history of the nation.

With a national reputation as an authority on the Constitution, and generally considered by his contemporaries as the most scholarly man in American public life, it was natural that Lamar should have been the recipient of a wide variety of honorary degrees. Of all of these, however, the one that he most valued was conferred by Harvard University during his secretaryship, in November, 1886. President Eliot had asked that—as one of the honored guests—he attend the exercises commemorating the two hundred and fiftieth year of the founding of the nation's oldest educational institution; and the Corporation, upon the recommendation of the President, had tendered him the degree of Doctor of Laws. Investing him before the assembly, Eliot referred to him as "teacher, orator, legislator, administrator."

"It was with feeling of great pleasure that in 1886 I saw Harvard confer her highest honor on this delightful Mississippian," remarked Senator Hoar concerning the occasion. "He was, in his time, I think, the ablest representative, certainly among the ablest, of the opinions opposed to mine. He had a delightful and original literary quality which, if the lines of his life had been cast amid other scenes than the tempest of a great Revolution and Civil War, might have made him a dreamer like Montaigne; and a chivalrous quality that might have made him a companion of Athos and D'Artagnan." [87]

Two months later, on the 5th of January, 1887, Lamar was wedded to a boyhood sweetheart, Mrs. Henrietta J. Holt, the widow of General William S. Holt, former President of the Southwestern Railroad Company. She was a native of Macon, Georgia, and as a young girl had been one of the famous beauties of that section. Born to affluence and social position—the daughter of James Dean, one of the State's wealthiest planters—she had had the advantage of considerable travel, and at an early age had married General Holt. At the time of her marriage to Secretary Lamar, she retained much of her beauty and was socially important in the most exclusive Washington circles. The union was in every respect fortunate, for she brightened Lamar's declining years and filled, to a remarkable degree, the awful void that had come into his life with the death of his first wife more than three years before.

The last occasion upon which Lamar delivered an address that might be considered in any degree political was upon the occasion of the unveiling of the Calhoun monument in Charleston on the 26th of April, 1887, the anniversary of the day, almost forty years before, when the committee of Congress delivered the remains of the great Carolinian to the people of his State. The unveiling was attended with the most ambitious celebration undertaken by the citizens of Charleston since the Civil War, and before an audience of many thousands Lamar delivered his oration upon Calhoun's life and character. To the preparation of the address he had given much thought, and his life-long study of the principles of American Government had fitted him to do something more than perform a mere perfunctory task of eulogy. Moreover, this was to be, as he intended, his valedictory to the people of the South and the nation, and it was to be expected that he would renew his plea for the death of sectional animosities and for the fostering of the broadest nationalism.

Let it be noted, too, that in his discussion of the evolution of our political system, and the forces that have worked to modify it, Lamar advanced (and developed fully) the theory of the influence of the American frontier. All that Dr. Frederick J. Turner, the eminent historian, was to say on the subject five years later (and which—despite his own recognition of his indebtedness to Lamar—has so frequently been labeled as his original contribution to the philosophy of history) was but a repetition and expansion of what Lamar had previously pointed out with admirable clearness and brevity. Our political literature, let it be said, presents no more profound or lucid exposition of the principles that governed the growth of the American nation.

Too, Lamar did not hesitate to point out certain respects in which Calhoun's political philosophy failed to take into consideration important social and political forces that are operative in all organized society. "This whole subject [the evolution of American nationalism] was well presented by Lamar in his oration in Charleston in 1887," says William M. Meigs in the preface to his monumental "Life" of the Carolinian, "and the orator intimated very plainly to his Southern audience the opinion that Calhoun had entirely neglected to take into view essential matters in our history, which were entitled to great weight against his theories. It was a bold and manly view for a man of the South to present to so highly Southern a community, but it seems to have been well received. Charles Francis Adams and others have since presented much the same view." [88]

In this his valedictory speech—one of the greatest in our history and one which has done more than anything else to present

Calhoun in proper perspective and evaluation—Lamar gave his confession of faith and his final admonition to the section which for four decades he had single heartedly served. "I believe if he were here to-day," said Lamar, "and could see his own South Carolina, the land of Rutledge, Moultrie, Laurens, Hayne, Lowndes, Sumter, and Marion, restored largely through the efforts of her lion-hearted Hampton to her proud position of dignity and equality in the Union, he would say to her that, the great controversy being closed at the ballot box, closed by the arbitrament of war, and, above all, closed by the constitution, always deemed sacred and inviolable by her, she sacrifices no principle and falsifies no sentiment in accepting the verdict, determined, henceforth, to seek the happiness of her people, their greatness and glory, in the greatness and glory of the American Republic.

"He would have told her, if such counsel were necessary, that a people who in form surrender and profess to submit, yet continue secretly to nurse old resentments and past animosities and cherish delusive schemes of reaction and revenge, will sooner or later degenerate into baseness and treachery and treason. He would say that a heroic and liberty-loving State, like South Carolina, should cherish for the great Republic of which she is part that ardent, genuine patriotism which is the life and soul and light of all heroism and liberty. Ah, fellow-citizens, had he lived, his great talents would have been, as they had ever been before, directed to save this people from the horrors of disunion and war." The path of greatness for the Republic, said Lamar, lay in an indissoluble union and a common destiny for the whole people.

This address attracted much attention not only among Lamar's friends but from scholars, historians, and the press in general. Moreover, it was shortly published by the Calhoun Society in a very handsomely edited volume "to pay Mr. Lamar [according to the preface] the compliment of having his speech, delivered on the occasion of the unveiling of the monument, put in book form so that they can not only place it upon the shelves of their own libraries, but place it upon the shelves of many of the libraries of the schools, colleges, and public institutions of the country as an exponent of two great men—the subject of the oration and the orator himself, men whose voices will speak on forever." [89]

"As to the address on Calhoun," wrote Lamar on the 11th of May to Hon. H. S. Van Eaton, member of Congress, who, like so many others, had written to him concerning it, "it was not the result of any immediate or continuous preparation, but simply noting down, through my private secretary, the result of long years of reflection upon politics generally, and as expounded by Calhoun especially. I tried to throw the whole doctrine into a consistent whole, very much as Cousin, in his criticism of Locke's philosophy, was enabled to develop his own system of philosophical eclecticism. In other words, the speech was the result of years of reflection. I do not think in the whole time I had one hour of continuous, unbroken preparation." [90]

"It would be worse than useless to attempt a review of Mr. Lamar's oration," commented the *Charleston News and Courier* of April 27th. "His analysis of the sentiments and motives which were the inspiration of Mr. Calhoun's public conduct and the guide of his private life affords a clear and luminous reflection of the great Carolinian. But there is so much that throws a new light upon the history of the exciting questions associated with the development of the theory of popular government, that the oration comprises in itself a complete text-book upon our Republican institutions."

On the 6th of October Lamar received an invitation (in no sense political) to address the One Hundred and Nineteenth Annual Banquet of the New York Chamber of Commerce, to be held at Delmonico's on the 15th of the next month. "You shall have the place of honor at the table and make the leading speech," he was informed. "You are no doubt aware that this is a conspicuous occasion, and corresponds very nearly to the dinner of the Lord Mayor of London. They are very anxious to have you make the speech of the evening. It would be a good thing for the country, the South, the chamber, and yourself. You know that this is the first and greatest chamber of commerce of the country. Your address will go all over the country." [91]

After some hesitation because of the press of official business, Lamar signified his acceptance on the 23rd and on the evening of November 15th he delivered the address, as arranged, before an audience which included Hon. Joseph Chamberlain (Special Commissioner of the British Government), Secretary Fairchild, of the Treasury, and others as well known. Afterwards, brief remarks were heard from Hon. Joseph Chamberlain, Chauncey M. Depew, George W. Curtis, Abram S. Hewitt (the Mayor), James C. Carter, and William R. Creamer, M.P. The press notices that appeared in the New York papers were uniformly complimentary.

XIX

THE SUPREME COURT

Since Associate Justice Woods of the Supreme Court, who died on the 14th of May, 1887, had been appointed from Georgia, the presumption was that his successor would be selected from the same Judicial Circuit, the fifth. Every Southern State forthwith presented its candidate for the position, Mississippi putting forward Senator George, former Chief Justice of the State Supreme Court.

Immediately, however, and without the suggestion either of Lamar or his close friends, his name began to be mentioned as the probable appointee. As early as the 6th of June, 1887, an account of an interview which Congressman Oates of Alabama had had with President Cleveland was published widely in the press. "I feel quite certain that if Secretary Lamar desired the position he could get it," said Oates after discussing the prospects of a number of candidates whose names had been urged upon the President. "The President, I know, has the very highest opinion of Lamar. He told me so himself. I heard him say that Secretary Lamar had the clearest and most comprehensive intellect that he had ever known."[1]

Without respect to party or section, the suggestion that Lamar might be appointed as the new Justice was hailed with acclaim by the press. Said the Republican *New York Mail and Express:* "The story comes from Washington by way of an administration organ, that Secretary Lamar is to quit the Cabinet for the Bench, and that next autumn he will be appointed to the vacancy caused by the death of Mr. Justice Woods.... In the first place, Mr. Lamar is a sound lawyer.... [He is] a dreamer, but a dreamer over the practical concerns of life"; and his "administration of the Interior Department has shown that he can transact business in a masterful way, and he is probably better

469

fitted for a judgeship than for an executive office. He is a student and has a student's habit of investigating subjects to the bottom.... There is no question of constitutional or statute law to the consideration of which Mr. Lamar could not materially contribute.... No one who has been named so nearly approaches the high standard of the court as Mr. Lamar. We trust that the prediction of his appointment will be verified." [2]

"He is a man of broad learning, both legal and other, and of a philosophical and judicial mind," said the Republican *Providence Journal.* "The habit of strict constitutional construction which he would bring to the decision of his cases is something for which there is no small need in these times, when the tendency of legislation, as regards the extension of the central authority, is so obviously away from the wise precedents of the fathers." [3] Again, the Independent *Boston Herald*, remarking that every one in Washington took it for granted that Lamar would be appointed to fill the vacancy, thought that the appointment would be notable, but that Mr. Cleveland would lose the strongest member of his Cabinet: "The President will part with the man who has been perhaps in all respects the most satisfactory of his Cabinet appointments. The work of the Interior Department under Mr. Lamar has been well done, and he has at the same time had an influence in Congress which has not been possessed by his Cabinet associates." To the Independent *Washington National View* of June 18th, it seemed that Lamar's appointment would "satisfy the country North and South, East and West," for "we know that he is eminently fitted for the place; that he has a judicial mind, which opens a broad and liberal outlook, free from all local prejudice, or partial, contracted sentiment." By the 27th of June the press generally agreed with the *Memphis Avalanche* of that date that "the elevation of Secretary Lamar to the bench of the Supreme Court may be regarded as only a question of time," not because there had been any public announcement from the President, but because of "the splendid abilities of the distinguished Mississippian, the broadness and liberality of his views, his deep knowledge of national law and his blameless record."

Just how Lamar himself reacted to the situation is seen in his letters of this period. On the 7th of July, in answering an enthusiastic assurance of support, he was writing to an acquaintance, the Hon. J. F. King of Louisiana, that in the spirit of "open-hearted frankness which has always characterized our intercourse, you must permit me to express my regret at one thing, and that is that you should have sent letters to your numerous friends upon the subject. If the position is offered me, I wish it done with the promptings of the President's free and unconstrained choice, and in accordance with the spontaneous and unsolicited manifestations of public opinion." [4] Two days later he wrote to Senator Walthall that the proposal of his name "was wholly unexpected to me.... The publication of my name ...arose from the impressions which Congressmen, making applications for aspirants from their respective States, carried with them after conversing with the President himself. Not a word has ever been exchanged between the President and myself on the subject of *myself* for the position, nor has any one at my suggestion ever approached him." [5] In this letter is found the first note of discord in regard to his prospective appointment: "The objection made to me by Garland and Vest, which is spreading around a little and perhaps making its impression on the President's mind, is that I am not a practical lawyer and not fit for the ordinary business and drudgery of the position, though amply qualified now and then to write a good opinion on constitutional law." As a matter of fact, it was commonly known that the one great ambition of Garland's life was to serve upon the bench of the Supreme Court (where, indeed, he would probably have been a most useful and even brilliant figure), but by his too ardent advocacy of his own cause he effectively eliminated himself from any considerations to which his eminent abilities might have entitled him.

Other letters that passed between Lamar and his friends indicate the progress of the matter. "I am more inclined to-day than I was when I wrote you to think that the President's mind has been pretty well made up to offer me the place," he wrote to Walthall on July 30th. "With reference to the work and drudgery necessary for the Bench, I have no fear whatever."

"This morning for the first time the President informed me that he was considering gravely the propriety of offering me the Judgeship on the Supreme Bench," he wrote on August 17th to Postmaster General William F. Vilas. "The generous appreciation of my fitness & the recognition of my past services in the Cabinet which he expressed touched me profoundly, and my feelings were too strong for adequate expression. I could not say a word about my sense of his goodness without seeming effusive & therefore said nothing that did justice to my sentiments." The one problem that had appeared at the conference, said Lamar, was that of finding a suitable individual who could take over the conduct of the Interior Department with the many grave responsibilities that the secretaryship, at this time particularly, entailed. "It will not surprise you," he continued, "to learn that in such a discussion the first suggestion in both our minds was whether you would be willing to contribute your assistance to the proposed change.... My own belief is that the President will not be satisfied with any other selection than the selection of you." Cleveland had suggested, said Lamar, that he approach Vilas on the question of his acceptance, and it was the sincere hope of them both that he would take over the reins of the department. It would be well, he remarked, for Mr. Vilas to write to the President as soon as he could come to a decision.[6]

"I need hardly write of the joy with which I read in your letter the information that the good President has definitely determined upon your selection for the vacancy on the Supreme Bench," Vilas replied on September 5th in a most touching personal letter wherein he signified his purpose of accepting the place which Lamar was vacating. "I am persuaded, not by love —which gives me such gratification—but by a clear and discriminating judgment, a perception of your qualities which lighted the way for my affection, that no one could have been chosen with greater satisfaction to the country, nor could the place have been more suitably a reward for great deserving. Your education, your experience of affairs, and your observation of men, have generously aided to accomplish a mind naturally adapted, in a peculiar degree, to deal with the great questions which will invoke profound political forecast and a lofty, impartial judgment. Your value in that seat will be vast to your countrymen." [7]

There was much more in the letter, too, in regard to Lamar's service to the nation which, Secretary Vilas thought, would make his selection pleasing to all of the people, and would raise it above sectional and party animosities. The letter ended on the following personal note: "It is impossible for me to withhold expression of my pain at parting with you as my associate. It has been such a source of pride and honor to possess your friendship in that collaboration we have enjoyed. It has been such a solace to feel unquestioning assurance of your sympathy and kindness when you took your seat at our table, and I have had such timely help in my inexperience and many lacks when help was so grateful, that I melt at the thought of your loss to our official concord and to my personal support and delight. It has been, as you say, a warmer bond between you and me than perhaps between any other two. My attachments have been peculiarly to the ends of our table [at which during Cabinet meetings always sat Cleveland and Lamar], and all must cling with equal reception to the great head of it. I shall have no longer an especial grasp on the love of any one beside, by which my errors and shortcomings may be tenderly considered and relieved; but this cannot qualify, after all, the profound joy and gratitude with which I contemplate your well-merited honors of the gown."

One letter of particular interest received under date of October 29th was from his gifted disciple, Henry W. Grady, editor of the *Atlanta Constitution*, in reference to a conversation which he had recently held with President Cleveland upon the occasion of the latter's visit to Atlanta. "While riding with the President," wrote Grady, "we passed [the home of a certain prominent lawyer]. I mentioned it to the President" who commented upon the lack of wisdom shown by the individual in question in arranging for public meetings to support his candidacy for a position so exalted as that of a seat on the Supreme Bench. Another self-appointed adviser, Cleveland remarked, had urged "that in appointing a man who would be retired on a pension the President ought to get a man young enough to have the guarantee of several years of service before pensioning. I knocked that out, remarked the President, by saying: 'Yes, unless we get a man of such overweening ability that one year's service is worth ten of an ordinary man's, and unless we could get a man who has given his whole life already to the public service.'

"I then said that I thought Lamar the best equipped man, living or dead, the South had given to the public," Grady reported further of his conversation. "He said: 'I think certainly the best of the living men.' I replied that I did not except Clay or Calhoun; for, while they may have been abler, I thought no man from the South had ever been so perfectly equipped for public life as Lamar. He then made this significant remark: 'I have noticed one thing about him: he cannot decide a thing wrong. His temperament is such that when he considers a question he is obliged to decide it right. I have never seen this quality so marked in any other man. The truth is, his mind and heart are right, and he cannot decide anything wrong.'" [8]

Despite the warm and almost unanimous approbation that had been showered upon Lamar's proposed elevation to the Supreme Court, it so resulted that he was not to be seated without a struggle. Mr. Henry Jones Ford, in his *The Cleveland Era*, finds it impossible to assign the reason for the delay in confirmation. "He had been an eminent member of the Senate, with previous distinguished service in the House," says Mr. Jones, who praises highly his record as Secretary of the Interior, "so that the Senate must have had abundant knowledge of his character and attainments. It is impossible to assign the delay that ensued to reasonable need of time for inquiry as to his qualifications." [9] As a matter of fact, the opposition that arose will be seen to have had a two-fold basis which is not far to seek: the realization of the Republicans that they must begin to make ammunition for the approaching Presidential campaign; and the natural Republican opposition that would fall to the lot of any prominent ex-Confederate who might have been nominated for a seat in the Supreme Court. Indeed, it is unlikely that any other man who had been high in the councils of the Confederacy could have been seated at this time.

Throughout September the factionalism increased, and, headed by the *New York Tribune*, a number of the arch-Republican organs began to make war upon Lamar. Reiterating his alleged "gross and insolent defiance of the court at whose bar he stood as attorney and officer"[10] during reconstruction days, and proclaiming that he had previously "devoted about five years to the work of trying to break up the Union, during which time it is not likely that he practiced much law,"[11] that radical organ said that "Mr. Cleveland's candidate for the Supreme Court represents more perfectly than most of his surviving comrades the treason which they once practiced and still preach.... His course of conduct before, during, and since the war entitles him to the distinction." Again, "he has never recanted. He is an unrepentant bulldozer just as he is an unrepentant rebel."[12]

The *New York Tribune*, remarked the *Memphis Appeal* of January 7th, 1888, "has taken advantage of the opportunity to wave the bloody shirt for all it was worth. In order to fire the Northern Republican heart, particularly the hearts of those Republican Senators who have shown a disposition to accept Mr. Lamar, it has set forth the facts of his prominence in the Southern Confederacy in such lurid colors as it could command, and, by distorting sentences of old speeches, by malicious interpretation of motives and by ungenerous perversion of history it has sought to make party capital which would produce dividends next November." So far as was in his power, Lamar allowed no answer to be made. Even when George Ticknor Curtis, the prominent liberal, suggested to him in a letter of September 16th that he write an article in correction of the misrepresentations that had been broadcast concerning his life and career, particularly those in the *New York Tribune*, Lamar expressed his sincere appreciation but refused as he had been accustomed to do throughout his life when such situations arose.

Probably a just evaluation of the main-spring of the opposition is to be found in a letter, under date of December 20th, 1887, that Lamar received from Mr. A. T. Britton, who said of himself: "I believe that I was nearly, if not quite, the first man that crossed to Southern soil in 1861 with a federal uniform on my back and a hostile gun in my hand. As you are very well aware, I am a stalwart Republican, and shall always contribute my individual efforts to the success of that party." Beyond his personal admiration for Lamar, he remarked that he had a professional reason for wishing to see him seated upon the Bench: "because, having been at the bar for thirty years, and having a professional income exceeded by but few if any lawyers in the United States, I can truthfully say that I prefer to argue a case before you rather than any other judge I have ever addressed [he had appeared before Lamar in important land cases]. You will, I am confident, be assured of the sincerity of this remark, because I never asked a favor at your hands, and have no other possible relation to you than that of esteem for your character and ability." [18]

Britton hoped that he had contributed somewhat to the defeat of the proposed resolutions against Lamar's confirmation that had been presented before the Blaine convention in New York the past week. "I have also," he said, "during the past week met representative men from all parts of the country; and I am assured that the opposition to you is not personal, but sectional. Under whatever pretexts your opponents may pretend to speak, the true motive is to defeat the confirmation of any ex-Confederate to the Supreme Bench. Any other Southern man of like antecedents would meet with the same opposition; and, in my opinion, the antagonism to you is less than would be directed against any other Southern man who could be named for the same position. So that the South might just as well understand that they must stand shoulder to shoulder in pressing your confirmation to a successful result, if they ever intend to break down and surmount the bitter prejudices of the 'bloody shirt' faction."

On the 6th of December the President submitted Lamar's name to the Senate for action, and the nomination was sent to the Committee on the Judiciary—this chairmaned by George F. Edmunds—a majority of which were Republicans. They, feeling sure that the tide was running against confirmation, determined to withhold action as long as possible with the idea of whipping the Republican members of the Senate unanimously in line with the opposition. "I take the same view," wrote Senator Sherman, who, it will be recalled, Lamar had demolished in debate a few days before entering the Cabinet, to the Buckeye Club, of Springfield, Ohio, which had protested Lamar's confirmation. "You may be sure I shall do all I can to prevent his confirmation. I regret to say, however, that I fear my efforts will be unsuccessful," [14] and Senator Ingalls was writing to the Young Republican Club of Lawrence, Kansas: "My relations with Mr. Lamar are entirely friendly; but there can be no doubt that he represents everything that is bad in the past, dangerous in the present, and menacing in the future, of the history of this country. His nomination is still pending before the Committee on the Judiciary, of which I am a member, and will probably be disposed of at an early date. I regret to say that, in my opinion, there is little doubt of his confirmation." [15]

Much of the opposition to Lamar was allegedly on account of his age. On December 21st we find him writing to his sister, Mrs. Ross, of Oxford, Mississippi, and requesting a certified transcript of the date of his birth from the old family Bible. "They have not only alleged that I am sixty-seven years old," he wrote, "but they *prove* it by an old book purporting to be biographical sketches of Congressmen in 1857, by a man by the name of Lanman, who put me down five years older than I am.... Three months ago I would have been confirmed unanimously; but since then political passions have been aroused, and the conviction seems to be strong upon the mind of the

Republicans that their only chance of success in the next contest is sectional excitement." [16]

"Three months ago as many perhaps as one-half of the Republican Senators had congratulated me on the nomination, and assured me of the pleasure with which they would co-operate in the confirmation," he wrote on December 23rd to Mrs. Kate W. Freeman, sister of Senator Walthall. "But always on the eve of a Presidential election parties maneuver for choice of position; and in the struggle passions arise and influences are put in force not anticipated, and men find themselves hurried by the force of events in a direction entirely opposite to what they had intended and expected.... My friends are still quite confident of victory; but," humorously, "in that judicial frame of mind for which I am so eminent (in my own esteem) I observe indications that escape the most sanguine, and do not feel confident at all." [17]

January arrived, and with it the open secret that the majority report of the judiciary committee would be opposed to Lamar's confirmation. Moreover, the situation for the latter was most trying. He felt that his position in the Cabinet might seem to give him undue power to coerce the opposition in the Senate, and he believed that the increasingly frequent assaults upon the President, made under color of opposition to himself, would cease if he severed all official connection with the administration. These considerations had caused him, as early as November 11th, to tender Cleveland his resignation; [18] and only the strongest representations on the part of the President and his associates in the Cabinet had brought about a reconsideration. Now, on the 7th of January, 1888, writing from the offices of the Department of the Interior, he addressed to the President a letter in which he unequivocally surrendered his secretaryship.

"When, some months ago," he wrote, "you invited me to accept the vacant judgeship in the Supreme Court of the United States, you expressed the wish that, as the court was not in session, I should postpone the resignation of my present office, as there were certain matters before the department, inaugurated by me, which it was therefore desirable that I should close before leaving; and, as I would have been very reluctant to take the place upon the Bench until your nomination had been confirmed by the Senate, I cheerfully consented to your request. My nomination has now been submitted to the Senate, and recognizing both their right and their duty to subject its fitness to the most critical examination, I would still wait in my present position their decision; but I think that I am warranted in supposing that the final decision may be delayed for some time. As you have at the same time nominated both my successor in this department and his successor in the Postoffice Department, this delay may, to some extent at least, embarrass the administration of the public business in the departments affected. To avoid such embarrassment, which is my duty to you and to the country, and to leave before the Senate in its final judgment upon my nomination the sole question of my fitness for the position, dissociated from any other nomination and unaffected by any other considerations, I now respectfully ask you to accept my resignation as Secretary of the Interior, which I hereby tender.

"In terminating my relations to you as a member of your official family, I desire to express my grateful sense of the obligation that I am under to you personally for the consideration and kindness which have always characterized your treatment of me, and for the generous confidence and support which you have steadily given me in the trying and arduous administration of this department. I shall always be proud to have been associated with the honorable record which you will leave upon the page of your country's history." [19]

On the same day, January 7th, Mr. Cleveland answered Lamar's letter of resignation in a communication which reveals the depth of affection which had grown up between the two men. "When I determined to nominate you to a position upon the Bench of the Supreme Court," he wrote, "the personal gratification afforded by the tender to you of so honorable and suitable a place, and the satisfactory conviction that an important executive duty would thus be well performed, led me almost to forget that my action involved the loss of your conscientious and valuable aid and advice in Cabinet counsel, which for nearly three years I have so much enjoyed and appreciated.

"Your note of to-day forces me to contemplate this contingency with the most profound and sincere regret. But since I know that the separation which you now insist upon arises from that conception of public duty which has always so entirely guided your conduct in our official relations, I am constrained to accept the resignation that you tender, hoping that it only anticipates your entrance upon the discharge of higher and more congenial functions than those now relinquished.

"What I have thus far written seems formal indeed. I intended this, because I am sure that the close confidence and the relations of positive affection which have grown up between us need no expression or interpretation.

"And yet I find it utterly impossible for me to finish this note without assuring you that the things which have characterized your conduct and bearing in the position from which you now retire—all your devotion to your country and your chief, all your self-sacrificing care and solicitude for public interests, all the benefit which your official service had conferred upon your fellow-countrymen, and all the affection and kindness so often exhibited toward me personally—I shall constantly remember with tenderness and gratitude." [20] Accompanying this personal note was a formal acceptance of the resignation "to take effect on Tuesday, January 10th, at twelve o'clock noon."

Thus for a few days Lamar passed again into private life. His resignation had been his own decision, and had been strongly opposed by his friends, especially by Secretary of State Bayard who felt that he should hold the Cabinet post until the Senate had actually passed upon his nomination to the Supreme Court. When, however, he had decided it to be for the best interests both of the country and of his party, he acted in that singularly disinterested fashion that had been typical of his whole public life.

Even the Republican press was forced to join with the Democratic papers in their praise of Lamar's brave action. "Let the Senate decide upon his nomination as the oaths and the highest duty of Senators demand, without favor or prejudice," editorialized the Independent *New York Herald* of January 9th in a representative press notice. "This act of his will fix the eyes of the country upon his judges; and the people, honest and brave themselves, and cherishing above all other qualities courage and honesty in public men, will require that the Senate do no injustice in this case."

"The correspondence between the President and Mr. Lamar," continued this paper, "is removed from the ordinary routine of public communication by the grace and delicacy of their letters, and especially the tenderness and appreciation shown in the letter of the President. We are reminded in their tone of those between Washington and Hamilton, as well as those between Jackson and the men whom he trusted. To have inspired so high a feeling in the heart of a man as resolute and perhaps as severe as Mr. Cleveland, shows the possession by Mr. Lamar of rare personal traits of loyalty which are the reserve of true character. Mr. Cleveland in his tenderness and sincerity shows the same qualities. It is this capacity for strong sincere friendship which gives the President so firm a hold upon the public heart. The people like a man who feels like a man."

The warm friendship that existed between Lamar and General Walthall has been repeatedly commented upon in the course of this study. We have seen that Lamar exerted all his influence to have the other man chosen by Mr. Cleveland for the position in his Cabinet, and that when the President made it clear that he would accept only Lamar himself, it was largely through the influence of the new Cabinet member that General Walthall was selected to succeed him in the Senate. No sooner had Lamar resigned his secretaryship than Senator Walthall insisted that he must return to the Senate, and began to make immediate arrangements for his own resignation. As he explained to a friend, no one from the State could so powerfully serve Mississippi and the nation, and his election to the legislative body would act as his vindication in the face of the delay in the ratification of his nomination to the Supreme Court. "Sir," remarked Lamar, when Assistant Secretary Muldrow communicated to him Walthall's plans, "before I would permit Walthall to do that I would go upon the streets of Washington and break rock for a living!"[21] This incident sheds interesting light upon Lamar's strongest friendship, either personal or public.

Shortly before the middle of January, the Judiciary Committee of the Senate presented its findings, with the majority report opposing Lamar's confirmation on the grounds that he was too old and that he had been too long separated from actual practice in the legal profession. As had been predicted, the vote in the committee was strictly along party lines with all of the Republicans voting against confirmation.

On the face of the matter, it seemed improbable that he would be confirmed, for the Senate was composed of thirty-eight Republicans, one Independent—Senator Riddleberger (a Virginian, it will be remembered), and thirty-seven Democrats. Unless party lines could be broken, Lamar's seating would inevitably fail, for even if Riddleberger should vote with the Democrats he would be defeated because the resultant tie would automatically count as failure of confirmation.[22] Most of the Republican Senators, at least half of whom had four months before made a special trip to the Interior Building to congratulate Lamar and assure him of their support, were known to have been won over to the view that political expediency demanded his defeat. But the Democrats had strong hopes that Senator Stanford of California and Senators Jones and Stewart of Nevada would refuse to follow the dictates of their own party leaders and would, instead, throw in their votes with the Democracy.

It is impossible to determine precisely how much of the Republican opposition to Lamar was really based upon the alleged grounds reported by the majority of the Senate Judiciary Committee. The report, as we have seen, claimed that his age unfitted him for the heavy duties of the Court. As a matter of fact, though with the exception only of Mr. Chief Justice Hunt, who had been nominated when some two months older, he was the oldest man that had up to that time been nominated for the Supreme Court, he was only slightly past his sixty-third birthday, and—as statesmen go—could not be considered as aged. The second count in opposition was upon the score that his years in the actual practice of law were too brief to fit him for a seat upon the highest tribunal in the land. Some, there almost certainly were, who actually believed that this second consideration should bar him from the Supreme Court. All credit should be accorded them for the honesty of their belief. As a matter of fact they were wrong, as Hoar, who led the fight in committee and on the floor of the Senate, later confessed. "I voted against him—in which I made a mistake," he was later to write. "...He...showed his great intellectual capacity for dealing with the most complicated legal questions." [23]

Students of our judicial system have come to recognize that, though a knowledge of the technique of actual practice—of which Lamar was, in reality, the master—is desirable and, indeed, necessary, this knowledge is far from being the most important qualification for distinctive service upon the Supreme Bench. This point needs to be elaborated to some extent. There are, it is generally conceded, many practicing lawyers with a wide and successful practice who are nevertheless totally lacking in that extensive knowledge of legal principles, in that catholicity of sympathy and understanding that fit one for a judgeship in the Supreme Court. Rather, it has become increasingly evident that the important things are not merely a technical mastery of the law—although that is a prerequisite—but, more fundamental still, the quality of one's thinking, the judicial temperament that weighs and balances the evidence, and the training and the habits of the scholar whose inclination is to study exhaustively each case and each problem that is presented. No characteristic is so commonly attributed to the greatest of our Justices, such as Marshall, Taney, and Holmes, as the ability to understand great legal principles and to give them actual and concrete application. Characteristic, too, of our greatest Justices is the philosophical bent that enables one to see life clearly and see it whole, and the ability to express ideas lucidly and illuminatingly.

Thus it is evident that all Lamar's life had been, in a sense, a preparation for this, the crowning office of his public career. Always, since popular interest had been centered in him, he had been called the "philosopher," the "scholar," the "dreamer," the "thinker," the "most profound of our living interpreters of constitutional law." Much of his early life had been devoted to actual practice in the courts of Georgia and Mississippi, though with the exception of a very few years it had been in connection with some legislative office or with a professorship at the University of Mississippi, where he had deepened and broadened his knowledge by a study of man's social institutions and the intricacies of constitutional and international law. It is only to be regretted that the crowning honor of his life, in the form of an office for which by temperament and training he was preëminently fitted, was to come at a time when his physical energy was being sapped by the organic heart trouble which had been the dread foe of his entire manhood.

Despite the almost solid Republican opposition, there had been some reasons for encouragement to those who hoped that Lamar would be confirmed. For instance, on January 7th, the precise day that Lamar had resigned the secretaryship, Senator Stewart, of Nevada, had sent to one of his friends and constituents an open letter in which he stated very frankly that he would not coöperate in the Republican attempt to defeat Lamar's seating: "The public press has so framed the issue that the rejection of Mr. Lamar will be construed both in the North and South as a declaration that his participation in the war disqualifies him and all others occupying the same position for a place on the Supreme Bench. It is unreasonable to expect that the people of eleven States of the Union shall, during all the present generation, be excluded from participation in the judicial determinations of the highest court of the United States."

Meanwhile the weakness of the charge that he had not for some time actually practiced law and was hence incompetent for a place on the Supreme Bench was being aired in the press.

As the *New York Evening Telegram* said, "The absurd notion that a man can't be a great lawyer unless he passes his entire time in a musty office with a professional sign on the door would disqualify Hon. Theodore Dwight, one of the profoundest jurists in America."[24] Interesting in this connection are the words of Hon. T. C. Catchings spoken before the Supreme Court after Lamar's death: "The brilliance and magnitude of his political achievements had obscured the fact that no man was better trained or more profoundly versed in the science and philosophy of the law. There are to-day...many able and accomplished lawyers who were educated by him while Professor of Law in the University of Mississippi, which position he filled with great dignity and distinguished ability."[25]

On January 16th, Lamar's confirmation came before the Senate for consideration. "At one o'clock," according to a "special" of that date which appeared in the *New York World*, "Senator Riddleberger, who by common consent has been accorded the privilege of offering the resolution to go into executive session upon the Cabinet nominations, rose in his seat and said: 'If the business of the morning hour is over, I move that the Senate now proceed to the consideration of executive business.'

"The motion was at once agreed to, and it was not until half past four o'clock that the doors were finally reopened and the announcement made that after three and a half hours spent in executive session the Senate had confirmed the nominations of Mr. Lamar to the Supreme Court Bench, Mr. Vilas to the Interior, and Mr. Dickinson as Postmaster General. Though the proceedings of the Senate were shrouded in the veil of mystery which hides from the public gaze all the incidents of executive sessions, it is known that Mr. Lamar's nomination was confirmed by a vote of thirty-two to twenty-eight, Senators Riddleberger, Stanford, Stewart and Sawyer [as a matter of fact the latter was paired in the negative] voting in the affirmative.

"Senator Stewart had already distinctly defined his position in his lengthy argument given to the press some days since. Senator Riddleberger had expressed himself in Mr. Lamar's favor in the most unmistakable terms upon the floor of the Senate, and his action did not consequently occasion any particular surprise. Senators Sawyer and Stanford have been regarded as Mr. Lamar's friends from the time of his nomination, and in casting their votes for him to-day they have evoked little comment. As foreshadowed in *The World* some time ago, the Republicans abandoned the attempt to coerce their colleagues by insisting upon a caucus which should bind all by its instructions. They recognized the futility of such action after the outspoken utterances of Senators Stewart and Riddleberger, and thus saved themselves the embarrassment and chagrin which would have been occasioned by the failure of the caucus to hold the Republicans together.

"In the session to-day the ground which had been gone over in the public prints and in private Senatorial debate was again reviewed, and the old straw thrashed over again. The Republicans who spoke in opposition to Mr. Lamar recited the oft-repeated charges that he had not been a practicing lawyer for many years, and that his views upon the important question as to the constitutionality of the thirteenth, fourteenth, and fifteenth amendments, were not strictly orthodox. These charges were warmly combated by Mr. Lamar's friends. In the course of the debate every Senator who has taken any prominent part in the discussion grasped the opportunity to express himself at considerable length. No new views of the case were advanced; and the final outcome did not greatly surprise any one, though in some quarters it was not expected that a confirmation would be reached to-day." [26]

Although the *New York Tribune* characterized the action of the Republican senators who voted for Lamar's confirmation as "poor patriotism and *the worst kind of politics*," [27] almost the entire press without regard to party affiliation—once the matter was settled—expressed editorial pleasure at the outcome as well as the belief that it marked the definite end of sectionalism. The prevailing note, too, was one of high praise for the great ability that Lamar would carry into his duties. The Democratic *New York Star* thought that "in character, in natural endowments, and in acquirements, he is above the standard of the Supreme Court," while the *Richmond Whig* remarked: "Mr. Lamar, in native ability, learning, and attainments, is the peer of any man upon the Supreme Bench; and, notwithstanding the silly charges that have been made against him by malignants, he is equal to any of them in patriotism and devotion to the Union and the constitution. He goes upon the Bench in the fullness of his years and the maturity of his intellect, and with a ripe experience in law and in public life that cannot fail to place him among the most distinguished jurists that ever graced the Bench of the Supreme Court." [28] It is not to be doubted that most of the opposition that had developed against Lamar's confirmation was political in nature, and that once he had taken his seat upon the Bench, most of those who had opposed him were glad.

It should be remarked that many papers as well as people saw the struggle over the confirmation as something more than a matter of one man's future and his usefulness to the country. This feeling is mirrored in many of the articles dealing with the controversy. The Republican *Cincinnati Commercial-Gazette* thought that it would have a "serious influence in teaching the people of the United States who do care for our nationality, and who do mistrust the Confederate Democratic party, that the Supreme Court is in danger as well as the Senate of the United States, which is first in the place of peril, and that the only salvation for them is to elect the next Republican candidate for President of the United States." [29] Likewise, remarked the Republican *Cleveland Leader*: "Little ground now remains for the South to win back in order to regain all its lost prestige and posts of honor and emolument. The Army and Navy will doubtless soon be attacked by the Democrats in behalf of ex-Confederate officers; and if the assault succeeds, everything will be captured." [30]

Such, too, was the opinion of the old harlequin, Ben Butler, according to a letter of April 1st of this year, written by General Sherman to his brother, Senator John Sherman, who had so bitterly opposed Lamar's confirmation. That morning, it seems, General Sherman had received a note from Butler with the request for an interview. After some preliminary conversation the latter had come to the point with the statement "that the country was in real danger, revealed by the death of the Chief Justice, that there was a purpose clearly revealed for the old rebels to capture the Supreme Court, as shown by the appointment of Lamar and the equal certainty of Waite being succeeded by a Copperhead or out and out rebel; that in the next four years Miller and Bradley would create vacancies to be filled in like manner, thus giving the majority in the court to a party which fought to destroy the Government, thereby giving those we beat in battle the sacred fruits of victory. There is a real danger...."[31]

Such were the views of the irreconcilable radicals. But the most common expressions both on the part of the Republican and Democratic papers were far otherwise. "In the broader aspect of his record and his attitude toward the government and the North since the war," said the Independent *New York Evening Post* editorially, "no representative Southern man was so fit for the place. Mr. Lamar was one of the first 'to accept the situation,' and has always been the most conspicuous among former 'rebels' in urging the South forward in the new career of freedom. His eulogy upon Charles Sumner was an act which showed the character of the man. This act and other acts of the same sort have made him as offensive to the irreconcilables of the South as they have made him admired by progressive men at the North. It is an instructive coincidence that when he left the Interior Department the other day he was waited upon by a delegation of employees who had served on the Union side during the war, and who, through their spokesman, 'expressed their appreciation of the kindness and consideration which he had always shown toward the members of the Grand Army,' while, at the same time, the *New Mississippian*, a Bourbon sheet, was complaining of 'the extraordinarily conservative course which he has pursued at Washington, the preference which he has shown to the Grand Army of the Republic, and the tenderness with which he has dealt with the negro Republicans from Mississippi.'"[32]

The *Memphis Daily Appeal* of January 17th, saying that Lamar "has shown no shadow of turning nor has he tampered with his principles for a second," thought his seating "a great triumph" both for him and for the President. He will "take his place upon the bench made illustrious by Marshall, Taney, and Campbell. He is there now, and is there to stay, without any apology for his record in or out of Congress, before, during, or since the war, and without abating a jot or tittle from the words of his masterful and almost exhaustive eulogy of Calhoun at Charleston last year. . . . Mr. Lamar has earned his promotion, and will always, we feel assured, be found on the side of right and justice, and fairly interpreting the constitution, which no man knows better or is more competent to construe."

Lamar, it has been seen, had a tremendous following throughout the nation as well as in the South and in Mississippi which latter he carried like a "pocket borough." Playing upon this fact in an attempt to arouse antagonisms within the Democracy, certain radical organs tried to make it appear that Cleveland had come to believe that he had presidential ambitions and for that reason had appointed him to the Supreme Court in order to remove him from the stage of active politics. Such was the propaganda fostered by the *New York Tribune* and a number of lesser papers which looked to it for guidance. There was, of course, no truth in the assertion. Lamar, as his letters abundantly show, did not believe that the time was yet ripe for a Southern man to aspire to the Presidency. Moreover, he had the most profound regard for and loyalty to his chief, and desired nothing quite so much as to see him serve a second term. Some papers, it is true, had sincerely and honestly sponsored Lamar's name for the ensuing Democratic nomination for the Presidency, but he, with characteristic good sense, had lent no heed to their siren song. Certainly there was nothing in the situation to lend the slightest credibility to the propaganda sponsored by the *New York Tribune*.

When the press of the 16th and 17th of January carried the news of Lamar's confirmation as a Justice of the Supreme Court, he was immediately the recipient of a flood of telegrams and letters, and for days his home was crowded with distinguished visitors. None of the messages did he appreciate more than those from the Justices themselves who gave him a warm welcome. "The newspapers this morning give me the good news of your confirmation," wrote Chief Justice Waite on the 17th. "Come to us as soon as you can, for we want you. I wish you could be on the Bench to-day, when we take up some Arkansas bond cases, which are important in amount at least. By Thursday we shall reach an interesting California land case, in which I hope we may have your help. You will have a hearty welcome from us all; and don't keep away from us any longer than is absolutely necessary." [33]

"The *World* correspondent called upon Mr. Lamar at his home on K Street this evening," reported that paper in a news letter of January 16th. "Upon a small table in the hallway lay a pile of congratulatory dispatches and many cards of distinguished visitors who had called to pay their respects to Judge Lamar. Several of the telegrams were addressed 'Mr. Justice Lamar.' The correspondent was cordially received by Judge Lamar, who was surrounded by friends. Among them were Secretary Vilas, Senator and Mrs. Walthall, and Mr. and Mrs. Lamar, Jr. Intense gratification beamed from every lineament of Judge Lamar's countenance....

"Judge Lamar then asked Secretary Vilas if it would be convenient for him to be inducted into the mysteries of the Interior Department to-morrow. 'I suppose,' replied Mr. Vilas, 'that the Cabinet commissions will be speedily issued, and I may as well begin to-morrow as at any other time. I realize fully that the hardest task that will confront me in my new office will be the necessity for constant endeavor to keep the department up to the high standard which you have established. I can but do my best, however.'

"'You will not find the task so difficult,' replied Mr. Lamar, while a glow of pleasure suffused his countenance, and his eye kindled at the compliment so gracefully tendered. 'It is true, I have left many things undone, that you might not be in any way hampered in assuming charge of the department; but I do not doubt that you will soon have everything well in hand. I have devoted my energies of late more particularly to keeping up the legal decisions of the office, and believe they are quite up to date."

As a matter of fact, Lamar had exerted every effort to leave the affairs of the Interior Department in commendable condition, and when he surrendered his post (even in the short interval following his resignation he had remained in active control) he left a clear desk. "The Department has some important vacancies which you will fill to suit yourself," he had written to Mr. Vilas in the letter in which he had tendered him the portfolio of the Interior in the President's behalf. "Among these are the Chief Clerk of the Department, three & perhaps four members of the law division & one of the Pensions Board of Appeals. I will advise you of the other changes which you can make to great advantage—so that you can have your own friends near to you. [Henry L.] Muldrow [an ex-Confederate Colonel—as was another of Lamar's chief assistants, John Dewitt Clinton Atkins, of Tennessee, Indian Commissioner—and an unusually capable administrator] will be a great comfort to you. He knows the Department thoroughly, so much so that you will have but little trouble."

After Vilas signified his willingness to head the Interior Department, Lamar had canvassed with him every subject of importance connected with his future work. Only one major change did the new Secretary desire, and this—the resignation of Land Commissioner William A. J. Sparks, the explosive Illinois Democrat who served as Land Commissioner—Lamar had already decided upon because of his intransigent attitude relative to the adjustment of the Chicago, St. Paul, Minneapolis, and Omaha R. R. Land Grants. Sparks was an entirely sincere and in many respects extraordinarily able administrator, but in his zeal for prosecuting the work of his bureau he had continually embarrassed himself and the Department by his failure to observe the indispensable legal requirements in cases that came before him for attention.

On November 11th, Lamar had received a lengthy communication from Sparks relative to the so-called "Omaha cases," in which he had vehemently protested the carrying out of certain of the Secretary's decisions. That same day, explaining that he had already given Sparks his "carefully matured instructions," [34] and that "in no other way can the functions of a great department be successfully executed than for the chief to command and the subordinates to obey," Lamar called for the Commissioner's resignation. On the 15th Sparks handed his resignation to Mr. Cleveland, presenting at the same time an elaborate defense of his own position in the obvious hope that he would be sustained. The President's reply in accepting the resignation evidences the close bond of love and respect that existed between himself and Secretary Lamar, and contains what is probably a correct statement of the situation in respect to the controversy.

"I have read your letter of resignation left with me to-day," replied Mr. Cleveland, "and also the communication addressed to you by the Secretary of the Interior accompanying the same. In the present situation I do not feel called upon to determine the merits of the controversy which has arisen between the Secretary and yourself further than to say that my impressions touching the legal question involved incline me to rely, as I naturally would do even if I had no impression of my own, upon the judgment of the Secretary. It presents a case of interpretation where two perfectly honest men may well differ.... This policy [of conserving the public domain] will continue to be steadfastly pursued, limited and controlled, however, by the law and the judgment of the courts by which we may be at times unwillingly restrained but which we cannot and ought not to resist." [35]

There is no evidence either in Lamar's public utterances or in his private correspondence that he ever entertained the least prejudice or ill will toward those Senators who had opposed his confirmation. "Senator Edmunds and Justice Lamar met, for the first time since the former tried to defeat the latter's confirmation, at the Thursday reception at the White House," reported the *Philadelphia Public Ledger* of the 26th. "They collided at the entrance of the Green Room, and those who stood around and knew how bitterly Edmunds had fought the nomination wondered what would happen. A repetition of the scene that occurred when Blaine and Edmunds met at the funeral of President Arthur was expected, but it did not occur. Justice Lamar is too much of a gentleman. The two men shook hands as cordially as ever, and chatted for a while in the best of temper." Justice Lamar would have shown perfect courtesy to any of his political opponents; but nothing that Senator Edmunds could have done would ever have erased the memory of his sympathetic understanding evinced three years before when the grave closed on the woman who, for almost forty years, had furnished the inspiration and sweetest associations of Lamar's life.

On the morning of the 18th, at the time appointed for Lamar to be sworn in, that section of the court room reserved for the general public was crowded with visitors. Having taken the ordinary oath of office privately in the Justices' room, at twelve o'clock he followed the members of the court into the chamber where he was formally inducted into office, and, clad in robes of black silk, he took his seat upon the bench.

It was indeed a historic moment, for it marked the end of a period of disunion and signalized the reception of the Southern commonwealths into full fellowship in the sisterhood of American States. Just how much more than the personality of one man was involved in Lamar's seating was well expressed in the memorial address of Senator Stewart at the time of the Justice's death. "The Senate by its voice recognized the equal rights of all citizens of this Republic," he said. "The beneficial results of that action of the Senate were immediately felt both North and South. Confidence, respect, and good-fellowship were increased in every section of our common country. It was an object lesson for the world. It marked the contrast between the methods of despotic governments, which never forgive a fallen foe, and our own free government, which, entertaining malice toward none, has charity for all." [36]

Lamar, although possessed of that self-confidence so often seen in men of unusual ability who have been accustomed invariably to succeed in what they attempt, was devoid of the slightest taint of egotism. Probably that was the secret of the deep love and loyalty that he inspired in others, and that made them willing to follow him and serve him. Characteristically, he accepted without elation (and in this instance with some trepidation) the honor of his elevation to the Bench of the Supreme Court, though he prized it deeply, appreciated the support of those who had urged his nomination, and was determined to shed luster upon the robes which he wore. "As to the Judgeship of the Supreme Court," he had written to Edward Mayes on December 13th, 1887, shortly after he had definitely signified his acceptance of the nomination, "it has cost me a struggle to accept it which I hope you will never have. I have always acted on the principle that a man should not undertake the duties of any position to which he is not consciously equal, until this matter came up. I had no more idea of it than I had of the dukedom of Argyle. The suggestion originated with the President, and was seconded by my associates in the Cabinet. I do not feel qualified for the place. I have been too long out of the atmosphere of practical jurisprudence, and my misgivings are so painful that I have sleepless nights....As it is, the position was too exalted for me to resist the temptation to accept it, when it was tendered by those who did not share my doubts as to my competency."[37]

On the 18th of January, the very day that Lamar was sworn in, the executive business of the court was resumed. The next day saw the arguing of the first case after his seating, that of Porter *vs.* Beard, 124 U. S., and shortly afterwards he delivered his first opinion in the case of the Hannibal and St. Joseph Railroad Co. *vs.* Missouri River Packet Co., 125 U. S., decided on the 19th of March. When the time arrived for the writing of opinions upon the first group of decided cases, the Chief Justice, as was customary in respect to one just seated, assigned Lamar somewhat fewer than were given to the senior members on the Bench. He, however, insisted that he was prepared to

LAMAR MEMORIAL WINDOW IN SIGMA ALPHA EPSILON TEMPLE

assume his share of the work from the first, and consequently received his full quota.

Notice has already been taken of the quickness with which Lamar had attracted the attention of the nation in every position of trust and honor which he had held : in the House of Representatives his eulogy over the dead body of Sumner in the first Congress after his return to public life ; in the Senate, soon after he entered that body, the notable Silver Speech which had riveted the attention of the entire country, and in its bearing upon questions of finance had attracted international comment ; in the Cabinet his efforts during his first year which led to the recovery of hundreds of millions of dollars worth of the Public Domain. He was, likewise, to sit on the Supreme Bench for only a short time before he had written the dissenting opinion *in re* Neagle (Cunningham *vs.* Neagle, 135 U. S. 1 ; decided April 14th, 1890), which immediately became historic in judicial literature.

The situation in respect to this case was as follows : Mr. Justice Field had been threatened with a violent and perhaps mortal attack by Judge Terry of California who had become angered in connection with certain decisions rendered by the Justice. The threats in question caused the Attorney General to order Deputy Marshal Neagle to accompany the Justice as a bodyguard and to defend him from personal attack. Judge Terry, as was feared, dangerously assaulted the Justice in a public restaurant in California, whereupon the Deputy Marshal killed the assailant. Neagle was arrested in accordance with a warrant issued by a local State court, but he quickly recovered his freedom through a writ of *habeas corpus* issued by the federal court on the grounds that he had been arrested because of the performance of a duty incumbent upon him under the *laws* of the United States.

The question at issue before the Supreme Court was the legality of the grounds upon which the writ had been issued. The majority of the Supreme Court held that, although there was no actual law imposing such a duty upon a Marshal, or empowering the Attorney General to issue an order, the duty and power were in fact implied for the protection of the Court, and the maintenance of its dignity and authority. From this view the Chief Justice and Justice Lamar—pointing out that the question of the guilt or innocence of Neagle was entirely ir-relevant—dissented, they holding that he was subject to the laws of the State of California and a trial before a State court because it was impossible to show any law, act, or statute that would furnish authoritative justification for the interference of the federal authorities.

Both majority and minority opinions were reviewed widely in the nation's press with the newspapers of the South solidly approving Lamar's position, whereas in the North and East there was a decided difference of opinion. Such criticism as there was of the minority opinion was aimed at Lamar on the grounds that the question of States' Rights had been involved and that he had allowed his alleged Southern and Confederate sympathies unduly to influence him. There was, of course, no truth in the charges. In the first place, he was influenced in the performance of his duties by no such bias as was suggested; secondly the charge falls when it is considered that the Chief Justice, who certainly was not subject to any such influences, concurred in his minority opinion. Moreover, those acquainted with the law in the case saw that in fact no question of States' Rights was really involved. In his minority report, Lamar was at pains to concede that *all the authority claimed could have been conferred by Congress;* but he pointed out that Congress had not conferred such authority either upon the Marshal or the Attorney General, and that such authority and such powers were not delegated or implied to the Department of Justice by the Constitution. Hence he held that the jurisdiction in the case lay with the courts of the State in which the affair oc-curred. The basis of the dissent, it has been said, lay not in "any denial of implied power in the Federal Government, but only upon a denial of implied powers in the Department of Justice as distinguished from the Legislative Department." [38]

The criticisms came largely from certain representatives of the radical Republican press, but the consensus of opinions of

most trained legal observers agreed with that of Judge E. S.
Hammond, United States District Judge for the Western District of Tennessee who, writing on April 23rd, had this to say:
Such objections to the minority opinion are "very shabby nonsense. I repeat that in a very important view of the case there
is no question of Federal and State conflict in it; possibly not
in any proper view does such a conflict necessarily present itself. The result of Neagle's release on *habeas corpus* is that he
is not amenable *anywhere* according to our laws, to any form
of trial *before a jury*, which is the essential thing. In England,
possibly, where jury trial may be suspended, such power may
be exercised by a judge alone, if parliament shall authorize it;
but not in a State where the constitution guarantees jury trial.
So, if a *State* should grant such a power to a judge, would it
not be void? No State secures the right of trial by jury so
thoroughly as our Federal Constitution." [39]

From many lawyers and judges about the country Lamar
received letters approving his dissent and the forceful way in
which he had written the opinion. Most of them agreed with the
United States Circuit Judge for the Fifth District, Hon. Don. A.
Pardee who, writing from Savannah, Georgia, on the 22nd of
April agreed "with you and the Chief Justice," saying further:
"The power of the Government of the United States to protect its officers in the execution of its laws is undoubted; but
in the matter of protection, extent, mode, and manner, the government talks, if at all, by statutes, and not by orders of any
person or department." [40] Many there were who felt as did
Hon. Roger A. Pryor of New York who wrote on June 3rd:
"Will you suffer me to avow the admiration with which I read
your opinion in the Neagle case, and more generally my gratification at the ability and learning you display in the discharge
of the duties of your high office?" [41] "It has been the subject of
most general commendation both among lawyers and laymen,
in which I most heartily join," wrote Lamar's relative, the learned
A. O. Bacon, who was soon to begin his more than a score of
years in the United States Senate.

The estimate of Justice Lamar held by legal historians, with particular reference to the dissenting opinion *in re* Neagle, is perhaps best seen in the excellent *History of the Supreme Court of the United States*, by Hampton L. Carson, where, among other things, it is said: "The logical power of Mr. Justice Lamar, his striking talents as a rhetorician, his clearness of vision in detecting the true point in controversy, and his tenacious grasp upon it through all the involutions of argument, his familiarity with adjudged cases, his well-defined conceptions of the nature of the general government and the distribution of its powers under the constitution, are best displayed in his dissenting opinion *in re* Neagle, in which, unswayed by horror or resentment at the atrocious attempt to assassinate Mr. Justice Field, he insisted that, before jurisdiction of the crime of murder could be withdrawn from the tribunals of the State where the act was perpetrated into the Federal Courts, it was necessary to show some law, some statute, some Act of Congress, which could be pleaded in authoritative justification for the prisoner's act; and that no implied power existed in the President or one of his subordinates to substitute an order or direction of his own, no matter how lofty the motive or commendable the result." [42]

Only a few of the great body of opinions handed down by Justice Lamar can be mentioned here. For the scholar who desires an adequate conception of his legal prescience and acumen, it is necessary to read the corpus of his reported opinions beginning with his first—Hannibal & St. Joseph Railroad Co. *vs.* Missouri River Packet Co., 125 U. S. 260, through his last—The People, etc., of New York *vs.* Squire, 145 U. S., decided May 2nd, 1892. Perhaps he felt more pride in the case of Clement *vs.* Packer, 125 U. S. 309, than in any of his other early opinions. This involved some troublesome questions about the Pennsylvania law in reference to surveys of land and evidence of boundaries, and his opinion made what was, and is, considered as important law.

Repeatedly in this study we have noticed the precision and beauty with which Lamar used the English language. His ability as a literary artist was never more notable than in the more important opinions that he wrote as a member of the Supreme Court. Hon. Wiley P. Harris, of Jackson, Mississippi, in a letter of November 3rd, 1888, in reference to the opinion in Kidd *vs.* Pearson, 128 U. S., characterized it as a "very good specimen of sound judicial thought, portrayed with a clearness of exposition that is charming to the legal mind, and an almost faultless grace of diction. I read it with genuine pleasure. Our courts are not, ordinarily, schools of *belles-lettres.* I must confess, however, that this piece of composition from a young judge is encouraging." [43] Likewise, wrote Mr. Henry Craft, an eminent lawyer of Memphis, in a letter of December 18th in reference to the same case : "I stop in the preparation of a brief for your court to express the pleasure that I have found in reading that opinion." [44]

The most striking evidence of the high position that Lamar at once assumed among his associates in the Supreme Court is to be found in the criticisms noted upon the printed drafts of the opinions that were customarily submitted to each of the other Justices for suggestion and criticism.[45] These comments, the evidence of which can be accepted without discount because they were intended only for the eyes of the Court itself, are striking. On the copy of Justice Lamar's opinion in Bullitt County *vs.* Washer, 130 U. S., delivered in March, 1889, the conclusiveness whereof the author had expressed some doubt, Mr. Justice Bradley noted: "I have read this carefully, and cannot see ground for your scruples ; you prove the conclusion, it seems to me, almost demonstratively." "This is an admirable opinion, and a lucid review of the law on the subject of it," likewise inscribed Justice Bradley upon the first copy of Lamar's opinion in the case of Howard *et al vs.* Stillwell & Bierce Mfg. Co., 139 U. S., delivered in March, 1891. "I back down ; you are too much for me," Justice Brewer noted upon Lamar's opinion in the case of St. Paul, etc., Railway Co. *vs.* Phelps, 137 U. S., this decided in December, 1890. "Your argument I cannot answer ; and so, though I think it ought to be otherwise, I am convinced against my wish, and must concur."

"Upon another occasion," says Carson, "one of his judicial

associates remarked: 'Your differentiation of cases where a State may and may not be sued is the best that I have seen. The case [Pennoyer *et al vs.* McConnaughy, April 20th, 1891] seemed to me a difficult one, and I should not have suspected that you did not enjoy writing opinions. This is excellent.' Of the same case the oldest Justice now on the Bench [Mr. Justice Field] wrote as follows: 'I think that your summary of the constitutional principles applicable to the reciprocal relations of Article I, Section 10, and the Eleventh Amendment of the Constitution, is so clear that it would suffer from abridgement'; while of a recent case [Howard *et al vs.* The Stillwell & Bierce Mfg. Co., March 16th, 1891] involving the question of contingent or prospective profits, it was said: 'Your enunciation of the principles applicable to the question of profits is unusually clear and concise.'" "Lamar," remarked one of the Justices to ex-Senator Blanche K. Bruce, is "one of the ablest and most clear-headed members of the Court."[46]

"After you had finished reading your opinion this morning," Hon. William A. Maury, Assistant Attorney General of the United States, informed Lamar in a brief note that was representative of many others that he received from time to time, "Senator Hoar turned to me and said: 'That was a beautiful opinion.' I hope that I am not presuming in communicating this incident, which I do with the hope that it may be pleasing to you as it was to myself." Again, Dean Edmund H. Bennett, of the Boston University School of Law, under date of March 27th, 1890, wrote to Lamar in respect to his opinion in Dent *vs.* Ferguson, 132 U. S.: "I have read with great satisfaction the opinion....I do not wonder that the Court were unanimous. It is strong as 'proofs of Holy Writ.' I must also say that I fail to recognize a single phrase or word in it."

Attorney General Olney who, of course, had appeared before Lamar many times in the arguing of important cases, and who may be considered to have known whereof he spoke, thought him possessed of a "rare judicial mind,"[47] while Carson, in his *History of the Supreme Court,* asserts that "as a jurist he has taken high rank, his opinions being marked by scholarly

and careful study of principles and of cases. One of his colleagues, upon being asked whether he had met the expectation
of his friends, replied: 'Fully. Mr. Cleveland made no mistake
in appointing him.... He has sound judgment, a calm temperament, and a strong sense of justice. He possesses the judicial
faculty in a very high degree. He takes broad, comprehensive
views of legal and constitutional questions, and states his conclusions with unusual clearness and force, and in language most
aptly chosen to express the precise idea of his mind. His brethren
are greatly attached to him.' " [48]

Another distinguished jurist, Judge James M. Arnold, in discussing the importance of Justice Lamar's legal decisions, remarked that during his service on the bench, "some of the most
important cases in the annals of our independence, and with
which his name will be forever associated, were decided by the
court," in several of the cases Lamar writing, he said, dissenting opinions of great force and beauty. "The case of Pennoyer
vs. McConnaughy, 140 U. S., maintained the inviolability of
contracts as against State laws, and accurately defined the extent
to which a State officer under our system may be impleaded
in, or enjoined and restrained by, the Federal Courts; the
Neagle case, in 135 U. S., submitted for decision the question
whether or not a Federal officer who commits homicide in one
of the States while in the discharge of his official duties is
amenable to the criminal laws of the State for the offense, or
can be held to answer for the offense under the laws of the
State; and Fields vs. Clark, in 143 U. S., involved the power
of Congress to appropriate money to pay bounties on domestic
products, and to delegate legislative functions to the President
under the reciprocity statute, etc.

"These grave and dangerous questions, particularly those
presented by the Neagle case, brought out the strong convictions and judicial powers of Judge Lamar. The opinion of the
court delivered by him in one of these cases, and his dissenting
opinions in the other two, show his mastery of constitutional
law and familiarity with the nature and principles of constitutional government." [49]

Between Lamar and President Cleveland there had sprung up during the former's Cabinet days, as we have seen, a powerful and tender attachment. Some of the former Executive's love for his appointee, and pride in his achievements, is to be found in a most affecting letter of March 28th, 1891. "My Dear Friend," he wrote, "I am, for some reason, thinking much of you to-night. Though this is not uncommon, I believe that you are specially in my thoughts because I have just returned from a dinner at Mr. Fairchild's, where you were somewhat discussed.

"Mr. Vilas showed me some opinions, with the indorsements thereon of your brethren on the Bench, a few days ago; and you must allow me the satisfaction of telling you how much they pleased me, though they did not inspire a new confidence, nor disclose any new or unexpected condition." [50]

In February, 1889, just before the close of Mr. Cleveland's first term, Lamar had been interviewed for the *Baltimore Sun* in regard to the results of the Cleveland administration, especially in reference to the President's Southern policy and its effects. He had stipulated, because of his own position upon the Bench, that the interview not be published at that time. On the 28th of September, 1895, almost three years after his death, this document was given to the public. In it is evident the depth of affection that existed between the two men, and it is notable in that for insight and moderation its evaluation of Cleveland's personality and accomplishments is acceptable at the present time.

Space does not permit of further discussion of individual opinions written by Lamar, and they are easily accessible to the interested student of our legal history. A few general statements of fact will serve to place his judicial career in proper perspective. It will be recalled that when he was appointed it had been more than six years since a Justice had been added to the Court. Hence it is evident that in preparing opinions Lamar entered into competition with men who had not only spent a lifetime in legal work, but who had enjoyed many years of experience in the actual writing of opinions and in the operation of the court. Nevertheless, from the day of his seating, on the 18th of January, 1888, he assumed his full share of work and for two full years showed no evidence of slackening in the fast pace that he had set for himself. In 1890, however, came a slight recurrence of his old apoplectic trouble and throughout that year and 1891 he continued slowly to decline in strength.

Despite his failing health, however, a review of the total number of cases handled by the Supreme Court during the first four years of Lamar's incumbency (from January 18th, 1888, to January 18th, 1892, when he was in the grasp of his last illness) shows a remarkable number of major opinions written by him. The reference is to "major" opinions in contradistinction to the many short announcements which present neither the authorities nor the reasoning of the court but merely state, succinctly, the decision. An analysis of the nine hundred and eighty major opinions shows that Justice Lamar delivered precisely the same number as Mr. Justice Gray; that he delivered more than Mr. Justice Matthews and Mr. Justice Brewer together (the two being properly thus taken as one succeeded the other); and more than either Mr. Justice Field or Mr. Justice Bradley. Moreover, when the dissenting and individual concurring opinions are included, it is found that his relative standing in the writing of opinions is as high. The independence of his thinking is to be seen in the fact that while none of the Justices wrote many dissenting opinions, Lamar's percentage of dissents was higher than the average, presenting as many as Mr. Justice Field and more than Chief Justices Waite and Fuller, and Justices Blatchford and Gray.

The value of a man's services upon the Supreme Bench is not, of course, to be computed in the number of opinions which he prepares. That Lamar carried his full share of the load has been stressed because such an achievement was remarkable when it is considered that for only the first two years of his service was his health comparable to what it had been in the preceding years of his public life. For the two succeeding years he held his own in the work of the court in the face of rapidly failing health, and in the last year he was struggling with a mortal illness.

Undoubtedly, like so many men of tremendous mental and physical energy, he burned out his vital forces by driving himself too relentlessly, often working throughout the night upon important cases. It cannot be denied that—while by native talents, habits of thought, and training he was eminently fitted for a seat in the Supreme Court of the nation—he in a sense entered a new and untried field after having exhausted much of his energy in notable careers both in the legislative and executive branches of the government. That he achieved distinguished eminence as a jurist, no one who studies his opinions can deny; but it is painfully evident that in doing so he broke down his physical resistance that had already been ravaged by organic apoplectic illnesses. In this connection Secretary Vilas, speaking in the memorial meeting called by the bar of the Supreme Court after Justice Lamar's death, had this to say: "Being honored with his intimacy, it has been mine to know —nor should I withhold the testimony—how faithfully, how fervidly that ardor of duty to his country glowed in his breast to his latest days. It drove him, after his accession to this Bench, to such extremes of toil—he with his feeble, disease-struck, and shattered frame—as few men in the prime of natural vigor will submit to. It took from him, beyond all question, and piled upon the altar of self-sacrifice, days, months, years, it is even probable, of life. For what to him was life when in the path of duty—to him who had many a time and oft proffered it to fate unflinchingly, who cared for nothing on earth as for his friends, his country, and his honor? He seemed even to spurn the measures which prudence commended for his safety, not less than those for his comfort, with a seeming pride that he could thus mark more clearly to himself his devoted discharge of the high duties intrusted to him."

In discussing the opinions written by Justice Lamar the high estimates of his judicial ability held by his associates upon the Bench have been cited. That he would be an able judge had been conceded from the first by all of those who were in a position to know intimately the quality of his thinking. "Lamar is a man of magnificent surprises," Postmaster General Vilas had said during the period when his confirmation was pending in the Senate. "I did not know him until we met in the Cabinet, and during the past two years I have been very intimate with him. I think that I have never met any man whose intellect has grown upon me so overwhelmingly as has Lamar's. At times he has consulted with me about matters of public policy which only the decision of a question of law would settle." "Once," said Vilas in connection with a certain legal matter before the Department of the Interior, "he had a most important decision to make. He had not written it—for I believe that he does not write his decisions until the last minute—but he had the whole matter revolving in his mind. He began at the beginning and stated the facts. Such a faculty of clear, limpid statement is seldom met. I think that in my time no man that I have known has possessed it so well as Mr. Lamar, unless it was the late Matt. Carpenter of Wisconsin. Then he began to unfold the principles of law which he thought applicable. As his mind rolled on from position to position it was simply wonderful....

"Without making invidious comparisons, it is my judgment that Mr. Lamar will add strength and adornment to the Supreme Bench. I believe that he possesses some qualifications that the Bench needs, and as the years go on the wisdom of his appointment will establish itself far above the reach of criticism." [51]

As a matter of fact, Vilas' prophecy was triumphantly vindicated. Senator Hoar, who had so bitterly opposed his confirmation, was to write more than once of the "marvelous beauty and felicity of style" of his judgments, while Chief Justice Fuller was to remark that "his was the most suggestive mind that I ever knew, and not one of us but has drawn from its inexhaustible store." [52]

Too, when Lamar's days on the Bench were ended, many of the Republican organs that had warred upon his confirmation were most lavish in praise of his services in the judiciary. It was almost startling and certainly amusing to find the *New York Tribune* editorializing that "his rectitude and sincerity were universally recognized,...he more than satisfied the expectations which his appointment suggested...he was not deficient in moral any more than in physical courage," [53] and philosophizing that "appointments to the Supreme Court have been severely criticized and motives...sometimes called in question; but the selections made have almost invariably turned out to be wise." [54]

"He was the equal of his associates in learning and judicial capacity," said the *Philadelphia Evening Telegraph;* "and his retirement by the great reaper will be the occasion of sincere regret by those with whom he labored, and he will be everywhere spoken of with profound respect." [55] In the remarks of the *Philadelphia Ledger* there was something of prophecy: "Among the many distinguished men who have honored the Supreme Bench, Justice Lamar will hold high rank in future histories. A learned and most upright judge, he bore himself with dignity and honor. Before his elevation to the Bench he was a strong, and at times even a bitter partisan; but in that position he knew neither political friend nor foe." [56]

Perhaps there was no work of Lamar's life that he enjoyed so thoroughly as that of the Supreme Court, for his temperament was ideally suited to the judiciary, and the cultural associations were such that his whole environment was entirely congenial. As he once said in an address before a law class: "My acquaintance with them [his associates on the Bench] constitutes the most impressive incident in my entire intellectual and moral life." [57]

None of the Justices did he admire more thoroughly than Judge Bradley, concerning whom, in his inimitable fashion he once related the following episode: "I had been upon the Bench but a little while before I heard a keen, sharp, glib-tongued patent lawyer hold forth upon a case of an extended patent, which he claimed to have been infringed by the defendant. It seems that the reissued patent differed in some way from the original patent; and so the argument was made that, although the reissued patent might have been infringed, the original had not been. I sat there listening to the shrill whir of the attorney's talk, conscientiously doing my best, but with the conviction that if I sat there until the world melted into its original elements I would never be able to understand the ins and outs of patent law. Still, as the case went on, I began to feel that, though there might be, and was, a verbal difference in the original and reissued patent, the two really covered the same matter, when suddenly Justice Bradley broke in:

" 'Doesn't this reissue drawing show a tin spout somewhere at the bottom of the machine [whatever it was]?'

" 'Yes, sir.'

" 'And it isn't shown in the original?'

" 'No—no, sir, that is, this is a simple mechanical device, and nothing is claimed upon it.'

"I felt somewhat alarmed, but in spite of doubts held pretty firmly to my own opinion that there was an infringement. Afterwards, in conclave of the Justices, I was called upon to give my opinion first. It was a great trial to me, as I was then the junior Justice upon the Bench; but I gathered myself together and expressed my conviction, with considerable courage, that the two letters patent covered the same matter. The next Justice, in order was called upon, and this was Justice Blatchford; and he promptly said: 'Oh, reverse, of course' (which was an agreement with my vote, reversing the decision of Judge ——). And so they all fell into line after me. I was somewhat elated at this result, but the unforgettable tin spout was heavy upon my mind, and my conscience troubled me. Could there be anything of obscure but weighty import in that tin spout? I took Justice Bradley aside and said to him:

" 'See here; what did you mean by asking that question about the tin spout?' And he said: 'Oh, to tell the truth, I had been asleep for ten minutes, and I didn't want the counsel to know it.' " [58]

As was formerly the custom in respect to the Justices, Lamar spent a part of the summers of 1888, 1889, 1890, and 1891 in holding court on the circuit. He endeared himself greatly to the local bars of the sections which he visited and received many marks of their esteem, such as the note of January 1st, 1891, from District Judge William T. Newman of Atlanta. "I shall always regard your visit here," he wrote, "as one of the pleasantest events in my experience not only officially, but personally; and I know that the bar and your friends here regard it in the same way." [59]

SILENCE

LAMAR, throughout all the strenuous years of his public career, had never lost interest—his letters show—in the members of his family connection. Both of his brothers, in fact almost the whole generation that had played about the old Lamar homestead and fished and swum in the waters of Little River, had, as we have seen, perished in the Civil War—surely the "lost generation"; and only himself and J. L. M. Curry still survived. But there was evidence that the descendants of Thomas the emigrant had not perished from the earth. Among them, James Lamar, of Missouri, was making a brilliant legal reputation which he was soon to increase in Congress; the Justice's own nephew, William B. Lamar, of Florida, was serving as Attorney-General of his State and was preparing for his years of honorable service in the National Legislature; and Lamar's kinsman, Andrew J. Cobb, recognized as a lawyer of eminent talents, was soon to take his seat upon the Supreme Court of the State of Georgia.[1] Meanwhile, Justice Lamar was writing encouragingly to his brilliant young cousin, Joseph Rucker Lamar, of Augusta, Georgia, who had started on the legal career that was to lead to the Supreme Court of Georgia and to his elevation by a Republican President (Mr. Taft) to the Supreme Court of the Nation.[2]

The persistence of certain traits of mind and physique in successive generations of the family is remarkable. Between no members of the family, however, have the results of their common inheritance been so striking as between Justices L. Q. C. Lamar and Joseph Rucker Lamar. The latter, as a child, had been a schoolmate and an intimate of Woodrow ("Tommy") Wilson, in Augusta. At the University of Georgia, which he attended for a time, the memories still lingered of a dozen or more leaders who had passed through the University and gone out to serve the South and the nation, notably Thomas R. R. Cobb, Howell Cobb, Benjamin H. Hill, and Henry W. Grady. Like his older cousin, Joseph Rucker Lamar was possessed of certain mental traits that had been frequently recurrent in the family—that, indeed, for more than a hundred years had appeared in every generation: a rapier wit, kindly humor, the scholarly temperament which results in a love of research, and a flair for abstract thinking and delving into the principles and laws that govern human society. Where the elder Justice had been an intimate of Henry Adams and his circle, the other —a half generation later—was to be an associate of Charles Francis and Brooks Adams and a warm personal friend of Lord Brice. The physical constitution of the two men was curiously the same. Each was to serve upon the bench of the Supreme Court for within a few weeks of the same length of time; each, while in the discharge of his duties suffered a paralytic stroke that impaired the use of the left leg; and the death of each was occasioned, within considerably less than a decade of the same age, by a complication of high blood-pressure and hardening of the arteries.[3]

Always, too, Lamar recalled with great pleasure his student days at Emory College. Indeed, with certain of his classmates he kept up a lifelong correspondence, and his letters bear frequent witness to the veneration in which he held his Alma Mater. On June 24th, 1890, at the annual commencement, he delivered the principal address to the Society of the Alumni at the College in Oxford. "He possessed a marvelously retentive memory," said President (later Bishop) Candler in commenting upon this occasion. "In the course of the address..., he reproduced with almost literal accuracy sermons and addresses delivered in his hearing during his college days, from 1841-1845. A debate between two distinguished Georgians who were students with him at Emory, which he heard when they and he were sophomores, was reproduced with microscopic fidelity. This uncommon recollection was a prime factor in the triumphs of his political life."[4]

Lamar, we have seen, was reared in an intensely religious home, and received his education in a Methodist college. By nature and by environment he was himself a man with a strong religious bias. Despite his environment and his mystical turn of mind, however, he never allowed himself to be swept into the religious frenzy so characteristic of the Georgia Methodism of his youth. A thinker and profoundly dissatisfied with certain aspects of his own religious life as well as the contemporary orthodoxy that was his inheritance, it was not until almost twenty years after his graduation from college, in July of 1862, that he could feel satisfied to assume the vows of the Southern Methodist Church. "On Commencement Sunday at Wesleyan Female College, after an excellent sermon from Rev. Dr. Houston, of Nashville, the doors were opened, and my husband joined," Mrs. Lamar wrote of this event to her mother, Mrs. Longstreet. "I am so rejoiced that he has united himself with the Church, and believe that he will be a consistent and devout Christian. He has purchased a number of religious books, and reads, and prays a great deal." [5]

It was not difficult for Lamar, with his imaginative mind and mystical temperament, to conceive of a God; but he was frank to admit that his belief was an act of faith and was not reached by a rationalizing approach. "The union of divinity with humanity in the person of Jesus Christ we cannot explain or comprehend; at least I cannot," he once said. "The incomprehensibility of a fact, however, is, to a philosophical mind no proof of its nonexistence. There are a thousand facts around us whose existence is undoubted and indubitable, and yet whose natures are utterly incomprehensible." [6]

For a time, at least, during his College days and after, he had considered entering the Methodist ministry. The idea recurred to him even after he had made a place for himself at the Bar, and had held a professorship at the University of Mississippi. "I remember a casual conversation I held with him during his first years in Oxford, in which, as we spoke of his future, he remarked that he would not be surprised if he should end his life work in the ministry of the Methodist Church," recorded ex-Chancellor J. N. Waddell in his *Academic Memorials.* "My reply: 'No, sir; you will surely pass your life in the world of politics.' My own impression is that Mr. Lamar had from his early manhood kept steadily in view the career of statesmanship." It is significant that even after Lamar, in the postwar years, had made for himself a conspicuous place in the counsels of the nation, the fear recurred more than once that "after all he had probably mistaken the path of duty." But the nearest he was ever to come to a ministerial career was his founding, during his period of retirement after the Civil War, of a Bible class in Oxford where his brilliance as a speaker and his power as an expounder of the gospel drew large audiences that cut across all sectarian lines.

With his speculative and philosophical bent, combined with an insatiable intellectual curiosity, Lamar, as we have seen, was possessed of a remarkable capacity for analytical and practical thinking. Something of this appears in the course of a personal reference which he made in Congress on March 9th, 1876, in explanation of a vote that he had cast. "I have all my life," he said, "cultivated a deep and abiding sense of the importance, sanctity, and authority of truth. If I could reach my ideal, it would be an absolute surrender to it as the law of my life, to be severed from it by neither temptation, interest, passion, nor ambition."[7]

Among his many friends—and his acquaintance included most of the leading men in the nation's public life—was the self-professed infidel, Ingersoll. Lamar always felt that the other man's thinking was shallow. In 1886 the papers carried an account of a friendly argument between the two in which the Cabinet officer expressed impatience with Ingersoll's blatant and sensational professions of atheism. "He has no intellectual organ which gives him any avenue to the infinite or supernatural," Lamar wrote to a friend who had sent him the press clipping, "but his heart is full of a sort of piety; and his life, so far as I know it, is one of moral rectitude, humanity, and tender love."[8]

His own belief he stated frankly and simply in an address

before the Young Men's Christian Association of Washington, delivered in April, 1890. "I give them without figure of rhetoric or form of argument," he said of his own sentiments, "and simply declare that I believe that there is a God—a personal, infinitely gracious Creator and father of all; a God of goodness, justice, and holiness; the God of the Bible. I also declare my belief that the Bible is the Word of God, and that the central idea of his inspired revelation is Christ."[9]

American literature, moreover, presents few more genuine lyrics or impressive confessions of faith than his strangely beautiful little poem, published after his death, which begins:

> They are not ours
> The fleeting flowers
> But lights of God....[10]

To him, it is clear, the President of the Immortals was something more than Hardy's dumb and dreaming master of this show. Perhaps his conceptions of God and immortality are best to be compared with those of the poet Browning, though his faith was based on somewhat more subtle and philosophical grounds.

Many of Lamar's letters during the most strenuous years of his public life reveal his deeply religious nature. "I eat my breakfast, dinner, and supper always in the presence of some two or three eager applicants for office," he wrote to a member of his family while Secretary of the Interior; "go to bed with their importunities in my ears; and, what is of much greater inconvenience to me, and one that I feel more than any other, I hardly have time to say my prayers. You know that breaks up a cherished habit of mine." And during the same period to his lifelong friend, Chief Justice James Jackson, of Georgia: "That is a terrible question of yours about the 'roll call.' No; I am not ready. I have tried to 'tote fair' in this world, and have done my duty toward men honestly and bravely, and to my country; but to my God I am one of the most remiss, and could not stand before him and say that I have done my duty to him."[11]

In the previously mentioned address before the Society of the Alumni of Emory College, in June, 1890, Justice Lamar expressed his "profound conviction of the worthlessness and moral inadequacy of all science, literature, art, historical knowledge, and intellectual culture, unaccompanied by faith in duty and immortality, in God and Christ, as springs of motive and the inspiration of life." All his critical studies into the philosophy and theology of Christianity, he said, had left him "a firm and unwavering believer." He had his doubts, and there were mysteries that he could not fathom, Bishop Galloway remarked after Lamar's death, "but above these minor keys of sadness and fear rose his simple but sublime faith in essential truth"; and Bishop Fitzgerald believed that "It was his religious faith, that, more than anything else, gave unity, right direction, power, and success to his life. This was the mighty undercurrent that bore him onward in his course." [12]

In his years of public service in Washington, however, Lamar did not become an active communicant in any denomination until 1891 when, as a member of the Supreme Court, he joined the Mount Vernon Church, South. When the pastor, Reverend Dr. J. T. Wightman, asked—in view of the fact that he had been a member elsewhere—if he wished the simple entry of his name on the church rolls, he answered characteristically : "No ; I have been too far astray, and have too long neglected duty, to claim a place in the Church on an early confession of faith. I want to join *de novo*." "Well, Judge," said the pastor, "would you prefer to be received in the quiet of your own home?" "No," said he ; "I want to take the vows before the congregation as any other humble sinner, hoping thereby to encourage those who, like myself, have too long postponed this most important matter. I only ask that the reporters be not informed, and that we have no newspaper sensation." [13]

We have seen that Lamar, though a man of great physical strength and, in a sense, rugged health, had been threatened with apoplexy ever since the attack that he had suffered while encamped about Richmond in 1861. Repeatedly he had suffered minor seizures of this sort—once while Secretary of the Interior, but his last serious illness had been in 1880. Always with his medical advisers there had been the expectation that a sudden rupture of a blood vessel in the brain might bring instantaneous death; and yet he worked on with their warning constantly before him.

In the winter of 1889-90, under the stress of the prodigious labor to which all his life he had subjected himself, but which was now intensified by the arduous routine of the Supreme Court, his magnificent physical strength began to fail. On February 28th, 1890, he wrote to his sister, Mrs. Ross, that after a minor attack he had not recovered as fast as was to be expected. Further, "two doctors say, upon consultation, that one of the valves of my heart has ceased to act (I don't believe that) ;..."[14] But his decline in strength was henceforth perceptible.

In the summer of 1891, after holding a short term of Circuit Court at Oxford, Mississippi, he went to Danville, Kentucky, where he delivered the commencement address at Centre College on June 10th. Before a large audience, including a number of prominent guests, he spoke for slightly more than an hour. On the platform were Justices Lamar and Harlan, Chief Justice Holt, of Kentucky, Hon. W. C. P. Breckinridge, ex-Governor Proctor Knott, Hon. John Young Brown, Hon. A. P. McCormick of Texas, Colonel Elliott F. Shepard of the *New York Mail and Express*, and a number of others quite as distinguished. According to the *Courier-Journal*, it was a brilliant address "of great power and interest," which "was frequently applauded, and at the conclusion of his address [he] was cheered enthusiastically."[15]

By September he had lost more ground. "My debility is extreme, and seems to be lasting," he was writing to Mrs. Ross. "The work of the Court next month appalls me." In October, however, he had slightly improved, and, while carrying his share of the work of the Court, was accustomed to walk home after adjournment each day. Despite a slight set-back he was able to continue his labors and on the 5th of January, 1892, was writing to Mrs. Ross that "during the last preceding four days my health has been sensibly improving. Every one has said all the time that I am *looking* better, but now I *feel* such a decided improvement that I have postponed my trip South until the 1st of February. Of course there is a very general protest among all my friends against this conclusion, but the work that is upon this Court is not a mere matter of sentimental duty; it is a hard reality; and if I, to give myself a respite and relief, should suspend my share of it, I would be throwing upon my associates—some of whom are older and weaker than myself, and others more prostrated by sickness, who are staying here bravely at their post—an increase of the labor with which they are already burdened." [16]

In February, according to his plan, Lamar visited shortly in Macon, Georgia, and then went down to Pass Christian, on the Mississippi Coast. "I want to thank you, and tell you how much solace, comfort, and gratification your love for your brother gives him," he wrote Mrs. Ross from that place on the 17th. "My separation from you and my children is a sore trial to me, and becomes harder and harder to bear. Jennie's [Mrs. William Harmong Lamar] visits, with her two little cherubs, bring light into my household. She and they are treasures which ought to make any man grateful to God, and I am; but I feel the absence of the rest keenly....I wish I could accept your invitation to stop with you. In all my life I never wanted so much to see you. With no special reason for it, my thoughts frequently—yes, more than frequently—dwell upon the time when we shall cease to be with one another in life, and the time left me is increasing in preciousness with respect to my intercourse with those dear to my heart; but my duties as Judge leave me no respite, and I must go back without seeing any of you." [17]

On the morning after Lamar left for Washington, he felt severe pains in his back near the left kidney, and on the 8th of March, Dr. William Pepper of Philadelphia, with whom he had consulted, diagnosed his case as one of mild arterio-sclerosis complicated with renal trouble. "I think," said the specialist in advising against his resignation from the Bench, "that he is as well off at Washington, discharging with less than usual effort a less than usual portion of his judicial duties, as he would be elsewhere this season." Hence he returned to his duties. In April, while in the business of hearing a case, he suffered the long threatened stroke, complicated by a severe hemorrhage. After a few days in bed, however, he rallied his failing strength and returned to the Bench where he held on until the adjournment of court.

Throughout the spring of 1891, despite his illness, Lamar was in constant correspondence with Mr. Cleveland in connection with Southern affairs, and in anticipation of the ensuing Democratic National Convention and the Presidential election. "Our people are wretchedly poor," he was writing on April 3rd in explanation of the Southern "silver craze" and the recent visit to Mississippi of David B. Hill of New York, who was pushing his own candidacy for the Democratic nomination. "Their condition is not like that of Northern communities when a great financial disaster sweeps over them. It is individual poverty and distress which brood over plantations and fields and households, and consume their daily means of subsistence. They hear with almost despair that their most trusted Democratic leaders oppose the measures that are offered for their relief. The free coinage of silver and tariff reform have been regarded by them as the only measures of relief which the Democratic party has to propose. Your firm, and, as I think, wise stand against the free coinage of silver saddened their hearts and frustrated their expectations. Just then, Hill's Elmira speech came out, and was circulated under flaming capitals. Then followed his election to the Senate, and what was claimed to be his act fixing New York permanently in the Democratic column. An invitation was gotten up to him to address the Legislature of Mississippi—and the Southern tour." His invasion of Mississippi, Lamar said, had been a complete failure. The Southern leaders saw that he would not do. "When meetings have been called for Hill or any one else, the speaker does not call the name of Cleveland for fear of the applause. The avoidance of that name has got to be a joke.

"I am too weak to scribble more....I am sorry not to be able to give you a good account of my health. Have been down eleven days with frequent and copious hemorrhages, with no signs of an early recovery. I spend many of the silent and tedious hours of the night on my sick couch in thoughts of you, and in earnest aspirations for your happiness." [18]

The machinations for Senator Hill by none too ethical means throughout the lower South, Lamar informed the ex-President in this same letter, had been "seconded by men from whom better things might have been expected, but who yielded from a want of firmness to stand against what seemed to them to be the greater force." But he was convinced that only by the re-entrance of Cleveland into the arena could the gains made by the Democracy and for the nation be permanently assured. By May 1st, the date of the next letter which Lamar received from his former chief, the latter had apparently determined that it was his duty again to seek the Democratic nomination after having been out of office for one term: "I have within the last few months passed through much that has been trying and perplexing to me. The office of President has not to me personally a single allurement. I shrink from everything which another canvass means, and I know as well the dark depths that yawn at the foot of another defeat. I would avoid either if I should consult alone my peace, my comfort, or my desire.

"My discomforts arise from a sense of duty to honest people and devoted friends. I am alone with my own thoughts and with the apparent trust and confidence of my countrymen. Am I mistaken in all this, and are my country and my party prepared to discharge me from service? One thing I know. Forces are at work which certainly mean the complete turning back of the hands on the dial of democracy, and the destruction of party hopes....

"You shall know, my dear friend, my inmost thoughts. I shall be obedient to the call of my country and my party. Whatever happens, no one shall say that I refused to serve in time of evil, or abandoned those whom I have been instrumental in calling to the field, when is waged the battle for democratic principle. ...Our Southern friends, if they persist, will be left alone with their free coinage heresy. The west is slipping from their side. The danger is that another idea, and a charge of heedlessness for the public safety on the financial question, will do service in the place of the memories of the civil war.

"The question is often and justifiably put by friendly southerners, 'Can Cleveland carry New York?' The answer is ready as to Cleveland or any other man, if the democracy is at all weak on the coinage question. As one who loves his country and believes that her interest is bound up in democratic supremacy, I am most uncomfortable and unhappy in the fear that the south will not see until too late the danger of their marring all."[19] Cleveland, it should be noted, showed a remarkable premonition that if the Democracy allowed itself to be tied to the heresy of free silver coinage it would ensure long years of defeat, such as actually occurred in the period of Bryan domination from 1896 to 1912.

The summer of 1892 Lamar spent at Bethlehem in the White Mountains where, on September 9th, he wrote to Mrs. Ross that he had "not realized the sanguine hopes of restored health," and that he looked to the approaching October with dread lest it find him "unable to buckle on the harness for the resumption of judicial labors." "I am in doubt," he remarked, "whether I ought to undertake that work or resign a position the duties of which I do not feel able to discharge with credit to myself and those I love, or in a manner due to the public interests concerned....God bless you all! I wish you knew the insignificance of official rank and honors compared to the value to me of your affections."[20]

Nevertheless, he returned to Washington and resumed the functions of his office. That he was not without realization that his period of active service was nearing its close is evident in a touching letter of November 16th to his son. "I know," he said, "that the time is fast approaching when I can no longer be of much service to the children I love; that the horizon of my life stands still and awaits my approach, and that I shall soon pass beneath it from the sight of those for whom I wish to live. I do not shrink from it, and the only thing necessary to make me happy in the brief time that I have left me will be the happiness of knowing that you are resolute, happy, and possessed of a self-sustaining mind. May God bless you!" [21]

In a letter written in 1891 to Mr. Walter Barker, Lamar had expressed his love for Mississippi—an abiding affection which had not been dimmed by the years of separation—and, at the same time, had reiterated his faith in the tremendous future of the United States. "The greatness of this country in the past," he had remarked, "has been with the South. What it will be in the future should not, and must not, be without the South; but to be such a factor the South must hold to, and retain in the national life, her great and shining men. She must hurl contempt upon the miserable alternative of substituting them by the shallow, ignorant, self-seeking, upstart creatures of the hour." [22]

Continually in his last illness his mind turned back to the State of his adoption that had so often and so signally honored him. "How he clung to Mississippi and Mississippians in his last days of suffering it was my privilege to observe and appreciate," wrote Mr. Frank C. McGehee in a letter to the *Clarion-Ledger* of February 5th, 1893, in which he characterized Lamar as "a truly great and good man, a thinker, a philosopher, whose mind was cast in the mold from which only grand conceptions issue." "I had the opportunity of being with him, and of painfully observing the wreck which disease had made of his once powerful frame," continued Mr. McGehee. "His mind was as bright as ever. The body which held it had dwindled away, but in that shrinking the grand brain from which had come so many wise and brilliant thoughts had no part....

"I told him of my visit [to Mississippi] and of the many inquiries about him in the State that he loved so well. 'Ah!' he said, as a tinge of sadness swept over his features; 'I am so glad to hear it. I was afraid, since I have been away from them so long, that they were beginning to forget me.' It seemed to cheer him greatly to feel that the people whom he had served so long and so well still remembered and loved him."

Shortly before Christmas of 1892, Lamar with his wife started South for a visit in the milder climate of the Mississippi coast. On the first day of travel, however, he suffered a severe heart attack and was removed from the train at Atlanta and taken to the home of Mr. Hoke Smith (a family connection and son-in-law of Thomas R. R. Cobb)—the proprietor of the *Atlanta Journal* and soon to occupy Lamar's former post of Secretary of the Interior—where he was kindly entertained for two days. From here he went on to Macon where, among members of his family and surrounded by friends and associations of his young manhood, he died on the 23rd of January, 1893.

That he was seriously ill, every one had known; but the suddenness of his passing came as a severe shock to his family. At Macon they had gone to the home of Captain W. H. Virgin, a son-in-law of Mrs. Lamar, who lived in the little suburb of Vineville. Apparently Lamar had begun to show decided improvement, for on the very day of his death he had ridden into the city on the electric cars and that evening he had dined with the family and with "Doc" Flewellen, a friend of his student years at Emory, whom he had encountered in Macon and persuaded to return home with him. He had shown a lively interest in everything and every one, and in the course of the conversation had invited his friend to visit him in Washington the following summer.

At 7:45, fifteen minutes after Dr. Flewellen had left, remarking as he did so upon the improvement in his health, the Justice suffered the fatal stroke that for thirty years had threatened his life. When medical assistance arrived at about 8:40, his last spark of vitality was already ebbing, and as the physician, Dr. Parker, strove to revive him he passed quietly away.

The morning papers of the 24th carried throughout all the nation the news of Justice Lamar's death. Perhaps none of the telegrams of condolence would have so pleased the dead statesman, if he could have known, as that from Mayor John F. Brown of the little town of Oxford, Mississippi, where for so many years he had lived, teaching in the University, practicing law, and retaining his home after he had risen to national fame. "Oxford, the home of Justice Lamar for so many years," read the telegram, "is overwhelmed. Bells in the courthouse, churches and colleges are tolling. Business houses, residences, and the university chapel are draped in mourning. Expressions of deepest grief from all classes are universal. The profoundest statesman of the South, the noblest of gentlemen, the truest of patriots! Mississippi, whose fame has been so largely the product of his splendid services, is inconsolably stricken."[23]

Washington, too, was in mourning no less than the cities of his native section. When the Supreme Court assembled at noon on the 24th, the bar and the audience quarters were crowded, and the chair between Justices Gray and Brown was draped in black. Justice Fuller, after announcing Lamar's death and adjourning court, formally communicated the fact of his decease to both Houses of Congress. After a number of addresses (including those by Senators Walthall and Gordon in the Senate and by Mr. Allen of Mississippi in the House) both chambers adjourned out of respect to the man whose magic voice had for so many years been the death of factionalism among them. At the Department of the Interior, Secretary Noble issued an order in which he eulogized Lamar's administration and instructed that the department be "draped in mourning for twenty days on and from this date, the flag carried at half-mast, and the department closed on the day of his funeral."

For the passing of no other man had Mississippi shown such grief. In Oxford the United States Court adjourned "in honor of the greatest statesman of the South," and a mass-meeting, jointly presided over by the Mayor and the Chancellor of the University, assembled in the afternoon. Likewise, meetings for the making of speeches and the passing of resolutions took place in all of the larger towns of the State, and not a newspaper but carried editorials of eulogy and sorrow.

Perhaps the death of no statesman since the Civil War had

caused more genuine sorrow—such a feeling of personal bereavement—throughout the nation as well as in his native section.
Demonstrations such as those in Mississippi occurred in New
York City, Boston, Birmingham, Memphis, New Orleans, and
elsewhere, while a number of State legislatures that chanced to
be in session—as distant, even, as North Dakota—passed resolutions of praise for the dead statesman and sympathy for his
grieving family. Among the memorials placed on file by order
of the Chief Justice of the Supreme Court of the United States
was that of the Illinois Bar Association, which said, among other
things:

As a statesman, an orator, a scholar, and a judge, he is justly
regarded as a truly great American, and we desire to place on record
in this public manner our appreciation of his sterling worth and
public services.
We consider it becoming on this occasion to give expression to
the high esteem that we entertain for the character, learning, and
ability of the deceased judge.[24]

Georgia, only second to Mississippi, grieved at his passing.
The United States Courts in session in Atlanta and Savannah
adjourned, and memorial services were held, while at Emory
College, on the day of the funeral, classes were suspended and
a memorial meeting assembled in the college chapel in honor
of the passing of the institution's most distinguished alumnus.
"Among the mass of floral offerings banked about the casket
at the home of Mr. Virgin," said the *Macon Telegraph* of
January 28th, "was one composed of roses and hyacinths" forming the badge of Sigma Alpha Epsilon, the fraternity of which
Lamar was a member. Present, too, at the home, and later at
Mulberry Street Church, where the funeral services were held,
were Chief Justice Fuller, the Associate Justices Blatchford,
Brown, and Brewer, and a number of United States Senators
and Representatives, including Walthall and Gordon—Lamar's
closest friends in the National Legislature—together with the visitors representing the executive branches of the government.
In evidence, too, were the members of the Supreme Court of

Georgia, representatives of the American Bar Association, and a large group representing the alumni of Emory College.

In the city of Macon, all places of business and all offices were closed and the flags on the public buildings were placed at half-mast. Mulberry Church itself was draped in white and black from its dome to the smallest cornice, as was the choir loft and the interior. Shortly after 12 o'clock, the magnificent casket was carried down the center aisle, Dr. Candler, President of Emory College, preceding the pallbearers and reading the order of the burial: "I am the resurrection, and the life; he that believeth in me, though he were dead, yet shall he live; and whosoever liveth and believeth in me shall never die." President Candler delivered the address at the church—a tribute that in grace and eloquence is impressive forty years after its delivery:

...For nearly a half century, during stormy days, when passion was fierce and partisanism was bitter, he served his country in high public station; and today we lay him to rest in the soil of his native State, and no one can say as he lies down to his long sleep that he was ever charged with the slightest dishonor.... Mississippi, the State of his adoption, mourns for him as her Chevalier Bayard, the idol of her heart; Georgia, his native State, who in his long absence has never ceased to love him and wish him back home, presses her dead son to her bosom with unutterable sorrow, disconsolate as Rachel, refusing to be comforted, because he is not; all the nation mourns this knightly man, who lived without fear and died without reproach.... Sweet be his sleep in his sepulcher on the banks of the Ocmulgee, singing sadly to the sea, until the earth and the sea shall give up their dead, and God shall wipe away all tears from our eyes, and there shall be no more death, neither sorrow nor crying, nor any more pain! [25]

The body was placed in a vault on the north side of the redoubt built for the protection of the city during the Civil War, and overlooking the Ocmulgee River. In Lamar's right hand and just above his heart was placed the small copy of the Constitution of the United States which all his mature life he had carried in his inside vest pocket, and which—of all books next to his Bible—he loved best. "Lucius Quintus Cincinnatus Lamar's body has been called back to the bosom of mother earth," said the *Macon Telegraph* of the 28th; "but the spirit lives; it sweeps throughout the land with the same grand power for good; and for all time men will feel its influence whenever memory seeks an example of purity, unselfishness, or unassuming power."

On the 13th of March, the members of the bar of the Supreme Court assembled at the capitol to perfect plans for a memorial in honor of the departed jurist and statesman. Mr. Vilas, who was made the chairman, immediately appointed a committee to draft resolutions, and the meeting adjourned until the 18th of March.

Of all of the speeches delivered on the appointed day, perhaps that of Mr. Vilas himself was the most impressive. Quotation has already been made from that address, but one further passage must be cited here because it sums up so pertinently the chief significance of Lamar's services to the nation. "It was given to him to see, with a clearness which few besides him shared," said Mr. Vilas, "the true relations between his conquered people and the triumphant North; and there were added wisdom to guide their course, eloquence to win their hearts to follow it, patience and fortitude to bear its personal trials, and the manful spirit still to stand for what was their rightful due.

"Thus, in Lamar, to a degree unsurpassed, was displayed the magnanimity of the conquered which can nobly inspire and receive that other magnanimity which the conqueror may nobly show. It was he who could be tolerated, while yet the passions of civil war were still uncooled, to defend in Congress from reproach which he deemed unjust even Jefferson Davis himself, because it was he also who could, in the same body, reach to a just comprehension of the greatness of Charles Sumner, and dare to do his memory noble honor, reckless of the frowns of embittered critics behind him.

"And so it is that to none more upon his side is to be ascribed the achievement of that concord which has at last come to bless our land with such beneficence that he is now recognized its enemy who will touch the chord of remembrance for a single discordant tone to mar the harmony of our common love for our common country." [26]

Resolutions were passed at the close of the assembly, and on the 24th of April Attorney General Olney presented them to the Supreme Court in an address in which he reviewed Lamar's life and public services. The reply of the Chief Justice was chiefly a eulogy of the "marked judicial qualities" demonstrated by the deceased in his work upon the Supreme Bench. "With him," said Chief Justice Fuller, "the splendid visions attendant upon youth never faded into the light of common day; but they kept for him an ideal, the impossibility of whose realization, as borne in upon him from time to time, oppressed him with a sense of failure. Yet the conscientiousness of his work was not lessened, nor was the acuteness of his intellect obscured by these natural causes of his discontent; nor did a certain Oriental dreaminess of temperament ever lure him to abandon the effort to accomplish something that would last after his lips were dumb." [27]

They had laid him to rest in the bosom of his native State where for more than a hundred years his fathers had borne an honored name. But Mississippi was not willing that his ashes should take their long sleep beyond her boundaries. In the *Memphis Commercial-Appeal* of October 26th, 1894, was carried a dispatch from the town of Oxford. "There was laid to rest to-day," it read, "in the beautiful St. Peter's Cemetery, among a solid bank of flowers, all that was mortal of the late Justice L. Q. C. Lamar, the South's greatest orator and statesman." And there he yet sleeps in the shadow of the University that he loved, and close to the heart of the people whom, for almost four decades, he served in the highest councils of the nation.

NOTES

I

1. E. P. Oberholtzer, *History of the United States*, III, 41 ff., and 53 ff.
2. Claude G. Bowers, *The Tragic Era*, p. 418.
3. *New York World*, March 12th, 1874.
4. Moorfield Storey, *Ebenezer Rockwood Hoar: A Memoir*, p. 239; Ed. L. Pierce, *Memoir and Letters of Charles Sumner*, IV, 598.
5. Edward Mayes, *Lucius Q. C. Lamar: His Life, Times, and Speeches* (henceforth referred to as *Life and Times*), pp. 188, 372.
6. *Ibid.*, pp. 187 ff.; J. G. de Roulhac Hamilton, "Lamar of Mississippi," *The Virginia Quarterly Review*, VIII (Jan., 1932), 77. Henry A. Minor, in his *Story of the Democratic Party*, p. 309, says that Lamar "struck the truest national note" of any man of the post-war era.
7. *Congressional Record*, 43rd Cong., 1st sess., Vol. II, pt. 4, April 27th, 1874.
8. Cf. Pierce, *op. cit.*, p. 550. Because Sumner was ill at the time that this bill was called for consideration, it was not acted upon. In no case, however, could it have been passed at that time. On the contrary, the House adopted a drastic counter proposition by a strictly party vote. Sumner himself, for his advocacy of the measure, was severely censured by vote of the Massachusetts legislature; but before his death he saw this action rescinded by large majorities, this in February, 1874. Cf., J. F. Rhodes, *History of the United States*, VII, 100, and note.
9. Mayes, *Life and Times*, pp. 186 ff.
10. *Ibid.*, pp. 188 ff.
11. George F. Hoar, *Autobiography*, II, 176.
12. Mayes, *Life and Times*, p. 191.

13. Rhodes, *op. cit.*, VI, vii ; and VII, 103. Quoted with the permission of the Macmillan Co., publishers.
14. W. A. Dunning, *Reconstruction, Political and Economic*, pp. 267 ff. ; cf. James Schouler, *History of the United States*, VII, 242 n. 1.
15. E. W. Newman ("Savoyard"), *Essays on Men, Things, and Events*, p. 138.
16. Mayes, *Life and Times*, pp. 191-92.

II

1. Lantz in "The Lamar Lineage and Arms," *Baltimore Sun*, Oct. 22nd, 1905, p. 12.
2. *Ibid.*, cf. Edward Mayes, *Genealogical Notes*, C, 4 ff. ; Mayes, *Life and Times*, pp. 13 ff.
3. Lantz in *Baltimore Sun*, Oct. 22nd, 1905, p. 12.
4. Cf. C. P. Lamar, *The Life of Joseph Rucker Lamar*, pp. 5 ff.
5. *Baltimore Sun*, Oct. 22nd, 1905.
6. Land Records, Annapolis, Md., Vol. XX, folio 95 ; *Archives of Maryland*, III, 489 (Sept. 14th, 1663). A problem arises in the statement in the certificate of naturalization that Thomas and Peter Lamar were "subjects of the crown of France." The certificate was issued in 1663 (and the evidence is incontrovertible that Thomas and Peter were in England almost a decade before), whereas Wicre in Flanders, the family seat of the Lamars, did not come into possession of France until 1667. The explanation is that the branch with which we are concerned had dwelt for some time in France before the removal to England. In origin the family was Norman-French.
7. Land Records, Annapolis, Md., Vol. IX, folio 312 ; *Archives of Maryland*, XLIX, 338 (Nov. 8th, 1664).
8. Land Records, Annapolis, Md., Vol. IX, folio 312.
9. *Baltimore Sun*, Oct. 22nd, 1905.
10. Cf. Lantz, in *Baltimore Sun*, Dec. 3rd, 1905 ; Mayes, *Genealogical Notes*, C, 4 ff., for a discussion of the Lamar-Lamartine friendship.
11. *Archives of Maryland*, Proceedings of General Assembly from April, 1666-June, 1676, p. 400 (June, 1674).
12. *Baltimore Sun*, Oct. 22nd, 1905.
13. *Archives of Maryland*, II, 553 ; VII, 249 ; XV, 401.

14. *Baltimore Sun*, Oct. 22nd, 1905.
15. Cf. Mayes, *Genealogical Notes*, C, 4 ff. ; Mayes, *Life and Times*, pp. 13 ff. ; W. H. Lamar, "Thomas Lamar of the Province of Maryland," *Publications of Southern History Association*, I (July, 1897), 203-10.
16. Land Office of Maryland, Liber No. 19, folio 481.
17. *Baltimore Sun*, Oct. 22nd, 1905.
18. Mayes, *Life and Times*, p. 14.
19. *Baltimore Sun*, Oct. 22nd, 1905.
20. C. P. Lamar, *op. cit.*, p. 8 ; *Baltimore Sun*, Oct. 22nd, 1905.
21. Cf. Deed of Robert Lamar to the Rev. John Urquhart, Land Records of Frederick County, Maryland, Liber E, folios 639, 640, 641.
22. Mayes, *Life and Times*, p. 14 ; *Baltimore Sun*, Oct. 22nd, 1905.
23. C. P. Lamar, *op. cit.*, pp. 8, 165 ; *Baltimore Sun*, Oct. 22nd, 1905 ; Mayes, *Life and Times*, p. 14.
24. *Baltimore Sun*, Oct. 22nd, 1905 ; *Mayes, Life and Times*, p. 15 ; cf. *The Papers of Mirabeau Buonaparte Lamar*, ed. by Gulick and Elliott.
25. William Preston Johnston, *Farmer's World*, Feb. 5th, 1879, quoted in Mayes, *Life and Times*, p. 15.
26. L. L. Knight, *Reminiscences of Famous Georgians*, I, 162.
27. *Baltimore Sun*, Oct. 22nd, 1905.
28. Mayes (*Life and Times*, p. 15) thinks the house built in 1810, but my own investigation indicates the earlier date.
29. Mayes, *Life and Times*, pp. 21 ff.
30. Cf. Mrs. Clement C. Clay, *A Belle of the Fifties*, pp. 74 ff.
31. *New International Encyclopaedia*, XIII, 489 ; J. L. Carson, *History of the Supreme Court*, II, 530.
32. Garnett Andrews, *Reminiscences of an Old Georgia Lawyer*, p. 19.
33. Knight, *Reminiscences*, I, 159 ; cf. S. F. Miller, *The Bench and Bar of Georgia*, p. 139.
34. Mayes, *Life and Times*, p. 18 ; Knight, *Reminiscences*, p. 159.
35. R. M. Charlton, *Reports of Decisions*, pp. iii-iv.
36. Cf. Miller, *op. cit.*, pp. 133-150.
37. *Ibid.*
38. Carson, *op. cit.*, II, 530.
39. Knight, *Reminiscences*, I, 159. Cf. *The Green Bag*, V (1893), 164. According to Hon. Joel Crawford, the elder Lamar was

"distinguished for his attainments in *belles-lettres,* for the classic purity of his composition, and for his forensic eloquence."

40. In order of their birth: Susan Rebecca, Mary Elizabeth, Sarah Williamson, Lucius Q. C., Thompson Bird, Louisa Leonora, Mary Ann, and Jefferson Mirabeau.

III

1. Cf. L. L. Knight, *Georgia's Landmarks, Memorials, and Legends,* I, 836 ff.
2. Mayes, *Life and Times,* p. 27.
3. Knight, *Reminiscences,* I, 598.
4. *Appleton's Cyclopedia of American Biography,* ed. by James Grant Wilson and John Fiske (New York, 1887-1889, 6 Vols.), III, 598. Considerable MS. material, collected by the late Edward Mayes and concerned with all branches of the Lamar family including the South American, is now in the possession of George H. Lamar of Rockville, Md., and Washington, D.C. Also see the MS. family history left by the late Lucian Lamar Knight to the Georgia Department of Archives and History.
5. *Ibid.,* p. 597.
6. *Biographical Directory of the American Congress* (1928).
7. *Ibid.,* pp. 803 and 1198-99.
8. Knight, *Reminiscences,* I, 165; Knight, *Georgia's Landmarks,* II, 384; cf. U. B. Phillips, *American Negro Slavery,* 288-91; Lamar MS. in possession of Mrs. A. S. Erwin, Athens, Ga.
9. Knight, *Reminiscences,* I, 166; Knight, *Georgia's Landmarks,* II, 903, 917.
10. *Ibid.,* pp. 390, 947.
11. Cf. E. A. Anderson and A. C. Gordon, *J. L. M. Curry, A Biography.*
12. Knight, *Georgia's Landmarks,* I, 683; Mayes, *Life and Times,* p. 27.
13. Mayes, *Life and Times,* p. 29.
14. Cf. John Donald Wade, *Augustus Baldwin Longstreet,* pp. 254 ff.
15. Mayes, *Life and Times,* p. 31.
16. Cf. Dr. Few's letter of July 23rd, 1839, in the *Methodist Advocate* of August 2nd, 1839. The definitive "Life" of Augustus Baldwin Longstreet is the altogether admirable volume of Dr. John Donald Wade.

17. Cf. Wade's *op. cit.* on the early history of Emory College; G. G. Smith, *History of Georgia Methodism,* p. 378.
18. Cf. *Southern Christian Advocate,* Feb. 28th, 1840; June 25th, 1841; Sept. 30th, 1843.
19. Oscar P. Fitzgerald, *Judge Longstreet,* p. 47.
20. *Southern Christian Advocate,* Feb. 25th, 1842.
21. Mayes, *Life and Times,* pp. 33 ff.
22. *Ibid.,* p. 561.
23. *Ibid.,* pp. 33 ff.
24. *Southern Christian Advocate,* August 12th, 1842.
25. Wade, *op. cit.,* p. 243.

IV

1. Mayes, *Life and Times,* p. 37.
2. *Ibid.,* p. 42.
3. *Ibid.,* p. 40.
4. *Ibid.,* pp. 41 ff.
5. *Ibid.,* pp. 45-46.
6. Wade, *op. cit.,* pp. 299 ff.
7. John N. Waddell, *Memorials of Academic Life,* p. 276.
8. *Ibid.*
9. Lamar to Harper, A. C. Lunsford MS. Collection.
10. *Ibid.*
11. Mayes, *Life and Times,* p. 50.
12. Dunbar Rowland, *History of Mississippi,* I, 757 ff.
13. *Ibid.,* p. 757.
14. Mayes, *Life and Times,* p. 51.
15. *Ibid.,* p. 55.

V

1. Lamar to Harper, A. C. Lunsford MS. Collection.
2. Mayes, *Life and Times,* p. 57.
3. Hill, W. B., in *The Green Bag,* April, 1893.
4. Herbert Fielder, *Life, Times and Speeches of Joseph E. Brown,* p. 68.
5. Lamar to Harper, A. C. Lunsford MS. Collection.
6. *Ibid.*
7. Mayes, *Life and Times,* p. 60.

8. *Ibid.*

9. *Ibid.*, p. 62.

10. Lamar to Harper, A. C. Lunsford MS. Collection.

11. Rowland, *History* I, 759 ff.

12. *Ibid.*, quoting Mrs. N. D. Dupree from *Some Historical Homes of Mississippi*, published by Mississippi Historical Society.

13. Edward Channing, *A History of the United States*, VII, 156.

14. *Statutes at Large of the United States* (from Dec. 1, 1851-March 3, 1855), X, 277 ff.

15. Mayes, *Life and Times*, pp. 64 ff.

16. *Ibid.*, p. 69.

17. *Ibid.*, p. 70.

18. *Ibid.*

19. Rhodes, *op. cit.*, II, 276 ff.

20. Mayes, *Life and Times*, p. 71.

21. *Ibid.*

22. *Ibid.*, p. 72.

23. *Cong. Globe*, 1st sess., 35th Cong., Jan. 13th, 1858.

24. Henry Adams, *The Education of Henry Adams*, p. 246.

25. Mayes, *Life and Times*, p. 73.

26. *Ibid.*

27. *Ibid.*, p. 75.

28. *Cong. Globe*, 1st sess., 35th Cong., May 22nd, 1858.

29. *Cong. Globe*, 2nd sess., 35th Cong., Jan. 17th, 1859.

30. *Cong. Globe*, 2nd sess., 35th Cong., Feb. 21st, 1859.

31. Adams, *Education*, p. 185.

32. Clay, *op. cit.*, p. 48.

33. *Ibid.*, p. 48.

34. Mayes, *Life and Times*, p. 76.

35. *Ibid.*, p. 78.

36. *Ibid.*

37. Channing, *op. cit.*, VI, 203.

38. Mayes, *Life and Times*, p. 80 ; Rhodes, *op. cit.*, II, 419 ; Channing, *op. cit.*, VI, 203.

39. *Cong. Globe*, 1st sess., 36th Cong., Dec. 7th, 1859.

40. Mayes, *Life and Times*, p. 82.

VI

1. Rhodes, *op. cit.*, II, 243 ff.
2. *Ibid.*, p. 443.
3. R. M. Johnston and W. H. Browne, *The Life of Alexander H. Stephens*, p. 355.
4. Mayes, *Life and Times*, p. 83.
5. Rhodes, *op. cit.*, II, 475.
6. *Ibid.*, p. 454.
7. Mayes, *Life and Times*, p. 85.
8. Channing, *op. cit.*, VI, 252 ff.
9. Mayes, *Life and Times*, p. 92.
10. James G. Blaine, *Twenty Years in Congress*, I, 546.
11. Wade, *op. cit.*, p. 334.
12. Mayes, *Life and Times*, p. 86.
13. *Ibid.*, p. 87.
14. *Ibid.*, pp. 87-88.
15. S. S. Cox, *Three Decades of Federal Legislation*, pp. 74, 79.
16. Blaine, *op. cit.*, I, 243.
17. Cf. letters to his sister and his brother ; J. W. Jones, *Personal Reminiscences, Anecdotes, and Letters of Gen. Robert Edward Lee*, pp. 133 and 134.
18. Mayes, *Life and Times*, p. 89.
19. *Cong. Record*, 45th Cong., 2nd sess., vol. VII, pt. 1, Jan. 24th, 1878.
20. Thomas H. Woods, "A Sketch of the Mississippi Secession Convention," *Publications of the Mississippi Historical Society*, VI (1902), 91 ff.; Rowland, *History*, I, 778; Mayes, *Life and Times*, p. 90.
21. *Ibid.*, p. 91.
22. Rowland, *History*, I, 781.
23. Mayes, *Life and Times*, p. 92.

VII

1. Mayes, *Life and Times*, p. 94.
2. *Ibid.*, p. 96.
3. Mary B. Chesnut, *A Diary from Dixie*, p. 70.
4. *Ibid.*, pp. 72, 144.
5. Mayes, *Life and Times*, p. 96.

6. Chesnut, *op. cit.*, pp. 71-73.

7. Mayes, *Life and Times*, p. 96.

8. Chesnut, *op. cit.*, p. 82.

9. Mayes, *Life and Times*, p. 97.

10. *Ibid.*

11. Channing, *op. cit.*, VI, 467.

12. Rhodes, *op. cit.*, III, 492 ff., 616 ff.; Channing, *op. cit.*, VI, 467.

13. Channing, *op. cit.*, VI, 468; Rhodes, *op. cit.*, III, 4.

14. For the official reports of the Battle of Williamsburg, see *War of the Rebellion: Official Records* (hereafter cited as *O.R.*), ser. i, vol. XI, pt. 1.

15. Sara Agnes Pryor, *Reminiscences of Peace and War*, p. 173.

16. *O.R.*, ser. i, vol. XI, pt. 1, p. 593.

17. Cf. *ibid.*, pp. 597 ff. for Lamar's report.

18. *Ibid.*, p. 599.

19. *Ibid.*, p. 588.

20. *Ibid.*, p. 592.

21. Mayes, *Life and Times*, p. 101.

22. "Maryland and Heraldry," *Baltimore Sun*, Dec. 3rd, 1905; I. W. Avery, *History of Georgia*, pp. 263, 314.

23. *Ibid.*, pp. 198 ff.

24. Pryor, *Reminiscences*, p. 161.

25. Mayes, *Life and Times*, p. 102.

26. Fitzgerald, *op. cit.*, pp. 198-99.

27. Cf. A. B. Longstreet, "From Out the Fires," *Nineteenth Century*, December, 1869, p. 545.

28. Mayes, *Life and Times*, p. 103.

29. Confederate MS., Library of Congress.

30. Mayes, *Life and Times*, p. 106.

31. *Ibid.*

32. Letter in Confederate MS., Library of Congress.

33. Beckles Wilson, *John Slidell and the Confederates in Paris*, p. 69.

34. Mayes, *Life and Times*, p. 44.

35. No one has more truly caught the spirit of the Middle Ages than Lamar's intimate friend, Henry Adams, whose tastes were closely similar to his own. Cf. Adams, *Mont-Saint-Michel and Chartres*.

36. Mayes, *Life and Times*, p. 108.

37. *Ibid.*, p. 111.

38. *Ibid.*, p. 110.

39. Cf. Henry Watterson, *Marse Henry*, II, 18 ff.

40. Mayes, *Life and Times*, p. 587.

41. Adams, *Education*, pp. 184-88.

42. D. Jordan and E. Pratt, *Europe and the American Civil War*, pp. 170 ff.; Mayes, *Life and Times*, p. 112.

43. Adams, *Education*, p. 246.

44. Chesnut, *op. cit.*, 72.

45. Cf. Wilson, *op. cit.*, p. 276.

46. Cf. F. L. Owsley, *King Cotton Diplomacy*, pp. 495 ff. ; Letter : Slidell to Benjamin, June 12th, 1862, no. 37 ; *Official Records of the Union and Confederate Navies* (hereafter referred to as *O. R. N.*), Series 2, III, 806-7.

47. Pickett Papers, Benjamin to Lamar, No. 2, Jan. 11th, 1863 ; *O. R. N.*, Ser. 2, III, 796.

48. Mayes, *Life and Times*, p. 109.

49. *Ibid.*, p. 375.

50. *Ibid.*, p. 113.

51. Clay, *op. cit.*, p. 181.

52. Chestnut, *op. cit.*, p. 279.

53. *Ibid.*, p. 280.

54. Mayes, *Life and Times*, p. 113.

55. *Ibid.*, *Appendix* no. 7.

56. *Ibid.*, p. 114.

57. Clay, *op. cit.*, p. 204.

58. Mayes, *Life and Times*, p. 114.

59. *Ibid.*, p. 559.

60. *Ibid.*

61. *Ibid.*, p. 560.

62. *Ibid.*

63. *Ibid.*

64. *Ibid.*, p. 115.

65. Channing, *op. cit.*, VI, 435-636.

66. *Ibid.*, pp. 635 ff. ; cf. John B. Gordon, *Reminiscences of the Civil War*, p. 444 ; J. L. Chamberlain, *The Passing of the Armies*, p. 259.

VIII

1. Mayes, *Life and Times*, p. 115.

2. *New York Tribune*, Aug. 8th, 1865, citing *Columbia Phoenix*.

3. M. F. Maury Papers, Library of Congress ; Diana F. M. Corbin, *Life of Matthew Fontaine Maury* ; J. W. Jones, *Personal Reminiscences, Anecdotes, and Letters of Gen. Robert E. Lee*, pp. 202 ff.

4. Mayes, *Life and Times*, p. 121.

5. Mrs. J. G. Johnson, "The University War Hospital," *Publications of the Mississippi Historical Society*, XII (1912), 96 ; Mayes, *Life and Times*, p. 121.

6. Quoted in Clay, *op. cit.*

7. Mayes, *Life and Times*, p. 122.

8. Cf. *Life of Davis*, by his wife, II, 655 ; Rhodes, *op. cit.*, VI, 50 ff.

9. Dunbar Rowland, *Jefferson Davis, Constitutionalist*, VIII, 544-45.

10. Mayes, *Life and Times*, p. 123.

11. *Ibid.*

12. *Ibid.*, pp. 123-24.

13. W. D. Armes, ed., *The Autobiography of Joseph Le Conte*, p. 230.

14. Charles W. Ramsdell, *Reconstruction in Texas*, p. 44.

15. Walter L. Fleming, *Documentary History of Reconstruction*, I, 25-27.

16. Quoting Mrs. Brooks, MS. Diary, Bowers, *op. cit.*, pp. 45 ff.

17. *Annual Cyclopaedia*, 1865, p. 392.

18. Chesnut, *op. cit.*, p. 384.

19. Susan Dabney Smedes, *Memoirs of a Southern Planter*, p. 229.

20. *Ibid.*, p. 228.

21. Chesnut, *op. cit.*, 385, 394.

22. Fleming, *op. cit.*, I, 92, 93.

23. C. M. Thompson, *Reconstruction in Georgia*, p. 138.

24. Bowers, *op. cit.*, p. 59.

25. Whitelaw Reid, *After the War*, p. 245.

26. Mayes, *Life and Times*, p. 124.

27. Cf. Samuel E. Morison, ed., *Development of Harvard University*, pp. 479 ff.; 491 ff.

28. Mayes, *Life and Times*, p. 125.

29. *Ibid.*

30. *Ibid.*, p. 126.

31. *Ibid.*, p. 596.

32. S. H. Acheson, *Joe Bailey*, p. 8 (quoted with permission of the Macmillan Co., publishers).

33. *Ibid.*, p. 12.
34. Memorial address in *Cong. Record*, June 14th, 1932, 13, 351 ff.
35. Mayes, *Life and Times*, p. 128.
36. *Ibid.*, p. 129.
37. *Ibid.*, appendix 8.
38. *Ibid.*, pp. 131 ff.
39. J. S. McNeilly, "The Enforcement Act of 1871 and the Ku Klux Klan in Mississippi," *Publications of the Mississippi Historical Society*, IX (1906), 140 ff.
40. *Ibid.*, pp. 142 ff.
41. Mayes, *Life and Times*, p. 134.
42. *Ibid.*, p. 135.
43. Cf. Wade, *op. cit.*, p. 371.
44. Lamar to Bledsoe, Library of Congress MS.
45. Mayes, *Life and Times*, p. 57.
46. *Ibid.*, p. 135.
47. *Ibid.*, p. 136.
48. *Ibid.*, p. 135.

IX

1. Mayes, *Life and Times*, pp. 157-58.
2. *Ibid.*, p. 166.
3. Oberholtzer, *op. cit.*, III, 1 ff.
4. Quoted in *New York Tribune*, July 2nd, 1872.
5. Cf. *Harper's Weekly*, Aug. 10th, 1872.
6. Mayes, *Life and Times*, p. 170.
7. *The Nation*, July 11th, 1872, p. 17.
8. Mayes, *Life and Times*, pp. 171-73.
9. *Ibid.*, p. 174.
10. *Ibid.*
11. *Ibid.*, pp. 175-76.
12. *Ibid.*, p. 175.
13. Rhodes, *op. cit.*, VII, 93.
14. Cf. *House Reports*, 43rd Cong., 2nd sess., no. 265, xxxvi.
15. Mayes, *Life and Times*, p. 177 ; cf. Rhodes, *op. cit.*, VII, 95.
16. James W. Garner, *Reconstruction in Mississippi*, p. 293.
17. Cf. Wade, *op. cit.*, p. 169.
18. *Cong. Record*, 43rd Cong., 1st sess., vol. II, pt. 1 (Dec. 1, 1873-Jan. 29, 1874).

19. Mayes, *Life and Times*, pp. 179-80.
20. Quoted in *ibid.*, p. 189.
21. *Ibid.*, p. 190.
22. *Ibid.*, 189.
23. *Ibid.*, p. 190.
24. *Ibid.*
25. *Daily Memphis Avalanche*, May 6th, 1874.
26. Mayes, *Life and Times*, p. 182.
27. Quoted in *ibid.*, p. 189.
28. *Ibid.*, p. 189.
29. *Ibid.*, p. 190.
30. *North American Review*, Vol. 126 (January-February, 1878).
31. Blaine, *op. cit.*, II, 546.
32. Quoted in Mayes, *Life and Times*, p. 194 ; cf. Rhodes, *op. cit.*, VII, 99 ff.
33. Mayes, *Life and Times*, pp. 200-201.

X

1. *Cong. Record*, 43rd Cong. 1st sess., vol. II, pt. 5, June 8th, 1874.
2. Taylor, in *The Nation*, May 20th, 1873 ; cf. W. D. Foulke's *Life of Oliver P. Morton*, II, 284-85 ; Bowers, *op. cit.*, p. 43.
3. H. C. Warmoth, *War, Politics, and Reconstruction*, p. 206.
4. *Ibid.*, p. 208.
5. *Ibid.*, p. 252.
6. Mayes, *Life and Times*, p. 197.
7. Quoted in *ibid.*, p. 198.
8. *Ibid.*, p. 199.
9. *Ibid.*
10. *Ibid.*
11. J. S. McNeilly, "Climax and Collapse of Reconstruction in Mississippi," *Publications of the Mississippi Historical Society*, XII (1912), p. 296.
12. *Ibid.*
13. Mayes, *Life and Times*, pp. 199-200.
14. *Ibid.*, p. 375.

XI

1. Bowers, *op. cit.*, pp. 439 ff.
2. Ella Lonn, *Reconstruction in Louisiana after 1868*, p. 269.

3. Oberholtzer, *op. cit.*, II, 236 ; Mayes, *Life and Times*, p. 202.
4. Lonn, *op. cit.*, p. 271.
5. J. W. Jones, *op. cit.*, p. 228.
6. Mayes, *Life and Times*, pp. 203-4.
7. *Ibid.*, p. 204.
8. *Ibid.*, pp. 204-5.
9. Cf. *New York World*, Nov. 14th, 1874.
10. Mayes, *Life and Times*, p. 211.
11. *Cong. Record*, 43rd Cong., 2nd sess., Vol. III, pt. 2, Feb. 3rd, 1875.
12. Mayes, *Life and Times*, p. 211.
13. *Ibid.*, pp. 211-12.
14. Fleming, *op. cit.*, II, 387.
15. Bowers, *op. cit.*, 428 ff.
16. *The Nation*, Feb. 18th, 1875, p. 108.
17. *Cong. Record*, 43rd Cong. 2nd sess., Vol. III, pt. 3, Feb. 24th, 1875, pp. 1748, 1929.
18. Mayes, *Life and Times*, p. 215.
19. McNeilly, "Reconstruction in Mississippi," *Pubs. of the Miss. Hist. Soc.*, XII (1912), 357.
20. *Ibid.*, pp. 358 ff.
21. *Cong. Record*, 43rd Cong., 2nd sess., Vol. IV, pt. 2, Feb. 4, 1875.
22. *Ibid.*
23. *Cong. Record*, 44th Cong., 1st sess., Vol. IV, pt. 3, May 2nd, 1876.
24. Mayes, *Life and Times*, p. 507.
25. *Ibid.*, p. 223.
26. *Ibid.*, pp. 224-28.
27. Cf. Bowers, *op. cit.*, p. 434.
28. Mayes, *Life and Times*, p. 228.
29. Quoted in *ibid.*, p. 247.
30. *Ibid.*
31. *Ibid.*, p. 256.
32. *Ibid.*, pp. 259 ff.

XII

1. Garner, *op. cit.*, pp. 302-3.
2. *Ibid.*, pp. 293-366.
3. Rhodes, *op. cit.*, VII, 97.

4. *Ibid.*
5. Mayes, *Life and Times*, p. 231.
6. Rhodes, *op. cit.*, VII, 203.
7. McNeilly, "Reconstruction in Mississippi," *Pubs. of the Miss. Hist. Soc.*, XII (1912), 297.
8. *Ibid.*
9. Cf. Frank Johnston, "Suffrage and Reconstruction in Mississippi," *Publications of the Mississippi Historical Society*, VI (1902), 197.
10. Mayes, *Life and Times*, p. 232.
11. Quoted in McNeilly, "Reconstruction in Mississippi," *Pubs. of the Miss. Hist. Soc.*, XII (1912), 323.
12. Rhodes, *op. cit.*, VII, 103 ff.
13. Mayes, *Life and Times*, p. 235.
14. *Ibid.*, pp. 236-37.
15. *Cong. Record*, 43rd Cong., 2nd sess., vol. III, pt. 1, p. 77, Dec. 14, 1874.
16. Mayes, *Life and Times*, p. 238.
17. *Ibid.*, p. 239.
18. Rowland, *Hist. of Miss.*, II, 192.
19. McNeilly, "Reconstruction in Mississippi," *Pubs. of the Miss. Hist. Soc.*, XII (1912), 338-40.
20. Mayes, *Life and Times*, p. 251.
21. *Ibid.*
22. *Ibid.*, p. 258.
23. Quoted in McNeilly, "Reconstruction in Mississippi," *Pubs. of the Miss. Hist. Soc.*, XII (1912), 369.
24. Fleming, *op. cit.*, II, 394.
25. Cf., C. H. Brough, "The Clinton Riot," *Publications of the Mississippi Historical Society*, VI (1902), 56 ff. ; McNeilly, "Reconstruction in Mississippi," *Pubs. of the Miss. Hist. Soc.*, XII (1912), 385 ; Garner, *op. cit.*, p. 375.
26. *Ibid.*
27. Rhodes, *op. cit.*, VII, 131.
28. *Appleton's Annual Cyclopaedia*, 1875, p. 562.
29. *Ibid.*, p. 516.
30. McNeilly, "Reconstruction in Mississippi," *Pubs. of the Miss. Hist. Soc.*, XII (1912), 376; Dunbar Rowland, "The Rise and Fall of Negro Rule in Mississippi," *Publications of the Mississippi Historical Society*, II (1899), 195.

31. McNeilly, "Reconstruction in Mississippi," *Pubs. of the Miss. Hist. Soc.*, XII (1912), 377 ff.
32. Gray might threaten Ames, but in the face of the aroused citizenry he cringed and allowed his black troops to melt away.
33. Rhodes, *op. cit.*, VII, 138.
34. Garner, *op. cit.*, 394.
35. F. Bancroft, *Speeches, Correspondence, and Political Papers of Carl Schurz*, p. 63, note.
36. Reports of Committees of the United States Senate, 44th Cong., 1st sess. (1875-1876), I, xxxiii ff., lxxv.
37. Cf., Rhodes, *op. cit.*, VII, 139.
38. Reports of Committees of the United States Senate, 44th Cong., 1st sess. (1875-1876), I, 1015 ff., 1085 ; Garner, *op. cit.*, p. 399.
39. *Ibid.*, p. 396.
40. George J. Leftwich, "Reconstruction in Monroe County," *Publications of the Mississippi Historical Society*, IX (1906), 77.
41. Cf. Garner, *op. cit.*, p. 399 ; *New York World*, May 22nd, 1876.
42. Charles Nordhoff, *The Cotton States in the Spring and Summer of 1875*, p. 79 ; cf. Bowers, *op. cit.*, p. 457.
43. Mayes, *Life and Times*, pp. 263-4.
44. *Ibid.*, p. 264.
45. Cf. Rowland, *Hist. of Miss.*, II, 195 ; Rhodes, *op. cit.*, VII, 97 ff. ; Oberholtzer, *op. cit.*, III, 214 ff. ; Julia Kendel, "Reconstruction in Lafayette County," *Publications of the Mississippi Society*, XIII (1913), 263 ; *The South in the Building of the Nation*, II, 460.

XIII

1. Cf. Oberholtzer, *op. cit.*, III, 141 ff.
2. A. K. McClure, *Recollections of a Half Century*, p. 254 ; *World Almanac*, p. 63.
3. Rhodes, *op. cit.*, VII, 217.
4. Carson, *op. cit.*, II, 531.
5. Mayes, *Life and Times*, p. 265.
6. Quoted in *ibid.*, p. 268.
7. *Ibid.*
8. *Ibid.*, pp. 268-69.
9. *Ibid.*, p. 270.
10. *Memphis Appeal*, Dec. 1, 1876.

11. Quoted in Mayes, *Life and Times*, p. 271.
12. J. W. Garner, "The Senatorial Career of J. Z. George," *Publications of the Mississippi Historical Society*, VII (1903), 245 ff.
13. Rowland, *Hist. of Miss.*, II, 201.
14. Mayes, *Life and Times*, p. 273.
15. *Cong. Record*, 44th Cong., 1st sess., vol. III, pt. 1, p. 324, Jan. 10, 1876.
16. *Ibid.*, pp. 324-26.
17. Cf. Rhodes, *op. cit.*, VII, 180 ; Oberholtzer, op. cit., III, 257.
18. Cf. H. J. Pearce, *Benjamin H. Hill*, pp. 266 ff. ; *Cong. Record*, 44 Cong., 1st sess., vol. IV, pt. 1, pp. 345-51, Jan. 11, 1876.
19. Quoted in Mayes, *Life and Times*, pp. 274-75.
20. *Ibid.*, p. 275.
21. Gail Hamilton, *Biography of James G. Blaine*, p. 381.
22. *New York World*, Jan. 11th, 1876.
23. *Cong. Record*, 44th Cong., 1st sess., Vol. IV, pt. 1, Jan. 25th, 1876.
24. Quoted in Mayes, *Life and Times*, pp. 276-77.
25. *Ibid.*, p. 278.
26. *Ibid.*, pp. 278-79.
27. McNeilly, "Reconstruction in Mississippi," *Pubs. of the Miss. Hist. Soc.*, XII (1912), 435.
28. Cf. Rhodes, *op. cit.*, VII, 1 ff., for an interesting but inaccurate account. Better is Oberholtzer, *op. cit.*, II, 610-14. Cf. George S. Merriam, *Life and Times of Samuel Bowles*, II, 255-59.
29. Oberholtzer, *op. cit.*, IV, 143 ff.
30. *Ibid.*, p. 170 ff.
31. *Ibid.*, p. 160 ff.
32. *New York World*, March 7th, 1876 ; cf. Bowers, *op. cit.*, p. 470.
33. *Cong. Record*, 44th Cong., 1st sess., Vol. IV, pt. 2, March 7th, 1876.
34. George F. Hoar, *Autobiography of Seventy Years*, I, pp. 200-1.
35. Mayes, *Life and Times*, pp. 281-82.
36. Oberholtzer, *op. cit.*, III, 262 ff. ; Rhodes, *op. cit.*, VII, 194.
37. Walter Allen, *Governor Chamberlain's Administration in South Carolina*, pp. 321-25.
38. *Cong. Record*, 44th Cong., 1st sess., Vol. IV, pt. 5, July 18th, 1876.
39. *New York Tribune*, July 19th and 26th, 1876.

40. *Cong. Record*, 44th Cong., 1st sess., Vol. IV, pt. 5, July 25th, 1876.
41. *Ibid.*, pt. 6, August 2nd, 1876.
42. Cf. T. C. Smith, *James Abram Garfield*, pp. 607 ff.
43. Mayes, *Life and Times*, p. 289; cf. *New York Tribune*, Aug. 3rd, 1876.

XIV

1. *New York World*, August 22nd, 1876.
2. *Ibid.*, Oct. 24th, 1876.
3. *Ibid.*, Aug. 18th, 1876.
4. J. J. Eckenrode, *Rutherford B. Hayes*, pp. 178 ff. (cf. Oberholtzer, *op. cit.*, III, 279).
5. *Ibid.*, p. 178.
6. Bowers, *op. cit.*, p. 523.
7. Eckenrode, *op. cit.*, pp. 178 ff.
8. Cf. E. B. Andrews, *The United States in Our Times*, 215; Bowers, *op. cit.*, 524; Eckenrode, *op. cit.*, pp. 178 ff.
9. Rhodes, *op. cit.*, VII, 229.
10. Bowers, *op. cit.*, p. 526; Watterson, *Marse Henry*, I, 296.
11. Cf. *House Reports*, 44th Cong., 2nd sess., No. 156, pt. 1, p. 7; John Bigelow, *Letters and Literary Memorials of Samuel J. Tilden*, II, 39; Watterson, *Marse Henry*, I, 298-99; Paul L. Haworth, *The Hayes-Tilden Election*, pp. 97-98; Oberholtzer, *op. cit.*, II, 287.
12. Rhodes, *op. cit.*, VII, 232.
13. *Ibid.*, VII, 232 and n. 1; Bowers, *op. cit.*, p. 529.
14. Watterson, *Marse Henry*, I, 299.
15. Oberholtzer, *op. cit.*, III, 178 ff.
16. *Cong. Record*, 44th Cong., 2nd sess., vol. V, pt. 2, Jan. 26th, 1877.
17. Oberholtzer, *op. cit.*, III, 304 ff.
18. Mayes, *Life and Times*, p. 699.
19. *Diary and Letters of Rutherford Birchard Hayes*, ed. by C. R. Williams, III, 181, 383.
20. Cf. Eckenrode, *op. cit.*, pp. 219 ff.
21. Charles R. Williams, *Life of Rutherford B. Hayes*, I, 530.
22. Hayes Papers.
23. Relative to these conferences, see Oberholtzer, *op. cit.*, III, 311; *House Miscellaneous Documents*, 45th Cong., 3rd sess., No. 31,

pt. 1, pp. 875 ff. ; *ibid.*, pt. 3, 595-633 ; Eckenrode, *op. cit.*, pp. 219 ff. ; Reynolds, *Reconstruction in South Carolina*, p. 499 ; Haworth, *op. cit.*, 268 ff. ; Watterson, *Marse Henry*, I, 309-11 ; T. S. Smith, *The Life and Letters of James Abram Garfield*, I, 173 ff.

24. Hoar, *Autobiography*, II, 173 ff.
25. Mayes, *Life and Times*, p. 302.
26. *Ibid.*, pp. 303-4.
27. *Ibid.*, p. 303.
28. *Diary and Letters of Rutherford Birchard Hayes*, III, 427.
29. Oberholtzer, *op. cit.*, III, 328.
30. On Lamar's visit to Hayes, see *House Miscellaneous Documents*, 45th Cong., 3rd sess., no. 31, pt. 1, pp. 881, 896-973. Cf. *ibid.*, pp. 875 ff., 898 ff., for Hayes's opinion of Lamar as stated to William H. Roberts.
31. Mayes, *Life and Times*, pp. 307-9.
32. *Ibid.*, pp. 297-98.
33. Eckenrode, *op. cit.*, pp. 219 ff.
34. John Bigelow, *Retrospections of an Active Life*, V, 314.
35. Bowers, *op. cit.*, 537.
36. *Ibid.*
37. Curtis, in *Harper's Weekly*, June 23rd, 1888.
38. Mayes, *Life and Times*, p. 310.
39. H. P. Judson, "American Politics," *Review of Reviews*, VII (March, 1893).
40. Mayes, *Life and Times*, p. 311.
41. Lamar to Walthall ; cf. Mayes, *Life and Times*, p. 313.
42. Mayes, *Life and Times*, pp. 313-14.
43. *Ibid.*, pp. 316 ff.
44. *New York Tribune*, Jan. 20th, 1877.

XV

1. Mayes, *Life and Times*, p. 318.
2. *Cong. Record*, 45th Cong., 1st sess., Vol. VI, Nov. 30th, 1877.
3. Cf. Oberholtzer, *op. cit.*, IV, 1-9, 21-37.
4. James L. Laughlin, *Mill's Principles of Political Economy*, 323 ; Blaine, *op. cit.*, II, 608 ; Oberholtzer, *op. cit.*, IV, 27 ff.
5. *Cong. Record*, 45th Cong., 2nd sess., vol. VII, pt. 1, pp. 644-45, Jan. 29, 1878.

6. *Ibid.*, p. 607.
7. Mayes, *Life and Times*, p. 326.
8. Oberholtzer, *op. cit.*, IV, 30.
9. *Cong. Record*, 45th Cong., 2nd sess., Vol. VII, pt. 1, Jan. 24th, 1878.
10. Mayes, *Life and Times*, p. 331.
11. *Ibid.*, p. 332.
12. *Ibid.*, pp. 332-33.
13. *Ibid.*, p. 333.
14. Cong. Record, 45th Cong., 2nd sess., Vol. VII, pt. 2, Feb. 15th, 1878.
15. Quoted in Mayes, *Life and Times*, p. 334.
16. *The Nation*, Jan. 31st, 1878 ; *ibid.*, Feb. 21st, 1879. Cf. comments in *New York Tribune* of Aug. 9th, 1877 ; Jan. 25th and Feb. 17th, 1878.
17. Mayes, *Life and Times*, pp. 341-42.
18. *Ibid.*, p. 342.
19. *Ibid.*
20. *Ibid.*
21. *Ibid.*
22. Quoted in *ibid.*, pp. 342-48.
23. *Cong. Record*, 44th Cong., 2nd sess., Vol. V, pt. 2, Jan. 24th, 1877.
24. *Cong. Record*, 45th Cong., 2nd sess., Vol. VII, pt. 2, March 22nd, 1878.

XVI

1. For bitter attacks on Lamar, see *New York Tribune*, Nov. 29th, Dec. 13th, 30th, 1878.
2. *Cong. Record*, 45th Cong., 3rd sess., Vol. VIII, pt. 1, Dec. 11th, 1878.
3. *Ibid.*, Dec. 16th, 1878.
4. Quoted in Mayes, *Life and Times*, p. 362.
5. *Ibid.*, p. 364.
6. Rowland, *Jefferson Davis*, VIII, 297.
7. *Ibid.*, p. 217 ; cf. pp. 297-99.
8. *Ibid.*, p. 588.
9. *Cong. Record*, 45th Cong., 3rd sess., Vol. VIII, pt. 3, March 1st, 1879.

10. W. E. Connelley, *Ingalls of Kansas*, pp. 359 ff.
11. For the opposite view, see *New York Tribune*, March 4th, ·1879.
12. Mayes, *Life and Times*, p. 371.
13. Hoar, *Autobiography*, II, 173 ff.
14. *Diary and Letters of Rutherford Birchard Hayes*, III, p. 638.
15. Mayes, *Life and Times*, p. 379; cf. Watterson, *Marse Henry*, I, 296.
16. *Cong. Record*, 46th Cong., 1st sess., Vol. IX, pt. 1, June 18th, 1879.
17. Connelley, *Ingalls*, pp. 348 ff.
18. Mayes, *Life and Times*, pp. 388-89.
19. *Ibid.*, pp. 390-91.
20. Cf. *Memphis Avalanche*, March 5th, 1885.
21. Watterson, *Marse Henry*, I, pp. 65-66.
22. *Memphis Daily Avalanche*, May 24th, 1874.
23. Mayes, *Life and Times*, pp. 391-92.
24. *Ibid.*, p. 392.
25. *Ibid.*
26. Hoar, *Autobiography*, II, 173 ff.
27. W. C. Ford, ed., *Letters of Henry Adams*, p. 130.

XVII

1. Mayes, *Life and Times*, pp. 395-98.
2. *Ibid.*, p. 408.
3. Adams, *Education*, p. 184.
4. Hon. T. C. Catchings in a memorial address after Lamar's death.
5. Mayes, *Life and Times*, p. 411.
6. *Ibid.*, pp. 412-13.
7. *Ibid.*, p. 414.
8. For the best discussion of the "exodus," see Oberholtzer, *op. cit.*, IV, 526 ff.
9. *Senate Reports*, 46th Cong., 2nd sess., pt. 3, p. 289.
10. Mayes, *Life and Times*, pp. 415-16.
11. *Cong. Record*, 46th Cong., 2nd sess., Vol. X, pt. 5, June 14th, 1880.
12. Quoted in Mayes, *Life and Times*, pp. 419-20.
13. *Ibid.*

14. *Cong. Record*, 46th Cong., 3rd sess., Vol. XI, pt. 1, Jan. 25th, 1881.

15. *Cong. Record*, 46th Cong. (Special Session), vol. XII, pp. 154 ff., April 1st, 1881.

16. Cf. *New York Tribune*, April 8th, 1881.

17. Quoted in Mayes, *Life and Times*, p. 433.

18. *Ibid.*

19. Cf. *ibid.*, p. 434.

20. *Ibid.*, pp. 434-35.

21. *Ibid.*, p. 443.

22. *Ibid.*, p. 446.

23. *Ibid.*, pp. 446-47.

24. *Ibid.*, p. 447.

25. *Ibid.*, p. 449.

26. *Ibid.*

27. *Cong. Record*, 47th Cong., 2nd sess., Vol. XIV, pt. 3, Feb. 7th, 1883.

28. *Compilation of the Messages and Papers of the Presidents*, J. D. Richardson, ed., VIII, 49.

29. Oberholtzer, *op. cit.*, III, 146 ff.

30. *New York Tribune*, Feb. 9th, 1885.

31. *Cong. Record*, 48th Cong., 1st sess., Vol. XV, pt. 3, March 26th, 1884.

32. Mayes, *Life and Times*, pp. 453 ff.

33. *Ibid.*, p. 460.

34. *New York Tribune*, Dec. 12th, 1884.

35. Mayes, *Life and Times*, p. 712.

36. *Ibid.*, p. 462.

37. *Cong. Record*, 48th Cong., 2nd sess., Vol. XVI, pt. 1, Jan. 1885.

38. J. T. Adams, *America's Tragedy*, p. 362. Quoted with the permission of Charles Scribner's Sons.

39. Bishop Galloway, in *Memphis Appeal-Avalanche*, Jan. 25th, 1893.

40. B. K. Bruce, in *Boston Herald*, Jan. 28th, 1893.

41. Judge Arnold, before the Bar Association of Birmingham, Ala. Cf. Mayes, *Life and Times*, p. 599.

42. Cf. Mayes, *Life and Times*, p. 595.

43. Bishop Galloway, in *Memphis Appeal-Avalanche*, Jan. 25th, 1893.

44. Mayes, *Life and Times*, p. 607.
45. *Ibid.*, p. 586.

XVIII

1. Ford, ed., *Letters of Henry Adams*, p. 364.
2. Cf. letter in Cleveland Papers, Library of Congress.
3. White to Schurz, in Bancroft, *op. cit.*, IV, 350.
4. Cf. Bancroft, *op. cit.*, IV, 355 ff.
5. Clay, *op. cit.*, p. 75.
6. Lamar to Cleveland, Nov. 15th, 1884, Cleveland Papers.
7. Lamar to Cleveland, Jan. 1st, 1885, Cleveland Papers.
8. Lamar to Cleveland, Feb. 6th, 1885, Cleveland Papers.
9. Lamar to Bates, Dec. 18th, 1884, Cleveland Papers.
10. Mayes, *Life and Times*, pp. 469-70.
11. *Ibid.*, p. 470.
12. *Ibid.*
13. *Ibid.*, p. 471.
14. Lamar to Cleveland, Feb. 19th, 1885, Cleveland Papers.
15. Rhodes, *op. cit.*, VIII, 242-43.
16. Mayes, *Life and Times*, p. 471.
17. *Atlanta Constitution*, April 28th, 1883.
18. Let it be noted that confirmation now takes place in open Senate.
19. Cf. Mayes, *Life and Times*, pp. 471-72.
20. *Memphis Daily Avalanche*, March 5th, 1885.
21. Cf. *ibid.*, March 5th, 1885.
22. *Ibid.*, March 6th, 1885.
23. Harry T. Peck, *Twenty Years of the Republic*, pp. 52 ff.
24. Bancroft, *op. cit.*, IV, 354.
25. George F. Parker, *Recollections of Grover Cleveland*, p. 309.
26. Mayes, *Life and Times*, p. 472.
27. *Ibid.*, p. 473.
28. Hoar, *Autobiography*, II, 190.
29. Mayes, *Life and Times*, p. 476.
30. *Ibid.*, pp. 476-77.
31. *Ibid.*, p. 528.
32. *Ibid.*, p. 529.
33. Cf. *New York Tribune*, Dec. 6th, 1885.
34. Quoted in Mayes, *Life and Times*, pp. 479-86.

35. *Ibid.*, p. 478.
36. *Ibid.*, p. 480.
37. *Memphis Daily Avalanche*, March 4th, 1885.
38. Mayes, *Life and Times*, p. 593, quoting Bruce from the *Boston Herald* of Jan. 28th, 1893.
39. John R. Lynch, *The Facts of Reconstruction*, p. 249.
40. Mayes, *Life and Times*, pp. 480-81.
41. *Ibid.*, pp. 481-82.
42. *Ibid.*, p. 482.
43. *Ibid.*, p. 483.
44. *Ibid.*, pp. 485-86.
45. Cleveland Papers. Cf. Mayes, *Life and Times*, pp. 486-87.
46. Cleveland Papers, April 2nd, 1885.
47. Cleveland Papers, June 20th, 1885.
48. Cf. C. M. Fuess, *Carl Schurz*, p. 304.
49. *Ibid.*, p. 326.
50. Mayes, *Life and Times*, pp. 489-90.
51. Schurz to Lamar, June 18th, 1886 ; letters from Schurz dated Sept. 28th, 1886 ; Oct. 14th, 1886 ; Oct. 9th, 1886, in Schurz Papers, Library of Congress.
52. Mayes, *Life and Times*, pp. 488-89.
53. Schurz to Lamar, Oct. 9th, 1886, Schurz Papers.
54. Lamar to Lamont, Nov. 20th, 1885, Cleveland Papers.
55. *House Executive Documents*, 49th Cong., 1st sess. (*Report of the Sec. of the Int.*, 5 vols.), I, 3-91. Cf. Mayes, *Life and Times*, pp. 488-89.
56. *Ibid.*, p. 490.
57. *Ibid.*
58. Perhaps the best account of Lamar's historic work in the Department of the Interior is in Oberholtzer, *op. cit.*, IV (see index).
59. *Report of Sec. of Int.* for 1885, I, 35.
60. Oberholtzer, *op. cit.*, IV, 620 ff.
61. Cf. *Report of the Sec. of Int.* for 1886, I, 30.
62. Cf. Robert McElroy, *Grover Cleveland*, I, 104-5.
63. *House Reports*, 48th Cong., 2nd sess., no. 2683, pt. 1, pp. 103 ff.
64. *Ibid.*, p. 108.
65. Oberholtzer, *op. cit.*, IV, 354 ff.
66. *Ibid.*, p. 355.

67. Cf. *Report of the Sec. of Int.* for 1885, I, 111-12.
68. Mayes, *Life and Times*, pp. 497-98.
69. *House Executive Documents*, 49th Cong., 2nd sess. (*Report of the Sec. of the Int.*, 5 vols.).
70. Undated, Lamar to Cleveland, 1885, Cleveland Papers. Vol. 81.
71. Mayes, *Life and Times*, p. 207.
72. *Ibid.*, pp. 206-7.
73. *Ibid.*, p. 376.
74. *House Executive Documents*, 50th Cong., 1st sess. (*Report of the Sec. of the Int.*, 5 vols.).
75. Mayes, *Life and Times*, p. 505.
76. *Ibid.*
77. Carson, *op. cit.*, II, 532.
78. F. E. Goodrich, *The Life and Public Services of Grover Cleveland*, 441 ff.
79. *New York Tribune*, Aug. 19th, 1887.
80. Peck, *op. cit.*, pp. 52-53 ; Rhodes, *op. cit.*, VII, 242-43 ; McElroy *op. cit.*, I, 104-5 ; Oberholtzer, *op. cit.*, IV, 323, 329.
81. Memorial Address at meeting of Bar of Supreme Court of United States, March 18th, 1893.
82. Newman ("Savoyard"), *In the Pennyrile of Old Kentucky*, pp. 218 ff.
83. Quoted in Mayes, *Life and Times*, p. 532.
84. *Ibid.*
85. Clay, *op. cit.*, p. 48.
86. Quoted in Mayes, *Life and Times*, p. 530.
87. Hoar, *Autobiography*, II, 173 ff.
88. W. M. Meigs, *The Life of John Caldwell Calhoun*, I, 17 (preface).
89. Clarence Cuningham, ed., *History of the Charleston Monument*, pp. 67-103, and preface.
90. Mayes, *Life and Times*, pp. 511-12.
91. *Ibid.*, pp. 513-18.

XIX

1. Mayes, *Life and Times*, pp. 518-19.
2. Quoted in *ibid.*, p. 519.
3. *Ibid.*, p. 520.
4. *Ibid.*
5. *Ibid.*, pp. 520-21.

NOTES

6. Lamar to Vilas, August 17th, 1887, Vilas MS., Wisconsin Historical Society.
7. Mayes, *Life and Times*, pp. 521-22.
8. *Ibid.*, p. 522.
9. H. J. Ford, *The Cleveland Era*, pp. 112-13.
10. The *New York Tribune*, Nov. 14th, 1887.
11. *Ibid.*, Nov. 29th, 1887.
12. *Ibid.*, Nov. 14th, 1887.
13. Mayes, *Life and Times*, pp. 522-24.
14. *Ibid.*, p. 523.
15. *Ibid.*
16. *Ibid.*, pp. 524-25.
17. *Ibid.*
18. Lamar to Cleveland, Nov. 11th, 1887, Cleveland Papers.
19. Cleveland Papers and Mayes, *Life and Times*, pp. 526-27.
20. *Ibid.*
21. *Ibid.*, p. 533.
22. Because, since the death of Hendricks, a Republican was acting as President *pro tem.* of the Senate.
23. George F. Hoar, "Charles Sumner," *North American Review* (January-February, 1878), 1-26.
24. Quoted in Mayes, *Life and Times*, p. 534.
25. *Ibid.*
26. *Ibid.*, pp. 534-35.
27. *New York Tribune*, Jan. 17th, 1888.
28. Quoted in Mayes, *Life and Times*, p. 537.
29. *Ibid.*, p. 535.
30. *Ibid.*, p. 536.
31. R. S. Thorndike, *The Sherman Letters*, p. 378.
32. Quoted in Mayes, *Life and Times*, p. 536.
33. *Ibid.*, p. 538.
34. Cf. Lamar's letter in *New York Tribune*, Nov. 12th, 1887.
35. Cleveland to Sparks, Nov. 15th, 1887, Cleveland Papers. Cf. Allan Nevins, *Letters of Grover Cleveland*, p. 165.
36. Mayes, *Life and Times*, p. 540.
37. *Ibid.*, pp. 540-41.
38. *Ibid.*, p. 543.
39. *Ibid.*
40. *Ibid.*
41. *Ibid.*, p. 544.

42. Carson, *op. cit.*, II, 533.
43. Lamar correspondence (cf. Mayes, *Life and Times*, p. 544).
44. *Ibid.*
45. Cf. *ibid.*, 544 ff.
46. Cf. Bruce in *Boston Herald*, Jan. 28th, 1893.
47. Olney in *United States Reports*, CLVIII (Oct., 1892 term), 707.
48. Carson, *op. cit.*, II, 533 ff.
49. Mayes, *Life and Times*, p. 600.
50. *Ibid.*, p. 545.
51. *Ibid.*, pp. 545-46.
52. Cf. *United States Reports*, CLVIII, 707 ff.
53. *New York Tribune*, Jan. 25th, 1893.
54. *Ibid.*, Jan. 26th, 1893.
55. Quoted in Mayes, *Life and Times*, p. 605.
56. *Ibid.*
57. *Ibid.*, p. 548.
58. *Ibid.*, pp. 548-49.
59. Newman to Lamar ; cf. Mayes, *Life and Times*, p. 549.

XX

1. Cf. Knight, *Reminiscences*, II, 478-88 ; *Biographical Dictionary of the American Congress*, pp. 1198 ff.
2. See C. P. Lamar, *op. cit.*, pp. 32, 37 ff.
3. Cf. *ibid.*, and Mayes, *Life and Times*, pp. 596 ff.
4. Mayes, *Life and Times*, Appendix 24, p. 801.
5. *Ibid.*, p. 559.
6. *Ibid.*, p. 558.
7. *Cong. Record*, 44th Cong., 1st sess., Vol. IV, pt. 2, March 9th, 1876.
8. Mayes, *Life and Times*, p. 562.
9. *Ibid.*, p. 563.
10. Cf. W. B. Hill, "Lucius Q. C. Lamar," *The Green Bag*, V (1893), 165.
11. Mayes, *Life and Times*, p. 563.
12. *Ibid.*, p. 558.
13. *Ibid.*, pp. 564-65.
14. *Ibid.*, p. 567.
15. *Louisville Courier-Journal*, June 11th, 1891.

16. Cf. Mayes, *Life and Times*, p. 567.
17. *Ibid.*, pp. 567-68.
18. Lamar to Cleveland, April 3rd, 1892, Cleveland Papers; cf. Mayes, *Life and Times*, p. 554.
19. Cf. McElroy, *op. cit.*, p. 334.
20. Mayes, *Life and Times*, pp. 568-69.
21. *Ibid.*, p. 569.
22. *Ibid.*, p. 553.
23. *Ibid.*, p. 571.
24. *United States Reports*, CLVIII, 707.
25. Mayes, *Life and Times*, pp. 579 ff.
26. *United States Reports*, CLVIII, 707 ff. Cf. Mayes, *Life and Times*, pp. 584 ff.
27. *United States Reports*, CLVIII, 707 ff.

BIBLIOGRAPHY

1. MANUSCRIPTS

THE Vilas papers, in the possession of the Wisconsin Historical Society; the Cleveland, Confederate, Schurz, and Bledsoe MSS. in the Library of Congress; the Lamar-Harper letters (the A. C. Lunsford Memorial Collection) in the care of the Georgia Historical Society; MSS. in the possession of private individuals.

2. PUBLIC DOCUMENTS

Bibliographical Dictionary of the American Congress (Washington, 1928).
Compilation of the Messages and Papers of the Presidents, ed. by J. D. Richardson (Washington, 1896-99), 10 vols.
Congressional Globe and *Congressional Record*, 1857-1893.
House Executive Documents.
Maryland, Archives of; Proceedings and Acts of the General Assembly, series published in Baltimore.
Official Reports of Congressional Investigating Committees.
Official Records of the Union and Confederate Navies (Washington, 1894-1927), 31 vols.
Senate Executive Documents.
Statutes at Large of the United States.
United States Reports: Cases Adjudged in the Supreme Court, 1887-93.
War of the Rebellion, The; A Compilation of the Official Records of the Union and Confederate Armies (Washington, 1880-1901), 130 vols.

3. NEWSPAPERS

A large selection available at the Widener Library of Harvard University; the Atlanta Carnegie; the Tennessee State Library at Nashville, Tennessee; and the Library of Congress.

4. BOOKS AND ARTICLES

Acheson, Sam Hanna, *Joe Bailey : The Last Democrat* (New York, 1932). Quotations by permission of The Macmillan Co.

Adams, Henry, *The Education of Henry Adams* (Boston, 1918). Quotations by permission of Houghton Mifflin Co.

——, *Mont-Saint-Michel and Chartres* (Boston, 1924).

——, *Letters of Henry Adams*, ed. by W. C. Ford (Boston and New York, 1930).

Adams, James Truslow, *America's Tragedy* (New York, 1934).

Allen, Walter, *Governor Chamberlain's Administration in South Carolina* (New York, 1888).

Anderson, E. A., and Gordon, A. C., *J. L. M. Curry ; A Biography* (New York, 1911).

Andrews, E. B., *The United States in Our Times* (New York, 1903).

Andrews, Garnett, *Reminiscences of an Old Georgia Lawyer* (Atlanta, 1870).

Armes, W. D., editor, *The Autobiography of Joseph Le Conte* (New York, 1903).

Avery, I. W., *History of Georgia* (New York, 1881).

Bancroft, F., *Speeches, Correspondence, and Political Papers of Carl Schurz* (New York, 1913), 6 vols.

Bayard, Thomas F., *see* Spencer.

Bellows, Henry W., *Historical Sketch of the Union League Club* (New York, 1879).

Bigelow, John, *Letters and Literary Memorials of Samuel J. Tilden* (New York, 1902), 2 vols.

——, *Retrospections of An Active Life* (New York, 1909), 5 vols.

Blaine, James G., *Twenty Years in Congress* (Norwich, Conn., 1884), 2 vols.

Boutwell, George S., *Reminiscences of Sixty Years in Public Affairs* (New York, 1902), 2 vols.

Bowers, Claude G., *The Tragic Era* (Cambridge, 1929).

Brough, Charles H., "The Clinton Riot," *Publications of the Mississippi Historical Society*, VI (1902), 53-63.

Brown, Joseph E., *see* Fielder.

Burgess, John W., *Reconstruction and the Constitution* (New York, 1902).

BIBLIOGRAPHY

Butler, Benjamin F., *Butler's Book* (Boston, 1892).

Butler, Pierce, *Judah P. Benjamin* (Philadelphia, 1906).

Callahan, James M., *The Diplomatic History of the Southern Confederacy* (Baltimore, 1901).

Callender, E. B., *Thaddeus Stevens* (Boston, 1882).

Carpenter, Jesse T., *The South as a Conscious Minority* (New York, 1930).

Carson, Hampton L., *History of the Supreme Court* (prepared for the Judiciary Centennial Committee, 1893), 2 vols.

Chamberlain, Hope S., *Old Days in Chapel Hill* (Chapel Hill, N. C., 1926).

Chamberlain, Joshua L., *The Passing of the Armies* (New York, 1915).

Chandler, Zachariah, "Life and Public Services," *Detroit Post*, 1880.

Channing, Edward, *A History of the United States* (New York, 1926), Vol. VI. Quotations by permission of The Macmillan Co.

Charlton, Robert M., *Reports of Decisions* (Savannah, 1838).

Chesnut, Mary B., *A Diary from Dixie* (New York, 1905).

Clay, Mrs. Clement C., *A Belle of the Fifties* (New York, 1905).

Cleveland, Grover, *see* Nevins, Parker, Lynch, and McElroy.

Conkling, A. R., *Life and Letters of Roscoe Conkling* (New York, 1889).

Connelley, W. E., editor, *A Collection of the Writings of John James Ingalls* (Kansas City, 1902).

——, *Ingalls of Kansas* (Kansas City, 1909).

Corbin, Diana F. M., *Life of Matthew Fontaine Maury* (London, 1888).

Cox, S. S., *Three Decades of Federal Legislation* (Providence, 1888).

Cullom, Shelby M., *Fifty Years of Public Service* (Chicago, 1911).

Cuningham, Clarence, ed., *A History of the Charleston Monument* (Charleston, 1888).

Cutting, Elizabeth, *Jefferson Davis: Political Soldier* (New York, 1930).

Davis, Jefferson, *see* Davis, (Mrs.) Varina Howell.

Davis, S. L., *Authentic History of the Ku-Klux Klan* (New York, 1924).

Davis, (Mrs.) Varina Howell, *Jefferson Davis ... A Memoir by His Wife* (New York, 1890), 2 vols.

Dawson, Sarah Morgan, *A Confederate Girl's Diary* (Boston, 1913).

Devoto, Bernard, *Mark Twain's America* (Boston, 1932).

Dewitt, David M., *The Impeachment and Trial of Andrew Johnson* (New York, 1903).

Dunning, W. A., *Reconstruction, Political and Economic 1865-1877* (New York, 1907).

Duren, W. A., *Charles Betts Galloway* (Emory, 1932).

Eckenrode, J. J., *Rutherford B. Hayes: Statesman of Reunion* (New York, 1930).

Evarts, William M., *Arguments and Speeches* (New York, 1919), 3 vols.

Ficklin, John Rose, *History of Reconstruction in Louisiana* (Baltimore, 1910).

Fielder, Herbert, *Life, Times, and Speeches of Joseph E. Brown* (Springfield, 1883).

Fitzgerald, Oscar P., *Judge Longstreet: A Life Sketch* (Nashville, 1891).

Fleming, Walter L., *Documentary History of Reconstruction* (Cleveland, 1906-07), 2 vols.

Ford, Henry Jones, *The Cleveland Era* (New Haven, 1919). Chronicles of America Series.

Ford, W. C., *see* Henry Adams, *Letters.*

Foulke, William Dudley, *Life of Oliver P. Morton* (Indianapolis, 1899), 2 vols.

Fuess, Claude Moore, *Carl Schurz* (New York, 1932).

Garner, James W., *Reconstruction in Mississippi* (New York, 1901).

——, "The Senatorial Career of J. Z. George," *Publications of the Mississippi Historical Society*, VII (1903), 245-62.

Goodrich, F. E., *The Life and Public Services of Grover Cleveland* (Springfield, 1888).

Gordon, A. C., *see* Anderson, E. A.

Gordon, John B., *Reminiscences of the Civil War* (New York, 1903-05).

Grant, U. S., *Personal Memoirs* (New York, 1885).

Grice, Warren, *The Georgia Bench and Bar* (Macon, 1931).

Hamilton, Gail, pseudonym, *Biography of James G. Blaine* (Norwich, Conn., 1895).

Hamilton, J. G. de Roulhac, "Lamar of Mississippi," *Virginia Quarterly Review*, VIII (1932), 77-89.

Haworth, Paul L., *The Hayes-Tilden Election* (Indianapolis, 1927).

Hayes, Rutherford B., *see* Eckenrode, Williams.

Helper, Hinton Rowan, *The Impending Crisis* (New York, 1859).

Hill, Benjamin H., *see* Pearce.

Hill, Benjamin H., Jr., *Benjamin H. Hill: His Life, Speeches, and Writings* (Atlanta, 1891).

Hill, Walter B., "L. Q. C. Lamar," *The Green Bag*, April, 1893, pp. 153 ff.

Hoar, George F., *Autobiography of Seventy Years* (New York, 1903), 2 vols.

———, "Charles Sumner," *North American Review*, CXXV (January-February, 1878), 1-26.

Ingalls, J. J., *The Writings of John James Ingalls*, ed. by Wm. Connelley (Kansas City, 1902).

Johnson, Andrew, *see* Dewitt, Moore, Jones, Stryker, and Winston.

Johnston, Frank, "Suffrage and Reconstruction in Mississippi," *Publications of the Mississippi Historical Society*, VI (1902), 141-244.

Johnston, R. M., and Browne, W. H., *Life of Alexander H. Stephens* (Philadelphia, 1878).

Jones, Charles C., Jr., *Education in Georgia* (Washington, 1889).

Jones, James S., *Life of Andrew Johnson* (Greenville, Tenn., 1901).

Jones, J. W., *Personal Reminiscences, Anecdotes, and Letters of Gen. Robert E. Lee* (New York, 1874).

Jordan, D., and Pratt, E., *Europe and the American Civil War* (Boston, 1931).

Judson, Harry Pratt, "American Politics: A Study of Four Careers," *The Review of Reviews*, VII (March, 1893), 159-72.

Julian, George W., *Speeches on Political Questions* (New York, 1872).

———, *Political Recollections* (Chicago, 1884).

Kendel, Miss Julia, "Reconstruction in Lafayette County," *Publications of the Mississippi Historical Society*, XIII (1913), 223-64.

Knight, Lucian Lamar, *Georgia and Georgians* (Chicago, 1917), 6 vols.

———, *Georgia's Landmarks, Memorials, and Legends* (Atlanta, 1913), 2 vols.

———, *Reminiscences of Famous Georgians* (Atlanta, 1907), 2 vols.

Lamar, Clarinda P., *The Life of Joseph Rucker Lamar* (New York, 1926).

Lamar, Lucius Q. C., *see* Mayes.

Lamar, Mirabeau Buonaparte, *Papers*, ed. by C. A. Gulic and Katherine Elliott (Austin, 1922), 6 vols.

Lamar, W. H., "Thomas Lamar of the Province of Maryland," *Southern History Association Publications*, I (July, 1897), 203-10.

Laughlin, James L., *Mill's Principles of Political Economy* (New York, 1884).

Le Conte, Joseph, *see* Armes, W. D.

Lee, Capt. R. E., Jr., *Recollections of Robert E. Lee* (New York, 1926).

Leftwich, George J., "Reconstruction in Monroe County," *Publications of the Mississippi Historical Society*, IX (1906), 53-84.

Lingley, Charles R., *Since the Civil War* (New York, 1926).

Longstreet, Augustus Baldwin, "From Out the Fires," *The Nineteenth Century*, December, 1869.

Longstreet, A. B., *see* Wade ; Fitzgerald.

Lonn, Ella, *Reconstruction in Louisiana after 1868* (New York, 1918).

Lowry, Robert (with W. H. McCardle), *A History of Mississippi* (Jackson, 1891).

Lynch, Dennis T., *Life of Grover Cleveland* (New York, 1932).

Lynch, John R., *The Facts of Reconstruction* (New York, 1915).

McClure, Alexander K., *Recollections of a Half Century* (Salem, 1902).

McElroy, Robert, *Grover Cleveland : the Man and the Statesman* (New York, 1923).

McNeilly, J. S., "Climax and Collapse of Reconstruction in Mississippi," *Publications of the Mississippi Historical Society*, XII (1912), 283-474.

——, "The Enforcement Act of 1871 and the Ku Klux Klan in Mississippi," *Publications of the Mississippi Historical Society* IX (1906), 109-71.

Maury, M. F., *see* Corbin, Diana F. M.

Mayes, Edward, *Genealogical Notes on a Branch of the Family of Mayes and on the Related Families* (Jackson, 1928).

——, *Lucius Q. C. Lamar : His Life, Times, and Speeches* (Nashville, 1896).

Meigs, Wm. M., *The Life of John Caldwell Calhoun* (New York, 1917).

Merriam, George S., *Life and Times of Samuel Bowles* (New York, 1885), 2 vols.

Miller, Stephen F., *The Bench and Bar of Georgia* (Philadelphia, 1858).

Minor, Henry A., *The Story of the Democratic Party* (New York, 1928).

Morison, Samuel Eliot, ed., *The Development of Harvard University* (Cambridge, 1930).

Nevins, Allan, *Grover Cleveland: A Study in Courage* (New York, 1932).

——, *Letters of Grover Cleveland, 1850-1908* (Boston, 1933).

Newman, E. W. ("Savoyard"), *Essays on Men, Things, and Events* (New York and Washington, 1904).

——, *In the Pennyrile of Old Kentucky; and Men, Things and Events* (Washington, 1911).

Nordhoff, Charles, *The Cotton States in the Spring and Summer of 1875* (New York, 1875).

Oberholtzer, E. P., *History of the United States* (New York, 1917-1931), 4 vols.

Owsley, Frank L., *King Cotton Diplomacy* (Chicago, 1931).

Parker, George F., *Recollections of Grover Cleveland* (New York, 1909).

Pearce, Haywood J., *Benjamin H. Hill: Secession and Reconstruction* (Chicago, 1928).

Peck, Harry T., *Twenty Years of the Republic* (New York, 1926).

Phillips, U. B., *American Negro Slavery* (New York and London, 1918). Quoted with permission of D. Appleton and Co.

Pierce, Ed. L., *Memoir and Letters of Charles Sumner* (Boston, 1877-93), 4 vols.

Pierce, S., *The Freedmen's Bureau* (Iowa City, 1904).

Pratt, E. J., *see* Jordan, D.

Pryor, Sara Agnes (Mrs. Roger A.), *My Day: Reminiscences of a Long Life* (New York, 1909).

——, *Reminiscences of Peace and War* (New York, 1915).

Ramsdell, Charles W., *Reconstruction in Texas* (New York, 1910).

Reagan, John H., *Memoirs* (New York, 1906).

Reid, Whitelaw, *After the War; A Southern Tour* (Cincinnati, 1866).

Reynolds, John S., *Reconstruction in South Carolina* (Columbia, 1905).

Rhodes, James Ford, *History of the United States* (New York, 1893-1919), 8 vols. Quotations by permission of The Macmillan Co.

Riddle, A. G., *Life of Benjamin F. Wade* (Cleveland, 1886).

Ross, Edmund G., *History of the Impeachment of Andrew Johnson* (Santa Fé, 1896).

Rowland, Dunbar, *History of Mississippi* (Jackson, 1925).

——, *Jefferson Davis, Constitutionalist: His Letters, Papers, and Speeches* (Jackson, 1923), 10 vols.

——, "The Rise and Fall of Negro Rule in Mississippi," *Publications of the Mississippi Historical Society*, II (1899), 189-200.

"Savoyard," *see* Newman, E. W.

Schurz, Carl, *Reminiscences of Carl Schurz* (New York, 1907-08), 3 vols. (*See* Bancroft; Fuess).

Sherman, John, *Recollections of Forty Years* (New York and Chicago, 1895). 2 vols.

Schouler, James, *History of the United States* (New York, 1880-1913), 7 vols.

Smedes, Susan Dabney, *Memoirs of a Southern Planter* (Baltimore, 1888).

Smith, George G., Jr., *History of Georgia Methodism* (Atlanta, 1913).

Smith, T. C., *The Life and Letters of James Abram Garfield* (New Haven, 1925), 2 vols.

South in the Building of the Nation, The (Richmond, Virginia, 1909), 12 vols.

Spencer, Edward, *Public Life and Services of Thomas F. Bayard* (New York, 1880).

Storey, Moorfield (with E. W. Emerson), *Ebenezer Rockwood Hoar: A Memoir* (Boston, 1911).

Stryker, L. P., *Andrew Johnson: A Study in Courage* (New York, 1929).

Sumner, Charles, *see* Pierce, Ed. L.

Thompson, C. M., *Reconstruction in Georgia* (New York, 1915).

Thorndike, R. S., *The Sherman Letters* (New York, 1894).

Vallandigham, J. L., *A Life of Clement L. Vallandigham* (Baltimore, 1872).

Waddell, John N., *Memorials of Academic Life* (Richmond, 1891).

BIBLIOGRAPHY

Wade, John Donald, *Augustus Baldwin Longstreet: A Study of the Development of Culture in the South* (New York, 1924).

Warmoth, Henry Clay, *War, Politics, and Reconstruction* (New York, 1930).

Watterson, Henry, *Marse Henry: An Autobiography* (New York, 1919), 2 vols. Quoted with permission of Doubleday, Doran and Co.

——, "The Hayes-Tilden Contest for the Presidency," *The Century Magazine*, LXXXVI (May, 1913), 3-20; cf. (June, 1913), 193-201, "Another View of the 'Hayes-Tilden Contest'" by George F. Edmunds; and June, 1913, 285-87, Watterson's rejoinder to Edmunds.

Welles, Gideon, *Diary* (Boston, 1911), 3 vols.

Williams, Charles R., *Life of Rutherford B. Hayes* (Boston, 1914), 2 vols.

——, editor, *Diary and Letters of Rutherford Birchard Hayes* (Columbus, Ohio, 1926), 5 vols.

Wilson, Beckles, *John Slidell and the Confederates in Paris, 1862-1865* (New York, 1932). Quoted with permission of Minton, Balch and Co.

Winston, Robert W., *Andrew Johnson: Plebeian and Patriot* (New York, 1928).

Woodburn, James A., *Life of Thaddeus Stevens* (Indianapolis, 1913).

Woods, Thomas H., "A Sketch of the Mississippi Secession Convention of 1861," *Publications of the Mississippi Historical Society*, VI (1902), 91-104.

INDEX

Davis, Reuben, 60, 82 ; urges secession, 75-76 ; rebuked by audience for criticizing Lamar, 328

Dawes, H. L., places Lamar's credentials before the House, 148-49 ; demands censure or expulsion of John Young Brown, 190 ; on Bland Bill and Matthews Resolution, 309

De Kalb, Miss., Lamar speaks at, 390-91

Delane, John Thaddeus, Lamar writes article for, 101-2

Delano, Columbus, 245

Delmonico's, Grady's speech at, 398 ; Lamar's speech at, 467-68

De Morny, Count, opens his mind to Lamar, 96

Dennison, William, and the disputed presidential election, 280

Denniston, J. O., congratulates Lamar on silver vote, 318

Dent *vs.* Ferguson, 132 U. S. 50, Dean Edmund H. Bennett on Lamar's opinion, 500

Depew, Chauncey M., 468

Desert Land Acts, Lamar recommends repeal of, 448

De Trobriand, P. R., 214

Detroit Free Press, on Lamar's course in Congress, 203

Dickens, Charles, 98

Dickinson, Don M., 485

Disraeli, Benjamin, Lamar on, 96-97

Doolittle, J. R., and disputed presidential election, 270

Dorsey, A. W., 209-12

Douglas, Beverley B., 230

Douglas, Fred, 173-74

Douglas, Stephen A., 51-55, 68-71 ; his oratory compared with Lamar's, 460

Dowdell, James F., 62

Dred Scott decision, 65

Dudley, Colonel, his conduct of Pensions Bureau, 450-51

Dueling, Lamar on, 360-62

Dunning, W. A., on the Sumner eulogy, 6

Dupree, Mrs. N. D., 532

Durant, Thomas J., 228

Durell, E. H., takes unlawful interest in Louisiana election controversy, 165-71 ; resigns under fire, 168

Dwight, Theodore, 485

EARLY, J. A., 86

Eatonton, Ga., 21, 398. *See also* Old Lamar homestead.

Edmunds, George F., 341, 420 ; debates with Lamar, 333 ; writes to Lamar on death of latter's wife, 404-5 ; his oratory compared with Lamar's, 460 ; Lamar greets him courteously, 492-93 ; as chairman of judiciary committee, 477

Edmunds Amendment, 310. *See also* Matthews Resolution, Bland Silver Bill.

Education, Bureau of, Lamar on, 452-53 ; Lamar suggests founding of national university at Washington, 453

Electoral Commission, 272-95, 322, 366, 388

Eliot, Charles, confers degree on Lamar, 463-64

Eliot, George, Lamar on, 108

Ellis, E. J., and disputed presidential election, 281 ; Lamar and, 456

Emory, W. H., controls Federal troops in La., 166

Emory College, 20, 24-28 ; Lamar speaks to student body and is offered professorship, 136 ; Lamar recalls his student years, 510 ; religious atmosphere, 511 ; Lamar's address at, 514 ; alumni at Lamar's funeral, 524

Emory University, 27. *See also* Emory College.

Emporia (Kan.) *Saturday Evening News,* on Lamar's work as Secretary of the Interior, 462

Endicott, William C., 420

INDEX

English, William H., holds tariff views similar to Lamar's, 380-81

Eustis, J. B., congratulates Lamar on his reëlection to Senate, 394-95

Evarts, W. M., 286, 424

Everett, Edward, 71 ; his oratory compared with Lamar's, 410

Exodus, Negro, 373-79 ; Lamar's speech on, 376-79

FAIRCHILD, Charles S., 468, 502

Fearn, Walker, acts as Lamar's private secretary, 104, 107

Featherston, W. S., 132, 228 ; mentioned for Senate, 234

Ferry, T. W., supports silver bill, 322

Field, David Dudley, 322

Field, Stephen J., 495-96, 498, 503

Fields vs. Clark, 143 U. S. 649, Judge Arnold's estimate of Lamar's opinion, 501

Fifteenth Amendment, 139 ; Lamar on, 169, 221

Fisher, H. T., 222

Fitzgerald, O. P., on Lamar's religious life, 514

Fitzpatrick, Benjamin, 62, 71

Flewellen, "Doc," 521 ; Lamar on his friendship with, 405 ; with Lamar just before latter's death, 521

Flournoy, R. W., opposes Lamar for Congress, 147-48

Foote, H. S., debates with Lamar, 36-40

Force Bill, 236 ; Lamar defeats passage of, 184, 186-87

Ford, Henry Jones, on Lamar's elevation to the Supreme Court, 474

Forrest, N. B., 115

Forster, William Edward, 100-1

Fortress Monroe, 118

Foster, Charles, and disputed presidential election, 280-81

Foulke, W. D., 165

Fourteenth Amendment, 139 ; Lamar disqualified under terms of, 146-47 ; Lamar on, 169, 221

Franklin, F. E., radical leader, 150

Freeman, Mrs. Kate W., receives letter from Lamar, 478

Free Trade Club (New York), orders copies of Lamar's tariff speech, 396

French, O. C., supports Lamar's application for removal of his disabilities, 147

French Court, Lamar at, 94-95

Fuller, W. M., 503 ; on Lamar's fertility of mind, 505 ; attends Lamar's funeral, 523 ; on Lamar, 526

"Funders," Virginia, 384. See also "Readjusters."

Furlong, C. E., on the Vicksburg riot, 212

GALLOWAY, Charles B., on Lamar's influence on his career, 125 ; on Lamar's oratory, 410 ; on Lamar's religious life, 514

Gardner, ex-Governor, 197

Garfield, James A., 245, 280-81, 347, 394 ; suggests that Lamar be extended additional time for speech, 170 ; opposes Force Bill, 185 ; on Hamburg, S. C., race riot, 260 ; replies to Lamar, 263-64 ; and disputed presidential election, 270 ; opposes Electoral Commission, 273 ; writes to Hayes, 279 ; elected President, 383 ; death, 390, 396

Garland, A. H., 341, 420 ; battles carpetbag rule in Ark., 199 ; asks Lamar to intercede with Cleveland, 413-14 ; George F. Parker on, 423 ; strives for economy, 426 ; aspires to Supreme Court, 471

Gaskell, Milnes, 365

Geological Survey, 452

George, J. Z., 235, 265, 454, 469 ; serves on committee with Lamar to draw up ordinance of secession,

573

Halstead, Murat, and disputed presidential election, 279

Hamburg, S. C., race riot, Lamar's speech on, 258-63

Hamilton, Alexander, 481

Hamilton, Bermuda, 107

Hammond, Judge E. S., 497

Hammond, J. H., 79

Hampden, John, 343

Hampton, Wade, 304, 347, 466; on South's course after war, 114; and disputed presidential election, 279, 281-84, 290; and Gen. Sherman, 409

Hancock, W. S., 400; Lamar seconds his nomination, 380

Hanna, E. P., is reinstated by Lamar as private secretary, 433

Hannibal and St. Joseph Railroad Co. vs. Missouri River Packet Co., 125 U. S. 260, discussion of Lamar's opinion, 494, 498

Hardeman, Tom, 45

Hardy, Thomas, 513

Harlan, John M., 515

Harper, Robert G., corresponds with Lamar, 34, 41-42, 44-46, 49-50; practices law with Lamar, 43-46; his illness, 45

Harper's Weekly, 143; on Lamar's stand on the Silver Bill, 312, 320-22

Harris, Isham G., 344, 420; and Davis-Sherman controversy, 407

Harris, Joel Chandler, 23; on Lamar's career, 418-19

Harris, N. H., on Lamar's leadership of his regiment, 91; on Lamar's address to the soldiers, 112; writes to Lamar, 118-19

Harris, T. L., Lamar's tribute to, 61

Harris, Wiley P., corresponds with Lamar, 212-13; urges Lamar for the Senate, 234; on Lamar's judicial acumen, 499

Harrison, Benjamin H., 153

Harrison, Burton N., imprisoned after the war, 116; writes to Lamar, 417

Harvard University, 123-24; confers honorary degree upon Lamar, 124, 463-64

Harvey, Mrs. Evalina, 15. See also Miss Evalina Lamar.

Hawley, J. R., opposes Force Bill, 185; Mark Twain on, 266; and Davis-Sherman controversy, 407

Hayes, Rutherford B., 118, 300, 304; apprehensive over his presidential campaign, 265; the disputed election, 266-92; invites Lamar to Columbus, Ohio, 281, 288; his opinion of Lamar, 288, 544; Lamar demands that he fulfill promises, 289-90; his silver message, 308; revises Southern policy, 329-31; on Conkling and Butler, 349; Lamar discusses the Hayes-Tilden controversy, 366

Hayne, Robert Y., 466

Hazelhurst, Miss., Lamar speaks at, 393

Heiskell, A. Longstreet, ix

Heiskell, Mrs. Gussie Lamar (daughter), receives letter from Lamar, 416-17. See also Miss Sarah A. Lamar.

Helper, Hinton Rowan, writes The Impending Crisis, 65-66

Hendricks, Thomas A., 219, 347, 551; and disputed presidential election, 266, 269-70, 293; Lamar campaigns for, 399-403

Henry, Patrick, his oratory compared with Lamar's, 410

Hernando Press, supports Lamar's course in Congress, 175

Hewitt, Abram S., 468; and the disputed presidential election, 267; his wise leadership, 347-48

Hill, A. P., 112; at Battle of Williamsburg, 86-89; cites Lamar for gallantry under fire, 88

Hill, Benjamin H., 219, 230, 329, 349, 510; works in harmony with Lamar, 108-9; reply to Blaine on Amnesty Bill, 237-39; and disputed presi-